Music Express
Songbook

Series devised by **Maureen Hanke**

Songs arranged by **Michael Haslam**

Illustrations by **Alison Dexter**

Years 3-6

First published 2003
by A&C Black Publishers Ltd
37 Soho Square, London W1D 3QZ
© 2003 A&C Black Publishers Ltd
ISBN 0 7136 6783 4

Series devised by Maureen Hanke
Unit headings © Qualifications and Curriculum Authority, 2000
Series designed by Jocelyn Lucas
Cover illustration © Alex Ayliffe 2002
Inside illustrations © Alison Dexter 2003
Music setting by Jeanne Fisher
Edited by Marie Penny

A&C Black uses paper produced with elemental chlorine-free
pulp, harvested from managed sustainable forests.

Printed in Great Britain by Martins the Printers,
Berwick upon Tweed

Contents

Songs: Year 6

Roundabout

Songwriter

Stars, hide your fires (track from CD 2)

Acknowledgements

The publishers would like to thank everyone who assisted in the preparation of this book: Barrie Carson-Turner, Michael Haslam, Katherine Kermode, Jocelyn Lucas, Carla Moss, Sheena Roberts, Jane Sebba and Michelle Simpson.

The following have kindly granted permission for the reprinting of copyright material in this book:

A G-nu Words by Michael Flanders. Music by Donald Swann © 1974 The Estate of Michael Flanders and Donald Swann. Reproduced by permission of International Music Publications Ltd. All Rights Reserved.

Calypso by Jan Holdstock © 1980 Jan Holdstock.

Cats (poem) by Eleanor Farjeon from the *The Children's Bells* used by kind permission of David Higham Associates Ltd.

Cat and Mouse games music by Malcolm Abbs © 1995 Malcolm Abbs.

Day off © 1997 Malcolm Abbs.

Do-re-mi from 'The Sound of Music'. Lyrics by Oscar Hammerstein II. Music by Richard Rodgers © 1959 by Richard Rodgers and Oscar Hammerstein II. Copyright Renewed. WILLIAMSON MUSIC owner of publication and allied rights throughout the world. International Copyright Secured. All Rights Reserved.

Hard times blues by Buddy Moss © Columbia Records.

Horror hotel by Kaye Umansky.

Jelly on a plate music by Jane sebba © Jane Sebba.

Jibber jabber Music by Peter Gosling © Peter Gosling 1991. PFD on behalf of Michael Rosen for the adapted words from traditional © Michael Rosen.

Junkanoo by Jan Holdstock © Sing for Pleasure 0800 0184 164

Ki yo wah ji neh byJoseph Bruchac II.

Mice from *Fifty One New Nursery Rhymes* by Rose Fyleman © 1931,1932, Doubleday, a division of Random House Inc. used by permission of Random House Children's books, a division of Random House Inc for the rights in the USA.

Mice by Rose Fyleman. Used by kind permission of the Society of Authors as the Literary Representative of the estate of Rose Fyleman for the poem. Permission granted for the world excluding USA.

Ocean of Mystery © Niki Davies.

Relay race words and music by Ana Sanderson © 2002 A&C Black.

Silver and gold words and music by Ana Sanderson © 1997 A&C Black.

Sing it on the hillside (Christmas calypso) Words by Gerry Wakelin, music by Colin Evans. Words © 1999 Gerry Wakelin, music © 1999 Colin Evans. This arrangement by Jane Sebba © 1999 A&C Black.

The bellipong and **The zippi** by Jane Sebba © 2001 A&C Black.

The happiest time of year words and music © Jeremy Sams. Words © 1991, music © 1998 Jeremy Sams. This arrangement by Ana Sanderson © 1999 A&C Black.

Tortoise song words and music © David Sheppard 2002, A&C Black Publishers Ltd.

What you got? words and music by Ana Sanderson © 2002 Ana Sanderson, A&C Black.

You can do it words and music by Jane Sebba © 1986 Jane Sebba.

A sailor went to sea, sea, sea, Autumn leaves, Children of Africa, Come and sing together, Have you ever?, Hill an gully, Nanuma, Oh Danny Boy, Ol Mas Charlie, Old MacDonald had a glock, Over the garden wall, Pass the ball, Pass the pebble on, Shalom, Skye boat song, Suo-gân, The Blue Bell of Scotland, Which notes are these? and **What pattern's this?**, are all traditional songs, arranged and recorded by A&C Black.

Every effort has been made to trace and acknowledge copyright owners. If any right has been omitted, the publishers offer their apologies and will rectify this in subsequent editions following notification.

Using Music Express as a scheme of work

Music Express fulfils the requirements of the Music National Curriculum of England, of Wales and of Northern Ireland and the 5-14 National Guidelines for Scotland.

Learning with *Music Express*, children will gain a broad and balanced musical education.

A steady progression plan has been built into *Music Express*, both within each book and from one year to the next, ensuring consistent musical development.

Music Express songbooks

This songbook has been specially created for music readers. It is designed to be used alongside the Music Express scheme or on its own. Containing all the songs from Music Express Years 3-6, it is a useful reference and performance resource for music specialist teachers.

Using this book

This book contains all the songs that appear in the Music Express Year 3, 4, 5 and 6 books, arranged for voice(s) and piano/guitar.

The songs appear in the same order as in the Music Express scheme. The track number next to the song title refers to the CD track given in the scheme. (Where there are multiple tracks for a single song, the CD track number will be that of the complete or performance version.)

TORTOISE SONG

Vs 1 Orang-utans are big and hairy,
Kangaroos are always on the go,
Polar bears are kind of scary,
Give me something sensible and slow.

Ch A tortoise takes its time,
It tends to travel in a slow,
straight line.
A tortoise takes its time,
A friend of a tortoise is a
friend of mine.

Vs 2 Porcupines are plump and prickly,
Roadrunners are raring for a race,
Quails are quaint at moving quickly,
I prefer a smooth and steady pace.

Ch A tortoise takes its time ...

Then sing both verses again, with the chorus as a
second voice part. (You will need to repeat the final
section of the music FOUR times.)

Vs 1 Orang-utans are big and hairy ...

Ch A tortoise takes its time ...

Vs 2 Porcupines are plump and prickly ...

Ch A tortoise takes its time ...

Words and music: David Sheppard

THE HAPPIEST TIME OF YEAR

Ding ding-a-ding-a-ding-a-dong,
The bells are ringing loud and clear.
Ding ding-a-ding-a-ding-a-dong,
This is the happiest time of year.

Merry Christmas, Merry Christmas,
    one and all,
Joy to each and ev'ry creature,
    great and small, singing:

Ding ding-a-ding-a-ding-a-dong,
The bells are ringing loud and clear.
Ding ding-a-ding-a-ding-a-dong,
This is the happy time of year.
Ding ding-a-ding-a-ding-a-dong! Yeah!

Words and music: Jeremy Sams

HILL AN GULLY

Call:

Hill an gully rida,
Hill an gully rida,
An ah ben dung low dung,
An a low dung bessy dung,

Response:

Hill an gully.
Hill an gully.
Hill an gully.
Hill an gully.

OL MAS CHARLIE

Ol Mas Charlie,
Him got a *bulldog*
Ina him *back-yahd,*
An when him get mad,
Chain have fe chain him,
Chain have fe chain him.

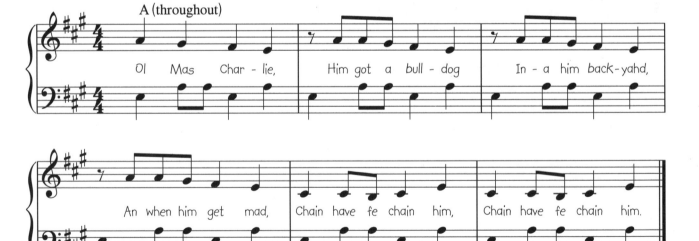

OLD MACDONALD HAD A GLOCK

Old MacDonald had a glock,
  E E D D C.
And on that glock he had some Cs,
  E E D D C.
With a C C here, and a C C there,
Here a C, there a C, ev'rywhere a C C,
Old MacDonald had a glock,
  E E D D C.

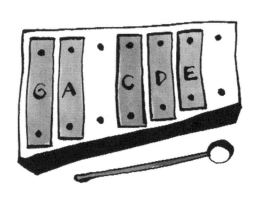

WHAT YOU GOT?

What you got cooking in the pot?
Is it sweet and sour, or spicy and hot?
Is it crunchy? Is it chewy?
Is it runny? Is it gooey?
Oh what?
I can't believe it,
You've eaten the lot!

Words and music: Ana Sanderson

WHICH NOTES ARE THESE?

Which notes are these?
? ? ? ?
Which notes are these?
Can you tell me which they are?

Words: Jane Sebba

WHAT PATTERN'S THIS

What pattern's this?
? ? ? ?
What pattern's this?
? ? ? ?

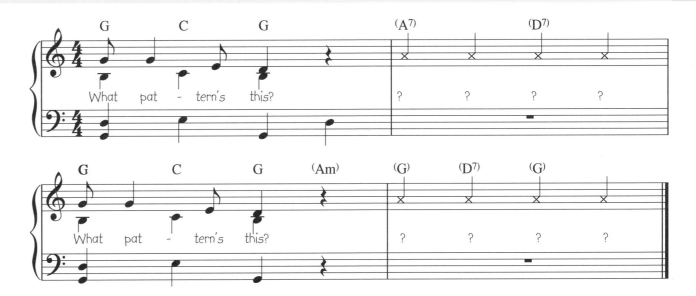

Photocopying is illegal **11**

Turn right down Sinister Street
Then cut through Panicky Park,
Turn left at Cold Feet Lane,
Where it's always dim and dark,
Head then for Horror Hotel
Arising from the gloom,
You can be sure that you won't sleep well
But you'll always get a room, for
The Spooky Duke runs this town's hotel,
What a laugh, it's an empty shell,
The roof's long gone and the walls as well,
And your host's a ghost!

Words and music: Kaye Umansky

A SAILOR WENT TO SEA, SEA, SEA

Vs 1 A sailor went to *sea, sea, sea*
To *see* what he *see, see, see*
But all that he could *see, see, see*
Was the bottom of the deep blue
   sea, sea, sea.

Vs 2 A sailor went to chop, chop, chop
To *see* what he could chop, chop, chop
But all that he could chop, chop, chop
Was the bottom of the *dee blue*
   chop, chop, chop.

Vs 3 A sailor went to Knee, Knee, Knee ...

Vs 4 A sailor went to sea, chop, Knee ....

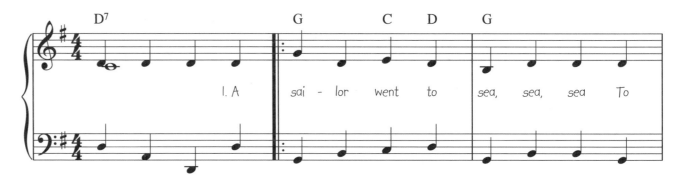

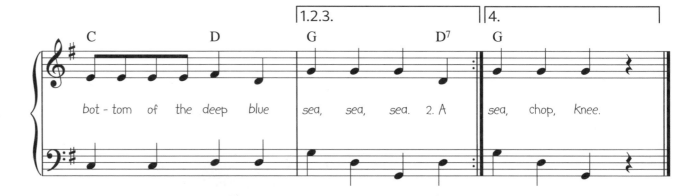

HAVE YOU EVER?

Vs 1 Have you ever, ever, ever in your
long-legged life,
Seen a long-legged sailor with a
long-legged wife?
No, I've never, ever, ever in my
long-legged life,
Seen a long-legged sailor with a
long-legged wife.

Vs 2 Have you ever, ever, ever in your
short-legged life ...
No, I've never, ever, eve in my
short-legged life....

Vs 3 Have you ever, ever, ever in your
one-legged life ...
No, I've never, ever, ever in your
one-legged life ...

OVER THE GARDEN WALL

Over the garden wall
I let my *baby* fall.
My mother came out,
She gave me a clout,
Over the garden wall.

Over the garden wall ...
She asked me what it was all about,
Over the garden wall.

Over the garden wall ...
She gave me another to match the other,
Over the garden wall

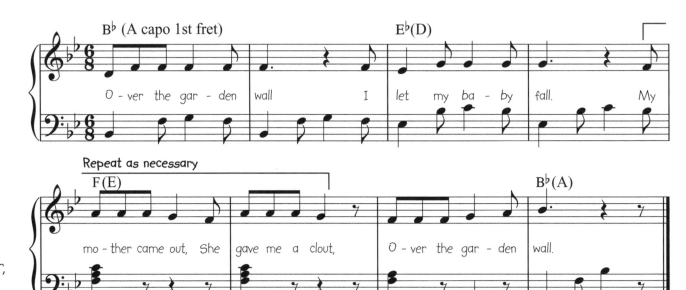

PASS THE BALL

Pass the *ball* and the *ball* go round,
Susie say that the *ball* go round.
Is the *ball* here? Is the *ball* there?
No, it isn't anywhere.

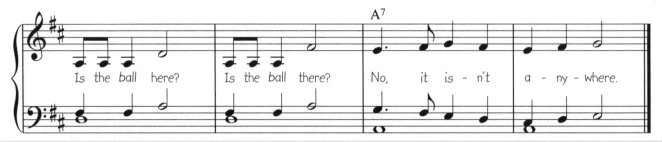

Pass the pebble on
Keep a steady rhythm
Pass the pebble on
Keep a steady rhythm
For you'll be out if you don't keep
In time to the beat,
For you'll be out if you don't keep
In time to the beat.

SUO GÂN

English lyrics:

Vs 1 Sleep, my baby, rest, my loved one,
Softly slumber now with me,
Clasped in mother's arms so tender,
Warm in mother's love for thee.

Vs 2 Naught shall ever come to harm thee,
While my loving watch I keep,
Thou, my pretty one, shall slumber
While I sing thy lullaby.

Welsh lyrics

Vs 1 Huna blentyn yn fy mynwes,
Clyd a chynnes ydyw hon;
Breichiau mam sy'n dyn am danat,
Cariad mam sy dan fy mron;

Vs 2 Ni cha dim amharu'th gyntun,
Ni wna undyn â thi gam;
Hu na'n dawel, anwyl blentyn,
Huna'n fwyn ar fron dy fam.

Traditional Welsh lullaby

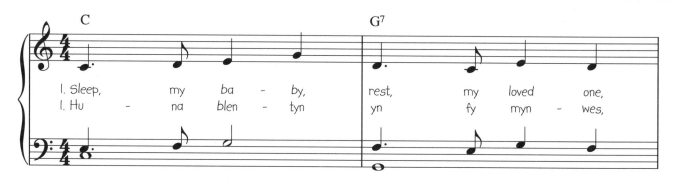

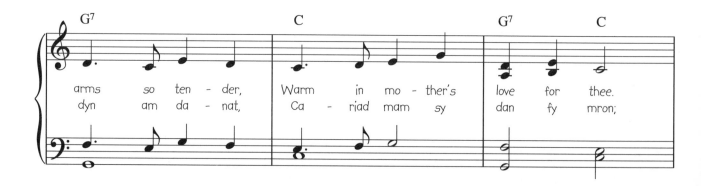

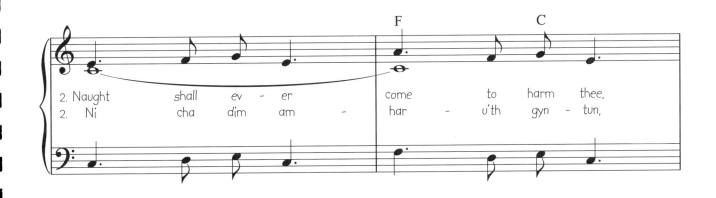

2. Naught   shall   ev - er   come   to   harm   thee,
2. Ni   cha   dim   am   -   har   -   u'th   gyn - tun,

While   my   lov - ing   watch   I   keep,   Thou,   my   pret - ty
Ni   wna un - dyn   â   thi gam,   Hu   na'n da - wel,

one,   shall slum - ber   While   I   sing   thy   lul - la - by.
an - wyl blen - tyn,   Hu - na'n fwyn   ar   fron   dy   fam.

JELLY ON A PLATE

Vs 1 Jelly on a plate,
Jelly on a plate,
Wibble, wobble, wibble, wobble,
Jelly on a plate.

Vs 2 Lassi in a glass,
Lassi in a glass,
Smooth and fruity, smooth and fruity,
Lassi in a glass.

Vs 3 Lolly on a stick,
Lolly on a stick,
Melting, dripping, melting, dripping,
Lolly on a stick.

Vs 1 Jelly on a plate ...

Words: Traditional
Music: Jane Sebba

KI YO WAH JI NEH

Ki yo wah ji neh
Yo ho hui ho,
Ki yo wah ji neh
Ki yo wah ji neh.
Ki yo wah ji neh
Yo ho hui,
Ki yo wah ji neh
Ki yo wah ji neh.

Words and music: Joseph Bruchac II

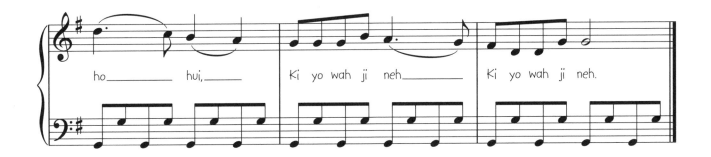

CHRISTMAS CALYPSO

Vs 1 Sing it on the hillside, sing on the mountains,
Christmas Day is almost here!
Sing it round the valleys, forests and fountains,
Christmas Day is near!

Ch So let the bells all ring,
Children sing, it's time for a holiday;
Let's all jump and shout,
Ev'ryone come out and sing!
So let the bells all ring,
Children sing, it's time for a holiday;
Let's all jump for joy,
Ev'ry girl and boy bringing gladness.

Sing it on the hillside, sing on the mountains ...

Vs 2 Decorate the house with tinsel and berry,
Christmas Day is almost here!
This'll be the time to give and be merry,
Christmas Day is near!

Ch So let the bells all ring ...

Decorate the house with tinsel and berry ...

Christmas Day is near!

Words: Gerry Wakelin
Music: Colin Evans

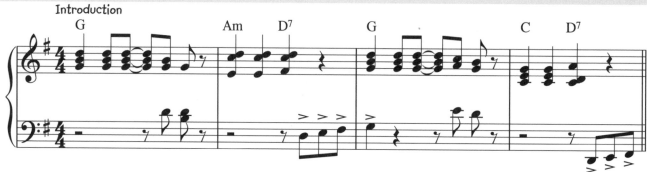

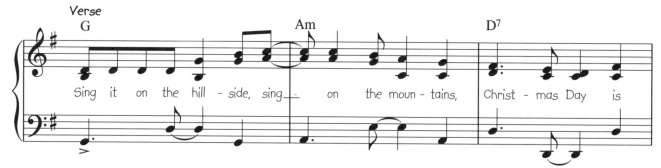

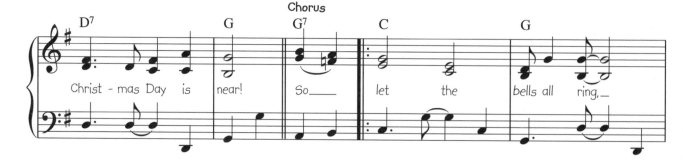

SKYE BOAT SONG

Ch 'Speed, bonnie boat,
  like a bird on the wing,
Onward,' the sailors cry.
'Carry the lad that's born to be King
Over the sea to Skye.'

Vs Loud the winds howl,
  loud the waves roar,
Thunder clouds rend the air;
Baffled, our foes stand on the shore,
Follow they will not dare.

Ch 'Speed, bonnie boat,
  like a bird on the wing, ...

Photocopying is illegal

For more songs like this visit www.acblack.com/musicexpress

YOU CAN DO IT

Ch You can do it,
You can do it,
You can do it if you really try.
You can meet that challenge,
Beat that challenge,
If you really try,
And when you've succeeded you'll feel
Nine feet high.

Vs Sums are hard with all that dividing,
Adding makes me feel like hiding,
I just want to take it all away,
Multiplying's even worse,
It makes me want to scream
and curse,
But then I hear a little voice inside
me say:

Ch You can do it ...

Words and music: Jane Sebba

First melody:

Doe - a deer, a female deer,

Ray - a drop of golden sun.

Me - a name I call myself

Far - a long, long way to run.

Sew - a needle pulling thread,

La - a note to follow sew.

Tea - a drink with jam and bread

That will bring us back to doe.

(last time only)

Do-re-mi-fa-so-la-ti-do. So doh!

Second melody:

Soh doh lah fah me doh ray,

Soh doh lah te doh ray doh.

When you know the notes to sing,

You can sing most anything.

Melodic Ostinato accompaniment:

Doh me me,

Me soh soh,

Ray fah fah,

Lah te te.

Words: Oscar Hammerstein II
Music: Richard Rodgers

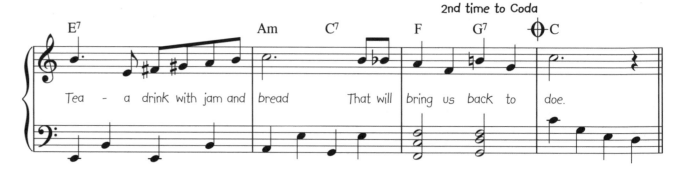

JIBBER JABBER

Vs Jibber jabber, gabble, babble, cackle, clack and prate,
Twiddle, twaddle, mutter, stutter, utter, splutter, blate,
Chatter, patter, tattle, prattle, chew the rag and crack,
Spiel and spout and spit it out, tell the world and quack.

Ch Jibber, jibber jabber,
Jibber jabber, jibber jabber,
you hoo hoo hoo.
Jibber, jibber jabber,
Jibber jabber, jibber jabber, YOU!

Second part
Doh me soh fah me ray doh,
Te ray fah me ray doh ray,
Doh me soh fah me ray doh,
Ray soh doh.

Words: Traditional; adapted by Michael Rosen
Music: Peter Gosling

Photocopying is illegal

For more songs like this visit www.acblack.com/musicexpress

Ch I've got a day off,
I know just where I'll be,
I've got a day off,
I know just what to see,
I've got a day off,
To take a trip or two round the world.

Vs 1 I'll watch the sun rise on the Great Wall
of China,
Play with a porpoise in the Caspian Sea,
I'm going to go to Nepal and climb a
mountain that's tall
And drop in to Darjeeling for tea.
I'll join a mariachi band in Mexico,
I'll write my name in soft Sahara sand,
I'll eat a biscuit in Nice and count the
islands of Greece,
And yodelay in Switzerland.

Ch I've got a day off ...

Words and music: Malcom Abbs

Am ... **D⁷sus** ... 3rd time to Coda ⊕ **G**

take a trip or two round the world.

Verse

1. I'll watch the sun rise on the Great Wall of Chi-
2. I'll take a long_____ cool_____ drink_____

E♭⁷

-na,_____ Play with a por-poise in the Cas-pi-an Sea,_____
Zan-zi-bar, I'll play a mean Ka-zoo in Ka-la-ma-zoo,_____

G ... **B⁷**

I'm going to go to Ne-pal_____ and climb a
I'll ride a hot air bal-loon_____ from Dun-oon_____

Vs 2 I'll take a long cool drink in Zanzibar,
I'll play a mean kazoo in Kalamazoo,
I'll ride a hot air balloon from Dunoon
to Kowloon
And walk from Chile up to Peru.
I'll wear a straw hat on the streets of
Panama,
Run up and down the Russian steppes
for fun,
I'll dance the limbo in style around a
tropical isle,
In Sweden see the midnight sun.

Ch I've got a day off ...

33

I'm a G-nu, I'm a G-nu,
The g-nicest work of g-nature in the zoo!
I'm a G-nu, how do you do?
You really ought to k-now w-ho's w-ho.
I'm a G-nu, spelt G.N.U.
I'm g-not a camel or a kangaroo,
So let me introduce,
I'm g-neither man or moose,
Oh, g-no, g-no, g-no,
I'm a G-nu!

I'm a G-nu, ag-nother G-nu,
I wish I could g-nash my teeth at you,
I'm a G-nu, how do you do?
You really ought to k-now w-ho's w-ho.
I'm a G-nu, spelt G.N.U.
Call me bison or okapi and I'll sue,
G-nor am I in the least
Like that dreadful hartebeest
Oh, g-no, g-no, g-no,
I'm a G-nu!

Words: Michael Flanders
Music: Donald Swann

The zippi

Thin and long,
  the zippi whizzes past,
She's going twice as fast
  as the old bellipong.

The bellipong

Fat and round,
  the bellipong is slow,
His tummy wobbles low,
  only just off the ground.

Words and music: Jane Sebba

Thin and long, the zip-pi whizz-es past, She's go-ing twice as fast as the old Bel-li-pong.

Fat and round, the bel - li - pong is slow, His

Thin and long, the Zip-pi whizz-ez past, She's go-ing twice as fast as the old bel-li-pong.

tum - my wob - bles low, on - ly just off the ground.

AUTUMN LEAVES

Autumn leaves are falling,
    orange, red and brown.
See them twirling in the wind,
    and floating to the ground.

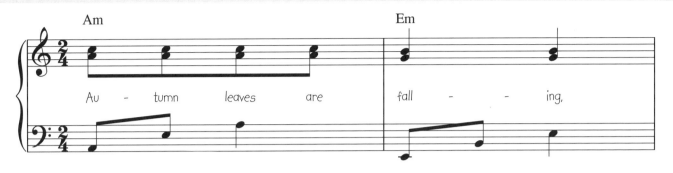

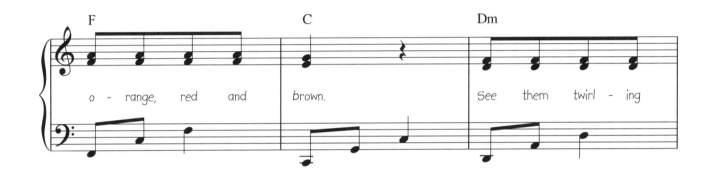

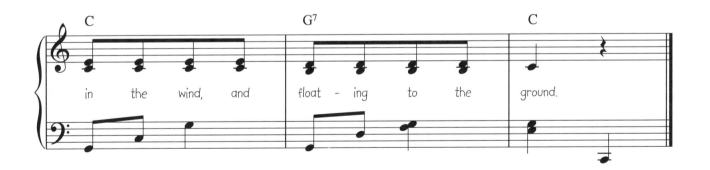

SHALOM (ROUND)

1 Shalom, my friend, shalom, my friend,
2 Shalom, shalom.
3 Until we meet again, my friend,
4 Shalom, shalom.

Words and music: Traditional Hebrew

COME AND SING TOGETHER (ROUND)

If you'd dance, then you must have
Boots of shining leather.
Money in your pocket book,
In your cap a feather.
But if you would sing with me,
You don't need a cent, you see, so
Come and sing together!
If you'd dance, then you must have
Boots of shining leather.

Hungarian folk round

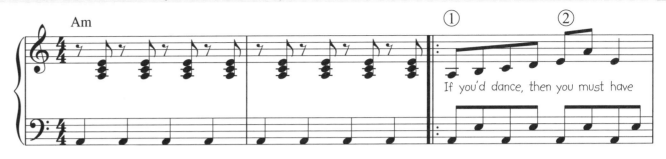

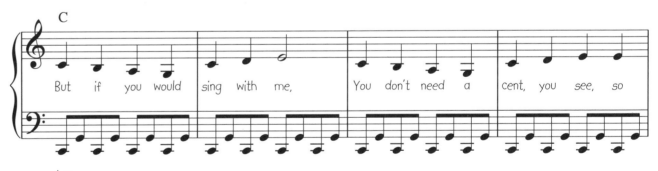

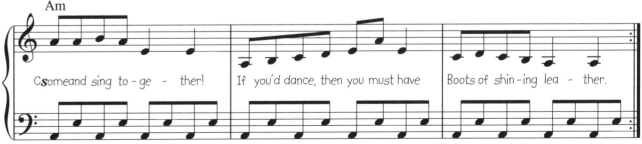

41

CALYPSO (ROUND)

1 Anytime you need a calypso,
   here is what you must do.
2 First of all you need a rhythm,
   so shake a little, shake a little,
   shake a little shaker, and you
3 Bang a drum and you sing and strum
   and then there's a calypso for you.

Words and music: Jan Holdstock

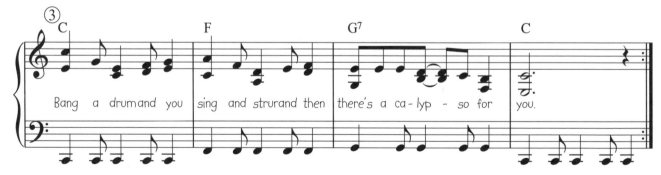

For more songs like this visit www.acblack.com/musicexpress

CHILDREN OF AFRICA

Vs 1 We are the children of Africa
And it's for freedom that
we're fighting.
We are the children of Africa
And it's for freedom that
we're fighting.

Ch A heavy load, a heavy load,
And it will take some real
strength.
A heavy load, a heavy load,
And it will take some real
strength.

Vs 2 In Soweto they shot us down,
But we will rise up united ...

Ch A heavy load ...

A street song from Soweto

OCEAN OF MYSTERY

Vs 1 A big blue giant cloaks the land;
He sprays the cliffs and hugs the sand,
With a mighty roar he crashes down,
And laughs from under his foamy crown.

Ch Ocean of mystery,
Deep your secrets lie.
Ocean of mystery,
Where the seagulls fly.

Vs 2 Swelling with his stormy power,
Waves as tall as any tower,
With a mighty roar he crashes down,
And laughs from under his foamy crown.

Ch Ocean of mystery ...

Words and music: Niki Davies

CAT AND MOUSE GAMES

First time:

Cats: Cats sleep anywhere,
Any table, any chair,
Top of piano, window ledge,
In the middle, on the edge.
Open drawer, empty shoe,
Anybody's lap will do,
Fitted in a cardboard box,
In the cupboard with your frocks.
Anywhere! They don't care!
Cats sleep anywhere.

Second time:

Mice: Their tails are long, their faces small,
They haven't any chins at all,
I think mice are rather nice.
Their ears are pink,
    their teeth are white,
They run about the house at night,
I think mice are rather nice.
They nibble things they shouldn't touch,
And no-one seems to like them much.
But I think mice are nice!

Third time: combine Cats and Mice:

Cats sleep ...   Their tails ...

Words of 'Mice': Rose Fyleman
Words of 'Cats': Eleanor Farjeon
Music: Malcom Abbs

RELAY RACE (ROUND)

1 Look at me, I'm lightning,
  I am *speedy*, I am *frightening*,
  I'm the leader of the pack,
  I'm tearing down the track
    to pass the *baton* on.

2 Go! Go! Go! Go!
  This is a relay race! No time to be slow!

3 See the crowd are on their feet,
  They loudly clap and cheer: hooray,

4 For we are the fastest!
  We are the winners!
  We are the champions!
  Keep on running! *(Second time)* Yes we are!

Words and music: Ana Sanderson

NANUMA (ROUND)

1 Nanuma wyaeh, Nanuma.

2 Nanuma wyaeh, Nanuma.

3 Nanuma wyaeh, Nanuma.

4 Nanuma wyaeh, Nanuma.

Traditional African

For more songs like this visit www.acblack.com/musicexpress

JUNKANOO (ROUND)

1 We've got a bell, we've got a drum,
  Junkanoo has begun.
2 Feel that Gombay beat,
  Giving life to your dancing feet.
3 Ev'rybody's on holiday,
  We'll dance the night away.
4 Now you know it's Junkanoo,
  Come on, let's go!

Words and music: Jan Holdstock

I WANNA SING SCAT

Part 1   **Part 2**

Vs 1 I wanna sing scat,   Cool cat, cool cat,
    sing scat,

    I wanna sing scat,   Cool cat, cool cat,
    sing scat,

    I wanna sing scat,   Cool cat, cool cat,
    sing scat,

    I wanna sing scat,   Cool cat, cool cat.
    sing scat, sing scat.

Vs 2 I wanna sing bop ...   Be bop ...

Vs 3 I wanna sing swing ...   Ring-a-ding ...

Vs 4 I wanna sing jazz ...   Jazza-ma-tazz ...

Vs 1 I wanna sing scat ...   Cool cat ...

Words and music: Malcolm Abbs

THE BLUE BELL OF SCOTLAND

Vs 1 Oh where, and oh where is your
　　Highland laddie gone?
　　Oh where, and oh where is your
　　Highland laddie gone?
　　He's gone to fight the foe for
　　King George upon the throne,
　　And it's oh, in my heart,
　　I wish him safe at home.

Vs 2 Oh where, and oh where does your
　　Highland laddie dwell?
　　Oh where, and oh where does your
　　Highland laddie dwell?
　　He dwells in merry Scotland at the
　　sign of the Blue Bell,
　　And it's oh, in my heart,
　　I love my laddie well.

Vs 3 Suppose, and suppose that your
　　Highland lad should die?
　　Suppose, and suppose that your
　　Highland lad should die?
　　The bagpipes should play o'er him and
　　I'll lay me down and cry,
　　But it's oh, in my heart,
　　I wish he may not die.

Words and music: Traditional Scottish

OH DANNY BOY

Vs 1

Oh, Danny Boy, the pipes, the pipes are calling
From glen to glen and down the mountain side.
The summer's gone, and all the roses falling,
It's you, it's you must go and I must bide.
But come you back when summer's in the
meadow,
Or when the valley's hushed and white with
snow.
It's I'll be there in sunshine or in shadow.
Oh, Danny Boy, oh, Danny Boy I love you so.

Vs 2

But when you come, and all the flow'rs are
dying,
If I am dead, as dead I may well be,
You'll come and find the place where I am
lying,
And kneel and say an Ave there for me;
And I shall hear, though soft you tread above
me,
And all my grave will warmer, sweeter be,
For you will bend and tell me that you love me,
And I shall sleep in peace until you come to
me.

Words: Fred E Weatherly
Music: Traditional Irish

Photocopying is illegal **55**

HARD TIMES BLUES

Hard times, hard times,
   how long are you gonna stay?
Hard times, hard times,
   how long are you gonna stay?
I'm here today, tomorrow,
   I may be goin' away.

Words and melody by: Buddy Moss
Accompaniment: Stephen Chadwick

Hard times,___ hard times,___ how long___ are you gon - na stay?___

Photocopying is illegal **57**

For more songs like this visit www.acblack.com/musicexpress

SILVER AND GOLD

Vs 1 You don't need a metal detector to
    find the greatest treasure,
You don't need a spade to dig
    deep into the ground,
You don't need to find a pirate's ship
    sailing across the ocean blue,
All you've got to do is open your eyes
    and look around.
Your world is full of treasures,
Your treasures are your friends;
So:

Ch Make new friends but keep the old.
The one is silver and the other is gold.
That's the wisest thing I've been told;
Make new friends but keep the old.
The one is silver and the other is gold.

Vs 2 Sometimes friends will argue and fight about things
    which aren't important,
Sometimes friends can let you down,
    leaving you upset.
If you feel that you don't understand,
    yet you don't want to lose your friend,
All you've got to do is try to forgive and to forget.
Just try to make amends.
Remember they're your friends.
And:

Ch Make new friends but keep the old ...

Rap - 1st part

Make new friends
but keep the old,
The one is silver
and the other gold.
That's the wisest
thing I've been told
About my silver and gold!

Rap - 2nd part

Yeah!
Yeah!
Silver!
Gold! Yeah!
Wisest!
Told! Yeah!
Yeah! Silver and gold!

(Sing twice:)

First part

Silver and gold,
My new friends and old.
They are my greatest treasure,
They are my hours of pleasure.
How sad it would be if
I never could be with
My most precious treasure,
My silver and gold.

Second part

Silver and gold,
My new friends and old.
Ooh
Ooh
How sad it would be if
I never could be with
My most precious,
Silver and gold.

Words and music: Ana Sanderson

63

(E) Leyenda	(F) Légende	(D) Zeichenerklärung
Autopista de doble vía sin peaje	Autoroute sans péage à chaussées séparées	Zweibahnige Autobahn ohne Gebühr
Autopista de una vía sin peaje	Autoroute sans péage à chaussée unique	Einbahnige Autobahn ohne Gebühr
Autopista de doble vía de peaje	Autoroute à péage et chaussées séparées	Zweibahnige Autobahn mit Gebühr
Autopista de una vía de peaje	Autoroute à péage et chaussée unique	Einbahnige Autobahn mit Gebühr
Acceso; acceso parcial; estación de servicio	Échangeur; échangeur partiel; aire de service	Anschlussstelle; Autobahnein- und/oder -ausfahrt; Tankstelle
Autopista en construcción (año de apertura)	Autoroute en construction (année d'ouverture)	Autobahn in Bau (Fertigstellungsjahr)
Túnel en autopista	Tunnel autoroutier	Autobahntunnel
Número de autopista; carretera europea; carretera nacional; carretera regional o local	Numéro d'autoroute; route européenne; route nationale; route régionale ou locale	Straßennummer: Autobahn; Europastraße; Nationalstraße; Regional- oder Lokalstraße
Carretera nacional de doble vía	Route nationale à chaussées séparées	Zweibahnige Nationalstraße
Carretera nacional de vía unica	Route nationale à chaussée unique	Einbahnige Nationalstraße
Carretera regional de doble vía	Route régionale à chaussées séparées	Zweibahnige Regionalstraße
Carretera regional de vía unica	Route régionale à chaussée unique	Einbahnige Regionalstraße
Carretera local de doble vía	Route locale à chaussées séparées	Zweibahnige Lokalstraße
Carretera local de vía unica	Route locale à chaussée unique	Einbahnige Lokalstraße
Carretera secundaria	Route secondaire	Nebenstraße
Carretera en construcción (año de apertura)	Route en construction (année d'ouverture)	Straße in Bau (Fertigstellungsjahr)
Túnel en carretera	Tunnel routier	Straßentunnel
Distancias en kilómetros (millas en Gran Bretaña e Irlanda) en autopista	Distances autoroutières en kilomètres (miles en Royaume-Uni et Irlande)	Autobahnentfernungen in Kilometern (Meilen in Großbritannien und Irland)
Distancias en kilómetros (millas en Gran Bretaña e Irlanda) en carretera	Distances routières en kilomètres (miles en Royaume-Uni et Irlande)	Straßenentfernungen in Kilometern (Meilen in Großbritannien und Irland)
Pendientes superiores al 14%; pendientes entre 6%–13%	Pente 14% et outre; pente 6%–13%	Steigungen über 14%; Steigungen 6%–13%
Rutas panorámicas	Routes panoramiques	Aussichtsstraßen
Puerto de montaña con altura y cierre invernal	Col avec altitude et fermeture en hiver	Pass mit Höhe und Wintersperre
Peaje	Barrière de péage	Gebührenstelle
Ferrocarril y túnel	Chemin de fer et tunnel	Eisenbahn und Tunnel
Línea marítima (con transporte de coches) y destino	Ligne de navigation (bac pour voitures) et destination	Schiffahrtslinie (Autofähre) und Ziel
Transporte de coches por ferrocarril	Transport de voitures par chemin de fer	Autoverladung per Bahn
Parque nacional, reserva natural	Parc national, réserve naturelle	Nationalpark, Naturschutzgebiet
Límites internacionales	Frontières internationales	Staatsgrenzen
Frontera en disputa; límite interno	Frontière en contestation; frontière intérieure	Strittige Grenze; Verwaltungsgrenze
Aeropuerto internacional	Aéroport international	Internationaler Flughafen
Edificio religioso; Castillo, fortaleza	Édifice religieux; Château, château-fort	Religiösgebäude; Schloss, Festung
Monumento aislado	Monument isolé	Alleinstehendes Denkmal
Ruinas, zona arqueológica; muralla	Ruines, site archéologique; vallum, muraille	Ruinen, archäologisches Ausgrabungsgebiet; Wall, Mauer
Cueva; paraje de interés natural	Grotte; curiosité naturelle	Höhle; Natursehenswürdigkeit
Vista panorámica	Vue panoramique	Rundblick
Otras curiosidades (jardín botánico, zoo, parque de atracciones etc.)	Autres curiosités (jardin botanique, zoo, parc d'attractions etc.)	Andere Sehenswürdigkeiten (Botanischer Garten, Zoo, Freizeitpark usw.)
LONDON — Ciudad o lugar de gran interés turístico	Localité ou site de grand intérêt touristique	Ortschaft oder Platz von großem touristischen Interesse
RAVENNA — Ciudad o lugar interesante	Localité ou site remarquable	Sehenswerte Ortschaft oder Platz
MONTPELLIER — Otra ciudad o lugar turístico	Autre localité ou site touristique	Andere touristischen Ortschaft oder Platz
Zermatt — Estación de esquí, localidad turística de montaña	Station de ski, localité touristique de montagne	Skistation, Touristenort in den Bergen
216 — Área geográfica cubierta y número de página de otros mapas más detallados en este atlas	Zone couverte et numéro de page pour des cartes plus détaillées dans cet atlas	Abgedecktes Gebiet und Seitennummer von ausführlicheren Karten in diesem Atlas

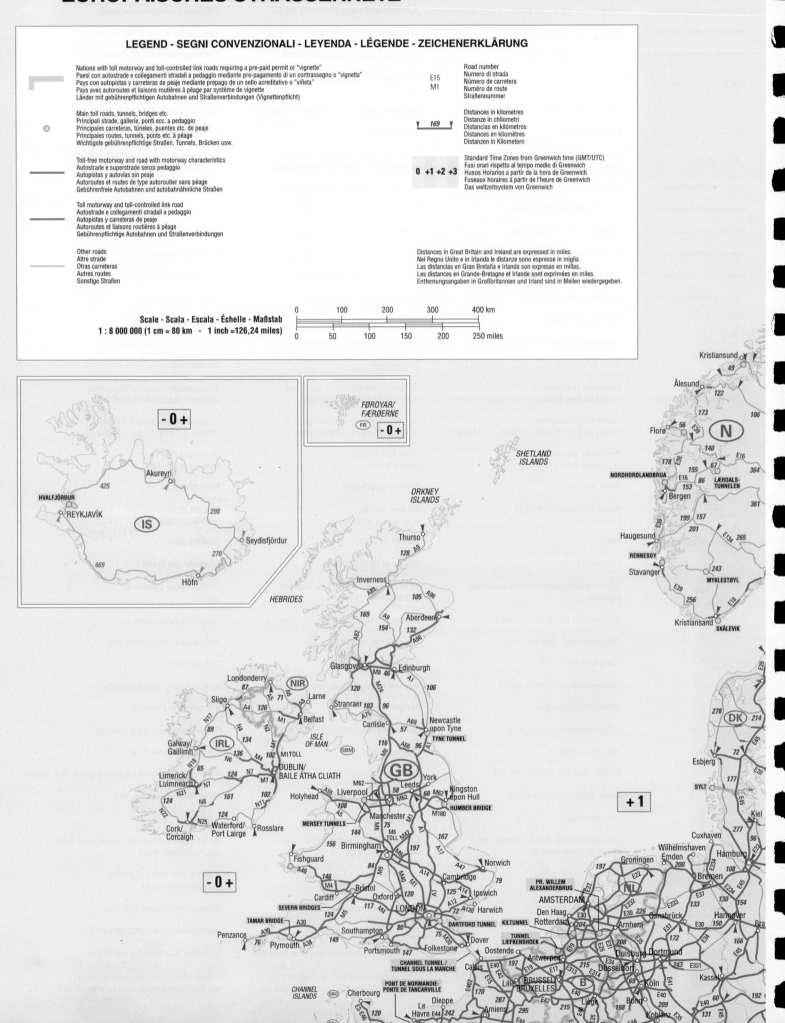

EUROPEAN ROAD NETWORK   RETE STRADALE EUROPEA
RED EUROPEA DE CARRETERAS   RÉSEAU ROUTIER EUROPÉEN
EUROPÄISCHES STRASSENNETZ

LEGEND - SEGNI CONVENZIONALI - LEYENDA - LÉGENDE - ZEICHENERKLÄRUNG

Nations with toll motorway and toll-controlled link roads requiring a pre-paid permit or "vignette"
Paesi con autostrade e collegamenti stradali a pedaggio mediante pre-pagamento di un contrassegno o "vignetta"
Pays con autopistas y carreteras de peaje mediante prepago de un sello acreditativo o "viñeta"
Pays avec autoroutes et liaisons routières à péage par système de vignette
Länder mit gebührenpflichtigen Autobahnen und Straßenverbindungen (Vignettenpflicht)

Main toll roads, tunnels, bridges etc.
Principali strade, gallerie, ponti ecc. a pedaggio
Principales carreteras, túneles, puentes etc. de peaje
Principales routes, tunnels, ponts etc. à péage
Wichtigste gebührenpflichtige Straßen, Tunnels, Brücken usw.

Toll-free motorway and road with motorway characteristics
Autostrade e superstrade senza pedaggio
Autopistas y autovías sin peaje
Autoroutes et routes de type autoroutier sans péage
Gebührenfreie Autobahnen und autobahnähnliche Straßen

Toll motorway and toll-controlled link road
Autostrade e collegamenti stradali a pedaggio
Autopistas y carreteras de peaje
Autoroutes et liaisons routières à péage
Gebührenpflichtige Autobahnen und Straßenverbindungen

Other roads
Altre strade
Otras carreteras
Autres routes
Sonstige Straßen

Road number
Numero di strada
Número de carretera
Numéro de route
Straßennummer

E15
M1

Distances in kilometres
Distanze in chilometri
Distancias en kilómetros
Distances en kilomètres
Distanzen in Kilometern

169

Standard Time Zones from Greenwich time (GMT/UTC)
Fusi orari rispetto al tempo medio di Greenwich
Husos Horarios a partir de la hora de Greenwich
Fuseaux horaires à partir de l'heure de Greenwich
Das weltzeitsystem von Greenwich

0 +1 +2 +3

Distances in Great Britain and Ireland are expressed in miles.
Nel Regno Unito e in Irlanda le distanze sono espresse in miglia.
Las distancias en Gran Bretaña e Irlanda son expresas en millas.
Les distances en Grande-Bretagne et Irlande sont exprimées en miles.
Entfernungsangaben in Großbritannien und Irland sind in Meilen wiedergegeben.

Scale - Scala - Escala - Échelle - Maßstab
1 : 8 000 000 (1 cm = 80 km - 1 inch =126,24 miles)

| 0 | 100 | 200 | 300 | 400 km |

| 0 | 50 | 100 | 150 | 200 | 250 miles |

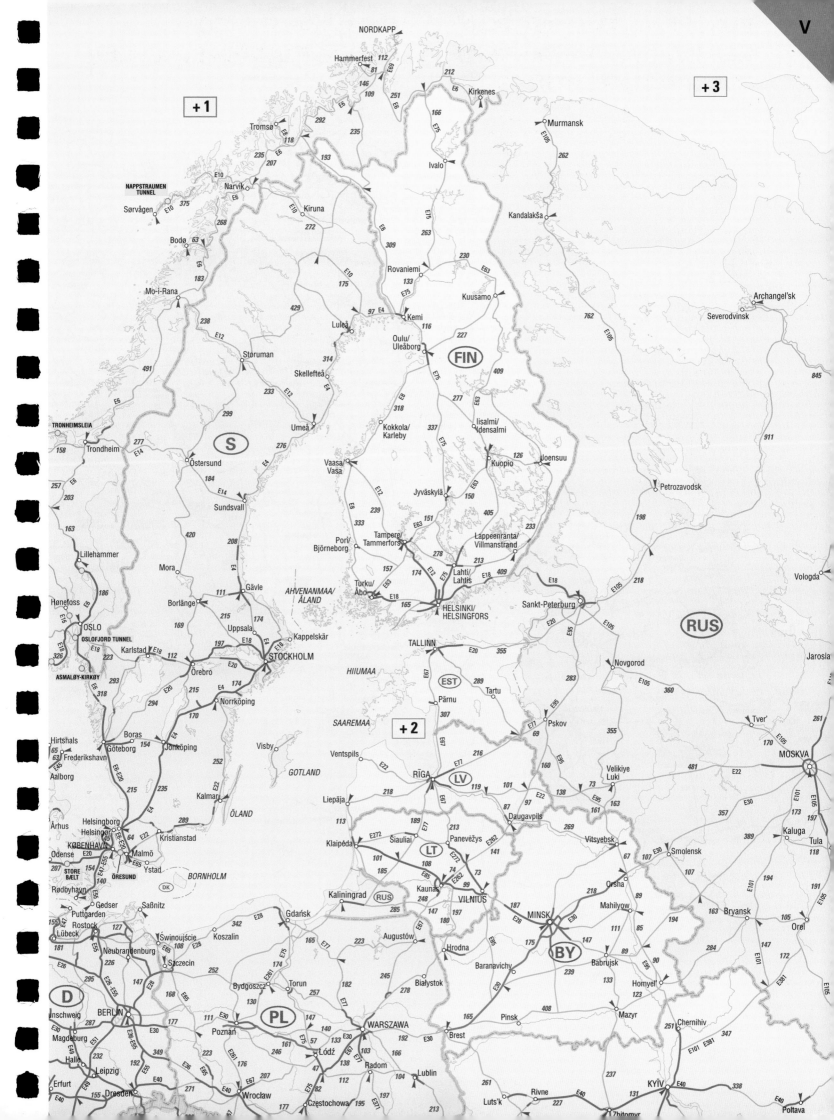

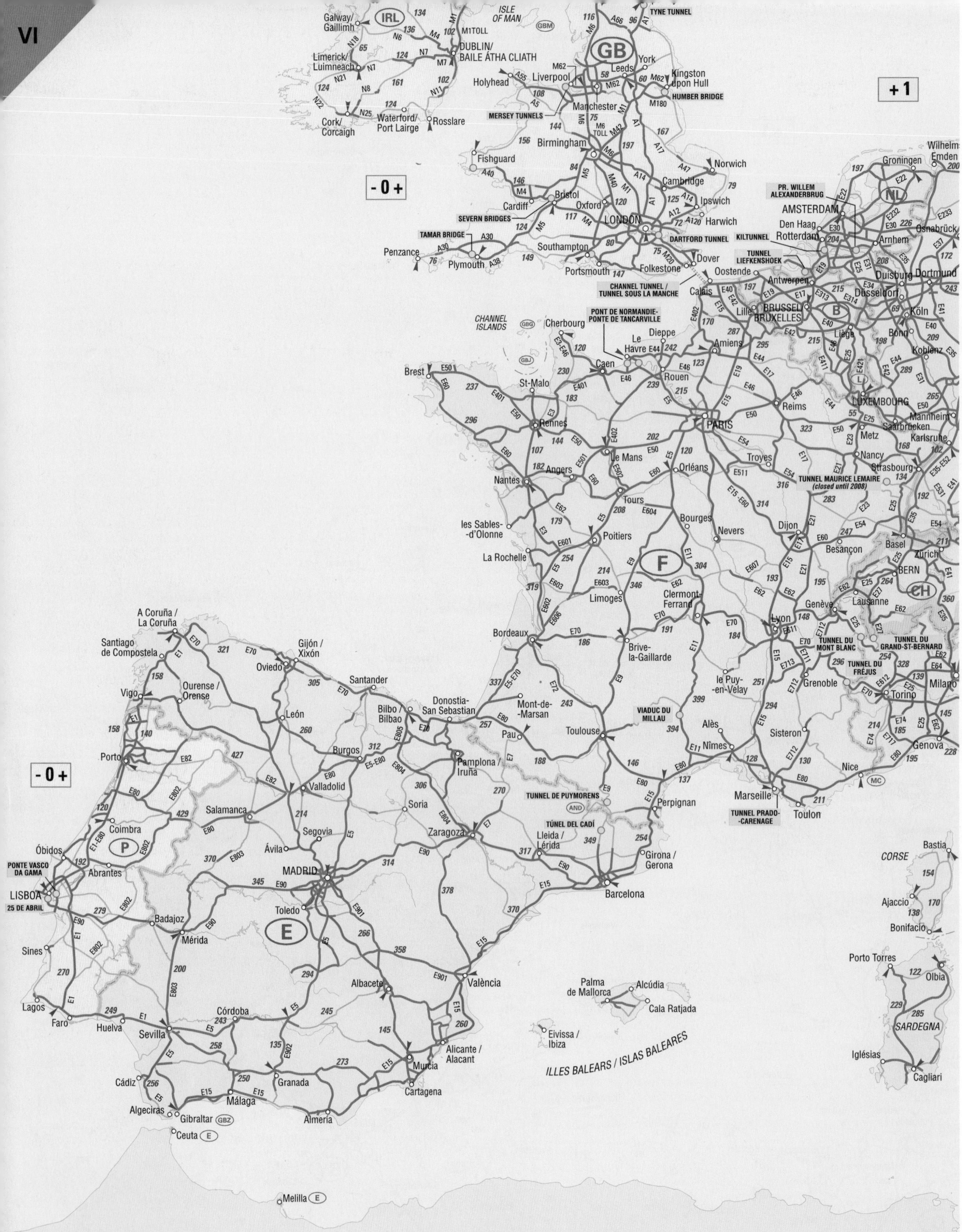

+1

-0+

Galway/ Gaillimh   IRL   134
ISLE OF MAN   GBM   116   A66   96   TYNE TUNNEL
136   M1   102   M1TOLL
N18   65   N6   124   M7   M7   102
Limerick/ Luimneach   124   N7   161   Holyhead   A55   Liverpool   58   60   York
N21   N8   M7   102   DUBLIN/ BAILE ÁTHA CLIATH   M62   Leeds   M62   Kingston upon Hull
N22   124   124   N11   M62   108   A5   75   M180   HUMBER BRIDGE
Cork/ Corcaigh   N25   Waterford/ Port Lairge   Rosslare   144   Manchester   M6 TOLL   M42   A1   167
156   Birmingham   84   M5   M40   M1   197   A12   Norwich   79
Fishguard   146   M4   120   Oxford   A1   125   A14   Ipswich
Cardiff   Bristol   117   M4   LONDON   A120   Harwich
SEVERN BRIDGES   124   M5   A120   Antwerpen
TAMAR BRIDGE   A30   80   M20   Dover   197   Lille   BRUSSEL/ BRUXELLES
Penzance   A30   Southampton   147   Folkestone   Oostende   Calais   E40
76   Plymouth   A38   149   Portsmouth   CHANNEL TUNNEL / TUNNEL SOUS LA MANCHE

AMSTERDAM   NL
Groningen   E22   Wilhelmshaven   Emden   200
PR. WILLEM ALEXANDERBRUG   197   E30   Osnabrück   E233
KILTUNNEL   Den Haag   204   Arnhem   226   E37   172
TUNNEL LIEFKENSHOEK   Rotterdam   208   Duisburg   Dortmund   243
B   E313   215   Düsseldorf   69   E41
Liège   198   Köln   E40   209
L   LUXEMBOURG   289   Koblenz   E35
287   Amiens   295   55   Mannheim   265
CHANNEL ISLANDS   GBG   Cherbourg   120   Le Havre   E44   242   Reims   E50   Metz   Karlsruhe   168   102
GBJ   Dieppe   230   Rouen   239   215   E54   Nancy   Strasbourg   134
Brest   E50   St-Malo   183   Caen   E46   Troyes   E17   Saarbrücken   192
237   E401   296   Rennes   144   E50   PARIS   323   TUNNEL MAURICE LEMAIRE (closed until 2008)   E35-E52
107   Le Mans   202   E50   Orléans   E511   316   283   Basel   211
182   Angers   E501   120   E54   Dijon   247   Zürich
Nantes   E62   179   Tours   208   E604   Bourges   Nevers   E60   Besançon   BERN   360
les Sables- d'Olonne   E601   254   Poitiers   214   E21   304   Limoges   193   195   Genève   Lausanne   E62   264   CH
La Rochelle   319   E603   346   Clermont- Ferrand   E62   Lyon   148   TUNNEL DU MONT BLANC   TUNNEL DU GRAND-ST-BERNARD
E602   Limoges   E70   191   E11   184   296   TUNNEL DU FRÉJUS   328   139   Milano
Bordeaux   E70   186   Brive- la-Gaillarde   le Puy- en-Velay   251   Grenoble   E25   Torino   E64
337   E72   243   VIADUC DU MILLAU   399   294   214   185   Genova   228
Mont-de- Marsan   257   Pau   188   Alès   394   Nîmes   128   Sisteron   130   Nice   195
Toulouse   146   E80   137   E9   Marseille   211   MC
TUNNEL DE PUYMORENS   AND   Perpignan   TUNNEL PRADO -CARENAGE   Toulon

A Coruña / La Coruña   E70   321   E70   Gijón / Xixón   Santander   BERN
Santiago de Compostela   E1   158   Oviedo   305   E70   Donostia- San Sebastian   CORSE   Bastia
Vigo   E1   Ourense / Orense   León   260   Bilbo / Bilbao   E20   Ajaccio   154   170
158   140   312   Burgos   Pamplona / Iruña   E804   306   270   138   Bonifacio
Porto   E82   427   Valladolid   E5-E80   Soria   E90   Porto Torres   Olbia
-0+   E80   E802   Salamanca   214   Segovia   Zaragoza   E7   317   Girona / Gerona   229   285   SARDEGNA
120   Coimbra   429   370   E803   Ávila   314   Lleida / Lérida   349   254   Barcelona   Iglésias   122
P   192   Abrantes   345   MADRID   378   E15   Cagliari
PONTE VASCO DA GAMA   E1-E80   E90   Toledo   370
LISBOA 25 DE ABRIL   279   E802   Badajoz   266   E5   E901
E90   Mérida   200   294   358   Albacete   València
Sines   270   E803   Córdoba   243   245   E15   ILLES BALEARS / ISLAS BALEARES
Lagos   249   E1   Sevilla   135   E902   145   260   Palma de Mallorca   Alcúdia   Cala Ratjada
Faro   Huelva   258   273   E15   Murcia   Eivissa / Ibiza
Cádiz   256   250   E15   Granada   Alicante / Alacant   Cartagena
Algeciras   E5   Málaga   Almería
Gibraltar   GBZ
Ceuta   E

Melilla   E

DRIVER INFORMATION - INFORMAZIONI UTILI
DIRECCIONES ÚTILES - INFORMATIONS UTILES
NÜTZLICHE AUSKÜNFTE

	Code	Country	🚗	☎	SOS	130	90	50	0,%‰	🚗
	A	Österreich	A, C	0043	112	130	100	50	0,5 ‰	✓
	AL	Shqipëria	B, C, D/E	00355	129	-	80	40	0,0 ‰	-
	AND	Andorra, Andorre	A, C	00376	110; 116	-	90	50	0,5 ‰	
	B	België, Belgique	A, C	0032	112	120	90-120	50	0,5 ‰	
	BG	Bălgarija	A, C, D/E	00359	166; 150	130	90	50	0,5 ‰	
	BIH	Bosna i Hercegovina	A, C, D/E	00387	92; 94	100	80	50	0,5 ‰	
	BY	Belarus'	B, C, D/E	00375	02; 03	110	90	60	0,0 ‰	
	CH	Schweiz, Suisse, Svizzera	A, C	0041	117; 144	120	80-120	50	0,5 ‰	
	CY	Kýpros, Kıbrıs	[a] A, C, E/D	00357	112	100	80	50	0,5 ‰	
	CZ	Česká Republika	A, C	00420	155	130	90	50	0,0 ‰	[b] ✓
	D	Deutschland	A, C	0049	110	130	100	50	0,5 ‰	✓
	DK	Danmark	A, C	0045	112	130	80	50	0,5 ‰	✓
	E	España	A, C	0034	112	120	90-120	50	0,5 ‰	-
	EST	Eesti	A/B, C	00372	112	110	90-110	50	0,0 ‰	✓
	F	France	A, C	0033	17; 112	130	90-110	50	0,5 ‰	✓
	FIN	Suomi, Finland	A, C	00358	112	120	80-100	50	0,5 ‰	✓
	FL	Fürstentum Liechtenstein	A, C	00423	117; 144	-	80	50	0,8 ‰	
	GB	Great Britain and N. Ireland	A, C	0044	999; 112	112 (70 mph)	96 (60 mph)	48 (30 mph)	0,8 ‰	
	GR	Hellas	A, C	0030	100; 112	120	90-110	50	0,5 ‰	-
	H	Magyarország	A, C	0036	104	130	90-100	50	0,0 ‰	✓
	HR	Hrvatska	A, C	00385	94; 92	130	80-90	50	0,0 ‰	✓
	I	Italia	A, C	0039	112; 118	130	90-110	50	0,5 ‰	✓
	IRL	Ireland	A, C	00353	112	120	100	50	0,8 ‰	-
	IS	Ísland	A, C	00354	112	-	80-90	50	0,5 ‰	✓
	L	Lëtzebuerg, Luxembourg	A, C	00352	112	130	90	50	0,8 ‰	✓
	LT	Lietuva	A, C	00370	112	110	90	50	0,0 ‰	✓
	LV	Latvija	A/B, C	00371	112	110	90	50	0,5 ‰	✓
	M	Malta	A, C	00356	191; 196	-	80	50	0,8 ‰	-
	MC	Principauté de Monaco	A, C	00377	17; 931 530 15	-	50	50	0,5 ‰	
	MD	Moldova	B, C, D	00373	902; 903	-	90	40	0,0 ‰	
	MK	Makedonija	A, C, D	00389	192; 194	120	80	50	0,5 ‰	✓
	MNE	Crna Gora	A, C, D	00381	92; 94	-	80	40	0,5 ‰	✓
	N	Norge	A, C	0047	112; 113	100	80	50	0,2 ‰	✓
	NL	Nederland	A, C	0031	112	120	80-100	50	0,5 ‰	-
	P	Portugal	A, C	00351	112	120	90-100	50	0,5 ‰	-
	PL	Polska	A, C	0048	112; 999	130	90-100	50	0,2 ‰	[b] ✓
	RO	România	A/B, C, D/E	0040	112; 955	120	90	50	0,0 ‰	
	RUS	Rossija	B, C, D/E	007	02; 03	110	90	60	0,0 ‰	✓
	S	Sverige	A, C	0046	112	110	70-90	50	0,2 ‰	✓
	SK	Slovensko	A, C	00421	112	130	90	60	0,0 ‰	[b] ✓
	SLO	Slovenija	A, C	00386	112	130	90-100	50	0,5 ‰	✓
	SRB	Srbija	[a] A, C, D	00381	92; 94	120	80-100	60	0,5 ‰	✓
	TR	Türkiye Cumhuriyeti	A, C, D	0090	155; 112	120	90	50	0,5 ‰	-
	UA	Ukraїna	B, C, D	0038	02; 03	130	90-110	60	0,0 ‰	-

EU

[a] Green cards are not accepted in Northern Cyprus and Kosovo (Serbia)

[b] in winter

	🕐	€	ℹ️	🌐
	+1	Euro (€)	0810 101 818	www.austria.info/
	+1	Lek (ALL)	4 258 323	www.albaniantourism.com/
	+1	Euro (€)	827 117	www.andorra.ad/
	+1	Euro (€)	25 040 390	www.visitbelgium.com/
	+2	Lev (BGN)	29 335 845	www.bulgariatravel.org/
	+1	Konvertibilna Marka (BAM)	33 252 924	www.bhtourism.ba/
	+2	Belarus Rouble (BYR)	172 269 971	www.belarus-misc.org/
	+1	Schweizer Franken (CHF)	432 105 500	www.myswitzerland.com/
	+2	Cyprus Pound (CYP)	22 691 100	www.visitcyprus.org.cy/
	+1	Koruna Česká (CZK)	221 580 111	www.czechtourism.com/
	+1	Euro (€)	(0)69 751 903	www.germany-tourism.de/
	+1	Danske Krone (DKK)	32 889 923	www.visitdenmark.com/
	+1	Euro (€)	913 433 500	www.spain.info/
	+2	Kroon (EEK)	645 7777	www.visitestonia.com/
	+1	Euro (€)	(0)142 967 000	other.franceguide.com/
	+2	Euro (€)	(0)106 058 000	www.visitfinland.com/
	+1	Schweizer Franken (CHF)	2 396 300	www.tourismus.li/
	0	Pound Sterling (GBP)	020 8846 9000	www.visitbritain.com/
	+2	Euro (€)	2 108 707 000	www.gnto.gr/
	+1	Forint (HUF)	1 4388080	www.hungary.com/
	+1	Kuna (HRK)	1 469 9333	www.croatia.hr/
	+1	Euro (€)	06 49711	www.enit.it/
	0	Euro (€)	1850230330	www.ireland.ie/
	0	Íslensk Króna (ISK)	5 355 500	www.visiticeland.com/
	+1	Euro (€)	42 82821	www.ont.lu/
	+2	Litas (LTL)	52 629 660	www.travel.lt/
	+2	Lats (LVL)	67 224 664	www.latviatourism.lv/
	+1	Maltese Lira (MTL)	22915000	www.visitmalta.com/
	+1	Euro (€)	92166166	www.visitmonaco.com/
	+2	Leu (MDL)	22 227 620	www.turism.md/
	+1	Denar (MKD)	fax: (0)23 075 333	www.exploringmacedonia.com/
	+1	Euro (€)	812 351 558	www.visit-montenegro.com/
	+1	Norsk Krone (NOK)	24144600	www.visitnorway.com/
	+1	Euro (€)	(0)703 705 705	www.holland.com/
	0	Euro (€)	848391818	www.visitportugal.com/
	+1	Złoty (PLN)	22 63 01 736	www.poland.travel/
	+2	Leu (ROL)	0 213 149 957	www.romaniatourism.com/
	c+3	Russian Rouble (RUB)	095 207 7117	www.russiatourism.ru/
	+1	Svensk Krona (SEK)	620 150 10	www.visitsweden.com/
	+1	Slovenská Koruna (SKK)	48 41 36146	www.slovakiatourism.sk/
	+1	Euro (€)	13 064 775	www.slovenia.info/
	+1	Srpski Dinar (RSD)	0 113 230 566	www.serbia-tourism.org/
	+2	Türk Lirası (TRL)	3 122 128 300	www.tourismturkey.org/
	+2	Hrivna (UAH)	(202)2 232 228	www.traveltoukraine.org/

c Moskva

Key to table
Legenda
Leyenda
Légende
Zeichenerklärung

Required driver's papers
Documenti di guida richiesti
Documentos requeridos para conducir
Papiers de conduire requis
Erforderliche Fahrzeugpapiere

A Driver's licence
   Patente di guida
   Carné de conducir
   Permis de conduire
   Führerschein

B International driver's licence
   Patente di guida internazionale
   Carné de conducir internacional
   Permis international de conduire
   Internationaler Führerschein

C Log-book
   Carta di circolazione
   Carné de circulación
   Permis de circulation
   Kraftfahrzeugschein

D Green card
   Carta verde
   Carta verde
   Carte verte
   Grüne Versicherungskarte

E Special insurance
   Assicurazione speciale
   Seguro especial
   Assurance spéciale
   Spezialversicherung

International code
Prefisso internazionale
Prefijo telefónico internacional
Indicatif international
Internationale Vorwahl

Emergency numbers
Numeri d'emergenza
Números de emergencia
Numéros d'urgence
Notrufnummern

Tourist office numbers
Numeri degli uffici turistici
Números de las oficinas de turismo
Numéros des bureaux de tourisme
Touristenämternummern

🌐

Tourist office websites
Siti web degli uffici turistici
Sitios web de las oficinas de turismo
Sites web des bureaux de tourisme
Touristenämterwebsites

 (km/h)

Speed limit on motorway
Limite di velocità in autostrada
Límite de velocidad en autopista
Limite de vitesse sur l'autoroute
Höchstgeschwindigkeit auf der Autobahn

 (km/h)

Speed limit outside the towns
Limite di velocità su strade extraurbane
Límite de velocidad en carreteras extraurbanas
Höchstgeschwindigkeit außerhalb der Städte
Limite de vitesse sur les routes extra-urbaines

 (km/h)

Speed limit in towns
Limite di velocità nei centri abitati
Límite de velocidad en ciudades
Limite de vitesse dans les villes
Höchstgeschwindigkeit innerhalb der Städte

Maximum permitted alcohol level
Tasso alcolemico massimo tollerato
Límite alcoólico màximo consentido
Taux d'alcoolémie maximum admis
Höchsterlaubte Blutalkoholgehalt

Lights on during the day
Obbligo luci accese di giorno
Encender los faros durante el dia
Feux allumés obligatoires de jour
Licht-Pflicht am Tag

Time zone from Greenwich
Fuso orario da Greenwich
Huso horario de Greenwich
Fuseaux horaires de Greenwich
Zeitzone gegenüber Greenwich

Local currency
Valuta locale
Divisa local
Devise locale
Lokalwährung

Note: the table is indicative; it is advisable to check the information before leaving.
Nota: la tabella è indicativa; si consiglia di verificare le informazioni prima della partenza.
Nota: el prospecto es indicativo; se aconseja verificar las informaciones antes de partir.
Nota: le tableau est indicatif; il est conseillé de vérifier les renseignements avant de partir.
Notiz: die Informationen sind als Hinweis gedacht; es empfiehlt sich,
   die Auskünfte vor der Abfahrt zu überprüfen.

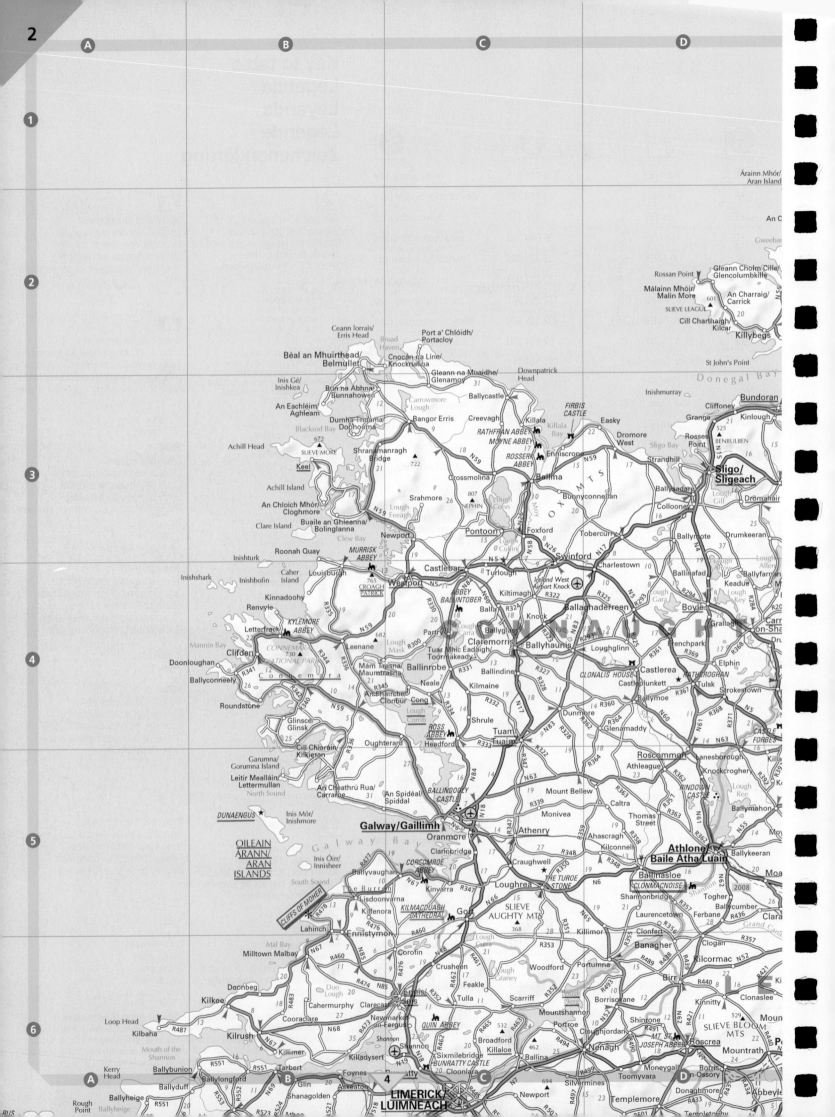

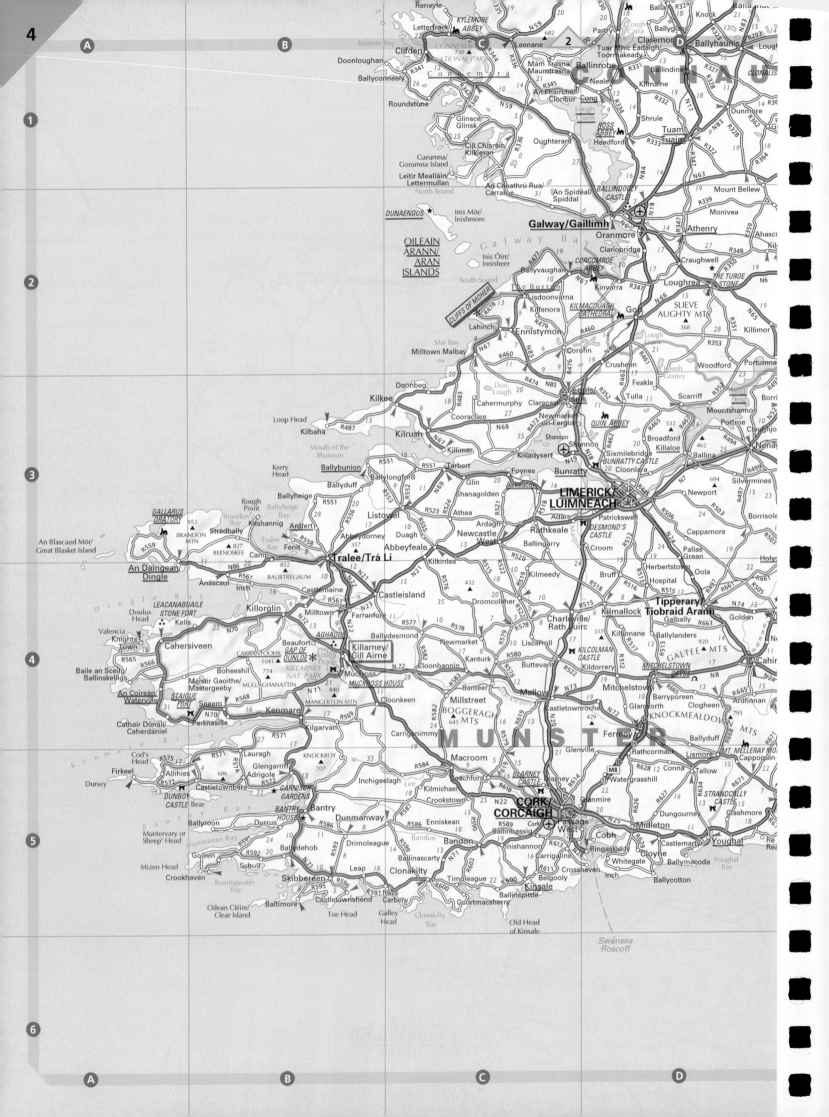

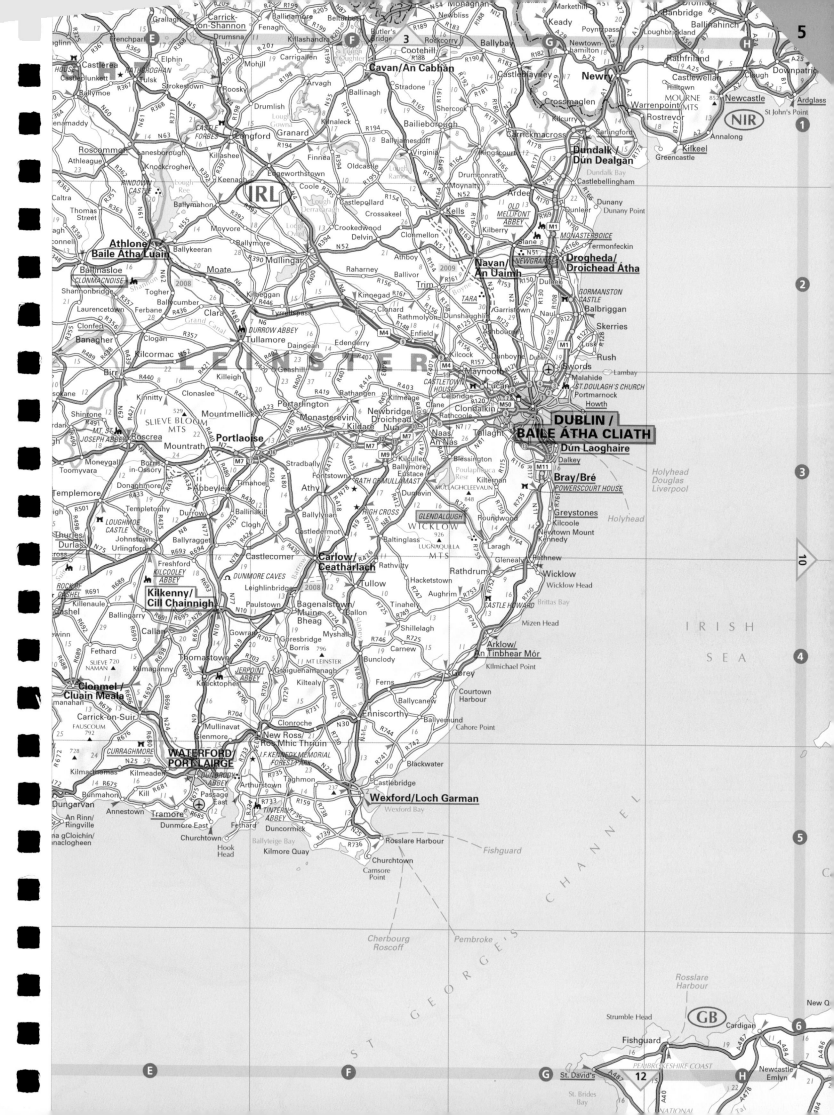

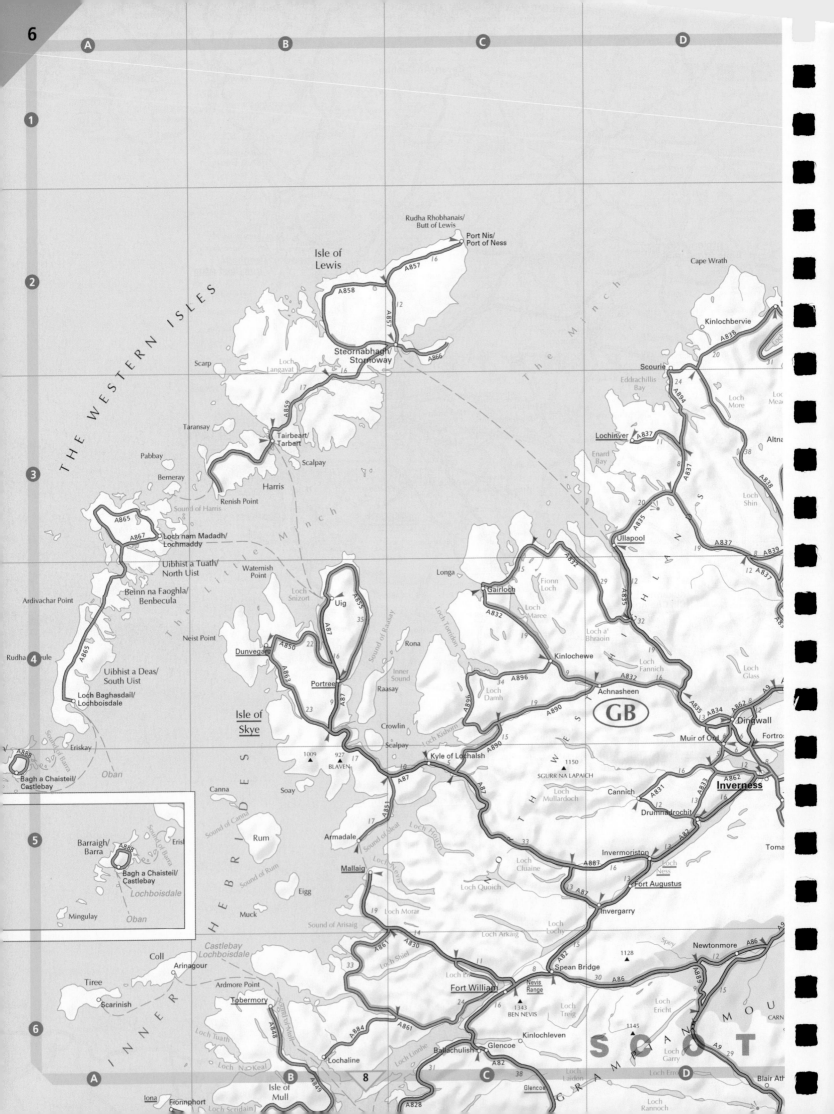

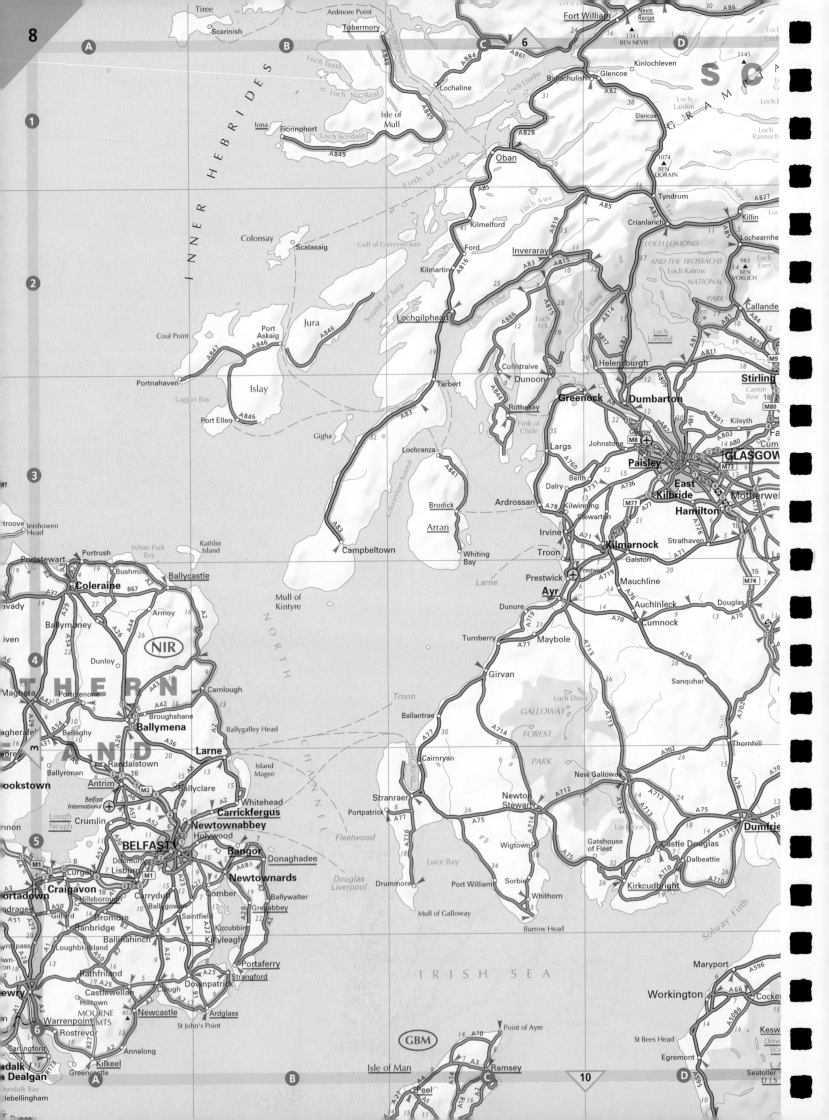

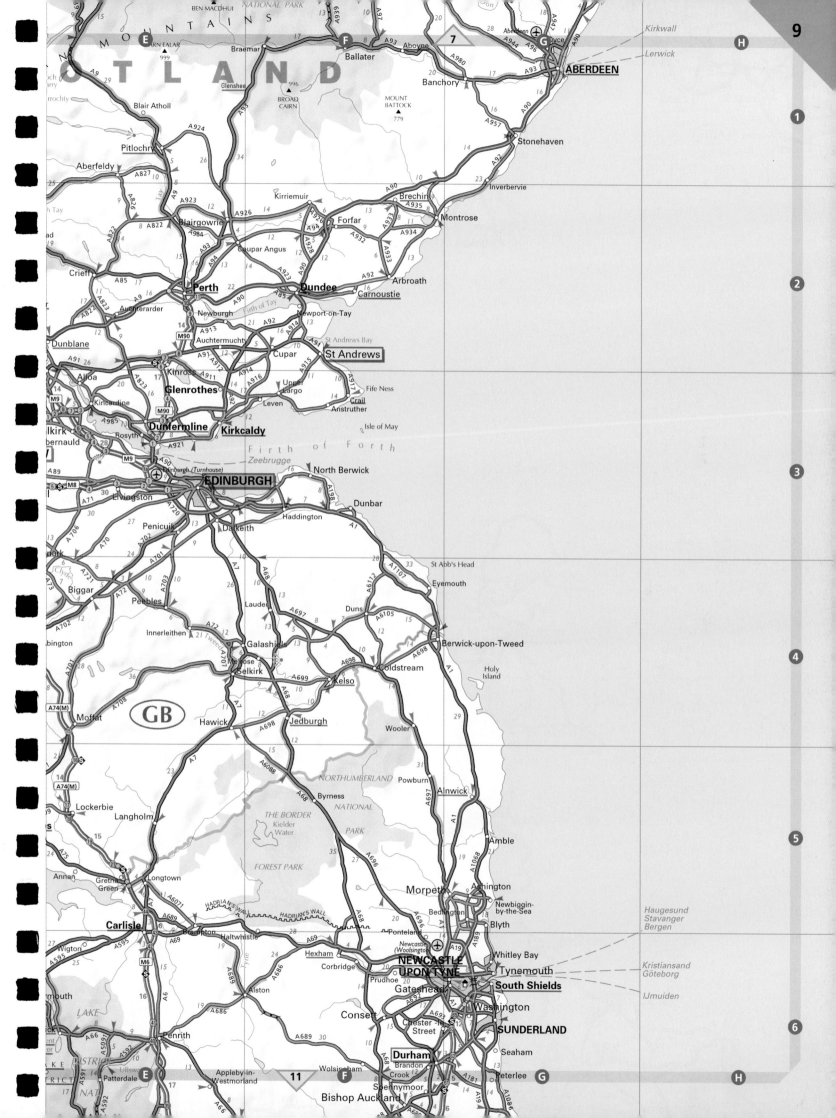

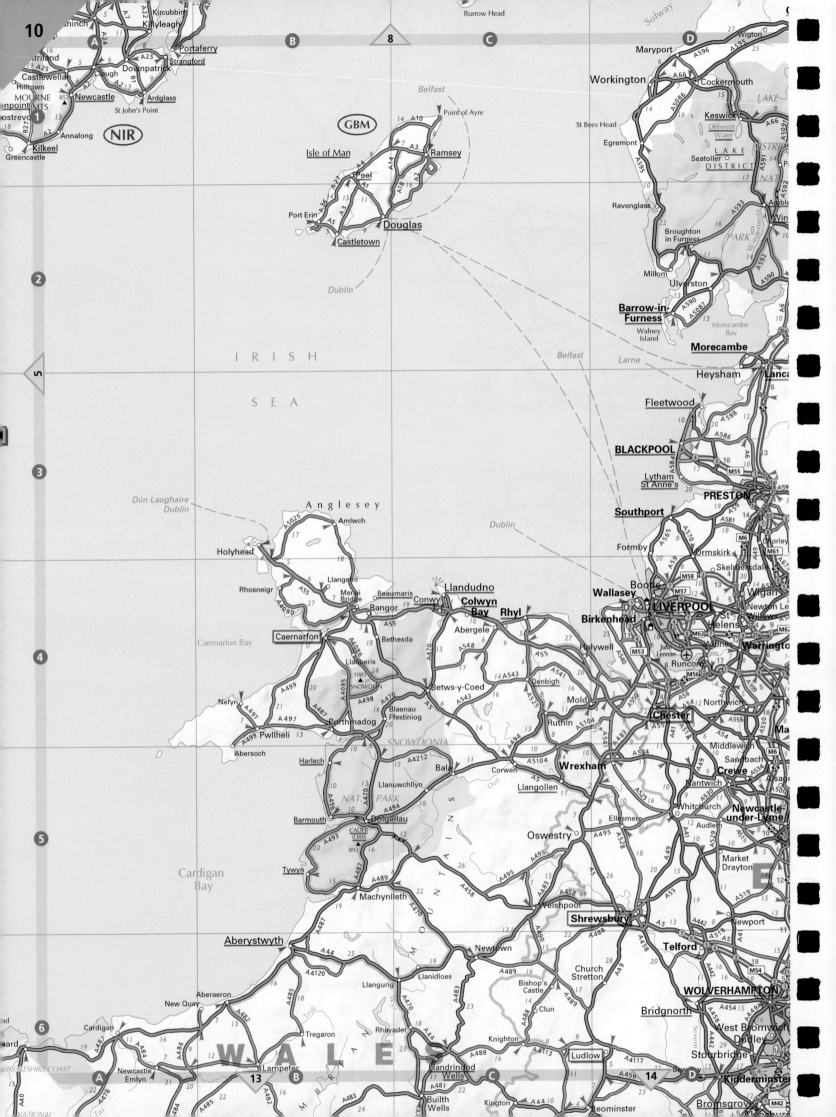

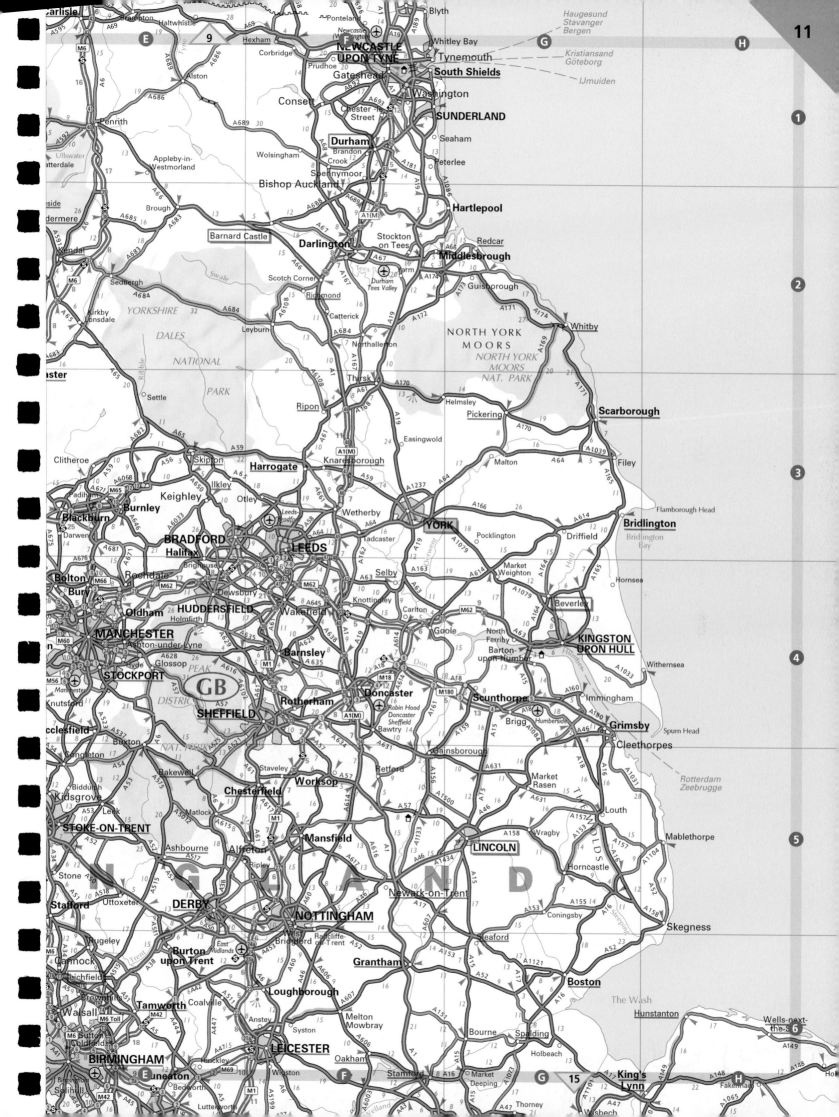

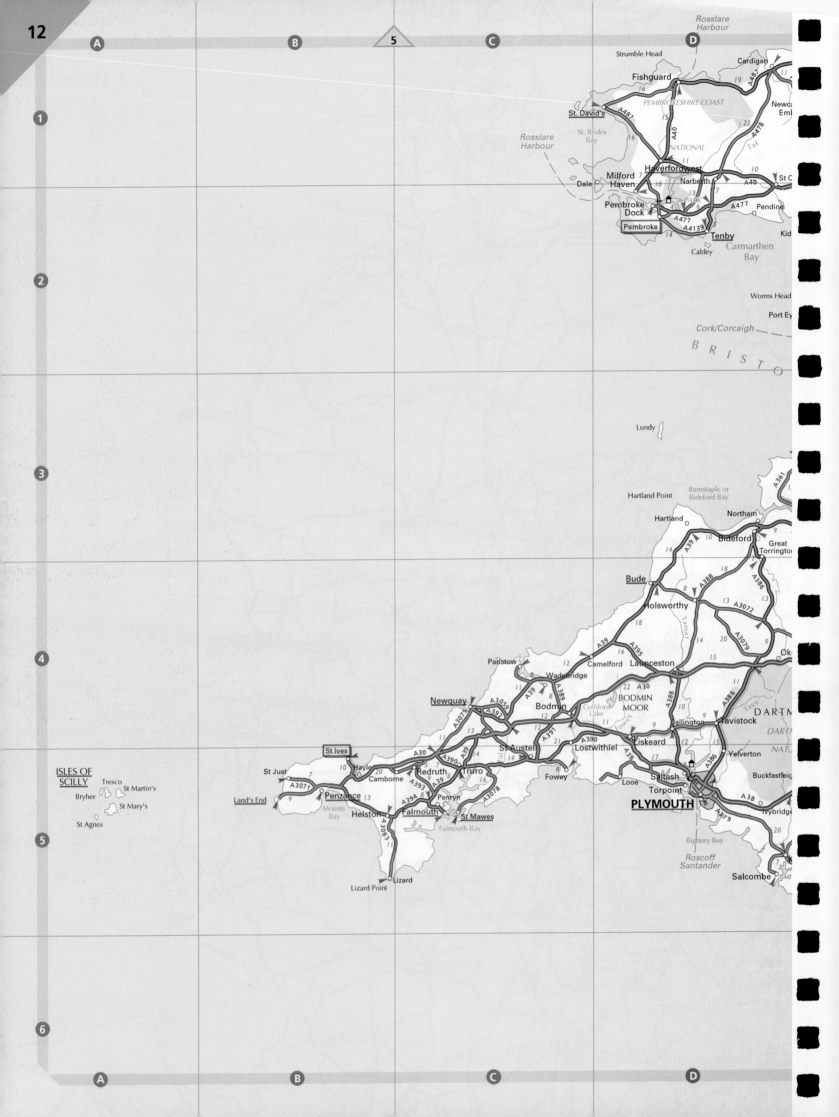

A **B** 5 **C** **D**

1

2

3

4

5

6

Rosslare
Harbour

Strumble Head
Fishguard
Cardigan
16
19 A487
St. David's
PEMBROKESHIRE COAST
A487
Newca
Emb
NATIONAL
22 A478
Haverfordwest
10
St C
Milford
Haven
10
Narberth
A40
7
Dale
A477
Pendine
Pembroke
Dock
A477
A4139
14
Pembroke
Tenby
Kid
Caldey
Carmarthen
Bay

Rosslare
Harbour

Worms Head

Port Ey

Cork/Corcaigh

B R I S T O

Lundy

Hartland Point
Barnstaple or
Bideford Bay

Hartland
Northam
10
Bideford
9
14 A39
Great
Torrington
A388
18
A386
Bude
8
13 A3072 13
Holsworthy
18
A39
16 A395
14
20 A3079 9
Ök
A388
15
11
Padstow
12
Camelford
Launceston
A386
Wadebridge
8
A39
22 A30
BODMIN
A388
10
Newquay
A3059
Bodmin
MOOR
DART
Colliford
Callington
Tavistock
A392
12
Lake
DART
13
11
A391
21
A390
Liskeard
12
15
NAT
St Ives
A30
A390
St Austell
Lostwithiel
A38
17
Yelverton
St Just
7
10
Hayle
Redruth
Truro
Fowey
Looe
Saltash
Buckfastleig
A3071
Camborne
A393 A39
16
Torpoint
ISLES OF
SCILLY
Penzance
13
A394 8
Penryn
A3078
PLYMOUTH
A38
Tresco
St Martin's
Land's End
9
Helston
Falmouth
St Mawes
A379
Ivybridge
Bryher
St Mary's
Mounts
Bay
Falmouth Bay
20
St Agnes
A3083
Bigbury Bay
Roscoff
Santander
Salcombe
Lizard
Lizard Point

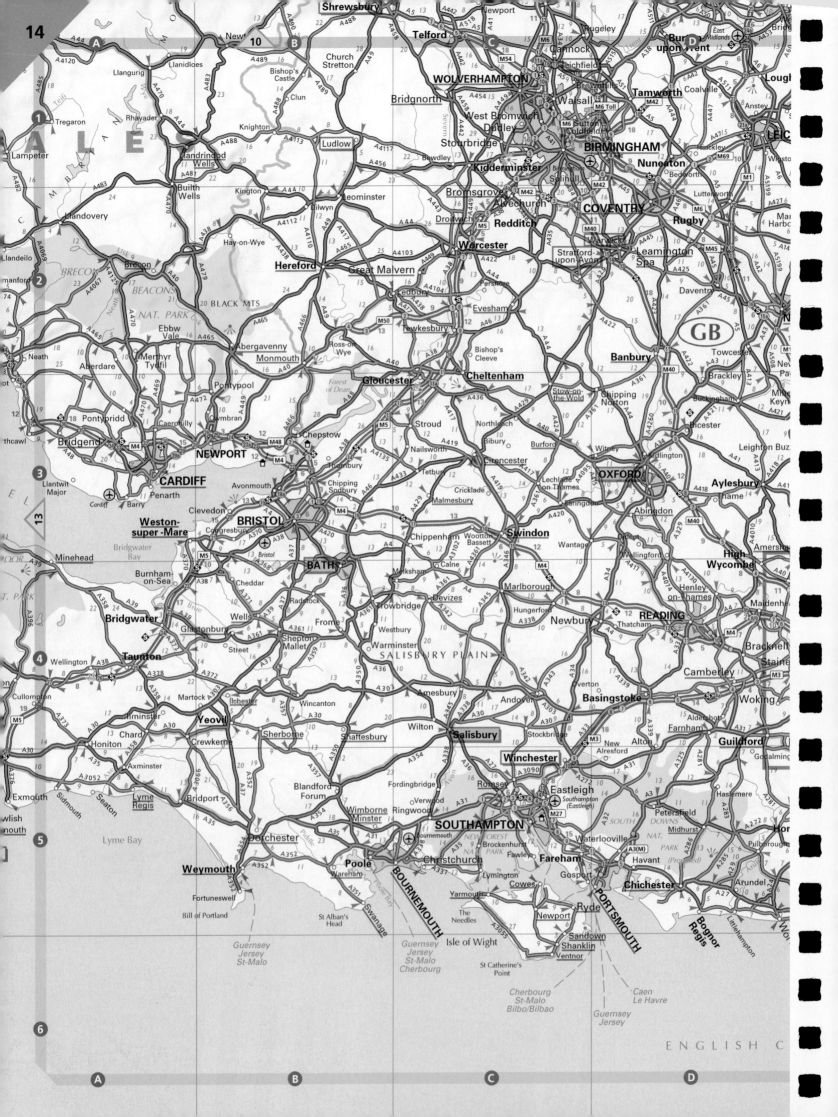

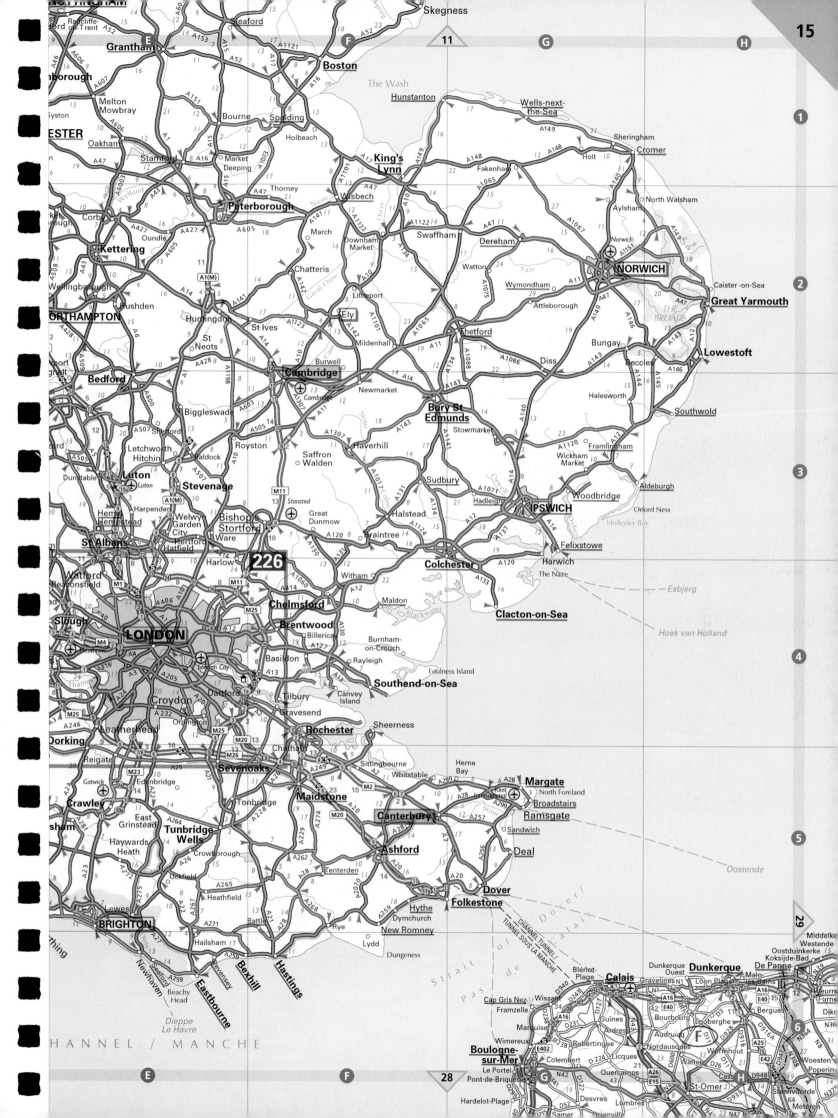

A B C D

1
2
3
4
5
6

Texel
De Koog
Den B
Qudes

Den Helder
De Kooy
Den
N250
N99
Anna
Paulow
N249
Schagen
N248

Bergen aan Zee
Bergen
Alkmaar
Huizen
N243
A9
E19
Castricum
13
N244
A7

Beverwijk
Wormerveer
Purm
IJmuiden
N8
40
207

*NATIONAAL PARK DE
KENNEMER DUINEN*

Newcastle upon Tyne

NOO
HOLL
N242

HAARLEM Zaandam
Zandvoort
101
116
Heemstede
103
115
AMSTERDAM
108
A10
Hillegom
14
A1
Noordwijk
aan Zee
Hoofddorp
A4
A9
Lisse
Schiphol
Aalsmeer
Naard
Sassenheim
Bussu
Katwijk
aan Zee
A44
Uithoorn
N201
A2
Wassenaar
Leiden
N207
N231
Wilsin
Alphen-
a/d Rijn
Hilversu
Scheveningen
Voorschoten
Harmelen
E35
Breukele
DEN HAAG
A4
Zoeterwoude
Bodegraven
E19
Zoetermeer
Poeldijk
A13
Boskoop
Woerden
A12
Hoek van
Holland
Delft
A12
E30
Oudewater
UTRECHT
Europoort
N209
E25 E30
11
Maasland
Rotterdam
E25
Gouda
Meerkerk
Brielle
A4
23
A20
Maassluis
35
N210
ROTTERDAM
Schoonhoven
Vianer
Goeree
Vlaardingen
Rhoon
Ridderkerk
Lek
N216
20
Culembo
Ouddorp
Hellevoetsluis
Barendrecht
*MOLENS VAN
KINDERDIJK*
A27
Leerdam
Spijkenisse
A15
Hendrik Ido
E311
A2
Schouwen
Stellendam
ZUID-
Ambacht
E31
Grevelingen
HOLL
Zwijndrecht
A29
Sliedrecht
A15
Burgh-Haamstede
N215
Gorinchem
Brouwershaven
Middelharnis
DORDRECHT
*NATIONA
PARK DE
BIESBOSCH*
N322
Zierikzee
N59
N59
Zaltbommel
30
A16 E19
Hank
Kingston upon Hull
Rosyth
Walcheren
Willemstad
Aalburg
Domburg
N287
Noord-
Beveland
Zijpe
N257
15
11
Made 15
Geertruidenberg
N57
Westkapelle
N288
Veere
Kamperland
A29 A59
12
Waalwijk
N286
Stavenisse
Steenbergen
N59
A27
Kaetsheuvel
Middelburg
A58
Goes
Halsteren
Zevenergen
Oosterhout
2008
Vlissingen
N254
Bergen
op Zoom
A17
BREDA
A261
Knokke-
Heist
N58
A58
Roosendaal
A16
Gilze
TILBURG
Zeebrug
R15
Kruiningen
30
A58
A65
Blankenberge
Breskens
oedeken-
skerke
A58 312
Zundert
De Haan
N34
Lissewege
Sluis
Schoondijke
Perkpolder
N133
Goirle
A58
Oostburg
N61
Hoogerheide
Oirschot

Kingston upon Hull
Harwich

ZEELAND

de

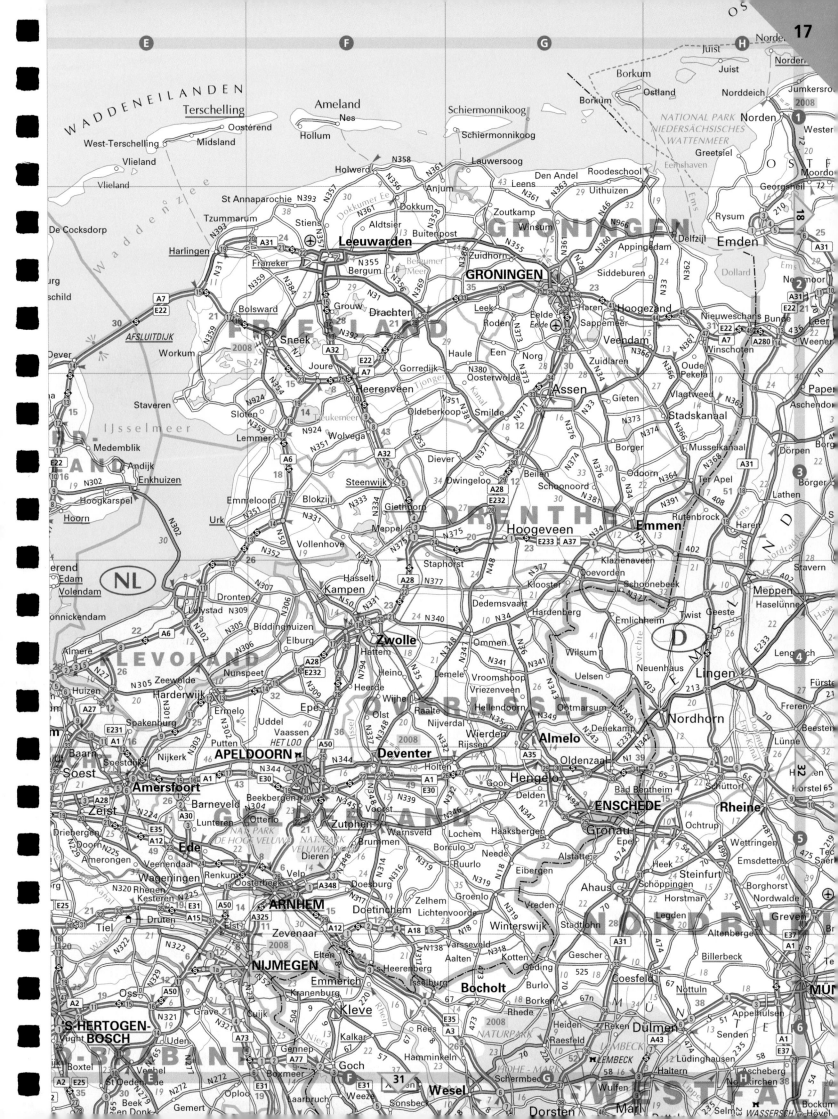

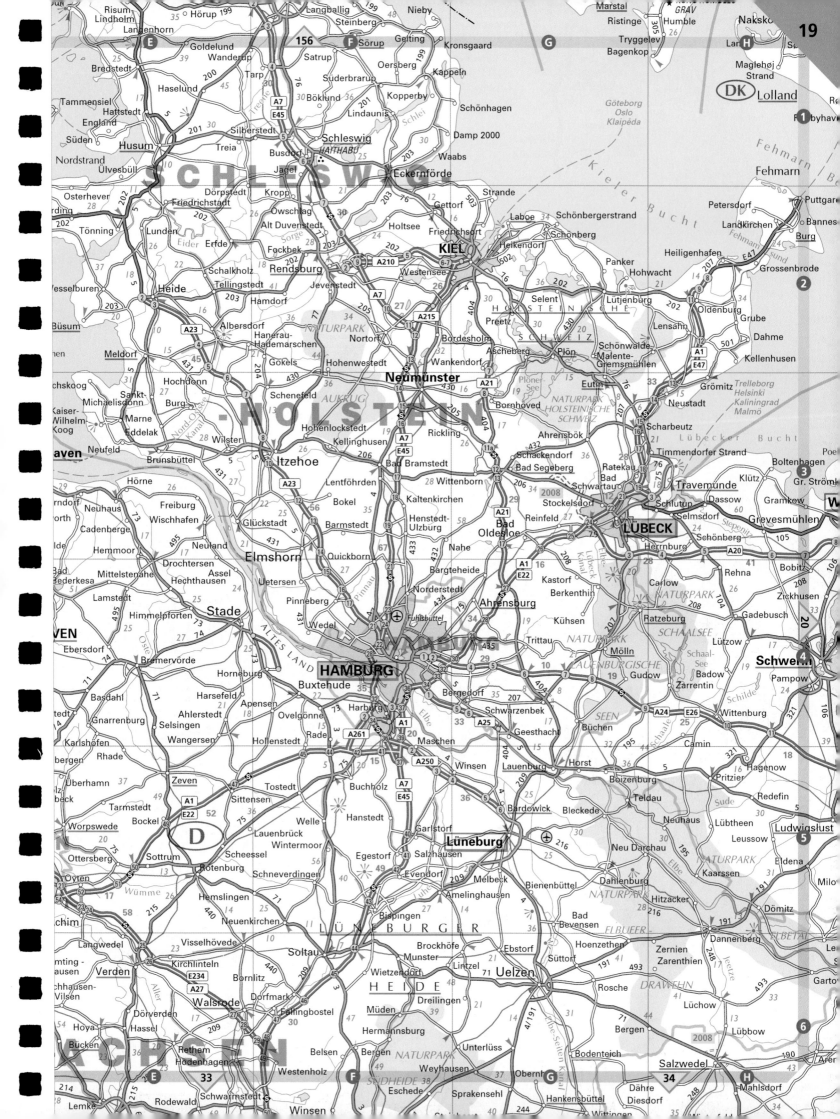

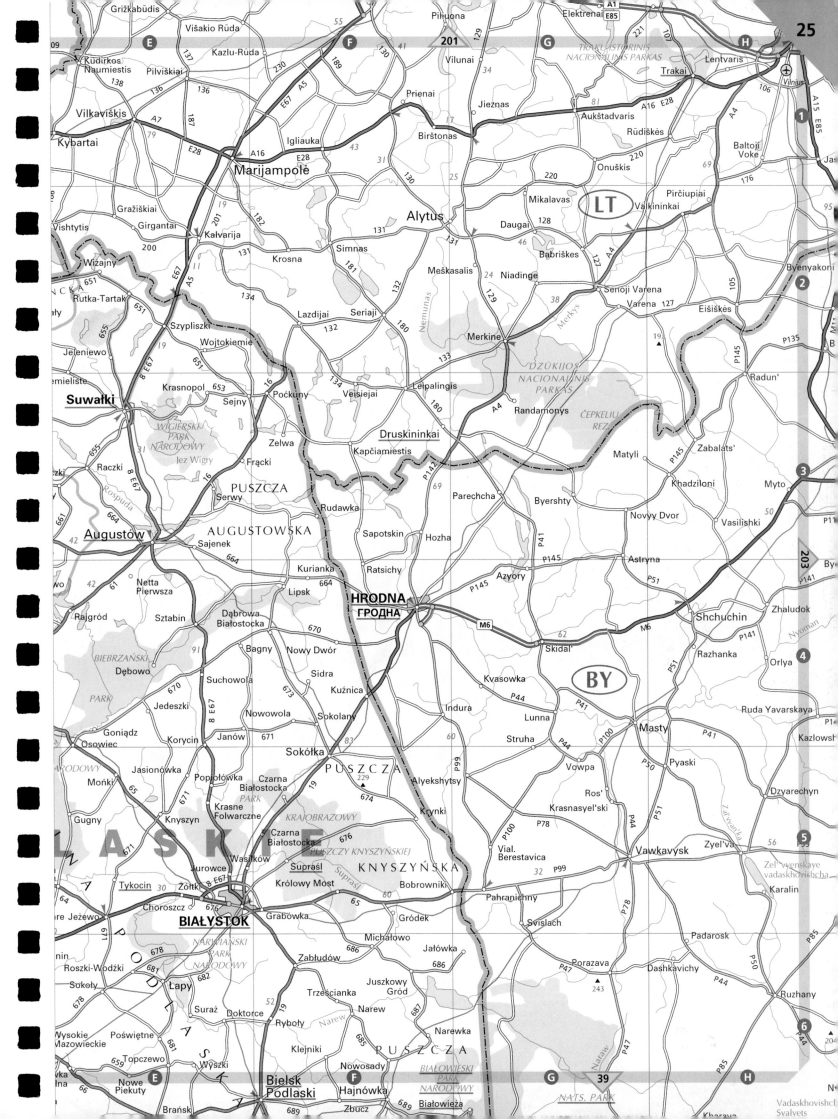

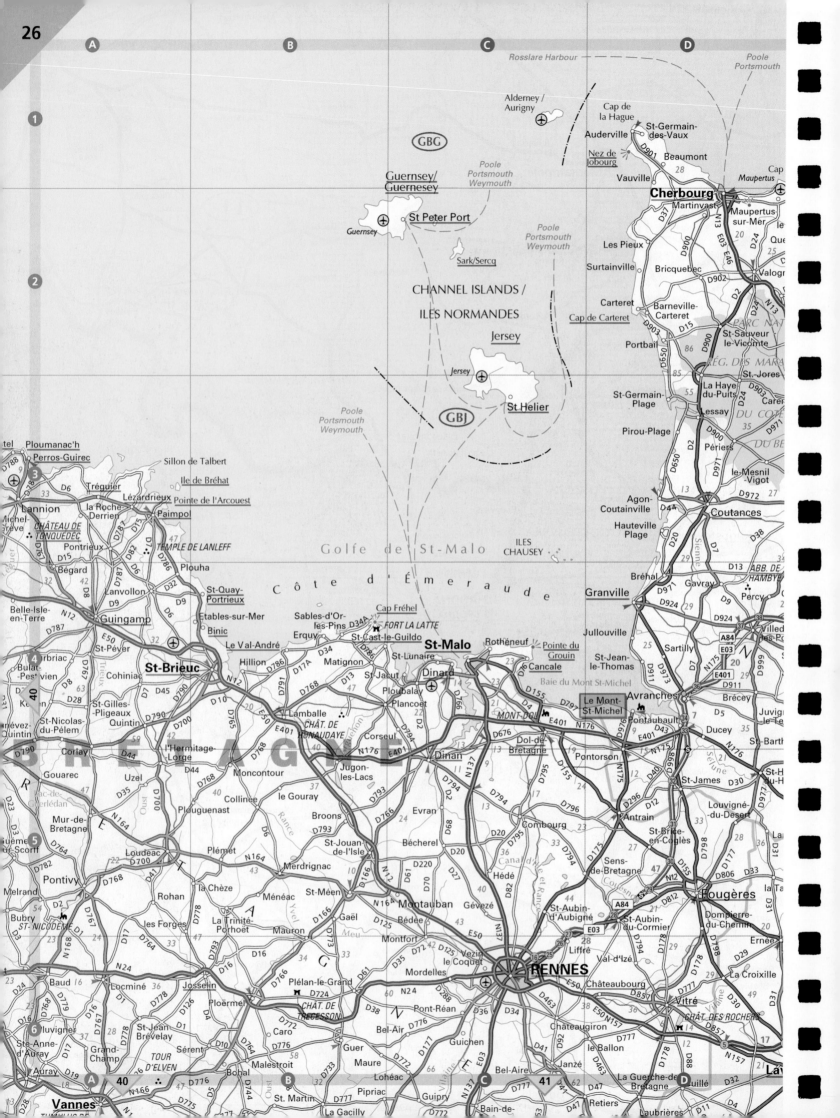

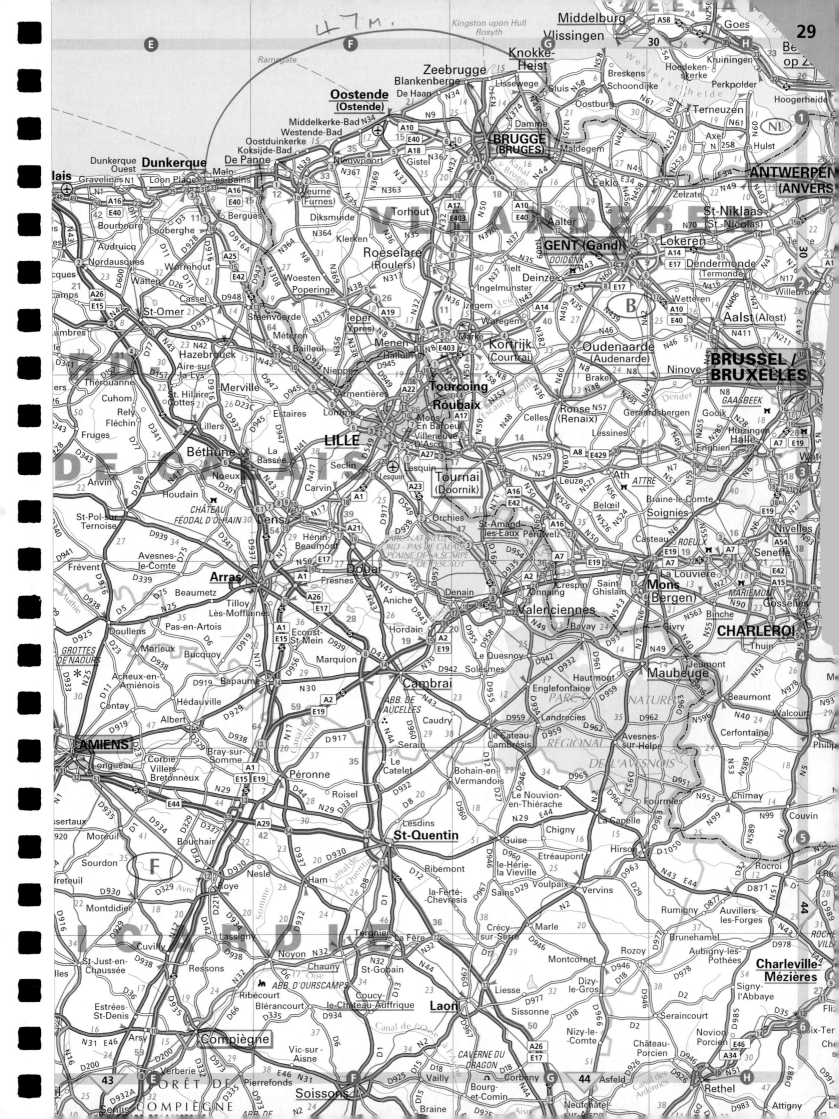

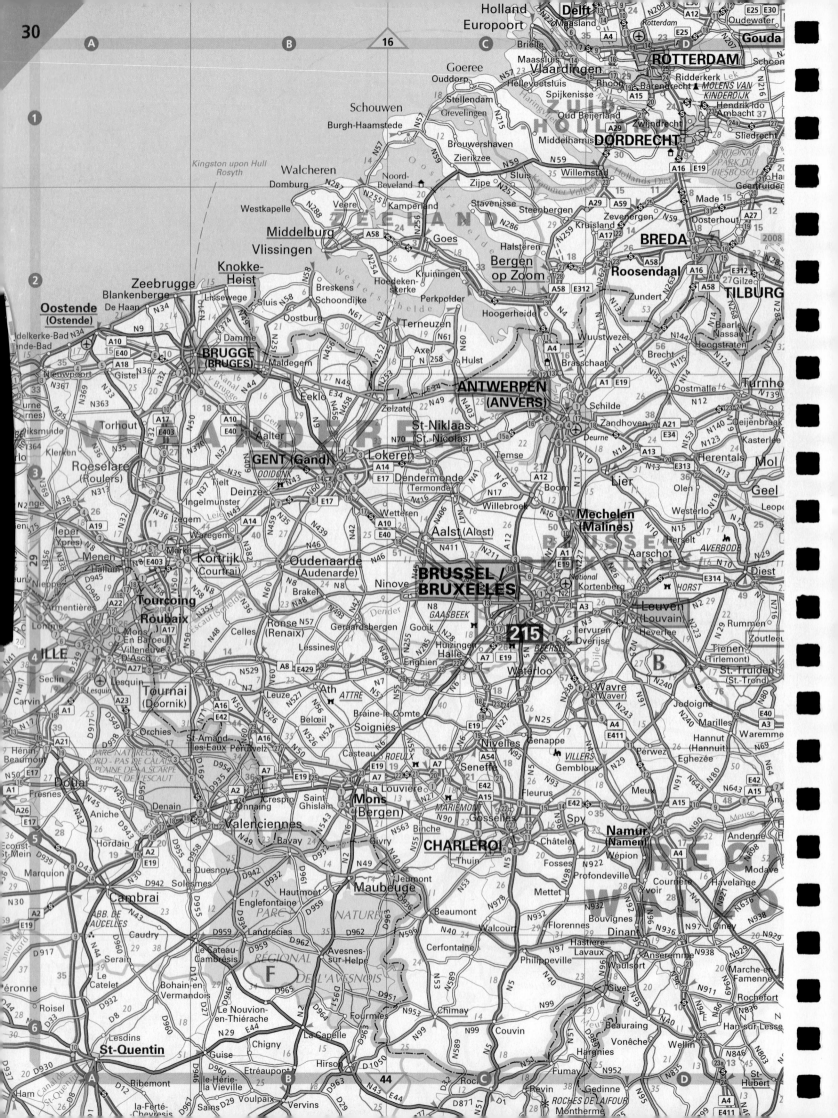

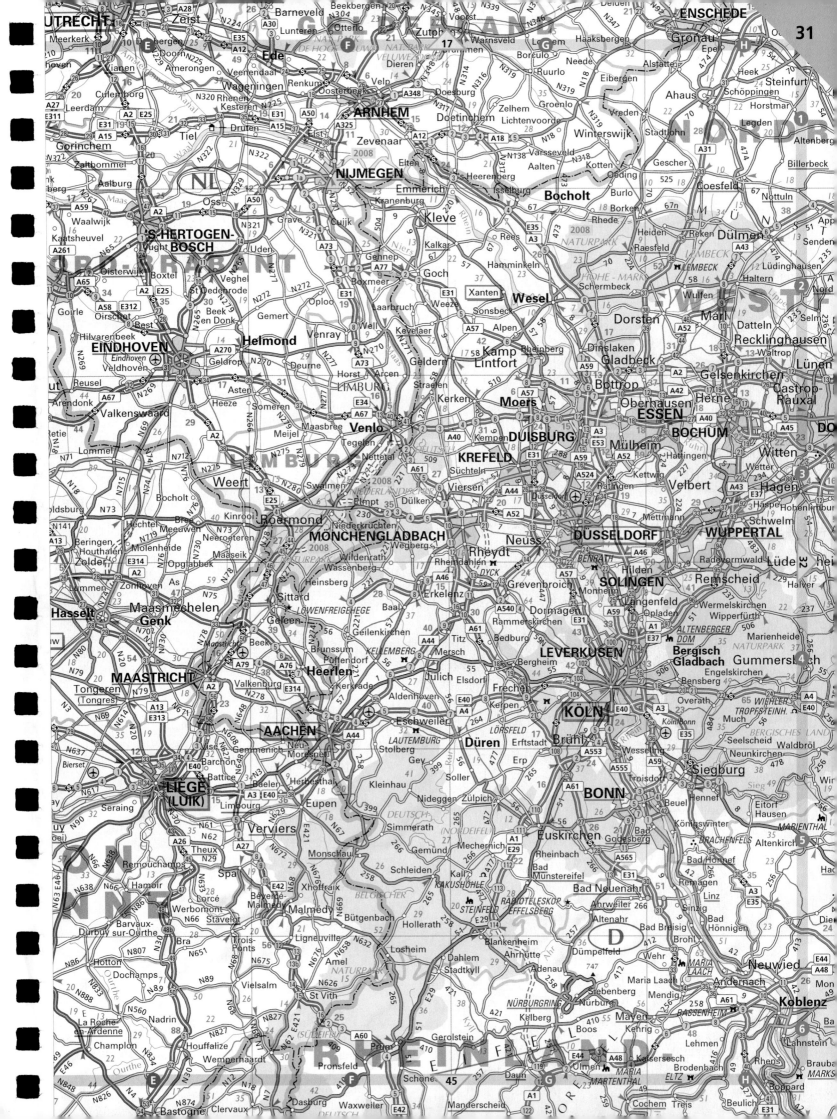

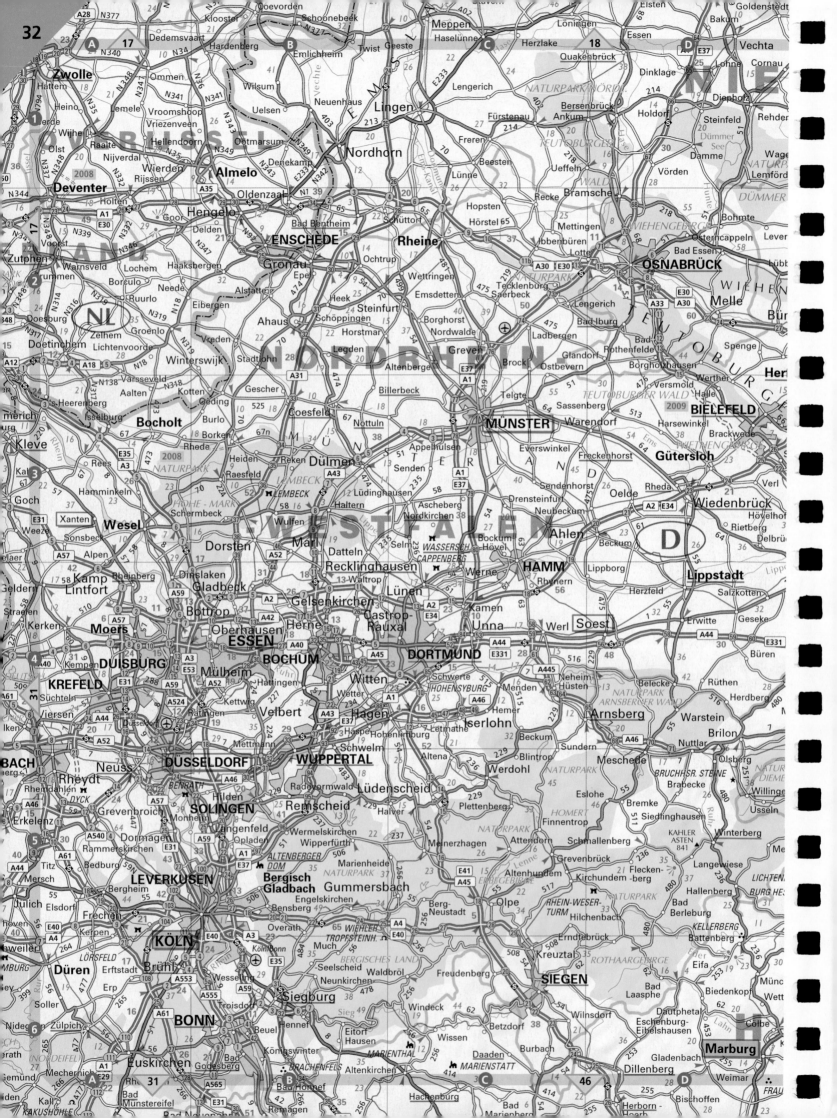

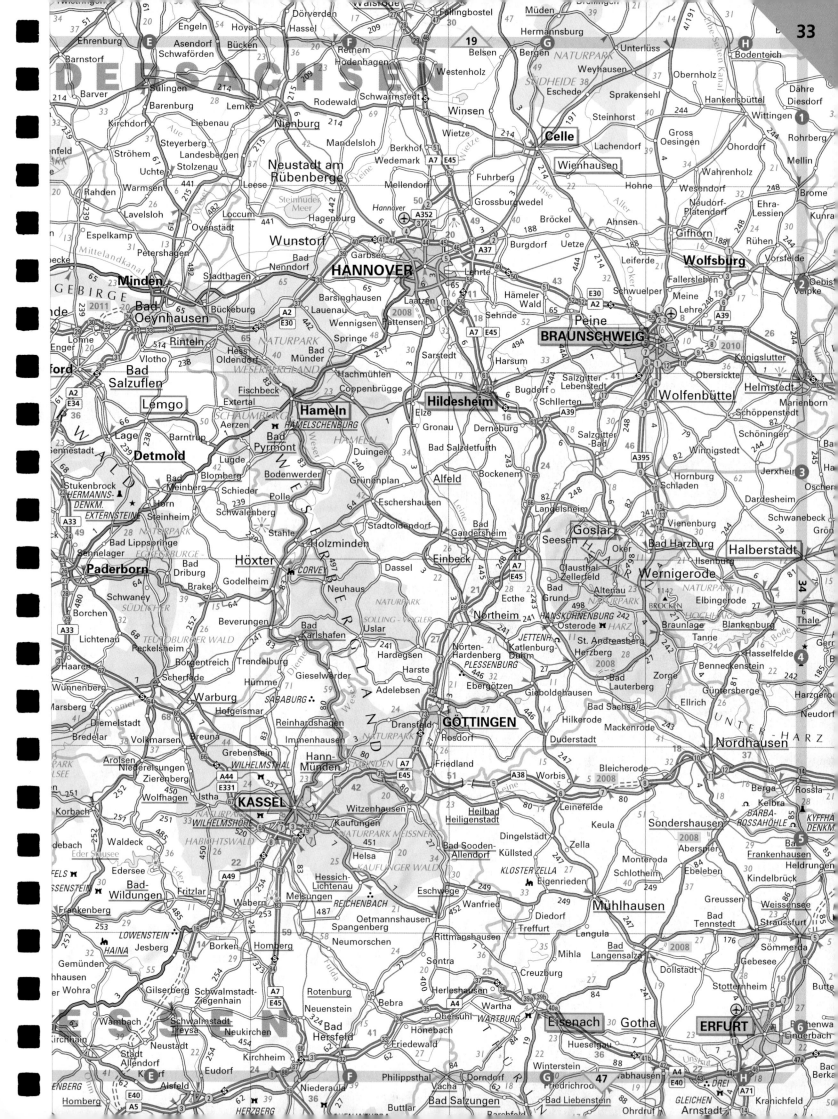

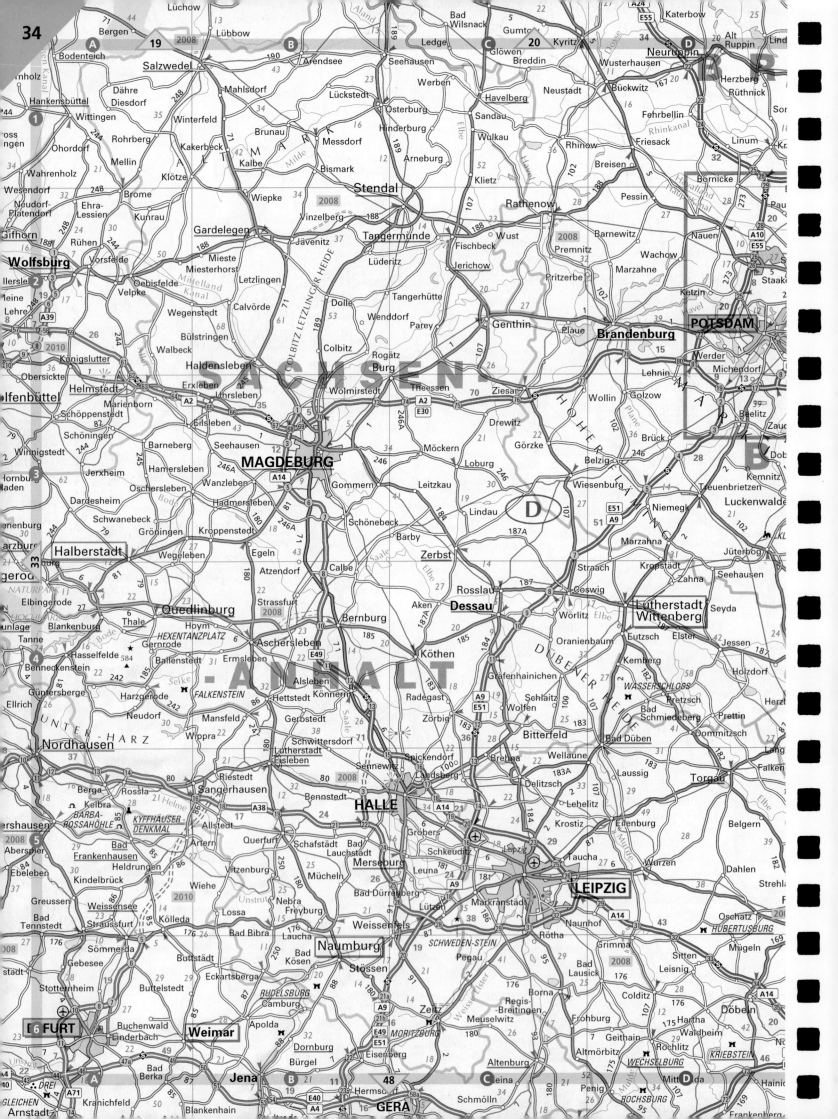

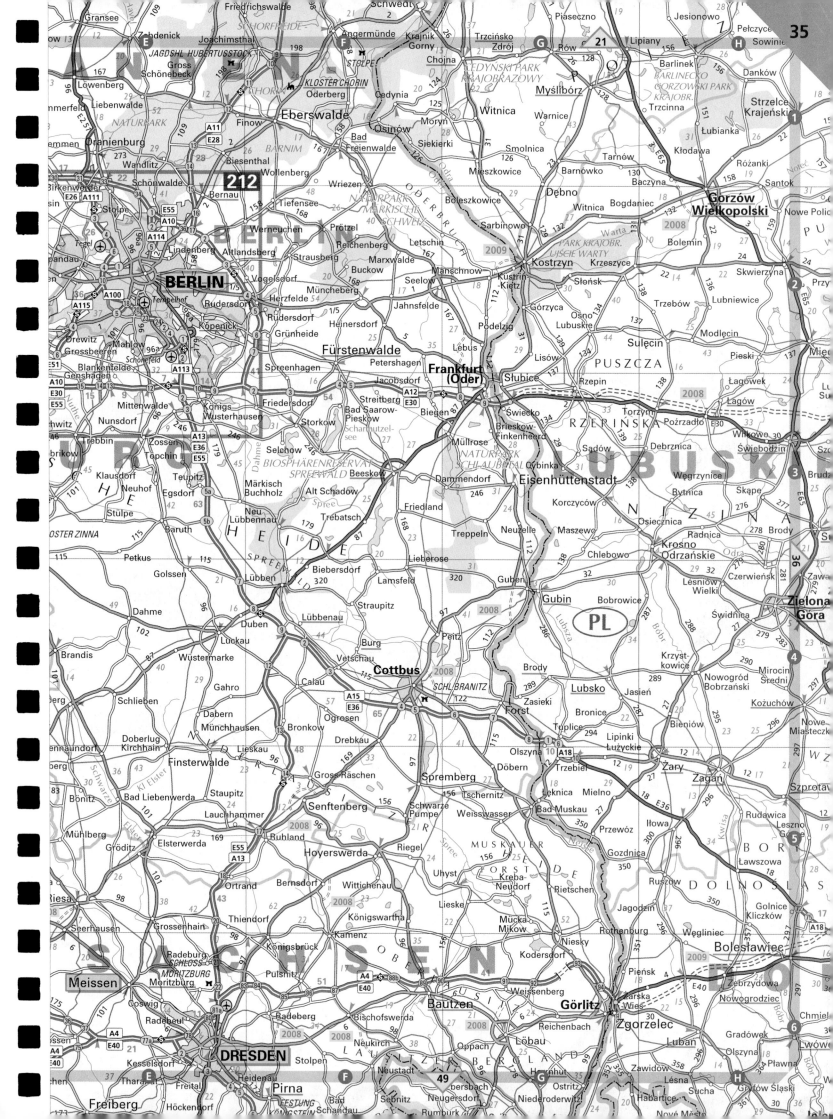

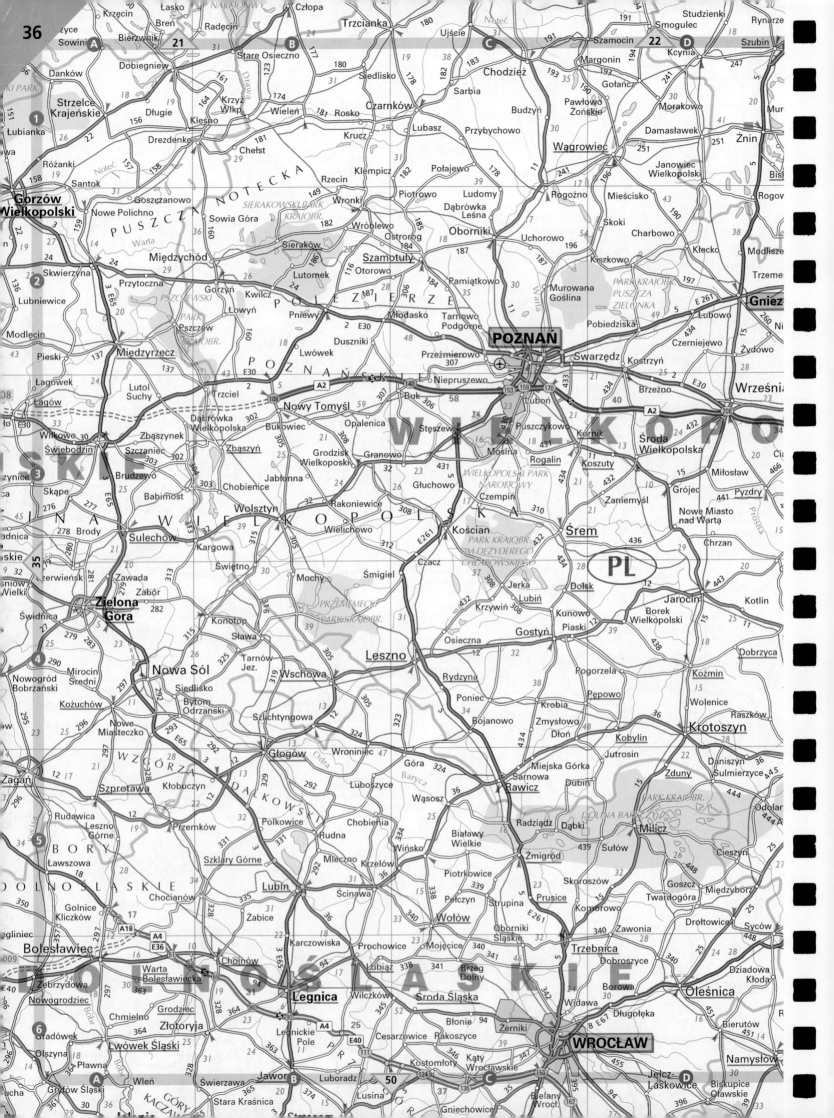

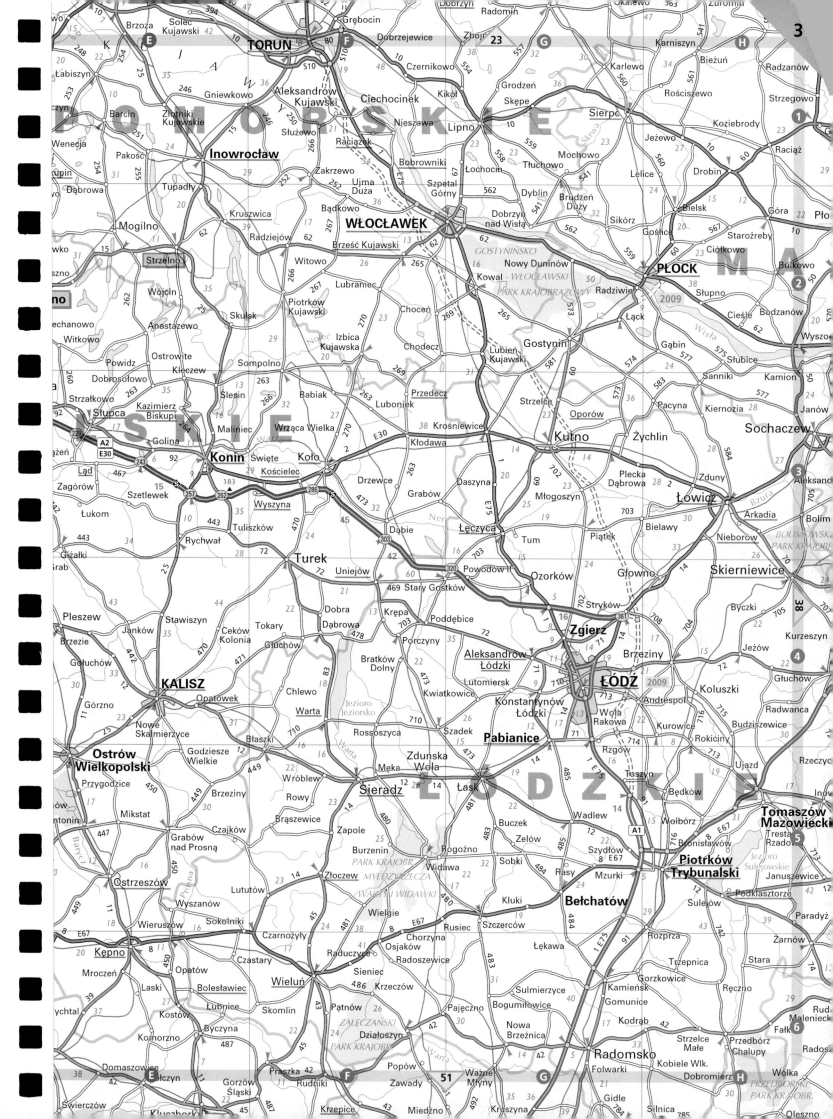

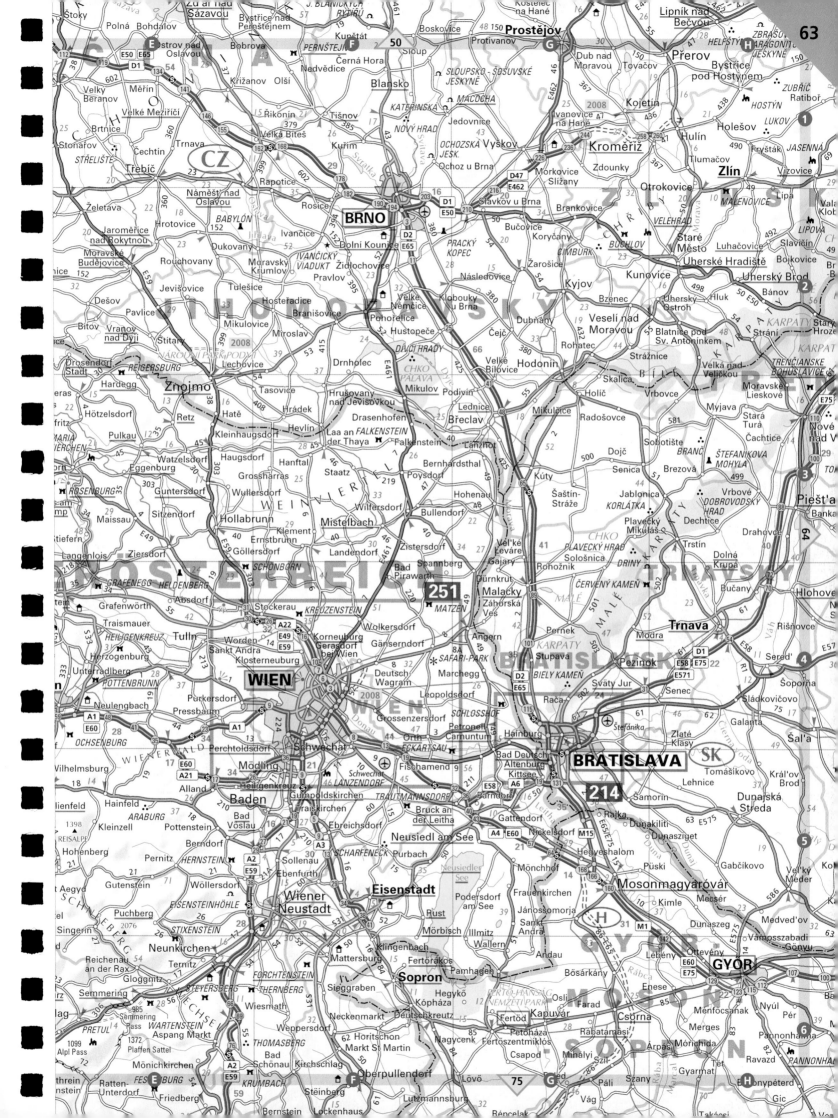

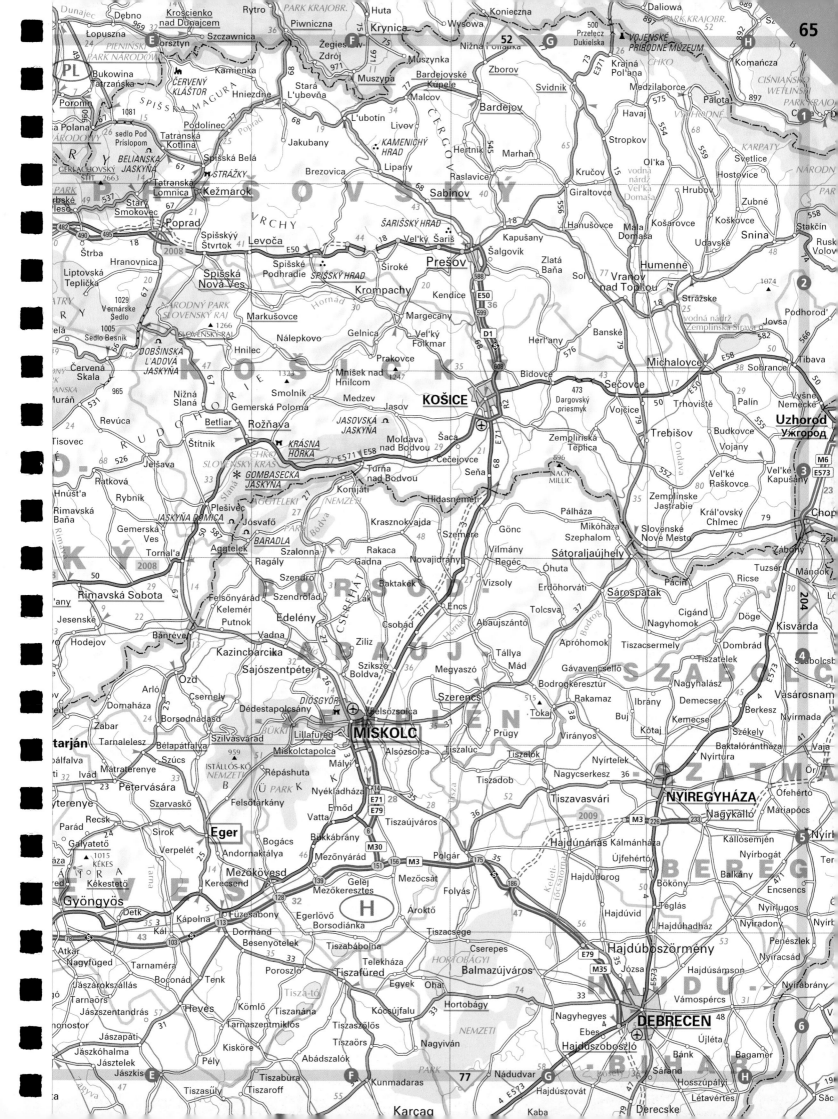

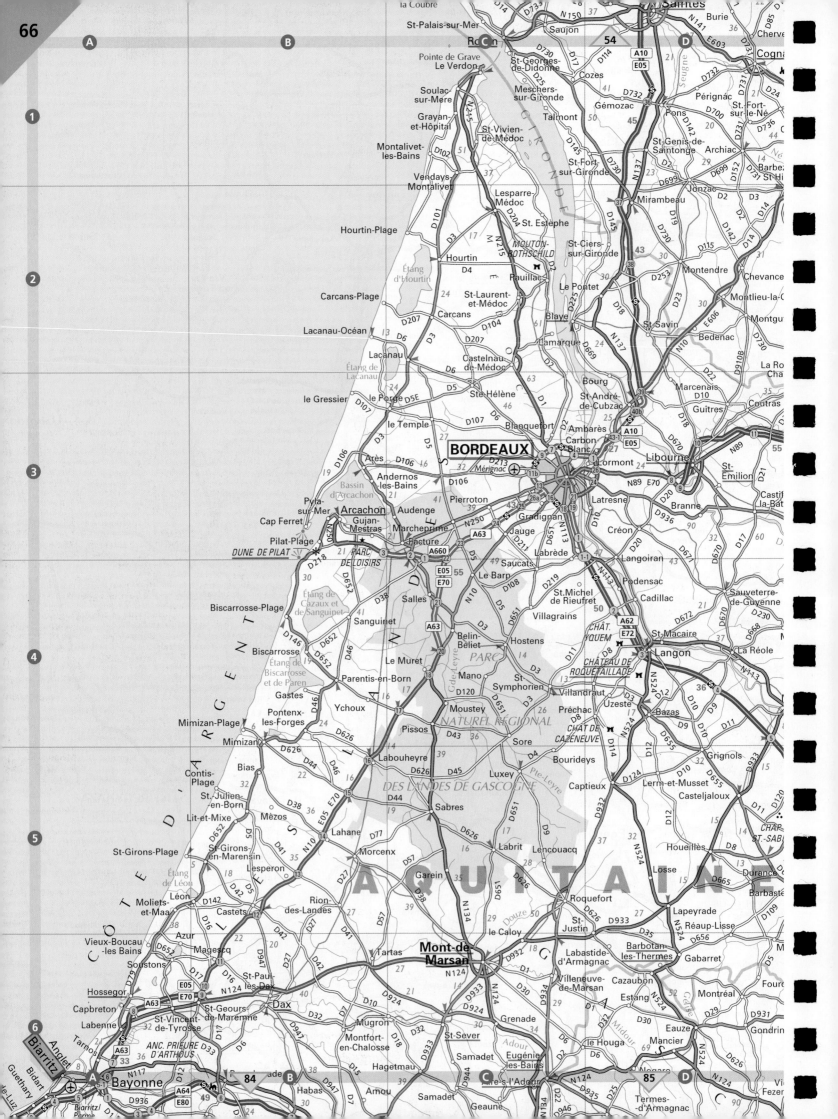

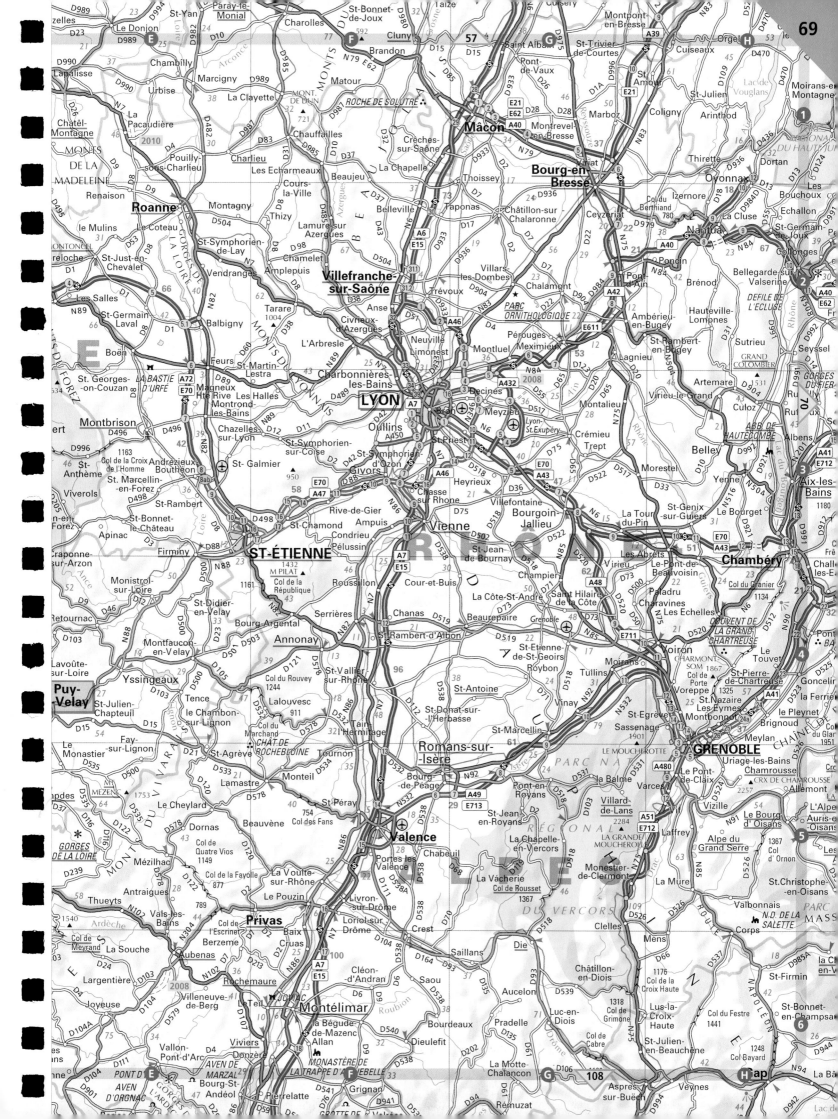

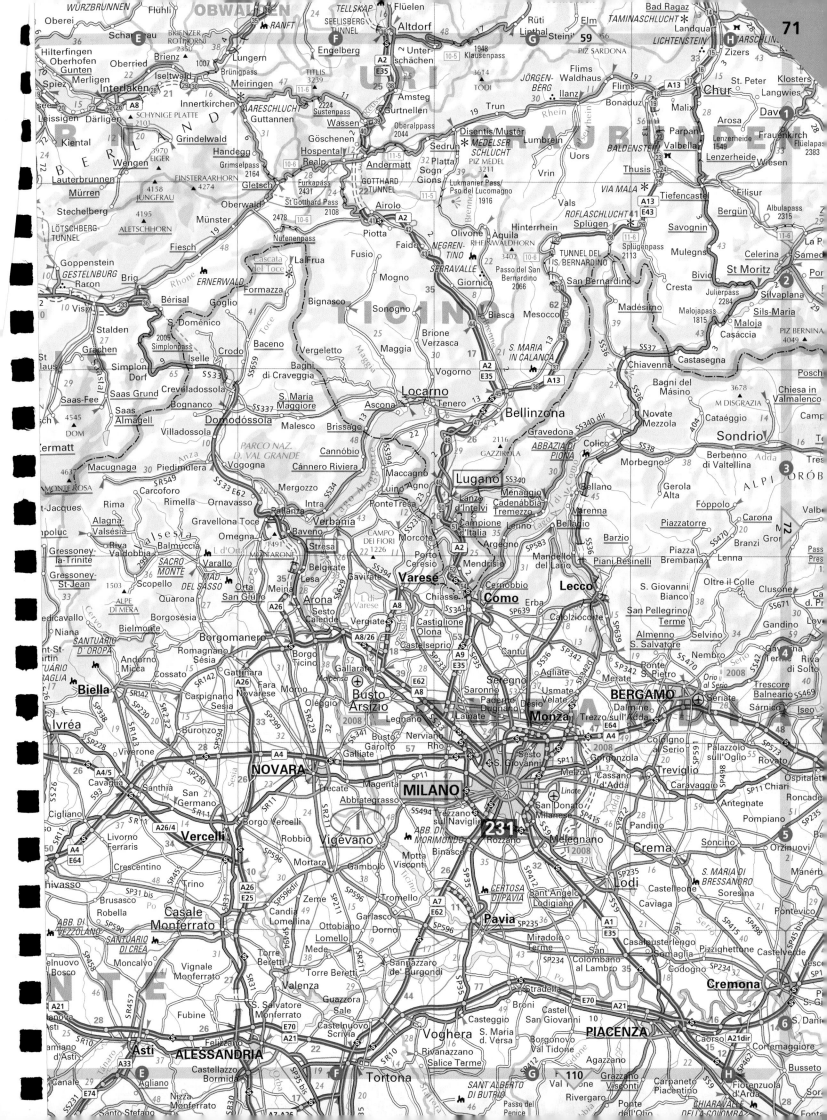

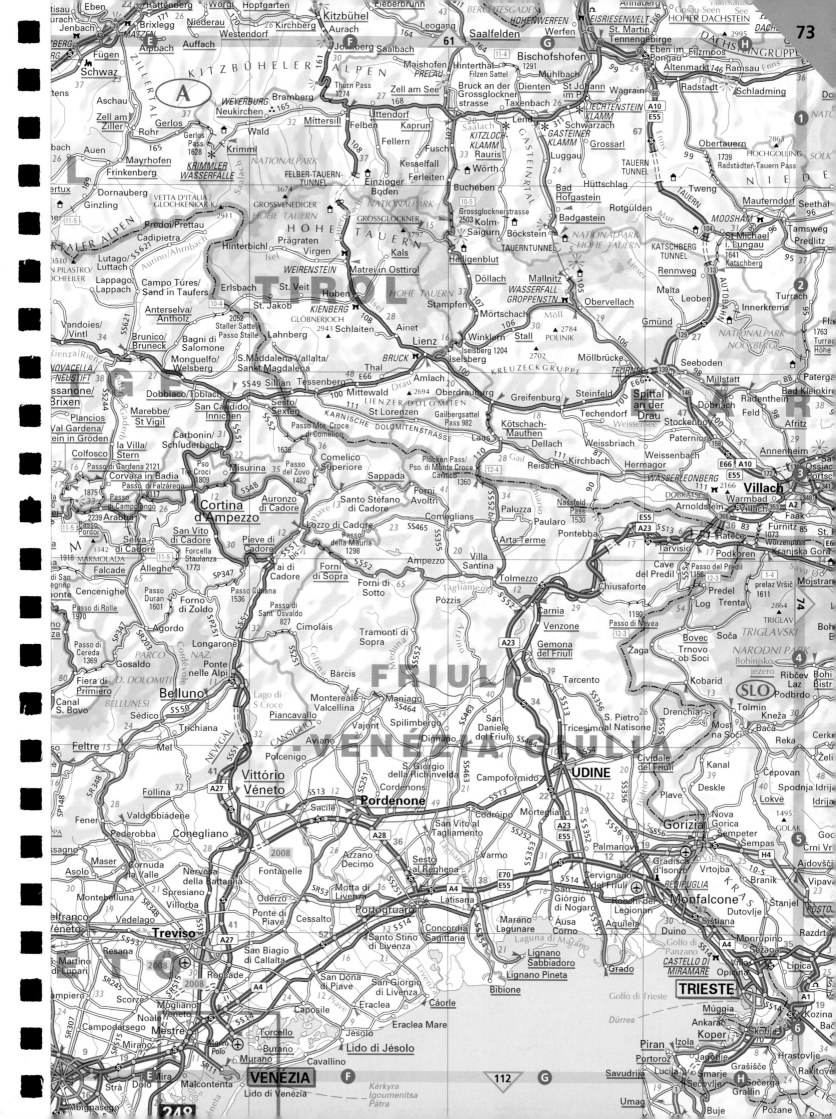

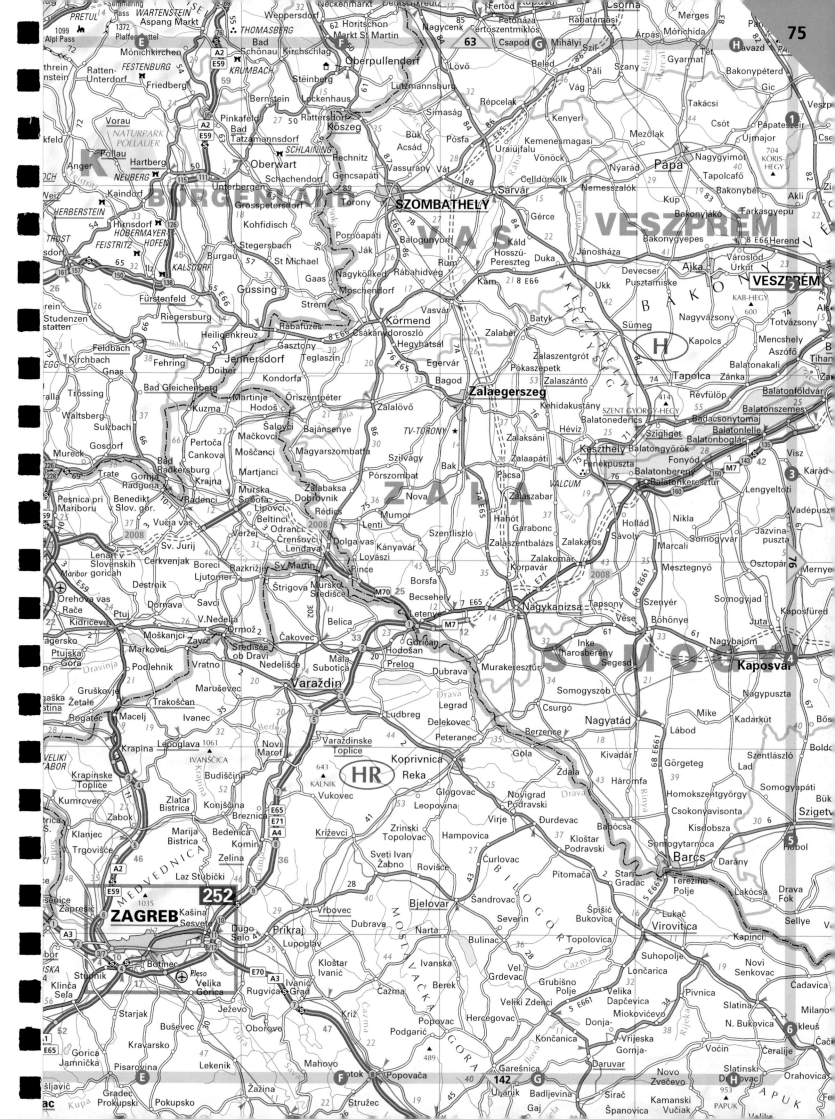

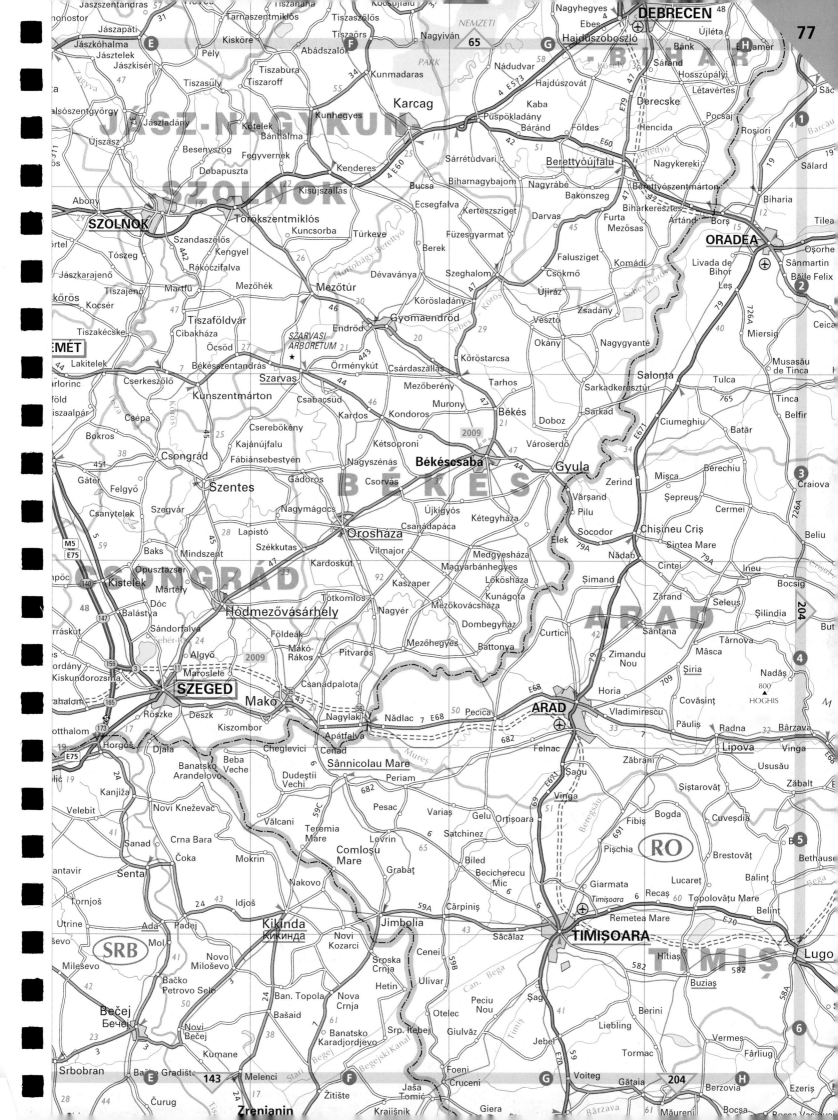

RÍAS BAIXAS
RÍAS
GALICIA
A CORUÑA/
LA CORUÑA
Ferrol
Santiago de
Compostela
Pontevedra
VIGO
OURENSE/
ORENSE
Lugo
Viana do
Castelo
VIANA DO CASTELO
Cabo Prior
Cabo Prioriño
Punta Candelaria
Cedeira
Valdoviño
Illas Sisargas
Cabo San Adrián
Malpica de Bergantiños
Punta del Roncudo
Laxe
Ponteceso
Cabo Vilán
Camariñas
Muxía
Cabo Touriñán
CEREIXO
DOLMEN DE DOMBATE
CASTRO DE BORNEIRO
Baio
San Roque
Carballo
Laracha
Arteixo
Cambre
Oleiros
Sada
Bergondo
Betanzos
Guisamo
Pontedeume
Miño
Cabañas
Ares
Mugardos
Neda
Fene
Xubia
San Sadurniño
MONASTERIO DE CAAVEIRO
CAST. DE ANDRADE
As Pontes de García Rodríguez
Puentes de García Rodríguez
Monfero
Vimianzo
Zás
Silva
Carral
Cerceda
Coirós
Irixoa
Pedreira
Fisterra/ Finisterre
Cee
Corcubión
Ézaro
Cabo Fisterra
Brandomil
Ponte Oliveras
Santa Comba
Mesón do Vento
Ordes
Curtis
Lourdes
Bembirre
Trazo
Lanzá
Guitiriz
Teixeiro
Baamonde
Pino do Val
A Baña
Carnota
Negreira
Portomouro
Oroso
Ru
SOBRADO DOS MONXES
STA. MARÍA DE MEZONZO
Sobrado
Begonte
Muros
Outes
Sigüeiro
Labacolla
Pastor
Friol
Rabade
Punta Carreiros
Porto do Son
Noia/ Noya
STA. MARÍA DE CONXO
Santiago
O Pino
Arzúa
Toques
CASTRO DE BAROÑA
Padrón
Teo
Ramallosa
Fontedias
Melide
Pobra do Caramiñal/ Puebla del Caramiñal
Boiro
Enfesta/ Pontecesures
Ponte Ulla
Embalse de Portodemouros
Palas de Rei
Cabo Corrubedo
Oleiros
Rianxo
Catoira
Vilagarcía de Arousa
Cuntis
A Estrada
PAZO DE OCA
Cruces
Guntín
Santa Uxía de Ribeira
Illa de Arousa
Punta de Couso
Vilanova de Arousa
Caldas de Reis
Silleda
Agolada
Monterroso
O Grove
Cambados
A Lagoa / Campo Lameiro
Lalín
Antas de Ulla
Narón
Portomarín
Illa de Sálvora
A Toxa
Forcarei
PARQUE NACIONAL
DAS ILLAS
ATLÁNTICAS
O Convento
Poio
Soutelo
Dozón
Castro
Rodeiro
Taboada
Paradela
Illa de Ons
Sanxenxo
Combarro
Cerdedo
Alto de Santo Domingo
SIERRA DO FARO
Embalse de Belesar
Marín
Ría de Pontevedra
Ponte-Caldelas
SERRA DO SUÍDO
Beariz
Chantada
STA. MARÍA DA REAL
MONASTERIO DE RIBAS DO MIÑO
Escairón
La Barrela
Piñor
Hío
Moaña
CAST. DE SOUTOMAIOR
Cea
Illas Cíes
Cangas
Avión
O Carballiño
Maside
Embalse dos Peares
Pantón
Redondela
Berducido
Ría de Vigo
MONASTERIO DE SAN CLODIO
Leiro
Mondariz-Balneario
Cambeo
Monforte de Lemos
Panxón
Nigrán
Punxín
Os Peares
Sober
Cabo Silleiro
Areas
Mondariz
Baiona
Ramallosa
Ponteareas
Ribadavia
Parada del Sil
Embalse de San Esteban
O Porriño
A Cañiza
SANTO ESTEVO
Arrabal/ Oia
Vilameán
Cortegada
Cartelle
MONASTERIO DE SANTO ESTEVO
Castro Caldelas
Puerto de A Cerdeira
Salvaterra de Miño
Ramirás
Esgos
Valença do Minho
Tui
A Merca
Maceda
Xunqueira de Espadanedo
A Guarda/ La Guardia
Monção
Melgaço
Padrenda
Puerto de Alto do Rodicio
A Pobra de Trives
Paredes
São Gregório
Celanova
Allariz
Xunqueira de Ambía
Embalse de Chandrexa
MTE. DE STA. TEGRA
Caminha
Vila Nova de Cerveira
Extremo
MANZANEDA
Moledo
Lanhelas
Verea
Vila Praia de Âncora
Paredes de Coura
Portela
Sandiás
Vilar de Barrio
Afife
SERRA DA PENEDA
SERRA DE QUEIXA
Bande
Arcos de Valdevez
Entrimo
Xinzo de Limia
Ginzo de Limia
Villariño de Conso
STA. LUZIA
Soajo
Muiños
Trasmiras
Laza
Lobios
Campobecerros
Ponte de Lima
Lindoso
PARQUE NACIONAL DA PENEDA-GERÊS
Puerto Estivadas
Cualedro
Darque
Ponte da Barca
Portela do Home
Baltar
A Gudiña
Deão
Randín
Castelo do Neiva
Balugães
SERRA DO GERÊS
Verín
Covide
Barragem de Paradela
Montalegre
N. S. D'ABADIA
Paradela
Ríos
Esposende
Feitos
Vila Verde
Caldelas
Gerês
Barragem de Venda Nova
Gralhos
Oímbra
Vilardevós
Barcelos
TIBÃES
BOM JESUS DO MONTE
Louredo
Barragem do Alto Rabagão
N. SENHORA DA AZINHEIRA
Vila Verde
80

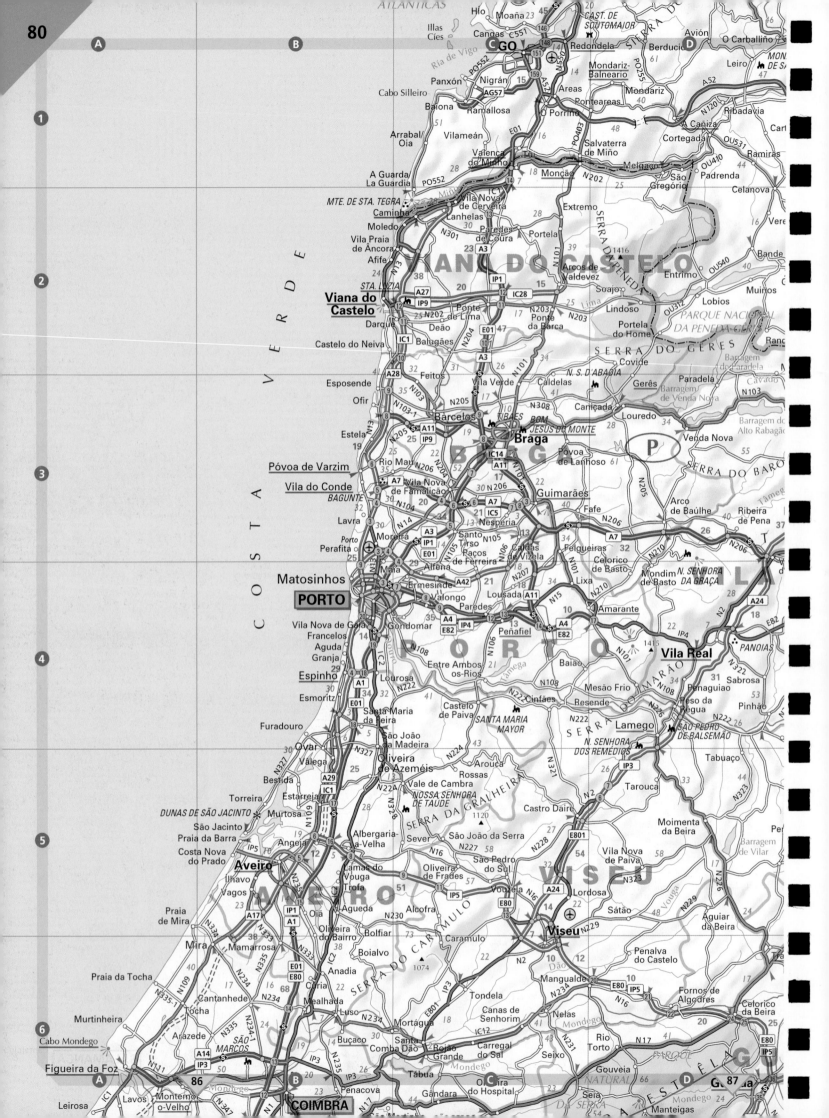

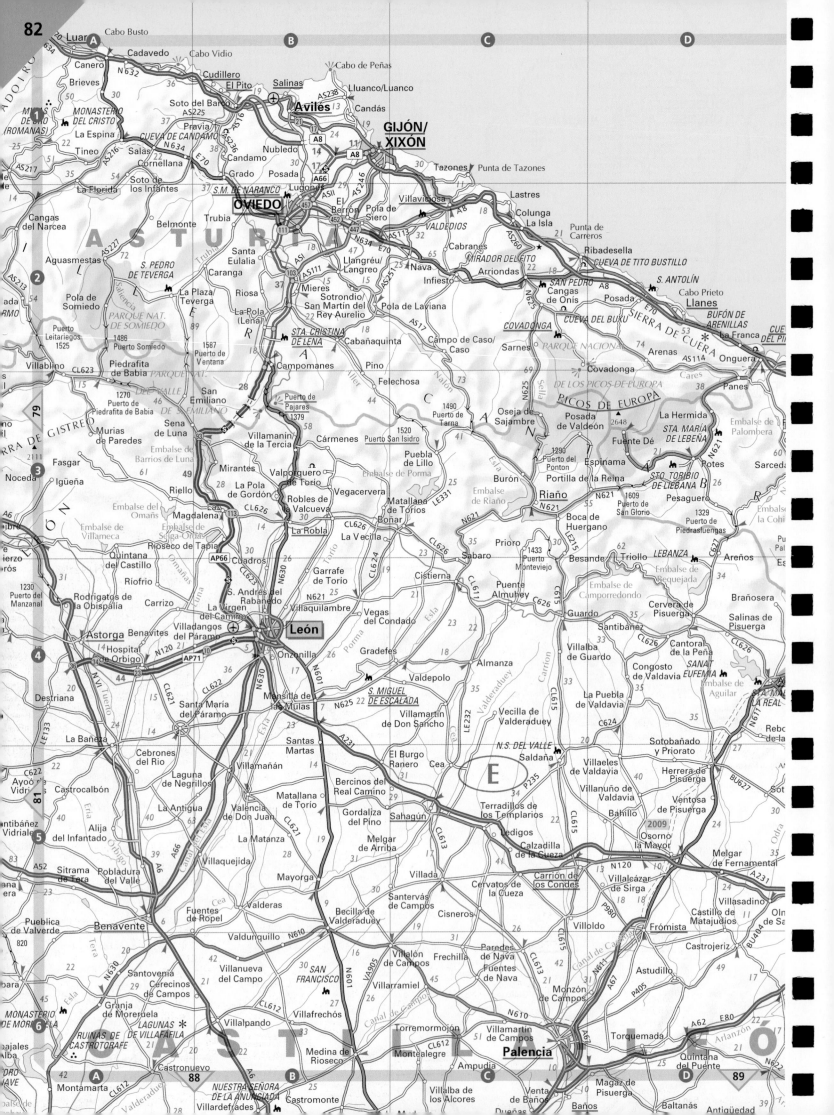

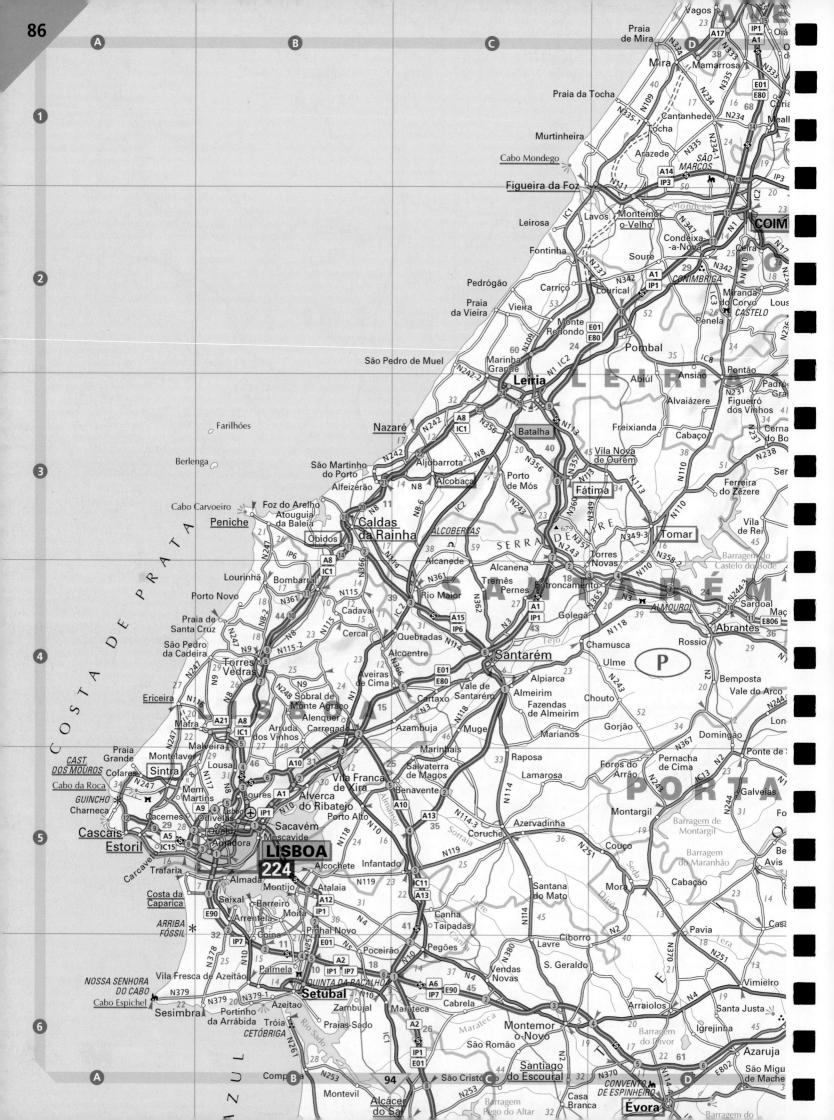

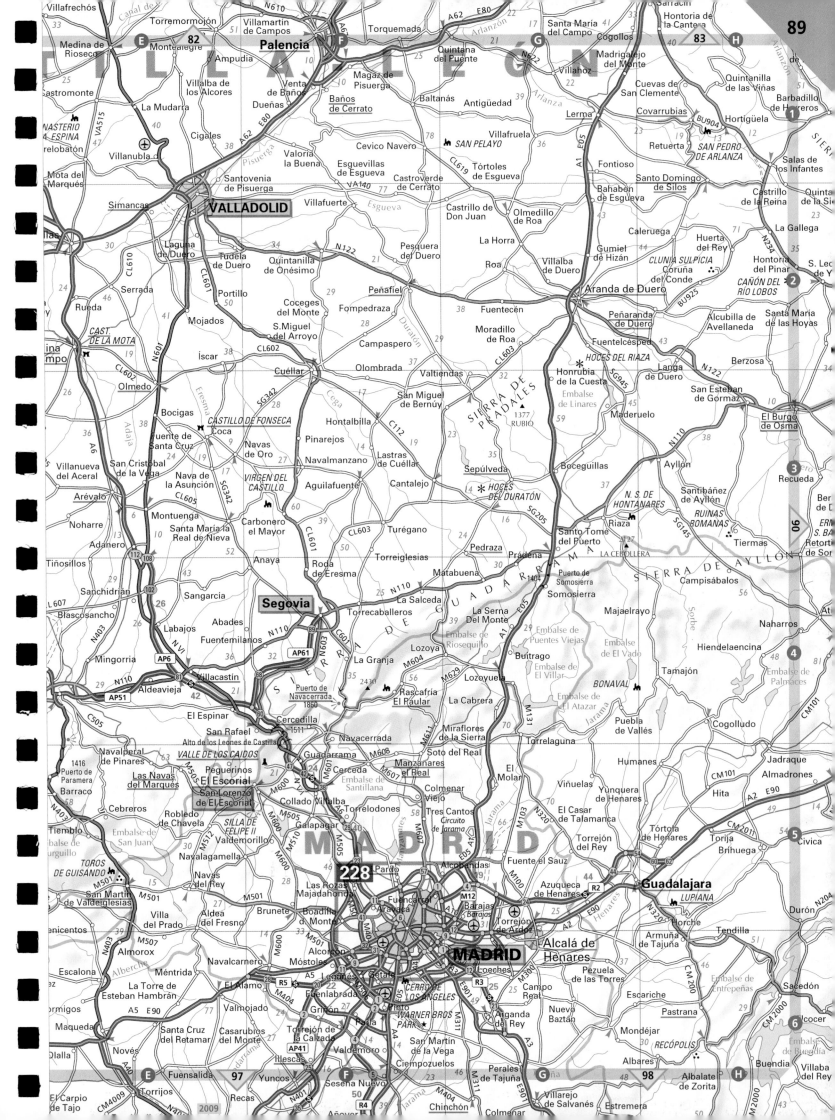

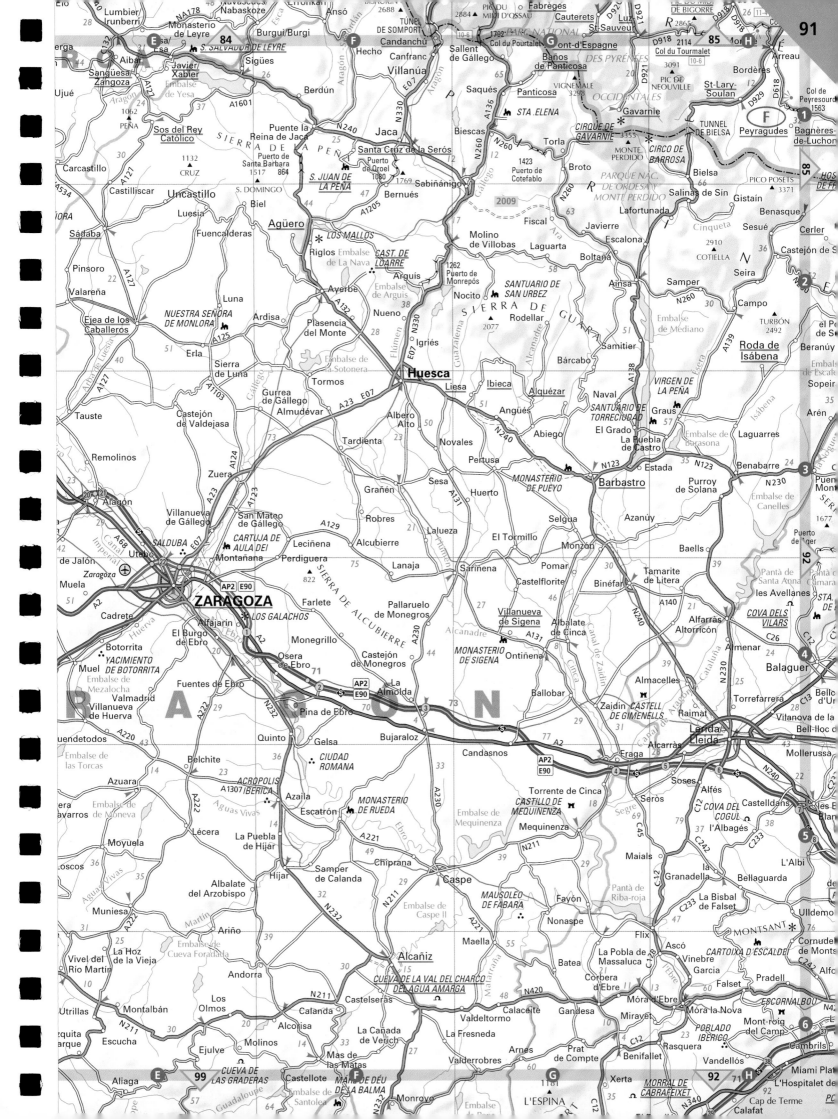

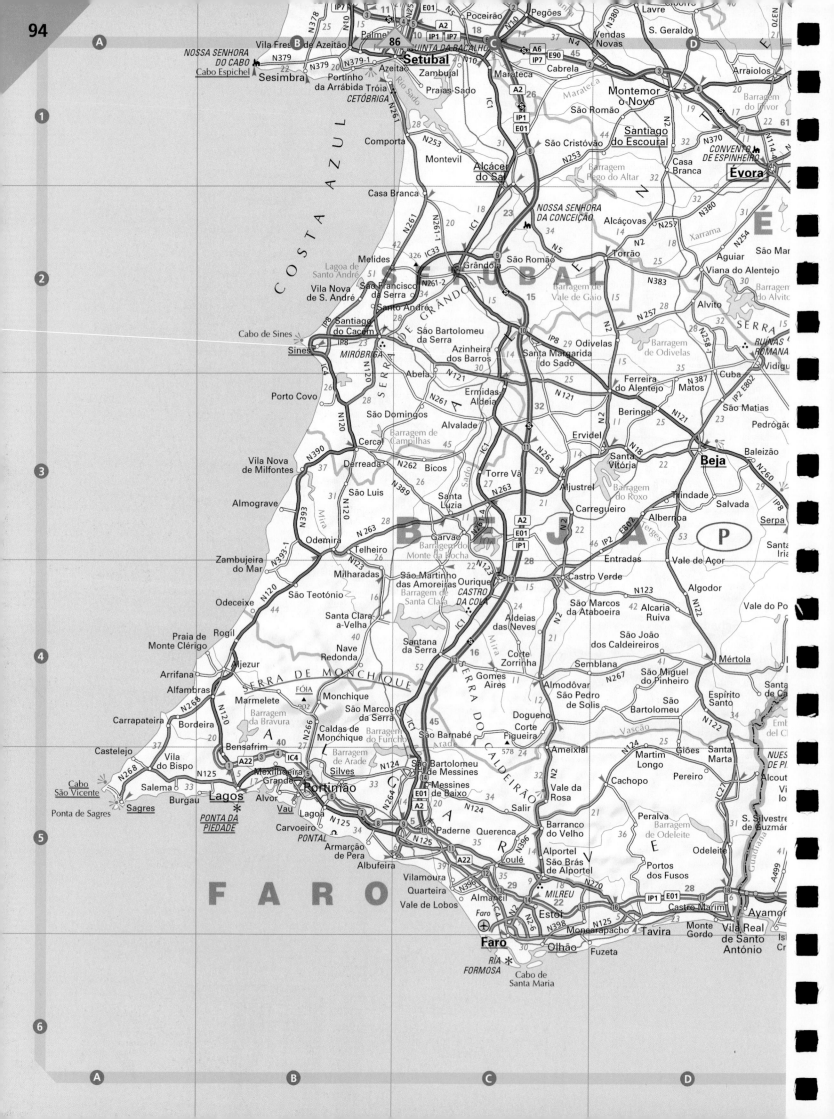

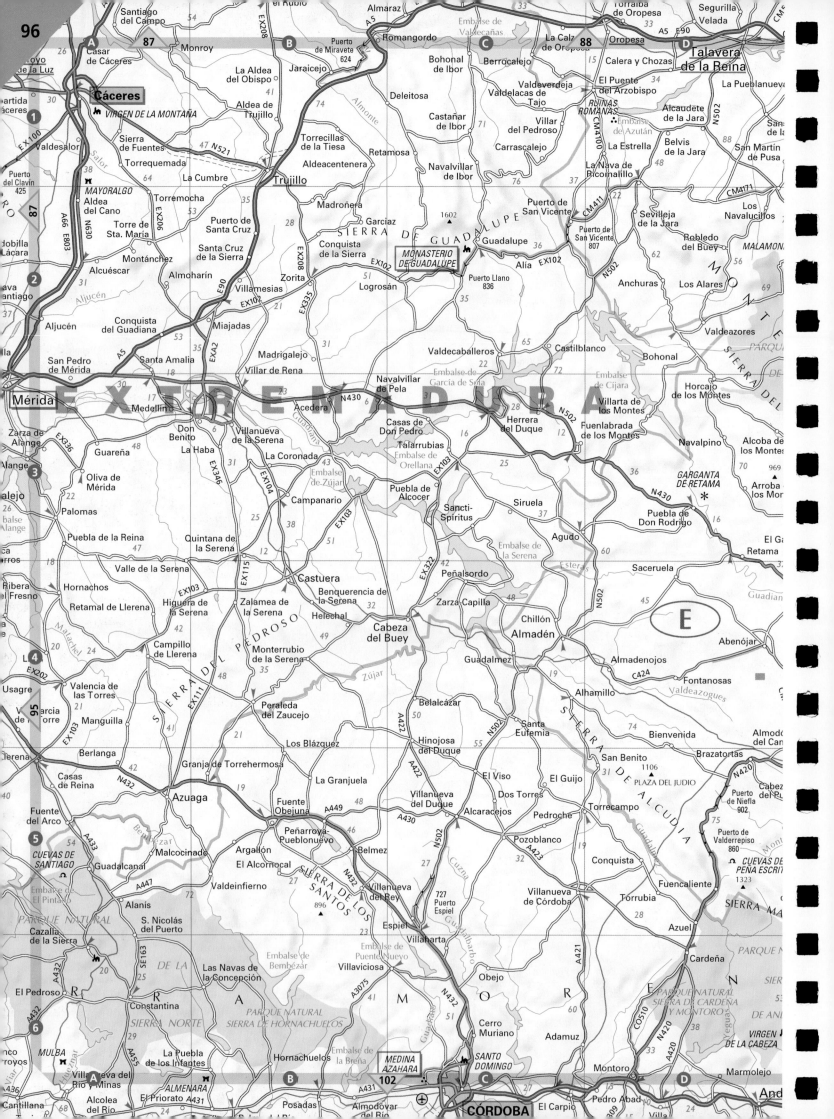

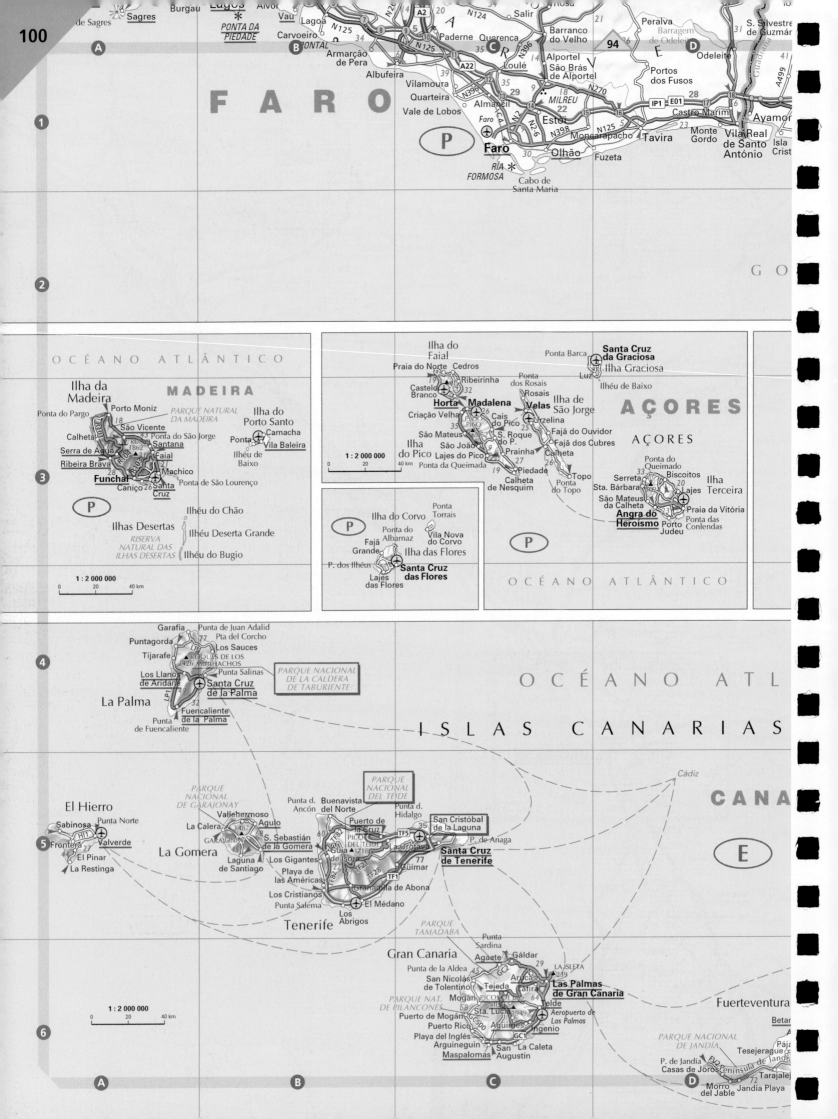

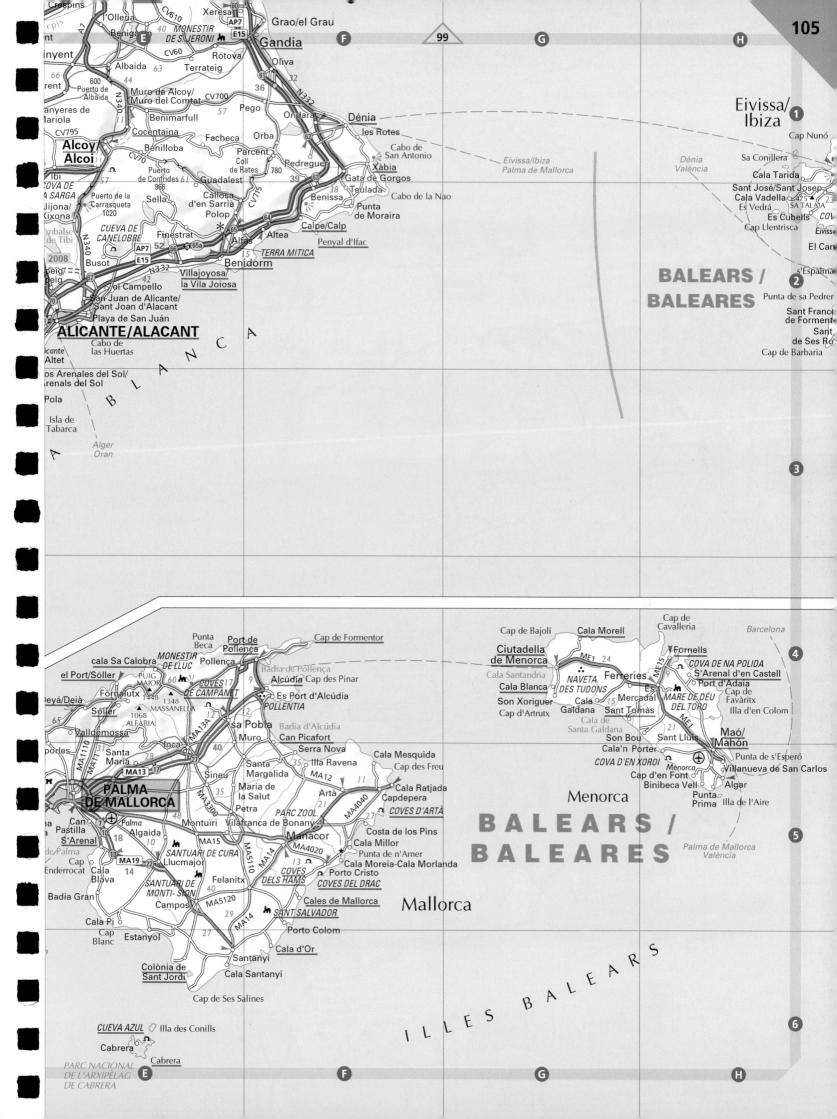

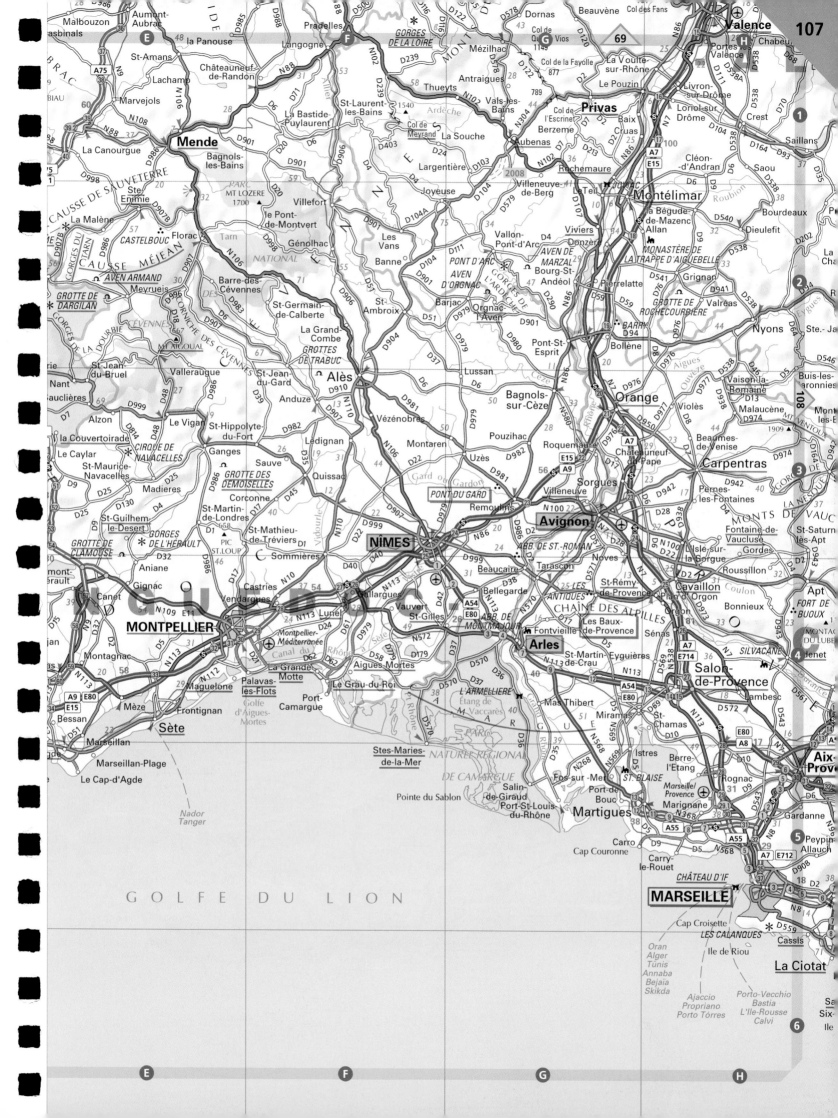

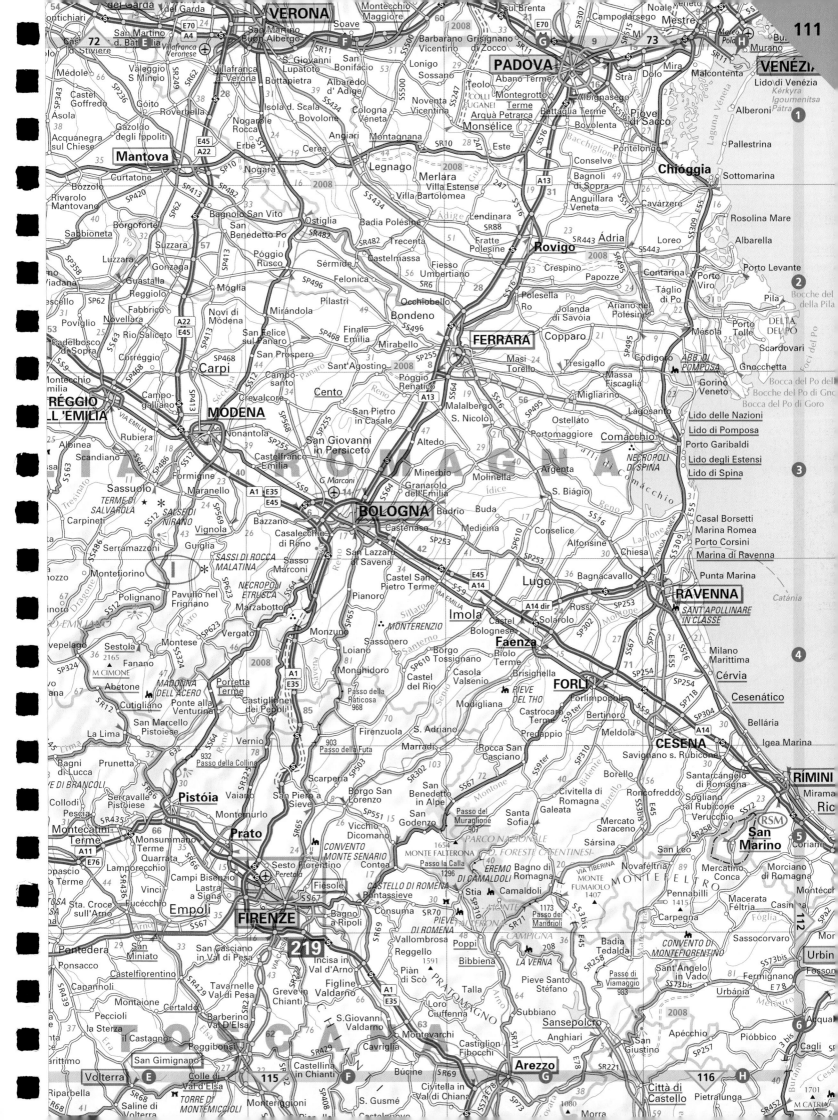

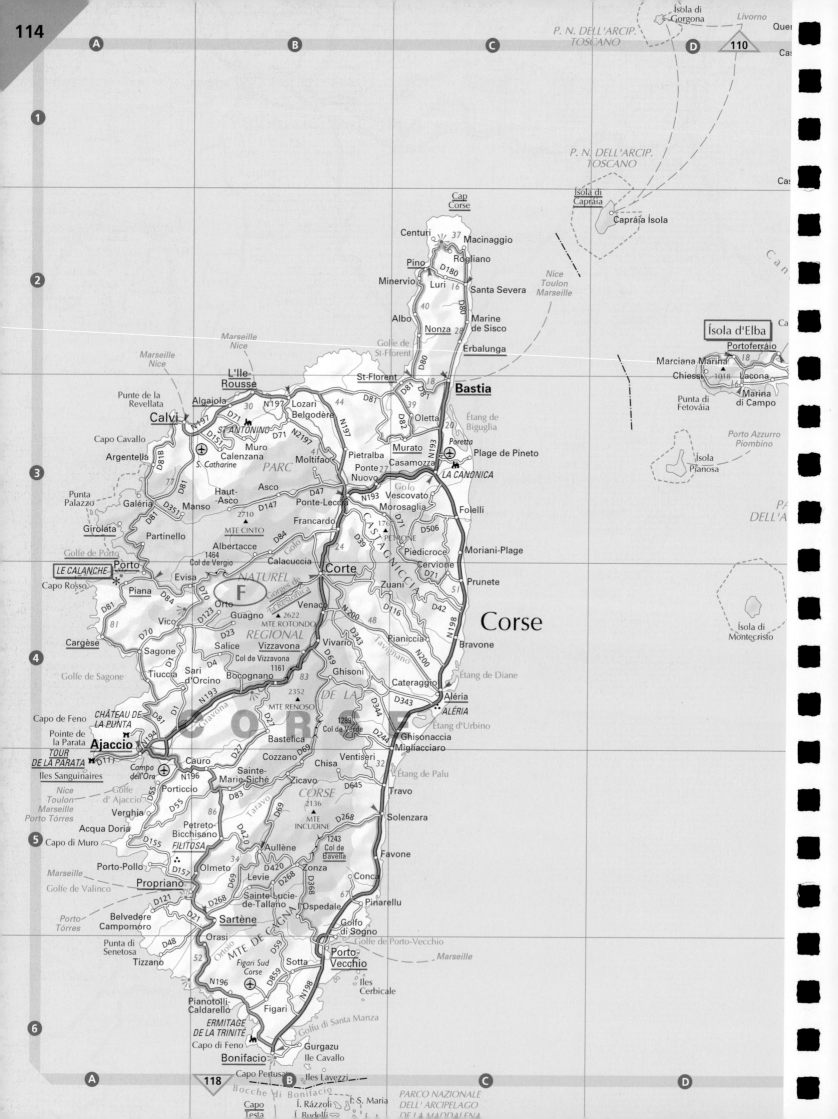

A   B   C   D

110

P. N. DELL'ARCIP.
TOSCANO

Ísola di
Gorgona

Livorno

Quer

Cas

1

P. N. DELL'ARCIP.
TOSCANO

Ísola di
Capráia

Capráia Ísola

Cap
Corse

Centuri   37   Macinaggio

Rogliano

Pino   D180

Minervio   Luri 16

2

Albo   40

Nonza   28

Marine
de Sisco

Santa Severa

Nice
Toulon
Marseille

Erbalunga

Ísola d'Elba

Portoferráio

Marciana Marina   18

Marseille
Nice

Golfe de
St-Florent

St-Florent   18

Bastia

Chiessi   1018   Lacona

Marina
di Campo

Marseille
Nice

L'Ile-
Rousse

Lozari
Belgodère   44   D81   39

D82   20

Oletta

Murato   Poretta

Étang de
Biguglia

Punta di
Fetováia

Porto Azzurro
Piombino

Punte de la
Revellata

Algaiola   30   N197

D71   N2197

Calvi   N197

Capo Cavallo

Muro   41
Calenzana   Moltifao

Pietralba   Casamozza

Plage de Pineto

Ísola
Pianosa

PA
DELL'A

Argentella   D81B

S. Catharine

PARC

Ponte
Nuovo   27

LA CANONICA

3

Punta
Palazzo

Galéria   D351

Manso   D81   77

Haut-
Asco   D147

Asco   D47

Ponte-Leccia   N193

Vescovato
Morosaglia

Golo

Folelli

2710

MTE CINTO

Francardo   D84

1765
PETRONE

Piedicroce   D506

Moriani-Plage

Girolata

Partinello

Albertacce   1464
Col de Vergio

Calacuccia

Corte

Cervione   D71

CASTAGNICCIA

Golfe de Porto

LE CALANCHE

NATUREL

Zuani   51

Prunete

Porto

Evisa   D70

F

Gorges de
la Restonica   Venaco

Capo Rosso

Piana   D84

Orto   2622

N200   48

D116

Pianiccia

Corse

Bravone

D81   81

Vico   D123

Guagno   MTE ROTONDO

REGIONAL

N193   Salice   D23

Vizzavona

Vivario   D343

Ghisoni

D42

Ísola di
Montecristo

Cargèse   D70

Sagone

Tiuccia   D4

Col de Vizzavona
1161

Bocognano   83

Tavignano

Pianiccia

N198

4

Golfe de Sagone

Sari
d'Orcino

2352

MTE RENOSO

DE   LA

Cateraggio

Étang de Diane

Aléria

ALÉRIA

Capo de Feno

CHÂTEAU DE
LA PUNTA

N193

Gravona

C O R S E

1289
Col de Verde

D344   D343

Étang d'Urbino

Pointe de
la Parata

D81

N194

Ghisonaccia
Migliacciaro

TOUR
DE LA PARATA

Ajaccio   D111

D27   Bastelica   D69

Cozzano

D244

Iles Sanguinaires

Cauro

Chisa   Ventiseri   32

Étang de Palu

Nice
Toulon
Marseille
Porto Tórres

Campo
dell'Ora   N196

Sainte-
Marie-Siché   D83

Zicavo

D645

Travo

Porticcio   D55

CORSE

Verghia   D55   86

Tarava

2136

MTE
INCUDINE

D268

Solenzara

5

Acqua Doria

Petreto-
Bicchisano

D420

1243
Col de
Bavella

Favone

Capo di Muro   D155

FILITOSA

Aullène

Porto-Pollo   D157

Olmeto   34

Levie   D268

Zonza   D368

Conca

Pinarellu

Propriano

D69

Sainte-Lucie-
de-Tallano   67

Marseille

Belvedere
Campomoro   D121

D268

L'Ospedale

Golfo
di Sogno

Porto
Tórres

D21   Sartène   D268

Golfe de Valinco

Orasi

MTE DE CAGNA

D59

Golfe de Porto-Vecchio

Marseille

Punta di
Senetosa

D48   52

Ortoio

Figari Sud
Corse   Sotta

Porto-
Vecchio

Tizzano

N196   D859   N198

Iles
Cerbicale

6

Pianotolli-
Caldarello   Figari

ERMITAGE
DE LA TRINITÉ

Golfu di Santa Manza

Capo di Feno

Gurgazu   Ile Cavallo

Bonifacio

A   B   118   Capo Pertusato   C   Iles Lavezzi   D

Bocche di Bonifacio

Capo
Testa

Í. Rázzoli   Í. S. Maria

PARCO NAZIONALE
DELL' ARCIPELAGO
DE LA MADDALENA

Kŭrba Vela

Zlarin Brodarica

E 113 G

Žirje

Primošten 60 Prapatnica

Bristvica

Rogoznica E65 Seget Split

Marina Trogir Kaštel Stari

Rt Okrug

Ploča Splitski kanal 1

HR Drvenik

Maslinica Rogač

Šolta Stomorsk

142

Split

2

Jabuka

Svetac Viški kanal Korčula

Komiža Vis

MODRA ŠPILJA Vis 19

Biševo

3

Marina

RA 4

ncavilla Palagruža
Mare

40 Ortona

A14

45 SS16

San Vito Chietino

SP538 SS84 SAN GIOVANNI IN VENERE

iano E55 5 Torino di Sangro Marina

Torino di Sangro Í Pianosa

SS652 15 Punta di Penna PARCO NAZIONALE
DEL GARGANO

Casalbordino Í. Capráia

54 Vasto

SP364 Marina di Vasto Í. S. Dómino ÍSOLE TRÉMITI

8 Í. S. Nicola

Atessa Cupello 5

Gissi SS86 24 SS16 Térmoli

SS652 San Salvo

Colledi- Montenero Lido di Rodi Péschici
mezzo di Bisáccia Campomarino Torre Mileto Gargánico

Villa 136 Guglionesi 28 Marina di Chiéuti SS89 40 SP52
nta Maria

MADONNA DI 97 SP483 Lago di Lésina 49 Lago di SS89 Vieste
otta CANNETO S. Martino Lésina Varano PARCO
Agnone Montefalcone in Pensilis Vico del NAZIONALE
nel Sannio 53 SS87 Serracapriola A14 Gargano SP144
Guardialfiera E55 31 Sannicandro Cagnano Carpino SS89 SS53
Trivento SP157 Larino 2008 Gargánico Varano
SS650 Ururi 23 Pugnochiuso
Lucito SS647 89 21 Apricena PROMONTORIO DEL GARGANO Baia
RUDERI ROMANI Casacalenda SP376 San Paolo 1055 SS272 delle Zagare
scolanciano Limosano di Civitate 47 SS272 Mattinata
Santa Croce San Marco San Giovanni Monte 6
Petrella di Magliano in Lamis Rotondo Sant'Angelo SS89b 59
Casalciprano Tifernina Bonefro Colletorto
rpinone 12 SP157 Torremaggiore San MANTE SANTA MARIA
E SS645 Sant'Elia Castelnuovo 121 Severo Granata DI SIPONTO Manfredónia H
solone a Pianisi SP212 Cárlantino della Dáunia SP160 22
Campobasso SS645 30 Lago SAN LEONARDO Golfo di
di Occhito

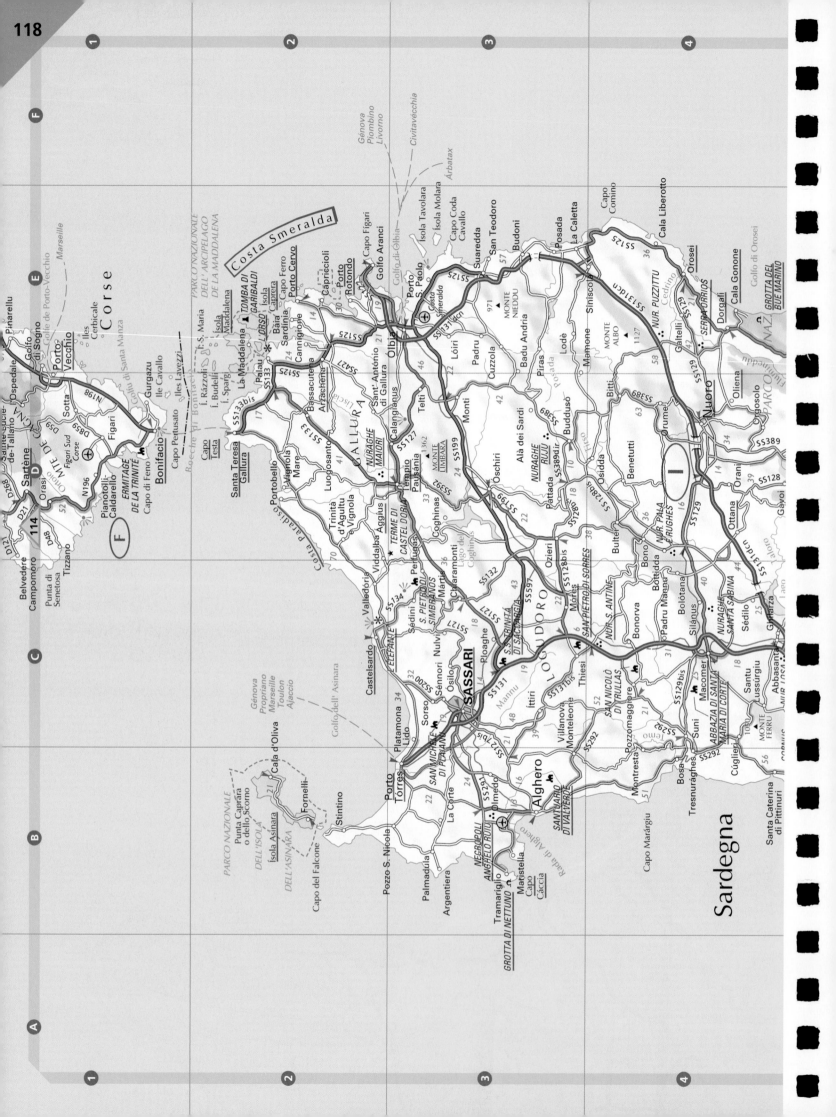

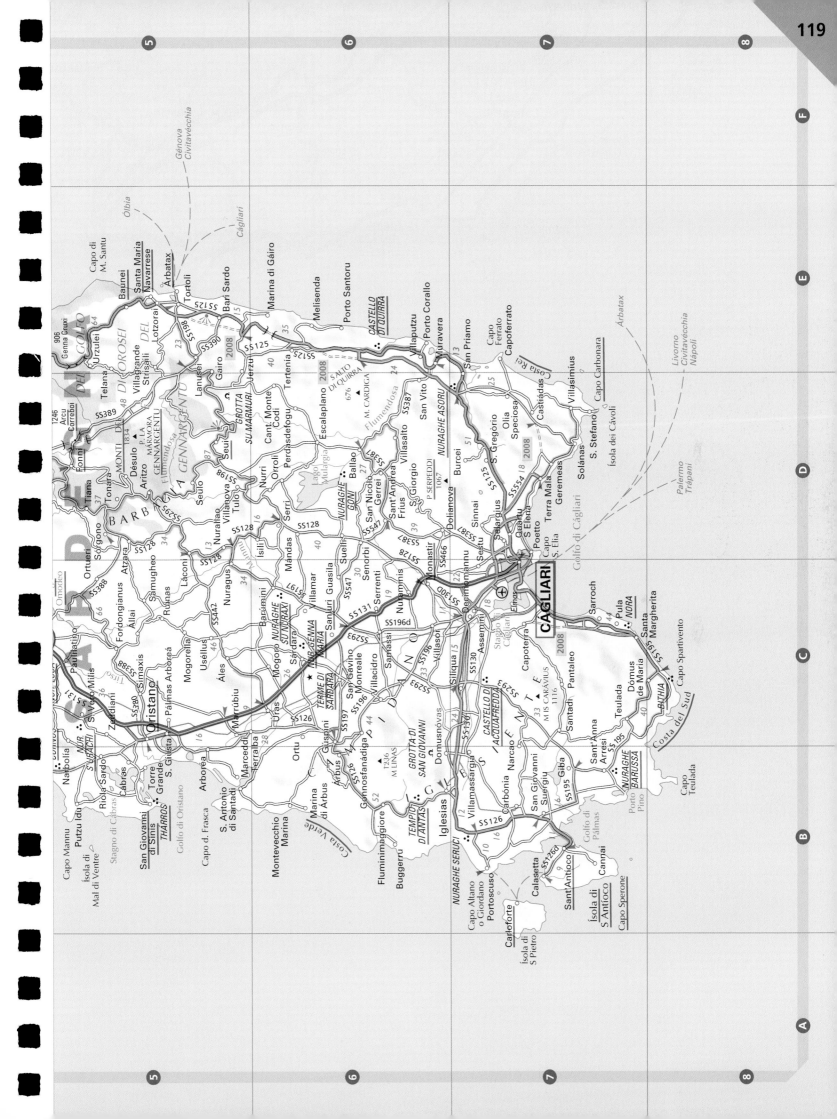

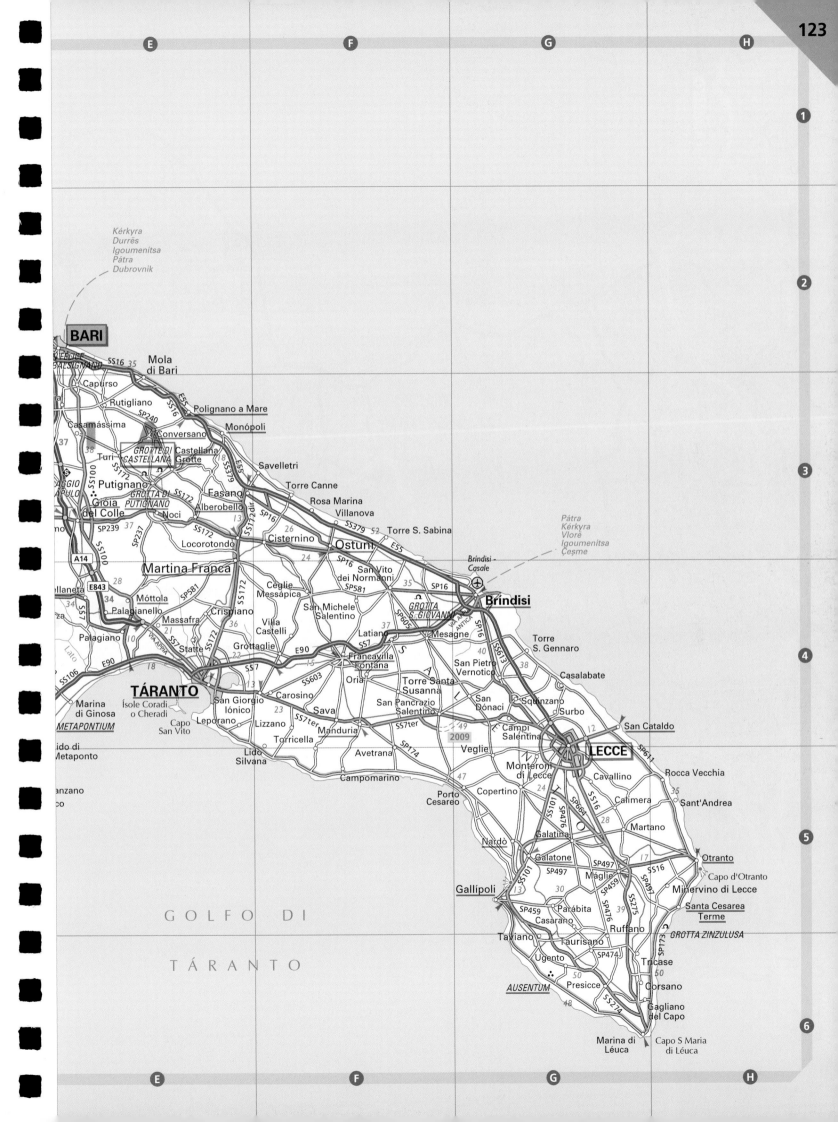

Kérkyra
Durrës
Igoumenítsa
Pátra
Dubrovnik

BARI

FELICE
BALSIGNANO

SS16 35 Mola
di Bari

Capurso

Rutigliano   Polignano a Mare

SP240

Casamássima   Monópoli

37   Conversano

Turi   Castellana/Grotte

38   GROTTE DI
CASTELLANA   Castellana Grotte

SS172   Savelletri

Putignano   SS172   Fasano   Torre Canne

AGGIO
APULO   Gioia   GROTTA DI
del Colle   Noci   Alberobello   Rosa Marina
PUTIGNANO   Villanova

SP239   37   SS172   SP16   SS379 52 Torre S. Sabina

A14   Locorotondo   Cisternino   Ostuni   E55

Martina Franca   24   SP16   San Vito
dei Normanni   35   SP16

E843   28   Ceglie
Messápica   SP581

Móttola   SS172   San Michele
Salentino   GROTTA
S. GIOVANNI   Bríndisi -
Casale

34   Palagianello   Crispiano   Villa
Castelli   Mesagne   **Bríndisi**

SS7   Massafra   36   37   SP605   SP16

Palagiano   21   Statte   Grottaglie   Latiano   40   SS613

E90   18   SS172   E90   Francavilla
Fontána   San Pietro
Vernotico   38

SS106   13   SS7   Oria   Torre Santa
Susanna   Casalabate

TÁRANTO   SS603   San Pancrazio
Salentino   San
Dónaci   Squinzano

Marina
di Ginosa   Ísole Coradi
o Cheradi   San Giorgio
Iónico   23   Sava   49   Surbo   San Cataldo

METAPONTIUM   Capo
San Vito   Leporano   Lizzano   SS7ter   2009   Campi
Salentina   12

Lido di
Metaponto   Torricella   Manduria   SS7ter   Veglie   **LECCE**

Lido
Silvana   Avetrana   SP174   Monteroni
di Lecce   SP611

anzano
co   Campomarino   47   Copertino   24   SS16   Cavallino   Rocca Vecchia

Porto
Cesareo   SP101   SP664   Calimera   35   Sant'Andrea

Nardò   Galatina   28   Martano

Galatone   SP497   17   SS16   Otranto

GOLFO DI   SP101   SP497   Máglie   SP459   SS16   Capo d'Otranto

13   30   SP459   SP497   Minervino di Lecce

Gallípoli   Parábita   SP476   39   SS275   Santa Cesarea
Terme

TÁRANTO   SP459   Casarano   Ruffano   SP173   GROTTA ZINZULUSA

Taviano   Taurisano   SP474   Tricase   50

Ugento   50   Corsano

AUSENTUM   Presicce   SS274   Gagliano
del Capo

48

Marina di
Léuca   Capo S Maria
di Léuca

GOLFO DI

TÁRANTO

Pátra
Kérkyra
Vlorë
Igoumenítsa
Çeşme

Lato

Lido di
Metaponto

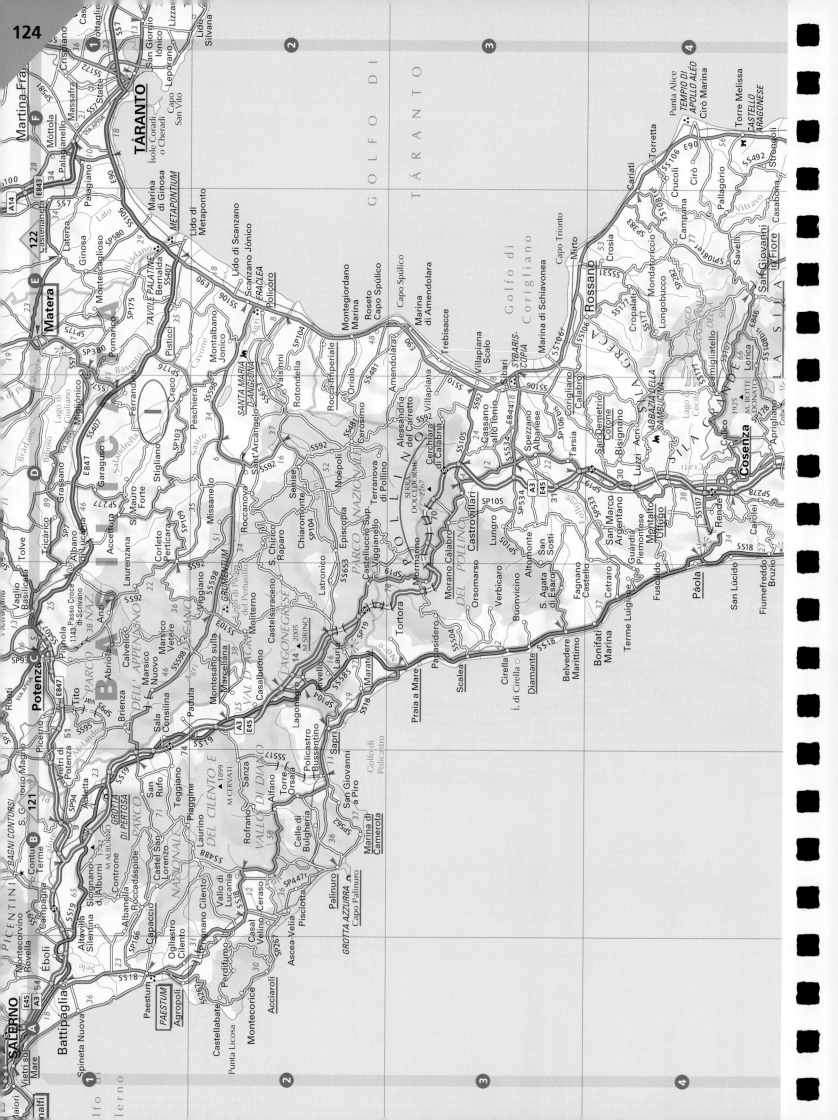

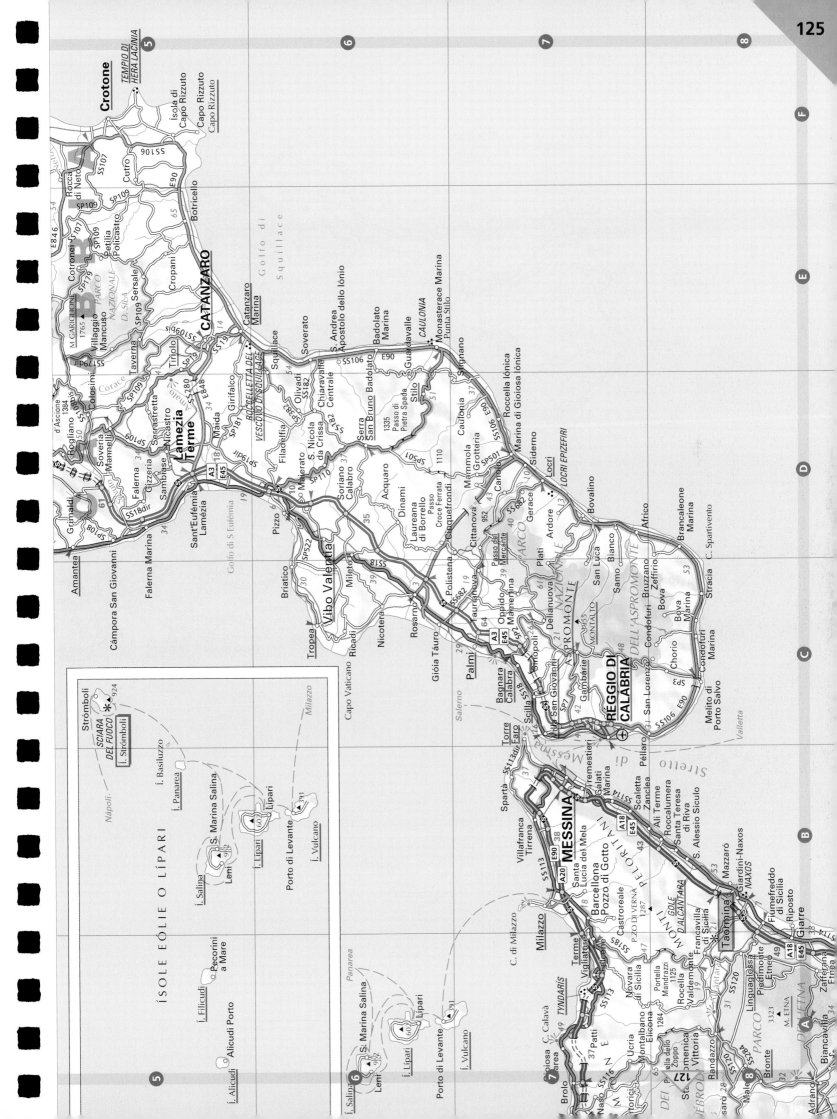

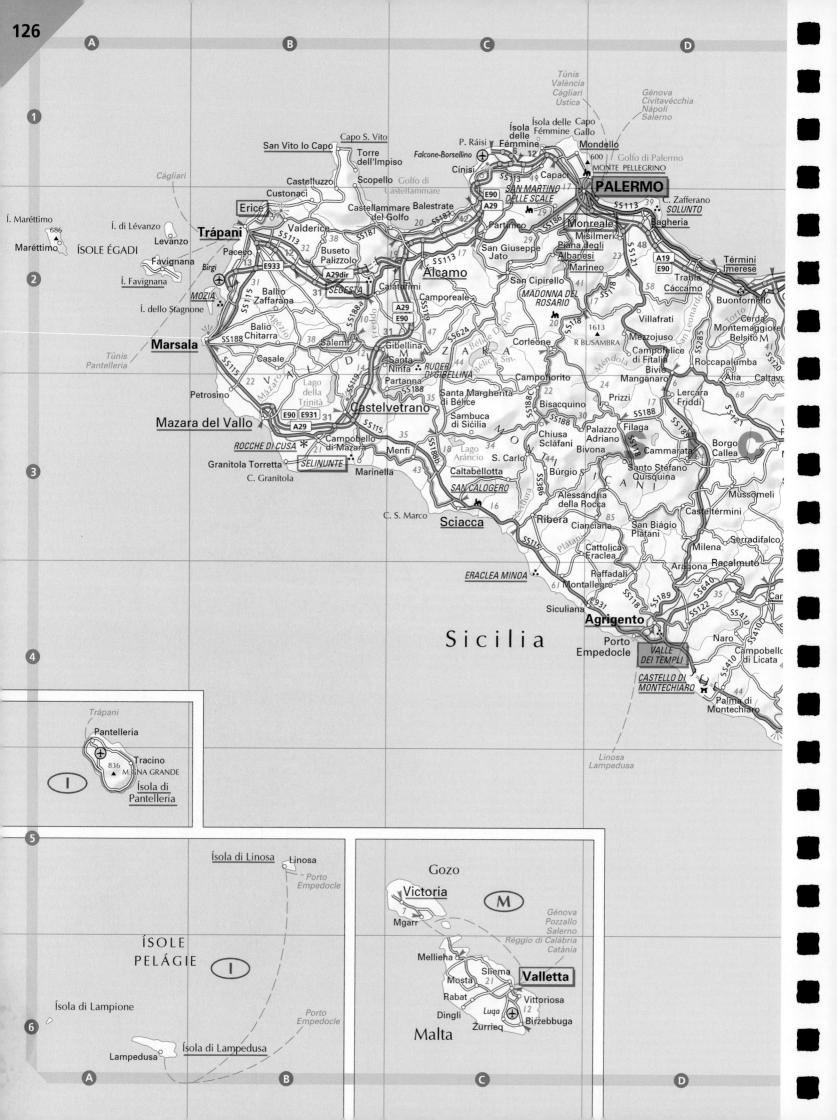

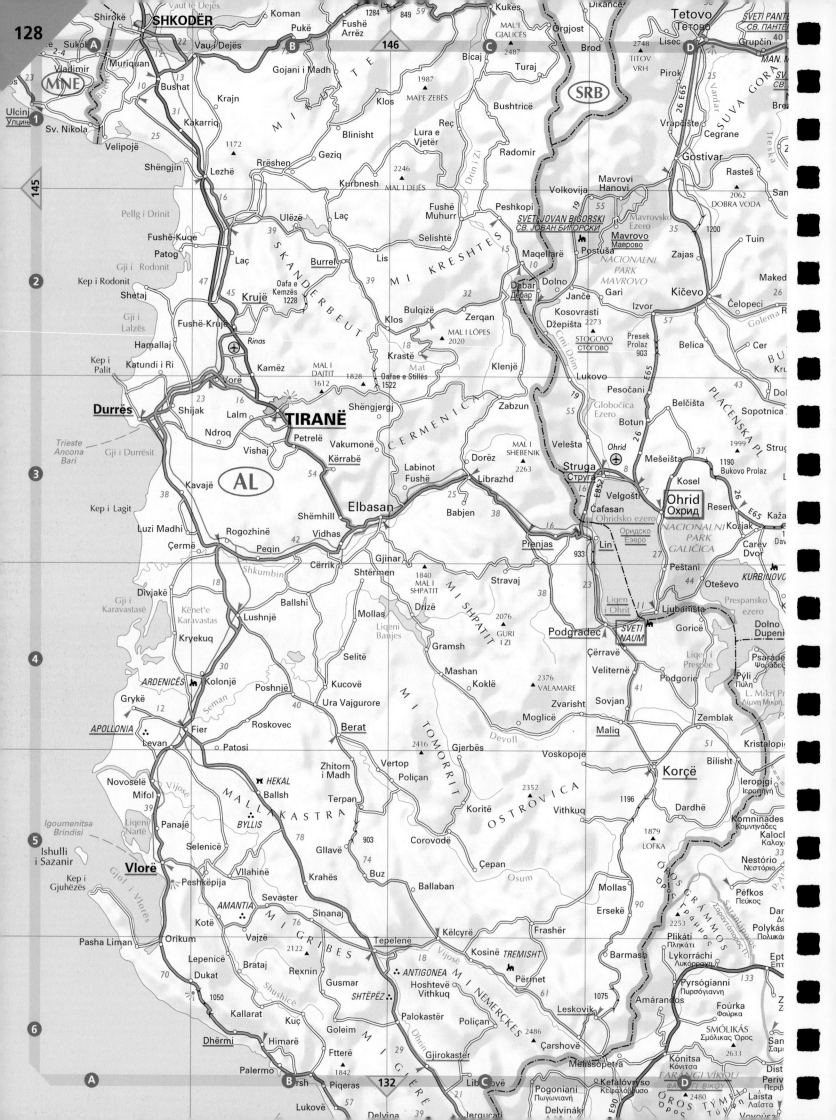

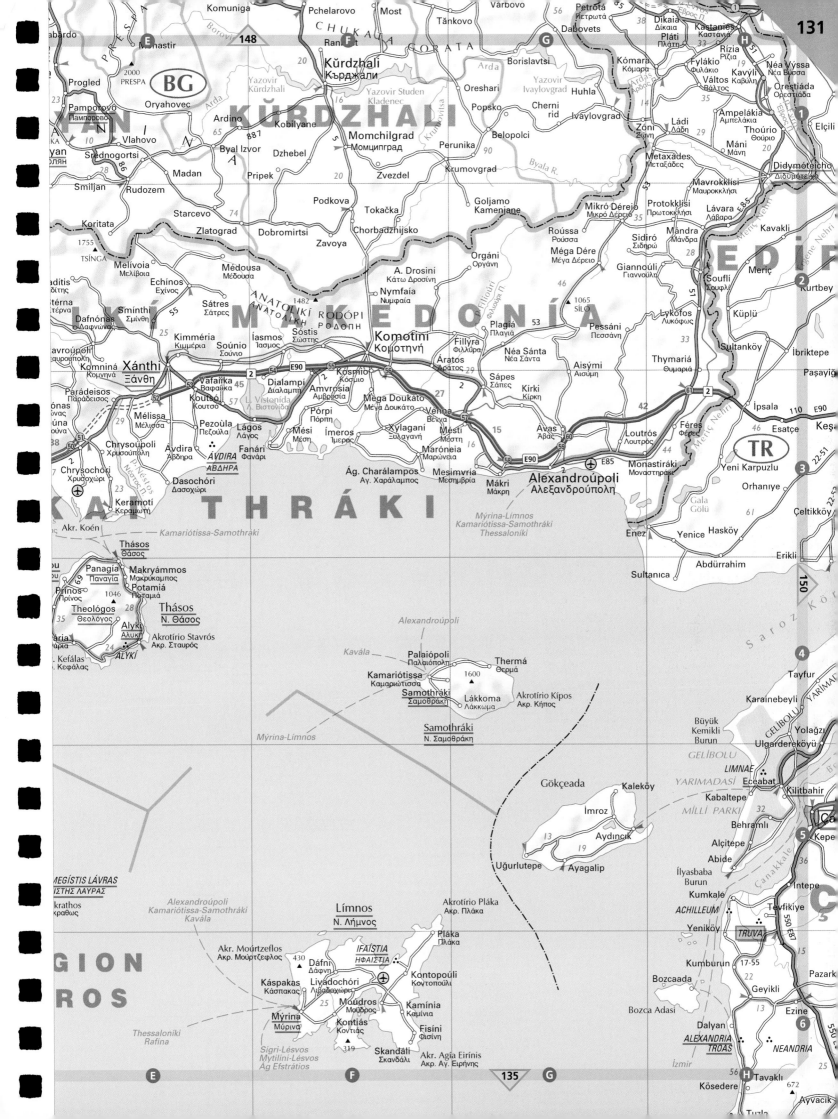

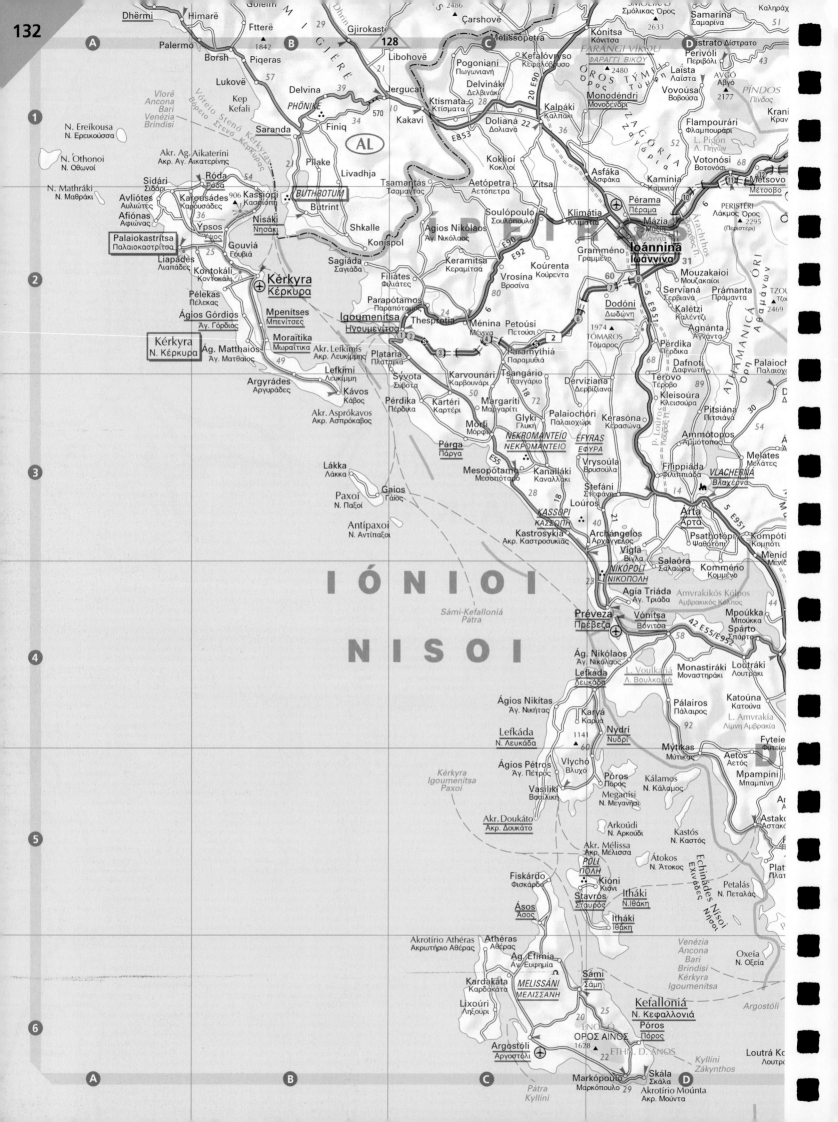

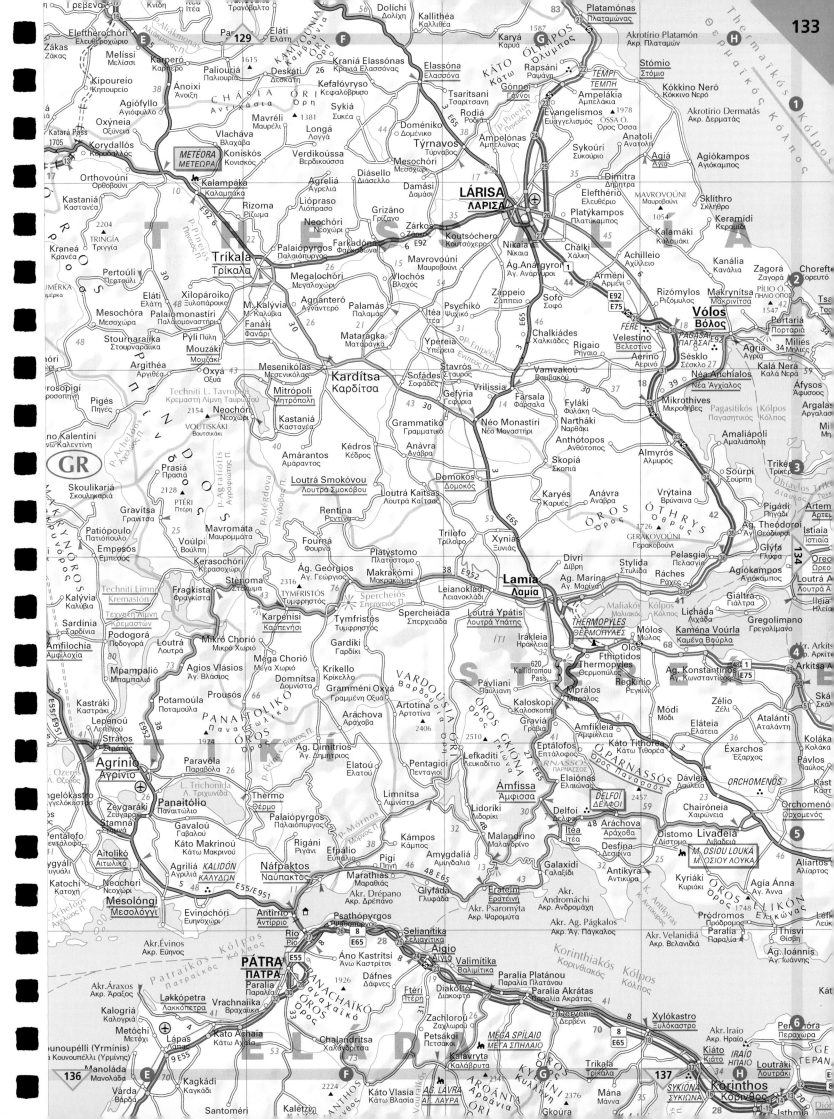

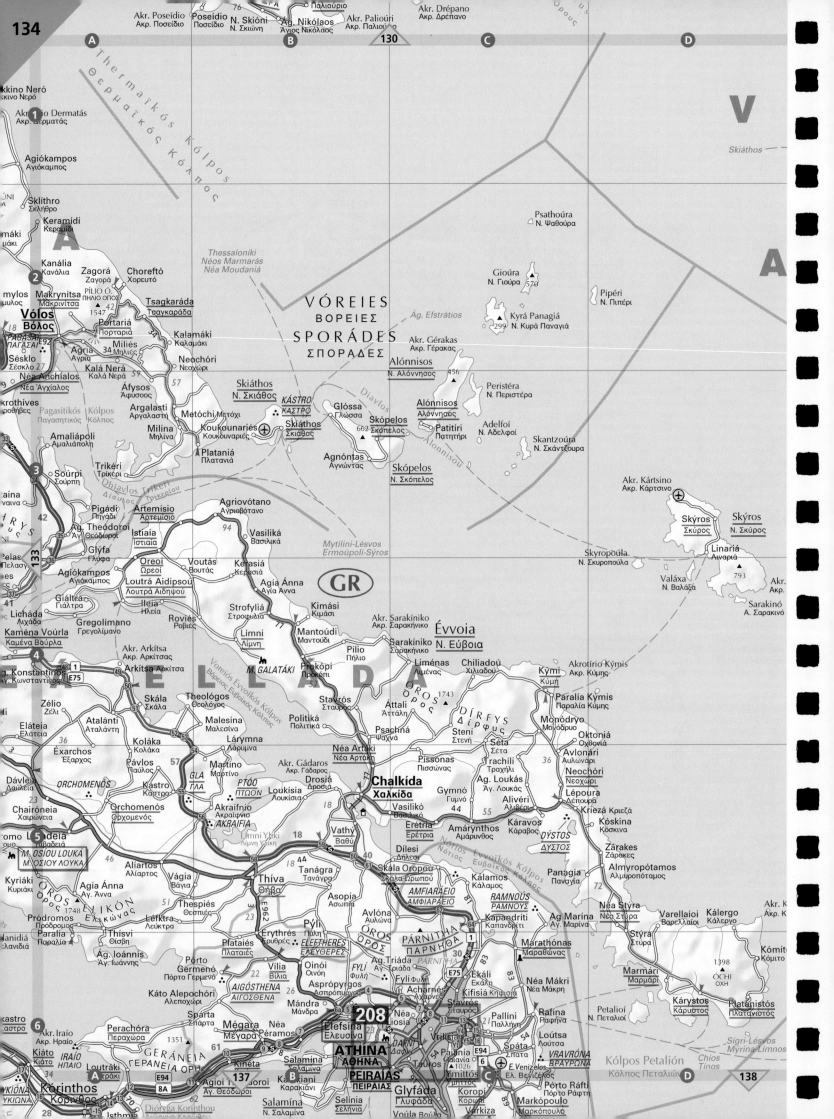

A — B — 138 C — D

Ádamas Φυλακωπή
Zefyría
Ζέφυρος
761 ▲
Akr. Psális
Akr. Ψάλις
Mílos
 Akr. Ψάλις
Akr. Psális
Akr. Ψάλη
N. Μήλος
Adámas-Mílos

Folégandros
Φολέγανδρος
Karavos
Καραβοστ

asía
ρασία

1 Apóstoloi
πόστολοι
Kastaniá
Καστανιά
Velanídia
Βελανίδια

Akrotírio Maléas
Ακρ. Μαλέας

137

agía
γία

2 Kythira
Ν. Κύθηρα

Avlémonas
Αυλέμονας

áli
άλι

NÓTIO

Agia Pelagía

3 Potamós
Ποταμός
Antikýthira
Ν. Αντικύθηρα

Gýtheio
Agia Pelagía

Akr. Spánta
Ακρ. Σπάντα

Peiraías

DIKTÝNAION
ΔΙΚΤΥΝΑΙΟΝ

Stavrós
Σταυρός
Akr. Mêrechas
Ακρ. Μέρεχας

GR

Akr. Voúcha
Ακρ. Βούξα

GONIÁ
ΓΩΝΙΑ

Kólpos Chaníon
Κόλπος Χανίων

Soúda
Σούδα
Stérnes
Στέρνες

Kolymvári
Κολυμβάρι

Chaniá
Χανιά

762 ▲
K. Kissámou
Kólpos
Κόλπος
Κισσάμου

Plataniás
Πλατανιάς

Soúda
Σούδα

Akr. Drápano
Ακρ. Δράπανο

Pánormos
Πάνορμος

Mpali
Μπαλι

4 FALÁSARNA
ΦΑΛΑΣΑΡΝΑ

Kastelli
Καστέλλι

90 E65
Máleme
Μάλεμε

23

90 E75
Kalámi
Καλάμι

Platanés
Πλατανές

78 90

Órmos Almyroú

7

Plátanos
Πλάτανος

21

Voukoliés
Βουκολιές

Fournés
Φουρνές

ÁPTERA
ΑΠΤΕΡΑ

Vámos
Βάμος

Réthymno
Ρέθυμνο

Pérama
Πέραμα

POLYRRINÍA
ΠΟΛΥΡΡΗΝΙΑ

Topólia
Τοπόλια

Néa
Roúmata
Νέα Ρούματα

Lákkoi
Λάκκοι

Mesklá
Μεσκλά

35

Vrýses
Βρύσες

Georgioúpoli
Γεωργιούπολη

67

Margarites
Μαργαρίτες

Prasiés
Πρασιές

ARKÁDI
ΑΡΚΑΔΙ

Ar

Kámpos
Κάμπος

Élos
Έλος

Stróvles
Στροβλές

LEFKÁ ÓRI
ΛΕΥΚΑ ΌΡΗ

Alikampos
Αλίκαμπος

77

Ó
ΟΡ

1182
45

Kántanos
Κάντανος

Omalós
Ομαλός

2452

72

Kournás
Κουρνάς

Epískopi
Επισκοπή

Arménoi
Αρμένοι

Spíli
Σπήλη

Amári
Αμάρι

Fourfourás
Φουρφουράς

2456 ▲

CHRYSOSKALÍTISSA
ΧΡΥΣΟΣΚΑΛΙΤΙΣΣΑ

ÉLYROS
ΕΛΥΡΟΣ

Anópoli
Ανώπολη

Askýfou
Ασκύφου

Argyroúpoli
Αργυρούπολη

79

1776 ▲

Kamáres
Καμάρες

Akrotírio Kríos
Ακρ. Κριός

Soúgia
Σούγια

Ag. Roúmeli
Αγ. Ρούμελη

Skalotí
Σκαλωτή

Sellía
Σελλία

Akoúmia
Ακούμια

97

VALSAM
ΒΑΛΣΑΜ

5 Palaiochóra
Παλαιόχωρα

FARÁNGI SAMARIÁS
ΦΑΡΑΓΓΙ ΣΑΜΑΡΙΑΣ

Sfakiá
Σφακιά

FRAGKOKÁSTELLO
ΦΡΑΓΚΟΚΑΣΤΕΛΛΟ

Plakiás
Πλακιάς

MONÍ PRÉVELI
ΜΟΝΗ ΠΡΕΒΕΛΗΣ

Mélampes
Μέλαμπες

Agía Galíni
Αγ. Γαλήνη

Tympáki
Τυμπάκι

AG. TRIÁDA
ΑΓ. ΤΡΙΑΔΑ

Paximádia
Ν. Παξιμάδια

Mátala
Μάταλα

FAISTÓS
ΦΑΙΣΤΟΣ

Órmos Mesáras

Akr. Líthino
Ακρ. Λίθινο

Gavdopoúla
Ν. Γαυδοπούλα

Kastri
Καστρί

6 Gávdos
Ν. Γαύδος

A — B — C — D

Ακρ. Αχλάδες

Ofidoúsa
Ν. Οφιδούσα

Astypálaia
Αστυπάλαια

Kálymnos
Kos
Aigiáli-Amorgós

E   F   139   G   H

tásis
πάσης

Íos
Ίος

Mýkonos
Katápola-Amorgós

Siteía-Kríti
Ágios Nikólaos-Krití

Syrna
Ν. Σύρνα

Oía
Οία

Thíra/ Santoríni
Ν. Θήρα/ Σαντορίνη

Thirasía
Ν. Θηρασία

Thíra/Firá
Θήρα/ Φηρά

Anáfi
Ν. Ανάφη

Stenó Kárpathou
Στενό Καρπάθου

Thessaloníki

24

THÍRA
ΘΗΡΑ

Anáfi
Ἀνάφη

Makrá
Ν. Μακρά

Akr. Paraspóri
Ακρ. Παρασπόρι

Ródos
Chálki

Akrotíri
Ακρωτήρι

Períssa
Περίσσα

Pacheiá
Ν. Παχειά

630

Saría
Ν. Σαρία

Irákleio-Kríti

Christianá
Ν. Χριστιανή

Diafáni
Διαφάνι

Ródos

A I G A Í O

Ólympos
Όλυμπος

Kárpathos
Ν. Κάρπαθος

Mesochóri
Μεσοχώρι

1215

Ródos

Voláda
Βωλάδα

Kárpathos
Κάρπαθος

K R Í T I

Kárpathos
Siteía-Kríti

Pylés
Πύλες

Armáthia
Ν. Αρμάθια

Menetés
Μενετές

Fry
Φρυ

Arkása
Αρκάσα

Siteía-Krití
Fry-Kásos

Ág. Marína
Αγ. Μαρίνα

Lemesos-Cyprus
Thessaloníki
Peiraias
Thíra

Kásos
Ν. Κάσος

Adámas-Milos
Astypálaia

Astypálaia

Fry-Kásos
Kárpathos

Día
Ν. Δία

Dragonáda
Ν. Δραγονάδα

Gianysáda
Ν. Γιανισάδα

Akr. Stavrós
Ακρ. Σταυρός

Ag. Pelagía
Αγ. Πελαγία

Akr. Ag.Ioánnis
Ακρ. Αγ. Ιωάννης

Akr. Síderos
Ακρ. Σίδερος

E75

Fódele
Φόδελε

**IRÁKLEIO
ΗΡΑΚΛΕΙΟ**

Gournes
Γούρνες

Limáni Chersonísou
Λιμάνι Χερσονήσου

Vrouchás
Βρουχάς

**SPINALÓGKA
ΣΠΙΝΑΛΟΓΚΑ**

ÍTANÓS
ΙΤΑΝΟΣ

Elása
Ν. Ελάσα

Vái
Βάι

Mílatos
Μίλατος

Karteros

9

Irákleio

Marathos
Μάραθος

Ammoudára
Αμμουδάρα

Nírou Kháni
Νίρου Χάνι

Goúves Stalida
Γούβες Σταλίδα

Mália
Μάλια

68

E75

Eloúnta
Ελούντα

Kólpos Mirampéllou
Κόλπος Μιραμπέλλου

TÓPLOU
ΤΟΠΛΟΥ

Siteía
ΣΗΤΕΙΑ

Palaíkastro
Παλαίκαστρο

Axós
Αξός

Tylisos
Τύλισος

Archánes
Αρχάνες

**KNOSÓS
ΚΝΩΣΟΣ**

Potamiés
Ποταμιές

Mochós
Μοχός

Neápoli
Νεάπολη

Ágios Nikólaos
Αγ. Νικόλαος

Móchlos
Μόχλος

90 E75

36

Akr. Pláka
Ακρ. Πλάκα

logeia

Ag. Mýron
Αγ. Μύρων

Kastélli
Κάστελλι

LATÓ
ΛΑΤΩ

Skopí
Σκοπή

Zakrós
Ζακρός

**ZAKRÓS
ΖΑΚΡΟΣ**

ID

IDAÍO ÁNTRO
ΙΔΑΙΟ ΑΝΤΡΟ

VATHÝPETRO
ΒΑΘΥΠΕΤΡΟ

45

DIKTAÍO ÁNTRO
ΔΙΚΤΑΙΟ ΑΝΤΡΟ

57

Psychró
Ψυχρό

Kritsá
Κριτσά

Kavoúsi
Καβούσι

Sfáka
Σφάκα

70

Praisós
Πραισός

Káto Zákros
Κάτω Ζακρός

Zarós
Ζαρός

Ag. Varvára
Αγ. Βαρβάρα

99

ÓROS DÍKTI
ΟΡΟΣ Δίκτη

Kaló Chorió
Καλό Χωριό

1237

Stavrochóri
Σταυροχώρι

Sykéa
Συκέα

Zíros
Ζίρος

ÓNERO
ΟΝΕΡΟ

GORTYS
ΓΟΡΤΥΣ

Arkalochóri
Αρκαλοχώρι

Panagiá
Παναγιά

2148

Máles
Μάλες

Pachiá Ámmos
Παχιά Αμμος

**GOURNIA
ΓΟΥΡΝΙΑ**

Koutsourás
Κουτσουράς

58

Moíres
Μοίρες

Askífu
700

Ag. Thomás
Αγ. Θωμάς

Teféli
Τεφέλι

Garípa
Γαρίπα

Áno Viánnos
Ανω Βιάννος

Ammoudára
Αμμουδάρα

Ag. Fotiá
Αγ. Φωτιά

Makrygialós
Μακρυγιαλός

Agioi Déka
Αγιοι Δέκα

Pyrgos
Πύργος

Skiniás
Σκινιάς

97

Péfkos
Πεύκος

57

Mýrtos
Μύρτος

**Ierápetra
Ιεράπετρα**

Koufonísi
Κουφονήσι

17

Árvi
Άρβη

18 Pómpia
Πόμπια

Vagionía
Βαγιονιά

1231

Tsoútsouros
Τσούτσουρος

Kerátokampos
Κερατόκαμπος

Chárakas
Χάρακας

Léntas
Λέντας

Chrysí
Ν. Χρυσή

Kaloí Liménes
Καλοί Λιμένες

Kríti
Ν. Κρήτη

1   154   2   3   4   5   6

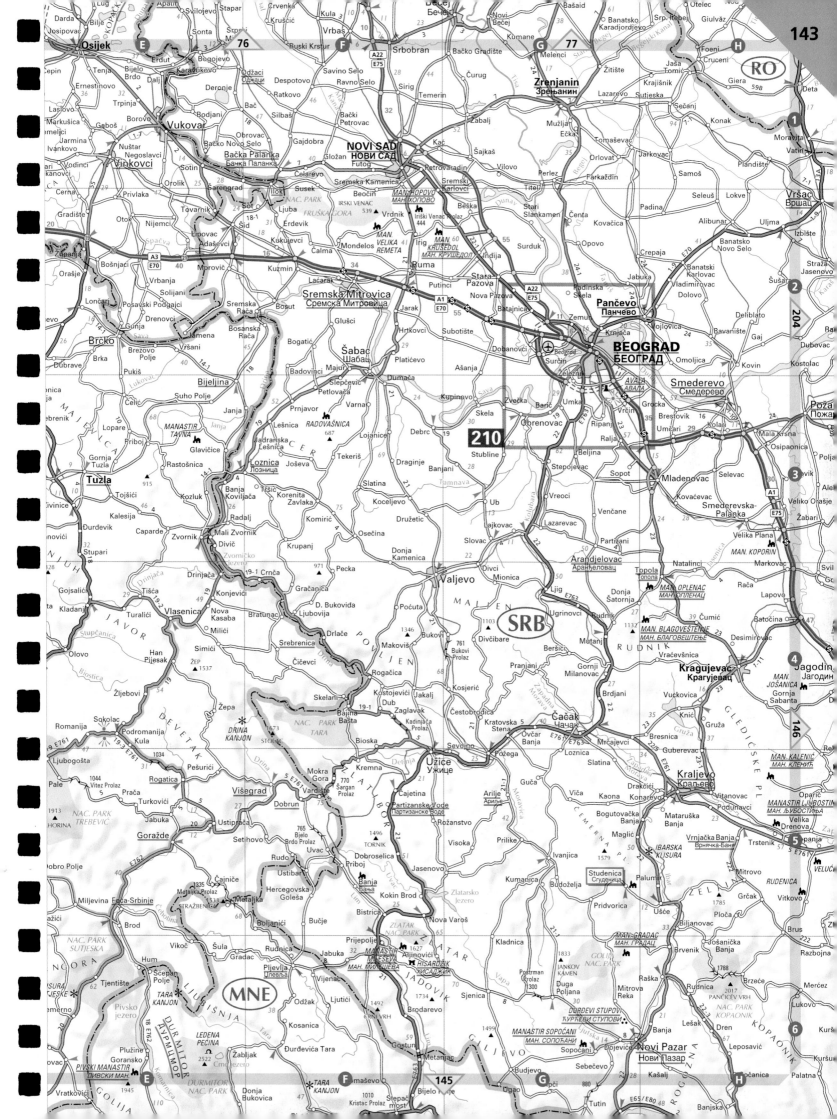

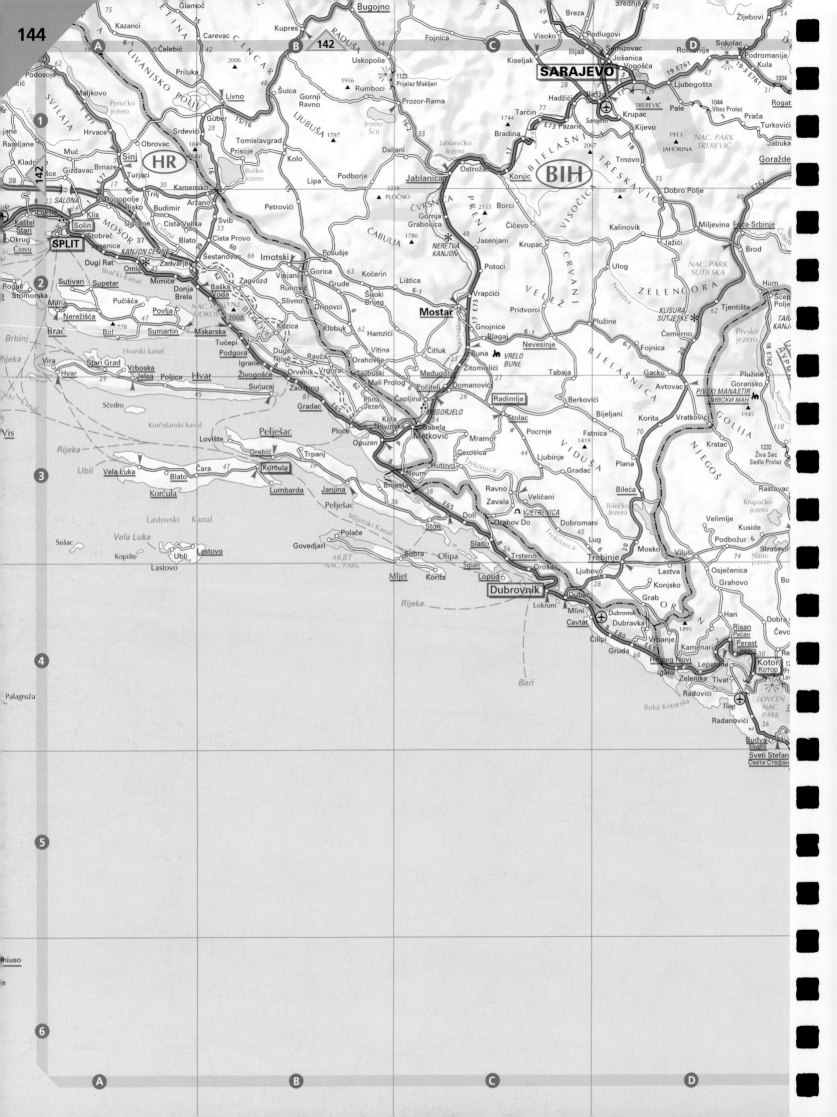

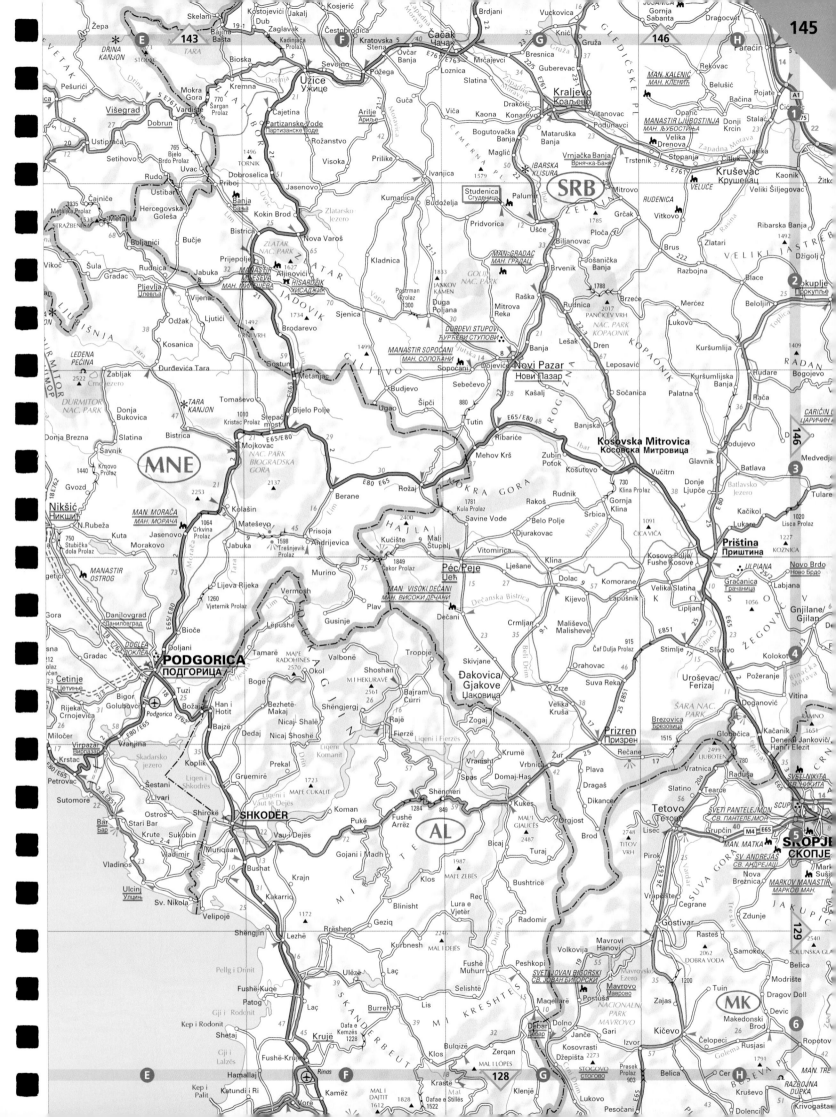

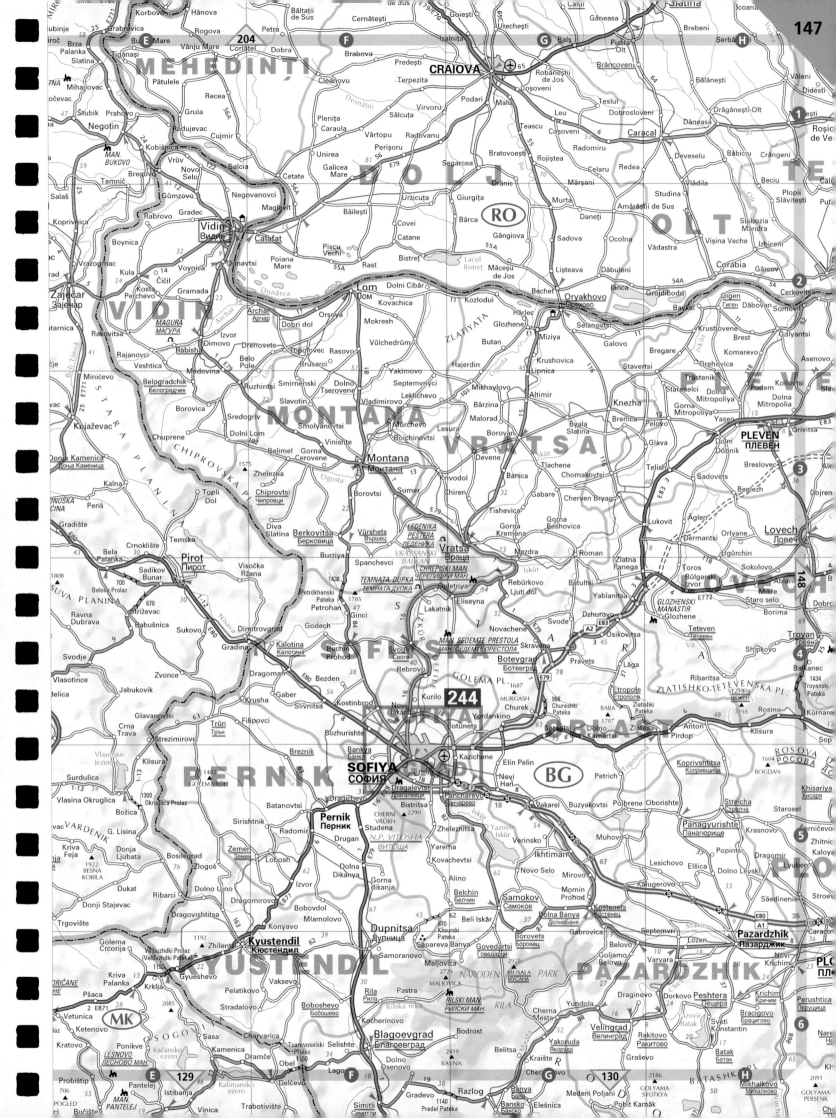

TR

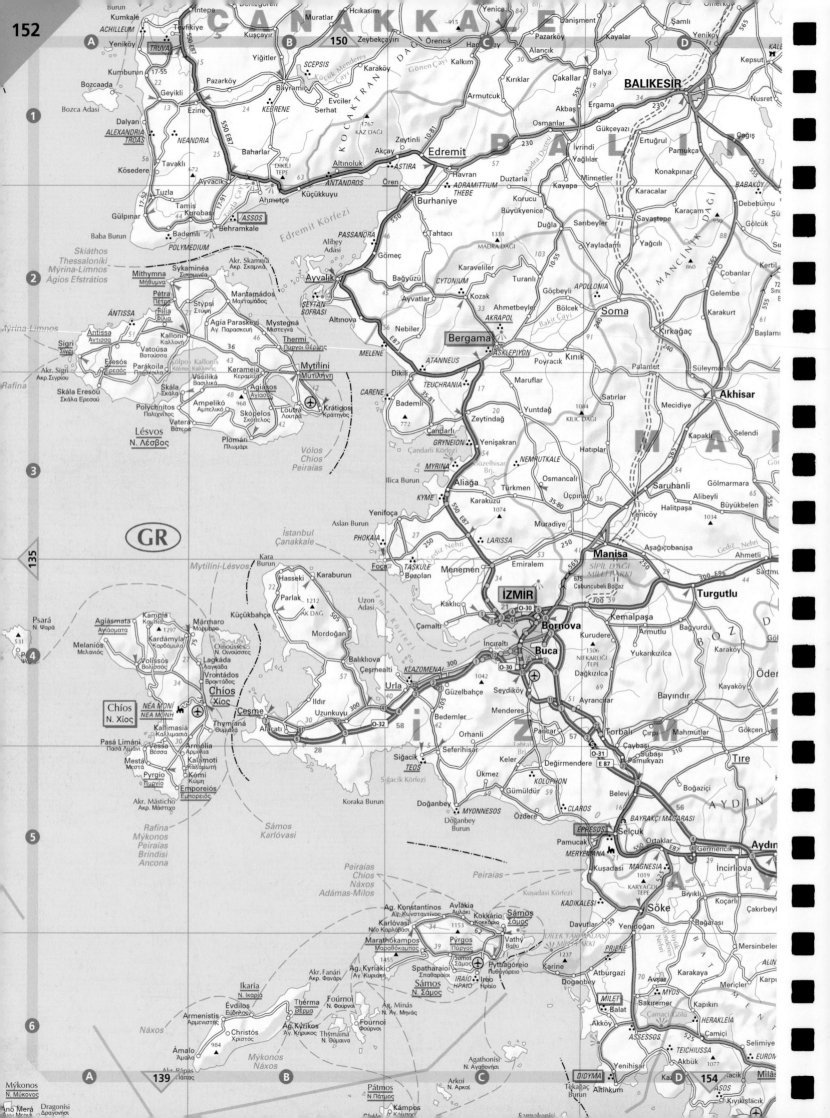

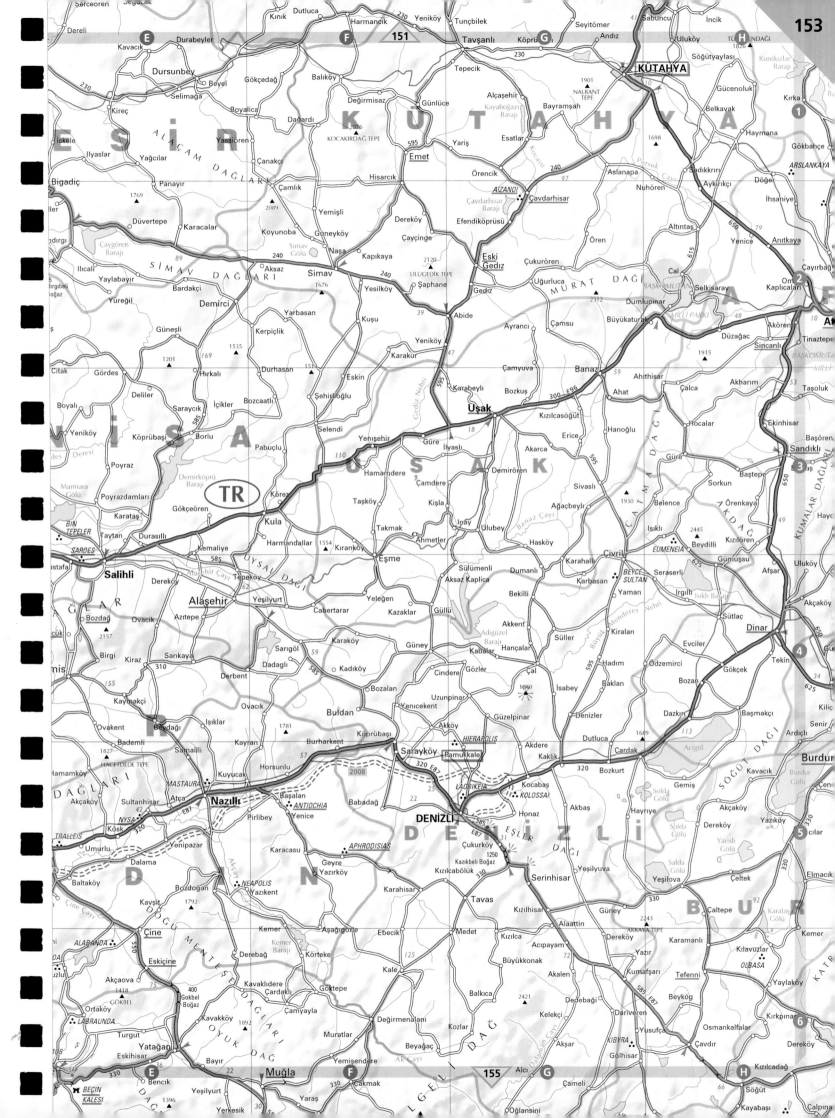

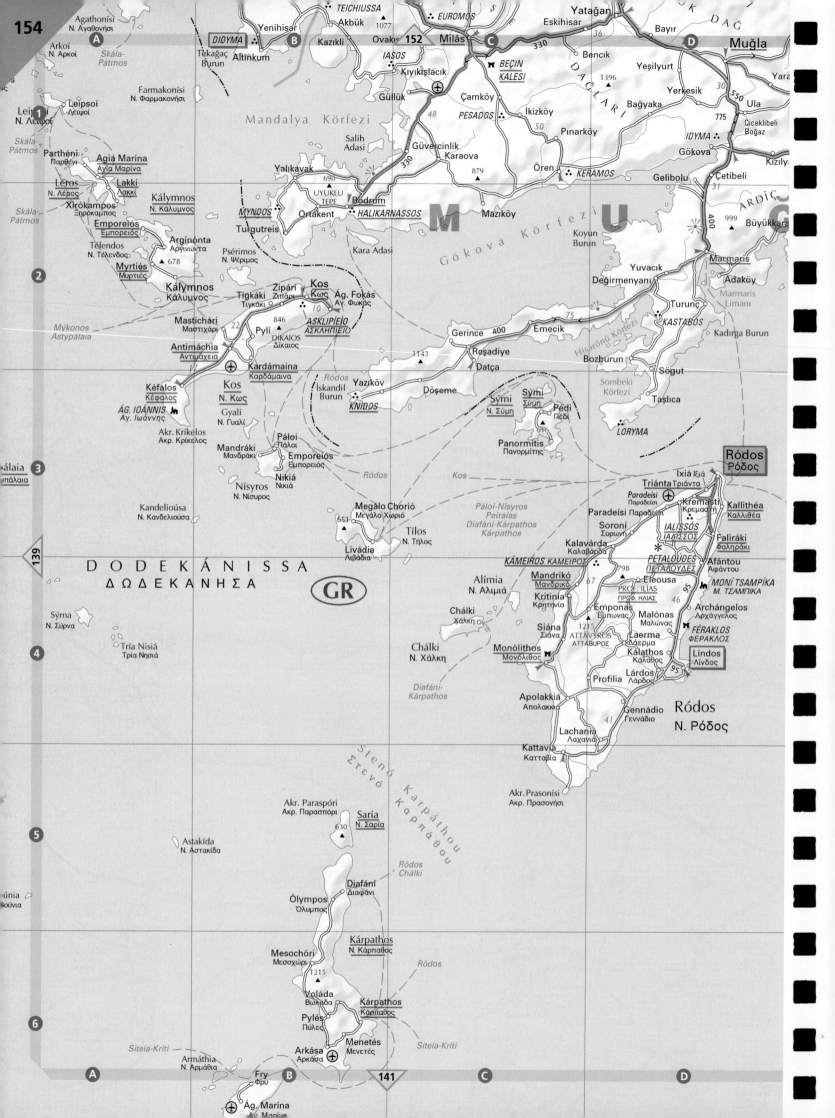

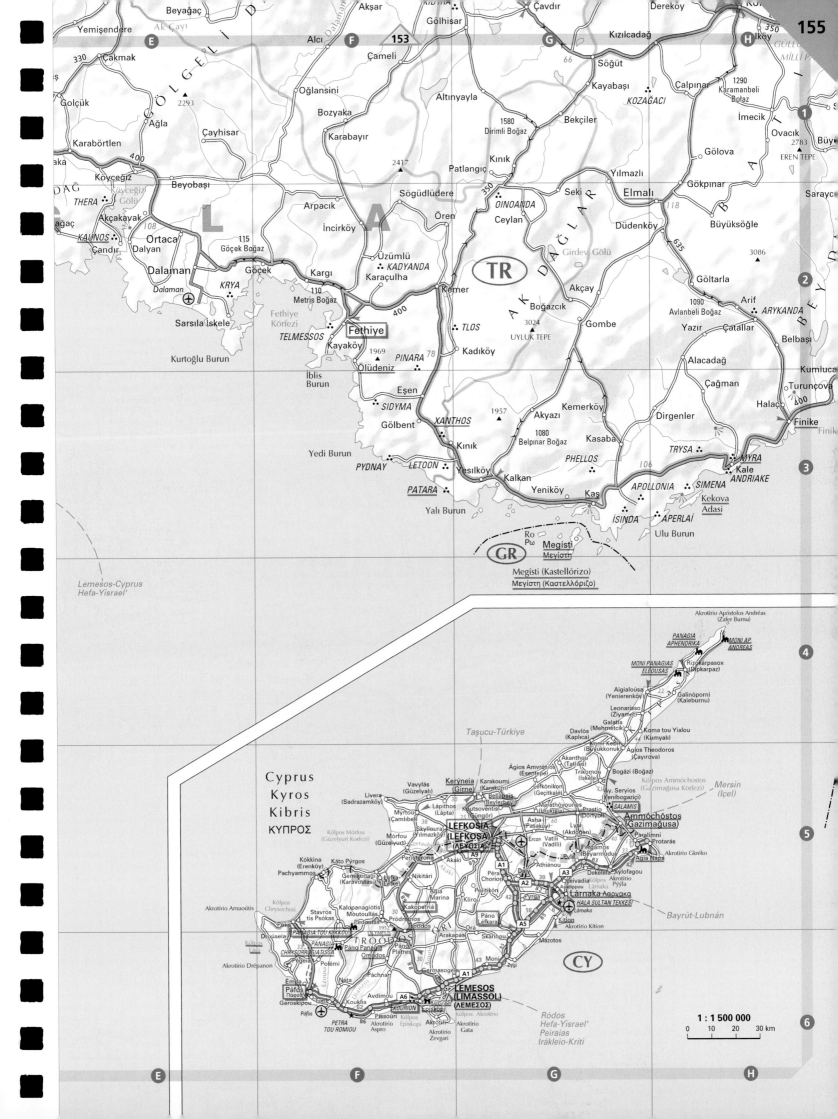

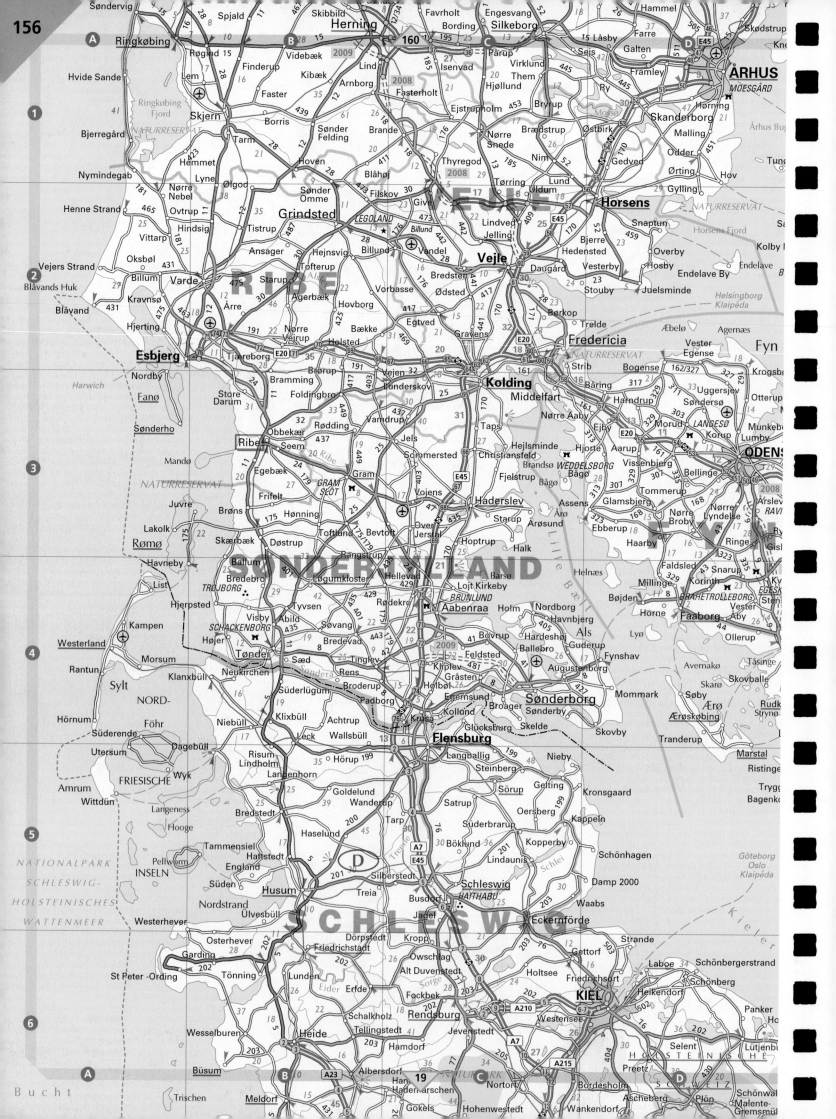

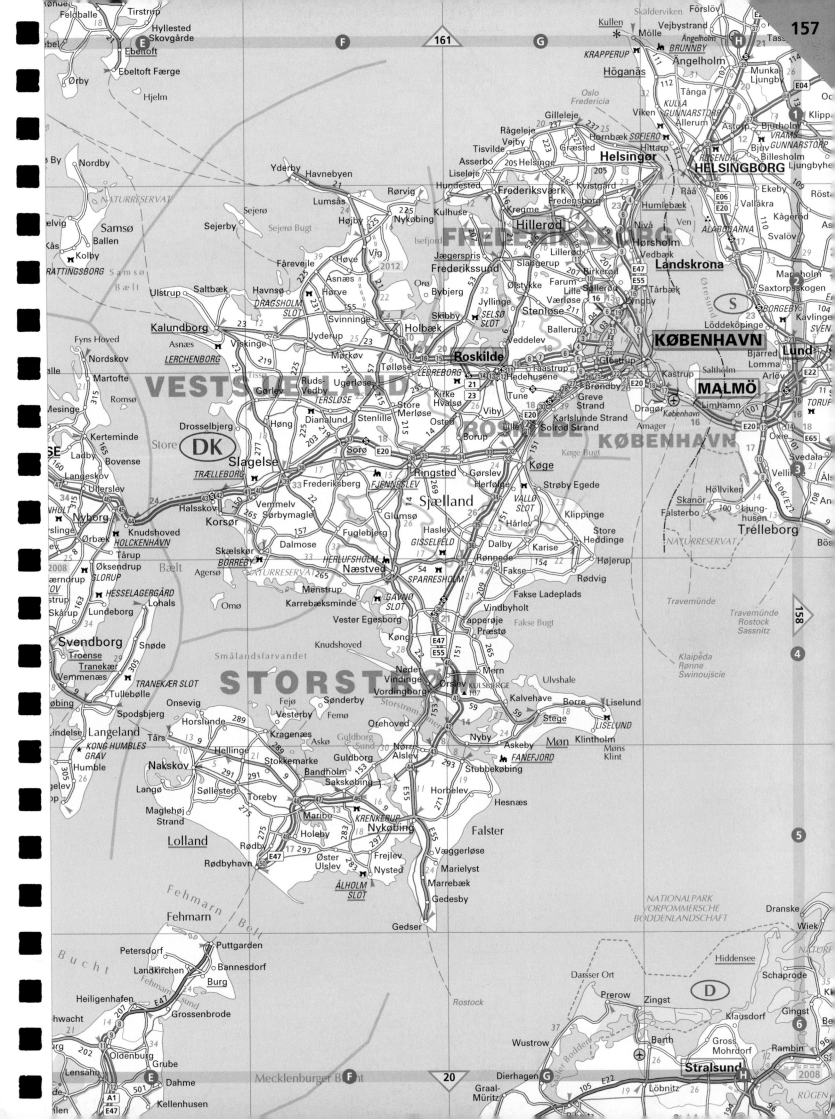

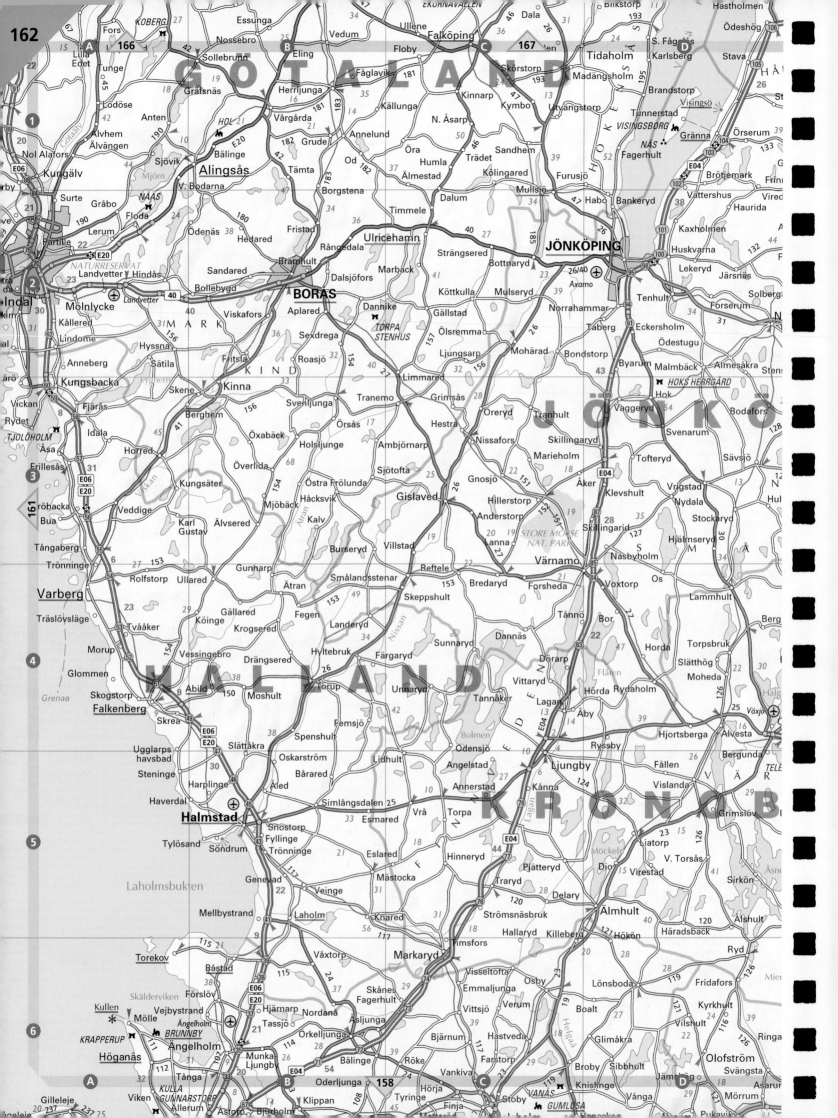

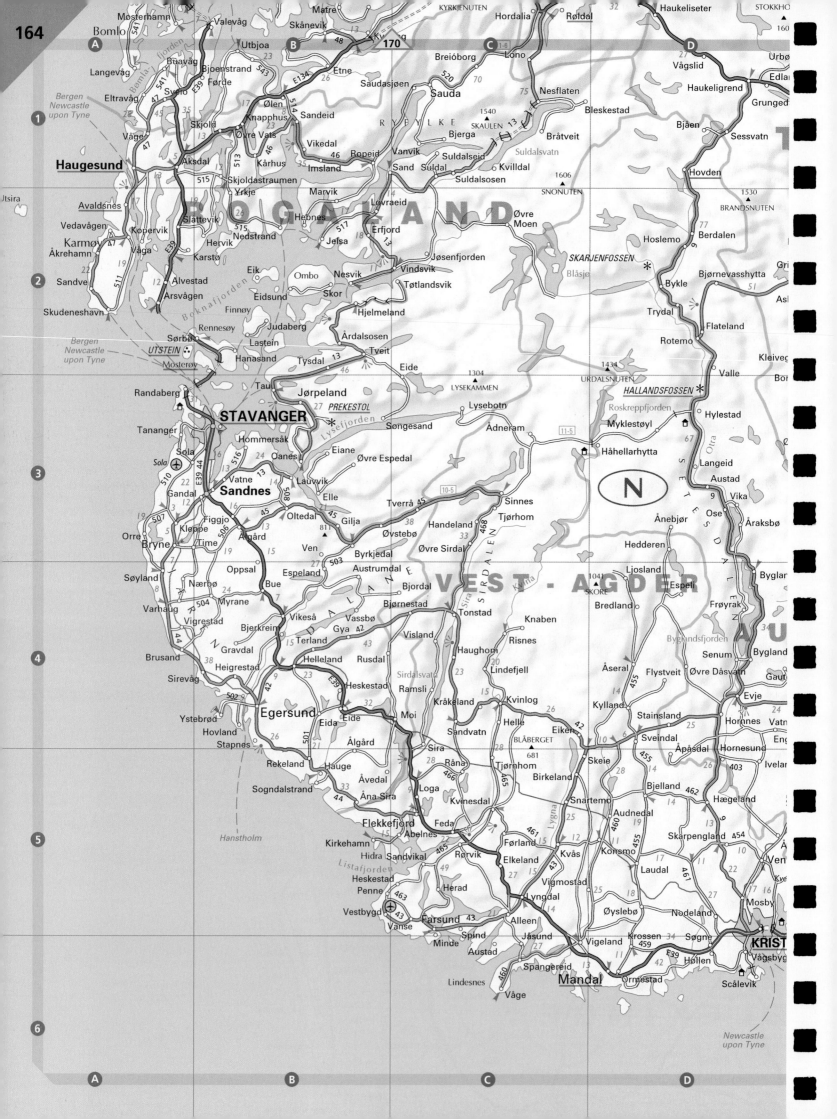

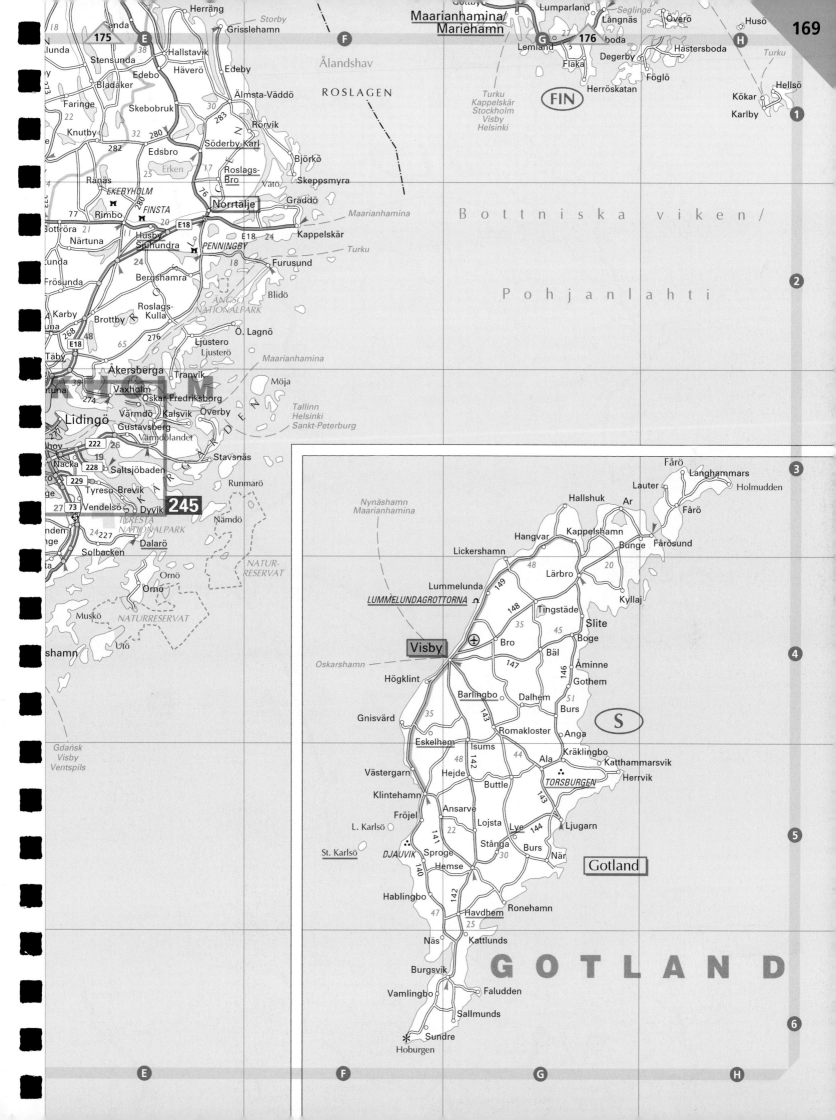

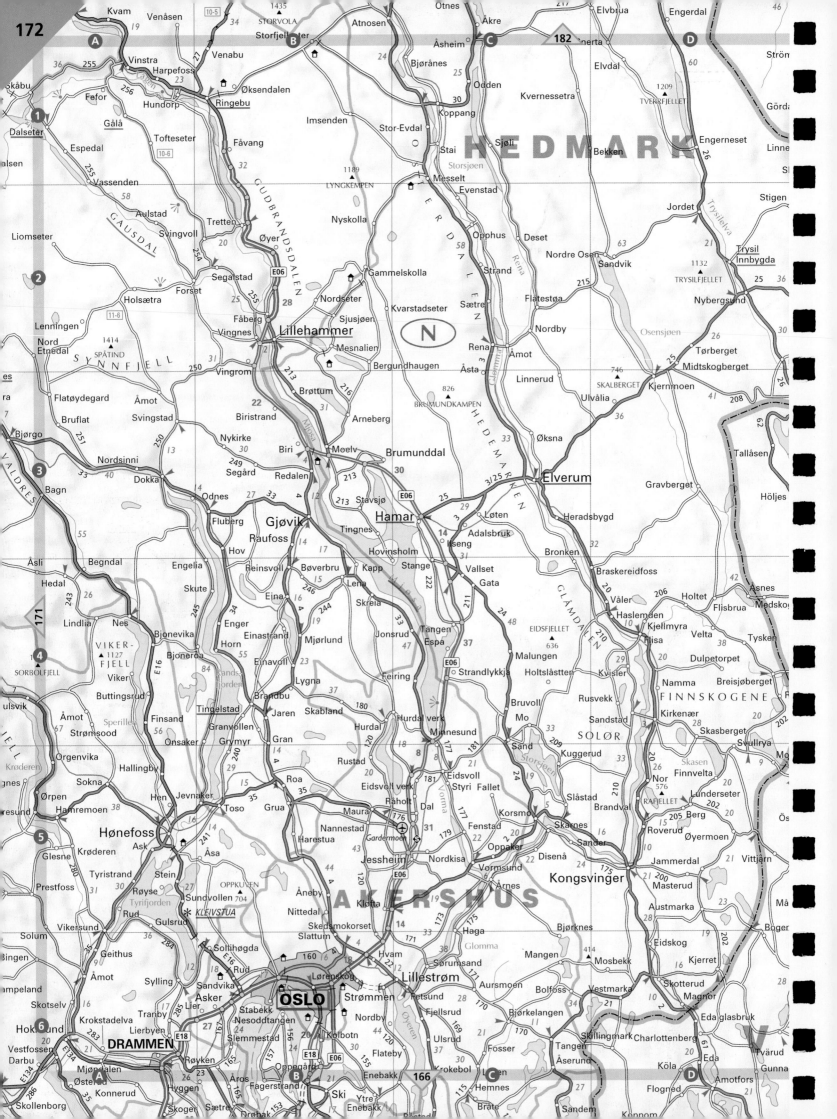

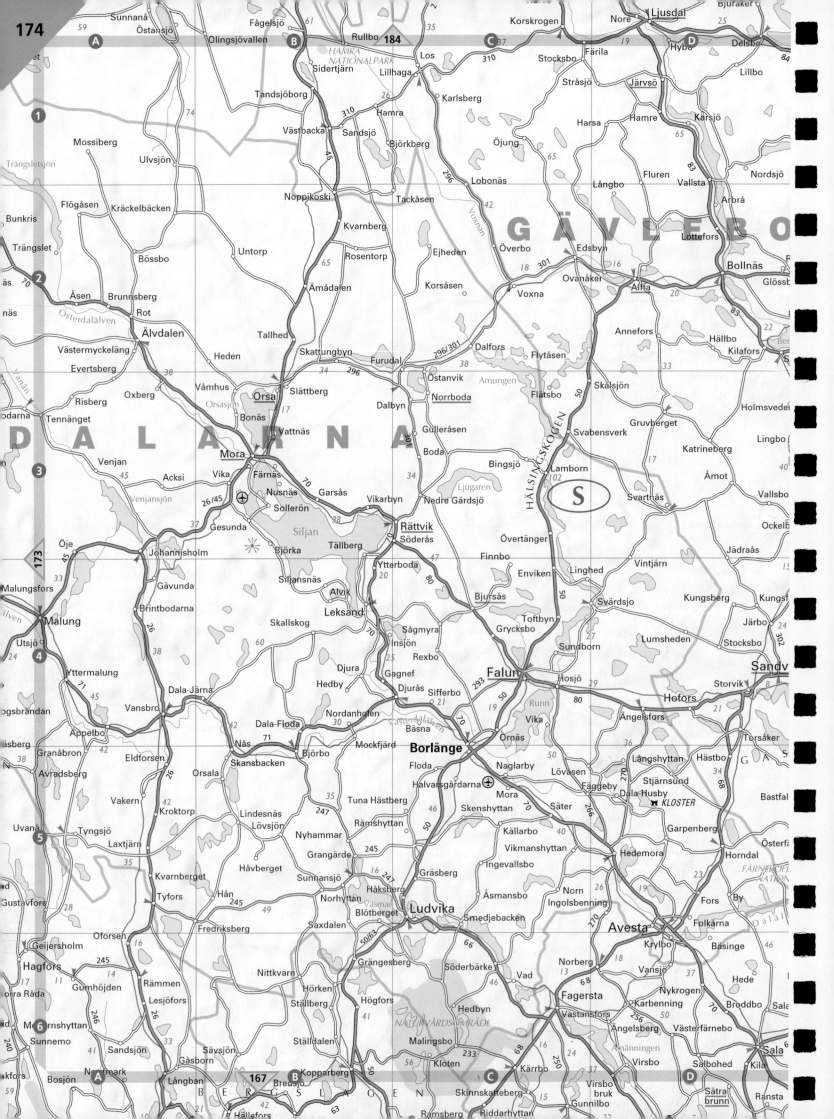

Bottniska viken/

Pohjanlahti

AHVENANMAA/

Ahvenanmaa/Åland

ÅLAND

BOLSTAHOLM

Geta

Bovik
Finström
Saltvik
Sund
Lövö
Vårdö

Storby
Godby
KASTELHOLMS
Hammarland
Gölby
Bomarsund
Delet
Teili

Eckerö
Torp
Jomala

Grisslehamn

Gottby

Maarianhamina/
Mariehamn

Lumparland
Långnäs
Övero
Husö

Lemland
Granboda

Lshav

Flaka
Degerby
Hastersboda

Föglö
Herröskatan

Turku
Kappelskär
Stockholm
Visby

Helsinki

Kökar
Karlby

LAGEN

Reposaari
Mäntyluoto
Pihlava

Kööritilä
Pohjansaha
Ahlainen

Pirltijärvi
Isojärvi
Honkakoski

Vaneskoski

Pomarkku/
Pämark
Lamppi

Kairila

Lessila

Haunia

Noormarkku/
Norrmark
Söörmarkku

Karhijärvi

256

Kuuminainen

PORI/
BJÖRNEBORG

Niittumaa

Palus
Ulvila/
Ulvsby
Käyhtiönmaa

Kullaa
11
72

Kiikoiner

257
44

Lankoori

2

Luvia
Peränkylä

Nakkila

Harjavalta

Sääksjärvi

246

Lievikoski
247
Säpilä

Saarenmaa

49

62

Kokemäk
Kumo

217

43

Peipohja

Eurajoki/
Euraåminne

Kiukainen
214

Sydanmää

Lähteenk

Rauma/
Raumo

Lutta
208
12

Eura
Köyliö/
Kjulo
Vu

Unaja

Lappi

Kauttua

211

Voiluoto

207

Mestilä

Säkylä

213

Reila
Vermuntila

43

Pyhäjärvi

Pyh

32

Pato

Hinnerjoki

21

Pyhämaa
Pyhäranta

196

8

Suontaka

Vaaljoki

204

Laajoki

2021

208

Uusikaupunki/
Nystad

43

Kalanti

Laitila

Nästi

Uusikartano

Karjala

2021

Kalela

Ran

Lahti

Sairinen

Juva

60

Tarvainen

Mattinen

Korvensuu

202

Tortinmäki

Lokalahti

Vehmaa

194

Mynämäki

8

Jurmo

Rautila

192

193

Mietoinen

196

Askainen/
Villnäs

190

Paatinen
Masku

Kustavi/
Gustavs

Taivassalo
Tövsala

192

Raisio/
Reso

9

Turku

222

Osnäs
Hakkenpää

193
E63

Avå

KULTARANTA

Fiskö

Merimasku

Naantali
Nådend

8

E18

Brändö

Velkua

Poikko

189

TURKU/
ÅBO

Kaarin

Enklinge
Björkö

Iniö

Velkuanmaa

Rymättylä/
Rimito

Lappo

Houtsala

Ylikla

Parainen/
Pargas

Kumlinge

Houtskari/
Houtskär

Lofsdal

Seglinge

Storlandet

180

Korppoo/
Korpo

180

Nauvo/
Nagu

180

Sottunga

1801

Korpoström

Dra

Stockholm
Maarianhamina
Kökar

Gullkrona Fjärd

Nötö

Turku

Hellsö

SAARISTOMEREN KANSALLISPUISTO /
SKÄRGÅRDSHAVETS NATIONALPARK

Jurmo

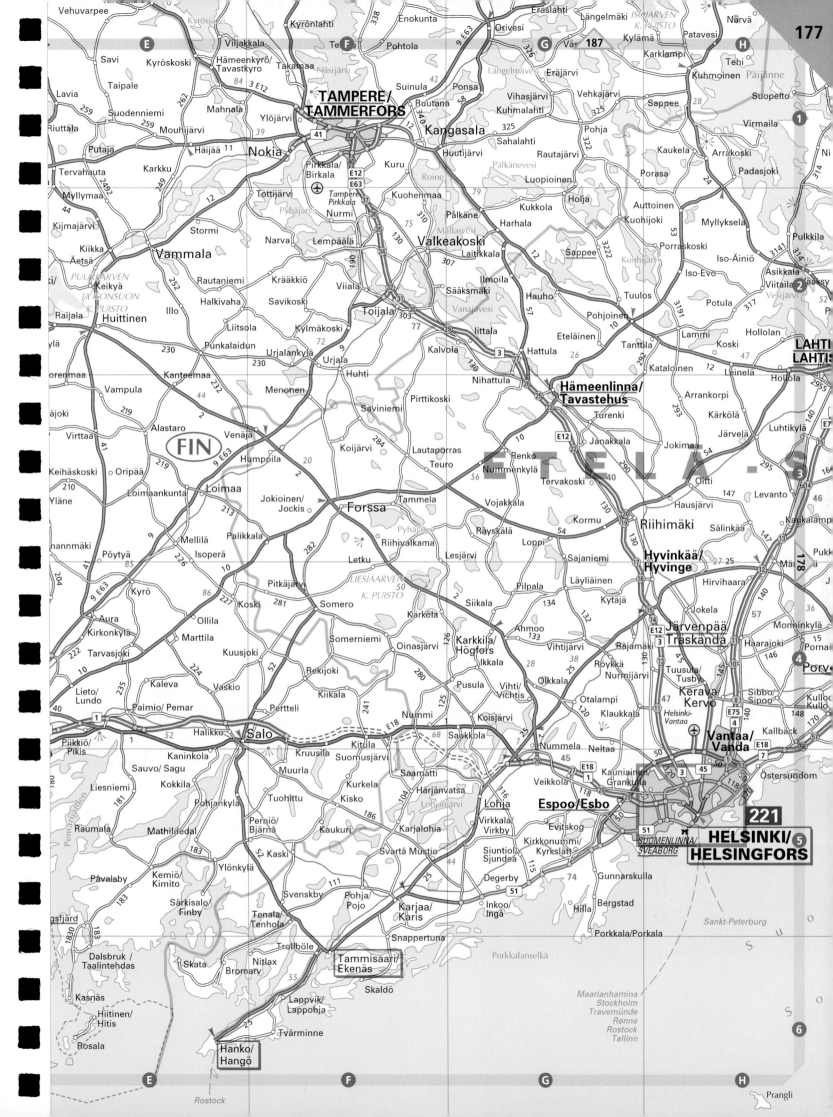

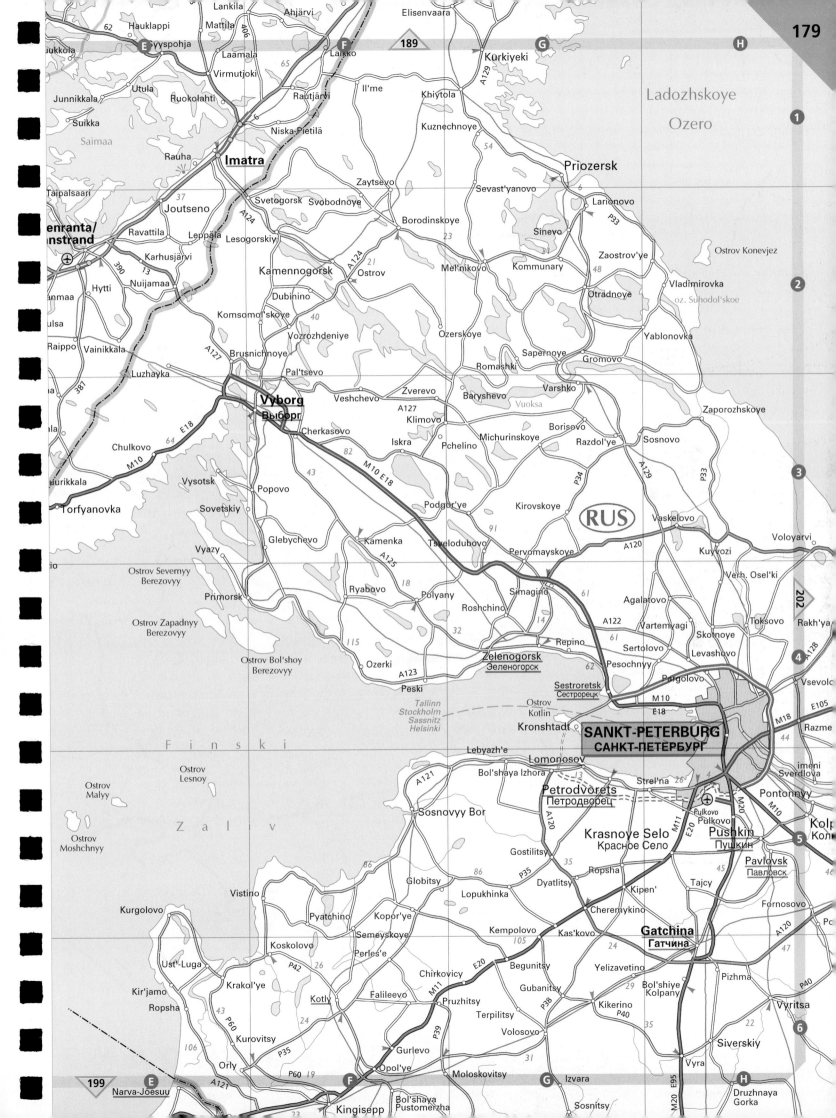

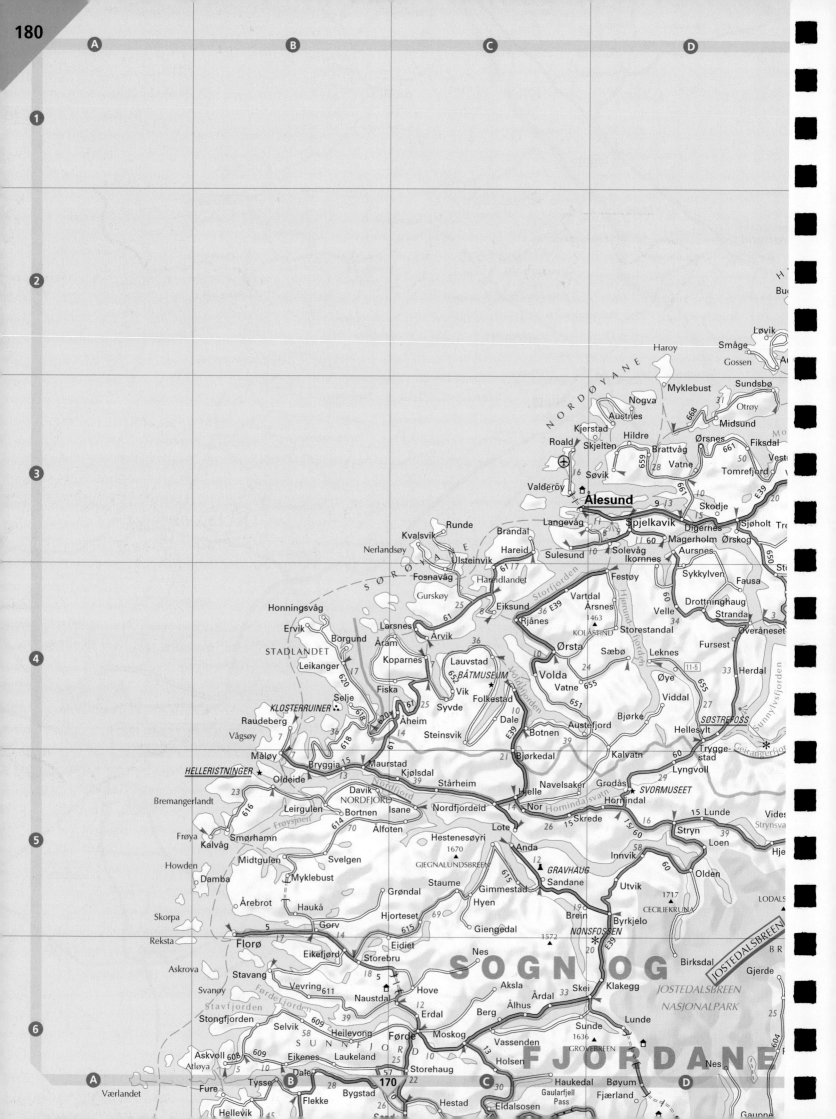

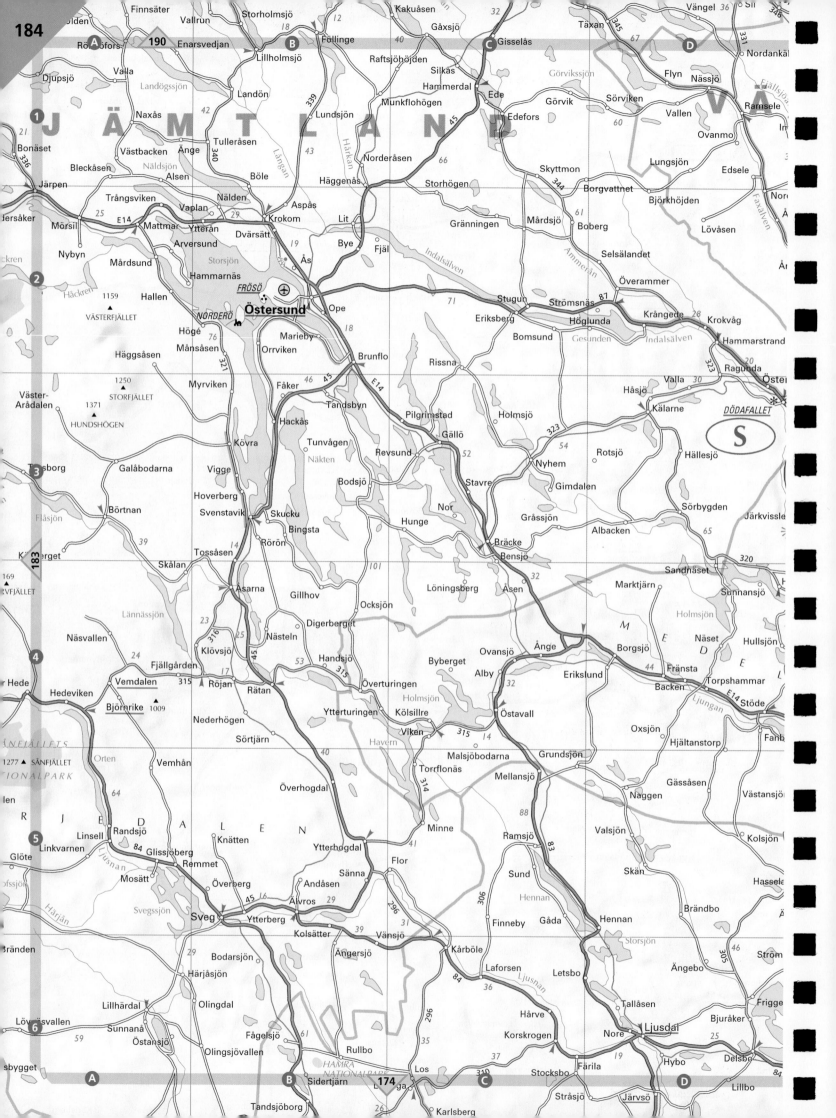

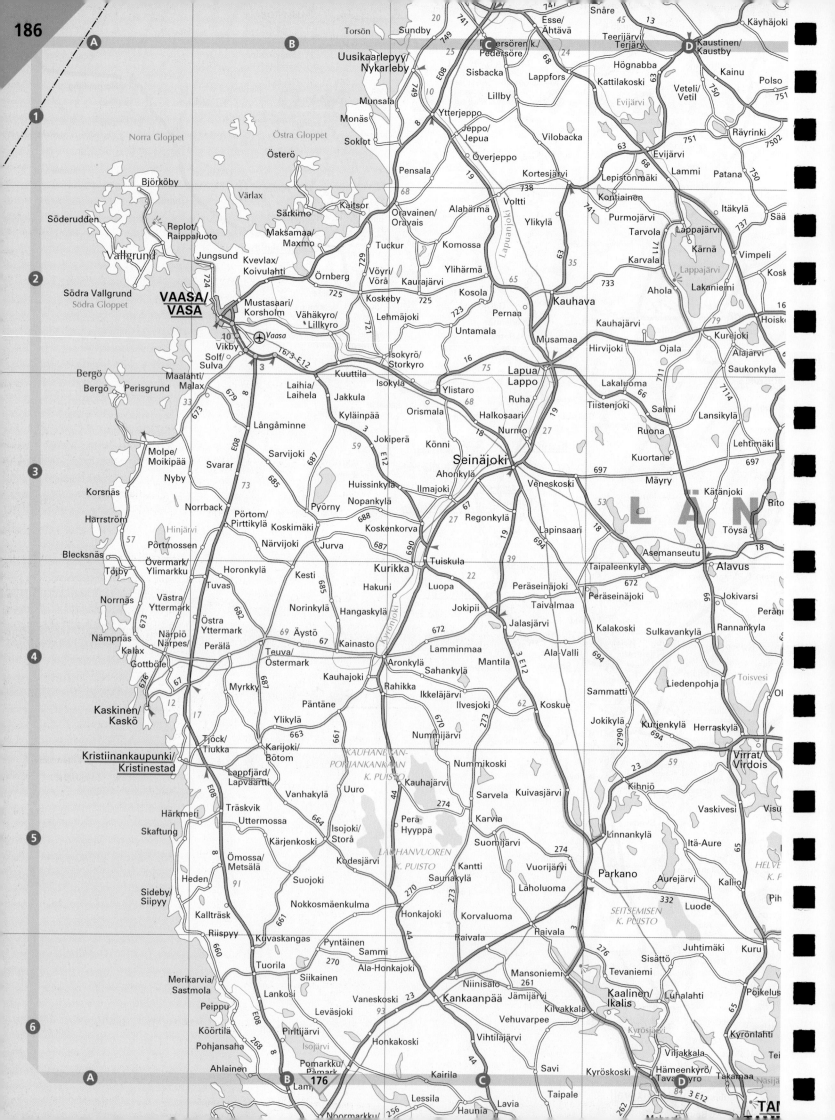

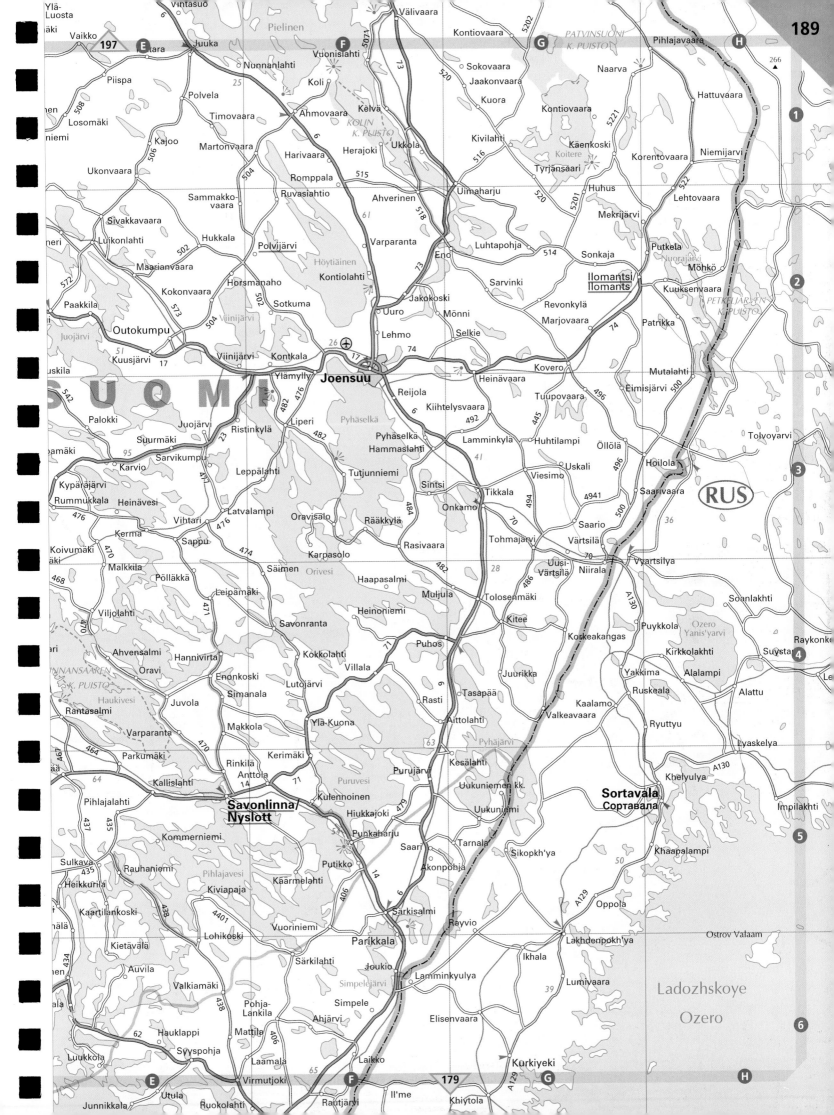

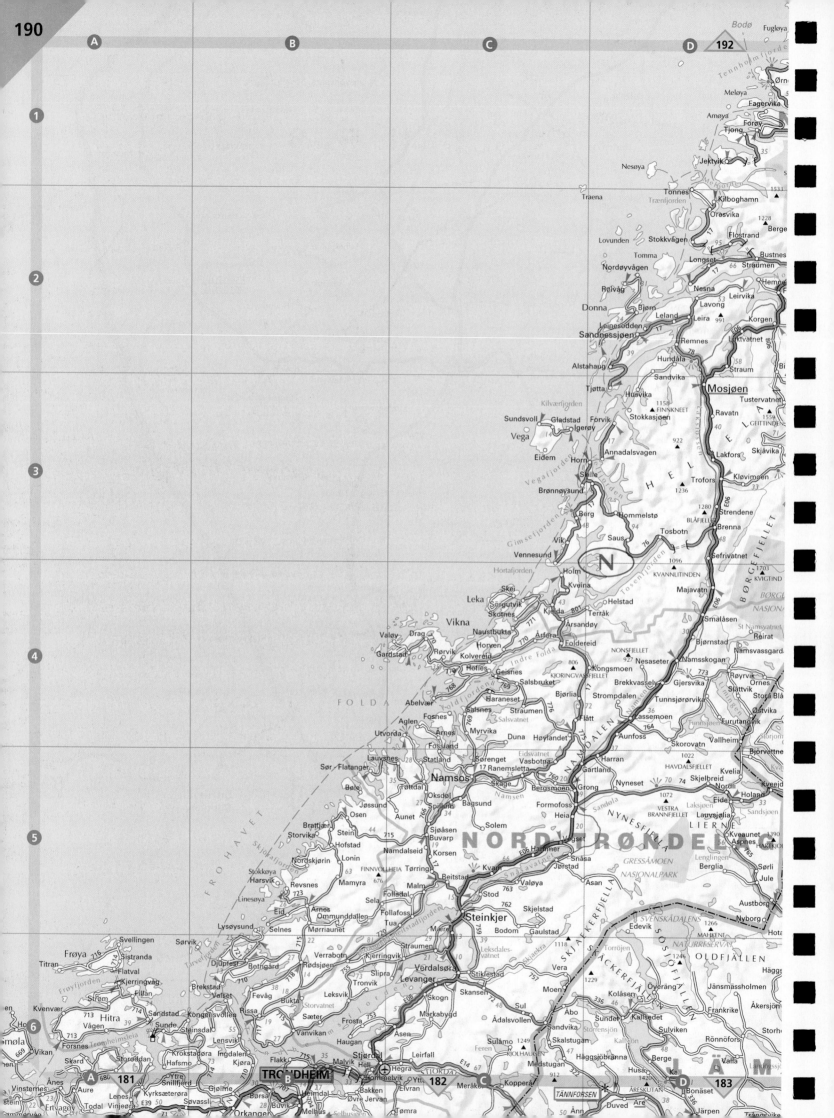

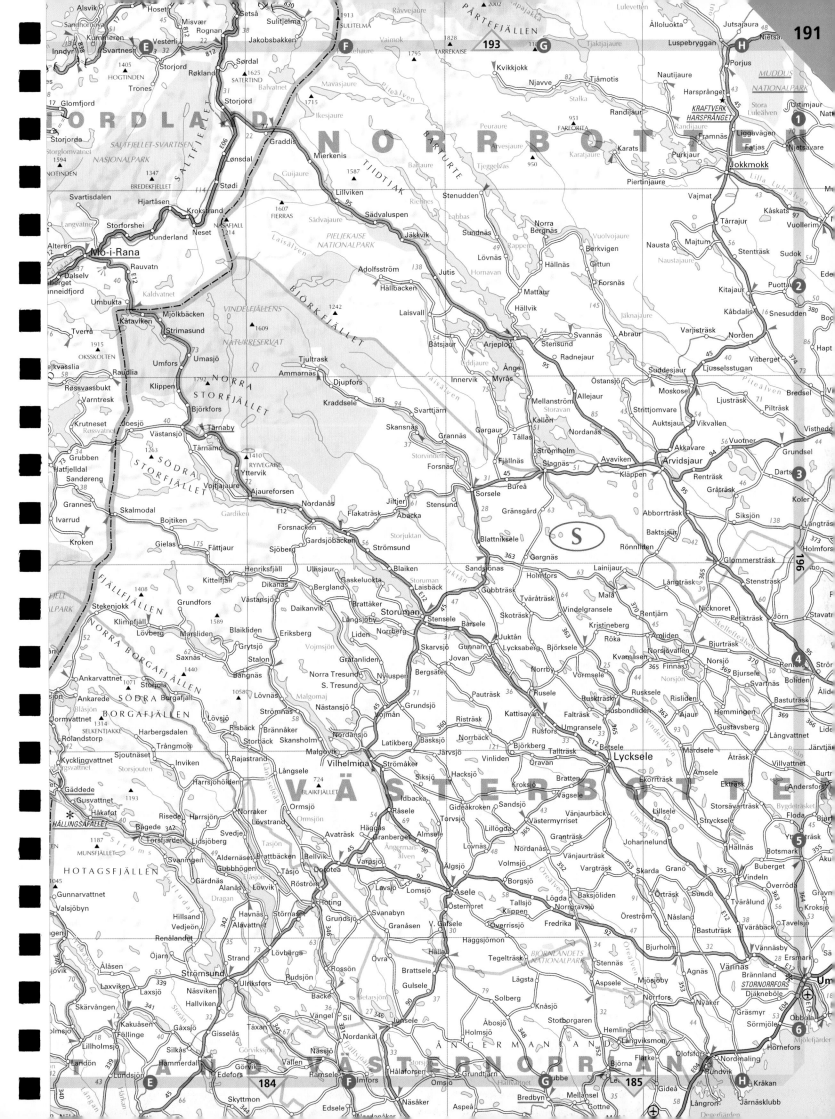

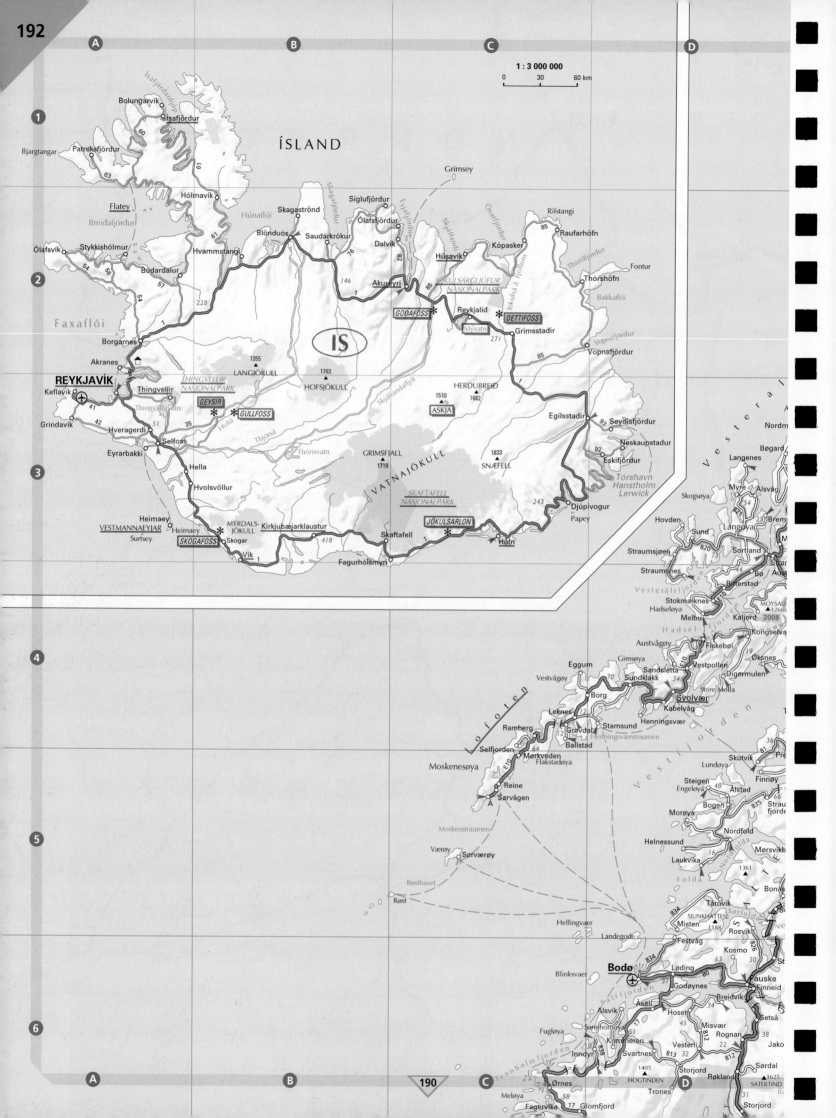

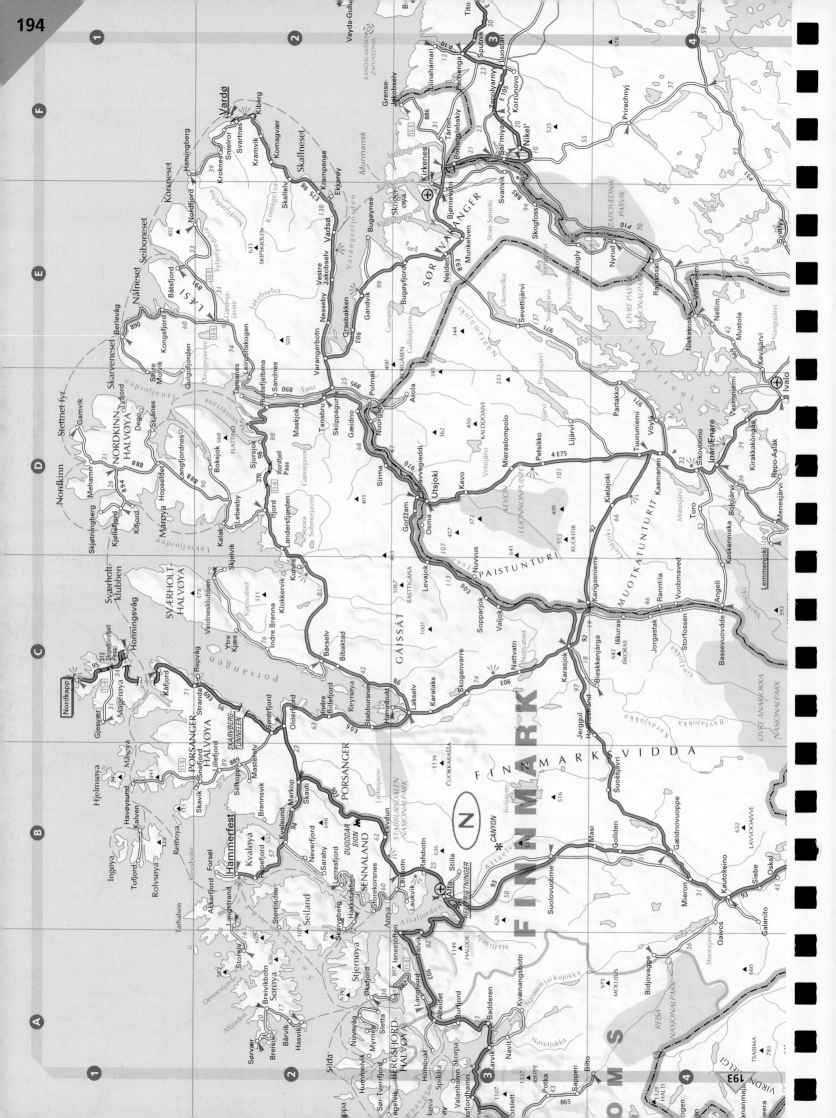

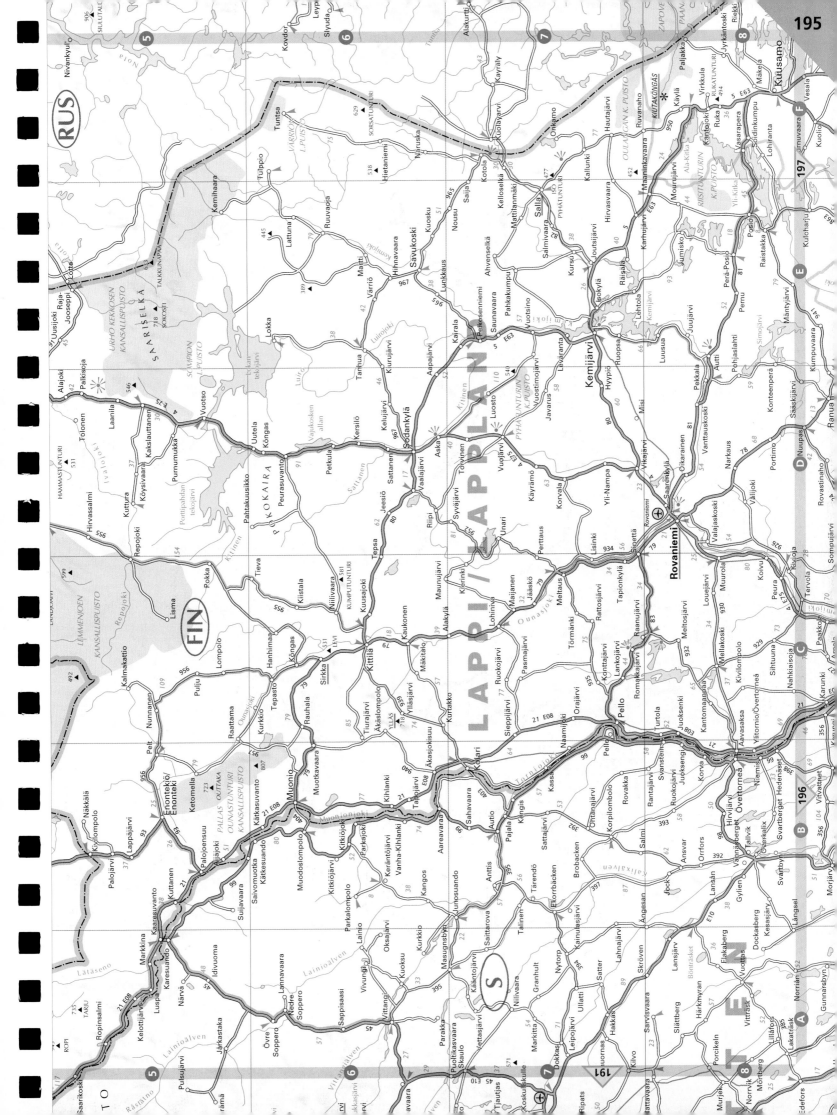

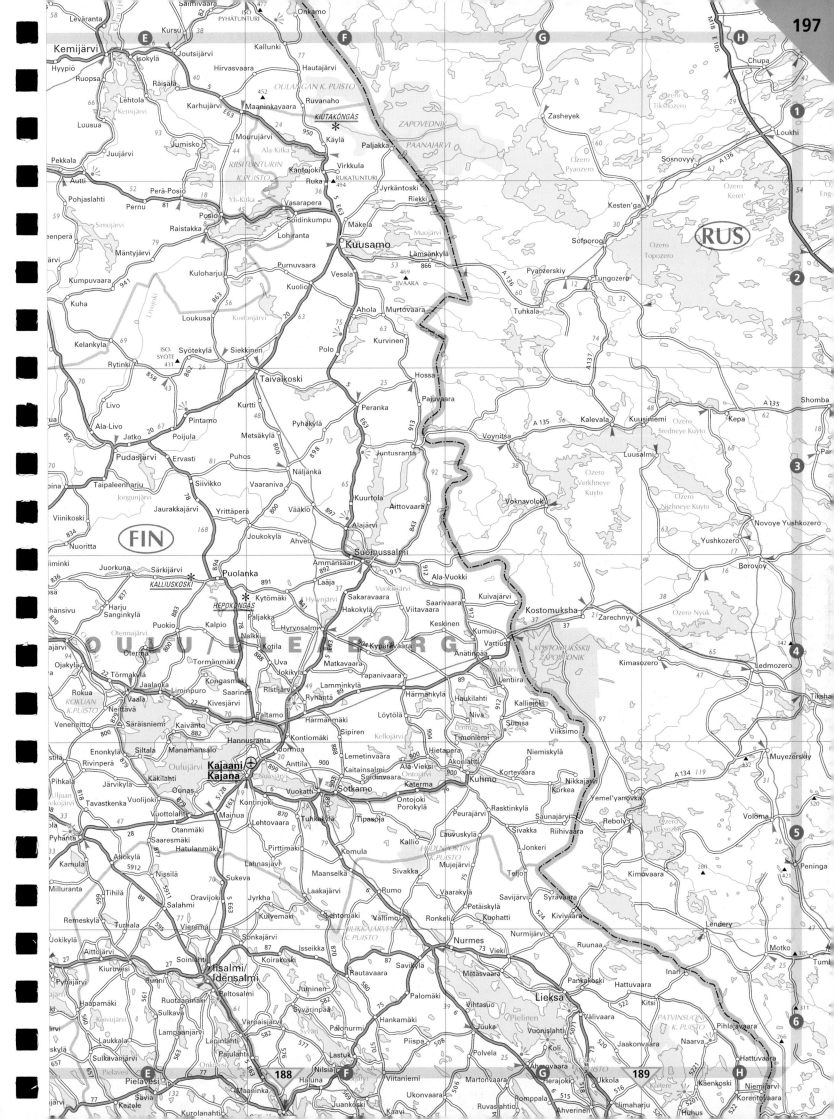

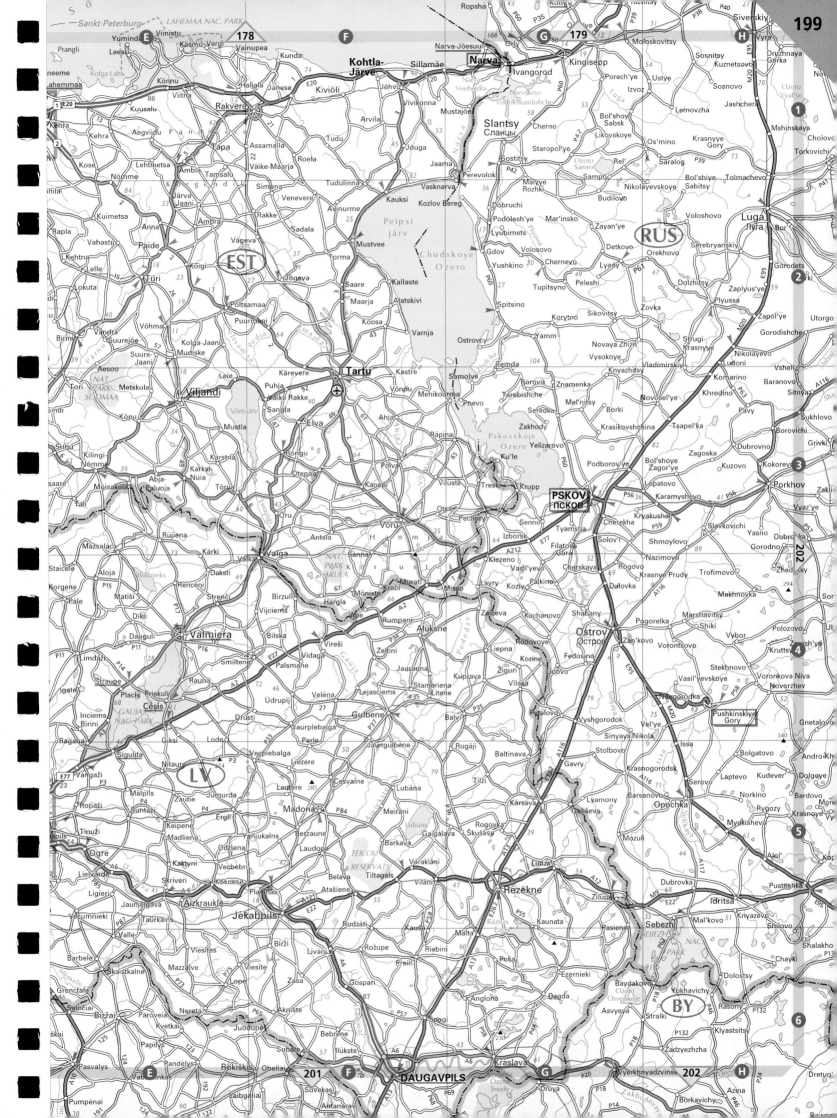

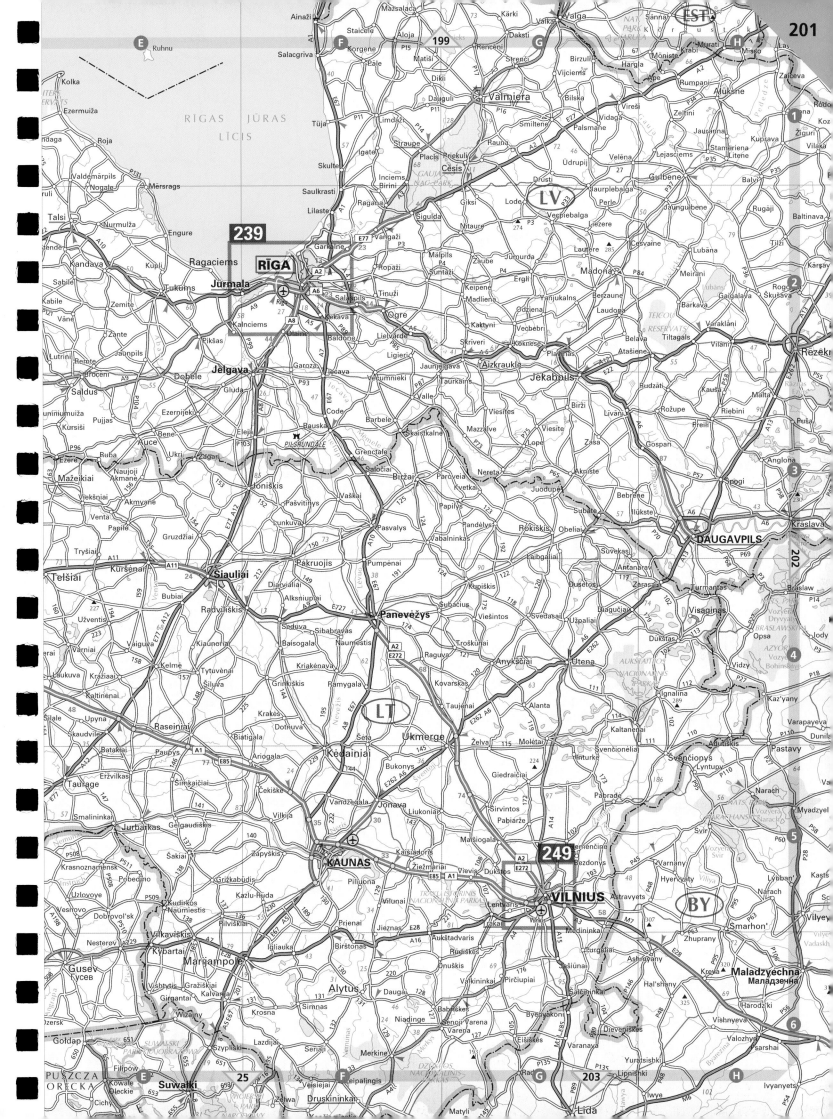

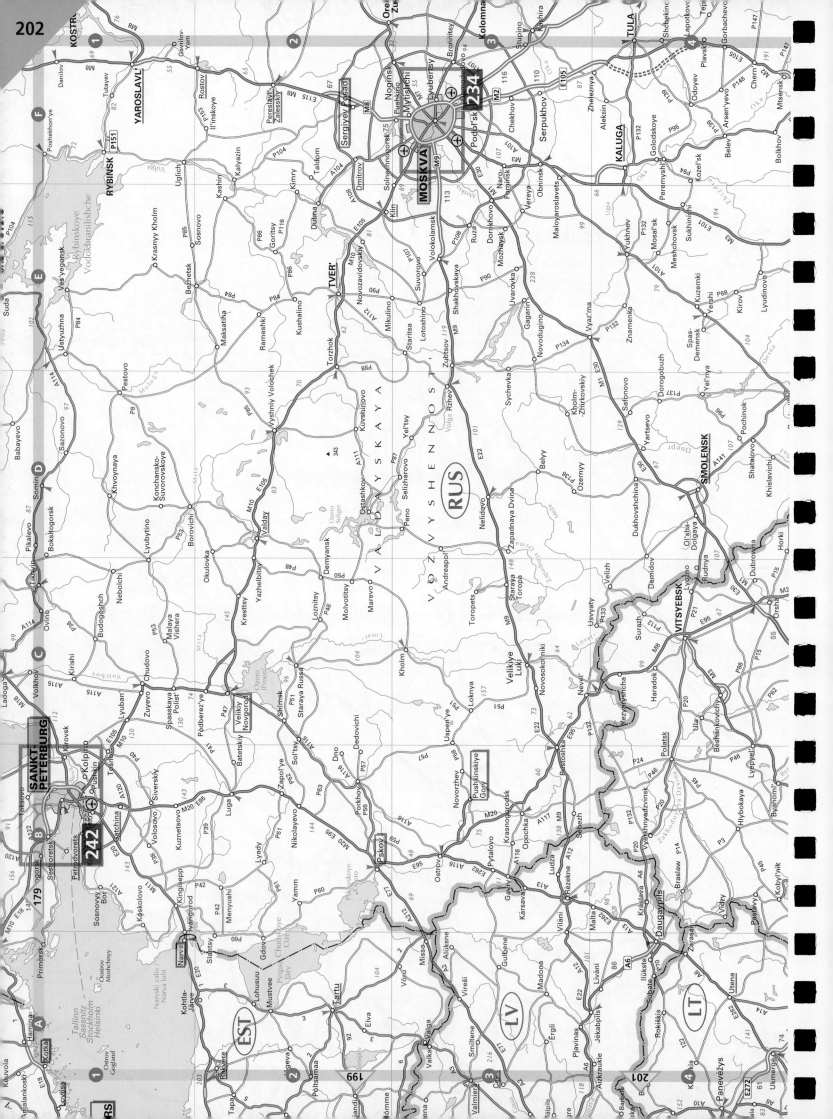

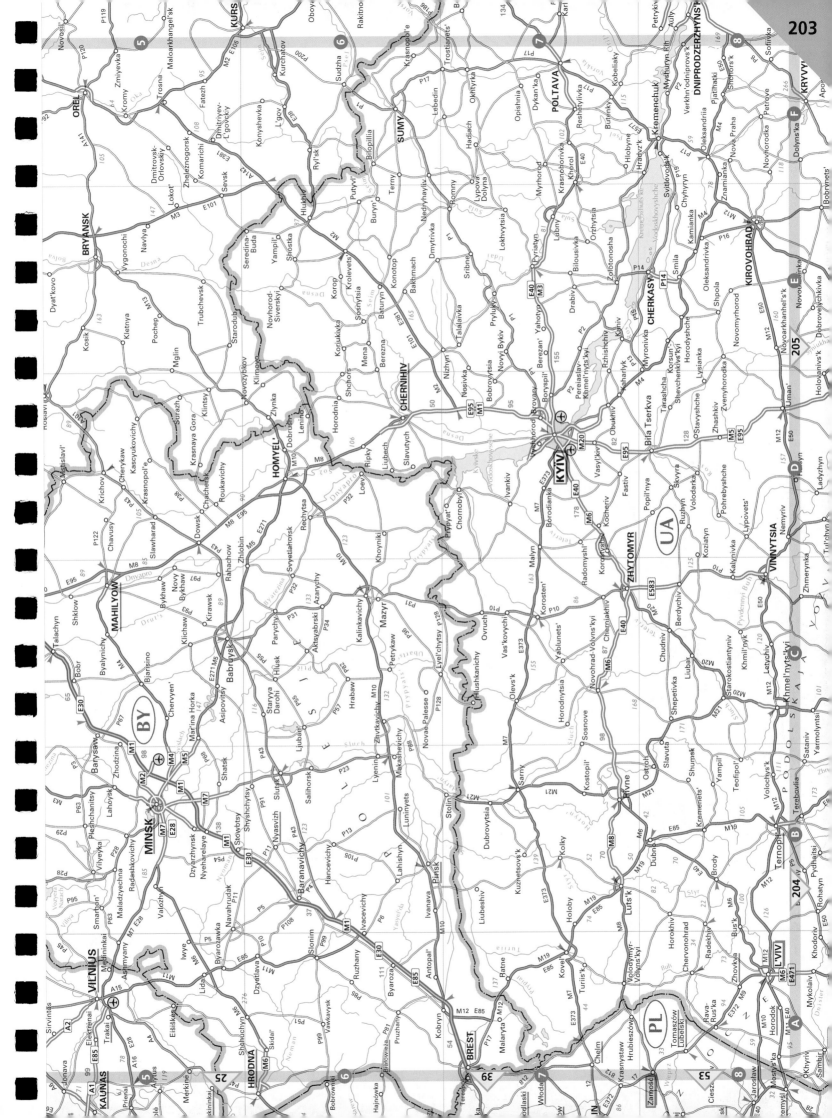

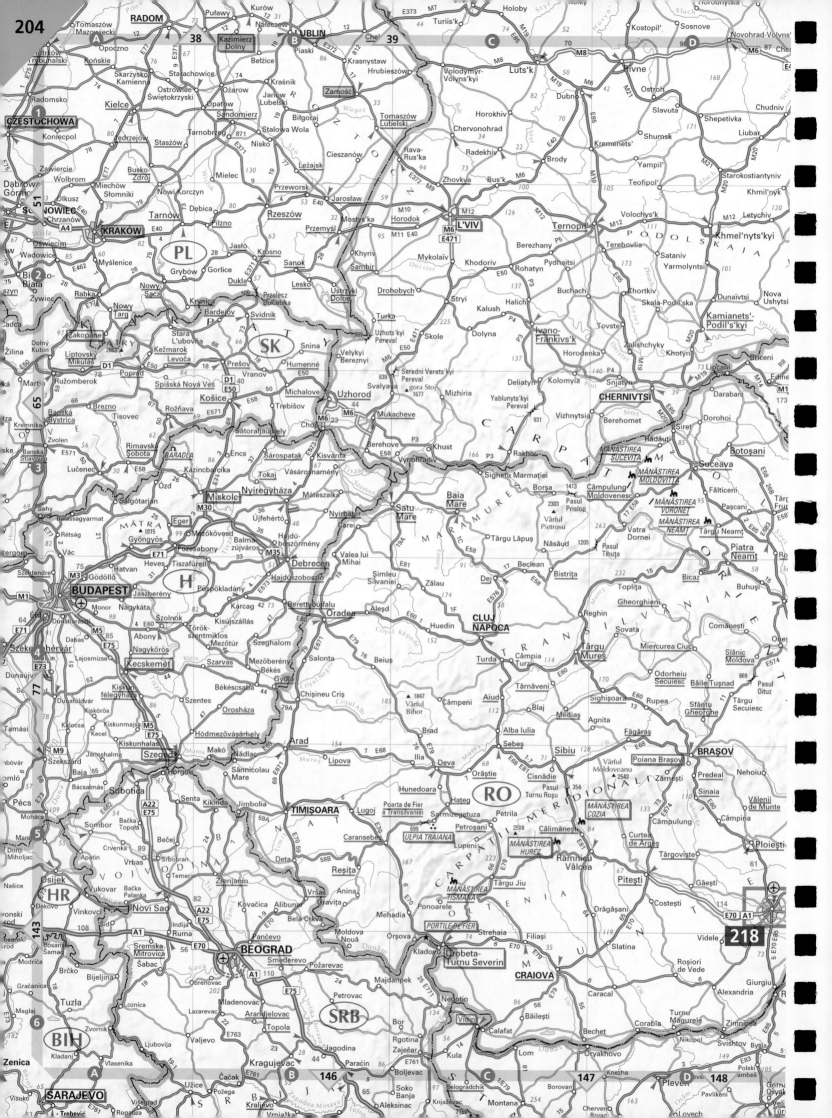

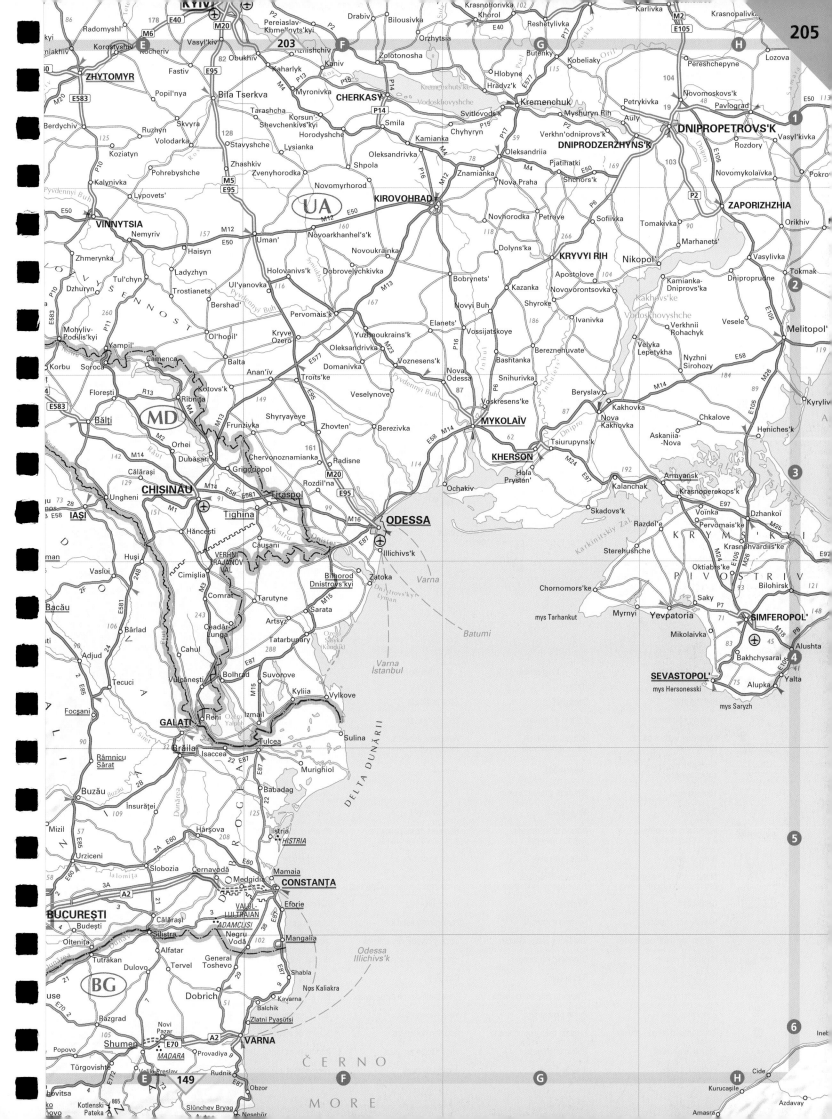

CITY AND URBAN ROUTES
CITTÀ E AREE URBANE
CIUDADES Y ÁREAS URBANAS
VILLES ET AIRES URBAINES
STÄDTE UND ZUFAHRTEN

● City plans / Piante di città / Planos de ciudades / Plans de villes / Stadtpläne

□ Urban route maps / Aree urbane / Áreas urbanas / Aires urbaines / Stadtdurchfahrtspläne

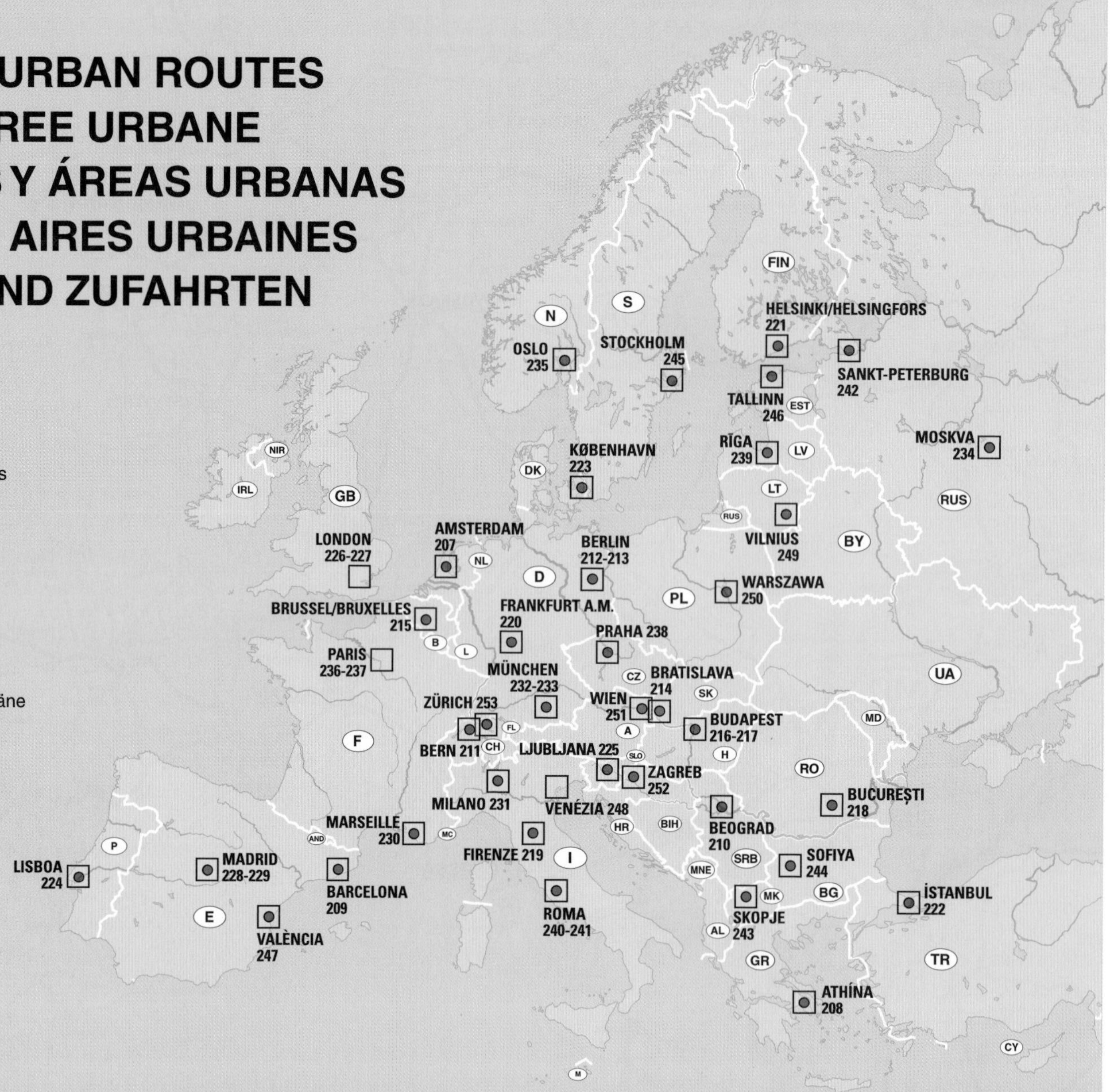

FIN
N
S
HELSINKI/HELSINGFORS 221
OSLO 235
STOCKHOLM 245
SANKT-PETERBURG 242
TALLINN 246
EST
KØBENHAVN 223
DK
RĪGA 239
LV
MOSKVA 234
NIR
IRL
GB
LT
RUS
RUS
AMSTERDAM 207
BERLIN 212-213
VILNIUS 249
BY
LONDON 226-227
NL
D
WARSZAWA 250
PL
BRUSSEL/BRUXELLES 215
FRANKFURT A.M. 220
B
L
PRAHA 238
PARIS 236-237
MÜNCHEN 232-233
CZ
BRATISLAVA 214
UA
SK
ZÜRICH 253
WIEN 251
MD
BUDAPEST 216-217
F
FL
A
BERN 211
CH
LJUBLJANA 225
SLO
H
RO
ZAGREB 252
MILANO 231
VENÉZIA 248
BUCUREȘTI 218
HR
BIH
MARSEILLE 230
AND
MC
BEOGRAD 210
P
FIRENZE 219
I
SOFIYA 244
MADRID 228-229
SRB
LISBOA 224
MNE
BARCELONA 209
ROMA 240-241
MK
BG
İSTANBUL 222
E
SKOPJE 243
VALÈNCIA 247
AL
GR
TR
ATHÍNA 208
CY
M

	GB Legend	I Legenda	E Leyenda	F Légende	D Zeichenerklärung
	Built-up area	Caseggiati	Zona edificada	Zones bâties	Bebauung
	Building of interest	Edificio d'interesse	Edificio relevante	Édifice remarquable	Bemerkenswertes Gebäude
6	Motorway, access points, service area	Autostrada, caselli, stazione di servizio	Autopista, accesos, estación de servicio	Autoroute, accès, aire de service	Autobahn, Anschlüsse, Tankstelle
	Road with motorway characteristics	Superstrada	Autovía	Route-express	Autobahnähnliche Schnellstraße
	Through road	Strada di attraversamento	Travesía	Route de traversée	Hauptdurchfahrtsstraße
	Other road	Altra strada	Otra carretera	Autre route	Sonstige Straße
A9 N202	Numbering of motorway and national roads	Numeri di autostrada e strade nazionali	Números de autopista y carreteras nacionales	Numéros d'autoroute et routes nationales	Autobahnnummer, Staatsstraßennummer
	Road in tunnel	Galleria stradale	Túnel en carretera	Tunnel routier	Straßentunnel
2009	Motorway and road under construction (opening year)	Autostrada e strada in costruzione (anno di apertura)	Autopista y carretera en construcción (año de apertura)	Autoroute et route en construction (année d'ouverture)	Autobahn und straße in Bau (Fertigstellungsjahr)
Utrecht	Destination	Direzione	Direccion	Direction	Richtung
	Railway and station	Ferrovia e stazione	Ferrocarril y estacion	Chemin de fer et gare	Eisenbahn und Bahnhöf
	Garden and park; cemeteries	Giardino e parco; cimiteri	Jardin y parque; cementerios	Jardin et parc; cimetières	Gärten und Park; Friedhöfe
P	Hospital; Parking	Ospedale; Parcheggio	Hospital; Aparcamiento	Hôpital; Parking	Krankenhaus; Parkplatz
	Camping site	Campeggio	Cámping	Camping	Campingplatz
	Vehicle ferry route	Trasporto auto su traghetto	Transbordador de automóviles	Bac pour autos	Autofähre
	Panoramic view	Punto panoramico	Vista panorámica	Vue panoramique	Aussichtspunkt
M	Underground railway station	Fermata della metropolitana	Estación del metro	Station de métro	U-Bahnhöfe
i	Tourist information	Ufficio informazioni	Información turística	Informations touristiques	Touristische Auskünfte
	Pedestrian area	Area pedonali	Área peatonales	Zone réservé aux piétons	Fußgängerzone

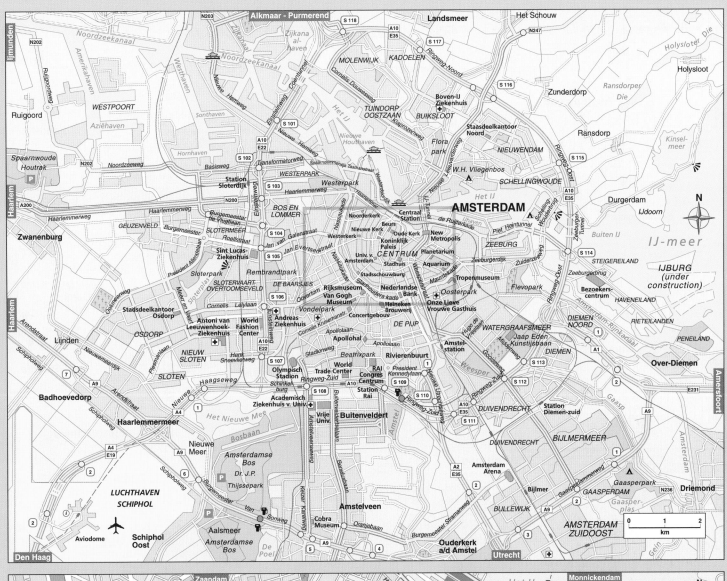

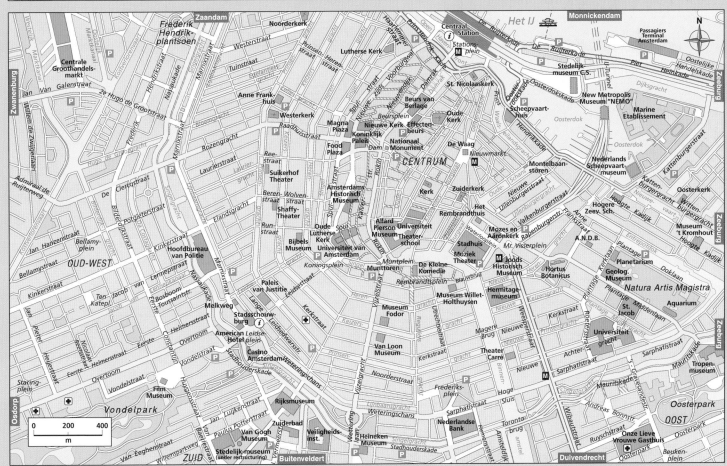

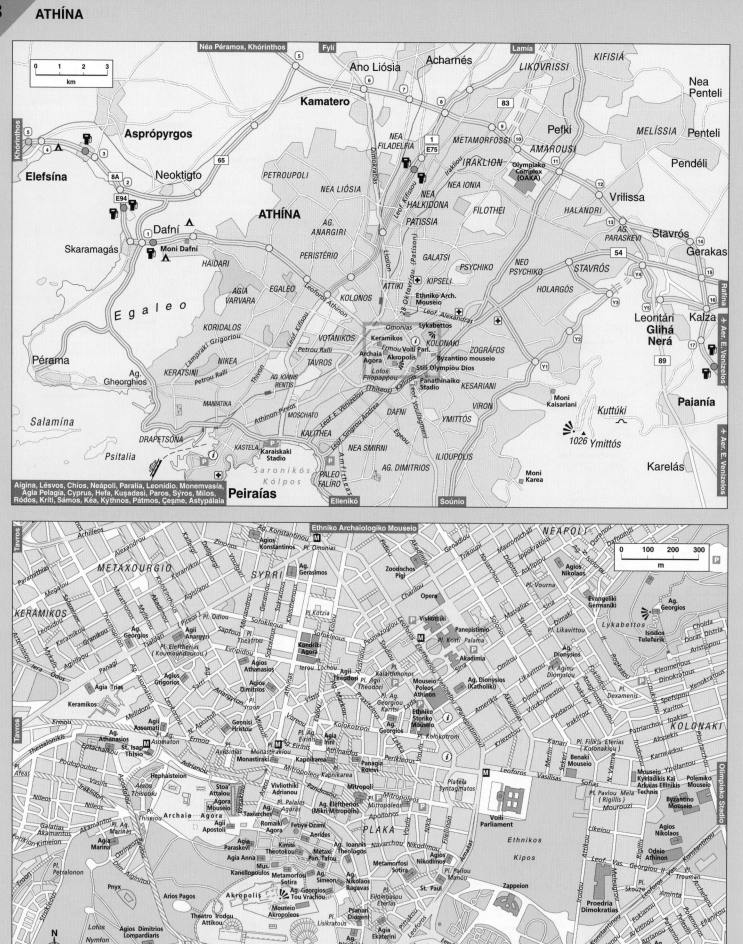

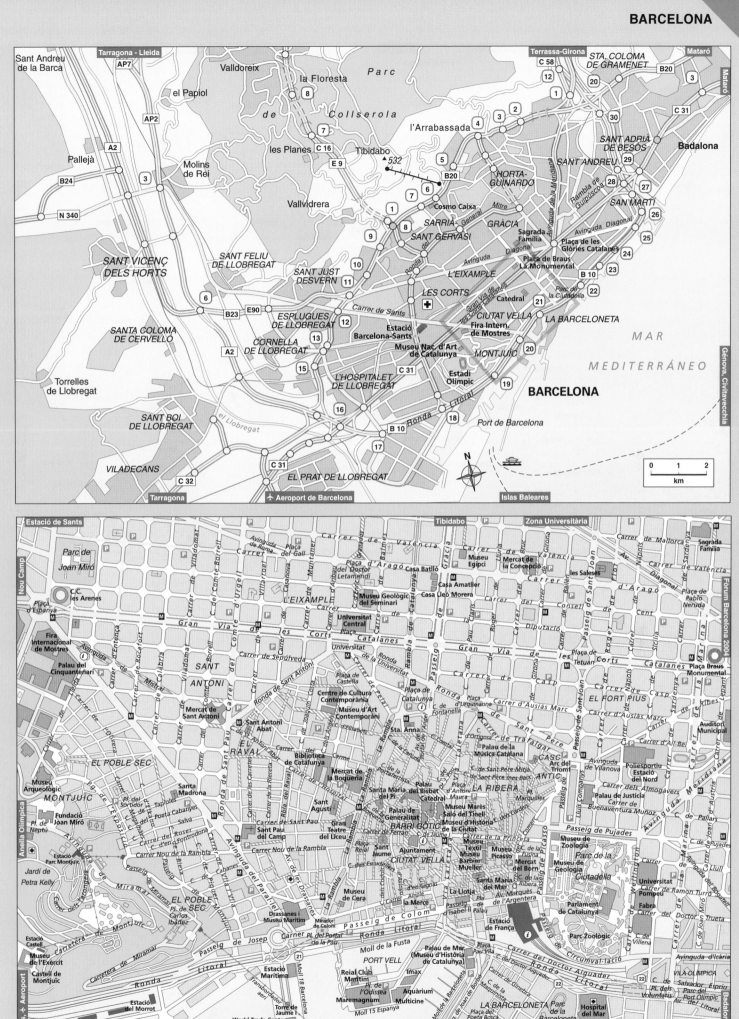

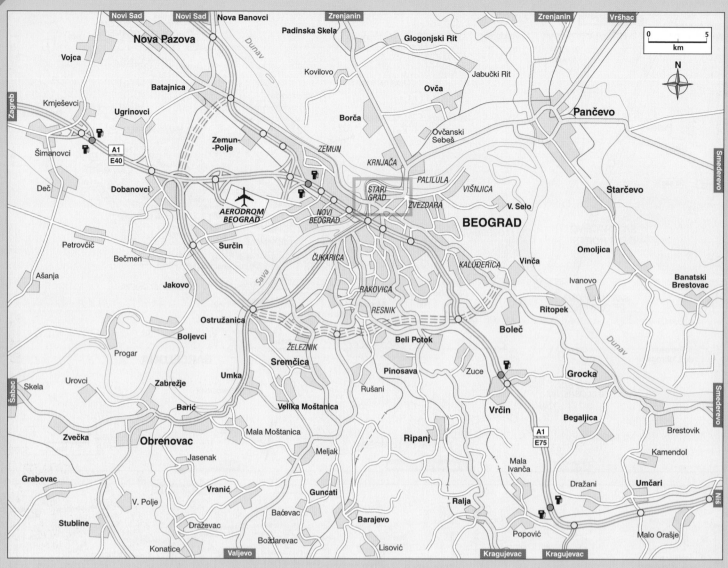

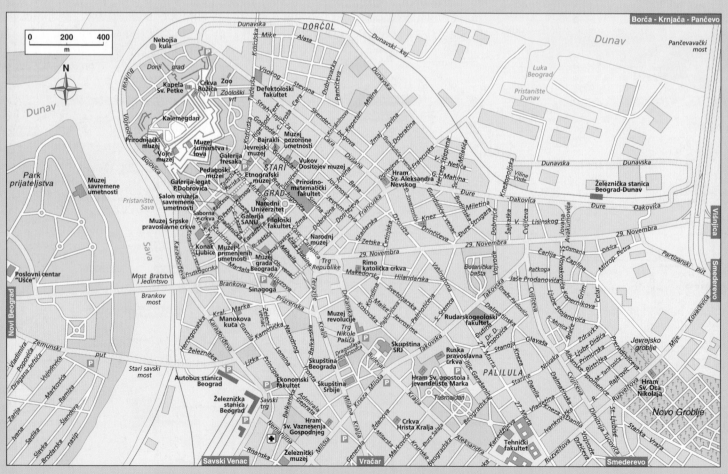

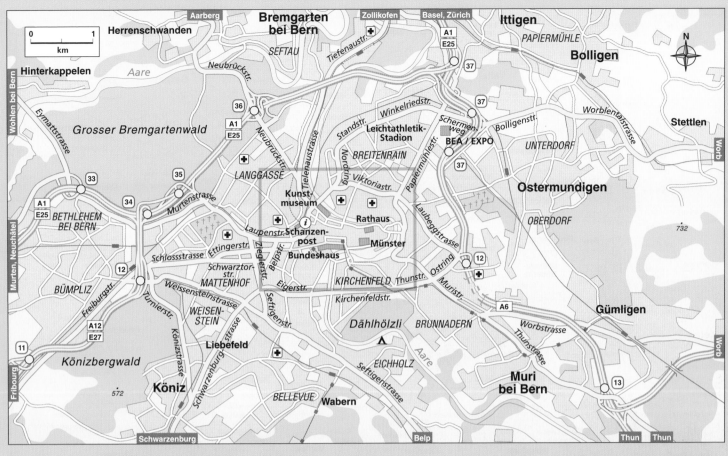

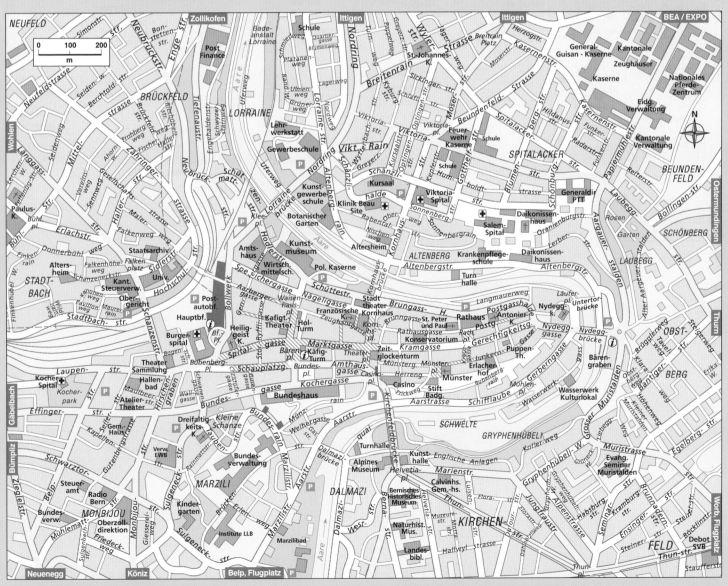

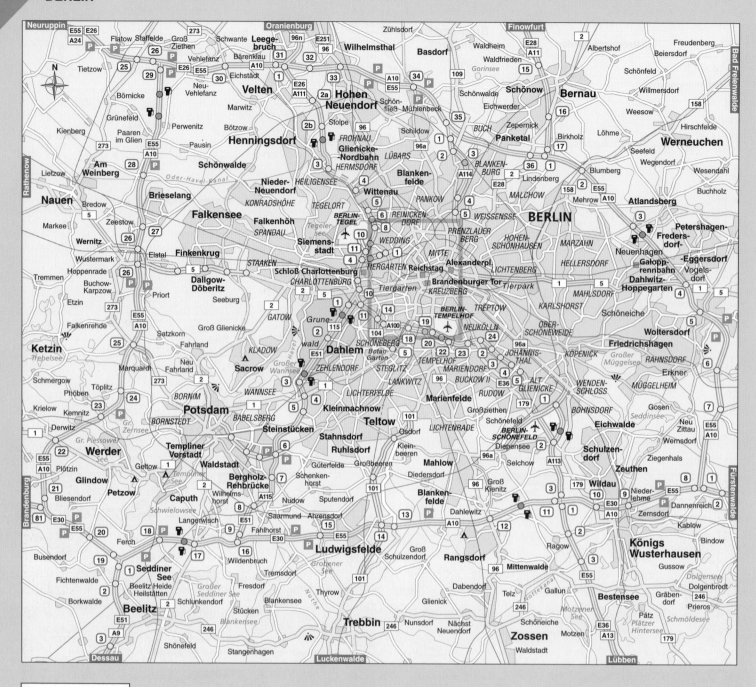

Neuruppin · Oranienburg · Finowfurt · Bad Freienwalde · Rathenow · Brandenburg · Fürstenwalde · Dessau · Luckenwalde · Lübben

0 3 6 9
km

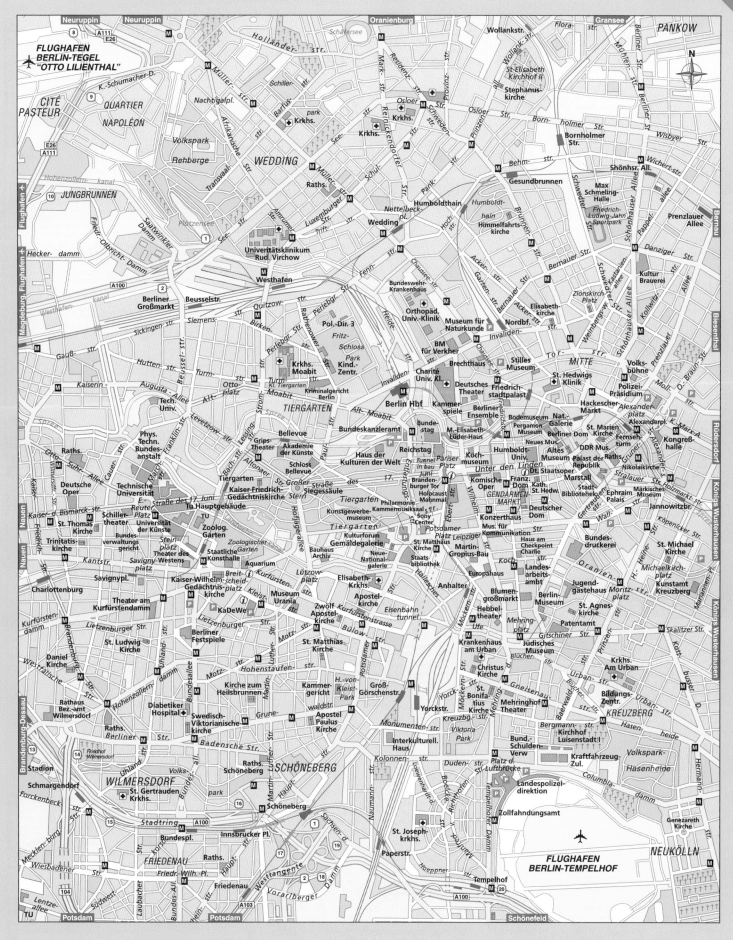

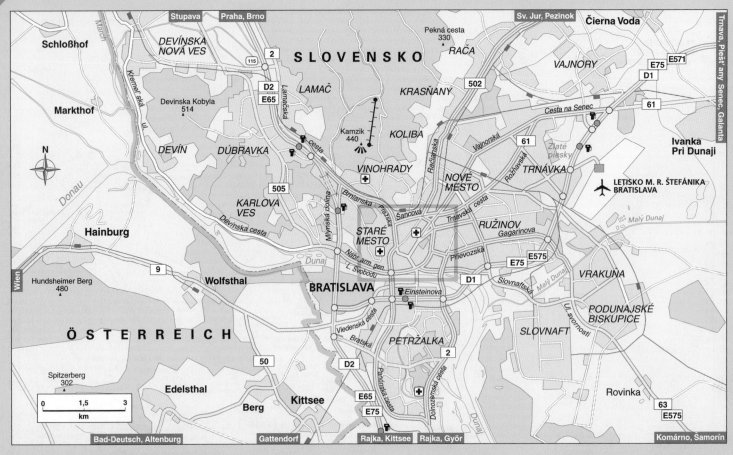

Stupava   Praha, Brno   Sv. Jur, Pezinok   Čierna Voda

Schloßhof   DEVÍNSKA
                   NOVÁ VES   Trnava, Piešť'any Senec, Galanta

Markthof   Devinska Kobyla
                            514   Pekná cesta
                                                   330   RAČA   VAJNORY   E75   E571
                            2   D1
                   115   D2   502
                          E65   LAMAČ   KRASŇANY   61
              DEVÍN   DÚBRAVKA   Cesta na Senec
                                                                                    Zlaté
                                    VINOHRADY   Račianska   61   piesky   Ivanka
          N   Vajnorská   Pri Dunaji
                                KARLOVA   Kamzik   Rožňavská
                                505   VES   440   NOVÉ   TRNÁVKA   LETISKO M. R. ŠTEFÁNIKA
              Donau   MESTO   BRATISLAVA
                                Devínska cesta   Mlynská dolina   Trnavská cesta   Malý Dunaj
          Hainburg   Brnianska Pražská   Sancová
                                                                  STARÉ   RUŽINOV
                            9   Dunaj   MESTO   Gagarinova
          Wien   Nábr. arm. gen.   Prievozská   E75   E575
              Hundsheimer Berg   L. Svobodu   Slovnaftská   Malý Dunaj   VRAKUŇA
              480   Wolfsthal   BRATISLAVA   Einsteinova   D1
                                                                                              PODUNAJSKÉ
          ÖSTERREICH   Viedenská cesta   BISKUPICE
                                                          Bratská   PETRŽALKA   SLOVNAFT
                                        50   2   Ul. svornosti
              Spitzerberg   D2
              302   Edelsthal   Panónska cesta   Rovinka
          0   1,5   3   Berg   Kittsee   E65   Dolnozemská cesta   63
              km   E75   E575

          Bad-Deutsch, Altenburg   Gattendorf   Rajka, Kittsee   Rajka, Györ   Komárno, Šamorín

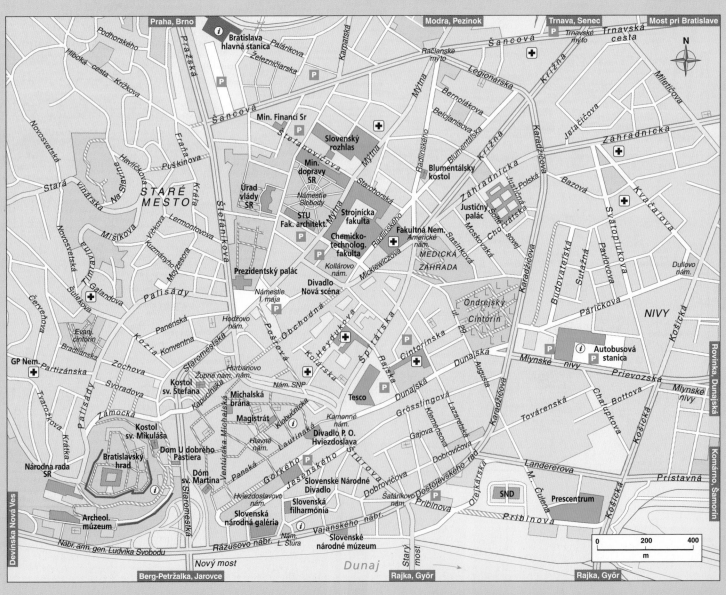

Praha, Brno   Modra, Pezinok   Trnava, Senec   Most pri Bratislave

                    Bratislava   Trnavské   Trnavská
                    hlavná stanica   Račlanske   mýto   cesta   N
          Podhorského   Palárikova   Karpatská   mýto   Šancová
          Hlboká cesta Železničiarska   Krížna   Miletičova
                    Krížkova   Mýtna   Legionárska   Záhradnícka
          Novosvetská   Šancová   Mýtna   Belojanisova   Karadžičova   Bazová
                    Štefanovičova   Radlinského   Kvačalova
          Stará   Min. Financí Sr   Blumentálska
                    Slovenský   Blumentálsky   Justičný
          STARÉ   Havlíčkova   rozhlas   Starohorská   kostol   palác
          MESTO   Puškinova   Min.   Fakultná Nem.   Záhradnícka
                    Úrad   dopravy   Námestie   Americké
          Mišíkova vlády   SR   Slobody   STU   nám.   Moskovská   Chorvátska
                    SR   Fak. architekt.   Strojnícka   MEDICKÁ
          Lermontovova Kuzmányho   fakulta   ZÁHRADA   Dullovo
          Na Slavíne Vlčkova Moyzesova   Chemicko-   Mickiewiczova   nám.
          T. Galandova   technolog.   Kollárovo
          Šulekova   fakulta   nám.   Ondrejský   NIVY
          Červeňova PALISÁDY   Prezidentský palác   cintorín
                    Panenská   Námestie   Hodžovo   Páričkova
          Evanj.   1. mája   nám.   Divadlo   Autobusová
          cintorín   Kozia   Konventná   Nová scéna   Cintorínska   stanica
          GP Nem. Bradlianska   Obchodná   Mlynské
                    Zochova   Heydukova   nivy   Prievozská
          Partizánska Svoradova   Staromestská   Kollárska   Špitálska   Rajská   Mlynské
                    Hurbanovo   Nám. SNP   Tesco   Dunajská   Augusta   nivy
          Kostol   Župné nám. nám.   Grösslingová   Lazaretská
          sv. Štefana   Michalská   Kamenné   Klemensova   Dostojevského rad
                    brána   Klobučnícka   nám.   Gajova
          Kostol   Magistrát   Divadlo P. O.   Dobrovičova
          sv. Mikuláša   Ventúrska-Michalská   Hlavné   Hviezdoslava   Landererova
          Národna rada   Dom U dobrého   nám.   Dobrovičova   M. Čulena
          SR   Pastiera   Laurinská   Slovenské Národné   Šafárikovo   SND   Prescentrum
          Bratislavský   Dóm   Panská   Gorkého   Divadlo   nám.   Pribinova
          hrad   sv. Martina   Jesénskeho   Slovenská   Vajanského nábr.   Pribinova
                    Hviezdoslavovo   filharmónia   Štúrova   Olejkárska   Košická
          Archeol.   nám.   Slovenská   Prístavná
          múzeum   národná galéria   Nám.
                    Rázusovo nábr.   L. Štúra   Slovenské
          Nábr. arm. gen. Ludvika Svobodu   národné múzeum   0   200   400
                    Nový most   Starý most   m
                              Dunaj
          Berg-Petržalka, Jarovce   Rajka, Györ   Rajka, Györ

          Devínska Nová Ves   Rovinka, Dunajská   Komárno, Šamorín

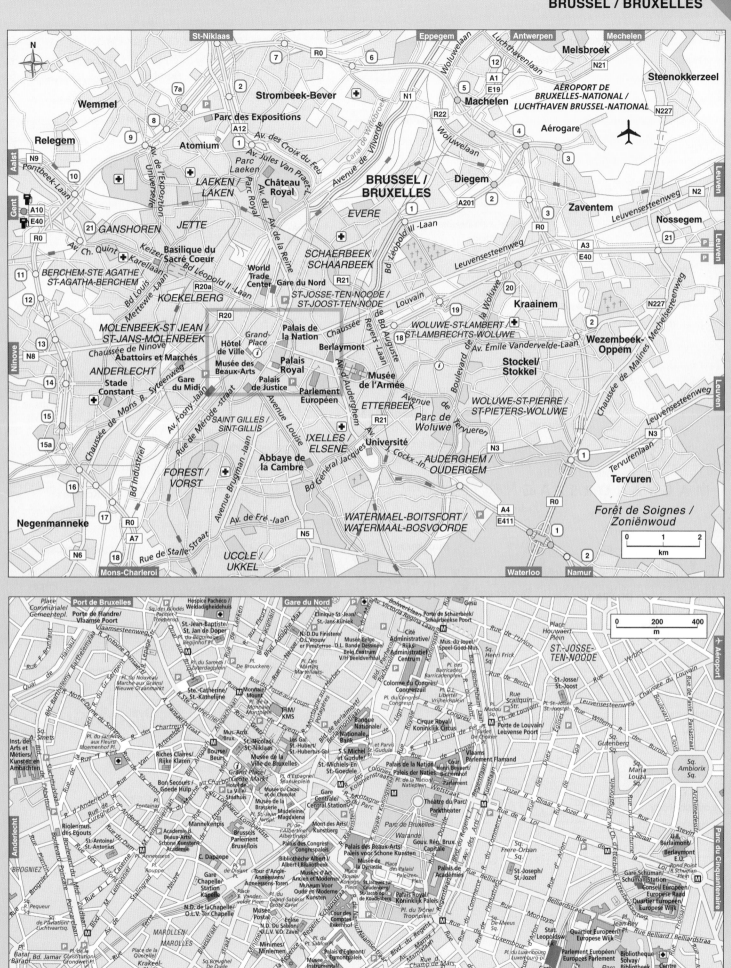

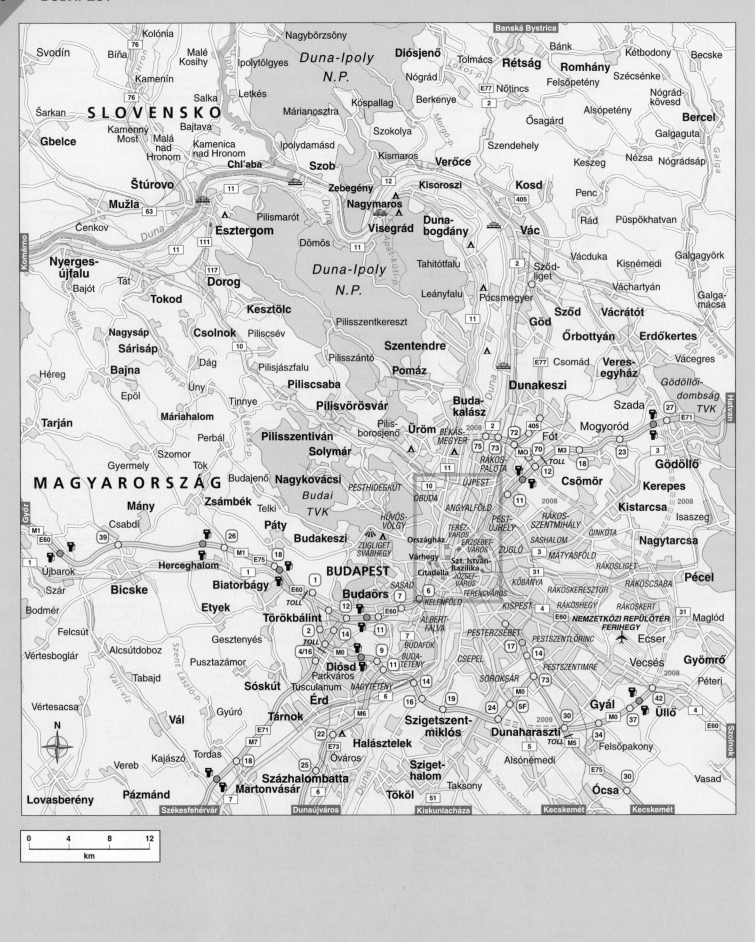

Kolónia
Svodín · Bína · 76 · Malé · Nagybörzsöny · Diósjenő · Tolmács · Rétság · Romhány · Kétbodony · Becske
Kosihy · Ipolytölgyes · Duna-Ipoly · Nógrád · Bánk · Felsőpetény · Szécsénke
Kamenín · N.P. · Berkenye · E77 · Nőtincs · Nógrád-

Malé · Salka · Kóspallag · Ősagárd · Alsópetény · Bercel · kövesd
Kamenný · Bajtava · Márianosztra · 2
SLOVENSKO · Most · Szendehely · Galgaguta

Šarkan · Malá · Kamenica · Ipolydamásd · Szokolya · Keszeg · Nézsa · Nógrádsáp
Gbelce · nad · nad Hronom · Chl'aba · Szob · Kismaros · Verőce
Hronom · 12 · Galga-
Čenkov · Zebegény · Kisoroszi · Kosd · mácsa
Štúrovo · Duna · 11 · Nagymaros · 405 · Penc · Rád · Püspökhatvan
Mužla · 63 · Pilismarót · Visegrád · Duna- · Vác · Galgagyörk
Esztergom · bogdány · Vácduka · Kisnémedi
Dömös · 11 · 2 · Sződ-
Nyerges- · 111 · Tahitótfalu · liget · Váchartyán
újfalu · 117 · Duna-Ipoly · Leányfalu · Sződ · Vácrátót · Galga-
Bajót · Tát · Dorog · N.P. · Pócsmegyer · mácsa
Tokod · Pilisszentkereszt · 11 · Göd · Őrbottyán · Erdőkertes
Nagysáp · Kesztölc · Szentendre · E77 · Csomád · Veres- · Vácegres
Sárisáp · Csolnok · Piliscsév · egyház · Gödöllői-
Héreg · Dág · Pilisszántó · Pomáz · Dunakeszi · Szada · 27 · dombság
Bajna · Pilisjászfalu · Buda- · E71 · TVK
Tarján · Úny · Tinnye · Piliscsaba · kalász · Mogyoród · Gödöllő
Epöl · Máriahalom · Pilisvörösvár · Pilis- · Üröm · 2008 · 2 · Fót · 3 · Kerepes
Perbál · borosjenő · BÉKÁS- · 75 · 73 · M0 · 70 · 18 · 23
MAGYARORSZÁG · Szomor · Pilisszentiván · MEGYER · RÁKOS- · TOLL · M3 · Kistarcsa
Gyermely · Tök · Solymár · 11 · PALOTA · 12 · Csömör · Isaszeg · 2008
Mány · Budajenő · Nagykovácsi · PESTHIDEGKÚT · 10 · ÚJPEST · Nagytarcsa
Csabdi · Zsámbék · Telki · Budai · ÓBUDA · 11 · 2008 · RÁKOS-
M1 · TVK · HŰVÖS- · ANGYALFÖLD · SZENTMIHÁLY · CINKOTA
E60 · 39 · Páty · VÖLGY · PEST- · MÁTYÁSFÖLD
Újbarok · 26 · Budakeszi · ZUGLIGET · Országház · TERÉZ- · ÚJHELY · 3 · RÁKOSLIGET · Pécel
1 · Herceghalom · M1 · 18 · SVÁBHEGY · VÁROS · ERZSÉBET- · ZUGLÓ · 31 · RÁKOSCSABA
Bicske · E75 · Várhegy · VÁROS · KŐBÁNYA · RÁKOSKERESZTÚR
Szár · 1 · Biatorbágy · BUDAPEST · Citadella · Szt. István- · RÁKOSHEGY · 31
Bodmér · Etyek · E60 · SASAD · 6 · Bazilika · JÓZSEF- · 4 · NEMZETKÖZI REPÜLŐTÉR · Maglód
Felcsút · TOLL · Budaörs · 7 · KELENFÖLD · VÁROS · FERIHEGY · Ecser
Gesztenyés · 12 · E60 · FERENCVÁROS · KISPEST · 17 · 14
Vértesboglár · Alcsútdoboz · Törökbálint · 14 · 11 · ALBERT- · PESTERZSÉBET · PESTSZENTLŐRINC · Vecsés · Gyömrő
Tabajd · 2 · FALVA · 7 · BUDAFOK · Péteri · 2008
Pusztazámor · TOLL · M0 · 9 · BUDA- · CSEPEL · PESTSZENTIMRE · 73 · 42
Vértesacsa · 4/16 · Diósd · 11 · TÉTÉNY · SOROKSÁR · Gyál · Üllő
Vál · Parkváros · 14 · M0 · 5F · 24 · 14 · 37
Gyúró · Sóskút · Tusculanum · NAGYTÉTÉNY · 6 · 19 · 2009 · 4
Érd · 6 · 16 · Szigetszent- · Dunaharaszti · 30 · 34 · E60
Gyömrő · Tárnok · M6 · miklós · 5 · TOLL · M5 · Felsőpakony
E71 · 22 · Alsónémedi
Kajászó · M7 · E73 · Óváros · 30 · E75
Vereb · Tordas · 18 · 25 · Halásztelek · Sziget- · Vasad
Pázmánd · 7 · Százhalombatta · halom · Taksony · Ócsa
Lovasberény · Martonvásár · 6 · Tököl · 51
Duna-Tisza csatorna

N

0 · 4 · 8 · 12
km

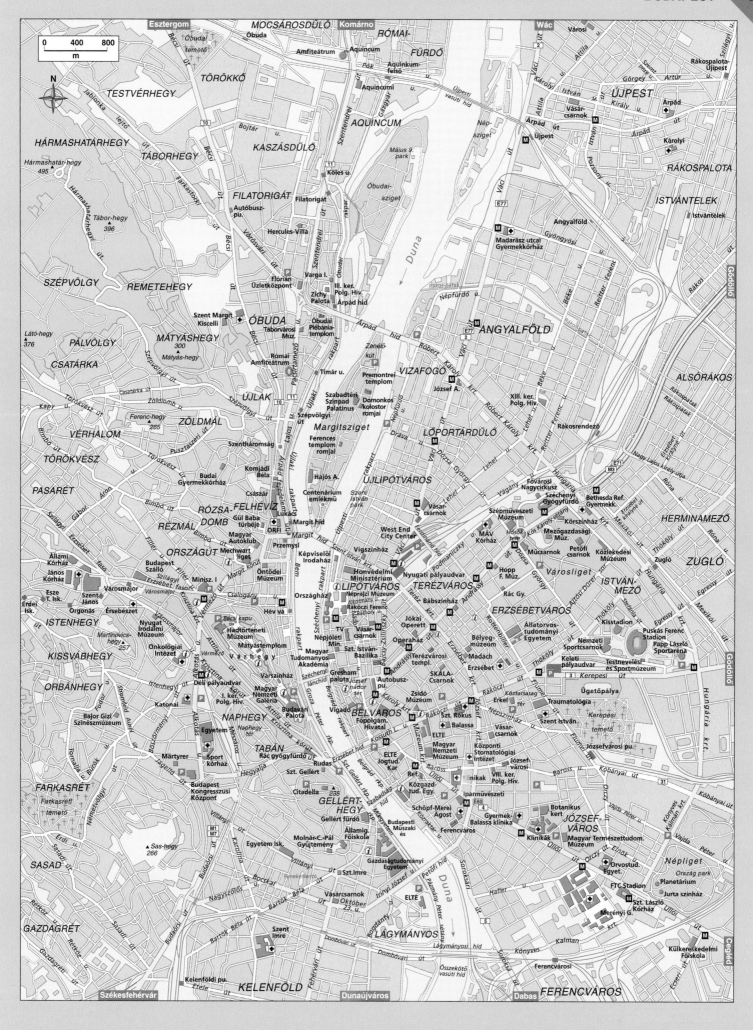

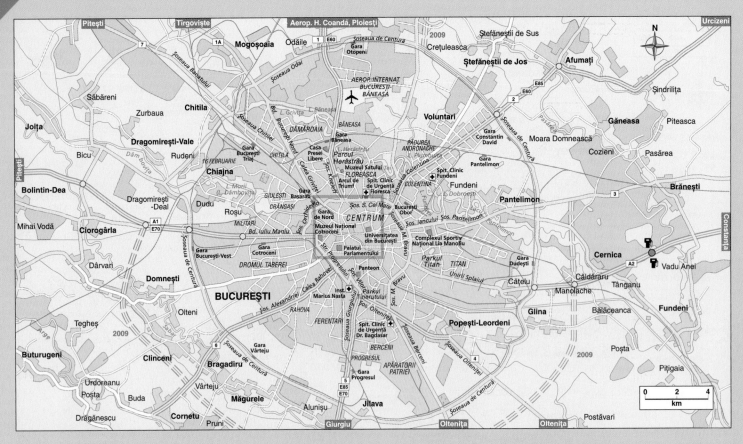

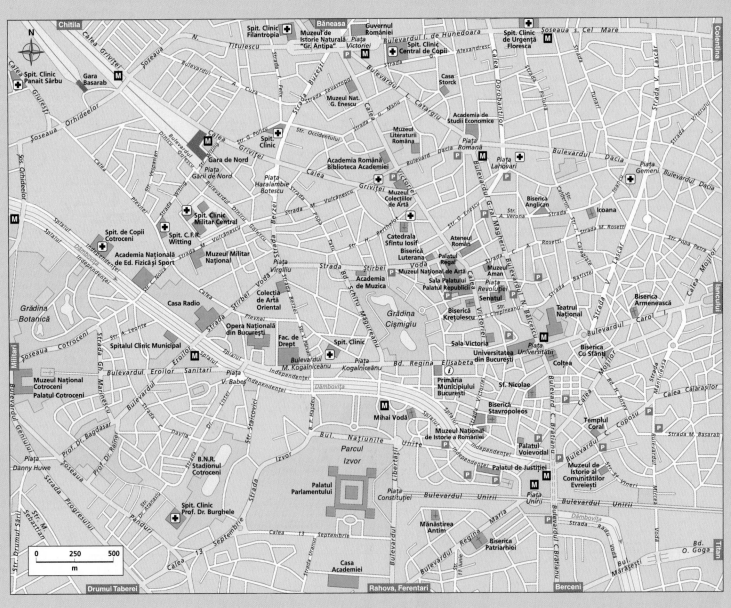

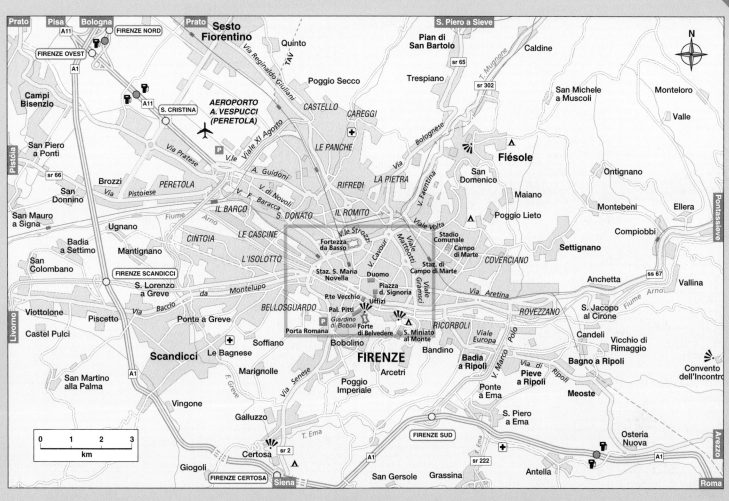

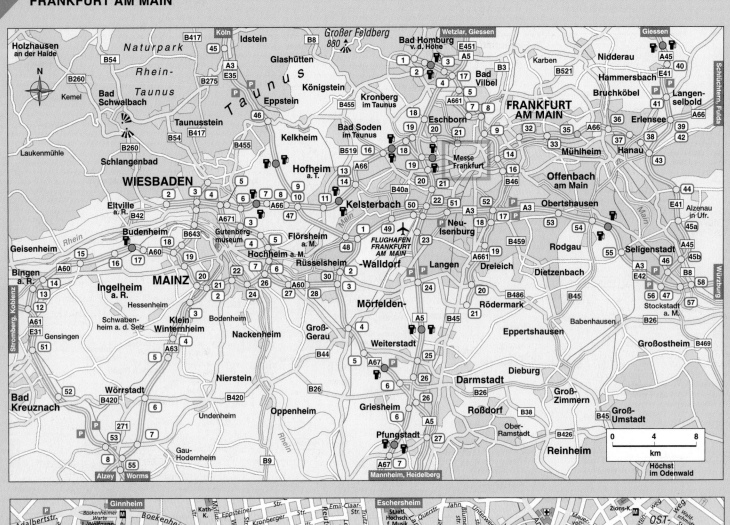

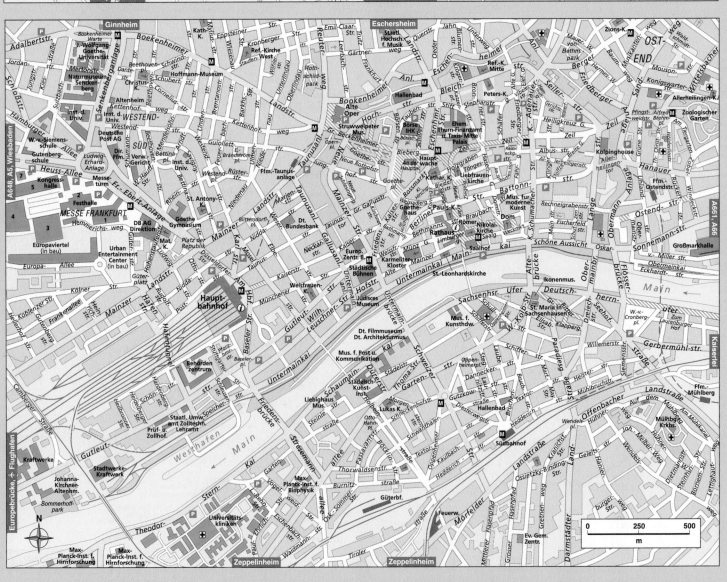

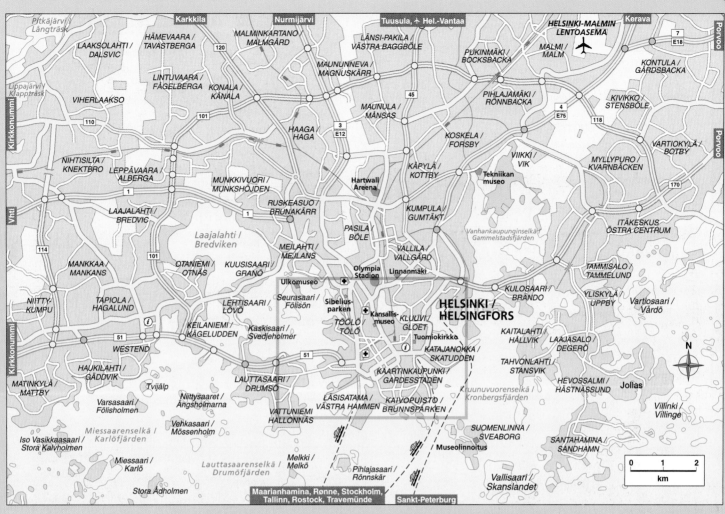

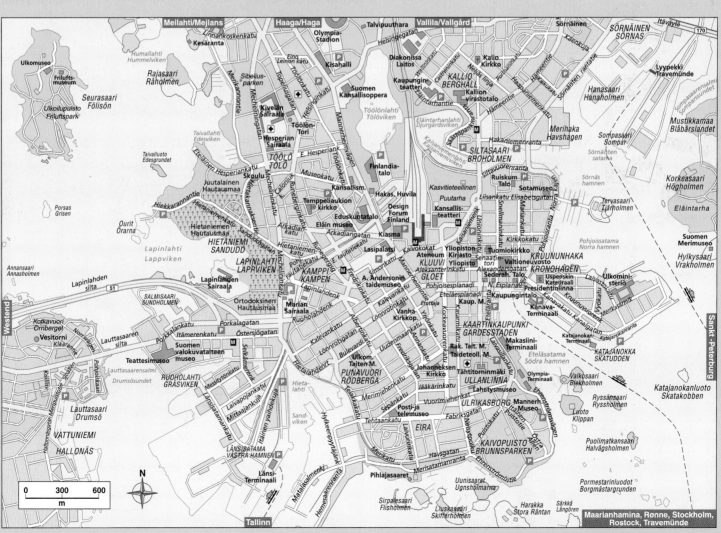

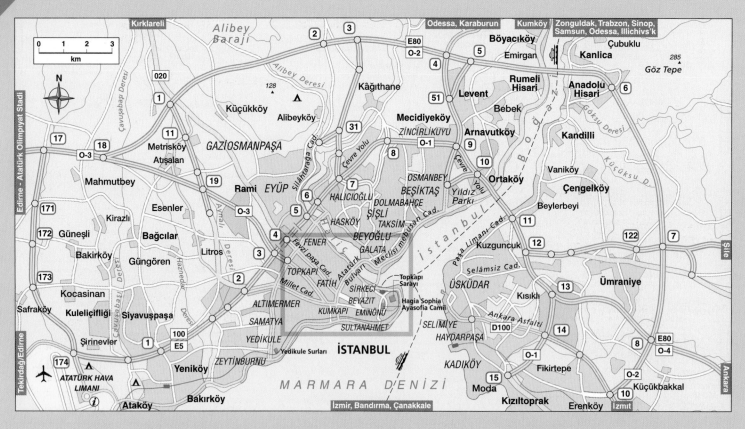

İSTANBUL

MARMARA DENİZİ

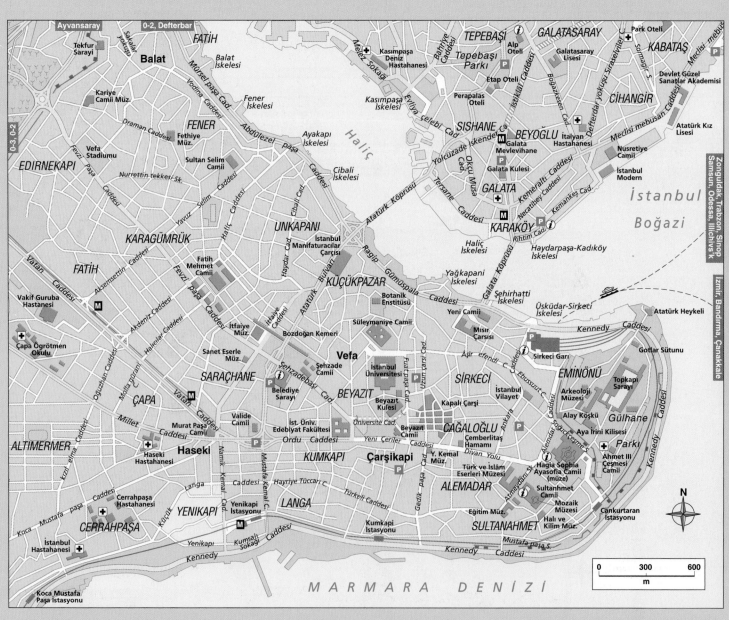

MARMARA DENİZİ

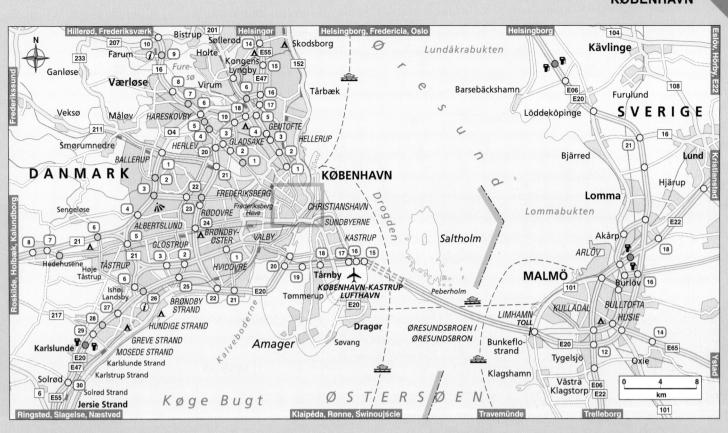

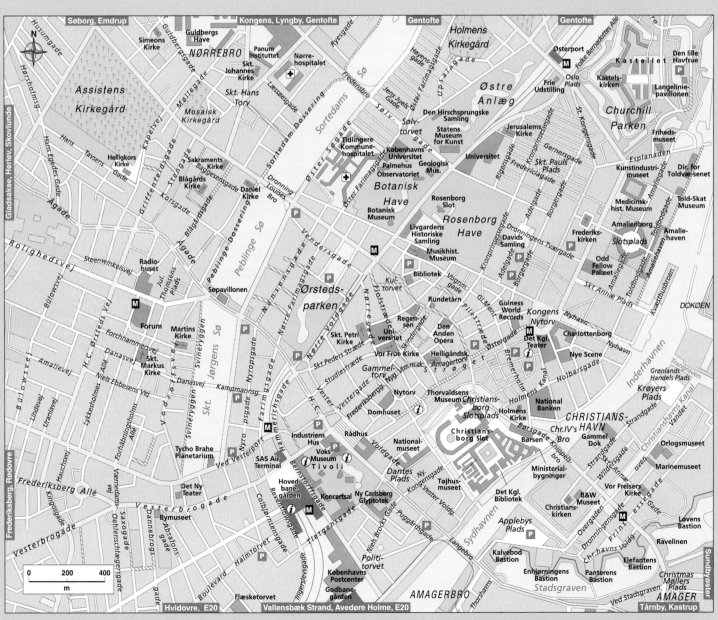

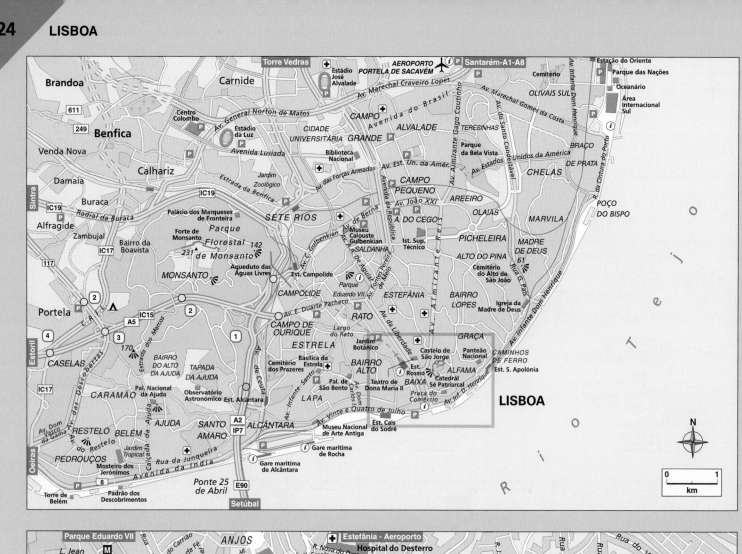

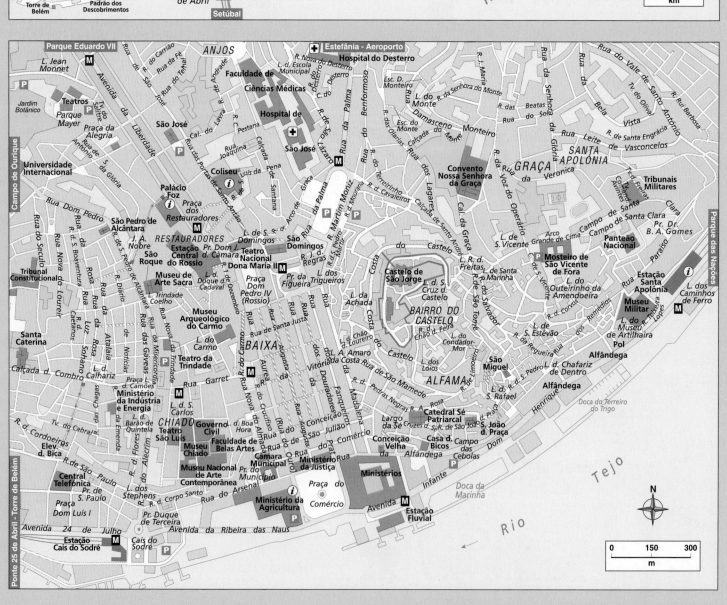

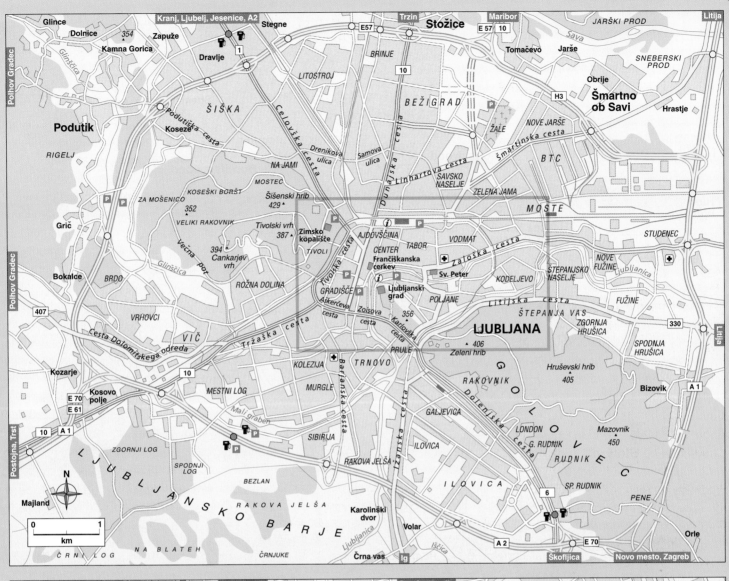

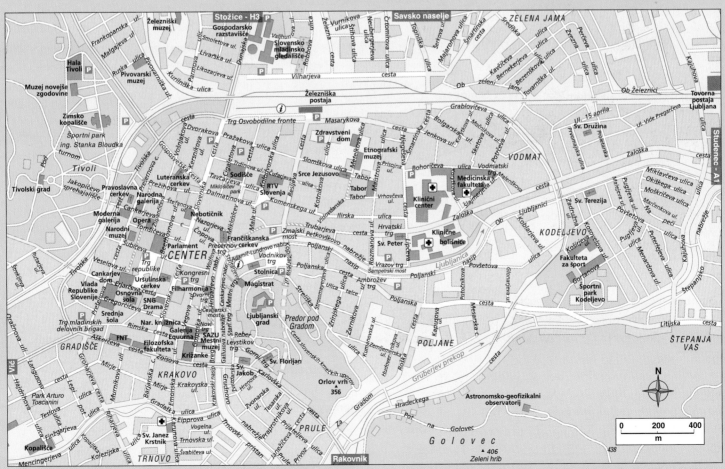

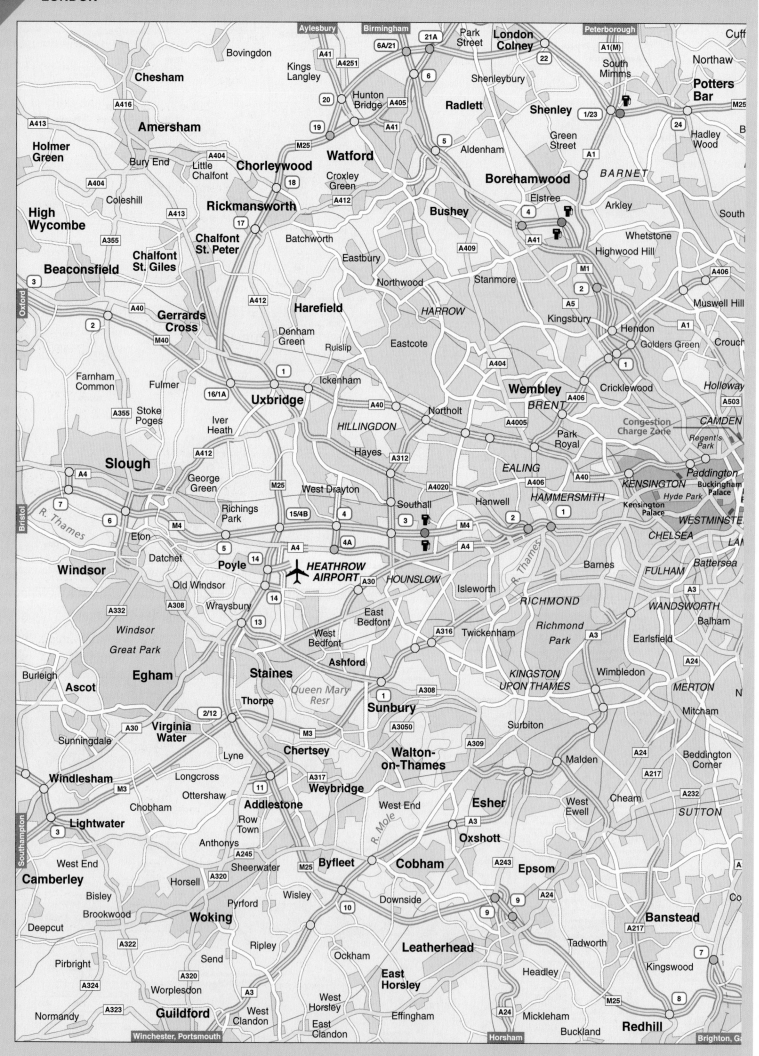

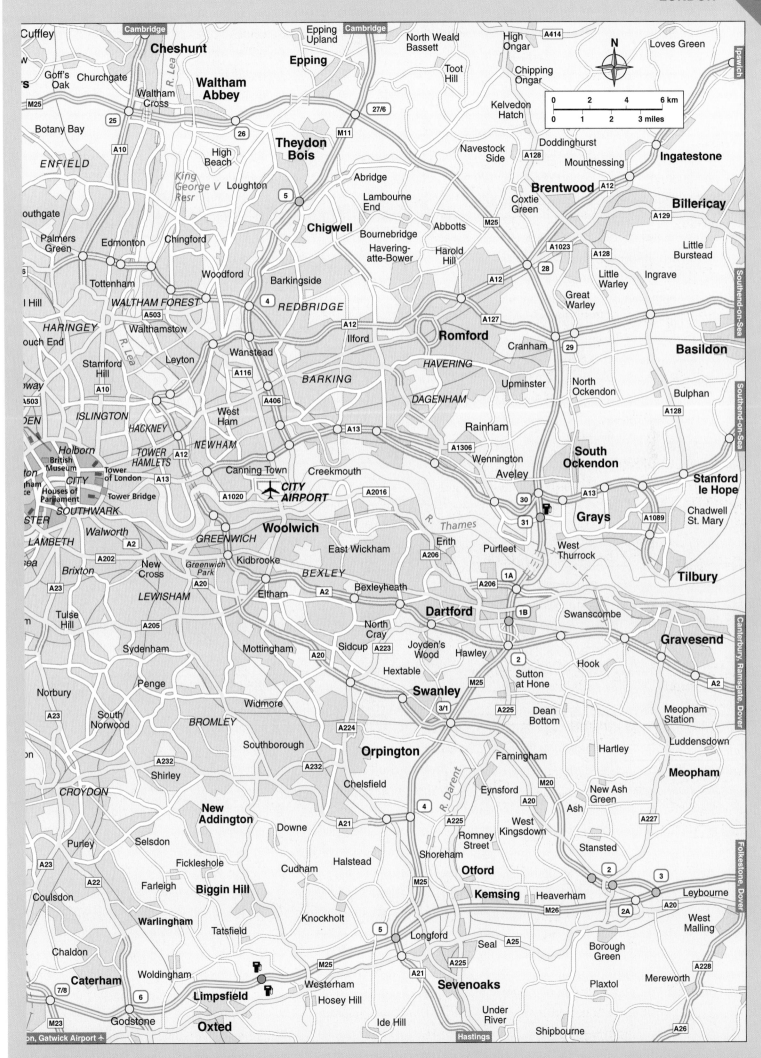

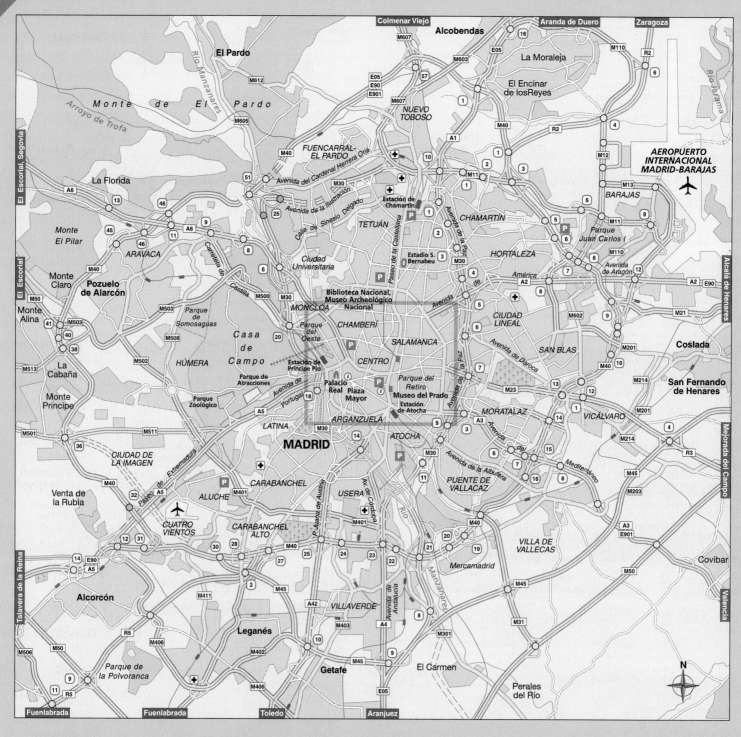

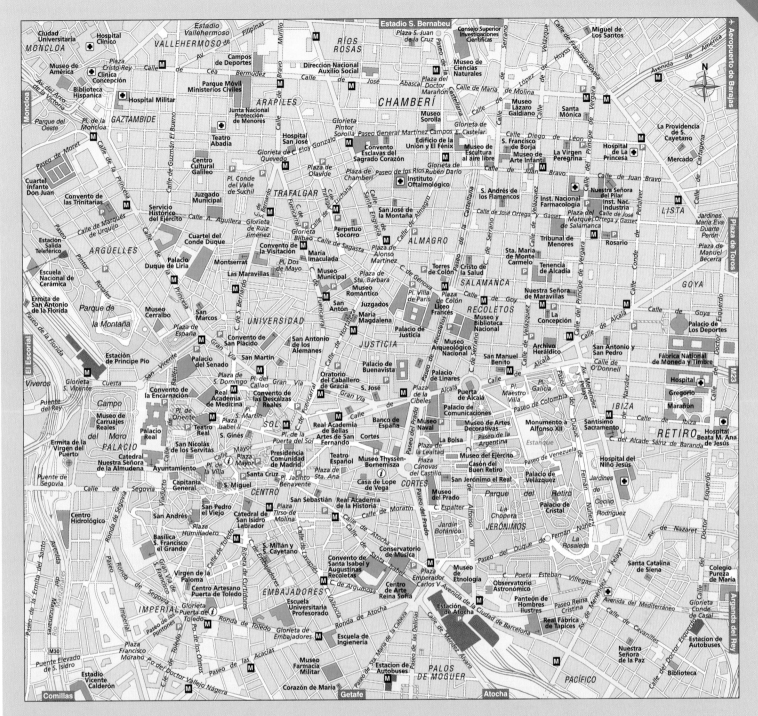

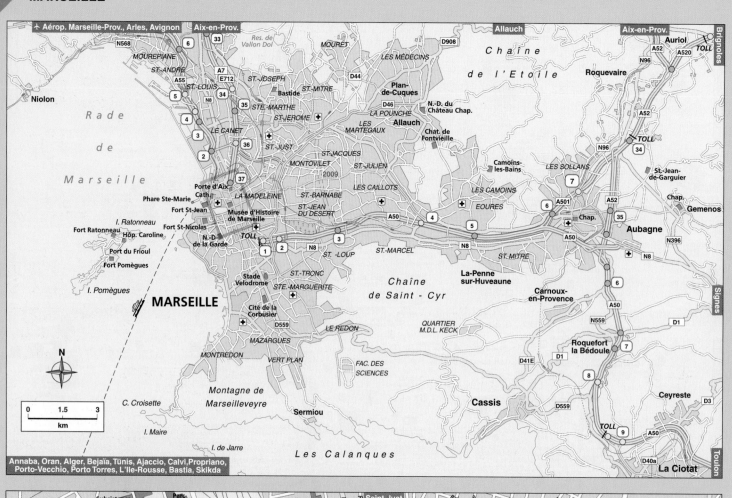

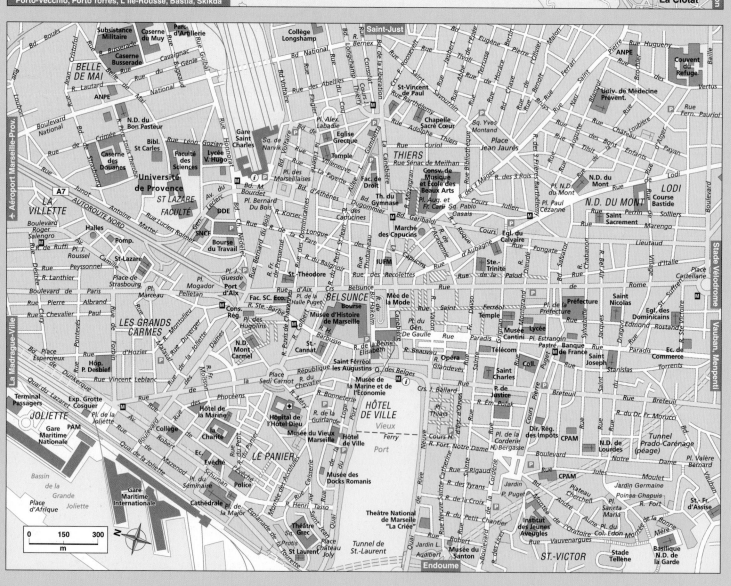

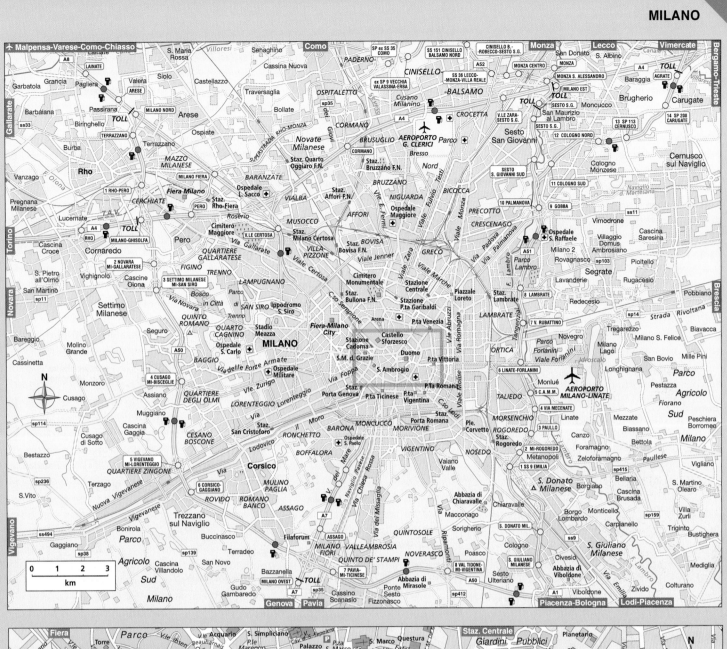

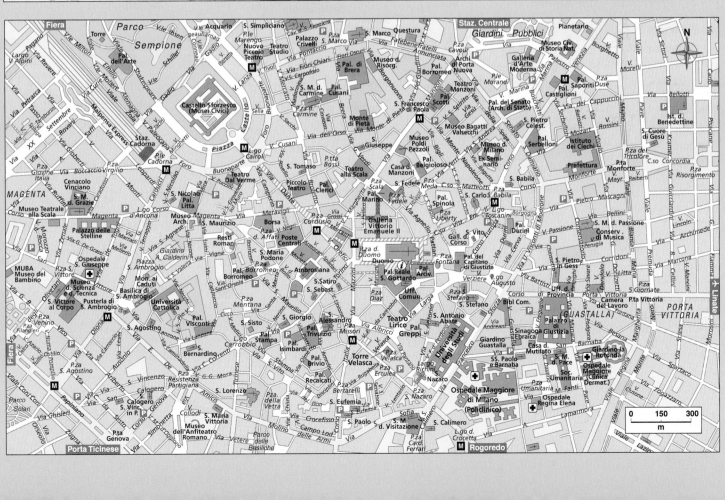

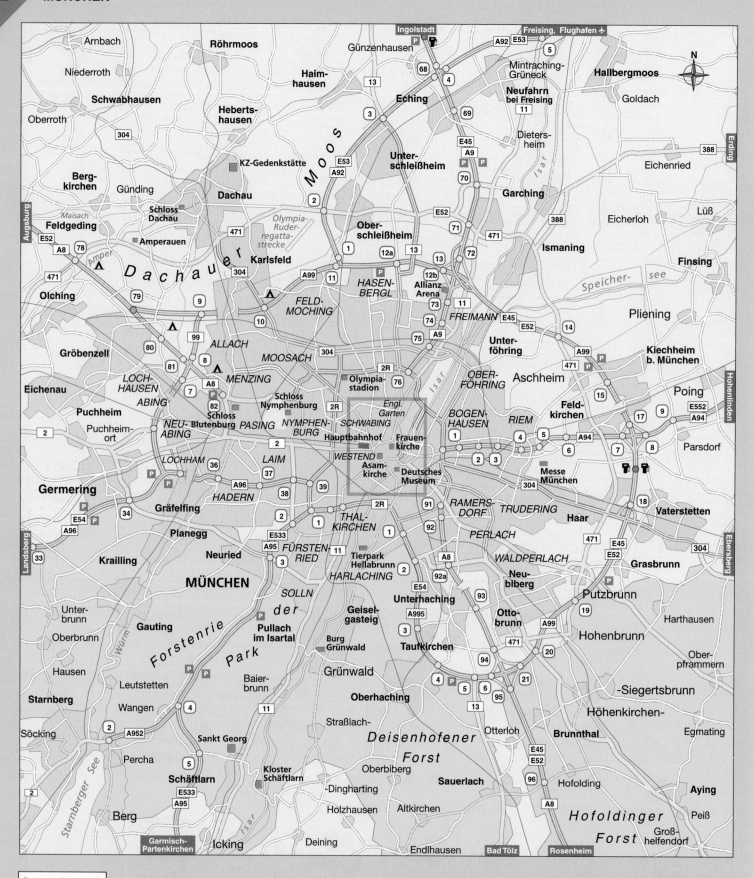

N

Arnbach
Röhrmoos
Ingolstadt
Günzenhausen
Freising, Flughafen
A92 E53
5
Niederroth
Haim-hausen
68
Mintraching-Grüneck
Hallbergmoos
Schwabhausen
13
Eching
4
Neufahrn bei Freising
Goldach
Oberroth
Heberts-hausen
3
69
11
Dieters-heim
388
304
KZ-Gedenkstätte
E53
Unter-schleißheim
E45
Garching
Eichenried
Berg-kirchen
Günding
A92
A9
Ismaning
Eicherloh
Lüß
Maisach
Dachau
70
Finsing
Feldgeding
Schloss Dachau
Olympia-Ruder-regatta-strecke
Ober-schleißheim
E52
71
388
E52
A8
78
Amperauen
471
Ober-schleißheim
12a
13
72
471
Karlsfeld
1
Speicher- see
Augsburg
471
Dachauer
304
A99
11
HASEN-BERGL
13
12b
Garching
Erding
Olching
79
9
FELD-MOCHING
Allianz Arena
73
11
FREIMANN
Pliening
10
ALLACH
304
74
E45
14
Kiechheim b. München
Gröbenzell
99
80
MOOSACH
75
A9
Unter-föhring
A99
471
81
8
2R
OBER-FÖHRING
Aschheim
Poing
Eichenau
7
A8
MENZING
76
Olympia-stadion
Isar
15
E552
LOCH-HAUSEN
82
Schloss Nymphenburg
2R
Engl. Garten
RIEM
17
9
A94
Puchheim
ABING
Schloss Blutenburg
NYMPHEN-BURG
SCHWABING
BOGEN-HAUSEN
5
A94
Parsdorf
Puchheim-ort
NEU-ABING
PASING
Hauptbahnhof
1
6
7
8
2
LOCHHAM
36
LAIM
WESTEND
Frauen-kirche
2
3
Messe München
18
Germering
37
Asam-kirche
Deutsches Museum
304
Vaterstetten
Gräfelfing
A96
38
39
91
RAMERS-DORF
TRUDERING
Haar
34
HADERN
2
2R
92
PERLACH
471
E45
Grasbrunn
Planegg
E533
1
1
WALDPERLACH
E52
304
Krailling
A95
FÜRSTEN-RIED
11
Tierpark Hellabrunn
A8
Neu-biberg
Putzbrunn
Neuried
3
THAL-KIRCHEN
2
92a
93
19
MÜNCHEN
HARLACHING
E54
Otto-brunn
Hohenbrunn
Harthausen
Unter-brunn
SOLLN
der
Geisel-gasteig
Unterhaching
A995
A99
Oberbrunn
Gauting
Pullach im Isartal
3
Taufkirchen
20
Siegertsbrunn
Oberpframmern
Hausen
Burg Grünwald
94
471
Starnberg
Leutstetten
Baier-brunn
Grünwald
4
5
6
21
95
Höhenkirchen-
Wangen
4
Oberhaching
13
Brunnthal
Egmating
Söcking
2
A952
Straßlach-
Otterloh
Deisenhofener
E45
Percha
Sankt Georg
Oberbiberg
E52
96
Hofolding
Aying
5
Kloster Schäftlarn
Forst
Sauerlach
Peiß
Schäftlarn
Dingharting
Hofoldinger
E533
Holzhausen
Altkirchen
A8
Groß-helfendorf
Berg
A95
Icking
Deining
Endlhausen
Forst
Garmisch-Partenkirchen
Bad Tölz
Rosenheim
Starnberger See
Wurm
Forstenrie
Park
Landsberg
Ebersberg
Hohenlinden
33
Eichenau

0   2   4
km

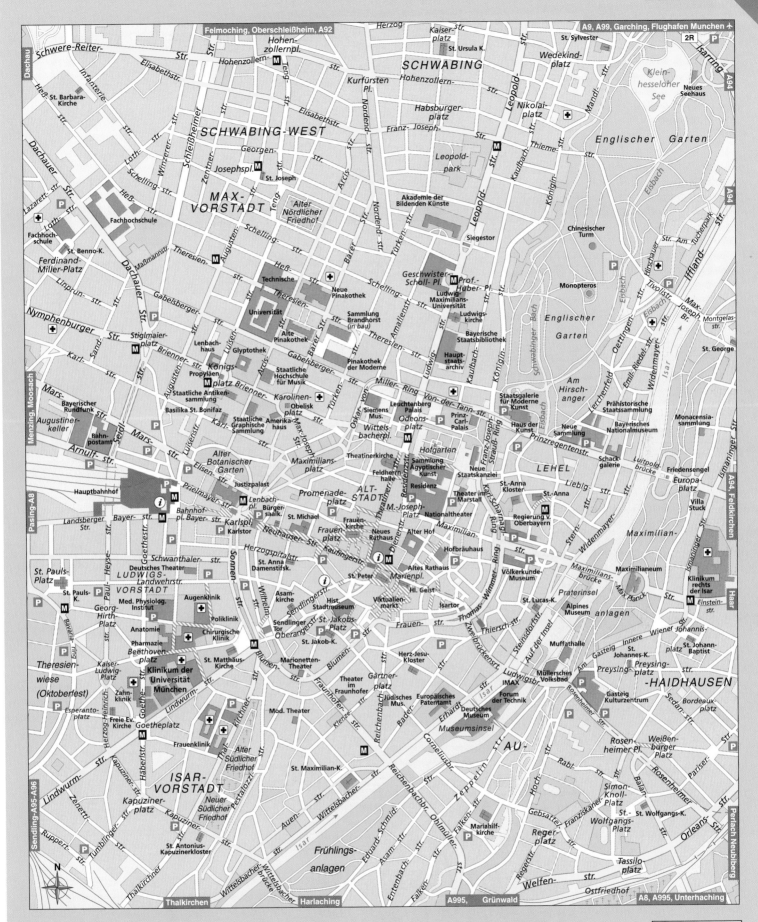

SCHWABING

SCHWABING-WEST

MAX-VORSTADT

Georgen-platz
Josephspl.
St. Joseph
Alter Nördlicher Friedhof
Akademie der Bildenden Künste

Leopold-park

Habsburger-platz

Nikolai-platz

Englischer Garten

Kleinhesseloher See
Neues Seehaus

Siegestor

Chinesischer Turm

Monopteros

Englischer Garten

Fachhochschule
Fachhochschule
St. Benno-K.
Ferdinand-Miller-Platz

Technische
Universität
Neue Pinakothek
Sammlung Brandhorst (in bau)
Alte Pinakothek
Geschwister-Scholl- Pl.
Prof.-Huber- Pl.
Ludwig-Maximilians-Universität
Ludwigs-kirche
Bayerische Staatsbibliothek
Hauptstaatsarchiv

Lenbach-haus
Glyptothek
Königs-platz
Propyläen
Staatliche Antiken-sammlung
Basilika St. Bonifaz
Staatliche Hochschule für Musik
Karolinen-platz
Obelisk
platz
Staatliche Graphische Sammlung
Amerika-haus
Pinakothek der Moderne

Haus der Kunst
Staatsgalerie für Moderne Kunst

Neue Sammlung

Prähistorische Staatssammlung
Bayerisches Nationalmuseum
Monacensia-sammlung

St. George

Bayerischer Rundfunk
Augustiner-keller
Bahn-postamt
Alter Botanischer Garten

Stiglmaier-platz

Maximilians-platz

Siemens Mus.
Wittels-bacherpl.
Leuchtenberg Palais
Odeons-platz
Prinz-Carl-Palais

Hofgarten
Theatinerkirche
Sammlung Ägyptischer Kunst
Neue Staatskanzlei
Residenz

St.-Anna Kloster
St. Anna

LEHEL

Schack-galerie
Luitpold-brücke
Friedensengel
Europa-platz
Villa Stuck

Maximilian-

Hauptbahnhof
Justizpalast
Feldherrn-halle
M.-Joseph-Platz
Nationaltheater
Regierung v. Oberbayern

Maximilianeum

Klinikum rechts der Isar

Bahnhof-pl.
Karlspl.
Karlstor
Lenbach-pl.
Bürger-saal.
St. Michael
Promenade-platz
ALT-STADT
Frauen-platz
Frauen-kirche
Neues Rathaus
Alter Hof
Hofbräuhaus
Altes Rathaus
Völkerkunde-Museum

Maximilians-brücke

St. Pauls-Platz
St. Pauls-K.
Deutsches Theater
LUDWIGS-VORSTADT
Schwanthaler- str.
St. Anna Damenstifsk.
Asam-kirche
Hist. Stadtmuseum
St. Jakobs-Platz
St. Peter
Marienpl.
Hl. Geist
Viktualien-markt
Isartor

Praterinsel
Alpines Museum

anlagen

Einstein-str.

Med. Physiolog. Institut
Augenklinik
Poliklinik
Georg-Hirth-Platz
Anatomie
Pharmazie
Beethoven-platz
Chirurgische Klinik
Sendlinger Tor
St. Jakob-K.
Herz-Jesu-Kloster
Muffathalle

Preysing-platz
HAIDHAUSEN

Theresien-wiese (Oktoberfest)
Klinikum der Universität München
Zahn-klinik
Kaiser-Ludwig-Platz
St. Matthäus-Kirche
Marionetten-Theater
Theater im Fraunhofer
Gärtner-platz
Jüdisches Mus.
Europäisches Patentamt
IMAX
Forum der Technik
Müllersches Volksbad
Gasteig Kulturzentrum
Bordeaux-platz

Esperanto-platz
Freie Ev. Kirche
Goetheplatz
Frauenklinik
Mod. Theater
Deutsches Museum
Rosen-heimer Pl.
Weißen-burger Platz

ISAR-VORSTADT
Kapuziner-platz
Alter Südlicher Friedhof
St. Maximilian-K.
Museumsinsel
AU-
Simon-Knoll-Platz
St. Wolfgangs-K.

Neuer Südlicher Friedhof
Mariahilf-kirche
Regerplatz
Wolfgangs-Platz
St. Johann-Baptist

St. Antonius-Kapuzinerkloster
Frühlings-anlagen
Tassilo-platz

0   200   400
m

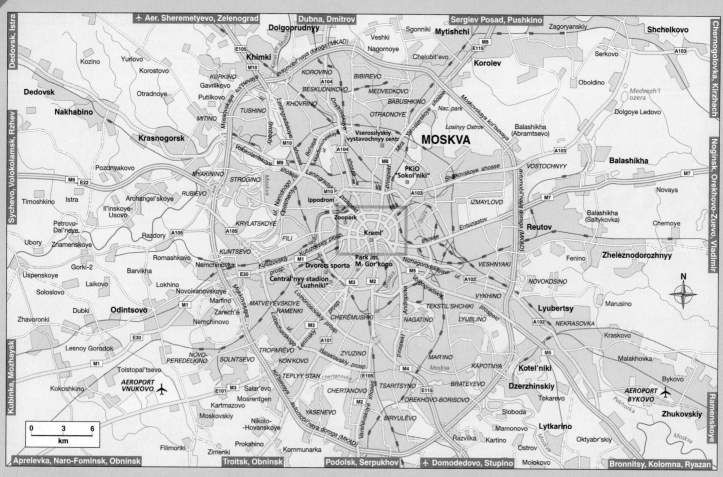

Dedovsk, Istra · Aer. Sheremetyevo, Zelenograd · Dubna, Dmitrov · Sergiev Posad, Pushkino · Shchelkovo

Chernogolovka, Kirzhach

Dolgoprudnyy
Sgonniki · Mytishchi · Zagoryanskiy

Veshki · Nagornoye
Chelobit'evo · E115 · Korolev

Khimki · M10 · KURKINO · KOROVINO · BIBIREVO · Serkovo · A103

Kozino · Yurlovo · Korostovo · BESKUDNIKOVO · MEDVEDKOVO · Oboldino

Dedovsk · Gavrilkovo · TUSHINO · KHOVRINO · BABUSHKINO · Dolgoye Ledovo

Nakhabino · Otradnoye · Putilkovo · OTRADNOYE · Nac. park

Krasnogorsk · MITINO · Vserossiyskiy vystavochnyy centr · Losinyy Ostrov · Balashikha (Abramtsevo)

MOSKVA · Balashikha

Pozdnyakovo · MYAKININO · STROGINO · PKiO "Sokol'niki" · VOSTOCHNYY · Novaya

Timoshkino · Istra · RUBIEVO · Ippodrom · IZMAYLOVO · Balashikha (Saltykovka) · Chernoye

Petrovo-Dal'neye · Archangel'skoye · KRYLATSKOYE · Zoopark · Kreml' · Reutov

Ubory · Il'inskoye-Usovo · Znamenskoye · FILI · Park im. M. Gor'kogo · Zheleznodorozhnyy

Romashkovo · KUNTSEVO · Dvorets sporta · VESHNYAKI · Fenino

Gorki-2 · Nemchinovka · Central'nyy stadion "Luzhniki" · NOVOKOSINO

Barvikha · MATVEYEVSKOYE · RAMENKI · TEKSTIL'SHCHIKI · VYKHINO · Lyubertsy · Marusino

Uspenskoye · Laikovo · Zarech'e · CHERÉMUSHKI · NAGATINO · LYUBLINO · NEKRASOVKA

Soloslovo · Novoivanovskoye · Nemchinov · Marfino

Dubki · Odintsovo · TROPARÉVO · ZYUZINO · MAR'INO · KAPOTNYA · Kotel'niki · Malakhovka

Zhavoronki · NOVO-PEREDELKINO · SOLNTSEVO · KON'KOVO · Balakiavskiy prosp. · Kraskovo

Lesnoy Gorodok · TEPLYY STAN · TSARITSYNO · BRATEYEVO · Dzerzhinskiy · Bykovo

Tolstopal'tsevo · YASENEVO · CHERTANOVO · OREKHOVO-BORISOVO · AEROPORT BYKOVO

AEROPORT VNUKOVO · Salar'evo · Mosrentgen · Sloboda · Tokarevo · Zhukovskiy

Kokoshking · Kartmazovo · Nikolo-Hovanskoye · Moskovskiy · BIRYULÉVO · Lytkarino · Oktyabr'skiy

Filimonki · Zimenki · Prokshino · Razvilka · Kartino · Ostrov

Kommunarka · Mamonovo · Molokovo

0 3 6 km

Kubinka, Mozhaysk · Aprelevka, Naro-Fominsk, Obninsk · Troitsk, Obninsk · Podolsk, Serpukhov · Domodedovo, Stupino · Bronnitsy, Kolomna, Ryazan

Ramenskoye

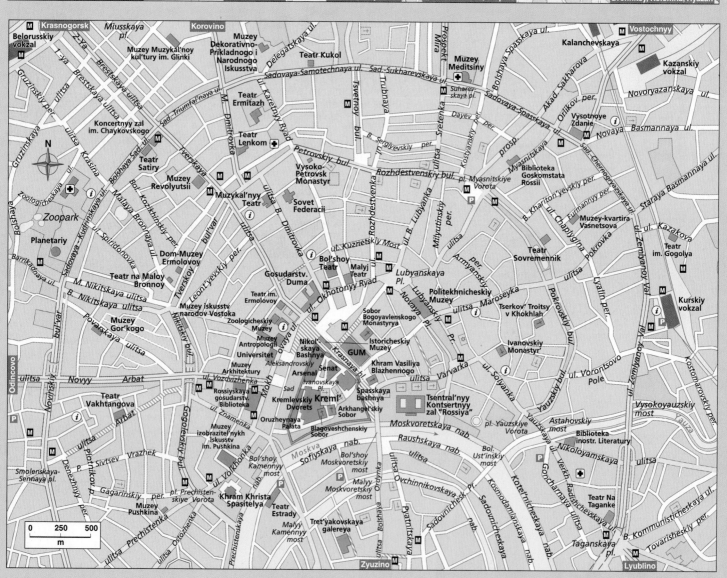

Krasnogorsk · Miusskaya pl. · Korovino · Vostochnyy

Belorusskiy vokzal · Muzey Muzykal'noy kul'tury im. Glinki · Muzey Dekorativno-Prikladnogo i Narodnogo Iskusstva · Teatr Kukol · Muzey Meditsiny · Kalanchevskaya · Kazanskiy vokzal

Sadovaya-Samotechnaya ul. · Sad-Sukharevskaya ul. · Novoryazanskaya ul.

Teatr Ermitazh · Suharevskaya pl. · Sadovaya-Spasskaya · Vysotnoye Zdanie · Novaya · Basmannaya ul.

Koncertnyy zal im. Chaykovskogo · Teatr Lenkom · Petrovskiy bul. · Myasnitskaya ul. · Biblioteka Goskomstata Rossii

Teatr Satiry · Muzey Revolyutsii · Vysoko-Petrovsk Monastyr · Rozhdestvenskiy bul. · pl. Myasnitskiye Vorota · Muzey-kvartira Vasnetsova

Zoopark · Muzykal'nyy Teatr · Sovet Federacii · ul. Kuznetskiy Most · Lubyanka · Teatr Sovremennik

Planetariy · Dom-Muzey Ermolovoy · Bol'shoy Teatr · Malyj Teatr · Lubyanskaya Pl. · Kurskiy vokzal

Teatr na Maloy Bronnoy · Gosudarstv. Duma · Politekhnicheskiy Muzey · Tserkov' Troitsy v Khokhlah

Muzey iskusstv narodov Vostoka · Teatr im. Ermolovoy · ul. Okhotonyy Ryad · Sobor Bogoyavlenskogo Monastyrya · Ivanovskiy Monastyr'

Muzey Gor'kogo · Zoologicheskiy Muzey · Nikol'skaya Bashnya · Istoricheskiy Muzey

Muzey Antropologii · Universitet · GUM · Khram Vasiliya Blazhennogo · ulitsa Varvarka

Novyy Arbat · Muzey Arkhitektury · Aleksandrovskiy Sad · Senat · Spasskaya bashnya · Tsentral'nyy Kontsertnyy zal "Rossiya" · pl. Yauzskiye Vorota

Teatr Vakhtangova · Rossiyskaya gosudarstv. Biblioteka · Kremlevskiy Dvorets · Kreml' · Arkhangel'skiy Sobor

Arbat · Muzey izobrazitel'nykh iskusstv im. Pushkina · Oruzheynaya Palata · Blagoveshchenskiy Sobor · Biblioteka inostr. Literatury

Smolenskaya-Sennaya pl. · Muzey Pushkina · Khram Khrista Spasitelya · Teatr Estrady · Tret'yakovskaya galereya · Teatr Na Taganke · Taganskaya pl.

0 250 500 m

Odincovo · Zyuzino · Lyublino

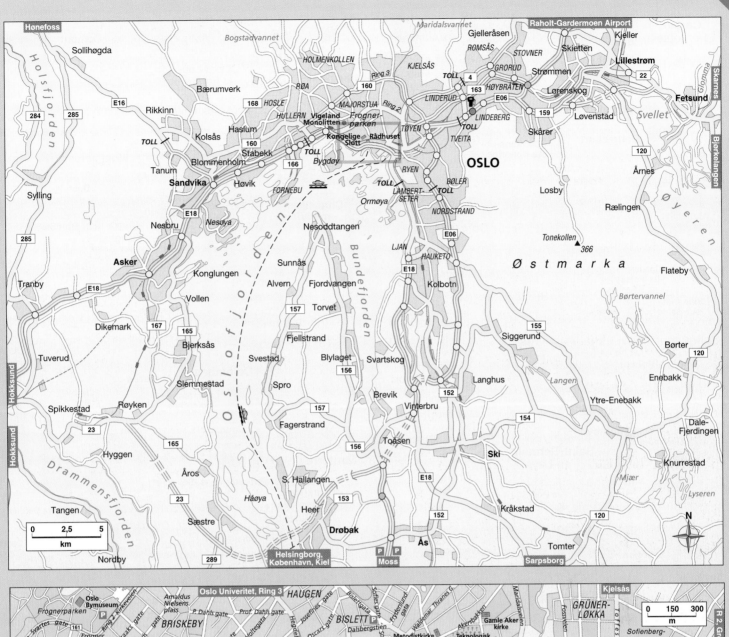

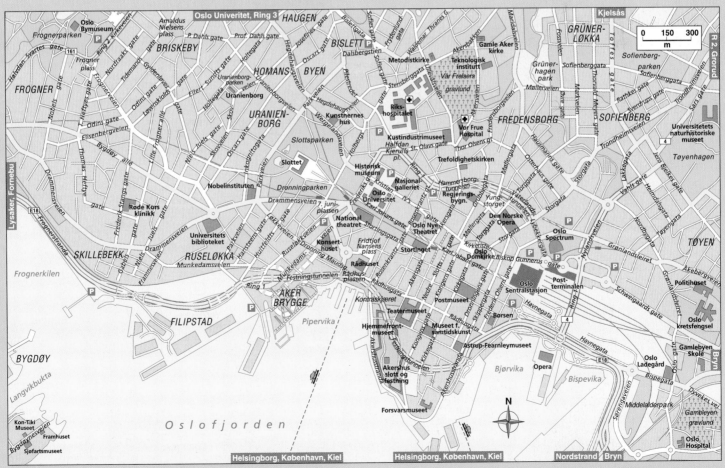

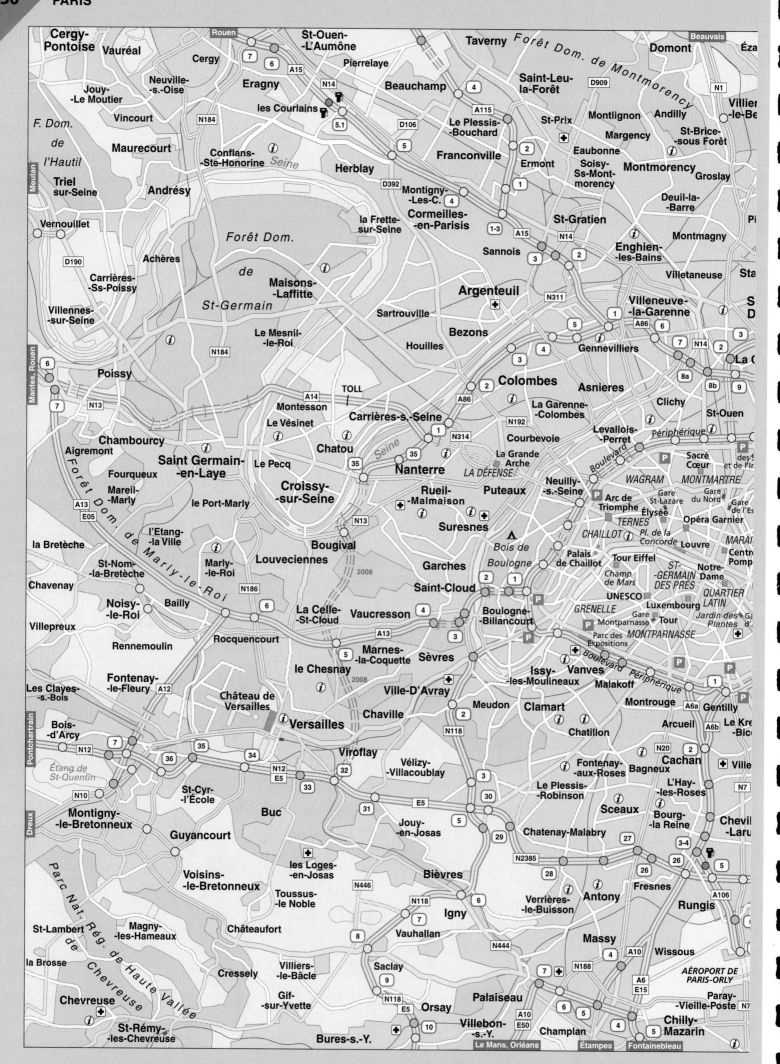

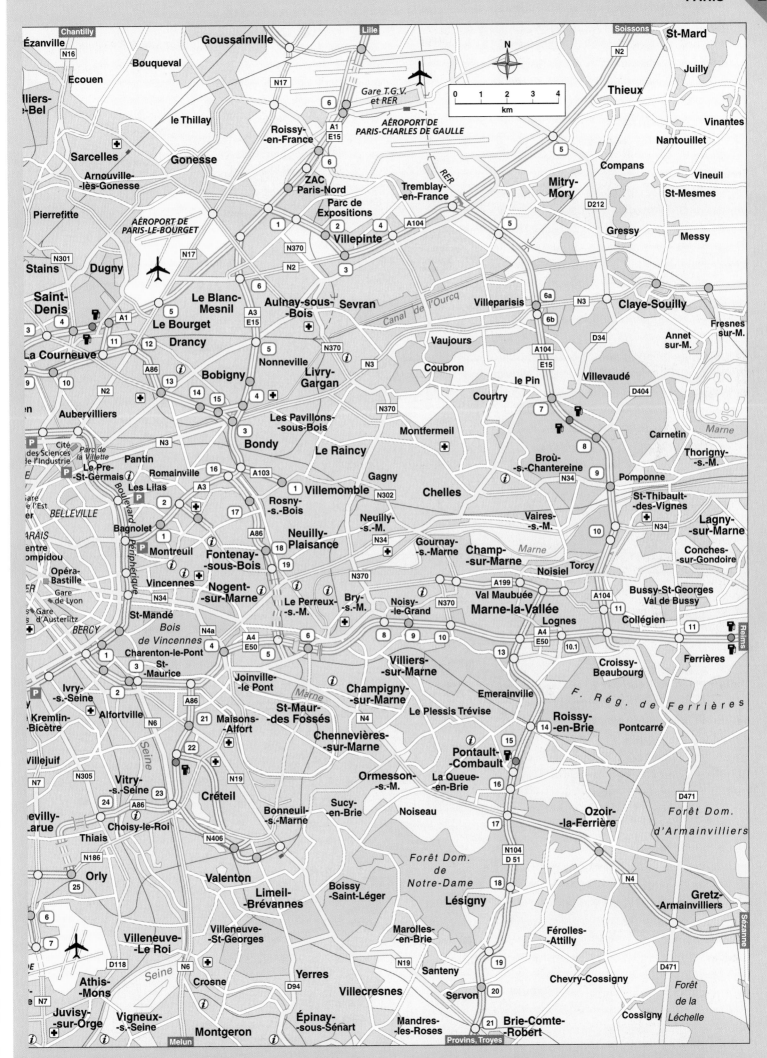

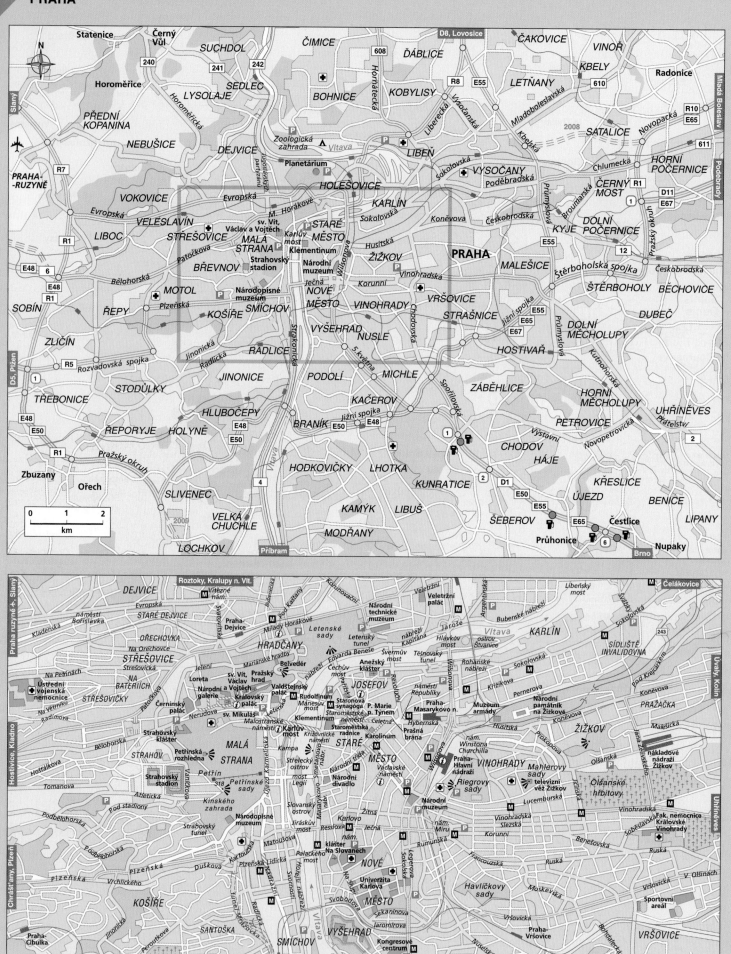

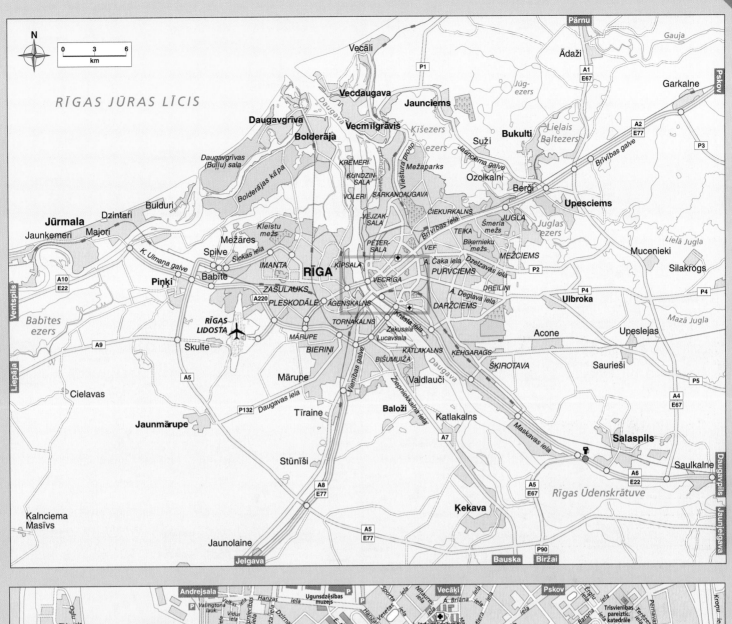

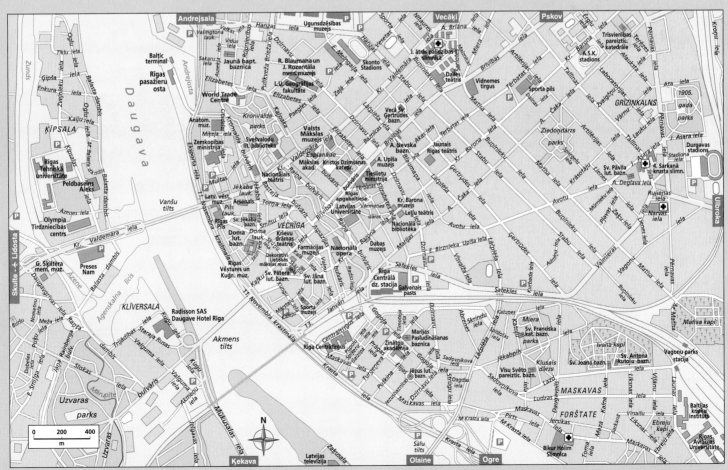

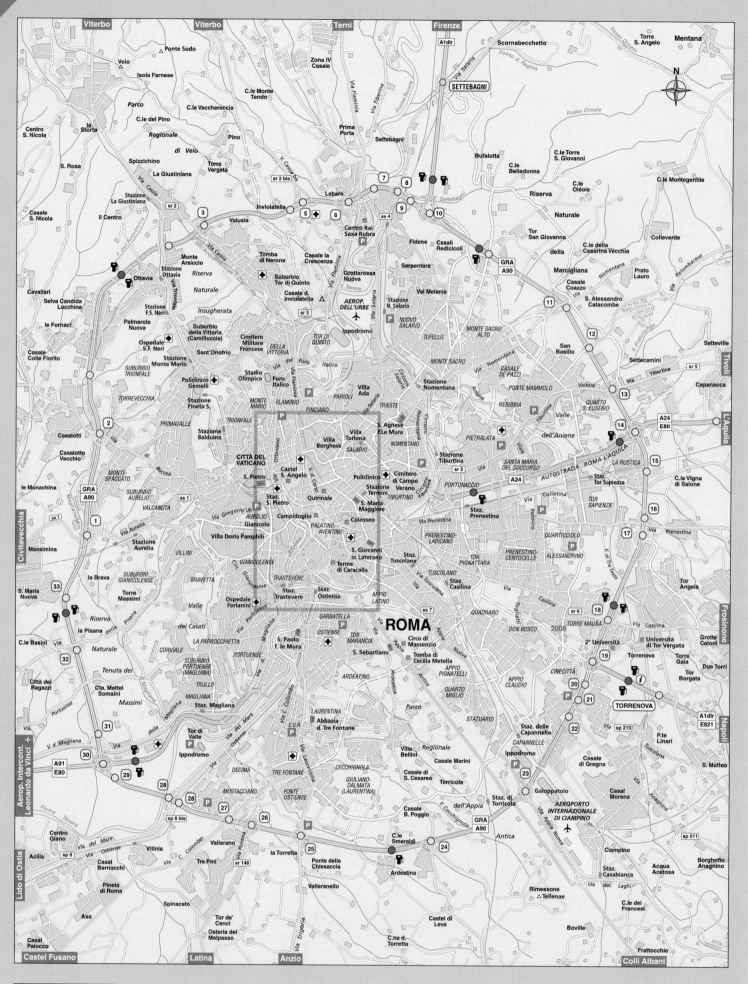

0   1   2   3
km

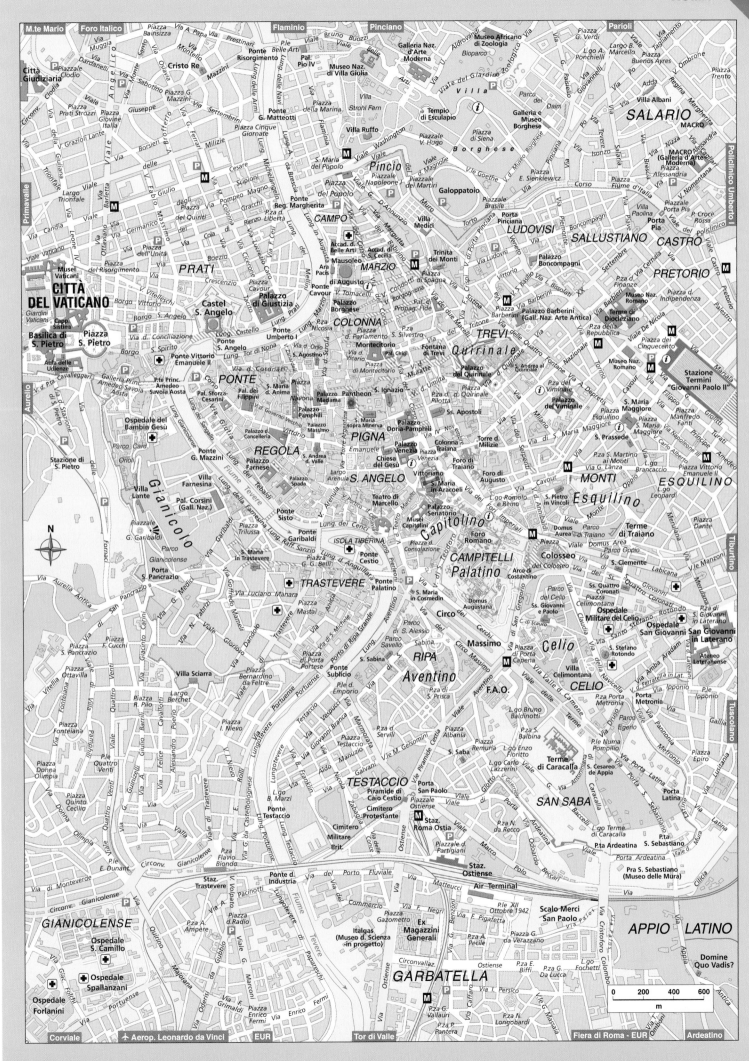

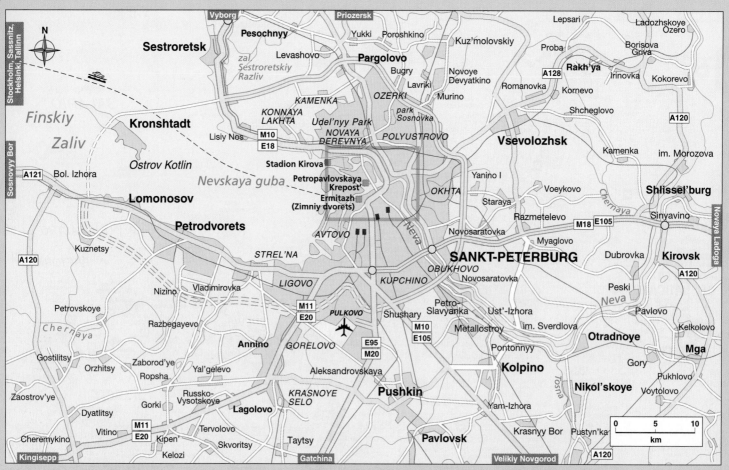

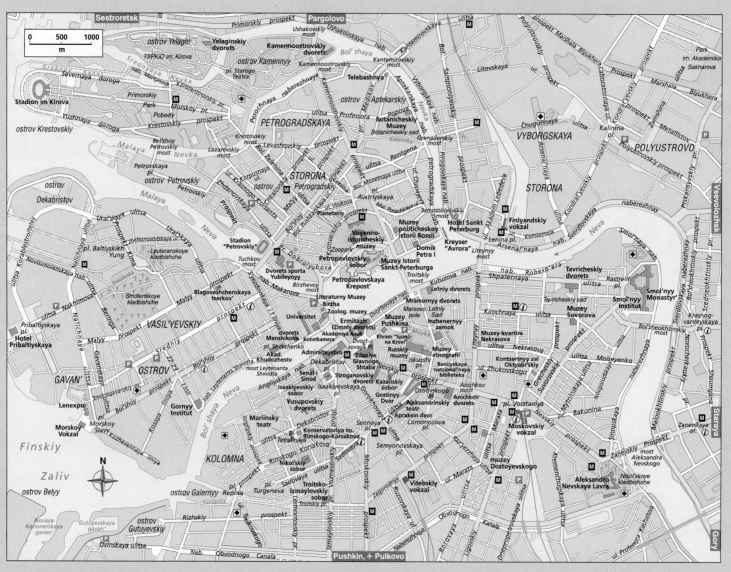

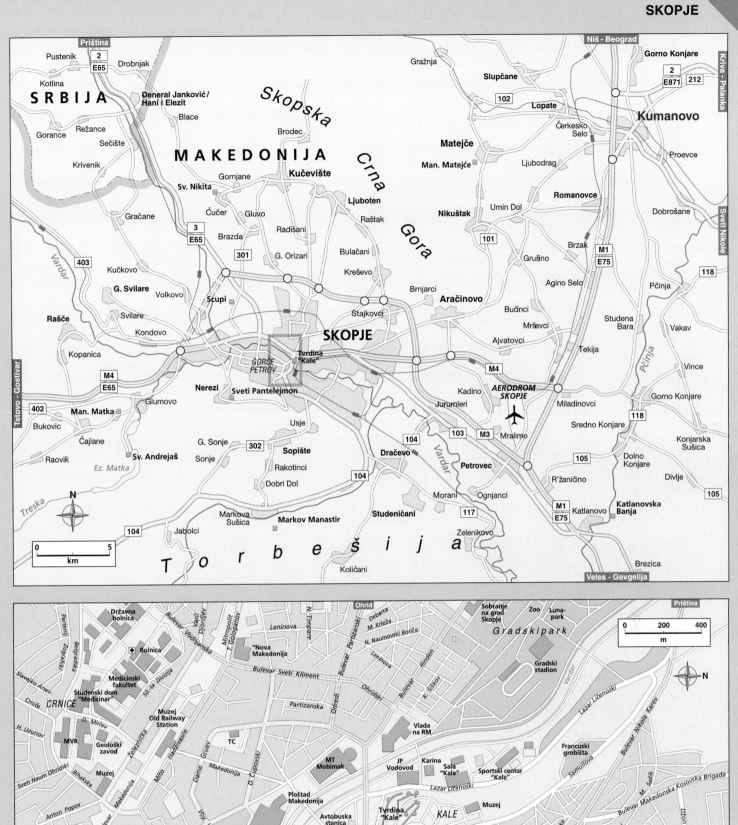

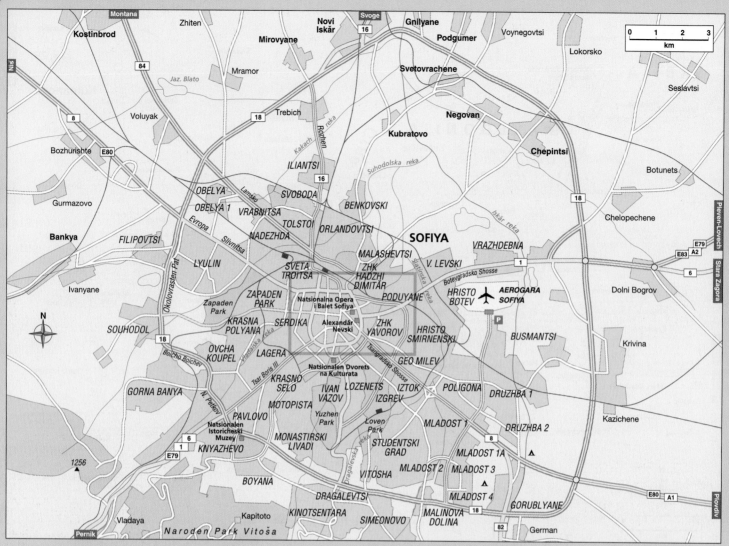

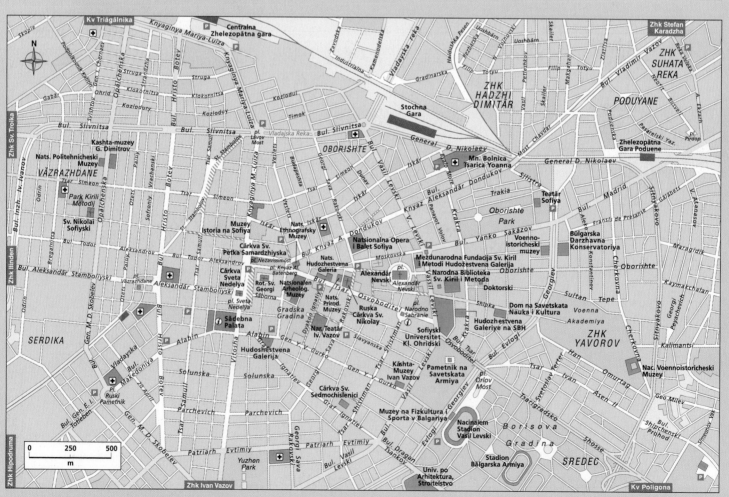

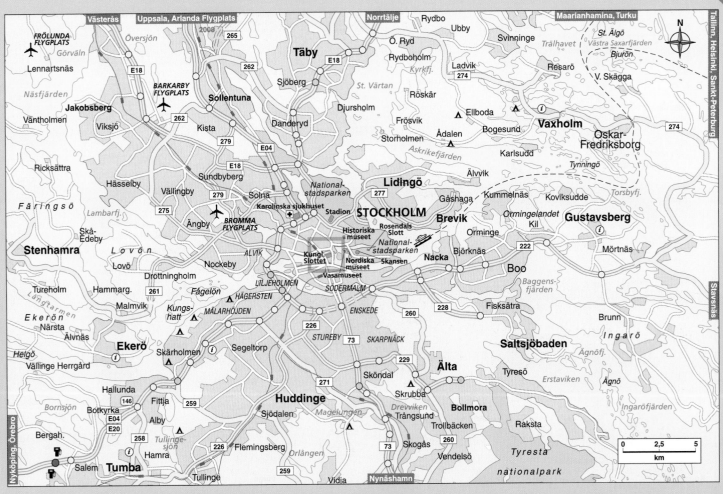

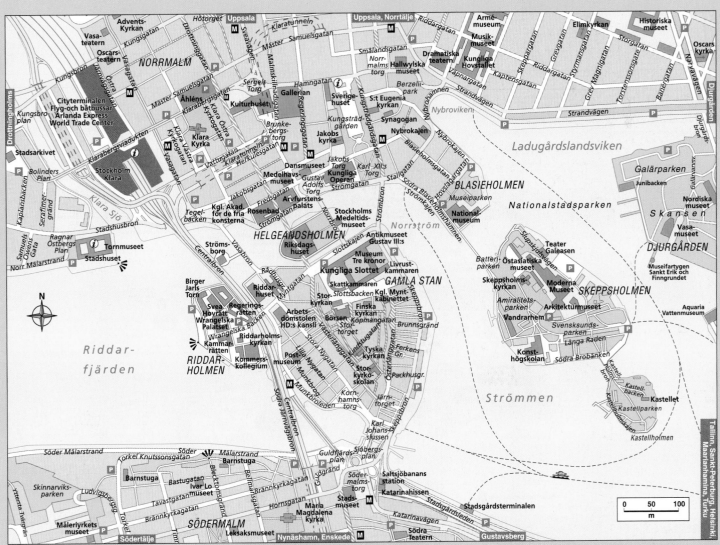

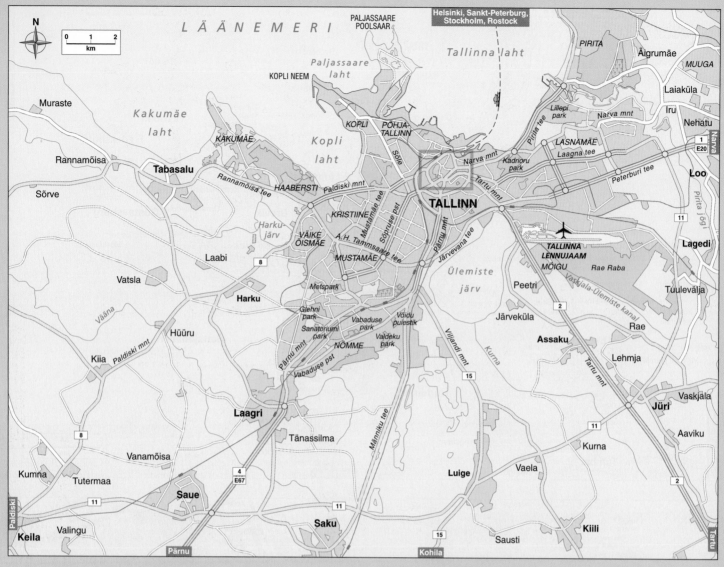

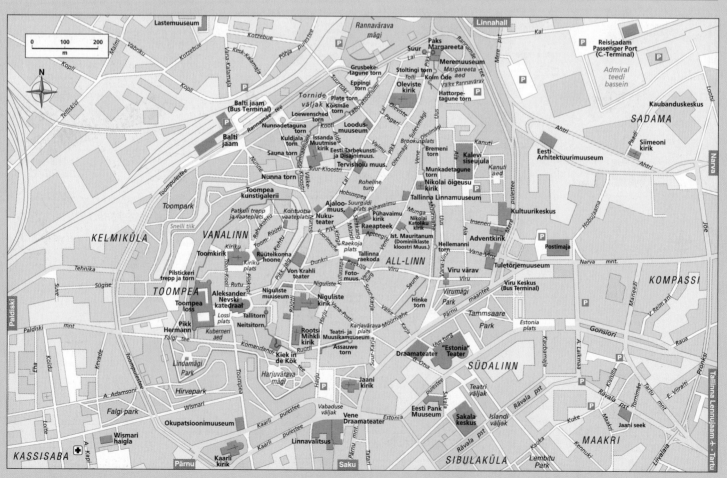

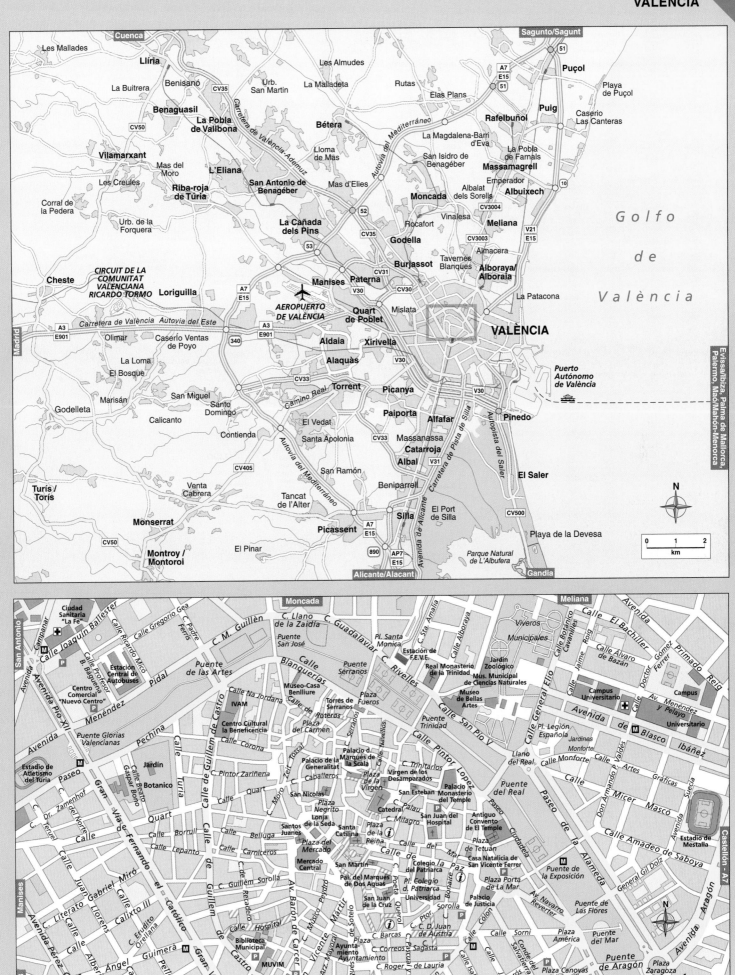

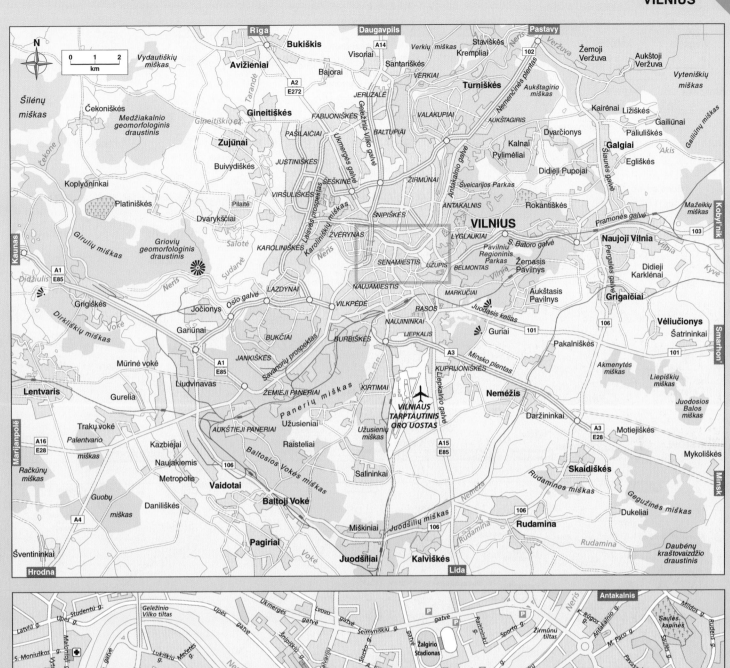

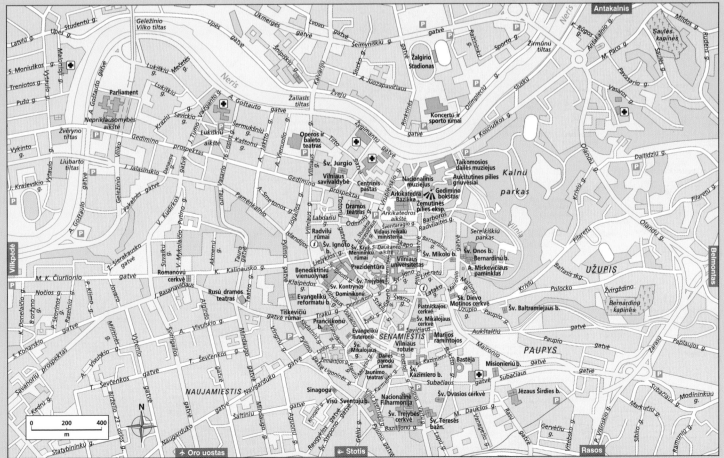

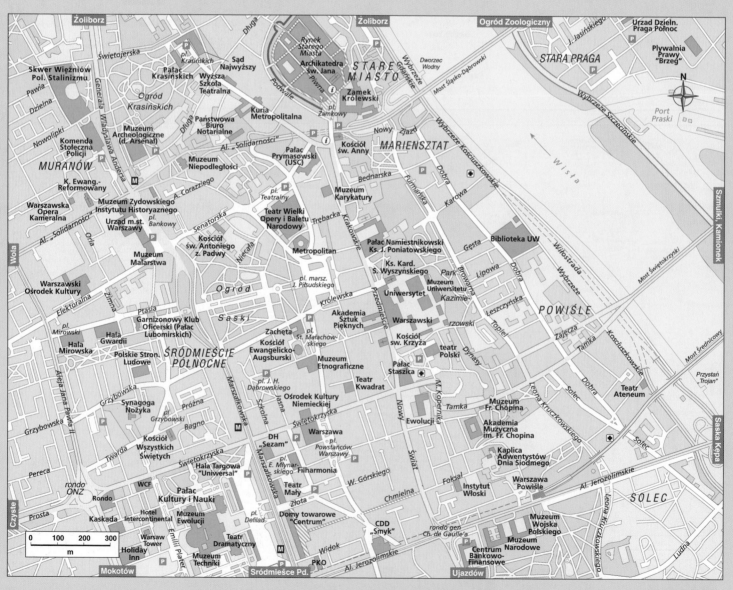

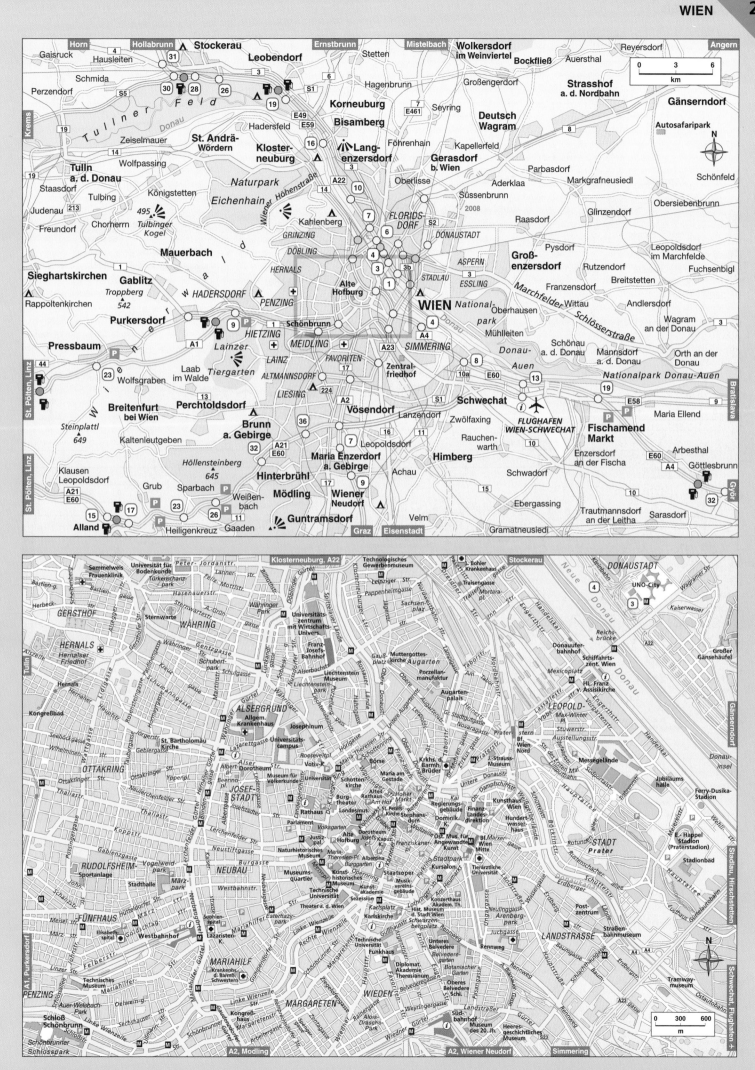

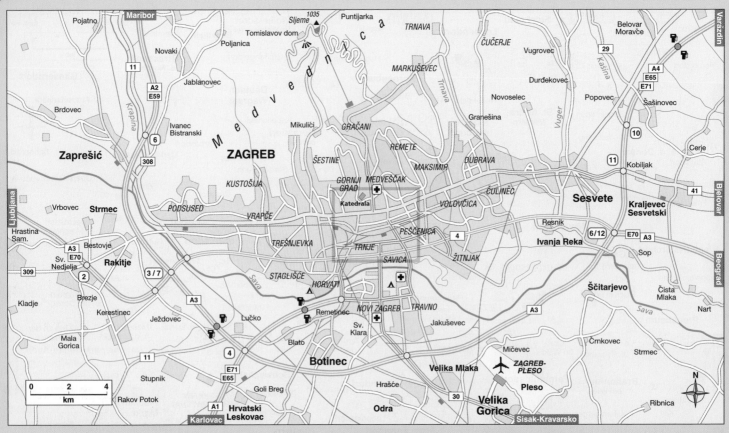

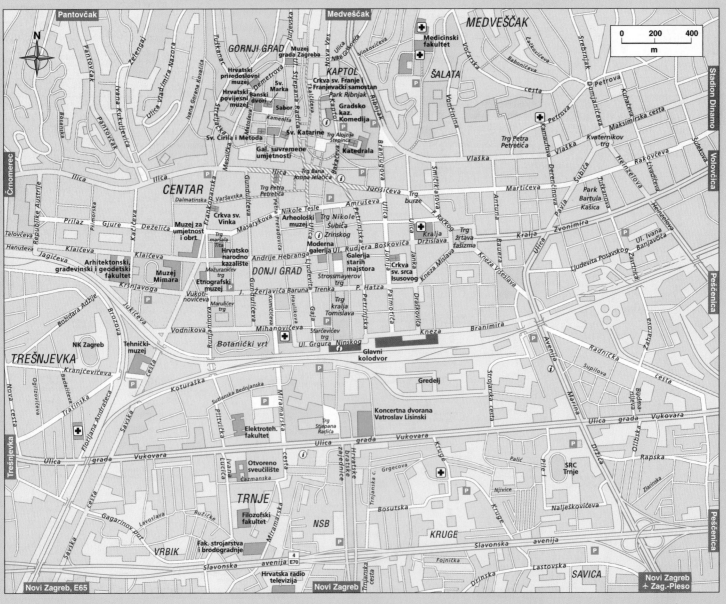

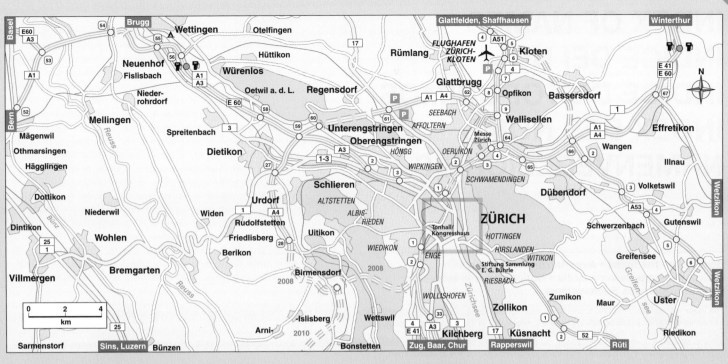

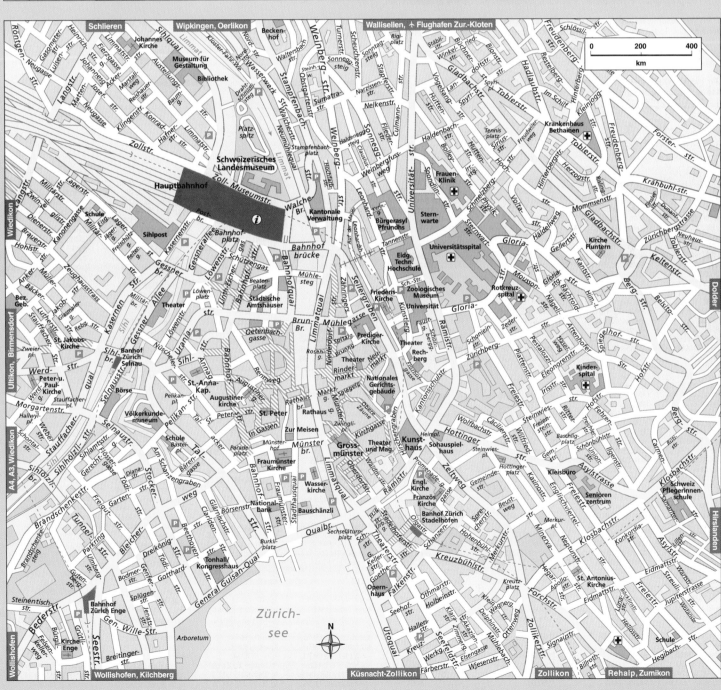

INDEX OF NAMES
INDICE DEI NOMI
ÍNDICE DE TOPÓNIMOS
INDEX DES NOMS
NAMENVERZEICHNIS

How to use the index • Avvertenze per la ricerca
Instrucciones para la consulta • Notices pour la recherche
Erläuterungen des Suchsystems

The index lists the place names, tourist sites, main tunnels and passes contained in the atlas, followed by the abbreviation of the country name to which they belong.
All names contained in two adjoining pages are referenced to the even page number.

L'indice elenca i toponimi dei centri abitati, dei siti turistici, dei principali tunnel e passi presenti nell'atlante, accompagnati dalla sigla della nazione di appartenenza.
Tutti i nomi contenuti in due pagine affiancate sono riferiti alla pagina di numero pari.

El índice presenta los topónimos de localidades, lugares turísticos, principales túneles y puertos de montaña que figuran en el atlas, seguidos de la sigla que indica el País de pertenencia. Todos los nombres contenidos en dos páginas juntas éstan referidos a la página de número par.

L'index récense les noms des localités, sites touristiques, principales tunnels et cols contenus dans l'atlas, suivis par le sigle qui indique le Pays d'appartenance.
Tous les noms contenus dans deux pages l'une à côté de l'autre sont rapportés à la page avec nombre pair.

Der Index enthält die im Atlas vorhandenen Ortsnamen, Sehenswürdigkeiten, wichtigsten Tunnels und Pässe, von dem zugehörigen Staatskennzeichen gefolgt.
Alle in zwei anliegenden Seiten enthaltenen Namen sind auf die Seite mit gerader Zahl bezogen.

Aianí [GR] 128 F6
Aibar [E] 84 C4
Aich [D] 60 F3
Aicha [D] 60 H3
Aichach [D] 60 D3
Aichstetten [D] 60 B5
Aidenbach [D] 60 G3
Aidone [I] 126 F4
Aigen [A] 62 B3
Aigiáli [GR] 138 G3
Aigialoúsa (Yenierenköy) [CY] 154 G4
Aígina [GR] 136 G2
Aigínio [GR] 128 G5
Aígio [GR] 132 F6
Aigle [CH] 70 C2
Aiglsbach [D] 60 E3
Aignay-le-Duc [F] 56 G2
Aigósthena [GR] 134 B6
Aigre [F] 54 D6
Aigrefeuille-d'Aunis [F] 54 C5
Aigrefeuille-sur-Maine [F] 54 C2
Aiguablava [E] 92 G3
Aiguebelle [F] 70 B4
Aiguebelle [F] 108 D6
Aigueperse [F] 68 D1
Aigues-Mortes [F] 106 F4
Aigues-Vives [F] 106 C4
Aiguevives [F] 54 G2
Aiguilles [F] 70 B6
Aiguillon [F] 66 E5
Aigurande [F] 54 H5
Äijäjoki [FIN] 194 B5
Äijälä [FIN] 186 G3
Ailefroide [F] 70 B6
Aillant-sur-Tholon [F] 56 E1
Aime [F] 70 B4
Ainaži [LV] 198 D4
Ainet [A] 72 F2
Ainhoa [F] 84 C2
Ainsa [E] 84 E6
Airaines [F] 28 D4
Airan [F] 26 F4
Airasca [I] 70 D6
Aire [F] 28 E3
Aire-sur-l'Adour [F] 84 E2
Aire-sur-la-Lys [F] 28 E3
Airolo [CH] 70 F2
Airvault [F] 54 E3
Aisey-sur-Armançon [F] 56 F2
Aisey-sur-Seine [F] 56 G2
Aïssey [F] 58 B5
Aistaig [D] 58 G2
Aisými [GR] 130 G3
Aiterhofen [D] 60 G2
Aitolikó [GR] 132 E5
Aitrach [D] 60 B4
Aitrang [D] 60 C5
Aittojärvi [FIN] 196 E6
Aittolahti [FIN] 188 F4
Aittoperä [FIN] 196 D5
Aittovaara [FIN] 196 F3
Aiud [RO] 204 C4
Äivo / Oivu [FIN] 196 C6
Aix-en-Othe [F] 42 H6
Aix-en-Provence [F] 108 B4
Aixe-sur-Vienne [F] 66 G1
Aix-les-Bains [F] 68 H3
Aizanoi [TR] 152 G2
Aizenay [F] 54 B3
Aizkraukle [LV] 198 E5
Aizpute [LV] 198 B5
Ajaccio [F] 114 A5
Ajaur [S] 190 H4
Ajaureforsen [S] 190 F3
Ajdovščina [SLO] 74 A5
Ajka [H] 74 H2
Ajnovce [SRB] 146 D5
Ajo [E] 82 F3
Ajos [FIN] 196 C3
Akáki [CY] 154 F5
Akalan [TR] 150 D2
Akalen [TR] 152 G6
Akanthoú (Tatlısu) [CY] 154 G5
Akarca [TR] 152 G3
Äkasjokisuu [FIN] 194 B6
Äkäslompolo [FIN] 194 C6
Akasztó [H] 76 C3
Akbaş [TR] 152 C1
Akbaş [TR] 152 G5
Akbük [TR] 152 D6
Akçakavak [TR] 154 E2
Akçakese [TR] 150 F2
Akçaköy [TR] 152 E5
Akçaköy [TR] 152 H5
Akçaova [TR] 150 G2
Akçaova [TR] 152 E6
Akçay [TR] 152 C1
Akçay [TR] 154 G2
Akdere [TR] 152 G5
Akdoğan (Lysi) [CY] 154 G5
Aken [D] 34 C4
Åker [S] 162 C3
Åkersberga [S] 168 E2
Åkersjön [S] 190 D6
Åkers styckerbruk [S] 168 C3
Akharım [TR] 152 H3
Akhisar [TR] 152 D3
Akhtopol [BG] 148 G5
Akine [TR] 154 F4
Akkarfjord [N] 194 B2
Akkavare [S] 190 H3
Akkaya [TR] 150 H5
Akkent [TR] 152 G4
Akköprü [TR] 154 E1
Akköy [TR] 152 D6
Akköy [TR] 152 F4
Akland [N] 164 F4
Akli [H] 76 A2
Akmeşe [TR] 150 G3
Akmyane [LT] 198 C6
Aknīste [LV] 198 F6
Akonlahti [FIN] 196 G5
Akonpohja [FIN] 188 F5
Akoúmia [GR] 140 D5
Akpınar [TR] 150 H5
Åkra [N] 170 B5
Akrai [I] 126 G5
Akraifia [GR] 134 B5
Akraífnio [GR] 134 B5
Akranes [IS] 192 A2
Akrapol [TR] 152 C2
Åkre [N] 182 C6
Åkrehamn [N] 164 A2
Akrogiáli [GR] 130 C4
Akropótamos [GR] 130 C4
Akrötiri [CY] 154 F6
Akrotíri [GR] 138 F5
Akrovoúni [GR] 130 D3
Aksakal [TR] 150 D5
Aksakovo [BG] 148 F2
Akşar [TR] 152 G6
Aksaz [TR] 150 C4
Aksaz [TR] 152 F2
Aksaz Kaplica [TR] 152 F4
Aksdal [N] 164 A1
Aksla [N] 180 C6
Aktsyabrski [BY] 202 C6
Åkullsjön [S] 196 A5
Akureyri [IS] 192 C2
Akyaka [TR] 154 F4
Akyazı [TR] 150 H3
Akyazı [TR] 154 G3
Ål [N] 170 F3
Ala [I] 72 C5
Ala [S] 168 G5
Alaattin [TR] 152 G5
Alabanda [TR] 152 E6
Alabodarna [S] 156 H2
Alacadağ [TR] 154 H2
Alacant / Alicante [E] 104 E2
Alacat [TR] 150 E5
Alaçatı [TR] 134 H5
Alà dei Sardi [I] 118 D3
Ala di Stura [I] 70 C5
Aladzha Manastir [BG] 148 G2
Alaejos [E] 88 D2
Alagna-Valsésia [I] 70 E3
A Lagoa / Campo Lameiro [E] 78 B4
Alagón [E] 86 H4
Alagón [E] 90 E3
Alahärmä [FIN] 186 C2
Ala-Honkajoki [FIN] 186 C6
Alajärvi [FIN] 186 D2
Alajärvi [FIN] 196 F3
Alajoki [FIN] 194 D5
Alajoki [FIN] 196 D5
Alakylä [FIN] 194 C7
Alakylä [FIN] 196 D3
Alalampi [RUS] 188 H4
Ala-Livo [FIN] 196 E3
Alamaa [FIN] 186 F2
Alameda [E] 102 C3
Alamedilla [E] 102 F3
Alanäs [S] 190 E5
Alancık [TR] 152 C1
Åland [S] 168 D1
Alandroal [P] 94 E1
Ålandsbro [S] 184 F4
Alange [E] 94 H2
Alanís [E] 94 H4
Alanta [LT] 200 G4
Alap [H] 76 B3
Alapitkä [FIN] 188 C1
Alaquàs [E] 98 E4
Alaraz [E] 88 D4
Alarcón [E] 98 B3
Alaşehir [TR] 152 E4
Ålåsen [S] 190 E6
Alássio [I] 108 G4
Alastaro [FIN] 176 E3
Ala-Temmes [FIN] 196 D4
Alatoz [E] 98 C5
Alatri [I] 116 C6
Alatskivi [EST] 198 F2
Alattu [RUS] 188 H4
Ala-Valli [FIN] 186 C4
Alavattnet [S] 190 E5
Alaveteli / Nedervetil [FIN] 196 C6
Ala-Vieksi [FIN] 196 F5
Alavieska [FIN] 196 C5
Ala-Vuokki [FIN] 196 F4
Alavus [FIN] 186 D4
Alba [I] 108 G2
Alba Adriatica [I] 116 D3
Albacete [E] 98 B5
Albaching [D] 60 F4
Albacken [S] 184 D3
Alba de Tormes [E] 88 C3
Ålbæk [DK] 160 E2
Alba Fucens [I] 116 C5
Albaida [E] 98 E6
Albaina [E] 82 G5
Alba Iulia [RO] 204 C4
Albaladejo [E] 96 G5
Albalate de Cinca [E] 90 G4
Albalate del Arzobispo [E] 90 E5
Albalate de las Nogueras [E] 98 B1
Albalate de Zorita [E] 98 A1
Alban [F] 106 C3
Albánchez [E] 102 H4
Albanella [I] 120 F4
Albano di Lucania [I] 120 H4
Albano Laziale [I] 116 A6
Albaredo d'Adige [I] 110 F1
Albarella [I] 110 H2
Albares [E] 88 H6
Albarracín [E] 98 D1
Albarracín, Cuevas de- [E] 98 D1
Albatana [E] 104 C1
Albena [BG] 148 G2
Albenga [I] 108 G4
Albens [F] 70 A3
Albentosa [E] 98 E3
Alberga [S] 168 B3
Albergaria-a-Velha [P] 80 B5
Alberic [E] 98 E5
Albernoa [P] 94 D3
Albero Alto [E] 90 F3
Alberobello [I] 122 E3
Alberoni [I] 110 H1
Albersdorf [D] 18 E2
Albert [F] 28 E4
Albertacce [I] 114 B3
Albertirsa [H] 76 D1
Albertville [F] 70 B3
Albeşti [RO] 148 G1
Albi [F] 106 B2
Albier Montrond [F] 70 B5
Albignasego [I] 110 G1
Albinea [I] 110 E3
Albissola Marina [I] 108 H3
Albo [F] 114 C2
Albocácer / Albocàsser [E] 98 G2
Albocàsser / Albocácer [E] 98 G2
Alböke [S] 162 G4
Alboraia / Alboraya [E] 98 E4
Alboraya / Alboraia [E] 98 E4
Alborea [E] 98 C4
Albox [E] 102 H4
Albrechtice nad Vltavou [CZ] 48 F6
Albrechtsburg [A] 62 D4
Albudeite [E] 104 C3
Albufeira [P] 94 C5
Albujón [E] 104 C4
Albuñol [E] 102 E5
Albuñuelas [E] 102 D4
Alburquerque [E] 86 F5
Alby [S] 162 G6
Alby [S] 184 C4
Alcácer do Sal [P] 94 C1
Alcáçovas [P] 94 D2
Alcadozo [E] 98 B6
Alcafores [P] 86 G3
Alcaide [E] 102 H3
Alcalá de Chivert / Alcalà de Xivert [E] 98 G2
Alcalá de Guadaira [E] 94 G6
Alcalá de Henares [E] 88 G6
Alcalá de la Selva [E] 98 E2
Alcalá del Júcar [E] 98 C5
Alcalá de los Gazules [E] 100 G4
Alcalá del Río [E] 94 G6
Alcalá del Valle [E] 102 A3
Alcalà de Xivert / Alcalá de Chivert [E] 98 G2
Alcalá la Real [E] 102 D3
Álcamo [I] 126 C2
Alcanar [E] 92 A6
Alcanede [P] 86 C4
Alcanena [P] 86 C4
Alcañices [E] 80 G4
Alcañiz [E] 90 F6
Alcántara [E] 86 G4
Alcantara, Gole d'- [I] 124 A8
Alcantarilla [E] 104 C3
Alcantud [E] 90 B6
Alcaracejos [E] 96 C5
Alcaraz [E] 96 H6
Alcaria Ruiva [P] 94 D4
Alcarràs [E] 90 H5
Alçaşehir [TR] 152 G1
Alcaudete [E] 102 D2
Alcaudete de la Jara [E] 96 D1
Alcázar de San Juan [E] 96 G3
Alçitepe [TR] 130 H5
Alcobaça [P] 86 C3
Alcoba de los Montes [E] 96 D3
Alcobendas [E] 88 F5
Alcobertas [P] 86 C3
Alcocèber / Alcossebre [E] 98 G3
Alcocer [E] 90 A6
Alcochete [P] 86 B5
Alcoentre [P] 86 B4
Alcofra [P] 80 C5
Alcoi / Alcoy [E] 104 E1
Alcolea [E] 102 F5
Alcolea del Pinar [E] 90 B4
Alcolea del Río [E] 94 H5
Alconchel [E] 94 F2
Alcora / l'Alcora [E] 98 F3
Alcorcón [E] 88 F6
Alcorisa [E] 90 F6
Alcossebre / Alcocèber [E] 98 G3
Alcoutim [P] 94 D5
Alcover [E] 92 C4
Alcoy / Alcoi [E] 104 E1
Alcubierre [E] 90 F3
Alcubilla de Avellaneda [E] 88 H2
Alcubillas [E] 96 G5
Alcublas [E] 98 E3
Alcúdia [E] 104 F4
Alcudia de Guadix [E] 102 F4
Alcuéscar [E] 86 H6
Alda [E] 82 H5
Aldeacentenera [E] 96 B1
Aldeadávila de la Ribera [E] 80 F5
Aldea del Cano [E] 86 H6
Aldea del Fresno [E] 88 E5
Aldea del Rey [E] 96 E5
Aldea de Trujillo [E] 96 B1
Aldealpozo [E] 90 C3
Aldeanueva de Ebro [E] 84 A5
Aldeaquemada [E] 96 F6
Aldeatejada [E] 88 C3
Aldeavieja [E] 88 E4
Aldeburgh [GB] 14 G3
Aldeia da Ponte [P] 86 G2
Aldeia do Bispo [P] 86 G2
Aldeias das Neves [E] 94 C4
Aldenhoven [D] 30 F4
Aldernäset [S] 190 F5
Aldershot [GB] 14 D4
Aldinci [MK] 128 E1
Aldtsier [NL] 16 F2
Aled [S] 162 B5
Aledo [E] 104 B3
Alegranza [E] 100 E5
Alekovo [BG] 148 C3
Alekovo [BG] 148 E1
Aleksandrovac [SRB] 146 C1
Aleksandrovo [BG] 148 B3
Aleksandrów [PL] 38 A3
Aleksandrów [PL] 38 B6
Aleksandrów [PL] 52 F2
Aleksandrów Kujawski [PL] 36 F1
Aleksandrów Łódzki [PL] 36 G4
Aleksin [RUS] 202 F4
Aleksinac [SRB] 146 D3
Ålem [S] 162 G4
Alemdağ [TR] 150 F2
Ålen [N] 182 C3
Alençon [F] 26 F6
Alenquer [P] 86 B4
Aléria [F] 114 C4
Aléria [F] 114 C4
Alès [F] 106 F3
Áles [I] 118 C5
Aleşd [RO] 204 B4
Alessandria [I] 70 F6
Alessandria del Carretto [I] 122 D6
Alessándria della Rocca [I] 126 D3
Ålesund [N] 180 C3
Alexándreia [GR] 128 G4
Alexandria [RO] 148 B1
Alexandria Troas [TR] 130 H6
Alexandroúpoli [GR] 130 G3
Alf [D] 44 G2
Alfafar [E] 98 E5
Alfaites [P] 86 G2
Alfajarín [E] 90 E4
Alfambra [E] 98 E1
Alfambras [P] 94 B4
Alfândenga da Fé [P] 80 F4
Alfano [I] 120 G5
Alfarela de Jales [P] 80 E4
Alfaro [E] 84 B5
Alfarràs [E] 90 H4
Alfas [E] 104 F2
Alfatar [BG] 148 E1
Alfedena [I] 116 D6
Alfeizerão [P] 86 B3
Alfeld [D] 32 F3
Alfeld [D] 46 H5
Alfena [P] 80 C4
Alfés [E] 90 H5
Alfonsine [I] 110 G3
Alford [GB] 6 F6
Alforja [E] 92 B4
Ålfoten [N] 180 C5
Alfoz [E] 78 E2
Alfreton [GB] 10 F5
Alfstad [N] 170 G5
Alfta [S] 174 D2
Algaida [E] 104 E5
Algajola [F] 114 B3
Algar [E] 100 G4
Algar [E] 104 H5
Älgarås [S] 166 F4
Ålgård [N] 164 B5
Ålgård [N] 164 B3
Algarinejo [E] 102 D3
Algarra [E] 98 D3
Algatocín [E] 100 H4
Algeciras [E] 100 G5
Algemesí [E] 98 E5
Älgered [S] 184 E5
Alghero [I] 118 B3
Älghult [S] 162 F4
Alginet [E] 98 E5
Algodonales [E] 100 H3
Algodor [P] 94 D4
Algora [E] 90 A5
Algoso [P] 80 F4
Älgsjö [S] 190 G5
Alguazas [E] 104 C3
Algutsrum [S] 162 G5
Algyő [H] 76 E4
Alhama de Almería [E] 102 G5
Alhama de Aragón [E] 90 C4
Alhama de Granada [E] 102 D4
Alhama de Murcia [E] 104 B3
Alhambra [E] 96 G5
Alhamillo [E] 96 C4
Alhaurín de la Torre [E] 102 B5
Alhaurín el Grande [E] 102 B4
Alhojärvi [FIN] 186 F5
Ålholm Slot [DK] 20 B1
Ålhus [N] 180 C6
Alía [E] 96 C2
Ália [I] 126 D3
Aliaga [E] 98 F1
Aliağa [TR] 152 C3
Aliártos [GR] 134 A5
Alibeyli [TR] 152 D3
Alibunar [SRB] 142 H2
Alibunar [SRB] 204 B5
Aliç [TR] 150 B3
Alicante / Alacant [E] 104 E2
Alicudi Porto [I] 124 A5
Äliden [S] 196 A4
Alife [I] 120 E2
Alifuatpaşa [TR] 150 G3
Alija del Infantado [E] 80 H3
Alijó [P] 80 E4
Alíkampos [GR] 140 C4
Alikanás [GR] 136 A2
Alil Abasi [MK] 128 G1
Alimena [I] 126 E3
Alinci [MK] 128 E3
Alinda [TR] 152 E6
Alingsås [S] 162 B1
Alino [BG] 146 F5
Alinya [E] 92 D2
Aliseda [E] 86 G5
Alistráti [GR] 130 C3
Ali Terme [I] 124 B7
Alivéri [GR] 134 C5
Aljaraque [E] 94 E5
Aljezur [P] 94 B4
Aljinovići [SRB] 146 A3
Aljubarrota [P] 86 C3
Aljucén [E] 86 G6
Aljustrel [P] 94 C3
Alkmaar [NL] 16 D3
Alkotz [E] 84 B3
Alkoven [A] 62 B4
Alkpınar [TR] 150 C2
Alksniupiai [LT] 200 F4
Alkvettern [S] 166 G2
Állai [I] 118 C5
Allaines [F] 42 E5
Allainville [F] 42 E4
Allan [F] 68 F6
Allanche [F] 68 C3
Alland [A] 62 E5
Allariz [E] 78 C5
Allauch [F] 108 B5
Alleen [N] 164 C5
Alleghe [I] 72 E4
Allejaur [S] 190 G3
Allemont [F] 68 H5
Allenbach [D] 44 G2
Allentsteig [A] 62 D3
Allepuz [E] 98 E1
Aller-Heiligen [D] 58 F1
Allersberg [D] 46 G6
Allershausen [D] 60 E3
Allerum [S] 156 H1
Alleuze, Château d'- [F] 68 C4
Allevard [F] 70 A4
Allgunnen [S] 162 F4
Allihies [IRL] 4 A5
Allingåbro [DK] 160 E5
Allinge [DK] 158 E4
Allo [E] 84 A4
Alloa [GB] 8 E3
Ålloluokta [S] 192 G6
Allonnes [F] 42 E5
Allonnes [F] 54 E2
Allonö [S] 168 B5
Allos [F] 108 D3
Alloue [F] 54 E5
Ållsjön [S] 184 E2
Allstedt [D] 34 B5
Almacelles [E] 90 H4
Almada [P] 86 B5
Almadén [E] 96 C4
Almadén de la Plata [E] 94 G5
Almadenes, Cañón de los- [E] 104 B2
Almadenejos [E] 96 D4
Almadrones [E] 90 A5
Almagreira [P] 100 E4
Almagro [E] 96 F4
Almancil [P] 94 C5
Almandoz [E] 84 B3
Almansa [E] 98 D6
Almanza [E] 82 C4
Almaraz [E] 88 B6
Almargen [E] 102 B3
Almarza [E] 90 B2
Almås [N] 182 C2
Almásfüzitő [H] 64 B6
Almassora / Almazora [E] 98 F3
Almazán [E] 90 B3
Almazora / Almassora [E] 98 F3
Almedina [E] 96 G5
Almeida [P] 80 E6
Almeida de Sayago [E] 80 G5
Almeirim [P] 86 C4
Almelo [NL] 16 G4
Almenar [E] 90 H4
Almenara [E] 98 F4
Almenara [E] 102 B1
Almenara de Tormes [E] 80 G6
Almenar de Soria [E] 90 C3
Almendinilla [E] 102 D3
Almendra [P] 80 E5
Almendral [E] 94 G2
Almendralejo [E] 94 G2
Almenno S. Salvatore [I] 70 H4
Almere [NL] 16 E4
Almería [E] 102 G5
Almerimar [E] 102 F6
Almesåkra [S] 162 D2
Almestad [S] 162 C1
Älmhult [S] 162 D5
Almodôvar [P] 94 C4
Almodóvar del Campo [E] 96 E4
Almodóvar del Pinar [E] 98 C3
Almodóvar del Río [E] 102 B1
Almogía [E] 102 C4
Almograve [P] 94 B3
Almoharín [E] 86 H6
Almonaster la Real [E] 94 F4
Almonte [E] 94 F6
Almoradí [E] 104 D3
Almoraima [E] 100 G5
Almorox [E] 88 E6
Almourol [P] 86 D4
Almsele [S] 190 F5
Älmsta-Väddö [S] 168 E1
Almudévar [E] 90 F3
Almuñécar [E] 102 D5
Almunge [S] 168 D1
Almuradiel [E] 96 F5
Almvik [S] 162 G2
Almyró [GR] 136 D4
Almyropótamos [GR] 134 D5
Almyrós [GR] 132 H3
Alness [GB] 6 E4
Alnwick [GB] 8 G5
Aloja [LV] 198 E4
Alol' [RUS] 198 H5
Alónnisos [GR] 134 C3
Álora [E] 102 B4
Alosno [E] 94 E5
Alost (Aalst) [B] 28 H2
Alozaina [E] 102 B4
Alp [E] 92 E2
Alpalhão [P] 86 E4
Alpbach [A] 60 E6
Alpedrinha [P] 86 F3
Alpe du Grand Serre [F] 68 H5
Alpen [D] 30 G2
Alpengarten [D] 60 D6
Alpera [E] 98 C5
Alphen-aan den Rijn [NL] 16 D5
Alpiarça [P] 86 C4
Alpirsbach [D] 58 F2
Alportel [P] 94 C5
Alpua [FIN] 196 D5
Alpuente [E] 98 D3
Alpullu [TR] 150 B2
Alqueva [P] 94 E3
Alquézar [E] 90 G3
Als [DK] 160 E4
Alsager [GB] 10 D5
Alsasua / Altsasu [E] 82 H5
Alsen [S] 182 G1
Alsenz [D] 46 B4
Alsfeld [D] 46 D1
Ålshult [S] 162 D5
Alsleben [D] 34 B4
Alsø [DK] 160 F6
Alsóörs [H] 76 A2
Alsótold [H] 64 D5
Alsózsolca [H] 64 F5
Ålstad [N] 192 D5
Ålstad [S] 158 C3
Alstahaug [N] 190 D2
Alstätte [D] 16 G5
Alsterbro [S] 162 F4
Alstermo [S] 162 F4
Alston [GB] 8 F6
Alsunga [LV] 198 B5
Alsvåg [N] 192 D3
Alsvik [N] 192 D6
Alta [N] 194 B3
Altafulla [E] 92 C5
Altamira, Cuevas de- [E] 82 E3
Altamura [I] 122 D3
Altarejos [E] 98 B2
Altaussee [A] 62 A6
Altavilla Silentina [I] 120 F4
Altdahn [D] 44 H4
Altdorf [CH] 58 F6
Altdorf [D] 46 G5
Alt Duvenstedt [D] 18 F2
Altea [E] 104 F2
Altedo [I] 110 F3
Alteidet [N] 192 H1
Altenahr [D] 30 G5
Altenau [D] 32 G4
Altenberg [D] 48 E2
Altenberge [D] 16 H5
Altenberger Dom [D] 30 H4
Altenburg [A] 62 D3
Altenburg [D] 34 C6
Altenfelden [A] 62 B3
Altenglan [D] 44 H3
Altenhundem [D] 32 C5
Altenkirchen [D] 20 D1
Altenkirchen [D] 32 C6
Altenklingen [CH] 58 G4
Altenmarkt [A] 62 C6
Altenmarkt [A] 72 H1
Altenmarkt [D] 60 F5
Altenstadt [D] 60 B4
Altenstadt [D] 60 D5
Altensteig [D] 58 G1
Altentreptow [D] 20 D4
Altenwalde [D] 18 D3
Alter do Chão [P] 86 E5
Alteren [N] 190 E2
Althegnenberg [D] 60 D4
Altheim [A] 60 H4
Althofen [A] 74 B2
Alti [TR] 154 B1
Altimir [BG] 146 G3
Altınoluk [TR] 152 B1
Altınova [TR] 150 F3
Altınova [TR] 152 B2
Altıntaş [TR] 152 H2
Altınyayla [TR] 154 G1
Altipiani di Arcinazzo [I] 116 B6
Altkirch [F] 58 D4
Altlandsberg [D] 34 E2
Altmörbitz [D] 34 C6
Altmünster [A] 62 A5
Altnaharra [GB] 6 E3
Alto de los Leones de Castilla [E] 88 F4
Altomonte [I] 124 D3
Alton [GB] 14 D4
Altopascio [I] 110 E5
Altorricón [E] 90 H4
Altötting [D] 60 G4
Altrier [L] 44 F2
Alt Ruppin [D] 20 C6
Altsasu / Alsasua [E] 82 H5
Alt Schadow [D] 34 F3
Altshausen [D] 58 H3
Altstätten [CH] 58 H5
Alttajärvi [S] 192 G5
Altuna [S] 168 C1
Altura [E] 98 E3
Altwarp [D] 20 E4
Altwindeck [D] 58 F1
Alūksne [LV] 198 F4
Ålum [DK] 160 D5
Ålund [S] 196 A4
Alunda [S] 168 D1
Aluokta [S] 192 F6
Alupka [UA] 204 H4
Aluste [EST] 198 E2
Alvaiázere [P] 86 D3
Alvajärvi [FIN] 186 F1
Alvalade [P] 94 C3
Älvan [S] 166 H5
Älvängen [S] 160 H1
Alvastra [S] 166 G6
Alvdal [N] 182 B5
Älvdalen [S] 172 F2
Alvechurch [GB] 12 H1
Alverca do Ribatejo [P] 86 B5
Alversund [N] 170 B3
Alvesta [S] 162 D4
Alvestad [N] 164 A2
Älvhem [S] 160 H1
Alvignac [F] 66 G4
Ålvik [N] 170 C4
Alvik [S] 172 G4
Alvik [S] 196 B3
Älviken [S] 190 E6
Alvito [I] 116 C6
Alvito [P] 94 D2
Älvkarleby [S] 174 E4
Alvor [P] 94 B5
Älvros [S] 182 E6
Älvros [S] 182 G5
Älvsbacka [S] 166 F2
Älvsbyn [S] 196 A3
Älvsered [S] 162 B3
Älvsund [S] 184 E5
Ålvundeid [N] 180 F3
Alyekshytsy [BY] 24 G5
Alykí [GR] 130 E4
Alykí [GR] 130 E4
Alykí [GR] 138 E3
Alytus [LT] 24 G2
Alzenall [D] 46 D3
Alzey [D] 46 B4
Alzira [E] 98 E5
Alzon [F] 106 E3
Alzonne [F] 106 B4
Åmådalen [S] 172 G2
Amadora [P] 86 B5
Åmål [S] 166 D4
Amalfi [I] 120 E4
Amaliáda [GR] 136 C2
Amaliápoli [GR] 132 H3
Ámalo [GR] 138 G1
Amance [F] 58 B3
Amancey [F] 58 B5
Amandola [I] 116 C2
Amantea [I] 124 D5
Amantia [AL] 128 B5
Amarante [P] 80 C4
Amárantos [GR] 132 F3
Amărăştii de Sus [RO] 146 G2
Amareleja [P] 94 E3
Amári [GR] 140 D5
Amárynthos [GR] 134 C5
Amatrice [I] 116 C3
Amay [B] 30 E5
Ambarès [F] 66 D3
Ambazac [F] 54 G6
Amberg [D] 46 H5
Ambérieu-en-Bugey [F] 68 G2
Ambert [F] 68 D3
Ambiörnarp [S] 162 B3
Ambjörby [S] 172 E4
Ambla [EST] 198 E1
Amble [GB] 8 G5
Ambleside [GB] 10 D2
Amboise [F] 54 G2
Ämbra [EST] 198 E2
Ambrières [F] 26 E5
Åmdal [N] 164 D5
Ameixial [P] 94 C4
Amel [B] 30 F6
Amélia [I] 116 A3
Amélie-les-Bains [F] 92 F2
Amelinghausen [D] 18 F5
Amendolara [I] 122 D6
Amer [E] 92 F3
A Merca [E] 78 C5
Amerongen [NL] 16 E5
Amersfoort [NL] 16 E5
Amersham [GB] 14 E3
Amesbury [GB] 12 G4
A Mezquita [E] 78 E6
Amfiaráeio [GR] 134 C5
Amfíkleia [GR] 132 G4
Amfilochía [GR] 132 D4
Amfípoli [GR] 130 C4
Ámfissa [GR] 132 G5
Amiens [F] 28 E5
Åmilden [S] 190 H4
Åminne [S] 168 G4
Amiternum [I] 116 C4
Amlach [LT] 72 F3
Åmli [N] 164 E3
Åmli [N] 164 E4
Amlwch [GB] 10 B3
Ammanford [GB] 12 E2
Ämmänsaari [FIN] 196 F4
Ammarnäs [S] 190 F2
Åmmeberg [S] 166 G4
Ammersricht [D] 48 B5
Ammóchostos (Gazimağusa) [CY] 154 G5
Ammótopos [GR] 132 D3
Ammoudára [GR] 140 E4
Ammoudára [GR] 140 F5
Åmnes [N] 164 F2
Amorbach [D] 46 D4
Amóreira, Acueducto de- [P] 86 E6
Amorgós [GR] 138 G4
Amorosi [I] 120 E2
Åmot [N] 164 E1
Åmot [N] 164 G1
Åmot [N] 170 G4
Åmot [N] 170 H3
Åmot [N] 172 C2
Åmot [S] 174 D3
Åmotfors [S] 166 D1
Åmotsdal [N] 164 E1
Amou [F] 84 D2
Ampelákia [GR] 132 G1
Ampelikó [GR] 134 H2
Ampelónas [GR] 132 G1
Ampezzo [I] 72 F4
Ampfing [D] 60 F4
Amphion [F] 70 B2

Åstan [N] 180 H1
Asten [A] 62 B4
Asten [NL] 30 F3
Asti [I] 70 E6
Astira [TR] 152 C1
Astorga [E] 78 G6
Åstorp [S] 156 H1
Åstrand [S] 172 E5
Astravyets [BY] 200 H5
Ástros [GR] 136 E3
Astrup [DK] 160 D4
Astryna [BY] 24 G3
Astudillo [E] 82 D6
Astura, Torre- [I] 120 B1
Astypálaia [GR] 138 H4
Asvyeya [BY] 198 G6
Ászár [H] 64 A6
Aszód [H] 64 D6
Aszófő [H] 76 A2
Atalaia [P] 86 B5
Atalánti [GR] 132 H4
Atanneus [TR] 152 C2
Atapuerca [E] 82 E6
Atarfe [E] 102 E4
Atašiene [LV] 198 F5
Atburgazi [TR] 152 D6
Atça [TR] 152 E5
Ateca [E] 90 C4
Atella [I] 120 G3
Atessa [I] 116 E5
Ath [B] 28 G3
Athboy [IRL] 2 E5
Athea [IRL] 4 C3
Athenry [IRL] 2 C5
Athéras [GR] 132 C6
Athiénou [CY] 154 G5
Athína [GR] 134 C6
Athleague [IRL] 2 D5
Athlone / Baile Átha Luain [IRL] 2 D5
Athy [IRL] 4 F3
Atienza [E] 90 A4
Atina [I] 116 C6
Atkár [H] 64 E6
Atnbrua [N] 180 H6
Atnosen [N] 182 B6
Atouguia de Baleia [P] 86 B3
A Toxa [E] 78 B4
Ätran [S] 162 B4
Åträsk [S] 190 H5
Atri [I] 116 D3
Atripalda [I] 120 F3
Áttali [GR] 134 C4
Attel [D] 60 F4
Attendorn [D] 32 C5
Attersee [A] 60 H5
Attigny [F] 44 C2
Attleborough [GB] 14 G2
Attmar [S] 184 E5
Attnang-Puchheim [A] 62 A5
Attre [B] 28 G3
Attrup [DK] 160 D3
Åtvidaberg [S] 168 B6
Atzara [I] 118 D5
Atzendorf [D] 34 B4
Atzeneta del Maestrat [E] 98 F3
Au [A] 62 D6
Au [D] 60 E3
Aub [D] 46 E4
Aubagne [F] 108 B5
Aubange [B] 44 E3
Aubenas [F] 68 E6
Aubérive [F] 44 C3
Auberive [F] 56 H2
Aubeterre-sur-Dronne [F] 66 E2
Aubiet [F] 84 G3
Aubigny [F] 54 B3
Aubigny-les-Pothées [F] 28 H6
Aubigny-sur-Nère [F] 56 C2
Auboué [F] 44 E4
Aubrac [F] 68 C5
Aubusson [F] 68 B1
Auce [LV] 198 C6
Aucelon [F] 68 G6
Auch [F] 84 G2
Auchinleck [GB] 8 D4
Auchterarder [GB] 8 E2
Auchtermuchty [GB] 8 E2
Audelange [F] 56 H4
Audenarde (Oudenaarde) [B] 28 G2
Audenge [F] 66 C3
Auderville [F] 26 D1
Audeux [F] 58 B4
Audierne [F] 40 A3
Audincourt [F] 58 C4
Audlem [GB] 10 D5
Audnedal [N] 164 D5
Audressein [F] 84 G5
Audru [EST] 198 D3
Audun-le-Roman [F] 44 E3
Aue [D] 48 D2
Auen [A] 72 E1
Auen [CH] 72 E1
Auer / Ora [I] 72 D4
Auerbach [D] 46 H4
Auerbach [D] 48 C2
Auerbacher Schloss [D] 46 C4
Auffach [A] 60 F6
Augher [NIR] 2 F3
Aughnacloy [NIR] 2 F3
Aughrim [IRL] 4 G4
Augsburg [D] 60 D3
Augusta [I] 126 G4
Augustenborg [DK] 156 C4
Augustów [PL] 24 E3
Augustusburg [D] 48 D1
Aukra [N] 180 D2
Aukštadvaris [LT] 24 G1
Auktsjaur [S] 190 H3
Auletta [I] 120 G4
Aulla [I] 110 C4
Aullène [F] 114 B5
Aulnay [F] 54 D5
Aulstad [N] 170 H2
Ault [F] 28 C4
Aulus-les-Bains [F] 84 H5
Auly [RUS] 204 G1
Auma [D] 48 B2
Aumale [F] 28 D5
Aumetz [F] 44 E3
Aumont-Aubrac [F] 68 C5
Aunay-sur-Odon [F] 26 E4
Auneau [F] 42 E4
Aunet [N] 182 D2
Aunet [N] 190 C5
Aunet [N] 190 D4
Auneuil [F] 28 D6
Aunfoss [N] 190 D4
Auning [DK] 160 E5
Aups [F] 108 D4
Aurach [A] 60 F6
Aurach [D] 46 F5
Auray [F] 40 D4
Aurdal [N] 170 G3
Aure [N] 180 G1
Aurejärvi [FIN] 186 D5
Aurich [D] 18 B4
Aurignac [F] 84 G4
Aurillac [F] 68 B4
Auriol [F] 108 B5
Auris-en-Oisans [F] 70 A5
Auritz / Burguete [E] 84 C3
Aurlandsvangen [N] 170 D2
Auron [F] 108 E3
Auronzo di Cadore [I] 72 F3
Aursjøhytta [N] 180 F4
Aursmoen [N] 166 C1
Aursnes [N] 180 D3
Àusa Corno [I] 72 G5
Ausejo [E] 84 A5
Ausentum [I] 122 G6
Aussernbrünst [D] 60 H3
Austad [N] 164 C6
Austad [N] 164 D3
Austanå [N] 164 E3
Austborg [N] 190 D5
Austbygda [N] 170 F5
Austefjord [N] 180 C4
Austmarka [N] 172 D5
Austnes [N] 180 D3
Austpollen [N] 192 E4
Austrumdal [N] 164 B4
Auterive [F] 84 H4
Authon [F] 108 D3
Authon-du-Perche [F] 42 C5
Autio [S] 194 B7
Autol [E] 84 A5
Autti [FIN] 194 E8
Auttoinen [FIN] 176 H2
Autun [F] 56 F4
Auve [F] 44 C4
Auvers-s-Oise [F] 42 F3
Auvila [FIN] 188 E6
Auvillers-les-Forges [F] 28 H5
Auxerre [F] 56 E2
Auxi-le-Château [F] 28 D4
Auxonne [F] 56 H4
Auxy [F] 56 F4
Auzances [F] 56 B6
Auzon [F] 68 D3
Avå [FIN] 176 C4
Ava [S] 184 H1
Avafors [S] 196 B2
Availles-Limouzine [F] 54 F5
Aval, Falaise d'- [F] 26 G2
Avala [SRB] 142 G3
Avaldsnes [N] 164 A2
Avallon [F] 56 E3
Ávas [GR] 130 G3
Avaträsk [S] 190 F5
Avaviken [S] 190 G3
Avcılar [TR] 150 E3
Avdímou [CY] 154 F6
Ávdira [GR] 130 E3
Ávdira [GR] 130 E3
Åvedal [N] 164 B5
A Veiga [E] 78 E6
Aveiras de Cima [P] 86 C4
Aveiro [P] 80 B5
Avelengo / Hafling [I] 72 D3
Avellino [I] 120 F3
Aven Armand [F] 106 E2
Avenches [CH] 58 C6
Aven de Marzal [F] 106 G2
Aven d'Orgnac [F] 106 G2
Avène [F] 106 D3
Averbode [B] 30 D3
Aversa [I] 120 D3
Avesnes-le-Comte [F] 28 E4
Avesnes-sur-Helpe [F] 28 G4
Avesta [S] 174 D5
Avetrana [I] 122 F4
Avezzano [I] 116 C5
Avgerinós [GR] 128 E6
Avía [GR] 136 D4
Aviano [I] 72 F5
Aviemore [GB] 6 E5
Avigliana [I] 70 D5
Avigliano [I] 120 G3
Avigna [I] 72 D3
Avignon [F] 106 G3
Ávila [E] 88 E4
Avilés [E] 78 H3
Avinurme [EST] 198 F2
Avinyó [E] 92 E3
Avio [I] 72 C5
Avión [E] 78 C4
Avis [P] 86 D5
Avlákia [GR] 152 C5
Avlémonas [GR] 136 F6
Avlí [GR] 130 D3
Avliótes [GR] 132 A2
Avlóna [GR] 134 C5
Avlonári [GR] 134 C5
Avlum [DK] 160 C6
Avola [I] 126 G5
Avonmouth [GB] 12 F3
Avord [F] 56 C4
Avoriaz [F] 70 C2
Avradsberg [S] 172 F5
Avramov [BG] 148 E4
Avranches [F] 26 D4
Avril [F] 44 E3
Avşar [TR] 152 D6
Avtovac [BIH] 144 D3
Axat [F] 106 B5
Axel [NL] 28 H1
Axioúpoli [GR] 128 G3
Ax-les-Thermes [F] 106 A6
Axmarby [S] 174 E3
Axminster [GB] 12 F4
Axós [GR] 140 E4
Axvall [S] 166 F5
Ay [F] 44 B3
Ayagalip [TR] 130 G5
Ayamonte [E] 94 D5
Ayas [I] 70 D3
Aydın [TR] 152 D5
Aydıncık [TR] 130 G5
Aydıncık [TR] 154 F4
Ayerbe [E] 84 D6
Aykırıkçı [TR] 152 H2
Aylesbury [GB] 14 D3
Ayllón [E] 88 H3
Aylsham [GB] 14 G2
Ayna [E] 98 B6
Ayoó de Vidriales [E] 80 H3
Ayora [E] 98 D5
Ayr [GB] 8 C4
Ayrancı [TR] 152 G2
Ayrancılar [TR] 152 C4
Ay. Seryios (Yenibogaziçi) [CY] 154 G5
Äyskoski [FIN] 186 H2
Äystö [FIN] 186 B4
Aytos [BG] 148 F4
Ayvacık [TR] 134 H1
Ayvalık [TR] 152 B2
Ayvatlar [TR] 152 C2
Azaila [E] 90 F5
Azambuja [P] 86 C4
Azannes-et-Soumazannes [F] 44 D3
Azanúy [E] 90 H3
Azaruja [P] 86 D6
Azath [TR] 150 D2
Azay-le-Ferron [F] 54 G3
Azay-le-Rideau [F] 54 F2
Azeitão [P] 86 B6
Azervadinha [P] 86 C5
Azinheira dos Barros [P] 94 C2
Azıtepe [TR] 152 E4
Aziziye [TR] 150 C1
Aznalcóllar [E] 94 G5
Azpeitia [E] 82 H4
Azuaga [E] 96 A5
Azuara [E] 90 E5
Azuel [E] 96 D5
Azul, Cueva- [E] 104 E6
Azuqueca de Henares [E] 88 G5
Azur [F] 66 A6
Azyory [BY] 24 G4
Azzano Decimo [I] 72 F5
Azzurra, Grotta- [I] 120 D4
Azzurra, Grotta- [I] 120 F5

B

Baad [A] 60 B6
Baal [D] 30 F4
Baamonde [E] 78 D3
Baar [D] 60 D3
Baarle Nassau [NL] 30 D2
Baarn [NL] 16 E4
Babadag [RO] 204 F5
Babadağ [TR] 152 F5
Babaeski [TR] 150 B2
Babaköy [TR] 152 D2
Babek [BG] 148 B5
Babenhausen [D] 46 D3
Babenhausen [D] 60 C4
Babiak [PL] 22 G3
Babiak [PL] 36 F3
Babica [PL] 52 D4
Babice [PL] 50 G4
Băbiciu [RO] 148 A1
Babięta [PL] 24 B4
Babigoszcz [PL] 20 F4
Babimost [PL] 36 A3
Babin Potok [HR] 112 G3
Babjen [AL] 128 C3
BabnoPolje [SLO] 74 B6
Bábócsa [H] 74 G5
Bábolna [H] 64 A6
Babriškes [LT] 24 G2
Babruysk [BY] 202 C5
Babušnica [SRB] 146 E4
Babylon [CZ] 48 D5
Babylón [CZ] 62 E2
Bač [MK] 128 E4
Bač [SLO] 74 A6
Bač [SRB] 142 E1
Bača [SLO] 72 H4
Bacău [RO] 204 D4
Baccarat [F] 44 F6
Baceno [I] 70 F2
Bacharach [D] 46 B3
Bachkovo [BG] 148 B6
Bachkovski Manastir [BG] 148 B6
Bachórz [PL] 52 E4
Bačina [SRB] 146 C3
Backåkra [S] 158 D3
Bačka Palanka [MNE] 204 A5
Bačka Palanka [SRB] 142 F1
Bäckaskog [S] 158 D1
Bačka Topola [MNE] 204 A5
Bačka Topola [SRB] 76 D5
Backe [S] 190 F6
Bäckebo [S] 162 F4
Bäckefors [S] 166 D4
Backen [S] 184 D4
Backen [S] 184 E4
Bäckhammar [S] 166 F3
Bački Breg [SRB] 76 C5
Bački Petrovac [SRB] 142 F1
Bački Sokolac [SRB] 76 D5
Backnang [D] 46 D6
Bačko Gradište [SRB] 142 G1
Bačko Novo Selo [SRB] 142 E1
Bačko Petrovo Selo [SRB] 76 E6
Bąćkowice [PL] 52 C1
Bacoli [I] 120 D3
Bacova mahala [BG] 148 B3
Bacqueville-en-Caux [F] 28 B4
Bácsalmás [H] 76 D5
Bácsbokod [H] 76 C5
Bácsborsód [H] 76 C5
Baczyna [PL] 34 H1
Bad Abbach [D] 60 F2
Badacsonytomaj [H] 74 H3
Bad Aibling [D] 60 F5
Badajoz [E] 86 F6
Badalona [E] 92 E4
Badalucco [I] 108 G4
Bad Aussee [A] 62 A6
Bad Bederkesa [D] 18 D4
Bad Bentheim [D] 16 H5
Bad Bergzabern [D] 46 B5
Bad Berka [D] 46 H1
Bad Berleburg [D] 32 D5
Bad Berneck [D] 46 H3
Bad Bertrich [D] 44 G1
Bad Bevensen [D] 18 G5
Bad Bibra [D] 34 B5
Bad Blankenburg [D] 46 H2
Bad Brambach [D] 48 C3
Bad Bramstedt [D] 18 F3
Bad Breisig [D] 30 H5
Bad Brückenau [D] 46 E2
Bad Buchau [D] 60 A4
Badderen [N] 192 H2
Bad Deutsch-Altenburg [A] 62 G5
Bad Doberan [D] 20 B3
Bad Driburg [D] 32 E4
Bad Düben [D] 34 D4
Bad Dürkheim [D] 46 B4
Bad Dürrenberg [D] 34 C5
Bad Dürrheim [D] 58 F3
Bad Elster [D] 48 C3
Bademli [TR] 134 G1
Bademli [TR] 152 C3
Bademli [TR] 152 E5
Bad Ems [D] 46 B2
Baden [A] 62 F5
Baden [CH] 58 F4
Baden-Baden [D] 58 F1
Bad Endorf [D] 60 F5
Badenweiler [D] 58 E3
Baderna [HR] 112 D2
Bädeshte [BG] 148 C5
Bad Essen [D] 32 D2
Bad Frankenhausen [D] 34 A5
Bad Freienwalde [D] 34 F1
Bad Friedrichshall [D] 46 D5
Bad Gandersheim [D] 32 G3
Badgastein [A] 72 G2
Bad Gleichenberg [A] 74 E3
Bad Godesberg [D] 30 H5
Bad Goisern [A] 60 H6
Bad Gottleuba [D] 48 F1
Bad Grund [D] 32 G4
Bad Hall [A] 62 B5
Bad Harzburg [D] 32 H3
Bad Herrenalb [D] 58 F1
Bad Hersfeld [D] 32 F6
Bad Hofgastein [A] 72 G1
Bad Homburg [D] 46 C2
Bad Honnef [D] 30 H5
Bad Hönningen [D] 30 H5
Badia Gran [E] 104 E5
Badia Polésine [I] 110 F2
Badia Tedalda [I] 110 G6
Bad Iburg [D] 32 D2
Bad Ischl [A] 60 H5
Bad Karlshafen [D] 32 F4
Bad Kissingen [D] 46 E3
Bad Kleinen [D] 20 A4
Bad Kleinkirchheim [A] 72 H3
Bad König [D] 46 D4
Bad Königshofen [D] 46 F2
Bad Kösen [D] 34 B6
Bądkowo [PL] 36 F2
Bad Kreuznach [D] 46 B3
Bad Krozingen [D] 58 E3
Bad Laasphe [D] 32 D6
Bad Langensalza [D] 32 H6
Bad Lauchstädt [D] 34 B5
Bad Lausick [D] 34 D6
Bad Lauterberg [D] 32 G4
Bad Leonfelden [A] 62 B3
Bad Liebenstein [D] 46 F1
Bad Liebenwerda [D] 34 E5
Bad Liebenzell [D] 58 G1
Bad Lippspringe [D] 32 E3
Badljevina [HR] 142 C1
Bad Marienberg [D] 46 B1
Bad Meinberg [D] 32 E3
Bad Mergentheim [D] 46 E5
Bad Mitterndorf [A] 62 B6
Bad Münder [D] 32 F2
Bad Münster Ebernburg [D] 46 B3
Bad Münstereifel [D] 30 G5
Bad Muskau [D] 34 G5
Bad Nauheim [D] 46 C2
Bad Nenndorf [D] 32 F2
Bad Neuenahr [D] 30 G5
Bad Neustadt [D] 46 F2
Bad Oeynhausen [D] 32 E2
Badolato [I] 124 E6
Badolato Marina [I] 124 E6
Bad Oldesloe [D] 18 G3
Badonviller [F] 44 F6
Bad Orb [D] 46 D2
Badovinci [SRB] 142 F2
Badow [D] 18 H4
Bad Peterstal [D] 58 F2
Bad Pirawarth [A] 62 F4
Bad Pyrmont [D] 32 E3
Bad Radkersburg [A] 74 E3
Bad Ragaz [CH] 58 H6
Bad Reichenhall [D] 60 G5
Bad Rippoldsau [D] 58 F2
Bad Rothenfelde [D] 32 D2
Bad Saarow-Pieskow [D] 34 F3
Bad Sachsa [D] 32 G4
Bad Säckingen [D] 58 E4
Bad Salzdetfurth [D] 32 G3
Bad Salzuflen [D] 32 E3
Bad Salzungen [D] 46 F1
Bad Schallerbach [A] 62 B4
Bad Schandau [D] 48 F1
Bad Schmiedeberg [D] 34 D4
Bad Schönau [A] 74 F1
Bad Schönborn [D] 46 C5
Bad Schussenried [D] 60 B4
Bad Schwalbach [D] 46 B2
Bad Schwartau [D] 18 G3
Bad Segeberg [D] 18 G3
Bad Sooden-Allendorf [D] 32 F5
Bad St. Leonhard [A] 74 C2
Bad Sülze [D] 20 C3
Bad Tatzamannsdorf [A] 74 F1
Bad Tennstedt [D] 32 H5
Bad Tölz [D] 60 E5
Badu Andria [I] 118 E3
Badules [E] 90 D5
Bad Urach [D] 58 H2
Bad Vöslau [A] 62 F5
Bad Waldsee [D] 60 B4
Bad Wiessee [D] 60 E5
Bad-Wildungen [D] 32 E5
Bad Wilsnack [D] 20 B6
Bad Wimpfen [D] 46 D5
Bad Windsheim [D] 46 F5
Bad Wörishofen [D] 60 C4
Bad Wurzach [D] 60 B5
Bad Zwischenahn [D] 18 C5
Bække [DK] 156 B2
Bækmarksbro [DK] 160 B5
Baelen [B] 30 F5
Baells [E] 90 H3
Baelo Claudia [E] 100 G5
Baena [E] 102 D2
Bæverfjord [N] 180 F2
Baeza [E] 102 F2
Bagà [E] 92 E2
Bagamér [H] 64 H6
Bağarası [TR] 152 D5
Bägarin [BG] 148 D6
Bågede [S] 190 E5
Bagenalstown / Muine Bheag [IRL] 4 F4
Bagenkop [DK] 18 H1
Baggård [S] 190 H6
Bagh a Chaisteil / Castlebay [GB] 6 A5
Bagheria [I] 126 D2
Bagn [N] 170 G3
Bagnacavallo [I] 110 G4
Bagnara Calabra [I] 124 C7
Bagnères-de-Bigorre [F] 84 F4
Bagnères-de-Luchon [F] 84 F5
Bagni Contursi [I] 120 F4
Bagni del Màsino [I] 70 H3
Bagni di Bormio [I] 72 B3
Bagni di Craveggia [I] 70 F3
Bagni di Lucca [I] 110 E5
Bagni di Rabbi [I] 72 C3
Bagni di Salomone [I] 72 E2
Bagni di Vinadio [I] 108 E3
Bagno a Ripoli [I] 110 F5
Bagno di Romagna [I] 110 G5
Bagnoles-de-l'Orne [F] 26 F5
Bagnoli di Sopra [I] 110 G1
Bagnolo Mella [I] 72 B6
Bagnolo Piemonte [I] 108 F1
Bagnolo San Vito [I] 110 E2
Bagnols-en-Forêt [F] 108 D5
Bagnols-les-Bains [F] 68 D6
Bagnols-sur-Cèze [F] 106 G3
Bagnone [I] 110 D4
Bagnoregio [I] 114 H3
Bagno Vignoni [I] 114 G2
Bagny [PL] 24 E4
Bågø [DK] 156 C3
Bagod [H] 74 F3
Bagolino [I] 72 B5
Bagrationovsk [RUS] 22 H2
Bagsund [N] 190 C5
Báguena [E] 90 D5
Bagunte [P] 80 B3
Bağyaka [TR] 154 D1
Bağyurdu [TR] 152 D4
Bağyüzü [TR] 152 C2
Bahabón de Esgueva [E] 88 G2
Baharlar [TR] 152 B1
Bahçecik [TR] 150 G3
Bahçeköy [TR] 150 B4
Bahçeköy [TR] 150 D2
Bahillo [E] 82 D5
Baia delle Zagare [I] 116 H6
Baia Domizia [I] 120 D2
Baia Mare [RO] 204 C3
Baiano [I] 120 E3
Baião [P] 80 C4
Báia Sardinia [I] 118 E2
Baiersbronn [D] 58 F2
Baigneux-les-Juifs [F] 56 G3
Baile an Sceilg / Ballinskelligs [IRL] 4 A4
Baile Átha Cliath / Dublin [IRL] 2 F6
Baile Átha Luain / Athlone [IRL] 2 D5
Băile Felix [RO] 76 H2
Bailén [E] 102 E1
Băileşti [RO] 146 F2
Băile Tuşnad [RO] 204 D4
Bailieborough [IRL] 2 F4
Bailleul [F] 26 H2
Bailleul [F] 28 F2
Bain-de-Bretagne [F] 40 F5
Bains-les-Bains [F] 58 C2
Baio [E] 78 B2
Baiona [E] 78 A5
Bais [F] 26 E6
Baisogala [LT] 200 F4
Baix [F] 68 F5
Baixas [F] 92 G1
Baja [H] 76 C4
Bajánsenye [H] 74 F3
Bajč [SK] 64 B5
Bajina Bašta [SRB] 142 F4
Bajmok [SRB] 76 D5
Bajna [H] 64 B6
Bajram Curri [AL] 146 A6
Bajša [SRB] 76 D6
Bajzë [AL] 144 E4
Bak [H] 74 G3
Bakacak [TR] 150 C5
Bakar [HR] 112 E1
Bakewell [GB] 10 E5
Bakhchysarai [UA] 204 H4
Bakhmach [UA] 202 E6
Bakio [E] 82 G3
Bakırköy [TR] 150 E3
Bakke [N] 164 F1
Bakke [N] 164 F4
Bakke [N] 166 C4
Bakkejord [N] 192 F2
Bakken [N] 182 C1
Bakko [N] 170 F5
Baklan [TR] 152 G4
Bakonszeg [H] 76 G1
Bakonybél [H] 74 H2
Bakonycsernye [H] 76 A1
Bakonygyepes [H] 74 H2
Bakonyjákó [H] 74 H2
Bakonypeterd [H] 76 A1
Bakonysárkány [H] 76 A1
Bakonyszombatheley [H] 76 A1
Bakovac [HR] 112 F3
Baks [H] 76 E3
Baksa [H] 76 A5
Baksjöliden [S] 190 G5
Baktakék [H] 64 F4
Baktalórántháza [H] 64 H5
Baktsjaur [S] 190 H3
Bakum [D] 18 C6
Bål [S] 168 G4
Bala [GB] 10 C5
Balaban [TR] 150 C1
Balabancik [TR] 150 B4
Balaguer [E] 92 B3
Balanegra [E] 102 F5
Bălăneşti [RO] 148 A1
Balassagyarmat [H] 64 C5
Balástya [H] 76 E4
Balat [TR] 152 D6
Balatonakali [H] 74 H2
Balatonalmádi [H] 76 A2
Balatonberény [H] 74 G3
Balatonboglár [H] 74 H3
Balatonederics [H] 74 H3
Balatonföldvár [H] 76 A3
Balatonfüred [H] 76 A2
Balatonfűzfő [H] 76 A2
Balatongyörök [H] 74 G3
Balatonkenese [H] 76 A2
Balatonkeresztúr [H] 74 H3
Balatonlelle [H] 74 H3
Balatonszemes [H] 76 A3
Balazote [E] 98 B5
Balbigny [F] 68 E2
Balboa [E] 78 E4
Balbriggan [IRL] 2 F5
Bålby [S] 166 G3
Balchik [BG] 148 G2
Balcılar [TR] 150 B5
Balcon de Europa [E] 102 D5
Baldenstein [CH] 70 H1
Balderschwang [D] 60 B6
Baldock [GB] 14 E3
Baldone [LV] 198 E5
Bale [HR] 112 D2
Baleines, Phare des- [F] 54 B4
Baleira [E] 78 E3
Baleizão [P] 94 D3
Balestrand [N] 170 C1
Balestrate [I] 126 C2
Balewo [PL] 22 F4
Bälgviken [S] 168 B3
Balice [PL] 50 H3
Balıkesir [TR] 152 D1
Balıklıova [TR] 152 B4
Balıköy [TR] 152 F1
Bälinge [S] 158 C1
Bälinge [S] 162 B1
Bälinge [S] 168 D1
Balingen [D] 58 G2
Balinţ [RO] 76 H5
Balio Chitarra [I] 126 B2
Baljvine [BIH] 142 B3
Balkanec [BG] 148 B4
Balkanski [BG] 148 D2
Balkány [H] 64 H5
Balkıca [TR] 152 G6
Balla [IRL] 2 C4
Ballaban [AL] 128 C5
Ballachulish [GB] 6 C6
Ballaghaderreen [IRL] 2 D4
Ballangen [N] 192 E4
Ballantrae [GB] 8 C4
Ballao [I] 118 D6
Ballater [GB] 6 E6
Ballebro [DK] 156 C4
Ballefors [S] 166 F5
Ballen [DK] 156 E2
Ballenstedt [D] 34 A4
Balleroy [F] 26 E3
Ballerup [DK] 156 G2
Ballı [TR] 150 B3
Ballina [IRL] 2 C3
Ballina [IRL] 2 C6
Ballinafad [IRL] 2 D4
Ballinagh [IRL] 2 E4
Ballinahinch [NIR] 2 G4
Ballinakill [IRL] 4 E3
Ballinamore [IRL] 2 E4
Ballinascarty [IRL] 4 C5
Ballinasloe [IRL] 2 D5
Ballindine [IRL] 2 C4
Ballindooly Castle [IRL] 2 C5
Ballingarry [IRL] 4 C3
Ballingarry [IRL] 4 E4
Ballinhassig [IRL] 4 C5
Ballinrobe [IRL] 2 C4
Ballinskelligs / Baile an Sceilg [IRL] 4 A4
Ballinspittle [IRL] 4 C5
Ballintober, Abbey- [IRL] 2 C4
Ballintra [IRL] 2 E3
Ballio Zaffarana [I] 126 B2
Ballivor [IRL] 2 E5
Ballobar [E] 90 G4
Ballon [F] 42 B4
Ballon [IRL] 4 F4
Ballsh [AL] 128 B5
Ballshi [AL] 128 B4
Ballstad [N] 192 C4
Ballum [DK] 156 B3
Ballybay [IRL] 2 F4
Ballybofey [IRL] 2 E2
Ballybunion [IRL] 2 B6
Ballycanew [IRL] 4 F4
Ballycastle [IRL] 2 C3
Ballycastle [NIR] 2 G2
Ballyclare [NIR] 2 G3
Ballyconneely [IRL] 2 B4
Ballycotton [IRL] 4 D5
Ballycumber [IRL] 2 D5
Ballydehob [IRL] 4 B5
Ballydesmond [IRL] 4 C4
Ballyduff [IRL] 4 B3
Ballyduff [IRL] 4 D4
Ballyemund [IRL] 4 F4
Ballyfarnan [IRL] 2 D4
Ballygawley [NIR] 2 F3
Ballyglass [IRL] 2 C4
Ballygowan [NIR] 2 G4
Ballyhaunis [IRL] 2 C4
Ballyheige [IRL] 4 B3
Ballyhillin [IRL] 2 F1
Ballyjamesduff [IRL] 2 E4
Ballykeeran [IRL] 2 D5
Ballylanders [IRL] 4 D4
Ballylongford [IRL] 2 B6
Ballylynan [IRL] 4 F3
Ballymacoda [IRL] 4 D5
Ballymahon [IRL] 2 D5
Ballymena [NIR] 2 G3
Ballymoe [IRL] 2 D4
Ballymoney [NIR] 2 G2
Ballymore [IRL] 2 E5
Ballymore Eustace [IRL] 2 F6
Ballymote [IRL] 2 D3
Ballyragget [IRL] 4 E3
Ballyronan [NIR] 2 G3
Ballyroon [IRL] 4 B5
Ballysadare [IRL] 2 D3
Ballyshannon [IRL] 2 E3
Ballyvaughan [IRL] 2 C5
Ballywalter [NIR] 2 H4
Balmaseda [E] 82 G4
Balmazújváros [H] 64 G6
Balme [I] 70 C5
Balmúccia [I] 70 E3
Balogunyom [H] 74 F2
Balş [RO] 146 G1
Balsareny [E] 92 D3
Balsfjord [N] 192 F2
Balsicas [E] 104 C4
Balsorano [I] 116 C6
Bålsta [S] 168 D2
Balsthal [CH] 58 E5
Balta [UA] 204 E2
Baltaköy [TR] 152 E5
Baltanás [E] 88 F1
Baltar [E] 78 C6
Bălţi [MD] 204 E3
Baltimore [IRL] 4 B5
Baltinava [LV] 198 G5
Baltinglass [IRL] 4 F3
Baltiysk [RUS] 22 G1
Baltoji Vokė [LT] 24 H1
Baltrum [D] 18 B3
Balugães [P] 78 A6
Balvan [BG] 148 C3
Balvany [SK] 64 A5
Balvi [LV] 198 G4
Balya [TR] 152 D1
Balzers [FL] 58 H6
Bamberg [D] 46 G4
Bamble [N] 164 G3
Ban [H] 64 A6
Banafjäl [S] 184 G2
Banagher [IRL] 2 D6
Banarli [TR] 150 C3
Banatski Karlovac [SRB] 142 H2
Banatsko Aranđelovo [SRB] 76 E5
Banatsko Karadjordjevo [SRB] 76 F6
Banatsko Novo Selo [SRB] 142 H2
Banaz [TR] 152 G3
Banbridge [NIR] 2 G4
Banbury [GB] 14 D2
Banchory [GB] 6 F6
Bandaksli [N] 164 E2
Bande [E] 78 C5
Bandholm [DK] 156 F5
Bandırma [TR] 150 D4
Bandol [F] 108 B5
Bandon [IRL] 4 C5
Băneasa [RO] 148 C1

Banff [GB] 6 F5
Bångnäs [S] 190 E4
Bangor [F] 40 C5
Bangor [GB] 10 B4
Bangor [NIR] 2 H3
Bangor Erris [IRL] 2 C3
Bangsbo [DK] 160 E3
Bánhalma [H] 76 F1
Banica [BG] 146 G3
Banie [PL] 20 F6
Banie Mazurskie [PL] 24 D2
Baniska [BG] 148 C2
Banja [SRB] 144 E2
Banja [SRB] 146 B4
Banja Koviljača [SRB] 142 E3
Banjaloka [SLO] 112 F1
Banja Luka [BIH] 142 C3
Banjani [SRB] 146 A1
Banjska [SRB] 146 C4
Bánk [H] 64 H6
Banka [SK] 64 A3
Bankeryd [S] 162 D2
Bankháza [H] 76 C2
Bankya [BG] 146 F5
Bannalec [F] 40 C3
Banne [F] 106 F2
Bannesdorf [D] 20 A2
Bañolas / Banyoles [E] 92 F3
Banon [F] 108 C3
Baños de Alicún de las Torres [E] 102 F3
Baños de Cerrato [E] 88 F1
Baños de la Encina [E] 96 E6
Baños de Montemayor [E] 88 B4
Baños de Panticosa [E] 84 E5
Baños de Rio Tobia [E] 82 G6
Bánov [CZ] 62 H2
Bánovce nad Bebravou [SK] 64 B3
Banovići [BIH] 142 D3
Bánréve [H] 64 E4
Bansin [D] 20 E3
Banská Bystrica [SK] 64 C3
Banská Štiavnica [SK] 64 C3
Banské [SK] 64 G2
Bansko [BG] 130 B1
Bansko [MK] 128 H2
Banteer [IRL] 4 C4
Bantheville [F] 44 D3
Ban. Topola [SRB] 76 F6
Bantry [IRL] 4 B5
Bantry House [IRL] 4 B5
Banya [BG] 148 B5
Banya [BG] 148 D4
Banya [BG] 148 G3
Banyalbufar [E] 104 D4
Banyeres de Mariola [E] 104 D1
Banyoles / Bañolas [E] 92 F3
Banyuls-sur-Mer [F] 92 G2
Banz [D] 46 G3
Bapaume [F] 28 F4
Bar [MNE] 144 E5
Bara [RO] 76 H5
Baradla [H] 64 E3
Barajas [E] 88 G5
Barajas de Melo [E] 96 H1
Barakaldo [E] 82 G3
Baralla [E] 78 E4
Baranavichy [BY] 202 B6
Baránd [H] 76 G1
Baranowo [PL] 24 C5
Baranów Sandomierski [PL] 52 D2
Baraona [E] 90 B4
Baraqueville [F] 68 A6
Bårared [S] 162 B5
Barásoain [E] 84 B4
Barbadillo de Herreros [E] 90 A1
Barban [HR] 112 D2
Barbarano Vicentino [I] 72 D6
Barbaros [TR] 150 C3
Barba-Rossahöhle [D] 32 H5
Barbaste [F] 66 E5
Barbastro [E] 90 G3
Barbat [HR] 112 F3
Barbate [E] 100 F5
Bārbele [LV] 198 E6
Barberino Val d'Elsa [I] 110 F6
Barbezieux-St-Hilaire [F] 66 E2
Barbing [D] 60 F2
Barbizon [F] 42 F5
Barbotan-les-Thermes [F] 66 D6
Barby [D] 34 C3
Bärbyborg [S] 162 G6
Bârca [RO] 146 G2
Bárcabo [E] 84 E6
Barca de Alva [P] 80 E5
Barcarrota [E] 94 F2
Barcellona-Pozzo di Gotto [I] 124 B7
Barcelona [E] 92 E4
Barcelonnette [F] 108 E2
Barcelos [P] 80 C3
Bárcena de Pie de Concha [E] 82 E3
Barchfeld [D] 46 F1
Barchon [B] 30 E5
Barciany [PL] 24 B3
Barcin [PL] 36 E1
Barcino [PL] 22 B3
Bárcis [I] 72 F4
Barcones [E] 90 A4
Barcs [H] 74 H5
Barczewo [PL] 22 H4
Bardakçi [TR] 152 E2
Bardejov [SK] 52 D6
Bardejovské Kúpele [SK] 52 C5
Bardi [I] 110 C3
Bardo [PL] 50 C2
Bardolino [I] 72 C6
Bardonécchia [I] 70 B5
Bardovo [RUS] 198 H5
Bardowick [D] 18 G5
Bardufoss [N] 192 F3
Bärenalm [A] 62 B6
Barenburg [D] 32 E1
Barendrecht [NL] 16 C5
Barentin [F] 26 H3
Barenton [F] 26 E5
Bärfendal [S] 166 C5
Barfleur [F] 26 E2
Barga [I] 110 D4
Bargas [E] 96 F1
Barge [I] 108 F2
Bargteheide [D] 18 G4
Bari [I] 122 E2
Barič [SRB] 142 G3
Båring [DK] 156 D3
Bari Sardo [I] 118 E5
Barisciano [I] 116 C4
Bariyevo [BG] 148 B4
Barjac [F] 106 G2
Barjas [E] 78 E5
Barjols [F] 108 C4
Barkåker [N] 164 H2
Barkald [N] 182 C5
Barkarö [S] 168 B2
Barkava [LV] 198 F5
Barkowo [PL] 22 C4
Bârlad [RO] 204 E4
Bar-le-Duc [F] 44 D5
Barles [F] 108 D3
Barletta [I] 122 C2
Barlinek [PL] 20 G6
Barlingbo [S] 168 G4
Barmash [AL] 128 D6
Barmouth [GB] 10 B5
Barmstedt [D] 18 F3
Barnard Castle [GB] 10 F2
Bärnau [D] 48 C4
Barneberg [D] 34 A3
Barneveld [NL] 16 E5
Barneville-Carteret [F] 26 D2
Barnewitz [D] 34 D2
Barnówko [PL] 34 G1
Barnsley [GB] 10 F4
Barnstaple [GB] 12 E3
Barnstorf [D] 18 D6
Barntrup [D] 32 E3
Baroña, Castro de- [E] 78 B3
Barovo [MK] 128 F2
Barquilla de Pinares [E] 88 C5
Barr [F] 44 G6
Barracas [E] 98 E3
Barraco [E] 88 E5
Barrafranca [I] 126 E4
Barranco do Velho [P] 94 C5
Barrancos [P] 94 F3
Barrax [E] 98 B5
Barre-des-Cévennes [F] 106 E2
Barreiro [P] 86 B5
Barreiros / San Cosme [E] 78 F2
Barrême [F] 108 D3
Barrosa [E] 100 F4
Barrow-in-Furness [GB] 10 D2
Barruecopardo [E] 80 F5
Barruera [E] 84 F6
Barry [F] 106 G2
Barry [GB] 12 F3
Barryporeen [IRL] 4 D4
Barsanovo [RUS] 198 H5
Barsele [S] 190 G4
Barsinghausen [D] 32 F2
Barssel [D] 18 C5
Barstyciai [LT] 200 D3
Bar-sur-Aube [F] 44 C6
Bar-sur-Seine [F] 44 B6
Barsviken [S] 184 F4
Barth [D] 20 C2
Barton-upon-Humber [GB] 10 G4
Bartoszyce [PL] 22 H2
Barúmini [I] 118 C6
Barussa, Nuraghe- [I] 118 B7
Baruth [D] 34 E3
Barvaux-sur-Ourthe [B] 30 E5
Barver [D] 32 E1
Bårvik [N] 194 A2
Barwice [PL] 22 A4
Barysaw [BY] 202 C5
Baryshevo [RUS] 178 G3
Bărzina [BG] 146 G3
Barzio [I] 70 G3
Bas [E] 92 F2
Bås [N] 164 E4
Bašaid [SRB] 76 F6
Başalan [TR] 152 F5
Basauri [E] 82 G4
Basconcillos del Tozo [E] 82 E5
Basdahl [D] 18 E4
Basel [CH] 58 E4
Baselga di Pinè [I] 72 D4
Båsheim [N] 170 G5
Bashtanka [UA] 202 F8
Basi [LV] 198 B5
Basildon [GB] 14 F4
Basilice [I] 120 F2
Bäsinge [S] 174 D6
Basingstoke [GB] 14 D4
Baška [HR] 112 F2
Baška Voda [HR] 144 B2
Baške Ostarije [HR] 112 G4
Bäsksjö [S] 190 F4
Başlamış [TR] 152 D2
Başmakçı [TR] 152 H4
Bäsna [S] 172 H4
Bassacutena [I] 118 D2
Bassano del Grappa [I] 72 D5
Bassenheim [D] 30 H6
Bassevuovdde [N] 194 C4
Bassoues [F] 84 F2
Bassum [D] 18 D6
Båstad [N] 166 C2
Båstad [S] 162 B6
Bastelica [F] 114 B4
Bastenaken (Bastogne) [B] 44 E1
Baştepe [TR] 152 H3
Bastfallet [S] 174 E5
Bastia [F] 114 C3
Bastia [I] 116 A2
Bastnäs [S] 166 E1
Bastogne (Bastenaken) [B] 44 E1
Bastuträsk [S] 190 H4
Bastuträsk [S] 190 H5
Batajnica [SRB] 142 G2
Batak [BG] 148 A6
Batakiai [LT] 200 E5
Batalha [P] 86 C3
Batanovtsi [BG] 146 F5
Batăr [RO] 76 H3
Bátaszék [H] 76 C4
Baté [H] 76 A4
Batea [E] 90 G6
Batelov [CZ] 48 H6
Batetskiy [RUS] 202 B2
Bath [GB] 12 G3
Batin [BG] 148 C2
Batina [HR] 76 C5
Batlava [SRB] 146 C4
Bátmonostor [H] 76 C5
Båtmuseum [N] 180 C4
Batnfjordsøra [N] 180 E2
Batočina [SRB] 146 C2
Bátonyterenye [H] 64 D5
Batorz [PL] 52 E1
Bátovce [SK] 64 B4
Batrina [HR] 142 C2
Båtsfjord [N] 194 E1
Båtsjaur [S] 190 G2
Battaglia Terme [I] 110 G1
Battenberg [D] 32 D6
Battice [B] 30 E5
Battipáglia [I] 120 F4
Battle [GB] 14 F5
Battonya [H] 76 G4
Batultsi [BG] 146 G4
Baturyn [UA] 202 E6
Bátya [H] 76 C4
Batyk [H] 74 G2
Batz-sur-Mer [F] 40 D6
Baud [F] 26 A6
Baugé [F] 42 A6
Baugy [F] 56 C3
Baume, Cirque de- [F] 56 H5
Baume, Grottes de la- [F] 58 B4
Baume-les-Dames [F] 58 B4
Baume-Les Messieurs, Abbeye de- [F] 56 H5
Baumholder [D] 44 H3
Baunei [I] 118 E5
Bauska [LV] 198 D6
Bautzen [D] 34 F6
Bavanište [SRB] 142 H2
Bavay [F] 28 G4
Baveno [I] 70 F3
Bavorov [CZ] 48 F6
Bawtry [GB] 10 F4
Bayard [F] 70 A4
Baydakovo [RUS] 198 H6
Bayerisch Eisenstein [D] 48 D6
Bayeux [F] 26 E3
Bayındır [TR] 150 F4
Bayındır [TR] 152 D4
Bayır [TR] 152 E6
Bayırköy [TR] 150 B5
Bayırköy [TR] 150 F4
Baykal [BG] 148 A2
Bayon [F] 44 E6
Bayonne [F] 84 C2
Bayrakçi Mağarasi [TR] 152 D5
Bayramdere [TR] 150 E4
Bayramiç [TR] 152 B1
Bayramşah [TR] 152 G1
Bayreuth [D] 46 H4
Bayrischzell [D] 60 F5
Baza [E] 102 G3
Bazas [F] 66 D4
Bazenheid [CH] 58 G5
Bazoches-sur-Hoëne [F] 26 G5
Bazolles [F] 56 E4
Baztan / Elizondo [E] 82 H4
Bazzano [I] 110 F3
Beaconsfield [GB] 14 D4
Béal an Mhuirthead / Belmullet [IRL] 2 B2
Beariz [E] 78 C4
Beas [E] 94 F5
Beasain [E] 84 A3
Beas de Segura [E] 102 G1
Beateberg [S] 166 F5
Beaucaire [F] 106 G4
Beaufort [IRL] 4 B4
Beaufort-en-Vallée [F] 54 E1
Beaufort-sur-Doron [F] 70 B3
Beaugency [F] 42 D6
Beaujeu [F] 68 F1
Beaulieu-sur-Dordogne [F] 66 H4
Beaulieu-sur-Mer [F] 108 F4
Beaumaris [GB] 10 B4
Beaumes de Venise [F] 106 H3
Beaumesnil [F] 26 H4
Beaumetz [F] 28 E4
Beaumont [B] 28 H4
Beaumont [F] 26 D1
Beaumont [F] 66 F4
Beaumont-de-Lomagne [F] 84 H2
Beaumont-le-Roger [F] 26 H4
Beaumont-sur-Sarthe [F] 26 F6
Beaune [F] 56 G4
Beaune-la-Rolande [F] 42 F6
Beaupréau [F] 54 C2
Beauraing [B] 30 D6
Beauregard, Manoir de- [F] 54 H2
Beaurepaire [F] 68 G4
Beaurepaire-en-Bresse [F] 56 H5
Beausite [F] 44 D4
Beauvais [F] 28 D6
Beauvallon [F] 108 D5
Beauvène [F] 68 E5
Beauvezer [F] 108 D3
Beauville [F] 66 F5
Beauvoir-sur-Mer [F] 54 B2
Beauvoir-sur-Niort [F] 54 D5
Beba Veche [RO] 76 E5
Bebenhausen [D] 58 G2
Bebra [D] 32 F6
Bebrene [LV] 198 F6
Bebrovo [BG] 148 D4
Beccles [GB] 14 H2
Becedas [E] 88 C4
Bečej [SRB] 76 E6
Bečej [SRB] 204 A5
Becerreá [E] 78 E4
Bécherel [F] 26 C5
Bechet [RO] 146 G2
Bechhofen [D] 46 F6
Bechyně [CZ] 48 F6
Becicherecu Mic [RO] 76 G5
Becilla de Valderaduey [E] 82 B5
Beçin Kalesi [TR] 154 C1
Beciu [RO] 148 A2
Beckenried [CH] 58 F6
Beckum [D] 32 C4
Beckum [D] 32 D3
Beclean [RO] 204 C4
Bécon-les-Granits [F] 40 G6
Bečov nad Teplou [CZ] 48 D3
Becsehely [H] 74 G4
Becske [H] 64 D5
Bédarieux [F] 106 D4
Bedburg [D] 30 G4
Beddingestrand [S] 158 C3
Bédée [F] 26 C5
Bedemler [TR] 152 C4
Beden [BG] 130 D1
Bedenac [F] 66 D2
Bedenica [HR] 74 F5
Bedford [GB] 14 E3
Będgoszcz [PL] 20 F5
Będków [PL] 36 H5
Bedlington [GB] 8 G5
Bednarka [PL] 52 D5
Bédole [I] 72 B4
Bedonia [I] 110 C3
Bédous [F] 84 D4
Bedsted [DK] 160 B4
Bedworth [GB] 14 D1
Będzin [PL] 50 G3
Będzino [PL] 20 H3
Beek [NL] 30 E4
Beekbergen [NL] 16 F5
Beek en Donk [NL] 30 E2
Beelitz [D] 34 D3
Beenz [D] 20 D5
Beerfelden [D] 46 D4
Beersel [B] 30 C4
Beeskow [D] 34 F3
Beesten [D] 32 C1
Befreiungshalle [D] 60 E2
Bégard [F] 26 A4
Beglezh [BG] 148 A3
Beg-Meil [F] 40 B3
Begndal [N] 170 G4
Begnecourt [F] 58 B2
Begonte [E] 78 D3
Begov Han [BIH] 142 D3
Begunitsy [RUS] 178 G6
Begur [E] 92 G3
Behramkale [TR] 134 H1
Behramlı [TR] 130 H5
Behringersmühle [D] 46 G4
Beilen [NL] 16 G3
Beilngries [D] 46 H6
Beinwil [CH] 58 E5
Beith [GB] 8 D3
Beitostølen [N] 170 F2
Beitstad [N] 190 C5
Beiuş [RO] 204 B4
Beja [P] 94 D3
Béjar [E] 88 B4
Bejís [E] 98 E3
Bekçiler [TR] 154 G1
Békés [H] 76 G3
Békéscsaba [H] 76 G3
Békésszentandrás [H] 76 F2
Bekilli [TR] 152 G4
Bekken [N] 172 D1
Bélâbre [F] 54 G4
Bela Crkva [SRB] 204 B5
Bel-Air [F] 26 C6
Bel-Air [F] 54 F5
Bel-Aire [F] 26 C6
Belalcázar [E] 96 C4
Bělá nad Radbuzou [CZ] 48 C5
Bela Palanka [SRB] 146 E4
Bélapátfalva [H] 64 E5
Bělá pod Bezdězem [CZ] 48 G2
Bělá pod Pradědem [CZ] 50 D3
Belava [LV] 198 F5
Belbaşı [TR] 154 H2
Belcaire [F] 106 A5
Bełchatów [PL] 36 G5
Belchin [BG] 146 G5
Belchite [E] 90 E5
Belčišta [MK] 128 D3
Belcoo [NIR] 2 E3
Belecke [D] 32 D4
Beled [H] 74 G1
Belej [HR] 112 E3
Belence [TR] 152 H3
Belene [BG] 148 B2
Bélesta [F] 106 B5
Belev [RUS] 202 F4
Belevi [TR] 152 D5
Belevren [BG] 148 F5
Belfast [NIR] 2 G3
Belfir [RO] 76 H3
Belfort [F] 58 C4
Belgern [D] 34 D5
Belgirate [I] 70 F4
Belgodère [F] 114 B3
Belgooly [IRL] 4 C5
Beli [HR] 112 E2
Belianes [E] 92 C3
Belianska Jaskyňa [SK] 52 B6
Belica [BG] 148 D1
Belica [HR] 74 F4
Belica [MK] 128 D2
Belica [MK] 128 E2
Beli Iskăr [BG] 146 G5
Belikij Novgorod [RUS] 202 C2
Belıkliçeşme [TR] 150 C5
Beli Manastir [HR] 76 B6
Belimel [BG] 146 F3
Belin-Béliet [F] 66 C4
Belinchón [E] 96 H1
Belinţ [RO] 76 H5
Belišće [HR] 76 B6
Belitsa [BG] 146 G6
Beljakovci [MK] 146 D6
Beljina [SRB] 142 G3
Belkavak [TR] 152 H1
Bella [I] 120 G3
Bellac [F] 54 F5
Bellaghy [NIR] 2 G3
Bellágio [I] 70 G3
Bellaguarda [E] 90 H5
Bellamont [D] 60 B4
Bellamonte [I] 72 D4
Bellano [I] 70 G3
Bellante [I] 116 D3
Bellapaïs (Beylerbeyi) [CY] 154 G5
Bellária [I] 110 H4
Bellcaire d'Urgell [E] 92 C3
Belleek [NIR] 2 E3
Bellegarde [F] 42 F6
Bellegarde [F] 106 G4
Bellegarde-en-Marche [F] 68 B1
Bellegarde-sur-Valserine [F] 70 A2
Belle-Isle-en-Terre [F] 40 D2
Bellême [F] 26 G6
Bellenaves [F] 56 D6
Bellencombre [F] 28 C5
Bellengreville [F] 28 C4
Bellevesvre [F] 56 H5
Belleville [F] 68 F2
Belleville-sur-Vie [F] 54 B2
Belley [F] 68 H3
Bellinge [DK] 156 D3
Bellinzona [CH] 70 G3
Bell-lloc d'Urgell [E] 90 H4
Bello [E] 90 D5
Bellö [S] 162 E2
Bellpuig [E] 92 C3
Belluno [I] 72 E4
Bellver, Castell de- [E] 104 E5
Bellver de Cerdanya [E] 92 E2
Bellvik [S] 190 F5
Belmez [E] 96 B5
Belmez de la Moraleda [E] 102 F2
Belmonte [E] 78 G3
Belmonte [E] 96 H3
Belmonte [P] 86 F2
Belmont-sur-Rance [F] 106 D3
Belmullet / Béal an Mhuirthead [IRL] 2 B2
Belœil [B] 28 G3
Belogradchik [BG] 146 E3
Belokamensk [UA] 204 H4
Beloljin [SRB] 146 C4
Belopolci [BG] 130 G1
Belo Pole [BG] 146 F2
Belo Polje [SRB] 146 B5
Belopol'ye [UA] 202 F6
Belorado [E] 82 F6
Bělotín [CZ] 50 E5
Belovec [BG] 148 D2
Belovo [BG] 148 A6
Belozem [BG] 148 B5
Belpasso [I] 126 G3
Belsen [D] 18 F6
Belsk Duży [PL] 38 B4
Beltinci [SLO] 74 F3
Belturbet [IRL] 2 E4
Beluša [SK] 64 B2
Belušić [SRB] 146 C2
Belvedere Campomoro [F] 114 A5
Belvedere du Cirque [F] 108 E2
Belvedere Marittimo [I] 124 C3
Belvedere Ostrense [I] 112 C6
Belver [P] 86 E4
Belvès [F] 66 F4
Belvis de la Jara [E] 96 D1
Belyy [RUS] 202 D3
Belz [F] 40 C4
Belz [UA] 52 H2
Bełżec [PL] 52 G2
Belzig [D] 34 D3
Bełżyce [PL] 38 D6
Bembibre [E] 78 F5
Bembirre [E] 78 C2
Bemposta [P] 80 F5
Bemposta [P] 86 D4
Benabarre [E] 90 H3
Benalmádena [E] 102 B5
Benalup [E] 100 G5
Benamaurel [E] 102 G3
Benaojón [E] 100 H4
Benasque [E] 84 F5
Benassal [E] 98 F2
Benassay [F] 54 E4
Benátky nad Jezerou [CZ] 48 G3
Benavente [E] 82 A5
Benavente [P] 86 C5
Benavila [P] 86 D5
Benavites [E] 78 G6
Bencik [TR] 154 C1
Bene [LV] 198 D6
Benedikt [SLO] 74 E3
Benediktbeuern [D] 60 D5
Benediktiner-Abtei [D] 60 F4
Beneixama / Benejama [E] 104 D1
Benejama / Beneixama [E] 104 D1
Benešov [CZ] 48 G4
Benešov [CZ] 62 C3
Benešov nad Ploučnicí [CZ] 48 F2
Benestad [S] 158 D3
Benetutti [I] 118 D4
Bénévent l'Abbaye [F] 54 G6
Benevento [I] 120 F2
Benfeld [F] 58 E2
Bengtsfors [S] 166 D4
Beničanci [HR] 76 B6
Benicarló [E] 98 H2
Benicasim / Benicàssim [E] 98 G3
Benicàssim / Benicasim [E] 98 G3
Benidorm [E] 104 E2
Beniel [E] 104 C3
Benifaió [E] 98 E5
Benifallet [E] 90 G6
Benifassá, Monestir de- [E] 98 G2
Beniganín [E] 98 E6
Benilloba [E] 104 E1
Benimarfull [E] 104 E1
Benissa [E] 104 F2
Benkovac [HR] 112 G5
Benkovski [BG] 148 F2
Benneckenstein [D] 32 H4
Bennstedt [D] 34 B5
Bénodet [F] 40 B3
Benòs [E] 84 F5
Benós [F] 84 F5
Benquerencia de la Serena [E] 96 B4
Benrath [D] 30 G4
Bensafrim [P] 94 B5
Bensberg [D] 30 H4
Bensersiel [D] 18 C3
Bensheim [D] 46 C4
Bensjö [S] 184 C3
Benzú [MA] 100 G6
Beočin [SRB] 142 F2
Beograd [SRB] 142 G2
Beograd [SRB] 204 B6
Bera / Vera de Bidasoa [E] 84 B2
Berane [MNE] 146 A5
Beranúy [E] 84 F6
Berat [AL] 128 B4
Beratón [E] 90 C3
Berbenno di Valtellina [I] 70 H3
Berberana [E] 82 G4
Bercedo [E] 82 F4
Bercel [H] 64 D5
Berceto [I] 110 D3
Berchem [L] 44 F3
Berching [D] 46 G6
Berchtesgaden [D] 60 G6
Bercinos del Real Camino [E] 82 C5
Berck-Plage [F] 28 D3
Berdalen [N] 164 D2
Berducedo [E] 78 F3
Berducido [E] 78 B4
Berdún [E] 84 C5
Berdychiv [UA] 202 C8
Berechiu [RO] 76 H3
Berehomet [UA] 204 D3
Berehove [UA] 204 B3
Berek [H] 76 F2
Berek [HR] 74 G6
Berest [PL] 52 C5
Berestowitsa [BY] 202 A6
Berettyószentmárton [H] 76 G1
Berettyóújfalu [H] 76 G1
Berezan' [UA] 202 E7
Berezhany [UA] 202 B8
Berezivka [UA] 204 F3
Berezna [UA] 202 D6
Berg [CH] 58 F4
Berg [D] 46 H2
Berg [D] 60 D5
Berg [N] 166 C3
Berg [N] 172 D5
Berg [N] 180 C6
Berg [N] 190 C3
Berg [S] 162 D4
Berg [S] 166 D4
Berga [D] 32 H5
Berga [E] 92 E2
Berga [S] 162 F4
Bergama [TR] 152 C2
Bergamo [I] 70 H4
Bergara [E] 82 H4
Berg bei Neumarkt [D] 46 H5
Bergby [S] 174 E3
Bergdala [S] 162 E5
Berge [N] 164 E1
Berge [S] 182 F1
Bergedorf [D] 18 G4
Bergeforsen [S] 184 E4
Bergen [D] 18 F6
Bergen [D] 18 H6
Bergen [D] 20 D2
Bergen [D] 44 F3
Bergen [D] 48 C3
Bergen [N] 170 B4
Bergen [NL] 16 D3
Bergen (Mons) [B] 28 G4
Bergen aan Zee [NL] 16 D3
Bergen op Zoom [NL] 16 C6
Berger [N] 164 H2
Bergerac [F] 66 E4
Berget [N] 190 E2
Bergfors [S] 192 G4
Bergheim [D] 30 G4
Berghem [S] 160 H3
Bergisch Gladbach [D] 30 H4
Bergkvara [S] 162 F6
Bergland [S] 190 F4
Berglern [D] 60 E3
Berglia [N] 190 D5
Bergliden [S] 196 A4
Berg-Neustadt [D] 32 C5
Bergö [FIN] 186 A3
Bergondo [E] 78 D2
Bergsäter [S] 190 F4
Bergshamra [S] 168 E2
Bergsjö [S] 166 F3
Bergsjö [S] 184 E6
Bergsjøstøl [N] 170 F4
Berg slussar [S] 166 H5
Bergsmoen [N] 190 C5
Bergstad [FIN] 176 G5
Bergstrøm [N] 166 C3
Bergues [F] 14 H6
Bergum [NL] 16 F2
Bergün [CH] 70 H2
Bergunda [S] 162 D5
Bergundhaugen [N] 172 B2
Bergvik [S] 174 E2
Berhida [H] 76 B2
Beringel [P] 94 D3
Beringen [B] 30 E3
Berini [RO] 76 G6
Bérisal [CH] 70 E2
Berja [E] 102 F5
Berkåk [N] 180 H3
Berkenthin [D] 18 G4
Berkesz [H] 64 H4
Berkheim [D] 60 B4
Berkhof [D] 32 F1
Berkovići [BIH] 144 C3
Berkovitsa [BG] 146 F3
Berkvigen [S] 190 G2
Berlanga [E] 94 H4
Berlanga de Duero [E] 90 A3
Berlevåg [N] 194 E1
Berlin [D] 34 E2
Berlingen [CH] 58 G4
Bermeo [E] 82 H3
Bermillo de Sayago [E] 80 G5
Bern [CH] 58 D6
Bernalda [I] 122 D4
Bernartice [CZ] 48 F5
Bernati [LV] 198 B6
Bernau [D] 34 E2
Bernau [D] 60 F5
Bernaville [F] 28 E4
Bernay [F] 26 G4
Bernburg [D] 34 B4
Berndorf [A] 62 E5
Berne [D] 18 D5
Bernedo [E] 82 H6
Bernek [A] 72 C1
Bernhardsthal [A] 62 G3
Bernkastel-Kues [D] 44 G2
Bernsdorf [D] 34 F5
Bernstein [A] 74 F1
Bernués [E] 84 D5
Beromünster [CH] 58 F5
Beronovo [BG] 148 E4
Beroun [CZ] 48 F4
Berovo [MK] 128 H1
Berre-l'Etang [F] 106 H5
Berrien [F] 40 C2
Berriozar [E] 84 B4
Berrocal [E] 94 F5
Berrocalejo [E] 88 C6
Berroquejo [E] 100 F4
Bersenbrück [D] 32 D1
Beršići [SRB] 146 B2
Bertinoro [I] 110 G4
Bertrix [B] 44 D2
Berwang [A] 60 C6
Berwick-upon-Tweed [GB] 8 F4
Beryslav [UA] 204 G3
Berzaune [LV] 198 F5
Berzeme [F] 68 E6
Berzence [H] 74 G4
Berzosa [E] 88 H2
Besalú [E] 92 F2
Besançon [F] 58 B5
Besande [E] 82 C3
Besenyőtelek [H] 64 E6
Besenyszög [H] 76 E1
Beşevler [TR] 150 H3
Beşevlet [TR] 150 G3
Besigheim [D] 46 D6
Běšiny [CZ] 48 D6
Beška [SRB] 142 G2
Bessan [F] 106 E4
Bessans [F] 70 C5
Bessay-sur-Allier [F] 56 D5
Besse-en-Chandesse [F] 68 C3
Besse-sur-Issole [F] 108 C5
Bessheim [N] 170 F1
Bessines-sur-Gartempe [F] 54 G6
Best [NL] 30 E2
Bestida [P] 80 B5
Bestorp [S] 168 A6
Beszowa [PL] 52 C2
Betancuria [E] 100 E6
Betanzos [E] 78 D2
Betelu [E] 84 B3
Bétera [E] 98 E4
Beteta [E] 90 B6
Bétharram, Grottes de- [F] 84 E4
Bethesda [GB] 10 B4
Béthune [F] 28 E3
Betliar [SK] 64 E3
Betna [N] 180 F2
Betsele [S] 190 H5
Bettenburg [D] 46 F3
Bettna [S] 168 C4

Bettola [I] 110 C2
Bettyhill [GB] 6 E2
Betws-y-Coed [GB] 10 C4
Betz [F] 42 G3
Betzdorf [D] 32 C6
Betzigau [D] 60 C5
Beuel [D] 30 H5
Beuil [F] 108 E3
Beulich [D] 44 H1
Beuron [D] 58 G3
Beuzeville [F] 26 G3
Bevagna [I] 116 A2
Bévercé-Malmedy [B] 30 F5
Beverley [GB] 10 G4
Beverstedt [D] 18 D4
Beverungen [D] 32 F4
Beverwijk [NL] 16 D4
Bevtoft [DK] 156 C3
Bewdley [GB] 12 G1
Bex [CH] 70 C2
Bexhill [GB] 14 E6
Beyağaç [TR] 152 F6
Beyarmudu (Pergamos) [CY] 154 G5
Beyazköy [TR] 150 C2
Beycayırı [TR] 150 B5
Beyce Sultan [TR] 152 G4
Beydağı [TR] 152 E4
Beydilli [TR] 152 H3
Beyel [TR] 152 E1
Beyköğ [TR] 152 H6
Beykoz [TR] 150 E2
Beylerbeyi (Bellapaïs) [CY] 154 G5
Beynac-et-Cazenac [F] 66 F4
Beynat [F] 66 H3
Beyobaşı [TR] 154 E1
Bezau [A] 60 B6
Bezdan [SRB] 76 C5
Bezden [BG] 146 F4
Bezděz [CZ] 48 G2
Bezdonys [LT] 200 G5
Bezhetë-Makaj [AL] 146 A6
Bezhetsk [RUS] 202 E2
Béziers [F] 106 D4
Béznar [E] 102 E4
Bezzecca [I] 72 C5
B. Hornberg [D] 46 D5
Biała [PL] 50 D3
Białaczów [PL] 38 A5
Biała Piska [PL] 24 D4
Biała Podlaska [PL] 38 F3
Biała Rawska [PL] 38 A4
Białawy Wielkie [PL] 36 C5
Białobrzegi [PL] 38 B4
Białogard [PL] 20 H3
Białogóra [PL] 22 D1
Białowieża [PL] 38 G1
Biały Bór [PL] 22 B4
Białystok [PL] 24 E5
Biancavilla [I] 126 G3
Bianco [I] 124 D7
Biar [E] 104 D1
Biarritz [F] 84 C2
Bias [F] 66 B5
Biasca [CH] 70 G2
Biasteri / Laguardia [E] 82 G6
Biatigala [LT] 200 E4
Biatorbágy [H] 76 C1
Bibaktad [N] 194 C2
Bibbiena [I] 110 G6
Bibbiona [I] 114 E1
Biberach [D] 58 F2
Biberach an der Riss [D] 60 B4
Biberwier [A] 60 D6
Bibione [I] 72 G6
Bibury [GB] 12 H3
Bič [SLO] 74 C5
Bicaj [AL] 128 C1
Bicaz [RO] 204 D4
Bicester [GB] 14 D3
Bichl [D] 60 D5
Bicos [P] 94 C3
Bicske [H] 76 B1
Bidache [F] 84 C2
Bidalite [S] 162 F6
Bidart [F] 84 C2
Biddinghuizen [NL] 16 F4
Biddulph [GB] 10 E5
Bideford [GB] 12 D3
Bidjovagge [N] 192 H2
Bidovce [SK] 64 G3
Bidziny [PL] 52 D1
Bie [S] 168 B4
Bieber [D] 46 D3
Biebersdorf [D] 34 F4
Biecz [PL] 52 C4
Biedenkopf [D] 32 D6
Biegen [D] 34 F3
Biegen [D] 34 F3
Biejkvasslia [N] 190 D2
Biel [E] 84 C5
Biel / Bienne [CH] 58 D5
Bielany Wrocł. [PL] 50 C1
Bielawa [PL] 50 C2
Bielawy [PL] 36 G3
Bielczyny [PL] 22 E5
Bielefeld [D] 32 D3
Bielino [PL] 38 C1
Biella [I] 70 E4
Bielmonte [I] 70 E4
Bielopolje [HR] 112 H3
Bielowy [PL] 52 D4
Bielsa [E] 84 E5
Bielsa, Tunnel de- [E/F] 84 E5
Bielsk [PL] 36 H2
Bielsko-Biała [PL] 50 G4
Bielsk Podlaski [PL] 38 F1
Biely Kameň [SK] 62 G4
Bienenbüttel [D] 18 G5
Bieniów [PL] 34 H4
Bienne / Biel [CH] 58 D5
Bienvenida [E] 94 G3
Bienvenida [E] 96 D4
Bierberchren [D] 46 E5
Bierdzany [PL] 50 E2
Biermé [F] 40 H5
Bierre-Lès-Semur [F] 56 F3
Bierutów [PL] 36 D6
Bierzwnik [PL] 20 G6
Biescas [E] 84 D5
Biesenthal [D] 34 E1
Biesiekierz [PL] 20 H3
Bieskkenjárga [N] 194 C4
Bietigheim [D] 46 D6
Bieżuń [PL] 22 G6
Biga [TR] 150 C5
Bigadiç [TR] 152 D2
Bigastro [E] 104 D3
Biggar [GB] 8 E4
Biggleswade [GB] 14 E3
Bignasco [CH] 70 F2
Bigor [MNE] 144 E4
Bihać [BIH] 112 H3
Biharia [RO] 76 H2
Biharkeresztes [H] 76 H2
Biharnagybajom [H] 76 G1
Bijambarska Pećina [BIH] 142 D4
Bijeljani [BIH] 144 D3
Bijeljina [BIH] 142 F3
Bijelo Brdo [HR] 142 E1
Bijelo Polje [MNE] 146 A4
Bikava [LV] 198 G5
Bikovo [SRB] 76 D5
Bílá [CZ] 50 F5
Bila Tserkva [UA] 202 D8
Bilbao / Bilbo [E] 82 G4
Bilbo / Bilbao [E] 82 G4
Bileća [BIH] 144 D3
Bilecik [TR] 150 G4
Biled [RO] 76 G5
Bilenec [CZ] 48 E3
Biłgoraj [PL] 52 F2
Bilhorod Dnistrovs'kyi [UA] 204 F4
Bílina [CZ] 48 E2
Bilisht [AL] 128 D5
Biljanovac [SRB] 146 B3
Bilje [HR] 76 C6
Bilka [BG] 148 F3
Billdal [S] 160 G2
Billerbeck [D] 16 H6
Billericay [GB] 14 F4
Billesholm [S] 156 H1
Billingen [N] 180 E5
Billingsfors [S] 166 D4
Billom [F] 68 D2
Billsta [S] 184 G2
Billum [DK] 156 A2
Billund [DK] 156 C2
Bilopillia [UA] 202 E7
Bilousivka [UA] 202 E7
Bílovec [CZ] 50 E4
Bilska [LV] 198 F4
Bilsko [PL] 52 B4
Bilto [N] 192 H2
Biňa [SK] 64 B5
Binas [F] 42 D6
Binasco [I] 70 G5
Binche [B] 28 H4
Bindslev [DK] 160 E2
Binéfar [E] 90 G4
Bingen [D] 46 B3
Bingen [N] 170 G6
Binghöhle [D] 46 G4
Bingsjö [S] 174 C3
Bingsta [S] 182 G3
Binibeca Vell [E] 104 H5
Binic [F] 26 B4
Binkos [BG] 148 D4
Bin Tepeler [TR] 152 E3
Binz [D] 20 D2
Binzen [D] 58 E4
Bioče [MNE] 144 E4
Biograd [HR] 112 G5
Bionaz [I] 70 D3
Bioska [SRB] 144 F1
Bircza [PL] 52 E4
Birgi [TR] 152 E4
Birgittelyst [DK] 160 D5
Biri [N] 172 B3
Birini [EST] 198 E2
Birini [LV] 198 E4
Biristrand [N] 172 B3
Birkala / Pirkkala [FIN] 176 F1
Birkeland [N] 164 C5
Birkeland [N] 164 E5
Birkenfeld [D] 44 G3
Birkenfeld [D] 46 E4
Birkenhead [GB] 10 D4
Birkenwerder [D] 34 E2
Birkerød [DK] 156 G2
Birkfeld [A] 74 E1
Birksdal [N] 180 D6
Birmingham [GB] 10 E6
Birnau [D] 58 H4
Biron, Château de- [F] 66 F4
Birr [IRL] 2 D6
Birstein [D] 46 D2
Birštonas [LT] 24 F1
Biržai [LT] 198 E6
Birżebbuga [M] 126 C6
Birži [LV] 198 F6
Birzuli [LV] 198 F4
Bisaccia [I] 120 G3
Bisacquino [I] 126 C3
Biscarrosse [F] 66 B4
Biscarrosse-Plage [F] 66 B4
Bisceglie [I] 122 D2
Bischoffen [D] 46 C1
Bischofsgrün [D] 46 H3
Bischofsheim [D] 46 E2
Bischofshofen [A] 72 G1
Bischofswerda [D] 34 F6
Biscoitos [P] 100 D3
Biserci [BG] 148 D1
Bishop Auckland [GB] 10 F2
Bishop's Castle [GB] 10 C6
Bishop's Cleeve [GB] 12 G2
Bishop's Stortford [GB] 14 F3
Bisignano [I] 124 D4
Bisko [HR] 144 A2
Biskupice Oławskie [PL] 50 D1
Biskupice Radłowskie [PL] 52 C3
Biskupiec [PL] 22 F5
Biskupiec [PL] 22 H4
Biskupin [PL] 36 D1
Bisław [PL] 22 D5
Bislev [DK] 160 D4
Bismark [D] 34 B1
Bismo [N] 180 F5
Bispgården [S] 184 D3
Bispingen [D] 18 F5
Bistrec [BG] 148 E5
Bistreț [RO] 146 F2
Bistrica [MNE] 144 E3
Bistrica [SRB] 146 A3
Bistrica ob S. [SLO] 74 D5
Bistrița [RO] 204 C4
Bistritsa [BG] 146 F5
Bisztynek [PL] 22 H3
Bitburg [D] 44 F2
Bitche [F] 44 G4
Bitetto [I] 122 D3
Bithia [I] 118 C8
Bitola [MK] 128 E3
Bitonto [I] 122 D2
Bitov [CZ] 62 E2
Bitterfeld [D] 34 C4
Bitterstad [N] 192 D4
Bitti [I] 118 D4
Bıvıkali [TR] 150 C3
Bivio [CH] 70 H2
Bivio Manganaro [I] 126 D2
Bivona [I] 126 D3
Bıyıklı [TR] 152 D5
Bizovac [HR] 76 B6
Bjåen [N] 164 D1
Bjala Cherkva [BG] 148 C3
Bjalizvor [BG] 148 C5
Bjår [N] 164 F1
Bjarisino [BY] 202 C5
Bjärklunda [S] 166 E6
Bjärnå / Perniö [FIN] 176 F5
Bjärnum [S] 158 D1
Bjärred [S] 156 H2
Bjärtrå [S] 184 F3
Bjästa [S] 184 G2
Bjelland [N] 164 D5
Bjelovar [HR] 74 G5
Bjerga [N] 164 C1
Bjergby [DK] 160 C5
Bjerkreim [N] 164 B4
Bjerkvik [N] 192 E4
Bjerre [DK] 156 D2
Bjerregård [DK] 156 A1
Bjerringbro [DK] 160 D5
Bjoenstrand [N] 164 B1
Bjølstad [N] 180 G6
Bjoneroa [N] 170 H4
Bjonevika [N] 170 H4
Bjørånes [N] 172 C1
Björbo [S] 172 G5
Bjordal [N] 164 C4
Bjordal [N] 170 B2
Bjørgo [N] 170 G3
Björka [S] 172 G3
Bjørkåsen [N] 192 F3
Björkberg [S] 172 H1
Björkberg [S] 190 G4
Bjørke [N] 180 D4
Bjørkedal [N] 180 C4
Björkefors [S] 162 F1
Bjørkelangen [N] 166 C1
Bjørkflåta [N] 170 F4
Björkfors [S] 190 E3
Björkhöjden [S] 184 D2
Björkliden [S] 192 F4
Björklinge [S] 168 D1
Bjørknes [N] 172 C6
Björkö [FIN] 176 C5
Björkö [S] 162 E3
Björkö [S] 168 F1
Björköby [FIN] 186 A2
Björksele [S] 190 G4
Björksjön [S] 184 F2
Björkvattnet [S] 190 D5
Björkvik [S] 168 B4
Bjørlia [N] 190 C4
Björna [S] 184 G1
Björneborg [S] 166 G3
Björneborg / Pori [FIN] 176 D1
Bjørnestad [N] 164 C4
Bjørnevasshytta [N] 164 D2
Bjørnevatn [N] 194 E3
Björnhult [S] 162 G3
Björnlunda [S] 168 C4
Björnrike [S] 182 F4
Björnsholm [S] 162 G1
Björnsjö [S] 184 G1
Bjørnstad [N] 190 D4
Björsäter [S] 166 F5
Björsäter [S] 168 B6
Bjørsvik [N] 170 B3
Bjuråker [S] 184 D6
Bjurberget [S] 172 E4
Bjurfors [S] 196 A5
Bjurholm [S] 156 H1
Bjurholm [S] 190 H6
Bjuröklubb [S] 196 B5
Bjurön [S] 174 G5
Bjursås [S] 172 H4
Bjursele [S] 190 H4
Bjurträsk [S] 190 H4
Bjuv [S] 156 H1
Blace [SRB] 146 C3
Blachownia [PL] 50 F2
Blackburn [GB] 10 E3
Blacklion [IRL] 2 E3
Blackpool [GB] 10 D3
Blackstad [S] 162 G2
Blackwater [IRL] 4 F5
Bladåker [S] 168 E1
Blaenau Ffestiniog [GB] 10 B4
Blagaj [BIH] 144 C2
Blagaj Japra [BIH] 142 A2
Blagoevgrad [BG] 146 F6
Blagoevo [BG] 148 D2
Blagoveštenje, Manastir- [SRB] 146 B2
Blagovica [SLO] 74 C4
Blåhøj [DK] 156 B1
Blaiken [S] 190 F4
Blaikliden [S] 190 F4
Blain [F] 40 F5
Blair Atholl [GB] 8 E1
Blairgowrie [GB] 8 E2
Blaisy-Bas [F] 56 G3
Blaj [RO] 204 C4
Blajan [F] 84 G4
Błąkały [PL] 24 D2
Blåmont [F] 44 F6
Blanca [E] 104 C2
Blandford Forum [GB] 12 G4
Blanes [E] 92 F4
Blangy-sur-Bresle [F] 28 D4
Blanických Rytířů, Jeskyně- [CZ] 50 C5
Blankaholm [S] 162 G2
Blankenberge [B] 28 G1
Blankenburg [D] 32 H4
Blankenfelde [D] 34 E2
Blankenhain [D] 46 H1
Blankenheim [D] 30 G6
Blanquefort [F] 66 C3
Blansko [CZ] 50 C6
Blanzac [F] 66 E2
Blarney [IRL] 4 C5
Blarney Castle [IRL] 4 C5
Blascosancho [E] 88 E4
Błaszki [PL] 36 F5
Blatná [CZ] 48 E5
Blatnica [BIH] 142 C3
Blatnica [SK] 64 C2
Blatnice pod Sv. Antonínkem [CZ] 62 H2
Blato [HR] 144 A3
Blato [HR] 144 A2
Blattniksele [S] 190 G3
Blaubeuren [D] 60 B3
Blaufelden [D] 46 E5
Blaustein [D] 60 B3
Blåvand [DK] 156 A2
Blåvik [S] 162 E1
Blaye [F] 66 C2
Błażowa [PL] 52 E4
Blazquez [E] 96 B5
Bleckåsen [S] 182 F1
Bleckede [D] 18 G5
Blecksnäs [FIN] 186 A3
Bled [SLO] 74 B4
Bleiburg [A] 74 C3
Bleicherode [D] 32 G5
Bleik [N] 192 E3
Bleisfjord [N] 192 F4
Blendija [SRB] 146 D3
Bléneau [F] 56 D2
Blentarp [S] 158 C3
Blera [I] 114 H4
Blérancourt [F] 28 F6
Bléré [F] 54 G2
Blériot-Plage [F] 14 G6
Bleskestad [N] 164 C1
Blesle [F] 68 C3
Blessington [IRL] 2 F6
Bletterans [F] 56 H5
Blévy [F] 26 H5
Blexen [D] 18 D4
Bliesbruck-Reinheim, Parc Archéol. de- [F] 44 G4
Blieskastel [D] 44 G4
Bligny-sur-Ouche [F] 56 G4
Blikstorp [S] 166 F6
Blinisht [AL] 128 B1
Blinja [HR] 142 A1
Blintrop [D] 32 C5
Bliznaci [BG] 148 E2
Bliznak [BG] 148 F5
Bliznak [BG] 148 F3
Blizne [PL] 52 E4
Błogoszów [PL] 52 A2
Blois [F] 54 H1
Blokhus [DK] 160 D3
Blokzijl [NL] 16 F3
Blombacka [S] 166 F2
Blomberg [D] 32 E3
Blomsholms-Skeppet [S] 166 C4
Blomstermåla [S] 162 G4
Blönduós [IS] 192 B2
Błonie [PL] 36 C6
Błonie [PL] 38 B3
Błonie [PL] 38 F3
Bloška Polica [SLO] 74 B6
Blötberget [S] 172 H5
Błotnica [PL] 20 G3
Błotnica [PL] 38 B6
Błotno [PL] 20 F4
Blovice [CZ] 48 E5
Bludenz [A] 72 A1
Bludov [CZ] 50 C4
Blumberg [D] 58 F3
Blyth [GB] 8 G5
Bø [N] 164 F2
Bø [N] 164 G2
Bø [N] 170 B3
Bø [N] 170 B1
Bø [N] 192 D4
Bø [N] 192 E2
Bo [S] 166 H4
Boadilla del Monte [E] 88 F5
Boal [E] 78 F2
Boalt [S] 162 D6
Boário Terme [I] 72 B5
Bóbbio [I] 110 C2
Bobbio Pellice [I] 70 C6
Boberg [S] 184 C2
Bobice [PL] 52 E4
Bobin [PL] 52 B3
Bobingen [D] 60 D4
Bobitz [D] 20 A4
Böblingen [D] 58 G1
Bobolice [PL] 22 B3
Boboshevo [BG] 146 F6
Bobovdol [BG] 146 F5
Bobr [BY] 202 C5
Bobrová [CZ] 50 B5
Bobrovytsia [UA] 202 D7
Bobrowice [PL] 34 H4
Bobrowniki [PL] 24 F5
Bobrowniki [PL] 36 F1
Bobrynets' [UA] 204 G2
Bočac [BIH] 142 B3
Boca de Huergano [E] 82 C3
Bocairent [E] 104 E1
Boceguillas [E] 88 G3
Böçen [TR] 150 F5
Bochnia [PL] 52 B4
Bocholt [B] 30 E3
Bocholt [D] 16 G6
Bochov [CZ] 48 D3
Bochum [D] 30 H3
Bocigas [E] 88 E3
Bockara [S] 162 G3
Bockel [D] 18 E5
Bockenem [D] 32 G3
Boćki [PL] 38 E1
Böcksholm [S] 162 E4
Böckstein [A] 72 G2
Bockum Hövel [D] 32 C3
Bocognano [F] 114 B4
Boconád [H] 64 E6
Bócsa [H] 76 D3
Bocsig [RO] 76 H4
Böda [S] 162 H3
Boda [S] 166 E2
Boda [S] 172 H3
Boda [S] 184 E3
Bodaczów [PL] 52 F1
Bodafors [S] 162 D3
Boda glasbruk [S] 162 F5
Bodarsjön [S] 182 G6
Bodegraven [NL] 16 D5
Boden [S] 196 B3
Bodenmais [D] 48 D6
Bodenteich [D] 18 G6
Bodenwerder [D] 32 F3
Bodenwöhr [D] 48 C6
Bodjani [SRB] 142 E1
Bodman [D] 58 G4
Bodmin [GB] 12 C4
Bodø [N] 192 D6
Bodom [N] 190 C5
Bodrogkeresztúr [H] 64 G4
Bodrum [TR] 154 B2
Bodsjö [S] 182 H3
Bodsjöedet [S] 182 E1
Bodzanów [PL] 36 H2
Bodzanowice [PL] 50 F1
Bodzentyn [PL] 52 C1
Boëge [F] 70 B2
Boën [F] 68 E2
Bogács [H] 64 F5
Bøgard [N] 192 D3
Bogarra [E] 98 A6
Bogatić [SRB] 142 F2
Bogatovo [RUS] 22 G2
Bogatynia [PL] 48 G1
Boğaz (Bogázi) [CY] 154 G5
Boğazcık [TR] 154 G2
Bogázi (Boğaz) [CY] 154 G5
Boğaziçi [TR] 152 D5
Boğazköy [TR] 150 F4
Bogda [RO] 76 H5
Bogdana [RO] 148 B2
Bogdanci [MK] 128 G3
Bogdaniec [PL] 34 H2
Bogë [AL] 146 A6
Boge [S] 168 G4
Bogen [D] 60 G2
Bogen [N] 192 D5
Bogen [N] 192 E4
Bogen [S] 172 D6
Bogense [DK] 156 D2
Bogetići [MNE] 144 E4
Bogge [N] 180 F3
Böglosa [S] 168 C2
Bognanco [I] 70 E3
Bognes [N] 192 E4
Bognor Regis [GB] 14 D5
Bogojevo [SRB] 142 E1
Bogojevo [SRB] 146 D4
Bogoria [PL] 52 C2
Bogorodica [MK] 128 G3
Bogovina [SRB] 146 D2
Bogovinska Pećina [SRB] 146 D2
Bograngen [S] 172 E4
Boguchwałów [PL] 50 E3
Bogumiłowice [PL] 36 G6
Boguszów-Gorce [PL] 50 B2
Bogutovačka Banja [SRB] 146 B3
Bohain-en-Vermandois [F] 28 F5
Bohal [F] 26 B6
Bohdalov [CZ] 50 A5
Boheeshil [IRL] 4 B4
Bohinjska Bela [SLO] 74 B4
Bohinjska Bistrica [SLO] 74 A4
Böhmenkirch [D] 60 B2
Bohmte [D] 32 D2
Bohonal [E] 96 D2
Bohonal de Ibor [E] 88 B6
Böhönye [H] 74 H4
Bohula [MK] 128 F3
Boialvo [P] 80 B6
Boichinovtsi [BG] 146 F3
Bois-du-Four [F] 68 B6
Boitzenburg [D] 20 D5
Bòixols [E] 92 C2
Boizenburg [D] 18 G5
Böja [S] 166 F5
Bojano [I] 120 E1
Bojanów [PL] 52 D2
Bojanowo [PL] 36 C4
Bøjden [DK] 156 D4
Bojkovice [CZ] 62 H2
Bojnica [BG] 146 E2
Bojnice [SK] 64 B3
Bojnik [SRB] 146 D4
Bojtiken [S] 190 E3
Bokel [D] 18 F3
Bökemåla [S] 162 E6
Bokenäs [S] 166 C6
Bokinić [HR] 112 E3
Boklund [D] 18 F1
Bokod [H] 64 B6
Bokod [H] 64 B6
Bököny [H] 64 H5
Bokros [H] 76 E3
Boksitogorsk [RUS] 202 D1
Boksjök [N] 194 D2
Bol [HR] 144 A2
Bolaños de Calatrava [E] 96 F4
Bolayır [TR] 150 B4
Bolbec [F] 26 H3
Bolca [I] 72 C6
Bölcek [TR] 152 C2
Boldekow [D] 20 D4
Boldogasszonyfa [H] 76 A4
Boldva [H] 64 F4
Bøle [N] 190 B5
Böle [S] 182 G1
Bolekhiv [UA] 52 H6
Bolemin [PL] 34 H2
Bolesławiec [PL] 36 A6
Bolesławiec [PL] 36 E6
Bolesławów [PL] 50 C3
Boleszkowice [PL] 34 G2
Bolfiar [P] 80 B5
Bolfoss [N] 166 C1
Bolgatovo [RUS] 198 H5
Bolgheri [I] 114 E1
Bolhrad [UA] 204 E4
Boliden [S] 196 A4
Bolimów [PL] 38 A3
Bolinglanna / Buaile an Ghleanna [IRL] 2 B3
Boljanići [MNE] 144 E2
Boljevac [SRB] 146 D2
Boljevac [SRB] 204 B6
Boljun [HR] 112 E1
Bolkesjø [N] 164 G1
Bolkhov [RUS] 202 F4
Bolków [PL] 50 B1
Bollebygd [S] 162 B2
Bollène [F] 106 G2
Böllerkirche [D] 46 B3
Bollerup [S] 158 D3
Bollnäs [S] 174 D2
Bollstabruk [S] 184 F3
Bollullos de la Mitación [E] 94 G6
Bollullos Par del Condado [E] 94 F6
Bologna [I] 110 F3
Bologne [F] 44 C6
Bolótana [I] 118 C4
Bolsena [I] 114 H3
Bol'shakovo [RUS] 200 D5
Bol'shaya Izhora [RUS] 178 G5
Bol'shaya Yashchera [RUS] 198 H1
Bol'shie Sabicy [RUS] 198 H2
Bol'shiye Kolpany [RUS] 178 H6
Bol'shoye Zagor'e [RUS] 198 H3
Bol'shoy Sabsk [RUS] 198 G1
Bolstad [S] 166 D5
Bolstadøyri [N] 170 C3
Bolstaholm [FIN] 176 A5
Bolsward [NL] 16 E2
Bolszewo [PL] 22 D2
Boltaña [E] 84 E5
Boltenhagen [D] 18 H3
Boltigen [CH] 70 D1
Bolton [GB] 10 E4
Bolungarvík [IS] 192 A1
Bóly [H] 76 B5
Bolyarovo [BG] 148 E5
Bolyartsi [BG] 148 B6
Bolzano / Bozen [I] 72 D3
Bomarken [S] 166 C3
Bomarsund [FIN] 176 B5
Bomarzo [I] 114 H4
Bombarral [P] 86 B4
Bominago [I] 116 C4
Bom Jesus do Monte [P] 80 C3
Bomsund [S] 184 C2
Bonaduz [CH] 70 H1
Bonaguil, Château de- [F] 66 F5
Bonanza [E] 100 F3
Boñar [E] 82 C3
Bonar Bridge [GB] 6 E4
Bonares [E] 94 F6
Bonäs [S] 166 E2
Bonäs [S] 172 G3
Bonäset [S] 182 F1
Bonåsjøen [N] 192 D5
Bonassola [I] 110 C4
Bonaval [E] 88 G4
Bończa [PL] 38 B4
Bondal [N] 164 F1
Bondemon [S] 166 C4
Bondeno [I] 110 F2
Bondstorp [S] 162 C2
Bonefro [I] 116 F6
Bonete [E] 98 C6
Bonhamn [S] 184 G3
Bonhomme, Col du- [F] 58 D2
Bonifacio [F] 114 B6
Bonifati Marina [I] 124 C4
Bonilla [E] 98 B1
Bönitz [D] 34 E5
Bonlieu [F] 70 A1
Bonn [D] 30 G5
Bonnat [F] 54 H5
Bonndorf [D] 58 F4
Bønnerup Strand [DK] 160 F5
Bonnesvalyn [F] 42 H3
Bonnétable [F] 42 C5
Bonneuil-Matours [F] 54 F4
Bonneval [F] 42 D5
Bonneval-sur-Arc [F] 70 C4
Bonneville [F] 70 B2
Bonnières [F] 42 E3
Bonnieux [F] 106 H4
Bonnigheim [D] 46 D6
Bonny-sur-Loire [F] 56 D2
Bono [I] 118 D4
Bonorva [I] 118 C4
Bonport, Abbaye de- [F] 28 B6
Bonyhád [H] 76 B4
Boom [B] 30 C3
Boos [D] 30 G6
Boos [D] 60 B4
Boos [F] 28 C5
Booth of Toft [GB] 6 H3
Bootle [GB] 10 D4
Bopfingen [D] 60 C2
Boppard [D] 44 H1
Bor [CZ] 48 D4
Bor [RUS] 198 H2
Bor [S] 162 D4
Bor [SRB] 146 D2
Bor [SRB] 204 C6
Borås [N] 164 F4
Borås [S] 162 B2
Borba [P] 86 E6
Borbona [I] 116 B4
Borchen [D] 32 E4
Borci [BIH] 144 C2
Borculo [NL] 16 G5
Bordány [H] 76 E4
Bordeaux [F] 66 C3
Bordeira [P] 94 A4
Bordères [F] 84 F4
Bordesholm [D] 18 F2
Bordighera [I] 108 F4
Bording [DK] 160 C6
Bore [I] 110 C2
Boreci [SLO] 74 E3
Borek Wielkopolski [PL] 36 D4
Borello [I] 110 G5
Borensberg [S] 166 H5
Borg [N] 192 C4
Borgå / Porvoo [FIN] 178 B4
Borgafjäll [S] 190 E4
Borgarnes [IS] 192 A2
Borgeby [S] 156 H2
Borgen [N] 164 E3
Borgentreich [D] 32 E4
Börger [D] 18 B5
Borger [NL] 16 G3
Börgermoor [D] 18 B5
Borggård [S] 166 H5
Borghamn [S] 166 G6
Borghetto di Borbera [I] 110 B2
Borgholm [S] 162 G4
Borgholzhausen [D] 32 D2
Borghorst [D] 16 H5
Børglumkloster [DK] 160 D3
Borgo Callea [I] 126 D3
Borgoforte [I] 110 E2
Borgomanero [I] 70 F4
Borgond [H] 76 B2
Borgonovo Val Tidone [I] 70 G6
Borgorose [I] 116 B5
Borgo San Dalmazzo [I] 108 F3
Borgo San Lorenzo [I] 110 F5
Borgosésia [I] 70 E4
Borgo Ticino [I] 70 F4
Borgo Tossignano [I] 110 F4
Borgo Val di Taro [I] 110 C3
Borgo Valsugana [I] 72 D4
Borgo Vercelli [I] 70 F5
Borgsjö [S] 184 D4
Borgsjö [S] 190 G5
Borgstena [S] 162 B1
Borgund [N] 170 E2
Borgund [N] 180 B4
Borgvattnet [S] 184 C1
Borgvik [S] 166 E3
Borielsbyn [S] 196 B2
Borima [BG] 148 B4
Borino [BG] 130 D1
Borislavtsi [BG] 130 G1
Borisoglebskiy [RUS] 194 F3
Borisovo [RUS] 178 G3
Borja [E] 90 D3
Borken [D] 16 G6
Borken [D] 32 E6
Borkenes [N] 192 E3
Borki [RUS] 198 G3
Børkop [DK] 156 C2
Borków [PL] 52 B1
Borkum [D] 16 G1
Borlänge [S] 172 H4
Borlaug [N] 170 E2
Børlia [N] 182 B3
Borlu [TR] 152 E3
Bormes-les-Mimosas [F] 108 D6
Bórmio [I] 72 B3
Borna [D] 34 C6
Borneiro, Castro de- [E] 78 B2
Borne Sulinowo [PL] 22 B5
Bornhöved [D] 18 G3
Börnicke [D] 34 D1
Bornlitz [D] 18 F6
Bornos [E] 100 G3
Bornova [TR] 152 C4
Borodianka [UA] 202 D7
Borodinskoye [RUS] 178 F2
Boronów [PL] 50 F2
Borová Lada [CZ] 62 A2
Borovan [BG] 146 G3
Borovany [CZ] 62 C2
Borovets [BG] 146 G5
Borovica [BG] 146 E3
Borovichi [RUS] 198 H3
Borovik [RUS] 198 G3
Borovo [BG] 148 C2

Bundoran [IRL] 2 D3
Bungay [GB] 14 G2
Bunge [S] 168 G3
Bunić [HR] 112 G3
Bunkris [S] 172 F2
Bunleix [F] 68 B2
Bunmahon [IRL] 4 E5
Bun na Abhna / Bunnahowen [IRL] 2 B3
Bunnahowen / Bun na Abhna [IRL] 2 B3
Bunnyconnellan [IRL] 2 C3
Buñol [E] 98 E4
Bunratty [IRL] 2 C6
Bunratty Castle [IRL] 2 C6
Buonalbergo [I] 120 F2
Buonconvento [I] 114 G2
Buonfornello [I] 126 D2
Buonvicino [I] 124 C3
Buoux, Fort de– [F] 108 B3
Bur [DK] 160 B5
Burano [I] 72 F6
Burbach [D] 32 C6
Burcei [I] 118 D7
Bureå [S] 190 G3
Bureå [S] 196 A4
Burela [E] 78 E2
Büren [CH] 58 D5
Büren [D] 32 D4
Burfjord [N] 192 H1
Burford [GB] 12 H3
Burg [D] 18 E3
Burg [D] 18 H2
Burg [D] 34 C3
Burg [D] 34 F4
Burgas [BG] 148 F4
Burgau [A] 74 E2
Burgau [D] 60 C3
Burgau [P] 94 B5
Burgbernheim [D] 46 F5
Burgdorf [CH] 58 E5
Burgdorf [D] 32 G2
Burgebrach [D] 46 F4
Bürgel [D] 34 B6
Bürgeln [D] 58 E4
Burgelu / Elburgo [E] 102 B4
Burghaun [D] 46 E1
Burghausen [D] 60 G4
Burg Hessenstein [D] 32 E5
Burgh–Haamstede [NL] 16 B5
Búrgio [I] 126 C3
Burgistein [CH] 58 D6
Burgjoss [D] 46 E3
Burg Klam [A] 62 C4
Burgkunstadt [D] 46 G3
Burglengenfeld [D] 48 B6
Burg Metternich [D] 44 G1
Burgoberbach [D] 46 F5
Burgos [E] 82 E6
Burgsinn [D] 46 E3
Burg Stargard [D] 20 D5
Burgsvik [S] 168 G6
Burguete / Auritz [E] 84 C3
Burguillos [E] 94 G5
Burguillos del Cerro [E] 94 G3
Burhan [TR] 150 F5
Burhaniye [TR] 152 C2
Burharkent [TR] 152 F5
Burie [F] 54 D6
Burila Mare [RO] 146 E1
Burjassot [E] 98 E4
Burlada [E] 84 B4
Burladingen [D] 58 G2
Burlo [D] 16 G6
Burnham–on–Crouch [GB] 14 F4
Burnham–on–Sea [GB] 12 F3
Burnley [GB] 10 E3
Burón [E] 82 C3
Buron, Château de– [F] 68 D3
Buronzo [I] 70 E4
Burravoe [GB] 6 H3
Burrel [AL] 128 B2
Burriana / Borriana [E] 98 F3
Burs [S] 168 G4
Burs [S] 168 G5
Bursa [TR] 150 F4
Burseryd [S] 162 B3
Bürstadt [D] 46 C4
Burtenbach [D] 60 C3
Burton upon Trent [GB] 10 E6
Burträsk [S] 196 A5
Burvik [S] 196 B5
Burwell [GB] 14 F2
Bury [GB] 10 E4
Buryn' [UA] 202 E6
Bury St Edmunds [GB] 14 F3
Burzenin [PL] 36 F5
Burziya [BG] 146 F3
Busalla [I] 110 B3
Busana [I] 110 D4
Busca [I] 108 F2
Busdorf [D] 18 F1
Buseto Palizzolo [I] 126 B2
Buševec [HR] 74 E6
Bushat [AL] 128 A1
Bushmills [NIR] 2 G2
Bushtricë [AL] 128 C1
Bus'k [UA] 202 B8
Busko–Zdrój [PL] 52 B2
Bušno [PL] 38 G6
Busot [E] 104 E2
Busovača [BIH] 142 D4
Bussang [F] 58 D3
Bussang, Col de– [F] 58 D3
Busseto [I] 110 D2
Bussolengo [I] 72 C6
Bussoleno [I] 70 C5
Bussum [NL] 16 E4
Bustnes [N] 190 E2
Busto Arsizio [I] 70 F4
Busto Garolfo [I] 70 F4
Büsum [D] 18 E2
Butan [BG] 146 G2
Butenky [UA] 202 F7
Butera [I] 126 E4
Bütgenbach [B] 30 F5
Buthrotum [AL] 132 B2
Butler's Bridge [IRL] 2 E4
Butrint [AL] 132 B2
Butryny [PL] 22 H4
Butsyn [UA] 38 H5
Buttapietra [I] 110 F1
Buttelstedt [D] 34 A6
Buttevant [IRL] 4 C4
Buttingsrud [N] 170 H4
Buttlar [D] 46 E1
Buttle [S] 168 G5
Buttstädt [D] 34 B6
Butzbach [D] 46 C2
Bützow [D] 20 B3
Buvarp [N] 190 C5
Buvika [N] 182 B1
Buxtehude [D] 18 F4
Buxton [GB] 10 E5
Buxu, Cueva del– [E] 82 C2
Buxy [F] 56 F5
Büyükada [TR] 150 F3
Büyükaturak [TR] 152 H2
Büyükbelen [TR] 152 D3
Büyükçekmece [TR] 150 E3
Büyükkaraağaç [TR] 154 E2
Büyükkarıştıran [TR] 150 C2
Büyükkonak [TR] 152 G6
Büyükkonuk (Komi Kebir) [CY] 154 G4
Büyükorhan [TR] 150 F5
Büyüksöğle [TR] 154 H2
Büyükyenice [TR] 152 C2
Büyükyoncalı [TR] 150 D2
Buz [AL] 128 B5
Buzançais [F] 54 G3
Buzancy [F] 44 D3
Buzău [RO] 204 E5
Buzescu [RO] 148 B1
Buzet [HR] 112 D1
Buziaş [RO] 76 H6
Buzyakovtsi [BG] 146 G5
By [S] 166 E1
By [S] 174 D5
Byahoml' [BY] 202 B4
Byala [BG] 148 C2
Byala [BG] 148 F3
Byala Slatina [BG] 146 G3
Byal Izvor [BG] 130 E1
Byalynichy [BY] 202 C5
Byaroza [BY] 202 B6
Byarozawka [BY] 202 A5
Byarum [S] 162 D2
Byberget [S] 182 H4
Bybjerg [DK] 156 F2
Bychawa [PL] 38 E6
Byczki [PL] 36 H4
Byczyna [PL] 36 E6
Bydgoszcz [PL] 22 D6
Bye [S] 184 B2
Bye [S] 184 F4
Byenyakoni [BY] 200 G6
Byershty [BY] 24 G3
Bygdeå [S] 196 A5
Bygdeträsk [S] 196 A5
Bygdin [N] 170 F2
Bygdsiljum [S] 196 A5
Bygland [N] 164 D4
Byglandsfjord [N] 164 D4
Bygstad [N] 170 B1
Bykle [N] 164 D2
Byllis [AL] 128 B5
Byrkjedal [N] 164 B3
Byrkjelo [N] 180 D5
Byrknes [N] 170 A2
Byrness [GB] 8 F5
Byrum [DK] 160 F3
Byrum [S] 162 H3
Byšice [CZ] 48 G3
Byske [S] 196 A4
Bystré [CZ] 50 B5
Bystrianska Jaskyňa [SK] 64 D2
Bystřice [CZ] 48 G4
Bystřice nad Pernštejnem [CZ] 50 B5
Bystřice pod Hostýnem [CZ] 50 D6
Bystřička [CZ] 50 E5
Bystrzyca Kłodzka [PL] 50 C3
Byszki [PL] 22 B5
Byszyno [PL] 20 H4
Bytča [SK] 50 F6
Bytnica [PL] 34 H3
Bytom [PL] 50 F3
Bytom Odrzański [PL] 36 A4
Bytonia [PL] 22 D4
Bytów [PL] 22 C3
Byvattnet [S] 184 F1
Byxelkrok [S] 162 H3
Bzenec [CZ] 62 G2
Bzovík [SK] 64 C4

C

Caaveiro, Monasterio de– [E] 78 D2
Cabação [P] 86 D5
Cabaço [E] 86 D3
Cabaj–Čápor [SK] 64 A4
Cabañaquinta [E] 78 H4
Cabañas [E] 78 D2
Cabanes [E] 98 G3
Čabar [HR] 74 C6
Cabeço de Vide [P] 86 E5
Cabertarar [TR] 152 F4
Cabeza del Buey [E] 96 C4
Cabezamesada [E] 96 G2
Cabezarados [E] 96 E4
Cabezarrubias del Puerto [E] 96 E5
Cabezas Rubias [E] 94 E4
Cabezo de Torres [E] 104 C3
Cabezón de la Sal [E] 82 E3
Cabezuela del Valle [E] 88 B5
Cabo de Gata [E] 102 G6
Cabo de Palos [E] 104 D4
Cabourg [F] 26 F3
Cabra [E] 102 C2
Cabra del Santo Cristo [E] 102 F2
Cabranes [E] 82 C2
Cábras [I] 118 B5
Cabreiros [E] 78 D2
Cabrela [P] 86 C6
Cabrera [E] 104 E6
Cabrerets [F] 66 G5
Cabrillas [E] 88 B3
Cacabelos [E] 78 F5
Čačak [SRB] 146 B2
Čačak [SRB] 204 B6
Càccamo [I] 126 D2
Cacemes [P] 86 A5
Cáceres [E] 86 H5
Cachopo [P] 94 D5
Čachtice [SK] 62 H3
Čačini [HR] 76 A6
Cadaqués [E] 92 G2
Cadaval [P] 86 B4
Cadavedo [E] 78 G2
Čađavica [BIH] 142 B3
Čađavica [HR] 76 A6
Čadca [SK] 50 F5
Cadelbosco di Sopra [I] 110 E2
Cadenàbbia [I] 70 G3
Cadenberge [D] 18 E3
Cadenet [F] 106 H4
Cadeuil [F] 54 C6
Cadí, Túnel del– [E] 92 E2
Cádiar [E] 102 E5
Cadillac [F] 66 D4
Cadipietra [I] 72 E2
Cádiz [E] 100 F4
Cadrete [E] 90 E4
Caen [F] 26 F3
Caernarfon [GB] 10 B4
Caerphilly [GB] 12 F3
Čafasan [MK] 128 C3
Çağış [TR] 152 D1
Cagli [I] 112 B6
Cágliari [I] 118 C7
Çağman [TR] 154 H3
Cagnano Varano [I] 116 G6
Cagnes–sur–Mer [F] 108 E4
Caherdaniel / Cathair Dónall [IRL] 4 A4
Cahermurphy [IRL] 2 B6
Cahersiveen [IRL] 4 A4
Cahir [IRL] 4 D4
Cahors [F] 66 G5
Cahul [MD] 204 E4
Caiazzo [I] 120 E2
Cairnryan [GB] 8 C5
Cairo Montenotte [I] 108 G3
Cais do Pico [P] 100 C3
Caister–on–Sea [GB] 14 H2
Caivano [I] 120 E3
Cajarc [F] 66 G5
Ćajetina [SRB] 146 A3
Čajniče [BIH] 144 E2
Čakajovce [SK] 64 A4
Çakallar [TR] 152 C1
Çakılı [TR] 150 C2
Çakır [TR] 150 C5
Çakırbeyli [TR] 152 E5
Çakırlı [TR] 150 C4
Çakmak [TR] 154 E1
Čakovec [HR] 74 F4
Çal [TR] 152 G4
Cal [TR] 152 H2
Cala [E] 94 G4
Cala Blanca [E] 104 G4
Cala Blava [E] 104 E5
Calabor [E] 80 F3
Calabritto [I] 120 F3
Calaceite [E] 90 G6
Calacuccia [F] 114 B3
Cala d'Oliva [I] 118 B2
Cala d'Or [E] 104 F6
Calaf [E] 92 D3
Calafat [E] 92 B5
Calafat [RO] 146 F2
Calafell [E] 92 D5
Cala Galdana [E] 104 G4
Cala Gonone [I] 118 E4
Calahonda–Chaparral [E] 102 B5
Calahonda–Chaparral [E] 102 E5
Calahorra [E] 84 A5
Calais [F] 14 G6
Cala Liberotto [I] 118 E4
Cala Mesquida [E] 104 F5
Cala Millor [E] 104 F5
Calamocha [E] 90 D5
Calamonte [E] 94 H2
Cala Moreia–Cala Morlanda [E] 104 F5
Cala Morell [E] 104 G4
Calañas [E] 94 F5
Calanda [E] 90 F6
Calangiánus [I] 118 D3
Cala'n Porter [E] 104 H5
Cala Pi [E] 104 E5
Călăraşi [MD] 204 E3
Călăraşi [RO] 204 E5
Cala Ratjada [E] 104 F5
cala Sa Calobra [E] 104 E4
Cala Santanyí [E] 104 E6
Calascibetta [I] 126 E3
Calasetta [I] 118 B7
Calasparra [E] 104 B2
Calatafimi [I] 126 B2
Calatañazor [E] 90 B3
Cala Tarida [E] 104 B5
Calatayud [E] 90 D4
Calatorao [E] 90 D4
Calatrava, Convento de– [E] 96 E5
Calatrava la Vieja [E] 96 F4
Calau [D] 34 F4
Cala Vadella [E] 104 B5
Calbe [D] 34 B4
Çalca [TR] 152 H3
Caldarola [I] 116 C2
Caldas da Rainha [P] 86 B3
Caldas de Monchique [E] 94 B4
Caldas de Reis [E] 78 B3
Caldas de Vizela [P] 80 C3
Caldelas [P] 78 B6
Caldes de Boí [E] 84 F6
Caldes de Malavella [E] 92 F3
Caldes de Montbui [E] 92 E4
Caldes d'Estrac [E] 92 F4
Caldirola [I] 110 B2
Calella [E] 92 F4
Calella de Palafrugell [E] 92 G3
Calenzana [F] 114 B3
Calera y Chozas [E] 88 C6
Caleruega [E] 88 H2
Cales de Mallorca [E] 104 F5
Calheta [P] 100 A3
Calheta [P] 100 C3
Calheta de Nesquim [P] 100 C3
Çali [TR] 150 F5
Càlig [E] 92 A6
Calignac [F] 66 E5
Çalıklı [TR] 152 F3
Călimăneşti [RO] 204 C5
Calimera [I] 122 G5
Calitri [I] 120 G3
Calizzano [I] 108 G3
Callac [F] 40 D2
Callan [IRL] 4 E4
Callander [GB] 8 D2
Callington [GB] 12 D4
Callosa d'en Sarrià [E] 104 E2
Callosa de Segura [E] 104 D3
Čalma [SRB] 142 F2
Călmăţuiu [RO] 148 B2
Calne [GB] 12 G3
Calolziocorte [I] 70 G4
Calonge [E] 92 G3
Calpe / Calp [E] 104 F2
Calp / Calpe [E] 104 F2
Çalpınar [TR] 154 H1
Caltabellotta [I] 126 C3
Caltagirone [I] 126 F4
Caltanissetta [I] 126 E3
Caltavuturo [I] 126 E2
Çaltepe [TR] 152 H5
Çalti [TR] 150 H4
Çaltılıbük [TR] 150 E5
Caltra [IRL] 2 D5
Călugăreni [RO] 148 C1
Caluso [I] 70 D5
Calvello [I] 120 H4
Calvi [F] 114 A3
Calvià [E] 104 D5
Calvörde [D] 34 B2
Calw [D] 58 G1
Calzadilla de la Cueza [E] 82 C5
Camacha [P] 100 B3
Camaiore [I] 110 D5
Camaldoli [I] 110 G5
Camaldoli, Eremo di– [I] 110 G5
Çamaltı [TR] 152 C4
Camarena de la Sierra [E] 98 E2
Camarès [F] 106 D3
Camaret–sur–Mer [F] 40 B2
Camarillas [E] 98 E1
Camariñas [E] 78 B2
Camarzana de Tera [E] 80 H3
Camas [E] 94 G6
Cambados [E] 78 B4
Cambeo [E] 78 C5
Camberg [D] 46 C2
Camberley [GB] 14 D4
Cambo–les–Bains [F] 84 C2
Camborne [GB] 12 C5
Cambrai [F] 28 F4
Cambre [E] 78 C2
Cambremer [F] 26 G4
Cambridge [GB] 14 F3
Cambrils [E] 92 C5
Camburg [D] 34 B6
Çamdere [TR] 152 G3
Camelford [GB] 12 C4
Çameli [TR] 154 F1
Camenca [MD] 204 E2
Camerino [I] 116 B2
Çamiçi [TR] 152 D6
Camigliatello [I] 124 D4
Camin [D] 18 H4
Caminha [P] 78 A5
Caminomorisco [E] 88 A4
Caminreal [E] 90 D6
Çamkonak [TR] 150 G2
Çamköy [TR] 154 C1
Çamlıbel (Mýrtou) [CY] 154 F5
Çamlık [TR] 152 F2
Camlıpınar [TR] 154 F4
Cammarata [I] 126 D3
Camogli [I] 110 B3
Camp [IRL] 4 B3
Campagna [I] 120 F4
Campagnático [I] 114 F2
Campan [F] 84 F4
Campana [I] 124 E4
Campanario [E] 96 B3
Campanas / Kanpaneta [E] 84 B4
Campanet, Coves de– [E] 104 E4
Campaspero [E] 88 F2
Campbeltown [GB] 2 H2
Câmpeni [RO] 204 C4
Campi Bisenzio [I] 110 E5
Campiglia Marittima [I] 114 E2
Campiglia Soana [I] 70 D4
Campillo de Altobuey [E] 98 C3
Campillo de Arenas [E] 102 E3
Campillo de Llerena [E] 96 A4
Campillos [E] 102 B3
Câmpina [RO] 204 D5
Campione d'Italia [I] 70 G3
Campisábalos [E] 88 H4
Campi Salentina [I] 122 G4
Campo [E] 84 F6
Campo [P] 94 E2
Campobasso [I] 120 E1
Campobecerros [E] 78 D6
Campobello di Licata [I] 126 E4
Campobello di Mazara [I] 126 B3
Campocologno [CH] 72 B4
Campo Coy [E] 104 B3
Campodarsego [I] 72 E6
Campo de Caso / Caso [E] 82 C2
Campo de Criptana [E] 96 G3
Campofelice di Fitalia [I] 126 D2
Campofilone [I] 116 D2
Campofiorito [I] 126 C3
Campoformido [I] 72 G5
Campogalliano [I] 110 E3
Campohermoso [E] 102 G5
Campo Lameiro / A Lagoa [E] 78 B4
Campo Ligure [I] 108 H2
Campo Maior [P] 86 F6
Campomanes [E] 78 H4
Campomarino [I] 116 F5
Campomarino [I] 122 F5
Camponaraya [E] 78 F5
Campora San Giovanni [I] 124 D5
Campo Real [E] 88 G6
Camporeale [I] 126 C2
Camporrobles [E] 98 D3
Campos [E] 104 E5
Camposampiero [I] 72 E6
Camposanto [I] 110 F2
Campotejar [E] 102 E3
Campo Túres / Sand in Taufers [I] 72 E2
Camprodón [E] 92 F2
Câmpulung [RO] 204 D5
Câmpulung Moldovenesc [RO] 204 D3
Çamsu [TR] 152 G2
Çamyayla [TR] 152 F6
Çamyuva [TR] 152 G2
Çan [TR] 150 C5
Cañada de Benatanduz [E] 98 F1
Cañadajuncosa [E] 98 B3
Cañaíca del Calar [E] 102 H2
Çanak [HR] 112 G3
Çanakçı [TR] 152 F1
Çanakkale [TR] 150 B5
Canale [I] 108 G1
Canales de Molina [E] 90 C5
Canal S. Bovo [I] 72 E4
Canaples [F] 28 E4
Canas de Senhorim [P] 80 C6
Cañaveral [E] 86 H4
Cañaveral de León [E] 94 G4
Cañaveras [E] 98 B1
Canazei [I] 72 E3
Cancale [F] 26 C4
Cancon [F] 66 E4
Candamo [E] 78 G3
Candamo, Cueva de– [E] 78 H3
Candanchú [E] 84 D4
Çandarlı [TR] 150 G3
Çandarlı [TR] 152 C3
Candás [E] 78 H3
Candasnos [E] 90 G4
Candé [F] 40 G6
Candela [I] 120 G2
Candelario [E] 88 B4
Candeleda [E] 88 C5
Candia Lomellina [I] 70 F5
Çandır [TR] 154 E2
Canelli [I] 108 H2
Canelobre, Cueva de– [E] 104 E2
Canero [E] 78 G2
Canet [F] 106 E4
Canet de Mar [E] 92 F4
Cañete [E] 98 C2
Cañete la Real [E] 102 B3
Canet–Plage [F] 92 G1
Canfranc [E] 84 D4
Cangas [E] 78 B4
Cangas [E] 78 E2
Cangas del Narcea [E] 78 F3
Cangas de Onís [E] 82 C2
Canha [P] 86 C5
Caniçada [P] 80 D3
Canicatti [I] 126 D4
Canicattini Bagni [I] 126 G5
Caniço [P] 100 A3
Caniles [E] 102 G4
Canillas del Aceituno [E] 102 C4
Canino [I] 114 G4
Cañizal [E] 88 D2
Cañizares [E] 90 B6
Canjáyar [E] 102 F5
Cannai [I] 118 B7
Cannara [I] 116 A2
Canne [I] 120 H2
Cánnero Riviera [I] 70 F3
Cannes [F] 108 E5
Canneto [I] 114 E1
Canneto sull'Óglio [I] 110 D1
Cannich [GB] 6 D5
Canningione [I] 118 E2
Cannóbio [I] 70 F3
Cannock [GB] 10 E6
Canolo [I] 124 D7
Canosa di Púglia [I] 120 H2
Canossa [I] 110 D3
Canossa, Castello di– [I] 110 D3
Can Pastilla [E] 104 E5
Can Picafort [E] 104 F4
Cansano [I] 116 D5
Cantalapiedra [E] 88 D3
Cantalejo [E] 88 F3
Cantalpino [E] 88 D3
Cantanhede [P] 80 B6
Cantavieja [E] 98 F2
Čantavir [SRB] 76 D5
Canterbury [GB] 14 F5
Cantillana [E] 94 H5
Cantoral de la Peña [E] 82 D4
Cantoria [E] 102 H4
Cantù [I] 70 G4
Canvey Island [GB] 14 F4
Cany–Barville [F] 26 H2
Canyet de Mar [E] 92 G4
Canyon [N] 194 B3
Caoria [I] 72 D4
Cáorle [I] 72 F6
Caorso [I] 70 H6
Capaccio [I] 120 F4
Capaci [I] 126 C1
Capalbio [I] 114 F4
Capannoli [I] 110 E6
Caparde [BIH] 142 E3
Caparra, Ruinas de– [E] 88 B5
Caparroso [E] 84 B5
Capbreton [F] 66 A6
Cap–d'Ail [F] 108 F4
Capdella [E] 84 G6
Capdenac–Gare [F] 66 H5
Cap d'en Font [E] 104 H5
Capdepera [E] 104 F5
Capelas [P] 100 E2
Capellades [E] 92 D4
Capendu [F] 106 C5
Capens [F] 84 H4
Capestang [F] 106 D4
Capestrano [I] 116 C4
Cap Ferret [F] 66 B3
Capinha [P] 86 F2
Capistrello [I] 116 C5
Capizzi [I] 126 F2
Čapljina [BIH] 144 C3
Capmany [E] 92 G2
Capo Cavallo [F] 114 A3
Capodimonte [I] 114 G3
Capo di Ponte [I] 72 B4
Capodiponte [I] 110 D4
Capo d'Orlando [I] 124 B6
Capoferrato [I] 118 E7
Capolíveri [I] 114 E3
Capo Rizzuto [I] 124 F5
Caposile [I] 72 F6
Capoterra [I] 118 C7
Cappamore [IRL] 4 D3
Cappenberg [D] 32 C4
Cappoquin [IRL] 4 D5
Capracotta [I] 116 D6
Caprája [I] 114 D2
Capranica [I] 114 H4
Capri [I] 120 D4
Capriati a Volturno [I] 120 D1
Capriccioli [I] 118 E2
Captieux [F] 66 D5
Capua [I] 120 D2
Capurso [I] 122 E3
Čara [HR] 144 A3
Caracal [RO] 148 A1
Caracenilla [E] 98 B2
Caracovo [BG] 148 B5
Caracuel de Calatrava [E] 96 E4
Caraglio [I] 108 F2
Čarakovo [BIH] 142 B2
Caraman [F] 106 B3
Caramulo [P] 80 C6
Caranga [E] 78 G4
Caransebeş [RO] 204 B5
Carantec [F] 40 C1
Car Asen [BG] 148 D3
Carassai [I] 116 C2
Caraula [RO] 146 F1
Caravaca [E] 104 B2
Caravaggio [I] 70 H5
Carbajales de Alba [E] 80 H4
Carbajo [E] 86 F4
Carballo [E] 78 C2
Carbon–Blanc [F] 66 D3
Carboneras [E] 102 H5
Carboneras de Guadazaón [E] 98 C3
Carbonero el Mayor [E] 88 F3
Carbónia [I] 118 B7
Carbonin / Schluderbach [I] 72 E3
Carbonne [F] 84 H4
Carcaboso [E] 88 A5
Carcabuey [E] 102 C3
Carcaixent [E] 98 E5
Carcans [F] 66 C2
Carcans–Plage [F] 66 B2
Carcar [E] 84 A5
Carcare [I] 108 H3
Carcassonne [F] 106 B4
Carcastillo [E] 84 B5
Carcavelo [P] 86 A5
Carcelén [E] 98 C5
Carceri, Eremo delle– [I] 116 A2
Carcès [F] 108 C5
Carcoforo [I] 70 E3
Çardak [TR] 150 B5
Çardak [TR] 152 G3
Çardak [TR] 152 G5
Çardaklı [TR] 152 F6
Cardedeu [E] 92 E4
Cardejón [E] 90 C3
Cardelleda de Valdeorras [E] 78 E5
Cardeña [E] 96 D6
Cardenete [E] 98 C3
Cardiff [GB] 12 F3
Cardigan [GB] 4 H6
Cardito [I] 120 D1
Cardona [E] 92 D3
Carei [RO] 204 B3
Carene [TR] 152 C3
Carennac [F] 66 H4
Carentan [F] 26 E3
Carevac [BIH] 142 B4
Carev Dvor [MK] 128 D3
Carezza al Lago / Karersee [I] 72 D3
Cargèse [F] 114 A4
Carhaix–Plouguer [F] 40 C2
Caria [P] 86 F2
Cariati [I] 124 E4
Caričin Grad [SRB] 146 D4
Caričino [BG] 148 G2
Carignan [F] 44 D2
Carignano [I] 70 D6
Çarıklar [TR] 154 F4
Cariñena [E] 90 D4
Cariño [E] 78 E1
Carinola [I] 120 D2
Carlantino [I] 120 F1
Carlentini [I] 126 G4
Carlet [E] 98 E5
Carling [F] 44 F4
Carlingford [IRL] 2 G4
Carlisle [GB] 8 E6
Carloforte [I] 118 B7
Carlow [IRL] 4 F4
Carlow / Ceatharlach [IRL] 4 F4
Carlton [GB] 10 F4
Carmagnola [I] 70 D6
Carmarthen [GB] 12 E2
Carmaux [F] 106 C2
Cármenes [E] 78 H4
Carmona [E] 94 H6
Carnac [F] 40 D5
Carndonagh [IRL] 2 F1
Carnew [IRL] 4 F4
Carnia [I] 72 G4
Carnlough [NIR] 2 G3
Carnota [E] 78 B3
Carnoustie [GB] 8 F2
Caro [F] 26 B6
Carolei [I] 124 D4
Carolinensiel [D] 18 C3
Carona [I] 70 H3
Caronia [I] 126 F2
Carosino [I] 122 F4
Carpaneto Piacentino [I] 110 C2
Carpegna [I] 110 H5
Carpenédolo [I] 72 B6
Carpentras [F] 106 H3
Carpi [I] 110 E2
Carpignano Sesia [I] 70 E4
Carpineti [I] 110 E3
Carpineto Romano [I] 116 B6
Cărpiniş [RO] 76 F5
Carpino [I] 116 G6
Carpinone [I] 120 E1
Carpio [E] 88 D2
Carquefou [F] 40 F6
Carqueiranne [F] 108 C6
Carraig Airt / Carrickart [IRL] 2 F1
Carral [E] 78 C2
Carranza / Karrantza [E] 82 F3
Carrapateira [P] 94 A4
Carrara [I] 110 D4
Carraroe / An Cheathrú Rua [IRL] 2 B5
Carrascalejo [E] 96 C1
Carrascosa del Campo [E] 98 A2
Carrazeda de Ansiães [P] 80 E4
Carrazedo [P] 80 E3
Carrbridge [GB] 6 E5
Carregado [P] 86 B4
Carregal do Sal [P] 80 C6
Carrega Ligure [I] 110 B3
Carregueiro [P] 94 C3
Carrick / An Charraig [IRL] 2 D2
Carrickart / Carraig Airt [IRL] 2 F1
Carrickfergus [NIR] 2 G3
Carrickmacross [IRL] 2 F4
Carrick–on–Shannon [IRL] 2 D4
Carrick–on–Suir [IRL] 4 E4
Carriço [P] 86 C2
Carrigaline [IRL] 4 C5
Carrigallen [IRL] 2 E4
Carriganimmy [IRL] 4 C4
Carrigans [IRL] 2 F2
Carrión de Calatrava [E] 96 F4
Carrión de los Condes [E] 82 C5
Carrizo [E] 78 G5
Carrizosas [E] 96 G5
Carros [F] 106 G5
Carros [F] 108 E4
Carrouges [F] 26 F5
Carrowkeel [IRL] 2 F2
Carrù [I] 108 G2
Carryduff [NIR] 2 G4
Carry–le–Rouet [F] 106 H5
Çarshovë [AL] 128 C6
Carsoli [I] 116 B5
Carsulae [I] 116 A3
Cartagena [E] 104 C4
Cártama [E] 102 B4
Cartaxo [P] 86 C4
Cartaya [E] 94 E5
Cartelle [E] 78 C5
Carteret [F] 26 D2
Cartoixa de Porta Coeli [E] 98 E4
Cartoixa d'Escaldei [E] 90 H6
Cartuja de Aula Dei [E] 90 E3

Carviçais [P] 80 F5
Carvin [F] 28 F3
Carvoeiro [P] 94 B5
Carwitz [D] 20 D5
Casabermeja [E] 102 C4
Casabona [I] 124 E4
Casa Branca [P] 86 D5
Casa Branca [P] 94 C2
Casa Branca [P] 94 D1
Casacalenda [I] 116 E6
Casáccia [CH] 70 H2
Casalabate [I] 122 G4
Casalarreina [E] 82 G6
Casalbordino [I] 116 E5
Casal Borsetti [I] 110 H3
Casalbuono [I] 120 G5
Casalciprano [I] 116 E6
Casale [I] 126 B2
Casalecchio di Reno [I] 110 F3
Casale Monferrato [I] 70 E5
Casalmaggiore [I] 110 D2
Casalpusterlengo [I] 70 H6
Casal Velino [I] 120 F5
Casamáina [I] 116 C4
Casamari, Abbazia di– [I] 116 C6
Casamássima [I] 122 E3
Casamicciola Terme [I] 120 D3
Casamozza [F] 114 C3
Casarabonela [E] 102 B4
Casarano [I] 122 G5
Casar de Cáceres [E] 86 H5
Casar de las Hurdes [E] 88 A4
Casares [E] 100 H5
Casares, Cueva de los– [E] 90 B5
Casariche [E] 102 B3
Casarubios del Monte [E] 88 F6
Casas Cueva [E] 102 F3
Casas de Benítez [E] 98 B4
Casas de Don Pedro [E] 96 C3
Casas de Fernando Alonso [E] 98 B4
Casas de Jorós [E] 100 D6
Casas de Juan Núñez [E] 98 C5
Casas del Puerto [E] 104 C2
Casas de Reina [E] 94 H4
Casas-Ibáñez [E] 98 C4
Casatejada [E] 88 B6
Cascais [P] 86 A5
Cascante [E] 84 B6
Cascia [I] 116 B3
Casciana Terme [I] 110 E6
Cáscina [I] 110 D5
Căscioarele [RO] 148 D1
Casekow [D] 20 E5
Caselle [I] 70 D5
Caserta [I] 120 E2
Cashel [IRL] 4 D4
Cashel, Rock of– [IRL] 4 D4
Casillas del Ángel [E] 100 E6
Casina [I] 110 E3
Casinina [I] 110 H5
Casino di Terra [I] 114 E1
Casinos [E] 98 E4
Čáslav [CZ] 48 H4
Caso / Campo de Caso [E] 82 C2
Casola Valsenio [I] 110 G4
Casoli [I] 116 D5
Casoria [I] 120 E3
Caspe [E] 90 F5
Cassà de la Selva [E] 92 F3
Cassagnes-Bégonhès [F] 68 B6
Cassano allo Ionio [I] 122 C6
Cassano d'Adda [I] 70 G5
Cassano delle Murge [I] 122 D3
Cassel [F] 28 E2
Cassibile [I] 126 G5
Cassine [I] 108 H2
Cassino [I] 120 D1
Cassis [F] 108 B5
Cassuéjouls [F] 68 B5
Castagneto Carducci [I] 114 E1
Castalla [E] 104 D2
Castañar de Ibor [E] 96 C1
Castanet-Tolosan [F] 106 A3
Castanheira de Pera [P] 86 E2
Castasegna [CH] 70 H2
Casteau [B] 28 H3
Casteggio [I] 70 G6
Castejón de Monegros [E] 90 F4
Castejón de Sos [E] 84 F5
Castejón de Valdejasa [E] 90 E3
Castel Bolognese [I] 110 G4
Castelbouc [F] 68 C6
Castelbuono [I] 126 E2
Casteldelfino [I] 108 E2
Castel del Piano [I] 114 G2
Castel del Rio [I] 110 F4
Castel di Iúdica [I] 126 F3
Castel di Sangro [I] 116 D6
Castel di Tora [I] 116 B4
Castel Doria, Terme di– [I] 118 D3
Castelejo [P] 94 A5
Castelfidardo [I] 116 C1
Castelfiorentino [I] 110 E6
Castelflorite [E] 90 G4
Castelfranco Emilia [I] 110 F3
Castelfranco in Miscano [I] 120 F2
Castelfranco Véneto [I] 72 E6
Castel Goffredo [I] 110 E1
Casteljaloux [F] 66 D5
Castellabate [I] 120 F5
Castellammare del Golfo [I] 126 C2
Castellammare di Stábia [I] 120 E3
Castellamonte [I] 70 D5
Castellana, Grotte di– [I] 122 E3
Castellana Grotte [I] 122 E3
Castellana Sícula [I] 126 E3
Castellane [F] 108 D4
Castellaneta [I] 122 E4
Castellar [E] 102 F1
Castellar de la Frontera [E] 100 G5
Castellar de la Muela [E] 90 C5
Castellar de Santiago [E] 96 F5
Castell'Arquato [I] 110 C2
Castell'Azzara [I] 114 G3
Castellazzo Bormida [I] 108 H2
Castelldans [E] 90 H5
Castell d'aro [E] 92 G3
Castell de Cabres [E] 98 G1
Castelldefels [E] 92 D5
Castell de Ferro [E] 102 E5
Castell de Mur / Cellers [E] 92 C2
Castelleone [I] 70 H5
Castelletto d'Orba [I] 110 A2
Castellfollit de la Roca [E] 92 F2
Castellina in Chianti [I] 110 F6
Castelló de la Plana / Castellón de la Plana [E] 98 F3
Castelló de la Ribera [E] 98 E6
Castelló d'Empúries [E] 92 G2
Castellón de la Plana / Castelló de la Plana [E] 98 F3
Castellote [E] 90 F6
Castello Tesino [I] 72 D4
Castellterçol [E] 92 E3
Castellúccio dei Sáuri [I] 120 G2
Castelluccio Sup. [I] 120 H5
Castelluzzo [I] 126 B2
Castelmagno [I] 108 F2
Castelmassa [I] 110 F2
Castelmauro [I] 116 E6
Castelmoron [F] 66 E5
Castelnau [F] 66 H4
Castelnaudary [F] 106 B4
Castelnau-de-Médoc [F] 66 C2
Castelnau-de-Montmiral [F] 106 B2
Castelnau d'Estretefonds [F] 84 H2
Castelnau-Magnoac [F] 84 F3
Castelnau-Montratier [F] 66 F5
Castelnovo ne' Monti [I] 110 D3
Castelnuovo Berardenga [I] 114 G1
Castelnuovo Berardenga [I] 114 G1
Castelnuovo della Dáunia [I] 120 F1
Castelnuovo di Garfagnana [I] 110 D4
Castelnuovo di Porto [I] 116 A5
Castelnuovo di Val di Cecina [I] 114 F1
Castelnuovo Don Bosco [I] 70 E6
Castelnuovo Monterotaro [I] 116 F6
Castelnuovo Scrívia [I] 70 F6
Castelo [P] 86 D2
Castelo Branco [P] 80 F5
Castelo Branco [P] 86 F3
Castelo Branco [P] 100 C3
Castelo de Paiva [P] 80 C4
Castelo de Vide [P] 86 F4
Castelo do Neiva [P] 78 A6
Castel Porziano [I] 114 H6
Castelraimondo [I] 116 B2
Castel San Giovanni [I] 70 G6
Castel San Lorenzo [I] 120 F4
Castel San Pietro Terme [I] 110 F4
Castelsaraceno [I] 120 H5
Castelsardo [I] 118 C2
Castelsarrasin [F] 66 F6
Castelseprio [I] 70 F4
Castelserás [E] 90 F6
Casteltérmini [I] 126 D3
Castelvecchio Subequo [I] 116 C5
Castelverde [I] 70 H6
Castelvetere in Val Fortore [I] 120 F1
Castelvetrano [I] 126 B3
Castel Volturno [I] 120 D2
Castenaso [I] 110 F3
Castets [F] 66 B5
Castiádas [I] 118 D7
Castiglione d'Orcia [I] 114 G2
Castiglioncello [I] 110 D6
Castiglione dei Pepoli [I] 110 F4
Castiglione del Lago [I] 114 H2
Castiglione della Pescáia [I] 114 E3
Castiglione delle Stiviere [I] 72 B6
Castiglione Messer Marino [I] 116 E6
Castiglione Olona [I] 70 F4
Castiglion Fibocchi [I] 110 G6
Castiglion Fiorentino [I] 114 H1
Castilblanco [E] 96 C2
Castilblanco de los Arroyos [E] 94 G5
Castillejo de Martín Viejo [E] 86 H2
Castilliscar [E] 84 C5
Castillo de Locubín [E] 102 D3
Castillo de Matajudíos [E] 82 D5
Castillo de Tajarja [E] 102 D4
Castillo de Villamalefa [E] 98 F3
Castillon-la-Bataille [F] 66 D3
Castillonnès [F] 66 E4
Castillo Pasiega las Chimenas, Cuevas el– [E] 82 E3
Castione della Presolana [I] 72 A5
Castlebar [IRL] 2 C4
Castlebay / Bagh a Chaisteil [GB] 6 A5
Castlebellingham [IRL] 2 F5
Castleblayney [IRL] 2 F4
Castlebridge [IRL] 4 F5
Castlecomer [IRL] 4 E3
Castledermot [IRL] 4 F3
Castle Douglas [GB] 8 D5
Castleisland [IRL] 4 B4
Castlemaine [IRL] 4 B4
Castlemartyr [IRL] 4 D5
Castleplunkett [IRL] 2 D4
Castlepollard [IRL] 2 E5
Castlerea [IRL] 2 D4
Castletown [GBM] 10 B2
Castletownbere [IRL] 4 B5
Castletown House [IRL] 2 F6
Castletownroche [IRL] 4 D4
Castletownshend [IRL] 4 B5
Castlewellan [NIR] 2 G4
Castrejón [E] 88 D2
Castres [F] 106 B3
Castricum [NL] 16 D3
Castries [F] 106 F4
Castril [E] 102 G3
Castrillo de Don Juan [E] 88 G2
Castrillo de la Reina [E] 88 H2
Castrillón [E] 78 F3
Castro [I] 114 G3
Castro / Dozón [E] 78 C4
Castrobarto [E] 82 F4
Castrocalbón [E] 80 H3
Castro Caldelas [E] 78 D5
Castrocaro Terme [I] 110 G4
Castrocontrigo [E] 78 F6
Castro da Cola [P] 94 C4
Castro Daire [P] 80 C5
Castro dei Volsci [I] 120 C1
Castro del Río [E] 102 C2
Castro de Rei [E] 78 E3
Castrojeriz [E] 82 D6
Castro Marim [P] 94 D5
Castromil [E] 78 E6
Castromonte [E] 88 E1
Castronuevo [E] 88 D1
Castronuño [E] 88 D2
Castropol [E] 78 F2
Castrop-Rauxal [D] 30 H3
Castroreale [I] 124 B7
Castro-Urdiales [E] 82 G3
Castroverde [E] 78 E3
Castro Verde [P] 94 C4
Castroverde de Cerrato [E] 88 F2
Castrovillari [I] 122 C6
Castuera [E] 96 B4
Cataéggio [I] 70 H3
Çatalca [TR] 150 D2
Çatallar [TR] 154 H2
Catane [RO] 146 F2
Catánia [I] 126 G3
Catanzaro [I] 124 E5
Catanzaro Marina [I] 124 E5
Catarroja [E] 98 E5
Catenanuova [I] 126 F3
Cateraggio [F] 114 C4
Cathair Dónall / Caherdaniel [IRL] 4 A4
Catoira [E] 78 B3
Catterick [GB] 10 F2
Cattolica [I] 112 B5
Cattolica Eraclea [I] 126 C3
Catus [F] 66 G5
Caudebec-en-Caux [F] 26 H3
Caudete [E] 104 D1
Caudeval [F] 106 B5
Caudry [F] 28 F4
Caulonia [I] 124 D7
Caulonia [I] 124 E6
Caumont [F] 26 E3
Caumont [F] 84 G4
Caunes-Minervois [F] 106 C4
Cauro [F] 114 B5
Căuşeni [MD] 204 F3
Caussade [F] 66 G6
Cauterets [F] 84 E4
Cauville [F] 26 G2
Cava [E] 92 B6
Cava de' Tirreni [I] 120 E3
Cava d'Ispica [I] 126 F5
Cavaglià [I] 70 E5
Cavaillon [F] 106 H4
Cavalaire-sur-Mer [F] 108 D6
Cavalese [I] 72 D4
Cavalière [F] 108 D6
Cavallino [I] 72 F6
Cavallino [I] 122 G5
Cavalls, Cova dels– [E] 98 G2
Cavan / An Cabhán [IRL] 2 E4
Cavárzere [I] 110 G2
Çavdarhisar [TR] 152 G2
Çavdır [TR] 152 H6
Cave del Predil [I] 72 H4
Cavi [I] 110 B3
Caviaga [I] 70 H5
Cavo [I] 114 E2
Cavour [I] 70 C6
Cavriglia [I] 110 F6
Cavtat [HR] 144 C4
Çayağzi [TR] 150 F2
Çaybaşı [TR] 152 D4
Çayçinge [TR] 152 F2
Çayhisar [TR] 154 E1
Çayırova (Ágios Theodoros) [CY] 154 G5
Caylus [F] 66 G6
Cayrols [F] 68 A4
Çayyaka [TR] 150 F5
Cazalegas [E] 88 D6
Cazalla de la Sierra [E] 94 H5
Cazals [F] 66 F4
Cazaubon [F] 66 D6
Cazeneuve, Château de– [F] 66 D4
Cazères [F] 84 G4
Cazin [BIH] 112 H2
Čazma [HR] 74 F6
Cazorla [E] 102 F2
Cea [E] 78 C4
Cea [E] 82 C5
Ceatharlach / Carlow [IRL] 4 F4
Cebolla [E] 96 E1
Čebovce [SK] 64 C4
Cebreiro [E] 78 E4
Cebreros [E] 88 E5
Cebrones del Rio [E] 78 G6
Ceccano [I] 120 C1
Cece [H] 76 B3
Čečejovce [SK] 64 F3
Čechtice [CZ] 48 G5
Čechtín [CZ] 50 A6
Cécina [I] 114 E1
Ceclavín [E] 86 G4
Cecos [E] 78 F4
Cedeira [E] 78 D1
Cedillo [E] 86 F4
Cedros [P] 100 C2
Cedynia [PL] 34 F1
Cee [E] 78 B2
Cefalù [I] 126 E2
Cegléd [H] 76 D2
Céglie Messápica [I] 122 F4
Cegrane [MK] 128 D1
Cehegín [E] 104 B2
Ceillac [F] 108 E2
Ceira [P] 86 D2
Čejč [CZ] 62 G2
Čekiške [LT] 200 F5
Ceków Kolonia [PL] 36 E4
Čelákovice [CZ] 48 G3
Celano [I] 116 C5
Celanova [E] 78 C5
Čelarevo [SRB] 142 F1
Celaru [RO] 146 G1
Celbowo [PL] 22 D1
Celbridge [IRL] 2 F6
Čelebić [BIH] 142 B4
Celerina [CH] 70 H2
Čelić [BIH] 142 E3
Celico [I] 124 D4
Čelinac [BIH] 142 C3
Celjahavi [BY] 202 B6
Celje [SLO] 74 D4
Cella [E] 98 D1
Celldömölk [H] 74 G1
Celle [D] 32 G1
Celle di Bulgheria [I] 120 G5
Celle Lígure [I] 108 H3
Cellers / Castell de Mur [E] 92 C2
Celles [B] 28 G3
Celles-sur-Belle [F] 54 D4
Čelopeci [MK] 128 D2
Celorico da Beira [P] 80 D6
Celorico de Basto [P] 80 D4
Celsoy [F] 58 A3
Çeltek [TR] 152 H5
Çeltikköy [TR] 150 B4
Čemerno [BIH] 144 D2
Cemke [TR] 150 F2
Cenad [RO] 76 F4
Cencenighe [I] 72 E4
Cenei [RO] 76 F6
Ceneköy [TR] 150 C3
Cenicentos [E] 88 E5
Cenicero [E] 82 G6
Cenizzate [E] 98 C4
Čenta [SRB] 142 G2
Centallo [I] 108 F2
Centelles [E] 92 E3
Cento [I] 110 F3
Centuri [F] 114 C2
Centúripe [I] 126 F3
Cepagatti [I] 116 D4
Çepan [AL] 128 C5
Čepin [HR] 142 D1
Cepos [P] 86 E2
Čepovan [SLO] 72 H5
Ceprano [I] 120 C1
Čer [MK] 128 D2
Čeralije [HR] 74 H6
Cerami [I] 126 F2
Ceranów [PL] 38 D2
Ceraso [I] 120 F5
Cerbère [F] 92 G2
Cercal [P] 86 B4
Cercal [P] 94 B3
Cerceda [E] 78 C2
Cerceda [E] 88 F5
Cercedilla [E] 88 F4
Cerchiara di Calábria [I] 122 D6
Cerda [I] 126 D2
Cerdedo [E] 78 C4
Cerdeira [P] 86 G2
Cerdon [F] 56 C2
Cerea [I] 110 F1
Cerecinos de Campos [E] 82 B6
Cered [H] 64 E4
Cereixo [E] 78 B2
Ceremosnja [SRB] 146 D1
Ceres [I] 70 D5
Ceresole Reale [I] 70 C4
Céret [F] 92 F2
Cerfontaine [B] 28 H4
Ceriale [I] 108 G3
Cerignola [I] 120 H2
Cérilly [F] 56 C5
Čerín [SK] 64 C3
Cerisiers [F] 42 H6
Cerizay [F] 54 D3
Çerkezköy [TR] 150 D2
Cerknica [SLO] 74 B6
Cerkno [SLO] 74 B5
Cerkovitsa [BG] 148 B2
Cerkvenjak [SLO] 74 E3
Cerkwica [PL] 20 G3
Çermë [AL] 128 B3
Cermei [RO] 76 H3
Cerna [HR] 142 E2
Cernache do Bom Jardim [P] 86 D3
Černá Hora [CZ] 50 C5
Cernavodă [RO] 204 E5
Černá v Pošumaví [CZ] 62 B3
Cernay [F] 58 D3
Cernégula [E] 82 E5
Černičevo [BG] 148 B5
Cerniébaud [F] 58 B6
Cernik [HR] 142 C1
Cernóbbio [I] 70 G4
Černookovo [BG] 148 G1
Černošín [CZ] 48 D4
Černovice [CZ] 48 G6
Černuc [CZ] 48 F3
Cerósimo [I] 122 C5
Cerovačke Špilje [HR] 112 H4
Cerovica [BIH] 144 C3
Çërravë [AL] 128 D4
Cerreto [I] 116 B5
Cërrik [AL] 128 B4
Cerro de los Angeles [E] 88 F6
Cerro de los Santos [E] 98 C6
Cerro Muriano [E] 96 C6
Certaldo [I] 110 E6
Cervatos [E] 82 E4
Cervatos de la Cueza [E] 82 C5
Červená [CZ] 48 F5
Červená Lhota [CZ] 48 G6
Červená-Řečice [CZ] 48 H5
Červená Skala [SK] 64 E2
Červená Voda [CZ] 50 C4
Červený Hrádek [CZ] 48 E2
Červený Hrádek [CZ] 48 F5
Červený Kameň [SK] 62 G4
Červený Kameň [SK] 64 A2
Červený Kláštor [SK] 52 B5
Červený Kostelec [CZ] 50 B2
Cervera [E] 92 C3
Cervera de la Cañada [E] 90 C4
Cervera del Llano [E] 98 B3
Cervera del Río Alhama [E] 84 A6
Cervera de Pisuerga [E] 82 D4
Cerveteri [I] 114 H5
Cérvia [I] 110 H4
Cervignano del Friuli [I] 72 G5
Cervinara [I] 120 E3
Cervione [F] 114 C4
Cervo [E] 78 E1
Cervo [I] 108 G4
Cesana Torinese [I] 70 B6
Cesarica [HR] 112 F3
Cesarò [I] 126 F2
Cesarzowice [PL] 36 C6
Cesena [I] 110 H4
Cesenático [I] 110 H4
Ceserhát-Suráni [H] 64 D5
Cēsis [LV] 198 E4
Česká Bělá [CZ] 50 A5
Česká Kamenice [CZ] 48 F2
Česká Lípa [CZ] 48 G2
Česká Skalice [CZ] 50 B3
Česká Třebová [CZ] 50 B4
České Budějovice [CZ] 62 C2
České Libchavy [CZ] 50 B4
České Velenice [CZ] 62 C3
Český Brod [CZ] 48 G4
Český Krumlov [CZ] 62 B2
Český Šternberk [CZ] 48 G4
Český Těšín [CZ] 50 F5
Çeşme [TR] 134 H5
Çeşmealti [TR] 152 C4
Cespedosa [E] 88 C4
Cessalto [I] 72 F5
Cessenon-sur-Orb [F] 106 D4
Čestimensko [BG] 148 E1
Čestobrodica [SRB] 146 A2
Cestona / Zestoa [E] 84 A2
Cesvaine [LV] 198 F5
Cetate [RO] 146 F1
Çetibeli [TR] 154 D1
Cetinje [MNE] 144 E4
Cetóbriga [P] 86 B6
Cetona [I] 114 G2
Cetraro [I] 124 C4
Ceuta [E] 100 G6
Ceutí [E] 104 C3
Ceva [I] 108 G3
Cevico Navero [E] 88 F1
Čevo [MNE] 144 E4
Cewków [PL] 52 F3
Ceylan [TR] 154 G2
Ceyrat [F] 68 C2
Ceyzériat [F] 68 G2
Chaalis, Abbaye de– [F] 42 G3
Chabanais [F] 54 F6
Chabeuil [F] 68 F5
Chablis [F] 56 E2
Chabreloche [F] 68 D2
Chabris [F] 54 H3
Chachersk [BY] 202 D5
Chagny [F] 56 G5
Chailland [F] 26 E6
Chaillé-les-Marais [F] 54 C4
Chailley-Turny [F] 42 H6
Chailluz, Fort de– [F] 58 B4
Chairóneia [GR] 132 H5
Chalabre [F] 106 B5
Chalais [F] 66 E2
Chalamont [F] 68 G2
Chalampé [F] 58 E3
Chalandrítsa [GR] 132 F6
Chálki [GR] 132 G2
Chálki [GR] 154 C4
Chalkiádes [GR] 132 G2
Chalkída [GR] 134 B5
Chalkidóna [GR] 128 G4
Challans [F] 54 B3
Challes-les-Eaux [F] 70 A4
Chalonnes-sur-Loire [F] 54 D1
Châlons-en-Champagne [F] 44 B4
Chalon-sur-Saône [F] 56 G5
Chalupy [PL] 36 H6
Châlus [F] 66 G2
Chalusset, Château de– [F] 66 G1
Cham [CH] 58 F5
Cham [D] 48 C6
Chamberet [F] 66 H2
Chambéry [F] 68 H3
Chambilly [F] 56 E6
Chambley-Bussières [F] 44 E4
Chambon-sur-Lac [F] 68 C2
Chambon-sur-Voueize [F] 56 B6
Chambord [F] 54 H2
Chambord, Parc de– [F] 54 H2
Chamelet [F] 68 F2
Chameregg [D] 48 C6
Chammünster [D] 48 C6
Chamonix-Mont-Blanc [F] 70 C3
Champagnac-le-Vieux [F] 68 D3
Champagne-Mouton [F] 54 E5
Champagnole [F] 58 B6
Champaubert [F] 44 A4
Champdeniers [F] 54 D4
Champ du Bataille, Château du– [F] 26 H4
Champ du Feu [F] 58 D2
Champeix [F] 68 C3
Champéry [CH] 70 C2
Champex [CH] 70 C3
Champier [F] 68 G4
Champigné [F] 40 H6
Champigny-sur-Veude [F] 54 F2
Champillon [F] 44 B3
Champlan [F] 42 F4
Champlitte [F] 58 A3
Champlon [B] 30 E6
Champoluc [I] 70 D3
Champorcher [I] 70 D4
Champrond-en-Gâtine [F] 26 H6
Champtoceaux [F] 40 F6
Champvent [CH] 58 C6
Chamrousse [F] 68 H5
Chamusca [P] 86 C4
Chanaleilles [F] 68 D5
Chanas [F] 68 F4
Chandrinós [GR] 136 C4
Chaniá [GR] 140 C4
Chaniótis [GR] 130 C6
Channel Tunnel / La Manche, Tunnel sous– [F/GB] 14 G5
Chantada [E] 78 D4
Chantelle [F] 56 D6
Chantemerle [F] 70 B6
Chantilly [F] 42 G3
Chantonnay [F] 54 C3
Chão de Codes [P] 86 D4
Chaource [F] 44 B6
Chapelle-Royale [F] 42 D5
Chárakas [GR] 140 E5
Charavgí [GR] 128 F5
Charavines [F] 68 G4
Charbonnières-les-Bains [F] 68 F3
Charbowo [PL] 36 D2
Chard [GB] 12 F4
Charenton-du-Cher [F] 56 C4
Charité, Abbaye de la– [F] 58 B4
Charleroi [B] 30 C5
Charlestown [IRL] 2 D4
Charleville / Rath Luirc [IRL] 4 C4
Charleville-Mézières [F] 44 C2
Charlieu [F] 68 E1
Charlottenberg [S] 166 D1
Charly [F] 42 H3
Charly [F] 56 C4
Charmes [F] 44 E6
Charnawchytsy [BY] 38 G2
Charneca [P] 86 A5
Charny [F] 56 D1
Charnyany [BY] 38 G3
Charolles [F] 56 F6
Charpentry [F] 44 D3
Charrières [CH] 70 C1
Charron [F] 54 C4
Charroux [F] 54 E5
Chartres [F] 42 E4
Charvarica [BG] 146 F6
Charzykowy [PL] 22 C4
Chassant [F] 42 D4
Chasseneuil-s.-Bonnieure [F] 54 E6
Chasse sur Rhone [F] 68 F3
Chassigny [F] 56 H3
Château-Arnoux [F] 108 C3
Châteaubourg [F] 26 D6
Châteaubriant [F] 40 F5
Château-Chinon [F] 56 E4
Château d'Oex [CH] 70 D1
Château-du-Loir [F] 42 B6
Châteaudun [F] 42 D5
Châteaugiron [F] 26 C6
Château-Gontier [F] 40 H5
Château-Landon [F] 42 F5
Château-la-Vallière [F] 42 B6
Château-l'Évêque [F] 66 F3
Châteaulin [F] 40 B2
Châteaumeillant [F] 56 B5
Châteauneuf [F] 66 E1
Châteauneuf-de-Randon [F] 68 D5
Châteauneuf-du-Faou [F] 40 C3
Châteauneuf-du-Pape [F] 106 G3
Châteauneuf-en-Thymerais [F] 26 H6
Châteauneuf-sur-Cher [F] 56 C4
Châteauneuf-sur-Sarthe [F] 40 H6
Châteauponsac [F] 54 G5
Château-Porcien [F] 28 H6
Château-Queyras [F] 70 B6
Château-Regnault [F] 44 C1
Châteaurenard [F] 42 G6
Château-Renault [F] 54 G1
Châteauroux [F] 54 H4
Château-Salins [F] 44 F5
Château-Thierry [F] 42 H3
Châteauvillain [F] 56 G2
Châtel [F] 70 C2
Châtelaillon-Plage [F] 54 C5
Châtelet [B] 30 C5
Châtelguyon [F] 68 C2
Châtellerault [F] 54 F3
Châtel-Montagne [F] 68 E1
Châtel-St-Denis [CH] 70 C1
Châtelus-Malvaleix [F] 54 H5
Châtenois [F] 44 E6
Chatham [GB] 14 F4
Châtillon [I] 70 D4
Châtillon-Coligny [F] 56 D1
Châtillon-en-Bazois [F] 56 E4
Châtillon-en-Diois [F] 68 G6
Châtillon-sur-Chalaronne [F] 68 G2
Châtillon-sur-Indre [F] 54 G3
Châtillon-sur-Loire [F] 56 D2
Châtillon-sur-Marne [F] 44 A3
Châtillon-sur-Seine [F] 56 G2
Châtre, Église de– [F] 54 D6
Chatteris [GB] 14 F2
Chaudes-Aigues [F] 68 C5
Chauffailles [F] 68 F1
Chaufour-lès-Bonnières [F] 42 E3
Chaumergy [F] 56 H5
Chaumont [F] 56 H1
Chaumont-sur-Aire [F] 44 D4
Chaumont-sur-Loire [F] 54 G2
Chaunay [F] 54 E5
Chauny [F] 28 F6
Chaussin [F] 56 H5
Chauvigny [F] 54 F4
Chaux-Neuve [F] 58 B6
Chavaleč [CZ] 50 B2
Chavdar [BG] 130 D1
Chaves [P] 80 E3
Chavusy [BY] 202 D5
Chayki [RUS] 198 H6
Chazelles-sur-Lyon [F] 68 F3
Cheb [CZ] 48 C3
Chęciny [PL] 52 B1
Cheddar [GB] 12 F3
Chef-Boutonne [F] 54 D5
Cheglevici [RO] 76 F5
Cheimarros [GR] 130 B3
Chekhov [RUS] 202 F3
Chekhovo [RUS] 22 H2
Cheles [E] 94 F2
Chełm [PL] 38 F6
Chełmek [PL] 50 G3
Chełmno [PL] 22 D5
Chelmsford [GB] 14 F4
Chełmża [PL] 22 E6
Chełst [PL] 36 B1
Cheltenham [GB] 12 G2
Chelva [E] 98 D3
Chémery-sur-Bar [F] 44 C2
Chemillé [F] 54 D2
Chemin [F] 56 H5
Chemnitz [D] 48 D1
Chenaux [CH] 58 C6
Chêne-Pignier [F] 54 F6
Chénérailles [F] 56 B6
Chenonceaux [F] 54 G2
Chepelare [BG] 130 E1
Chepstow [GB] 12 G3
Chera [E] 98 D4
Cherasco [I] 108 G2
Cherbourg [F] 26 D2
Cheremykino [RUS] 178 G5
Cherepovo [BG] 148 D6
Cherkasovo [RUS] 178 F3
Cherkasy [UA] 202 E8
Chern [RUS] 202 F4
Cherna Mesta [BG] 146 G6
Chernevo [RUS] 198 G2
Cherniakhiv [UA] 202 C7
Chernihiv [UA] 202 D6
Cherni rid [BG] 130 G1
Chernivtsi [UA] 204 D3
Chernomorets [BG] 148 F4
Chernyakhovsk [RUS] 24 C1
Chéroy [F] 42 G5
Cherskaya [RUS] 198 G4
Chérso [GR] 128 H3
Cherveix-Cubas [F] 66 G3
Chervena Voda [BG] 148 D2
Cherven Bryag [BG] 148 A3
Cherves-Richemont [F] 54 D6
Chervonohrad [UA] 52 H2
Chervyen' [BY] 202 C5
Cherykaw [BY] 202 D5
Cheste [E] 98 E4
Chester [GB] 10 D4
Chesterfield [GB] 10 F5
Chester-le-Street [GB] 8 F6
Chevagnes [F] 56 D5
Chevanceaux [F] 66 D2
Chevenez [CH] 58 D4
Chevilly, Château de– [F] 42 E6
Chevreuse [F] 42 F4

Chézal-Benoît [F] 56 B4
Chialamberto [I] 70 D5
Chiampo [I] 72 D6
Chianca, Dolmen di- [I] 122 D2
Chianciano Terme [I] 114 G2
Chiaramonti [I] 118 C3
Chiaramonti Gulfi [I] 126 F5
Chiaravalle [I] 112 C6
Chiaravalle [I] 112 C6
Chiaravalle Centrale [I] 124 D6
Chiaravalle della Colomba [I] 110 D2
Chiari [I] 70 H5
Chiaromonte [I] 122 C5
Chiasso [CH] 70 G4
Chiavari [I] 110 B3
Chiavenna [I] 70 G2
Chichester [GB] 14 D5
Chiclana de la Frontera [E] 100 F4
Chiclana de Segura [E] 102 G1
Chieming [D] 60 F5
Chieri [I] 70 D6
Chiesa [I] 110 G3
Chiesa in Valmalenco [I] 70 H3
Chiessi [I] 114 D2
Chieti [I] 116 D4
Chigny [F] 28 G5
Chiliadoú [GR] 134 C4
Chiliandaríou, Moní- [GR] 130 D5
Chiliomódi [GR] 136 F1
Chillarón de Cuenca [E] 98 B2
Chillon [CH] 70 C2
Chillón [E] 96 C4
Chimay [B] 28 H5
Chinadievo [UA] 204 B3
Chinchilla de Monte-Aragón [E] 98 C5
Chinchón [E] 96 G1
Chinon [F] 54 F2
Chióggia [I] 110 H1
Chíos [GR] 134 G4
Chipiona [E] 100 F3
Chippenham [GB] 12 G3
Chipping Norton [GB] 12 H2
Chipping Sodbury [GB] 12 G3
Chiprana [E] 90 F5
Chiprovtsi [BG] 146 F3
Chiren [BG] 146 G3
Chirivel [E] 102 H3
Chirpan [BG] 148 C5
Chisa [F] 114 B5
Chişinău [MD] 204 E3
Chişineu Criş [RO] 76 G3
Chiusa / Klausen [I] 72 D3
Chiusa di Pesio [I] 108 F3
Chiusaforte [I] 72 G4
Chiusa Scláfani [I] 126 C3
Chiusi [I] 114 H2
Chiva [E] 98 E4
Chivasso [I] 70 D5
Chkalove [RUS] 204 H3
Chkalovo [PL] 24 D3
Chkalovo [RUS] 24 D1
Chlebowo [PL] 34 G3
Chlemoútsi [GR] 136 B1
Chlewice [PL] 50 H2
Chlewiska [PL] 38 B6
Chlewo [PL] 36 F4
Chlmec [SK] 64 H3
Chlumec nad Cidlinou [CZ] 48 H3
Chlum u Třeboně [CZ] 62 C2
Chmielnik [PL] 52 B2
Chmielno [PL] 36 A6
Chobienia [PL] 36 B5
Chobienice [PL] 36 B3
Choceň [CZ] 50 B4
Choceń [PL] 36 F2
Chochołów [PL] 50 H5
Chocianów [PL] 36 B5
Chociwel [PL] 20 G5
Choczewo [PL] 22 D1
Chodecz [PL] 36 F2
Chodel [PL] 38 D6
Chodos / Xodos [E] 98 F2
Chodov [CZ] 48 D3
Chodová Planá [CZ] 48 D4
Chodzież [PL] 22 B6
Chojna [PL] 20 F6
Chojnice [PL] 22 C4
Chojnów [PL] 36 B6
Cholet [F] 54 D2
Chomakovtsi [BG] 146 G3
Chomęciska Małe [PL] 52 F1
Chomutov [CZ] 48 E2
Chop [UA] 204 B3
Chóra [GR] 136 C4
Chorbadzhijsko [BG] 130 F2
Choreftó [GR] 134 A2
Chorges [F] 108 D2
Chorio [I] 124 C8
Choristí [GR] 130 D3
Chorley [GB] 10 D3
Chornobyl [UA] 202 D7
Chornomors'ke [UA] 204 G4
Choroszcz [PL] 24 E5
Chorro, Garganta del- [E] 102 B4
Chorros, Cueva de los- [E] 96 H6
Chorros del Mundo [E] 96 H6
Chortkiv [UA] 204 D2
Chorzele [PL] 22 H5
Chorzów [PL] 50 G3
Chorzyna [PL] 36 F5
Choszczno [PL] 20 G6
Chotěboř [CZ] 50 A5
Chotětín [CZ] 48 E4
Choumnikó [GR] 130 C3
Chouto [P] 86 D4
Chouvigny, Gorges de- [F] 56 C6
Choye [F] 58 A4
Chozoviótissa [GR] 138 G3
Chrast [CZ] 50 B4
Chrastava [CZ] 48 G1
Chrepiski Manastir [BG] 146 G4
Christchurch [GB] 12 G5
Christianoúpoli [GR] 136 C3
Christiansfeld [DK] 156 C3
Christinehof [S] 158 D2
Christkindl [A] 62 B5
Christós [GR] 138 G1
Chrudim [CZ] 50 A4
Chrýsafa [GR] 136 E4
Chrysochóri [GR] 130 E3
Chrysoskalítissa [GR] 140 B5
Chrysoúpoli [GR] 130 E3
Chrząchówek [PL] 38 D5
Chrzan [PL] 36 D3
Chrzanów [PL] 50 G3
Chudenice [CZ] 48 D5
Chudniv [UA] 202 C8
Chudoba [PL] 50 E1
Chudomir [BG] 148 D3
Chudovo [RUS] 202 C1
Chulkovo [RUS] 178 E3
Chupa [RUS] 196 H1
Chuprene [BG] 146 E3
Chur [CH] 70 H1
Church Stretton [GB] 10 D6
Churchtown [IRL] 4 E5
Churchtown [IRL] 4 F5
Churek [BG] 146 G4
Chvagnes-en-Paillers [F] 54 C2
Chvylevo [RUS] 202 C1
Chwaszczyno [PL] 22 D2
Chyhyryn [UA] 202 E8
Chyňava [CZ] 48 F4
Chýnov [CZ] 48 G5
Chýnovská Jeskyně [CZ] 48 G5
Chyżne [PL] 50 H5
Cianciana [I] 126 D3
Ciasna [PL] 50 F2
Ciążeń [PL] 36 E3
Cibakháza [H] 76 E2
Ciborro [P] 86 D6
Ciboure [F] 84 B2
Cicciano [I] 120 E3
Cicerone, Tomba di- [I] 120 C2
Ćićevac [SRB] 146 C3
Čičevci [BIH] 142 F4
Čičevo [BIH] 144 C2
Cichy [PL] 24 D3
Čičil [BG] 146 E2
Čičiuk [SRB] 146 C3
Ciclopi, Isole dei- [I] 126 G3
Čičmany [SK] 64 B2
Cide [TR] 204 H6
Cidones [E] 90 B2
Ciechanów [PL] 38 B1
Ciechanowiec [PL] 38 D1
Ciechocinek [PL] 36 F1
Ciemnik [PL] 20 G5
Ciempozuelos [E] 96 G1
Ciepielów [PL] 38 C5
Cieplice Śląskie-Zdrój [PL] 50 A1
Čierny Balog [SK] 64 D3
Cierp-Gaud [F] 84 F4
Cieśle [PL] 36 H2
Cieszanów [PL] 52 F3
Cieszyn [PL] 36 D5
Cieszyn [PL] 50 F4
Cieszyno [PL] 20 H5
Cieza [E] 104 C2
Ciężkowice [PL] 52 C4
Çiftlikköy [TR] 150 F3
Cifuentes [E] 90 A5
Cifuentes [E] 90 A5
Cigales [E] 88 E1
Cigánd [H] 64 H4
Cigliano [I] 70 E5
Cihangazi [TR] 150 G5
Cilipi [HR] 144 D4
Cill Airne / Killarney [IRL] 4 B4
Cillas [E] 90 C5
Cill Chainnigh / Kilkenny [IRL] 4 E4
Cill Charthaigh / Kilcar [IRL] 2 D2
Cill Chiaráin / Kilkieran [IRL] 2 B4
Cilleros [E] 86 G3
Cimadevilla [E] 78 B3
Cimburk [CZ] 50 C5
Cimburk [CZ] 62 G2
Cimino, Monte- [I] 114 H4
Cimitero Militare Britannico [I] 120 D1
Cimochy [PL] 24 E3
Cimoláis [I] 72 F4
Cîmpeni [RO] 204 C4
Çınarcık [TR] 150 F3
Cinco Casas [E] 96 G4
Cindere [TR] 152 F4
Çine [TR] 152 E6
Činěves [CZ] 48 H3
Ciney [B] 30 D5
Cinfães [P] 80 C4
Cingoli [I] 116 C1
Cinigiano [I] 114 F2
Cinisi [I] 126 C1
Cínovec [CZ] 48 E2
Cinquefrondi [I] 124 D6
Cintegabelle [F] 84 H4
Cintei [RO] 76 H4
Cintruénigo [E] 84 A6
Ciółkowo [PL] 36 H2
Circo de Barrosa [E] 84 E5
Cirella [I] 124 C3
Cirencester [GB] 12 G3
Cirey [F] 44 G6
Ciria [E] 90 C3
Ciriè [I] 70 D5
Čirkovicy [RUS] 178 G6
Cirò [I] 124 F4
Cirò Marina [I] 124 F4
Ciron [F] 54 G4
Çırpı [TR] 152 D4
Ciruli [LV] 198 C4
Cisa, Passo della- [I] 110 C3
Cisna [PL] 52 E6
Cisnădie [RO] 204 C5
Cisneros [E] 82 C5
Cista Provo [HR] 144 B2
Cista Velika [HR] 144 A2
Cisterna di Latina [I] 116 B6
Cisternino [I] 122 F3
Cistierna [E] 82 C4
Ciszyca [PL] 38 C3
Citak [TR] 152 E2
Cîteaux, Abbaye de- [F] 56 G4
Çıtlık [TR] 154 D1
Čitluk [BIH] 144 C2
Cittadella [I] 72 D6
Città della Pieve [I] 114 H2
Città del Vaticano [V] 116 A5
Città di Castello [I] 114 H1
Cittaducale [I] 116 B4
Cittanova [I] 124 D7
Città Sant'Angelo [I] 116 D4
Ciudad Iberica [E] 90 C4
Ciudad Real [E] 96 E4
Ciudad Rodrigo [E] 86 H2
Ciudad Romana [E] 94 G4
Ciumeghiu [RO] 76 H3
Ciutadella de Menorca [E] 104 G4
Civica [E] 90 A5
Cividale del Friuli [I] 72 G5
Çivili [TR] 150 E5
Civita [I] 114 H3
Cívita Castellana [I] 116 A4
Civitanova Marche [I] 116 C1
Civitavécchia [I] 114 G5
Civitella del Tronto [I] 116 C3
Civitella di Romagna [I] 110 G5
Civitella in Val di Chiana [I] 114 G1
Civitella Paganico [I] 114 F2
Civitella Roveto [I] 116 C5
Civray [F] 54 E5
Civrieux-d'Azergues [F] 68 F2
Çivril [TR] 152 G4
Clacton-on-Sea [GB] 14 G4
Clairvaux-les-Lacs [F] 70 A1
Clamecy [F] 56 E3
Clamerey [F] 56 F3
Clamouse, Grotte de- [F] 106 E3
Clane [IRL] 2 F6
Clara [IRL] 2 D5
Clarecastle [IRL] 2 C6
Claremorris [IRL] 2 C4
Clarinbridge [IRL] 2 C5
Claros [TR] 152 C5
Clashmore [IRL] 4 D5
Classe [F] 54 D3
Claudy [NIR] 2 F2
Clausholm [DK] 160 E5
Clausthal-Zellerfeld [D] 32 G4
Claviere [I] 70 B6
Cleanovu [RO] 146 F1
Clécy [F] 26 F4
Cleethorpes [GB] 10 G4
Clefmont [F] 58 A2
Clefs [F] 42 B6
Clelles [F] 68 G5
Clementino, Porto- [I] 114 G4
Cléon-d'Andran [F] 68 F6
Clères [F] 28 C5
Clermont [F] 28 E6
Clermont-de-Beauregarde [F] 66 F3
Clermont-en-Argonne [F] 44 D4
Clermont-Ferrand [F] 68 C2
Clermont-l'Hérault [F] 106 E4
Clerval [F] 58 C4
Clervaux [L] 44 F1
Cléry [F] 42 E6
Cles [I] 72 C3
Clevedon [GB] 12 F3
Clifden [IRL] 2 B4
Cliffoney [IRL] 2 D3
Clisson [F] 54 C2
Clitheroe [GB] 10 E3
Clitunno, Fonti del- [I] 116 B3
Clitunno, Tempio del- [I] 116 B3
Clogan [IRL] 2 D6
Clogh [IRL] 4 F3
Clogheen [IRL] 4 D4
Cloghmore / An Chloich Mhór [IRL] 2 B3
Clohars-Carnöet [F] 40 C4
Clonakilty [IRL] 4 C5
Clonalis House [IRL] 2 D4
Clonard [IRL] 2 E5
Clonaslee [IRL] 2 D6
Clonbur / An Fhairche [IRL] 2 C4
Clondalkin [IRL] 2 F6
Clones [IRL] 2 E4
Clonfert [IRL] 2 D5
Clonmacnoise [IRL] 2 D5
Clonmany [IRL] 2 F1
Clonmel / Cluain Meala [IRL] 4 E4
Clonmellon [IRL] 2 E5
Clonroche [IRL] 4 F4
Cloonbannin [IRL] 4 C4
Cloonkeen [IRL] 4 B4
Cloonlara [IRL] 4 D3
Cloppenburg [D] 18 C6
Clough [NIR] 2 G4
Cloughjordan [IRL] 2 D6
Cloyes-sur-le-Loir [F] 42 D5
Cloyne [IRL] 4 D5
Cluain Meala / Clonmel [IRL] 4 E4
Cluina [E] 88 H2
Cluj Napoca [RO] 204 C4
Clun [GB] 10 C6
Cluny [F] 56 F6
Cluses [F] 70 B2
Clusone [I] 72 A5
Ćmielów [PL] 52 D1
Cmolas [PL] 52 D3
Cnocán na Líne / Knocknalina [IRL] 2 C2
Coachford [IRL] 4 C5
Coalville [GB] 10 E6
Coaña [E] 78 F2
Çobanısa [TR] 154 H1
Çobanlar [TR] 152 D2
Cobh [IRL] 4 D5
Coburg [D] 46 G3
Coca [E] 88 E3
Coceges del Monte [E] 88 F2
Cocentaina [E] 104 E1
Cochem [D] 44 G1
Cockermouth [GB] 8 D6
Code [LV] 198 D6
Codigoro [I] 110 G2
Codogno [I] 70 H6
Codos [E] 90 D4
Codróipo [I] 72 G5
Coesfeld [D] 16 H6
Coevorden [NL] 16 G4
Coflans [F] 70 B4
Cofrentes [E] 98 D5
Coghinas [I] 118 D3
Cognac [F] 54 D6
Cogne [I] 70 D4
Cogolin [F] 108 D5
Cogollos [E] 82 E6
Cogolludo [E] 88 H4
Cogul, Cova del- [E] 90 H5
Cohiniac [F] 26 A4
Coimbra [P] 86 D2
Coín [E] 102 B4
Coina [P] 86 B6
Coirós [E] 78 D2
Čoka [SRB] 76 E5
Colares [P] 86 A5
Cölbe [D] 32 D6
Colbitz [D] 34 B2
Colcerasa [I] 116 B1
Colchester [GB] 14 F3
Colditz [D] 34 D6
Coldstream [GB] 8 F4
Colembert [F] 14 G6
Colera [E] 92 G2
Coleraine [NIR] 2 G2
Colfiorito [I] 116 B2
Colfosco [I] 72 E3
Colico [I] 70 G3
Coligny [F] 56 H6
Colindres [E] 82 F3
Colintraive [GB] 8 C2
Collado Villalba [E] 88 F5
Coll de Nargó [E] 92 D2
Collécchio [I] 110 D2
Colledimezzo [I] 116 E5
Colle di Val d'Elsa [I] 114 F1
Colleferro [I] 116 B6
Collegno [I] 70 D5
Colle Isarco / Gossensass [I] 72 D2
Collesalvetti [I] 110 D6
Colle Sannita [I] 120 F2
Collesano [I] 126 E2
Colletorto [I] 116 F6
Colliano [I] 120 G3
Collinée [F] 26 B5
Cóllio [I] 72 B5
Collioure [F] 92 G2
Collodi [I] 110 E5
Collonges [F] 70 A2
Collonges-la-Rouge [F] 66 G3
Collooney [IRL] 2 D3
Colmar [F] 58 D3
Colmars [F] 108 D3
Colmenar [E] 102 C4
Colmenar de Oreja [E] 96 G1
Colmenar Viejo [E] 88 F5
Cologna Véneta [I] 110 F1
Cologne [F] 84 G2
Cologno al Serio [I] 70 H5
Colombey-les-Belles [F] 44 E5
Colombey-les-Deux-Églises [F] 44 C6
Colomiers [F] 84 H3
Colònia de Sant Jordi [E] 104 E6
Colonia Selladores [E] 96 E6
Colorno [I] 110 D2
Colosimi [I] 124 D5
Colunga [E] 82 C2
Colwyn Bay [GB] 10 C4
Comácchio [I] 110 H3
Comana [RO] 148 D1
Comana [RO] 148 G1
Comănești [RO] 204 D4
Comano Terme [I] 72 C4
Coma-ruga [E] 92 C5
Combarro [E] 78 B4
Combeaufontaine [F] 58 B3
Comber [NIR] 2 G4
Combourg [F] 26 C5
Combronde [F] 68 C1
Comburg [D] 46 E6
Comeglians [I] 72 G3
Comelico Superiore [I] 72 F3
Comillas [E] 82 E3
Cómiso [I] 126 F5
Comloşu Mare [RO] 76 F5
Commentry [F] 56 C6
Commequiers [F] 54 B2
Commercy [F] 44 D5
Como [I] 70 G4
Cómpeta [E] 102 D4
Compiègne [F] 28 E6
Comporta [P] 94 C1
Comps-sur-Artuby [F] 108 D4
Comrat [MD] 204 E4
Comunanza [I] 116 C2
Conca [I] 114 B5
Concarneau [F] 40 B3
Concesio [I] 72 B5
Conches-en-Ouche [F] 26 H4
Concordia Sagittaria [I] 72 F5
Condat [F] 68 C3
Condé-en-Brie [F] 42 H3
Condeixa-a-Nova [P] 86 D2
Condé-sur-Noireau [F] 26 E4
Condino [I] 72 B5
Condofuri [I] 124 C8
Condofuri Marina [I] 124 C8
Condom [F] 66 E6
Condove [I] 70 C5
Condrieu [F] 68 F3
Conegliano [I] 72 E5
Conflans en Jarnisy [F] 44 E4
Conflans-sur-Lanterne [F] 58 B3
Confolens [F] 54 F6
Cong [IRL] 2 C4
Congleton [GB] 10 E5
Congosto de Valdavia [E] 82 D4
Congresbury [GB] 12 F3
Conil de la Frontera [E] 100 F5
Conímbriga [P] 86 D2
Coningsby [GB] 10 G5
Conlie [F] 42 B5
Conna [IRL] 4 D5
Connantre [F] 44 B4
Connerré [F] 42 C5
Čonoplja [SRB] 76 D5
Conques [F] 68 B5
Conquista [E] 96 D5
Conquista de la Sierra [E] 96 B2
Conquista del Guadiana [E] 96 A2
Conselice [I] 110 G3
Conselve [I] 110 G1
Consett [GB] 8 F6
Constanța [RO] 204 F5
Constantí [E] 92 C5
Constantina [E] 96 A6
Constantine [F] 44 E3
Consuegra [E] 96 F3
Consuma [I] 110 F5
Contarina [I] 110 H2
Contay [F] 28 E4
Contea [I] 110 F5
Conțești [RO] 148 C2
Contigliano [I] 116 B4
Contis-Plage [F] 66 B5
Contres [F] 54 H2
Contrexéville [F] 58 B2
Controne [I] 120 F4
Contursi Terme [I] 120 F4
Conty [F] 28 D5
Conversano [I] 122 E3
Conwy [GB] 10 C4
Cookstown [NIR] 2 F3
Coole [IRL] 2 E5
Cooraclare [IRL] 2 B6
Cootehill [IRL] 2 F4
Cope [E] 104 B4
Copertino [I] 122 G5
Çöpköy [TR] 150 B3
Copparo [I] 110 G2
Coppenbrügge [D] 32 F3
Corabia [RO] 148 A2
Corato [I] 122 D2
Coray [F] 40 C3
Corbalán [E] 98 E2
Corbeil-Essonnes [F] 42 F4
Corbeny [F] 28 G6
Corbera d'Ebre [E] 90 G6
Corbie [F] 28 E5
Corbigny [F] 56 E3
Corbridge [GB] 8 F6
Corby [GB] 14 E2
Corcaigh / Cork [IRL] 4 C5
Corciano [I] 114 H2
Corcieux [F] 58 D2
Corcomroe Abbey [IRL] 2 C5
Corconne [F] 106 F3
Corconte [E] 82 E4
Corcubión [E] 78 B2
Cordenons [I] 72 F5
Cordes [F] 106 B2
Córdoba [E] 102 C1
Cordobilla de Lácara [E] 86 G6
Corella [E] 84 A6
Cori [I] 116 B6
Coria [E] 86 H3
Coria del Río [E] 94 G6
Coriano [I] 110 H5
Corigliano Calabro [I] 124 E3
Corinaldo [I] 112 C6
Coripe [E] 100 H3
Cork / Corcaigh [IRL] 4 C5
Corlățel [RO] 146 E1
Corlay [F] 26 A4
Corleone [I] 126 C2
Corleto Perticara [I] 120 H4
Çorlu [TR] 150 C3
Cormainville [F] 42 E5
Cormeilles [F] 26 G3
Cormery [F] 54 G2
Cornau [D] 18 D6
Cornellana [E] 78 G3
Córniglio [I] 110 D3
Cornimont [F] 58 D3
Cornuda la Valle [I] 72 E5
Cornudella de Montsant [E] 90 H6
Cornus [I] 118 B5
Corofin [IRL] 2 C6
Corovodë [AL] 128 C5
Corps [F] 68 H6
Corral de Almaguer [E] 96 G2
Corralejo [E] 100 E6
Corrales [E] 80 H5
Corral Rubio [E] 98 C6
Corre [F] 58 B3
Corréggio [I] 110 E2
Corridonia [I] 116 C2
Corsano [I] 122 G6
Corseul [F] 26 C4
Corte [F] 114 B4
Corte Brugnatella [I] 110 C2
Corte Figueira [P] 94 C4
Cortegada [E] 78 C5
Cortegana [E] 94 F4
Cortemaggiore [I] 70 H6
Cortemilia [I] 108 G2
Cortes [E] 90 D3
Cortes de la Frontera [E] 100 H4
Cortes de Pallás [E] 98 D5
Cortes de Peleas [E] 94 G2
Corte Zorrinha [P] 94 C4
Cortijos de Abajo [E] 96 E3
Cortina d'Ampezzo [I] 72 E3
Cortona [I] 114 H1
Coruche [P] 86 C5
Coruña del Conde [E] 88 H2
Corvara in Badia [I] 72 E3
Corvera [E] 104 C3
Corvey [D] 32 F4
Corwen [GB] 10 C5
Cosa [E] 90 D6
Cosa [I] 114 F4
Cosenza [I] 124 D4
Cosne-Cours-sur-Loire [F] 56 D3
Cosne d'Allier [F] 56 C5
Coşoveni [RO] 146 G1
Coşoveni [RO] 146 G1
Cospeito [E] 78 E3
Cossato [I] 70 E4
Cossé-le-Vivien [F] 40 G5
Cossonay [CH] 70 B1
Costa da Caparica [P] 86 A5
Costa de los Pins [E] 104 F5
Costa Nova do Prado [P] 80 B5
Costești [RO] 204 D5
Costigliole Saluzzo [I] 108 F2
Coswig [D] 34 C4
Coswig [D] 34 E6
Cote [E] 100 H3
Cotignac [F] 108 C5
Cotronei [I] 124 E5
Cottbus [D] 34 F4
Couches [F] 56 F5
Couço [P] 86 D5
Coucy-le-Château-Auffrique [F] 28 F6
Coudray-Montbault, Château de- [F] 54 D2
Couflenz [F] 84 G5
Cougnac, Grottes de- [F] 66 G4
Couhé [F] 54 E5
Couilly [F] 42 G3
Couiza [F] 106 B5
Coulanges-la-Vineuse [F] 56 E2
Coulmier-le-Sec [F] 56 G2
Coulommiers [F] 42 G4
Coulon [F] 54 D4
Coulonges [F] 54 D4
Coupar Angus [GB] 8 E2
Couptrain [F] 26 F5
Courboyer, Manoir de- [F] 26 G6
Courceau [F] 56 G3
Courchevel [F] 70 B4
Cour-Cheverny [F] 54 H2
Courçon [F] 54 C4
Cour-et-Buis [F] 68 G4
Courgains [F] 26 F6
Courmayeur [I] 70 C3
Courpière [F] 68 D2
Courriere [B] 30 D5
Coursan [F] 106 D5
Courseulles-sur-Mer [F] 26 F3
Cours-la-Ville [F] 68 F2
Courson-les-Carrières [F] 56 E2
Courtacon [F] 42 H4
Courtanvaux, Château de- [F] 42 C6
Courteilles [F] 26 G4
Courtelevant [F] 58 D4
Courtenay [F] 42 G6
Courtmacsherry [IRL] 4 C5
Courtomer [F] 26 G5
Courtown Harbour [IRL] 4 G4
Courtrai (Kortrijk) [B] 28 G2
Courville [F] 26 H6
Coutances [F] 26 D3
Couterne [F] 26 E5
Coutevroult [F] 42 G4
Coutras [F] 66 D3
Couvet [CH] 58 C6
Couvin [B] 28 H5
Covadonga [E] 82 C2
Covadonga [E] 82 C2
Covaleda [E] 90 B2
Covarrubias [E] 88 H1
Covarrubias [E] 90 B3
Covăsinț [RO] 76 H4
Covci [RO] 146 F2
Coventry [GB] 14 D2
Covide [P] 78 B6
Covilhã [P] 86 F2
Cowes [GB] 12 H5
Cox [F] 84 H2
Cózar [E] 96 G5
Cozes [F] 54 C6
Cozia, Mănăstirea- [RO] 204 C5
Cozzano [F] 114 B5
Craco [I] 122 D4
Craigavon [NIR] 2 G4
Crail [GB] 8 F3
Crailsheim [D] 46 E6
Craiova [RO] 76 H3
Craiova [RO] 146 G1
Crângeni [RO] 148 B1
Crângu [RO] 148 B2
Crans [CH] 70 D2
Craon [F] 40 G5
Craponne-sur-Arzon [F] 68 D3
Crato [P] 86 E5
Craughwell [IRL] 2 C5
Crawley [GB] 14 E5
Crea, Santuario di- [I] 70 E6
Crêches-sur-Saône [F] 68 F1
Crécy [F] 42 G4
Crécy-en-Ponthieu [F] 28 D3
Crécy-sur-Serre [F] 28 G6
Crediton [GB] 12 E4
Creevagh [IRL] 2 C3
Creglingen [D] 46 E5
Creil [F] 42 G2
Crema [I] 70 H5
Cremaste [TR] 150 B5
Crémieu [F] 68 G3
Cremona [I] 110 D1
Črenšovci [SLO] 74 F3
Créon [F] 66 D3
Crepaja [SRB] 142 G2
Crépy-en-Valois [F] 42 G3
Cres [HR] 112 E2
Crésantignes [F] 44 A6
Crescentino [I] 70 E5
Crespin [F] 28 G4
Crespino [I] 110 G2
Cressensac [F] 66 G3
Cresslough [IRL] 2 E1
Crest [F] 68 F6
Cresta [CH] 70 H2
Creussen [D] 46 H4
Creutzwald [F] 44 F4
Creuzburg [D] 32 G6
Crevalcore [I] 110 F3
Crevecœur-en-Auge [F] 26 G4
Crevecoeur [F] 28 D5
Crevillent / Crevillente [E] 104 D2
Crevillente / Crevillent [E] 104 D2
Crevoladossola [I] 70 E3
Crewe [GB] 10 D5
Crewkerne [GB] 12 F4
Criação Velha [P] 100 C3
Crianlarich [GB] 8 D2
Cricklade [GB] 12 H3
Crieff [GB] 8 E2
Crikvenica [HR] 112 F2
Crillon [F] 28 D5
Crimmitschau [D] 48 C1
Črišnjeva [HR] 112 F2
Crispiano [I] 122 E4
Crissolo [I] 108 F2
Cristo, Monasterio del- [E] 78 G3
Cristo del Espíritu-Santo [E] 96 E3
Crivitz [D] 20 A4
Crkvice [BIH] 142 D4
Crkvina [BIH] 142 D2
Crkvina Prolaz [MNE] 144 E3
Crmljan [SRB] 146 B5
Črmošnjice [SLO] 74 C6
Črna [SLO] 74 C4
Crna Bara [SRB] 76 E5
Crna Trava [SRB] 146 E4
Crnča [SRB] 142 F4
Crni Lug [BIH] 142 B4
Crni Vrh [SLO] 74 B5
Črnkovci [HR] 76 B6
Crnokliště [SRB] 146 E3
Črnomelj [SLO] 74 D6
Crocq [F] 68 B1
Crodo [I] 70 F2
Croithlí / Crolly [IRL] 2 E2
Croix Haute, Col de la- [F] 68 G6
Crolly / Croithlí [IRL] 2 E2
Cro-Magnon [F] 66 F3
Cromarty [GB] 6 E4
Cromer [GB] 14 G1
Crook [GB] 10 F1
Crookedwood [IRL] 2 E5
Crookhaven [IRL] 4 B5
Crookstown [IRL] 4 C5
Croom [IRL] 4 D3
Cropalati [I] 124 E4
Cropani [I] 124 E5
Crosia [I] 124 E4
Crossakeel [IRL] 2 E5
Crosshaven [IRL] 4 D5
Crossmaglen [NIR] 2 F4
Crossmolina [IRL] 2 C3
Crotone [I] 124 F5
Crowborough [GB] 14 E5
Croydon [GB] 14 E4
Crozant [F] 54 G5
Crozon [F] 40 B2
Cruas [F] 68 F6
Cruceni [RO] 142 H1
Cruces [E] 78 C3
Crucoli [I] 124 F4
Crumlin [NIR] 2 G3
Cruseilles [F] 70 B2
Crusheen [IRL] 2 C6
Cruzy [F] 56 F2
Cruzy [F] 106 D4
Crvenka [MNE] 204 A5
Crvenka [SRB] 76 D6
Csabacsüd [H] 76 F3
Csákánydoroszló [H] 74 F2
Csakvár [H] 76 B1
Csanádapáca [H] 76 F3
Csanádpalota [H] 76 F4
Csanytelek [H] 76 E3
Csapod [H] 62 G6
Csárdaszállás [H] 76 F2
Császártöltés [H] 76 C4
Csávoly [H] 76 C4

Csépa [H] 76 E3
Cserebökény [H] 76 E3
Cserepes [H] 64 G6
Cserkeszőlő [H] 76 E2
Csernely [H] 64 E4
Csesznek [H] 76 A1
Csobád [H] 64 F4
Csókakői Várrom [H] 76 B1
Csökmő [H] 76 G2
Csokonyavisonta [H] 74 H5
Csongrád [H] 76 E3
Csopak [H] 76 A2
Csór [H] 76 B2
Csorna [H] 62 G6
Csorvás [H] 76 F3
Csót [H] 74 H1
Csurgó [H] 74 G4
Cuadros [E] 78 H5
Cualedro [E] 78 D6
Cuba [P] 94 D2
Cubel [E] 90 C5
Cubells [E] 92 C3
Cubo de Bureba [E] 82 F5
Çubukdağı [TR] 152 F5
Çubuklu [TR] 154 F1
Cudillero [E] 78 G3
Cuéllar [E] 88 F2
Cuenca [E] 98 B2
Cuers [F] 108 C5
Cuerva [E] 96 E2
Cuesta Blanca de Arriba [E] 104 C4
Cuevas del Almanzora [E] 102 H4
Cuevas del Becerro [E] 102 B4
Cuevas de San Clemente [E] 88 H1
Cuevas de San Marcos [E] 102 C3
Cúglieri [I] 118 C4
Cugnon-sur-Semois [B] 44 D2
Cuhom [F] 28 E3
Cuijk [NL] 16 E6
Cuillé [F] 40 G4
Cuiseaux [F] 56 H6
Cuisery [F] 56 G6
Cujmir [RO] 146 E1
Çukurhisar [TR] 150 H5
Çukurköi [TR] 150 B2
Çukurköy [TR] 152 G5
Çukurören [TR] 152 G2
Culaccio [I] 110 D4
Culan [F] 56 B5
Culdaff [IRL] 2 F1
Culemborg [NL] 16 E5
Cúllar [E] 102 G3
Cullen [GB] 6 F5
Cullera [E] 98 F5
Cullompton [GB] 12 E4
Culoz [F] 68 H3
Cuma [I] 120 D3
Cumbernauld [GB] 8 D3
Cumbres de S. Bartolomé [E] 94 F4
Cumbres Mayores [E] 94 F4
Čumić [SRB] 146 B2
Cumnock [GB] 8 D4
Cunault [F] 54 E2
Cúneo [I] 108 F3
Čunište [BIH] 142 D4
Čunski [HR] 112 E3
Cuntis [E] 78 B3
Cuorgnè [I] 70 D5
Cupar [GB] 8 F2
Cupello [I] 116 E5
Cupra Marittima [I] 116 D2
Cupramontana [I] 116 B1
Ćuprija [SRB] 146 C2
Cura, Santuari de- [E] 104 E5
Cura Nuova [I] 114 E2
Curel [F] 108 C3
Curia [P] 80 B6
Ćurlovac [HR] 74 G5
Curon Venosta / Graun im Vinschgau [I] 72 B2
Curraghmore [IRL] 4 E5
Curtatone [I] 110 E1
Curtea de Argeş [RO] 204 D5
Curtici [RO] 76 G4
Curtis [E] 78 D2
Ćurug [SRB] 142 G1
Cusset [F] 68 D1
Custines [F] 44 E5
Custonaci [I] 126 B2
Cutigliano [I] 110 E4
Cutro [I] 124 F5
Cutting [F] 44 F5
Çüvenli [TR] 150 C2
Cuveşdia [RO] 76 H5
Cuvilly [F] 28 E6
Cuxhaven [D] 18 D3
Cuzzola [I] 118 E3
Cvikov [CZ] 48 G2
Cwmbran [GB] 12 F2
Cybinka [PL] 34 G3
Cyców [PL] 38 F5
Cytonium [TR] 152 C2
Czacz [PL] 36 C3
Czajków [PL] 36 E5
Czaplinek [PL] 22 A5
Czarna [PL] 38 D4
Czarna Białostocka [PL] 24 F5
Czarna Białostocka [PL] 24 F5
Czarna Dąbrówka [PL] 22 C2
Czarna Górna [PL] 52 F5
Czarna Woda [PL] 22 D4
Czarne [PL] 22 B4
Czarnków [PL] 36 C1
Czarnożyły [PL] 36 F6
Czarny Dunajec [PL] 50 H5
Czastary [PL] 36 E6
Czchów [PL] 52 B4
Czechowice-Dziedzice [PL] 50 G4
Czeladź [PL] 50 G3
Czemierniki [PL] 38 E4
Czempiń [PL] 36 C3
Czeremcha [PL] 38 F2
Czerniejewo [PL] 36 D2
Czernikowo [PL] 36 F1
Czernin [PL] 22 E4
Czersk [PL] 22 D4
Czersk [PL] 38 C3
Czerwieńsk [PL] 34 H4
Czerwionka-Leszczyny [PL] 50 F3
Czerwony-Dwór [PL] 24 D3
Częstochowa [PL] 50 G1
Człopa [PL] 20 H6
Człuchów [PL] 22 C4
Czorsztyn [PL] 52 B5
Czudec [PL] 52 D4
Czyżew-Osada [PL] 38 D1

D

Daaden [D] 32 C6
Dabarska Spilja [BIH] 142 B3
Dabas [H] 76 C2
Dabern [D] 34 E4
Dąbie [PL] 20 F5
Dąbie [PL] 36 F3
Dabilja [MK] 128 G2
Dąbki [PL] 22 A2
Dąbki [PL] 36 C5
Dabo [F] 44 G5
Dabo, Roch. de- [F] 44 G5
Dăbovan [BG] 148 A2
Dăbovo [BG] 148 C4
Dąbrowa [PL] 36 E1
Dąbrowa [PL] 36 F4
Dąbrowa [PL] 38 E2
Dąbrowa [PL] 50 E2
Dąbrowa Białostocka [PL] 24 F4
Dąbrowa Górnicza [PL] 50 G3
Dąbrowa Tarnowska [PL] 52 C3
Dąbrówca Warszawska [PL] 38 C5
Dąbrówka [PL] 52 E2
Dąbrówka Kościelna [PL] 24 E6
Dąbrówka Leśna [PL] 36 C2
Dąbrówka Wielkopolska [PL] 36 A3
Dąbrówno [PL] 22 G5
Dăbuleni [RO] 146 G2
Dachau [D] 60 E4
Dachnów [PL] 52 F3
Dachsteinhöhlen [A] 62 A6
Dačice [CZ] 62 D2
Dad [H] 64 B6
Dadaglı [TR] 152 F4
Dädesjö [S] 162 E4
Dáfnes [GR] 132 F6
Dáfni [GR] 130 D5
Dáfni [GR] 130 F6
Dafní [GR] 134 B6
Dáfni [GR] 136 D2
Dafnónas [GR] 130 E2
Dafnotí [GR] 132 D2
Dağakça [TR] 150 F5
Dagali [N] 170 F4
Dağardı [TR] 152 F1
Dagda [LV] 198 G6
Dagebüll [D] 156 B5
Dağkızılca [TR] 152 D4
Dahlem [D] 30 F6
Dahlen [D] 34 D5
Dahlenburg [D] 18 G5
Dahme [D] 18 H2
Dahme [D] 34 E4
Dahmen [D] 20 C4
Dahn [D] 44 H4
Dähre [D] 32 H1
Daia [RO] 148 C1
Daikanvik [S] 190 F4
Daimiel [E] 96 F4
Daimoniá [GR] 136 F5
Daingean [IRL] 2 E6
Đakovica / Gjakove [SRB] 146 B6
Đakovo [HR] 142 D1
Daksti [LV] 198 E4
Dal [N] 170 F6
Dal [N] 172 C5
Dala [S] 166 F6
Dalaas [A] 72 B1
Dala-Floda [S] 172 G4
Dala-Husby [S] 174 D5
Dala-Järna [S] 172 G4
Dalama [TR] 152 E5
Dalaman [TR] 154 E2
Dalarö [S] 168 E3
Dalbeattie [GB] 8 D5
Dalberg [D] 44 H2
Dalby [DK] 156 G3
Dalby [S] 158 C3
Dalbyn [S] 172 H3
Dale [GB] 12 D1
Dale [N] 164 E3
Dale [N] 170 B3
Dale [N] 170 B1
Dale [N] 180 C4
Dalen [N] 164 E2
Dalen [N] 180 H3
Daleszyce [PL] 52 C1
Dalfors [S] 172 H2
Dalhem [S] 162 F1
Dalhem [S] 168 G4
Dalholen [N] 180 H5
Dalías [E] 102 F5
Daliowa [PL] 52 D5
Dalj [HR] 142 E1
Daljani [BIH] 144 C1
Dalkeith [GB] 8 E3
Dalkey [IRL] 2 F6
Dalmine [I] 70 H4
Dalmose [DK] 156 F3
Daløy [N] 170 A2
Dalry [GB] 8 C3
Dalsbruk / Taalintehdas [FIN] 176 E6
Dalselv [N] 190 E2
Dalseter [N] 170 G1
Dalseter [N] 180 H4
Dalsjöfors [S] 162 B2
Dalskog [S] 166 D4
Dals Långed [S] 166 D4
Dals Rostock [S] 166 D4
Dalstein [F] 44 F3
Daluis, Gorges de- [F] 108 E3
Dalum [S] 162 C1
Dalvík [IS] 192 C2
Daly [CY] 154 G5
Dalyan [TR] 130 H6
Dalyan [TR] 154 E2
Damási [GR] 132 F1
Damaskiniá [GR] 128 E5
Damasławek [PL] 36 D1
Damba [N] 180 G5
Dambaslar [TR] 150 C3
Dambeck [D] 20 C5
Dammartin-en-Goële [F] 42 G3
Damme [B] 28 G1
Damme [D] 32 D1
Dammen [N] 164 G2
Dammendorf [D] 34 G3
Damno [PL] 22 C2
Damp 2000 [D] 18 F1
Damparis [F] 56 H4
Dampierre [F] 42 F4
Dampierre [F] 58 A5
Dampierre-sur-Boutonne [F] 54 D5
Dampierre-sur-Salon [F] 58 A4
Damville [F] 26 H5
Damvillers [F] 44 D3
D. Andrijevci [HR] 142 D2
Dăneasa [RO] 148 A1
Daneţi [RO] 146 G2
Dângebo [S] 162 E5
Dangé-St-Romain [F] 54 F3
Danilov [RUS] 202 F1
Danilovgrad [MNE] 144 E4
Danişment [TR] 150 D5
Daniszyn [PL] 36 D5
Danków [PL] 34 H1
Dannäs [S] 162 C4
Dannemarie [F] 58 D4
Dannenberg [D] 18 H5
Dannenwalde [D] 20 D6
Dannike [S] 162 B2
Dánszentmiklós [H] 76 D2
Daon [F] 40 H5
Daoulas [F] 40 B2
Darabani [RO] 204 D3
Darány [H] 74 H5
Darbėnai [LT] 200 D4
Darbu [N] 164 G1
Darda [HR] 76 C6
Dardesheim [D] 32 H3
Dardhë [AL] 128 D5
Darfo [I] 72 B5
Dargilan, Grotte de- [F] 106 E2
Dargun [D] 20 C3
Darıca [TR] 150 D5
Darıca [TR] 150 F3
Darıçayırı [TR] 150 H2
Dariveren [TR] 152 G6
Därligen [CH] 70 E1
Darlington [GB] 10 F2
Darłówko [PL] 22 A2
Darłowo [PL] 22 A2
Darmstadt [D] 46 C3
Darney [F] 58 B2
Darnius [E] 92 G2
Daroca [E] 90 D5
Darque [P] 78 A6
Darro [E] 102 E3
Dartford [GB] 14 E4
Dartmouth [GB] 12 E5
Dartsel [S] 190 H3
Daruvar [HR] 74 G6
Darvas [H] 76 G2
Darwen [GB] 10 E3
Dasburg [D] 44 F1
Dashkavichy [BY] 24 H6
Dašice [CZ] 50 B4
Dasing [D] 60 D3
Daskalovo [BG] 146 F5
Dasochóri [GR] 130 E3
Dassel [D] 32 F4
Dassow [D] 18 H3
Dasswang [D] 46 H6
Daszyna [PL] 36 G3
Datça [TR] 154 C2
Datteln [D] 30 H2
Daugai [LT] 24 G2
Daugård [DK] 156 C2
Daugavpils [LV] 200 H3
Dauguli [LV] 198 E4
Daun [D] 30 G6
Dautphetal [D] 32 D6
Daventry [GB] 14 D2
Daviá [GR] 136 D2
Davik [N] 180 B5
Daviot [GB] 6 D5
Davle [CZ] 48 F4
Davleia [GR] 132 H5
Davlós (Kaplıca) [CY] 154 G4
Davos [CH] 72 A2
Davutlar [TR] 152 D5
Dawlish [GB] 12 E5
Dax [F] 66 B6
Dazkırı [TR] 152 H4
D. Bukovina [SRB] 142 F4
Ddrinci [BG] 148 F2
Deal [GB] 14 G5
Deão [P] 78 A6
Deauville [F] 26 G3
Debar [MK] 128 C2
Debeburnu [TR] 152 D2
Debelets [BG] 148 C3
Dębe Wielkie [PL] 38 C3
Dębica [PL] 52 D3
Dębina [PL] 50 E3
Dęblin [PL] 38 D5
Debnevo [BG] 148 B4
Dębnica Kaszubska [PL] 22 B2
Dębno [PL] 34 G1
Dębno [PL] 52 B4
Dębno [PL] 52 B5
Debovo [BG] 148 B2
Dębowo [PL] 24 E4
Debrc [SRB] 142 F3
Debrecen [H] 64 G6
Debrznica [PL] 34 H3
Debrzno [PL] 22 C5
Debür [BG] 148 C6
Dęby [PL] 24 C5
Dečani [SRB] 146 B5
Decazeville [F] 68 A5
Dechtice [SK] 62 H3
Decimomannu [I] 118 C7
Děčín [CZ] 48 F2
Decines [F] 68 G3
Decize [F] 56 D4
De Cocksdorp [NL] 16 D2
Dedaj [AL] 144 E4
Dedebağı [TR] 152 G6
Dedelow [D] 20 E5
Dedemsvaart [NL] 16 G4
Dédestapolcsány [H] 64 E4
Dedinci [BG] 148 D3
Dedino [MK] 128 G2
Dedovichi [RUS] 202 B2
Defile de L'Ecluse [F] 70 A2
Dég [H] 76 B3
Degaña [E] 78 F4
Degeberga [S] 158 D2
Degerby [FIN] 168 G1
Degerby [FIN] 176 G5
Degerfors [S] 166 G3
Degerhamn [S] 162 G6
Degerndorf [D] 60 F5
Degernes [N] 166 C3
Deggendorf [D] 60 G2
Değirmenalanı [TR] 152 F6
Değirmendere [TR] 150 G3
Değirmendere [TR] 152 C5
Değirmenyan [TR] 154 D2
Değirmisaz [TR] 152 F1
Dego [N] 194 D1
De Haan [B] 28 F1
Dehesa de Campoamor [E] 104 D3
Deià / Deyá [E] 104 E4
Deidesheim [D] 46 B5
Deifontes [E] 102 E3
Deining [D] 46 H6
Deinze [B] 28 G2
Deizisau [D] 58 H1
Dej [RO] 204 C4
Deje [S] 166 F2
Dekéleia [CY] 154 G5
De Koog [NL] 16 D2
De Kooy [NL] 16 D2
Dekov [BG] 148 B2
Delary [S] 162 C5
Delbrück [D] 32 D3
Delčevo [MK] 128 G1
Delden [NL] 16 G5
Delebäck [S] 166 F4
Delégyháza [H] 76 C1
Deleitosa [E] 96 C1
Đelekovec [HR] 74 G4
Delémont [CH] 58 D5
Delfoí [GR] 132 G5
Delfoí [GR] 132 G5
Delft [NL] 16 C5
Delfzijl [NL] 16 H2
Délia [I] 126 E4
Delianuova [I] 124 C7
Deliatyn [UA] 204 C3
Deliblato [SRB] 142 H2
Deliceto [I] 120 G2
Deliler [TR] 152 E3
Delitzsch [D] 34 C5
Dellach [A] 72 G3
Delle [F] 58 D4
Delme [F] 44 F5
Delmenhorst [D] 18 D5
Delnice [HR] 112 F1
Delouze-Rosières [F] 44 D5
Delsbo [S] 184 D6
Delvin [IRL] 2 E5
Delvina [AL] 132 B1
Delvináki [GR] 132 C1
Demandice [SK] 64 C4
Demänová [SK] 64 D2
Demänovská Jaskyňa Slobody [SK] 64 D2
Demecser [H] 64 H4
Demidov [RUS] 202 C4
Demigny [F] 56 G5
Demirci [TR] 150 F5
Demirci [TR] 152 E2
Demirhanlı [TR] 150 B2
Demir Kapija [MK] 128 G2
Demirköy [TR] 150 C1
Demirköy [TR] 150 G5
Demirören [TR] 152 G3
Demirtaş [TR] 150 F4
Demjansk [RUS] 202 C2
Demmin [D] 20 C3
Demoiselles, Grotte des- [F] 106 E3
Demonte [I] 108 F3
Demre [TR] 154 H3
Demyansk [RUS] 202 C2
Denain [F] 28 G4
Den Andel [NL] 16 G1
Denbigh [GB] 10 C4
Den Burg [NL] 16 D2
Dendermonde (Termonde) [B] 28 H2
Denekamp [NL] 16 G4
Đeneral Janković [SRB] 146 C6
Den Haag [NL] 16 C5
Den Helder [NL] 16 D2
Dénia [E] 104 F1
Denizgören [TR] 150 B5
Denizkent [TR] 150 C5
Denizköy [TR] 150 H2
Denizler [TR] 152 G4
Denizli [TR] 152 G5
Denkendorf [D] 60 E2
Denkingen [D] 58 H3
Den Oever [NL] 16 E2
Denzlingen [D] 58 E3
De Panne [B] 28 F1
Derbent [TR] 152 E4
Derby [GB] 10 E5
Derebağ [TR] 152 E6
Derecske [H] 76 G1
Dereham [GB] 14 G2
Dereköy [TR] 150 C1
Dereköy [TR] 152 E4
Dereköy [TR] 152 F2
Dereköy [TR] 152 G6
Dereköy [TR] 152 H5
Dereli [TR] 150 E6
Dereli [TR] 150 H4
Deringaj [HR] 112 H4
Dermantsi [BG] 148 A3
Dermbach [D] 46 F1
Dermulo [I] 72 C4
Derneburg [D] 32 G3
Deronje [SRB] 142 E1
Derreada [P] 94 B3
Derry (Londonderry) [NIR] 2 F2
Deruta [I] 116 A2
Derval [F] 40 F5
Dervéni [GR] 132 G6
Derventa [BIH] 142 D2
Dervishka mogila [BG] 150 A1
Descartes [F] 54 F3
Desenzano del Garda [I] 72 B6
Deset [N] 172 C2
Desfina [GR] 132 G5
Desimirovac [SRB] 146 C2
Desio [I] 70 G4
Deskáti [GR] 132 F1
Deskle [SLO] 72 H5
Desmond's Castle [IRL] 4 D3
Desná [CZ] 48 H2
Dešov [CZ] 62 E2
Despeñaperros [E] 96 F6
Despotovac [SRB] 146 C2
Despotovo [SRB] 142 F1
Dessau [D] 34 C4
Deštné [CZ] 50 B3
Destriana [E] 78 G6
Destrnik [SLO] 74 E4
Désulo [I] 118 D5
Desvres [F] 28 D2
Deszk [H] 76 E4
Deta [RO] 204 B5
Detk [H] 64 E5
Detkovo [RUS] 198 G2
Detmold [D] 32 E3
Dětřichov nad Bystřicí [CZ] 50 D4
Dettelbach [D] 46 F4
Dettifoss [IS] 192 C2
Detva [SK] 64 D3
Deurne [NL] 30 F2
Deutschkreutz [A] 62 F6
Deutschlandsberg [A] 74 D3
Deutsch-Wagram [A] 62 F4
Deva [E] 82 H4
Deva [RO] 204 C5
Dévaványa [H] 76 F2
Devčići [HR] 112 F3
Devecikonağı [TR] 150 E5
Devecser [H] 74 H2
Devene [BG] 146 G3
Deventer [NL] 16 F5
Deveselu [RO] 148 A1
Devetaki [BG] 148 B3
Devic [MK] 128 E2
Devin [BG] 130 D1
Devizes [GB] 12 G3
Devnya [BG] 148 F3
Dewsbury [GB] 10 F4
Deyá / Deià [E] 104 E4
Deza [E] 90 C4
Dezzo [I] 72 B4
Dhërmi [AL] 128 B6
Diafáni [GR] 140 H2
Diagučiai [LT] 200 G4
Diakoftó [GR] 132 G6
Dialampí [GR] 130 F3
Diamante [I] 124 C3
Dianalund [DK] 156 F3
Diano Marina [I] 108 G4
Diarvialiai [LT] 200 F4
Diásello [GR] 132 F1
Diatlovo [BY] 202 A6
Diavatá [GR] 128 H4
Dicomano [I] 110 F5
Didcot [GB] 14 D3
Didesti [RO] 148 B1
Dídyma [GR] 136 F2
Didymóteicho [GR] 130 H1
Die [F] 68 G6
Dieburg [D] 46 C3
Diedorf [D] 32 G5
Diego Alvaro [E] 88 D4
Diekirch [L] 44 F2
Diemelstadt [D] 32 E4
Dienne [F] 68 B4
Dienten [A] 72 G1
Diepholz [D] 32 D1
Dieppe [F] 28 C4
Dierdorf [D] 46 B1
Dieren [NL] 16 F5
Dierhagen [D] 20 C2
Diesdorf [D] 32 H1
Diessen [D] 60 D5
Diest [B] 30 D4
Dietenheim [D] 60 B4
Dietfurt [D] 46 H6
Dietikon [CH] 58 F5
Dietmannsdorf [A] 74 D3
Dietmannsried [D] 60 C5
Dieue-sur-Meuse [F] 44 D4
Dieulefit [F] 68 F6
Dieulouard [F] 44 E5
Dieuze [F] 44 F5
Dieveniškės [LT] 200 G6
Diever [NL] 16 G3
Diez [D] 46 B2
Differdange [L] 44 E3
Digerberget [S] 182 G4
Digermulen [N] 192 D4
Digernes [N] 180 D3
Dignac [F] 66 E2
Dignano [I] 72 G4
Digne-les-Bains [F] 108 D3
Digny [F] 26 H6
Digoin [F] 56 E5
Dijon [F] 56 G4
Díkaia [GR] 150 A2
Dikanäs [S] 190 F4
Dikance [SRB] 128 C1
Dikili [TR] 152 C3
Dikli [LV] 198 E4
Diksmuide [B] 28 F2
Diktaío Ántro [GR] 140 F5
Diktýnaion [GR] 140 B4
Dílesi [GR] 134 C5
Dillenberg [D] 32 D6
Dillingen [D] 44 F3
Dillingen [D] 60 C3
Dílos [GR] 138 E2
Dilwyn [GB] 12 G1
Dímaina [GR] 136 F2
Dimaro [I] 72 C4
Dímitra [GR] 132 G1
Dimitrovgrad [BG] 148 C6
Dimitrovgrad [SRB] 146 E4
Dimmelsvik [N] 170 B5
Dimovo [BG] 146 E2
Dinami [I] 124 D6
Dinan [F] 26 C5
Dinant [B] 30 D6
Dinar [TR] 152 H4
Dinard [F] 26 C4
Dingelstädt [D] 32 G5
Dingle [S] 166 C5
Dingle / An Daingean [IRL] 4 A3
Dingli [M] 126 C6
Dingolfing [D] 60 F3
Dingwall [GB] 6 D4
Dinkelsbühl [D] 46 F6
Dinklage [D] 18 C6
Dinozé [F] 58 C2
Dinslaken [D] 30 G2
Dio [S] 162 D5
Díon [GR] 128 G6
Diosgyőr [H] 64 F4
Dipkarpaz (Rizokárpasox) [CY] 154 H4
Dipótamos [GR] 130 D2
Dippoldiswalde [D] 48 E1
Dirgenler [TR] 154 H3
Dirnaich [D] 60 F3
Disenå [N] 172 C5
Disentis / Mustér [CH] 70 G1
Disneyland [F] 42 G3
Dispílì [GR] 128 E5
Diss [GB] 14 G2
Dístomo [GR] 132 H5
Dístrato [GR] 128 D6
Ditzingen [D] 58 G1
Diva Slatina [BG] 146 F3
Divci [SRB] 146 A1
Divčibare [SRB] 146 A2
Dívčí Hrady [CZ] 62 F2
Dives-sur-Mer [F] 26 F3
Divič [SRB] 142 E3
Divínski Hrad [SK] 64 D4
Divjakë [AL] 128 A4
Divonne-les-Bains [F] 70 B2
Dívri [GR] 132 G4
Divuša [HR] 142 A2
Dixence [CH] 70 D3
Dizy-le-Gros [F] 28 G6
Djäkneböle [S] 190 H6
Djala [SRB] 76 E4
Djauvik [S] 168 F5
Djupfest [N] 190 B6
Djupfors [S] 190 F3
Djúpivogur [IS] 192 C3
Djupsjö [S] 182 F1
Djupvik [N] 192 G2
Djura [S] 172 H4
Djurakovac [SRB] 146 B5
Djuramåla [DK] 162 E6
Djurås [S] 172 H4
D. Kronovo [SLO] 74 D5
Dłoń [PL] 36 C4
Dlouhá Loučka [CZ] 50 D4
Długie [PL] 36 A1
Długołęka [PL] 36 D6
Długosiodło [PL] 38 C1
Dmitriyev-L'govckiy [RUS] 202 F5
Dmitrov [RUS] 202 F2
Dmitrovsk-Orlovskiy [RUS] 202 F5
Dniprodzerzhyns'k [UA] 204 G1
Dnipropetrovs'k [UA] 204 H1
Dniprorudne [UA] 204 H2
Dno [RUS] 202 B2
Dobanovci [SRB] 142 G2
Dobapuszta [H] 76 E1
Dobbiaco / Toblach [I] 72 E3
Dobbrikow [D] 34 D3
Dobczyce [PL] 52 A4
Dobel [D] 58 G1
Dobele [LV] 198 D5
Döbeln [D] 34 D6
Doberlug Kirchhain [D] 34 E4
Döbern [D] 34 G5
Dobersberg [A] 62 D2
Dobiegniew [PL] 20 H6
Doboj [BIH] 142 D3
Doboz [H] 76 G3
Dobra [PL] 20 G4
Dobra [PL] 36 F4
Dobra [PL] 52 B4
Dobra [RO] 146 F1
Dobra Gora [MNE] 144 D4
Dobrá Niva [SK] 64 C3
Dobřany [CZ] 48 D5
Dobrčane [SRB] 146 D5
Dobrcz [PL] 22 D5
Dobre [PL] 38 C2
Dobre Miasto [PL] 22 G3
Döbriach [A] 72 H3
Dobrich [BG] 148 F2
Dobřichovice [CZ] 48 F4
Dobri Do [SRB] 146 C4
Dobri dol [BG] 146 F2
Dobrin [BG] 148 F1
Dobrinishte [BG] 130 B1
Dobrinja [BIH] 142 B3
Dobříš [CZ] 48 F4
Dobrits [BG] 148 E5
Dobrna [SLO] 74 D4
Dobrodan [BG] 148 B4
Dobrodzień [PL] 50 F2
Döbrököz [H] 76 B4
Dobromani [BIH] 144 C3
Dobromierz [PL] 50 B1
Dobromierz [PL] 50 H1
Dobromirka [BG] 148 C3
Dobromirtsi [BG] 130 F2
Dobromyl' [UA] 52 F5
Dobro Polje [BIH] 144 D2
Dobroselica [SRB] 146 A3
Dobrošinci [MK] 128 G2
Dobrosloveni [RO] 148 A1
Dobrosołowo [PL] 36 E3
Dobrosyn [UA] 52 H3
Dobroszyce [PL] 36 D6
Dobroteşti [RO] 148 B1
Dobrotitsa [BG] 148 E1
Dobrovelychkivka [UA] 204 F2
Dobrovnik [SLO] 74 F3
Dobrovodsky Hrad [SK] 62 H3
Dobrovol'sk [RUS] 24 D1
Dobrš [CZ] 48 E6
Dobruchi [RUS] 198 G2
Dobrun [BIH] 144 E1
Dobrush [BY] 202 D6
Dobrush [UA] 202 D6
Dobruška [CZ] 50 B3
Dobrzany [PL] 20 G5
Dobrzejewice [PL] 22 E6
Dobrzeń Wielki [PL] 50 E2
Dobrzyca [PL] 36 D4
Dobrzyń nad Wisłą [PL] 36 G2
Dobšinská l'Adová Jaskyňa [SK] 64 E2
Dóc [H] 76 E4
Dochamps [B] 30 E6
Dockasberg [S] 196 B2
Docksta [S] 184 F2
Doclea [MNE] 144 E4
Dödafallet [S] 184 D3
Döderhult [S] 162 G3
Dodóni [GR] 132 D2
Dodši [HR] 142 A1
Dodurga [TR] 150 G5
Doe Castle [IRL] 2 E1
Doesburg [NL] 16 F5
Doetinchem [NL] 16 F5
Doganbey [TR] 152 C6
Doğanbey [TR] 152 C5
Doganović [SRB] 146 C6
Döge [H] 64 H4
Döğer [TR] 152 H1
Dogliani [I] 108 G2
Dogueno [P] 94 C4
Dohňany [SK] 50 E6
Doiber [A] 74 E2
Dojč [SK] 62 G3
Dojeviće [SRB] 146 B4
Dojrenci [BG] 148 B3
Dokka [N] 170 H3
Dokkas [S] 192 H6
Dokkedal [DK] 160 E4
Dokkum [NL] 16 F2
Doksy [CZ] 48 G2
Doktorce [PL] 24 E6
Dolac [SRB] 146 B5
Dólar [E] 102 F4
Dolceácqua [I] 108 F4
Dol-de-Bretagne [F] 26 C4
Dole [F] 56 H4
Dølemo [N] 164 E4
Dolenci [MK] 128 D3
Dolenja Vas [SLO] 74 C6
Dolga Vas [SLO] 74 F3
Dolgellau [GB] 10 B5
Dolgorukovo [RUS] 22 G2
Dolhobyczów [PL] 52 H2
Doli [HR] 144 C3
Dolianá [GR] 132 C1
Dolianova [I] 118 D6
Dolice [PL] 20 G6
Dolíchi [GR] 128 G6
Dolina [SLO] 74 B6
Doljani [HR] 112 H4
Doljani [MNE] 144 E4
Doljevac [SRB] 146 D4
Döllach [A] 72 G2
Döllbach [D] 46 E2
Dolle [D] 34 B2
Døllii [N] 180 H4
Döllstädt [D] 32 H6
Dolmen de Dombate [E] 78 B2
Dolna Banya [BG] 146 G5
Dolna Dikanya [BG] 146 F5
Dolna Grupa [PL] 22 E5
Dolná Krupá [SK] 62 H4
Dolna Mahala [BG] 148 B5

Dolna Mitropolia [BG] 148 B3
Dolna Mitropoliya [BG] 148 A3
Dolná Strehová [SK] 64 D4
Dolni Chiflik [BG] 148 F3
Dolni Cibăr [BG] 146 F2
Dolni Dŭbnik [BG] 148 A3
Dolní Dvořiště [CZ] 62 C3
Dolní Kounice [CZ] 62 F2
Dolní Krupá [CZ] 48 G2
Dolni Lom [BG] 146 E3
Dolní Ročov [CZ] 48 E3
Dolno Dupeni [MK] 128 E4
Dolno Kamartsi [BG] 146 G4
Dolno Kosovrasti [MK] 128 C2
Dolno Levski [BG] 148 A5
Dolno Novkovo [BG] 148 D3
Dolno Tserovene [BG] 146 F3
Dolno Ujno [BG] 146 E5
Dolný Kubín [SK] 50 G6
Dolo [I] 110 H1
Dolores [E] 104 D3
Doloscy [RUS] 198 H6
Dolovo [SRB] 142 H2
Dolsk [PL] 36 C4
Dołubowo [PL] 38 E1
Dolyna [UA] 52 H6
Dolyns'ka [UA] 202 F8
Dolzhicy [RUS] 198 H2
Dołżyca [PL] 52 E6
Dom [A] 74 B2
Domaháza [H] 64 E4
Domaj-Has [AL] 146 B6
Domaniç [TR] 150 G5
Domanovići [BIH] 144 C3
Domašov [CZ] 50 D3
Domaszowice [PL] 50 E1
Domažlice [CZ] 48 D5
Dombas [N] 180 G5
Dombasle [F] 44 F5
Dombegyház [H] 76 G4
Dombóvár [H] 76 B4
Dombrád [H] 64 H4
Dombrot-le-Sec [F] 58 B2
Domburg [NL] 16 B6
Doméniko [GR] 132 F1
Domèvre-en-Haye [F] 44 E5
Domfront [F] 26 E5
Domingão [P] 86 D4
Dömitz [D] 18 H5
Domme [F] 66 G4
Dommitzsch [D] 34 D4
Domnítsa [GR] 132 F4
Domnovo [RUS] 22 H2
Domodedovo [RUS] 202 F3
Domodóssola [I] 70 E3
Domokós [GR] 132 G3
Domousnice [CZ] 48 G3
Dompaire [F] 58 C2
Dompierre [F] 56 E5
Dompierre-du-Chemin [F] 26 D5
Dompierre-sur-Besbre [F] 56 E5
Dompierre-sur-Mer [F] 54 C4
Domrémy-la-Pucelle [F] 44 D6
Dömsöd [H] 76 C2
Domurcali [TR] 150 B1
Dómus de Maria [I] 118 C8
Domusnóvas [I] 118 B6
Domžale [SLO] 74 C5
Donado [E] 80 G3
Donaghadee [NIR] 2 H3
Donaghmore [IRL] 4 E3
Doña Mencía [E] 102 C2
Donaueschingen [D] 58 F3
Donaustauf [D] 60 F2
Donauwörth [D] 60 D2
Don Benito [E] 96 B3
Doncaster [GB] 10 F4
Dondurma [TR] 150 B5
Donegal / Dún na nGall [IRL] 2 E2
Donja Brela [HR] 144 B2
Donja Brezna [MNE] 144 D3
Donja Bukovica [MNE] 144 E3
Donja Kamenica [SRB] 146 A1
Donja Kamenica [SRB] 146 E3
Donja Ljubata [SRB] 146 E5
Donja Šatornja [SRB] 146 B2
Donja Suvaja [HR] 112 H4
Donja-Vrijeska [HR] 74 G6
Donje Ljupče [SRB] 146 C5
Donje Petrčane [HR] 112 F5
Donji Koričani [BIH] 142 C3
Donji Krcin [SRB] 146 C3
Donji Lapac [HR] 112 H4
Donji Lipovik [MK] 128 G2
Donji Miholjac [HR] 76 B6
Donji Milanovac [SRB] 146 D1
Donji Stajevac [SRB] 146 E5
Donji Vakuf [BIH] 142 C4
Donji Zemunik [HR] 112 G5
Don Juan, Cueva de- [E] 98 D5
Donnalucata [I] 126 F5
Donnersbach [A] 62 B6
Donnersbachwald [A] 74 B1
Donostia-San Sebastián [E] 84 B2
Donovaly [SK] 64 C2
Dontilly [F] 42 G5
Donzenac [F] 66 G3
Donzère [F] 68 F6
Donzy [F] 56 D3
Doohooma / Dumha Thuama [IRL] 2 B3
Doonbeg [IRL] 2 B6
Doonloughan [IRL] 2 B4
Doorn [NL] 16 E5
Doornik (Tournai) [B] 28 G3
Dörarp [S] 162 C4
Dorchester [GB] 12 F5
Dordives [F] 42 G5
Dordrecht [NL] 16 D5
Dorëz [AL] 128 C3
Dorfen [D] 60 F4
Dorfmark [D] 18 F6
Dorgali [I] 118 E4
Doria, Castello- [I] 110 A3
Dório [GR] 136 D3
Dorkáda [GR] 130 B4
Dorking [GB] 14 E5
Dorkovo [BG] 148 A6
Dormagen [D] 30 G4
Dormánd [H] 64 E6
Dormans [F] 44 A3
Dornas [F] 68 E5
Dornauberg [A] 72 E2
Dornava [SLO] 74 E4
Dornbirn [A] 60 B6
Dornburg [D] 34 B6
Dorndorf [D] 46 F1
Dornes [F] 56 D5
Dorno [I] 70 F5
Dornoch [GB] 6 E4
Dornstetten [D] 58 G2
Dornum [D] 18 B3
Dorog [H] 64 C6
Dorogobuzh [RUS] 202 D4
Dorohoi [RO] 204 D3
Dorohucza [PL] 38 F6
Dorokhovo [RUS] 202 E3
Dorotea [S] 190 F5
Dörpen [D] 16 H3
Dörpstedt [D] 18 E2
Dorsten [D] 30 H2
Dortan [F] 68 H1
Dortmund [D] 32 C4
Dörtyol (Prastio) [CY] 154 G5
Dorum [D] 18 D3
Dörverden [D] 18 E6
Dörzbach [D] 46 E5
Dosbarrios [E] 96 G2
Döşeme [TR] 154 C3
Dos Hermanas [E] 94 G6
Dospat [BG] 130 D1
Dos Torres [E] 96 C5
Døstrup [DK] 156 B3
Dotnuva [LT] 200 F4
Douai [F] 28 F4
Douamont, Fort du- [F] 44 D3
Douarnenez [F] 40 B3
Douchy [F] 42 G6
Doucier [F] 58 A6
Doudeville [F] 26 H2
Doué-la-Fontaine [F] 54 E2
Douglas [GB] 8 D4
Douglas [GBM] 10 B2
Doulaincourt [F] 44 D6
Doulevant-le-Château [F] 44 C6
Doullens [F] 28 E4
Dourdan [F] 42 F4
Dourgne [F] 106 B4
Doussard [F] 70 B3
Douvaine [F] 70 B2
Douzy [F] 44 D2
Dover [GB] 14 G5
Dovre [N] 180 G5
Downham Market [GB] 14 F2
Downings [IRL] 2 E1
Downpatrick [NIR] 2 G4
Dowra [IRL] 2 E3
Dowsk [BY] 202 D5
Doxáto [GR] 130 D3
Dozón / Castro [E] 78 C4
Dozulé [F] 26 G3
Drabiv [UA] 202 E7
Drac, Coves del- [E] 104 F5
Dračevo [MK] 128 E1
Drachenfels [D] 30 H5
Drachenwand [A] 60 H5
Drachselsried [D] 48 D6
Drachten [NL] 16 F2
Drag [N] 190 C4
Drag Ájluokta [N] 192 E5
Dragalevtsi [BG] 146 F5
Drăgăneşti de Vede [RO] 148 B1
Drăgăneşti-Olt [RO] 148 A1
Drăgăneşti-Vlaşca [RO] 148 C1
Dragaš [SRB] 146 B6
Drăgăşani [RO] 204 D5
Dragatuš [SLO] 112 G1
Dragichevo [BG] 146 F5
Draginje [SRB] 146 A1
Draginovo [BG] 148 A6
Dragocvet [SRB] 146 C2
Dragoevo [MK] 128 F1
Dragoman [BG] 146 F4
Dragomir [BG] 148 A5
Dragomirovo [BG] 146 F5
Dragomirovo [BG] 148 B2
Dragomirovo [BG] 148 C3
Dragon, Caverne du- [F] 44 B2
Dragør [DK] 156 H3
Dragotina [HR] 142 A1
Dragov Doll [MK] 128 E2
Dragovishtitsa [BG] 146 E5
Dragsfjärd [FIN] 176 E5
Dragsholm Slot [DK] 156 F2
Draguignan [F] 108 D5
Drahanovice [CZ] 50 C5
Drahonice [CZ] 48 F6
Drahovce [SK] 62 H3
Draka [BG] 148 E5
Drakčići [SRB] 146 B3
Drakseníć [BIH] 142 B2
Dráma [GR] 130 D3
Dramče [MK] 146 E6
Drammen [N] 164 H1
Drangedal [N] 164 F3
Drängsered [S] 162 B4
Drängsmark [S] 196 A4
Drânic [RO] 146 G1
Dransfeld [D] 32 F4
Dranske [D] 20 D1
Drasenhofen [A] 62 F3
Drava Fok [H] 74 H5
Drávaszabolcs [H] 76 B6
Dravískos [GR] 130 C3
Dravograd [SLO] 74 C3
Drawno [PL] 20 H6
Drawsko Pomorskie [PL] 20 H5
Drążdżewo [PL] 24 B6
Draženov [CZ] 48 D5
Drażniew [PL] 38 E2
Drebkau [D] 34 F4
Drégelypalánk [H] 64 C5
Drei [D] 46 G1
Dreilingen [D] 18 G6
Dren [MK] 128 F3
Dren [SRB] 146 B4
Drenchia [I] 72 H4
Drenovac [SRB] 146 D5
Drenovci [HR] 142 E2
Drenovets [BG] 146 F2
Drensteinfurt [D] 32 C3
Drépano [GR] 128 F5
Dresden [D] 34 E6
Dretyń [PL] 22 B3
Dreux [F] 42 E3
Drevsjø [N] 182 D6
Drewitz [D] 34 C3
Drewitz [D] 34 E4
Drezdenko [PL] 36 B1
Drežnica [HR] 112 F2
Dreznik-Grad [HR] 112 G2
Driebergen [NL] 16 E5
Drienovo [SK] 64 C4
Driffield [GB] 10 G3
Drimoleague [IRL] 4 B5
Drina Kanjon [BIH] 142 E4
Drinjača [BIH] 142 E4
Drinovci [BIH] 144 B2
Driny [SK] 62 G4
Drionville [F] 28 E2
Driva [N] 180 H4
Drivstua [N] 180 H4
Drizë [AL] 128 C4
Drlače [SRB] 142 F4
Drnholec [CZ] 62 F2
Drniš [HR] 142 A5
Drnovo [SLO] 74 D5
Drøbak [N] 166 B2
Drobeta-Turnu Severin [RO] 204 C6
Drobin [PL] 36 H1
Drochtersen [D] 18 E3
Drogheda / Droichead Átha [IRL] 2 F5
Drohiczyn [PL] 38 E2
Drohobych [UA] 52 G5
Droichead Átha / Drogheda [IRL] 2 F5
Droichead Nua / Newbridge [IRL] 2 E6
Droitwich [GB] 12 G1
Drołtowice [PL] 36 D5
Dromahair [IRL] 2 D3
Dromcolliher [IRL] 4 C4
Dromore [NIR] 2 G4
Dromore West [IRL] 2 D3
Dronero [I] 108 F2
Dronninglund [DK] 160 E3
Dronten [NL] 16 F4
Dropla [BG] 148 G2
Drosáto [GR] 128 H3
Drosbacken [S] 182 E6
Drosendorf Stadt [A] 62 E2
Drosiá [GR] 134 B5
Drosopigí [GR] 128 E4
Drosopigí [GR] 132 D3
Drosselbjerg [DK] 156 E3
Drottninghaug [N] 180 D4
Droúseia [CY] 154 F6
Drozdowo [PL] 22 B2
Drugan [BG] 146 F5
Drumconrath [IRL] 2 F5
Drumevo [BG] 148 E3
Drumkeeran [IRL] 2 D3
Drumlish [IRL] 2 E4
Drummore [GB] 8 C5
Drumnadrochit [GB] 6 D5
Drumshanbo [IRL] 2 D4
Drumsna [IRL] 2 D4
Drusenheim [F] 44 H5
Druskininkai [LT] 24 F3
Drusti [LV] 198 F4
Druten [NL] 16 E5
Družetic [SRB] 146 A1
Druzhba [BG] 148 G3
Druzhba [RUS] 24 B2
Druzhnaja Gorka [RUS] 198 H1
Drvar [BIH] 142 A3
Drvenik [HR] 144 B3
Dryanovo [BG] 148 C4
Drygały [PL] 24 D4
Drymós [GR] 128 H4
Drýopi [GR] 136 F2
Dryopída [GR] 138 C2
Dryós [GR] 138 E3
Drzewce [PL] 36 F3
Drzewiany [PL] 22 B3
Drzewica [PL] 38 B5
D. Stupnica [HR] 142 A2
Duagh [IRL] 4 C3
Duas Igrejas [P] 80 G4
Dub [SRB] 146 A2
Dubá [CZ] 48 G2
Dubac [HR] 144 C4
Dubăsari [MD] 204 E3
Dubechne [UA] 38 H4
Duben [D] 34 E4
Dubí [CZ] 48 E2
Dubica [HR] 142 B2
Dubienka [PL] 38 G6
Dubin [PL] 36 D5
Dubinino [RUS] 178 F2
Dubliany [UA] 52 G5
Dublin / Baile Átha Cliath [IRL] 2 F6
Dubna [RUS] 202 E2
Dub nad Moravou [CZ] 50 D5
Dubňany [CZ] 62 G2
Dubnica nad Váhom [SK] 64 A2
Dŭbnitsa [BG] 130 C1
Dubno [UA] 202 B8
Dubovsko [BIH] 112 H3
Dubrava [BIH] 142 C3
Dubrava [HR] 74 F5
Dubrava [HR] 74 G4
Dubrava [RUS] 24 D2
Dubrave [BIH] 142 E2
Dubravica [BIH] 142 C4
Dubravka [HR] 144 D4
Dubrovka [RUS] 198 H5
Dubrovnik [HR] 144 C4
Dubrovno [RUS] 198 H3
Dubrovytsia [UA] 202 B7
Dubrowna [BY] 202 C4
Ducey [F] 26 D4
Duchcov [CZ] 48 E2
Ducherow [D] 20 E4
Duclair [F] 26 H3
Dudar [H] 76 A1
Dudelange [L] 44 E3
Düdenköy [TR] 154 H2
Duderstadt [D] 32 G4
Dudeştii Vechi [RO] 76 F5
Dudince [SK] 64 C4
Düdingen [CH] 58 D6
Dudley [GB] 10 D6
Due Carrare [I] 110 G1
Dueñas [E] 88 F1
Duesund [N] 170 B2
Dueville [I] 72 D6
Dufftown [GB] 6 F5
Duga Poljana [SRB] 146 B4
Duga Resa [HR] 112 G1
Duge Njive [HR] 144 B2
Dugi Rat [HR] 144 A2
Duğla [TR] 152 C2
Dugopolje [HR] 144 A2
Dugo Selo [HR] 74 F6
Duhnen [D] 18 D3
Duingen [D] 32 F3
Duingt [F] 70 B3
Duino [I] 72 H5
Duisburg [D] 30 G3
Duka [H] 74 G2
Dukat [AL] 128 A6
Dukat [SRB] 146 E5
Dukhovshchina [RUS] 202 D4
Dukla [PL] 52 D5
Dukovany [CZ] 62 F2
Dūkštas [LT] 200 H4
Dukštos [LT] 200 G5
Dŭlbok Izvor [BG] 148 C6
Duleek [IRL] 2 F5
Dŭlgopol [BG] 148 F3
Dülken [D] 30 F3
Dülmen [D] 16 H6
Dulnain Bridge [GB] 6 E5
Dulovka [RUS] 198 G4
Dulovo [BG] 148 E1
Dulpetorpet [N] 172 D4
Dumača [SRB] 142 F3
Dumakömlöd [H] 76 C3
Dumanlı [TR] 152 G4
Dumbarton [GB] 8 D3
Dumbrăveni [RO] 148 F1
Dumfries [GB] 8 D5
Dumha Thuama / Doohooma [IRL] 2 B3
Dumlupınar [TR] 152 H2
Dümpelfeld [D] 30 G6
Dun [F] 44 D3
Duna [N] 190 C4
Dunaengus [IRL] 2 B5
Dunaff [IRL] 2 F1
Dunaföldvár [H] 76 C3
Dunaharaszti [H] 76 C1
Dunaïvtsi [UA] 204 D2
Dunajská Streda [SK] 62 H5
Dunakeszi [H] 64 C6
Dunakiliti [H] 62 G5
Dunany [IRL] 2 F5
Dunapataj [H] 76 C3
Dunas de São Jacinto [P] 80 B5
Dunaszeg [H] 62 H5
Dunaszekcső [H] 76 C5
Dunaszentbenedek [H] 76 C3
Dunasziget [H] 62 G5
Dunatetétlen [H] 76 C3
Dunaújváros [H] 76 C2
Dunavecse [H] 76 C2
Dunavtsi [BG] 146 E2
Dunbar [GB] 8 F3
Dunbeath [GB] 6 F3
Dunblane [GB] 8 E2
Dunboy Castle [IRL] 4 A5
Dunboyne [IRL] 2 F6
Dunbrody Abbey [IRL] 4 E5
Duncormick [IRL] 4 F5
Dundaga [LV] 198 C4
Dundalk / Dún Dealgan [IRL] 2 F4
Dún Dealgan / Dundalk [IRL] 2 F4
Dundee [GB] 8 F2
Dunderland [N] 190 E2
Dunfanaghy [IRL] 2 E1
Dunfermline [GB] 8 E3
Dungannon [NIR] 2 F3
Dungarvan [IRL] 4 E5
Dungiven [NIR] 2 F2
Dunglow / An Clochán Liath [IRL] 2 E2
Dungourney [IRL] 4 D5
Dunje [MK] 128 F3
Dunjica [MK] 128 G2
Dunker [S] 168 C3
Dunkerque [F] 14 H6
Dunkerque Ouest [F] 14 H6
Dunkineely [IRL] 2 D2
Duńkowice [PL] 52 F3
Dún Laoghaire [IRL] 2 F6
Dunlavin [IRL] 4 F3
Dunleer [IRL] 2 F5
Dun-le-Palestel [F] 54 H5
Dunloe, Gap of- [IRL] 4 B4
Dunloy [NIR] 2 G2
Dunmanway [IRL] 4 C5
Dunmore [IRL] 2 C4
Dunmore Caves [IRL] 4 E4
Dunmore East [IRL] 4 E5
Dunmurry [NIR] 2 G3
Dún na nGall / Donegal [IRL] 2 E2
Dunoon [GB] 8 C3
Duns [GB] 8 F4
Dunshaughlin [IRL] 2 F5
Dunstable [GB] 14 E3
Dun-sur-Auron [F] 56 C4
Dunure [GB] 8 C4
Dunvegan [GB] 6 B4
Duoddar Sion [N] 194 B2
Dupnitsa [BG] 146 F6
Duquesa, Castillo de la- [E] 100 H5
Durabeyler [TR] 152 E1
Durach [BG] 148 E2
Duran [BG] 148 E2
Durance [F] 66 D5
Durango [E] 82 H4
Durankulak [BG] 148 G1
Duras [F] 66 E4
Durasıllı [TR] 152 E3
Durban-Corbières [F] 106 C5
Durbe [LV] 198 B6
Durbuy [B] 30 E5
Dúrcal [E] 102 E4
Đurđenovac [HR] 142 D1
Đurđevac [HR] 74 G5
Đurđevića Tara [MNE] 144 E2
Đurđevik [BIH] 142 E3
Durdevi Stupovi [SRB] 146 B4
Düren [D] 30 G4
Durham [GB] 8 F6
Durhasan [TR] 152 F3
Durlas / Thurles [IRL] 4 E3
Durness [GB] 6 D2
Dürnkrut [A] 62 G4
Dürnstein [A] 62 D4
Durnstein [A] 74 B2
Durón [E] 90 A5
Durrës [AL] 128 A3
Durrow [IRL] 4 E3
Durrow Abbey [IRL] 2 E5
Durrus [IRL] 4 B5
Dursunbey [TR] 152 E1
Durtal [F] 42 A6
Duruelo de la Sierra [E] 90 A2
Dusetos [LT] 200 G4
Dŭskotna [BG] 148 E3
Dusnok [H] 76 C4
Dusocin [PL] 22 E5
Düsseldorf [D] 30 G3
Duszniki [PL] 36 B2
Duszniki-Zdrój [PL] 50 B3
Dutluca [TR] 150 F6
Dutluca [TR] 152 G5
Dutovlje [SLO] 72 H5
Duved [S] 182 E1
Düvertepe [TR] 152 E2
Düzağac [TR] 152 H2
Duztarla [TR] 152 C2
Dvärsätt [S] 182 G2
Dve Mogili [BG] 148 C2
Dvor [HR] 142 A2
Dvor [SLO] 74 C6
Dvorce [CZ] 50 D4
Dvory nad Žitavou [SK] 64 B5
Dvůr Králové nad Labem [CZ] 50 A3
Dwingeloo [NL] 16 G3
Dyat'kovo [RUS] 202 E5
Dyatlitsy [RUS] 178 G5
Dybäck [S] 158 C3
Dyblin [PL] 36 G2
Dyce [GB] 6 F6
Dyck [D] 30 G4
Dygowo [PL] 20 H3
Dylewo [PL] 24 C5
Dymchurch [GB] 14 F5
Dymniki [BY] 38 G2
Dynów [PL] 52 E4
Dyranut [N] 170 E4
Dyrnes [N] 180 F1
Dyrráchio [GR] 136 D3
Dysbodarna [S] 172 F3
Dýstos [GR] 134 C5
Dyulino [BG] 148 F3
Dyuni [BG] 148 F4
Dyvik [S] 168 E3
Džepište [MK] 128 C2
Dzhankoï [UA] 204 H3
Dzhebel [BG] 130 F1
Dzhurovo [BG] 146 G4
Dzhuryn [UA] 204 E2
Dziadkowice [PL] 38 E2
Dziadowa Kłoda [PL] 36 D6
Działdowo [PL] 22 G5
Działoszyce [PL] 52 B3
Działoszyn [PL] 36 F6
Dziemiany [PL] 22 C3
Dzierzgoń [PL] 22 F4
Dzierzki [PL] 22 H4
Dzierżoniów [PL] 50 C2
Dzietrzychowo [PL] 24 B2
Džigolj [SRB] 146 D3
Dzivin [BY] 38 H3
Dziwnów [PL] 20 F3
Dziwnówek [PL] 20 F3
Džul'unica [BG] 148 C3
Džumajlija [MK] 128 F1
Dźwierzuty [PL] 22 H4
Dźwirzyno [PL] 20 G3
Dzyarechyn [BY] 24 H5
Dzyarzhynsk [BY] 202 B5

E

Easingwold [GB] 10 F3
Easky [IRL] 2 D3
Eastbourne [GB] 14 E6
East Grinstead [GB] 14 E5
East Kilbride [GB] 8 D3
Eastleigh [GB] 12 H5
Eaux-Bonnes [F] 84 D4
Eaux-Chaudes [F] 84 D4
Eauze [F] 66 D6
Ebberup [DK] 156 D3
Ebbo / Epoo [FIN] 178 B4
Ebbw Vale [GB] 12 F2
Ebecik [TR] 152 F5
Ebeleben [D] 32 H5
Ebelsbach [D] 46 F3
Ebeltoft [DK] 156 E1
Ebeltoft Færge [DK] 156 E1
Eben [A] 60 E6
Ebenfurth [A] 62 F5
Eben im Pongau [A] 72 H1
Ebensee [A] 62 A5
Eberbach [D] 46 B3
Eberbach [D] 46 D5
Eberdingen [D] 46 C6
Ebergötzen [D] 32 G4
Ebermannstadt [D] 46 G4
Ebern [D] 46 G3
Eberndorf [A] 74 C3
Ebersbach [D] 48 G1
Ebersberg [D] 60 E4
Eberschwang [A] 60 H4
Ebersdorf [D] 18 E4
Ebersdorf [D] 60 H3
Eberstein [A] 74 C3
Eberstein [D] 58 F1
Eberswalde [D] 34 F1
Ebes [H] 64 G6
Ebeyli [TR] 150 G4
Ebingen [D] 58 G3
Éboli [I] 120 F4
Ebrach [D] 46 F4
Ebreichsdorf [A] 62 F5
Ebreuil [F] 56 C6
Ebstorf [D] 18 G6
Eceabat [TR] 130 H5
Echallens [CH] 70 C1
Echallon [F] 68 H2
Echarri / Etxarri [E] 84 A3
Échevennoz [I] 70 D3
Echínos [GR] 130 E2
Échourgnac [F] 66 E3
Echternach [L] 44 F2
Écija [E] 102 B2
Eck [A] 62 A6
Ečka [SRB] 142 G1
Eckartsau [A] 62 F5
Eckartsberga [D] 34 B6
Eckernförde [D] 18 F1
Eckerö [FIN] 176 A5
Eckersholm [S] 162 D2
Eckwarden [D] 18 D4
Ecole Valentine [F] 58 B4
Ecommoy [F] 42 B5
Ecouis [F] 28 C6
Ecoust-St-Mein [F] 28 F4
Ecsegfalva [H] 76 F2
Ecthe [D] 32 G4
Ecueillé [F] 54 G3
Ecury [F] 44 B4
Ed [S] 166 C4
Ed[S] 184 E2
Eda [S] 166 D1
Eda glasbruk [S] 166 D1
Edam [NL] 16 E4
Edane [S] 166 E2
Eddelak [D] 18 E3
Ede [NL] 16 E5
Ede [S] 182 H1
Edebäck [S] 172 F6
Edebo [S] 168 E1
Edeby [S] 168 E1
Edefors [S] 184 C1
Edefors [S] 196 A2
Edelény [H] 64 F4
Edenbridge [GB] 14 E5
Edenderry [IRL] 2 E6
Edenkoben [D] 46 B5
Edersee [D] 32 E5
Édessa [GR] 128 F4
Edevik [S] 190 D5
Edewecht [D] 18 C5
Edgeworthstown [IRL] 2 E5
Edhem [S] 166 F6
Edinburgh [GB] 8 E3
Edincik [TR] 150 D4
Edineţ [MD] 204 D3
Edirne [TR] 150 A2
Edland [N] 164 D1
Ēdole [LV] 198 B5
Édolo [I] 72 B4
Édon [F] 66 E2
Edremit [TR] 152 C1
Edsbro [S] 168 E1
Edsbruk [S] 162 G1
Edsbyn [S] 174 C2
Edsele [S] 184 D1
Edsleskog [S] 166 D4
Edsta [S] 184 E6
Edsvalla [S] 166 E2
Eeklo [B] 28 G1
Eelde [NL] 16 G2
Een [NL] 16 G2
Efendiköprüsü [TR] 152 G2
Eferding [A] 62 B4
Effeløt [N] 164 G2
Efkarpía [GR] 128 H3
Eforie [RO] 204 F5
Efpálio [GR] 132 F5
Efýra [GR] 136 C2
Éfyras [GR] 132 D3
Egebæk [DK] 156 B3
Egeln [D] 34 B3
Egense [DK] 160 E4
Eger [H] 64 E5
Egerlövő [H] 64 F5
Egernsund [DK] 156 C4
Egersund [N] 164 B4
Egervár [H] 74 G2
Egesheim [D] 58 G3
Egeskov [DK] 156 D4
Egestorf [D] 18 F5
Egg [A] 60 B6
Egg [A] 72 D2
Egg [CH] 72 D2
Eggedal [N] 170 G5
Eggenburg [A] 62 E3
Eggenfelden [D] 60 G3
Eggesin [D] 20 E4
Eggjaseteren [N] 190 D5
Egglham [D] 60 G3
Eggum [N] 192 C4
Eghezée [B] 30 D5
Egiertowo [PL] 22 D3
Egilsstaðir [IS] 192 C3
Egletons [F] 68 A3
Eglinton [NIR] 2 F2
Egmond aan Zee [NL] 16 D3
Egna / Neumarkt [I] 72 D4
Egremont [GB] 8 D6
Egsdorf [D] 34 E3
Egtved [DK] 156 C2
Eguzon [F] 54 G5
Egyek [H] 64 F6
Ehingen [D] 60 B3
Ehnen [L] 44 F3
Ehra-Lessien [D] 32 H2
Ehrenburg [A] 60 C6
Ehrenburg [D] 18 D6
Ehrenhausen [A] 74 D3
Ehrwald [A] 60 D6
Eiane [N] 164 B3
Eibar [E] 82 H4
Eibenstock [D] 48 C2
Eibergen [NL] 16 G5
Eibiswald [A] 74 D3
Eich [D] 46 C4
Eichendorf [D] 60 G3
Eichstätt [D] 60 D2
Eid [N] 190 B5
Eida [N] 164 B4
Eidanger [N] 164 G3
Eide [N] 164 B4
Eide [N] 164 C3
Eide [N] 170 B1
Eide [N] 180 E2
Eide [N] 190 D5
Eidem [N] 190 C3
Eidet [N] 180 H1
Eidfjord [N] 170 D4
Eiði [FR] 160 B1
Eidiet [N] 180 C6
Eidsborg [N] 164 E2
Eidsbugarden [N] 170 F1
Eidsbygda [N] 180 E3
Eidsdal [N] 180 E4
Eidsfoss [N] 164 G2
Eidskog [N] 172 D6
Eidslandet [N] 170 B3
Eidsøra [N] 180 F3
Eidstod [N] 164 E2
Eidsund [N] 164 B2
Eidsvåg [N] 180 F3
Eidsvoll [N] 172 C5
Eidsvoll verk [N] 172 C5
Eifa [D] 32 D6
Eigenrieden [D] 32 G5
Eik [N] 164 B2
Eikefjord [N] 180 B6
Eikelandsosen [N] 170 B4
Eiken [N] 164 C4
Eikenes [N] 180 B6
Eiksund [N] 180 C4
Eilenburg [D] 34 D5
Eilsleben [D] 34 A3
Eimisjärvi [FIN] 188 G3
Eina [N] 172 B4
Einastrand [N] 172 B4
Einavoll [N] 172 B4
Einbeck [D] 32 F3
Eindhoven [NL] 30 E2
Einsiedeln [CH] 58 G6
Einzinger Boden [A] 72 F1
Eisenach [D] 32 G6
Eisenbach [D] 46 D1
Eisenback [D] 58 F3
Eisenberg [D] 34 B6
Eisenerz [A] 62 C6
Eisenhüttenstadt [D] 34 G3
Eisenkappel [A] 74 C4
Eisenstadt [A] 62 F5
Eisensteinhöhle [A] 62 E5
Eisfeld [D] 46 G2
Eisgarn [A] 62 D2
Eišiškės [LT] 24 H2
Eislingen [D] 60 B2
Eisriesenwelt [A] 60 H6
Eitorf [D] 30 H5
Eivindvik [N] 170 B2
Eivissa / Ibiza [E] 104 C5
Ejby [DK] 156 D3
Ejea de los Caballeros [E] 84 C6
Ejheden [S] 172 H2
Ejstrupholm [DK] 156 C1
Ejulve [E] 90 E6
Ek [S] 166 F5
Ekáli [GR] 134 C6
Ekeby [S] 156 H2
Ekeby [S] 166 G6
Ekeby [S] 168 D3
Ekebyholm [S] 168 E2
Ekedal [S] 174 E6
Ekedalen [S] 166 F6
Ekenäs [S] 166 E4
Ekenäs / Tammisaari [FIN] 176 F6
Ekenässjön [S] 162 E3
Ekerö [S] 168 D3
Ekinhisar [TR] 152 H3

Ekinli [TR] 150 H3
Ekkerøy [N] 194 E2
Ekolsund [S] 168 D2
Ekornavallen [S] 166 F6
Ekorrbäcken [S] 194 B7
Ekorrträsk [S] 190 H5
Ekshärad [S] 172 F5
Eksingedal [N] 170 C3
Eksjö [S] 162 E2
Ekträsk [S] 190 H5
Ekzarh Antimovo [BG] 148 E4
Elaía [GR] 136 F4
Elaiochória [GR] 130 B5
Elaiónas [GR] 132 G5
El Alamo [E] 88 F6
El Alcornocal [E] 96 B5
El Altet [E] 104 D2
Elämäjärvi [FIN] 196 D6
Elanets' [UA] 204 F2
Elantxobe [E] 82 H3
Elassóna [GR] 132 F1
El Astillero [E] 82 F3
Eláteia [GR] 132 H4
Eláti [GR] 128 F6
Eláti [GR] 132 E2
Elatoú [GR] 132 F5
El Ballestero [E] 96 H5
El Barco de Ávila [E] 88 C5
El Barraco [E] 88 E5
Elbasan [AL] 128 B3
El Berrón [E] 78 H3
Elbeuf [F] 26 H4
Elbigenalp [A] 72 B1
Elbingerode [D] 32 H4
Elbląg [PL] 22 F3
El Bodón [E] 86 H2
El Bonillo [E] 96 H5
El Bosque [E] 100 H4
Elburg [NL] 16 F4
Elburgo / Burgelu [E] 102 B4
El Burgo de Ebro [E] 90 E4
El Burgo de Osma [E] 90 A3
El Burgo Ranero [E] 82 B5
El Cabaco [E] 88 B4
el Campello [E] 104 E2
El Canal [E] 104 C6
El Cañavate [E] 98 B3
El Carpio [E] 102 C1
El Carpio de Tajo [E] 96 E1
El Casar de Talamanca [E] 88 G5
El Castillo de las Guardas [E] 94 G5
El Castor [E] 100 H3
El Centenillo [E] 96 E6
El Cerro de Andévalo [E] 94 F4
Elche / Elx [E] 104 D2
Elche de la Sierra [E] 104 B1
Elçili [TR] 150 B2
El Coronil [E] 100 H3
El Cotillo [E] 100 E6
El Cubo de Don Sancho [E] 80 F6
El Cubo de Tierra del Vino [E] 80 H5
El Cuervo [E] 100 G3
El'cy [RUS] 202 D3
Elda [E] 104 D2
Eldalsosen [N] 170 C1
Eldena [D] 20 A5
Eldforsen [S] 172 G5
Eldrehaug [N] 170 E2
Elefsína [GR] 134 B6
Eleftherés [GR] 134 B6
Elefthério [GR] 132 G2
Eleftherochóri [GR] 128 E6
Eleftheroúpoli [GR] 130 D3
Eleja [LV] 198 D6
El Ejido [E] 102 F5
Elek [H] 76 G3
Elena [BG] 148 C4
Elenite [BG] 148 F4
Eleousa [GR] 154 D4
El Escorial [E] 88 F5
El Espinar [E] 88 E4
el Fondó dels Frares [E] 104 D2
Elgå [N] 182 D5
El Gargantón [E] 96 E3
El Garrobo [E] 94 G5
Elgg [CH] 58 G5
Elgin [GB] 6 E5
El Grado [E] 90 G3
El Grau [E] 98 F4
el Grau / Grao [E] 98 F6
Elgsnes [N] 192 E3
El Guijo [E] 96 C5
Eliaröd [S] 158 D2
Elimäki [FIN] 178 C3
Eling [S] 166 E6
Elin Pelin [BG] 146 G5
Elisenvaara [RUS] 188 H5
Eliseyna [BG] 146 G4
Elizondo [E] 84 C3
Elizondo / Baztan [E] 82 H4
Ełk [PL] 24 D4
Elkeland [N] 164 C5
Elkhovo [BG] 148 E5
Ellan [S] 174 G5
Elle [N] 164 B3
Ellenberg [D] 46 E6
Ellesmere [GB] 10 D5
Elling [DK] 160 E2
Ellinge [S] 158 C2
Ellingen [D] 46 G6
Ellmau [A] 60 F6
Ellon [GB] 6 G6
Ellös [S] 166 C6
Ellrich [D] 32 H4
Ellwangen [D] 46 E6
Elm [CH] 58 G6
Elmacık [TR] 150 B1
El Madroño [E] 94 F5
Elmalı [TR] 154 H2
El Masnou [E] 92 E4
El Médano [E] 100 B5
Elmen [A] 60 C6
El Minguillo [E] 96 G4
El Molar [E] 88 G5
El Molinillo [E] 96 E2
El Moral [E] 102 H2
Elmpt [D] 30 F3
Elmshorn [D] 18 F3
Elmstein [D] 46 B5
Elne [F] 92 G1
Elnesvågen [N] 180 E2
Elo / Monreal [E] 84 B4
Eloro [I] 126 G5
Elorz / Noain [E] 84 B4
Élos [GR] 140 B5
Előszállás [H] 76 C3
Eloúnta [GR] 140 F4
el Palmar [E] 98 F5
El Palmar de Troya [E] 100 G3
El Palmeral [E] 104 D2
El Palo [E] 102 C4
El Pardo [E] 88 F5
El Paular [E] 88 F4
El Pedernoso [E] 96 H3
El Pedroso [E] 94 H5
El Perelló [E] 92 B5
El Perelló [E] 98 F5
Elphin [IRL] 2 D4
El Pinar [E] 100 A5
El Piñero [E] 80 H5
el Pinós / Pinoso [E] 104 D2
El Pito [E] 78 G3
el Pla de Santa Maria [E] 92 C4
El Pobo de Dueñas [E] 90 C6
el Pont de Suert [E] 84 F6
el Port / Sóller [E] 104 E4
el Port de la Selva [E] 92 G2
El Portil [E] 94 E6
el Prat de Llobregat [E] 92 E5
El Priorato [E] 102 A1
El Puente del Arzobispo [E] 96 D1
El Puerto de Santa María [E] 100 F4
El Ramonete [E] 104 B4
El Real de la Jara [E] 94 G4
El Real de San Vicente [E] 88 D6
El Recuenco [E] 90 B6
El Retiro [E] 102 B5
El Robledo [E] 96 E3
El Rocío [E] 94 F6
El Rompido [E] 94 E6
El Ronquillo [E] 94 G5
El Royo [E] 90 B2
El Rubio [E] 102 B2
El Sabinar [E] 102 H2
El Saler [E] 98 E5
El Salobral [E] 98 B5
El Saucejo [E] 102 B3
Elsdorf [D] 30 G4
El Serrat [AND] 84 H6
Elsfleth [D] 18 D5
Elšica [BG] 148 A5
Elst [NL] 16 E5
Elsten [D] 18 C6
Elster [D] 34 D4
Elsterberg [D] 48 C2
Elsterwerda [D] 34 E5
El Tejar [E] 102 C3
Elten [D] 16 F6
El Tiemblo [E] 88 E5
Eltmann [D] 46 F3
El Toboso [E] 96 G3
El Tormillo [E] 90 G3
El Torno [E] 88 B5
El Torno [E] 100 G4
Eltravåg [N] 164 A1
El Tumbalejo [E] 94 F5
Eltville [D] 46 B3
Eltz [D] 44 H1
Elva [EST] 198 F3
Elvas [P] 86 F6
Elvbrua [N] 182 D6
Elvdal [N] 172 D1
Elven, Tour d'- [F] 40 D4
El Vendrell [E] 92 D5
Elverum [N] 172 C3
Elverum [N] 192 F3
Elvestad [N] 166 B2
El Villar de Arnedo [E] 84 A5
Elvira [E] 102 E3
Elviria [E] 102 B5
El Viso [E] 96 C5
El Viso del Alcor [E] 94 H6
Elvran [N] 182 C1
Elx / Elche [E] 104 D2
Ely [GB] 14 F2
Élyros [GR] 140 B5
Elzach [D] 58 F2
Elze [D] 32 F3
Emberménil [F] 44 F5
Embrun [F] 108 D2
Embūte [LV] 198 C6
Emden [D] 16 H2
Emecik [TR] 154 C2
Emese [TR] 150 C5
Emet [TR] 152 F1
Emiralem [TR] 152 C3
Emlichheim [D] 16 G4
Emmaboda [S] 162 F5
Emmaljunga [S] 162 C6
Emmaste [EST] 198 C2
Emmeloord [NL] 16 F3
Emmen [NL] 16 G3
Emmendingen [D] 58 E3
Emmerich [D] 16 F6
Emmingen-Liptingen [D] 58 G3
Emőd [H] 64 F5
Emona [BG] 148 G4
Émpa [CY] 154 F6
Empesós [GR] 132 E3
Empfingen [D] 58 G2
Empoli [I] 110 E5
Émponas [GR] 154 D4
Emporeiós [GR] 134 G5
Emporeiós [GR] 138 H5
Emporeiós [GR] 154 B3
Empúriabrava [E] 92 G2
Empúries [E] 92 G3
Emsdetten [D] 16 H5
Emsfors [S] 162 G4
Emskirchen [D] 46 F5
Emstek [D] 18 C6
Emting-hausen [D] 18 D6
Emyvale [IRL] 2 F4
Enafors [S] 182 E2
Enäjärvi [FIN] 178 C3
Enånger [S] 174 E1
Enare / Inari [FIN] 194 D4
Enarsvedjan [S] 182 G1
Encamp [AND] 84 H6
Encarnación, Sant. de la- [E] 98 B6
Encinas de Abajo [E] 88 C3
Encinasola [E] 94 F3
Encinedo [E] 78 F6
Enciso [E] 90 C2
Encs [H] 64 F4
Endelave By [DK] 156 D2
Enden [N] 180 H6
Endingen [D] 58 E2
Endrefalva [H] 64 D4
Endrinal [E] 88 C4
Endrőd [H] 76 F2
Enebakk [N] 166 C1
Enese [H] 62 H6
Enevo [BG] 148 E2
Enez [TR] 130 H3
Enfesta / Pontecesures [E] 78 B3
Enfield [IRL] 2 E6
Engelberg [CH] 70 F1
Engelhartszell [A] 62 A3
Engelia [N] 170 H4
Engeln [D] 18 D6
Engelskirchen [D] 30 H4
Engelsviken [N] 166 B3
Engen [D] 58 G3
Enger [D] 32 D2
Enger [N] 170 H4
Engerdal [N] 182 D6
Engerneset [N] 172 D1
Engesland [N] 164 E4
Engesvang [DK] 160 C6
Enghien [B] 28 H3
Engi [CH] 58 G6
Engjane [N] 180 F2
England [D] 18 E1
Englefontaine [F] 28 G4
Engstingen [D] 58 H2
Énguera [E] 98 E6
Enguídanos [E] 98 C3
Engure [LV] 198 D5
Enkhuizen [NL] 16 E3
Enklinge [FIN] 176 B5
Enköping [S] 168 C2
Enmo [N] 182 B3
Enna [I] 126 E3
Ennezat [F] 68 D2
Ennis / Inis [IRL] 2 C6
Enniscorthy [IRL] 4 F4
Enniscrone [IRL] 2 C3
Enniskean [IRL] 4 C5
Enniskillen [NIR] 2 E3
Ennistymon [IRL] 2 B5
Enns [A] 62 C4
Eno [FIN] 188 G2
Enokunta [FIN] 186 E6
Enonkoski [FIN] 188 E4
Enonkylä [FIN] 196 E5
Enonteki / Enontekiö [FIN] 194 B5
Enontekiö / Enonteki [FIN] 194 B5
Enschede [NL] 16 G5
Ensisheim [F] 58 D3
Entlebuch [CH] 58 E6
Entradas [P] 94 D3
Entraigues [F] 54 H3
Entranis-sur-Nohain [F] 56 D3
Entraygues-sur-Truyère [F] 68 B5
Entre Ambos-os-Rios [P] 80 C4
Entrevaux [F] 108 E4
Entrèves [I] 70 C3
Entrimo [E] 78 C6
Entroncamento [P] 86 D4
Enviken [S] 174 C4
En Xoroi, Cova d'- [E] 104 H5
Enying [H] 76 B2
Eoux [F] 84 G4
Epannes [F] 54 D4
Epanomí [GR] 128 H5
Epe [D] 16 G5
Epe [NL] 16 F4
Épernay [F] 44 B3
Epernon [F] 42 E4
Ephesos [TR] 152 D5
Epídavros, Arhéa- [GR] 136 F2
Épila [E] 90 D4
Épinal [F] 58 C2
Epiry [F] 56 E3
Episcopía [I] 120 H5
Episkopí [CY] 154 F6
Episkopí [GR] 140 C4
Epitálio [GR] 136 C2
Epléný [H] 76 A2
Epône [F] 42 E3
Epoo / Ebbo [FIN] 178 B4
Eppan / Appiano [I] 72 D3
Eppenstein [A] 74 C2
Eppingen [D] 46 C5
Eptachóri [GR] 128 D6
Eptálofos [GR] 132 G5
Epuisay [F] 42 C5
Eraclea [I] 72 F6
Eraclea [I] 122 D5
Eraclea Mare [I] 72 F6
Eraclea Minoa [I] 126 C4
Eräjärvi [FIN] 176 G1
Eräslahti [FIN] 186 F6
Erateiní [GR] 132 G5
Erátyrá [GR] 128 E5
Erba [I] 70 G4
Erbach [D] 46 D4
Erbach [D] 60 B3
Erbalunga [F] 114 C2
Erbè [I] 110 F1
Erbendorf [D] 48 B4
Ercolano [I] 120 E3
Ercsi [H] 76 C2
Érd [H] 76 C1
Erdal [N] 180 C6
Erdek [TR] 150 D4
Erdevik [SRB] 142 F2
Erding [D] 60 E4
Erdőhorváti [H] 64 G4
Erdut [HR] 142 E1
Eremitage [D] 46 H4
Erenköy (Kókkina) [CY] 154 F5
Eresós [GR] 134 G2
Erétria [GR] 134 C5
Erfde [D] 18 E2
Erfjord [N] 164 B2
Erftstadt [D] 30 G5
Erfurt [D] 32 H6
Ergama [TR] 152 D1
Ergili [TR] 150 D5
Ērgli [LV] 198 E5
Ergoldsbach [D] 60 F3
Erice [I] 126 B2
Erice [TR] 152 G3
Ericeira [P] 86 A4
Ericek [TR] 150 F4
Erikli [TR] 150 B4
Eriksberg [S] 168 B4
Eriksberg [S] 184 C2
Eriksberg [S] 190 F4
Eriksmåla [S] 162 E5
Erikstad [S] 166 D5
Eringsboda [S] 162 E6
Erka [N] 180 F5
Erkelenz [D] 30 F4
Erla [E] 84 C6
Erlangen [D] 46 G4
Erlenbach [D] 46 D4
Erlsbach [A] 72 E2
Ermelo [NL] 16 E4
Ermenonville [F] 42 G3
Ermesinde [P] 80 C4
Ermidas-Aldeia [P] 94 C3
Ermióni [GR] 136 F3
Ermitage, Grotte de l'- [F] 56 H4
Ermoúpoli [GR] 138 D2
Ermsleben [D] 34 B4
Erndtebrück [D] 32 D6
Ernée [F] 26 D6
Ernerwald [CH] 70 E2
Ernestinovo [HR] 142 E1
Ernstbrunn [A] 62 F3
Erp [D] 30 G5
Erquy [F] 26 B4
Erratzu [E] 84 C3
Errenteria / Rentería [E] 84 B2
Erro [E] 84 C3
Erronkari / Roncal [E] 84 C4
Ersekë [AL] 128 D5
Ersmark [S] 196 A6
Ersnäs [S] 196 B3
Erstein [F] 44 H6
Ertuğrul [TR] 152 D1
Ervasti [FIN] 196 E3
Ervedal [E] 86 D5
Ervedosa [P] 80 D4
Ervenik [HR] 112 H5
Ervidel [P] 94 D3
Ervik [N] 180 B4
Ervy-le-Châtel [F] 44 A6
Erwitte [D] 32 D4
Erxleben [D] 34 B3
Erythrés [GR] 134 B6
Erzsébet [H] 76 B5
Eržvilkas [LT] 200 E5
Esa / Yesa [E] 84 C4
Esatçe [TR] 130 H3
Esatlar [TR] 152 G1
Esbjerg [DK] 156 A2
Esblada [E] 92 C4
Esbo / Espoo [FIN] 176 G5
Escairón [E] 78 D4
Escalada [E] 82 E4
Escalaplano [I] 118 D6
Escalona [E] 84 E5
Escalona [E] 88 E6
Escalonilla [E] 96 E1
Escandón, Puerto de- [E] 98 E2
Escariche [E] 88 G6
Escároz / Ezkaroze [E] 84 C4
Escatrón [E] 90 F5
Eschede [D] 32 G1
Eschenbach [D] 46 H4
Eschenburg-Eibelshausen [D] 32 D6
Eschenlohe [D] 60 D6
Escherndorf [D] 46 F4
Eschershausen [D] 32 F3
Esch-sur-Alzette [L] 44 E3
Esch-sur-Sûre [L] 44 E2
Eschwege [D] 32 G5
Eschweiler [D] 30 F4
Escipions, Torre dels- [E] 92 C5
Escombreras [E] 104 C4
Escornalbou [E] 90 H6
Escos [F] 84 D2
Es Cubells [E] 104 C5
Escucha [E] 90 E6
Escúllar [E] 102 F4
Eşen [TR] 154 F3
Esence [TR] 150 E4
Esenköy [TR] 150 H4
Esens [D] 18 C3
Esentepe (Ágios Amvrósios) [CY] 154 G5
Esenyurt [TR] 150 E3
es Figueral [E] 104 C5
Esgos [E] 78 D5
Esguevillas de Esgueva [E] 88 F1
Eskelhem [S] 168 F4
Eskiçine [TR] 152 E6
Eskifjörður [IS] 192 D3
Eski Gediz [TR] 152 G2
Eskihisar [TR] 152 E6
Eskilstuna [S] 168 B3
Eskin [TR] 152 F3
Eskişehir [TR] 150 H5
Eskiyüregil [TR] 150 G5
Eskola [FIN] 196 C5
Eslared [S] 162 C5
Eslarn [D] 48 C5
Eslohe [D] 32 D5
Eslöv [S] 158 C2
Esmared [S] 162 B5
Eşme [TR] 152 F4
Es Mercadal [E] 104 H4
Esmoriz [P] 80 B4
Esnandes [F] 54 C4
Esnouveaux [F] 56 H1
Espa [N] 172 C4
Espadilla [E] 98 F3
Espalion [F] 68 B5
Esparreguera [E] 92 D4
Espås [N] 182 B1
Espe [S] 170 C4
Espedal [N] 170 G1
Espejo [E] 102 C2
Espeland [N] 164 B4
Espeland [N] 170 B4
Espelette [F] 84 C2
Espeli [N] 164 D4
Espelkamp [D] 32 E2
Espera [E] 100 G3
Esperia [I] 120 C1
Espezel [F] 106 B5
Espiel [E] 96 C5
Espinama [E] 82 D3
Espinheiro, Convento de- [P] 94 D1
Espinho [P] 80 B4
Espinilla [E] 82 E4
Espinosa de los Monteros [E] 82 F4
Espírito Santo [P] 94 D4
Esplantas [F] 68 D5
Esponellà [E] 92 F2
Espoo / Esbo [FIN] 176 G5
Esporles [E] 104 E4
Es Port d'Alcúdia [E] 104 F4
es Port d'Andratx [E] 104 D5
Esposende [P] 78 A6
Espot [E] 84 G6
Espot Esquí [E] 92 E2
Esprels [F] 58 C4
Esse / Ähtävä [FIN] 196 C6
Essen [D] 18 C6
Essen [D] 30 H3
Essenbach [D] 60 F3
Essertaux [F] 28 D5
Esslingen [D] 58 H1
Essoyes [F] 56 G1
Essuilles [F] 28 D6
Essunga [S] 166 D6
Estada [E] 90 G3
Estagel [F] 106 C6
Estaing [F] 68 B5
Estaires [F] 28 F3
Estang [F] 66 D6
Estanyol [E] 104 E5
Estarreja [P] 80 B5
Estavayer-le-Lac [CH] 58 C6
Este [I] 110 G1
Estela [P] 80 B3
Estella / Lizarra [E] 84 A4
Estellencs [E] 104 D5
Estepa [E] 102 B3
Estepar [E] 82 E6
Estepona [E] 100 H5
Esteras, Cuesta de- [E] 90 B4
Esternay [F] 42 H4
Esterri d'Àneu [E] 84 G5
Esterwegen [D] 18 C5
Estíbaliz, Santuario de- [E] 82 H5
Estissac [F] 44 A6
Estói [P] 94 C5
Estoril [P] 86 A5
Estrées-St-Denis [F] 28 E6
Estremera [E] 96 H1
Estremoz [P] 86 E6
Esztergom [H] 64 C5
Étables-sur-Mer [F] 26 B4
Etagnac [F] 54 F6
Etain [F] 44 E3
Étalans [F] 58 B5
Etalle [B] 44 E2
Étampes [F] 42 F4
Étang-sur-Arroux [F] 56 F4
Etaples [F] 28 D3
Ete [H] 64 A6
Eteläinen [FIN] 176 G2
Etili [TR] 150 B5
Etne [N] 164 B1
Etoges [F] 44 A4
Éton [F] 44 D3
Etréaupont [F] 28 G5
Etrepagny [F] 28 C6
Etretat [F] 26 G2
Etropole [BG] 146 G4
Etseri / Ähtäri [FIN] 186 E4
Ettelbruck [L] 44 F2
Ettenheim [D] 58 E2
Ettlingen [D] 46 B6
Etxarri / Echarri [E] 84 A3
Eu [F] 28 C4
Eudorf [D] 46 D1
Euerhausen [D] 46 E4
Eugénie-les-Bains [F] 66 C6
Eulate [E] 82 H5
Eumeneia [TR] 152 H3
Eunate [E] 84 B4
Eupen [B] 30 F5
Eura [FIN] 176 D2
Euraåminne / Eurajoki [FIN] 176 C2
Eurajoki / Euraåminne [FIN] 176 C2
Euratsfeld [A] 62 C5
Euríalo, Castello- [I] 126 G5
Euromos [TR] 152 D6
Europa-Brücke [A] 72 D1
Europoort [NL] 16 C5
Euskirchen [D] 30 G5
Eussenhausen [D] 46 F2
Eutin [D] 18 G3
Eutzsch [D] 34 D4
Eväjärvi [FIN] 186 F6
Evangelismos [GR] 132 G1
Evanger [N] 170 C3
Evaux-les-Bains [F] 56 B6
Evciler [TR] 152 B1
Evciler [TR] 152 H4
Evciler [TR] 154 F4
Évdilos [GR] 138 G1
Evendorf [D] 18 F5
Evenstad [N] 172 C2
Everöd [S] 158 D2
Everswinkel [D] 32 C3
Evertsberg [S] 172 F3
Evesham [GB] 12 H2
Evian [F] 70 C2
Evijärvi [FIN] 186 D1
Evinochóri [GR] 132 E5
Evisa [F] 114 A4
Evitskog [FIN] 176 G5
Evje [N] 164 D4
Evolène [CH] 70 D3
Évora [P] 94 D1
Évora Monte [P] 86 D6
Evran [F] 26 C5
Evrensekiz [TR] 150 C2
Evreux [F] 42 D2
Evron [F] 26 E6
Evry [F] 42 F4
Évzonoi [GR] 128 G3
Exaplátanos [GR] 128 F3
Éxarchos [GR] 132 H5
Excideuil [F] 66 G2
Exeter [GB] 12 E4
Exmes [F] 26 G5
Exmouth [GB] 12 E5
Exochí [GR] 128 G5
Exochí [GR] 130 C2
Exómvourgo [GR] 138 E2
Externsteine [D] 32 E3
Extertal [D] 32 E3
Extremo [P] 78 B5
Eydehavn [N] 164 F5
Eyemouth [GB] 8 F4
Eyguières [F] 106 H4
Eygurande [F] 68 B2
Eylie [F] 84 G5
Eymet [F] 66 E4
Eymoutiers [F] 66 H2
Eyrarbakki [IS] 192 A3
Ézaro [E] 78 B2
Ezcaray [E] 82 F6
Ezere [LV] 198 C6
Ezermuiža [LV] 198 C4
Ezernieki [LV] 198 G6
Ezernijeki [LV] 198 D6
Ezine [TR] 130 H6
Ezkaroze / Escároz [E] 84 C4

F

Faaborg [DK] 156 D4
Faak [A] 74 A3
Fabara, Mausoleo de- [E] 90 G5
Fabbrico [I] 110 E2
Fåberg [N] 172 B2
Fabero [E] 78 F4
Fábiánsebestyén [H] 76 F3
Fabriano [I] 116 B1
Facheca [E] 104 E1
Fačkov [SK] 64 B2
Facture [F] 66 C3
Fadd [H] 76 C4
Faenza [I] 110 G4
Faeto [I] 120 F2
Fafe [P] 80 C3
Făgăraş [RO] 204 D4
Fågelfors [S] 162 F4
Fågelsjö [S] 182 G6
Fågelsundet [S] 174 F4
Fågelvik [S] 162 G1
Fageole, Col de la- [F] 68 C4
Fagerås [S] 166 E2
Fagerhaugen [N] 180 H3
Fagerheim Fjellstue [N] 170 E4
Fagerhult [S] 162 D1
Fagerhult [S] 162 F4
Fagerhult [S] 166 C5
Fagernes [N] 170 G3
Fagernes [N] 192 F2
Fagersanna [S] 166 F5
Fagersta [S] 168 A1
Fagerstrand [N] 166 B1
Fagervika [N] 190 D1
Fäggeby [S] 174 D5
Faglävik [S] 162 B1
Fagnano Castello [I] 124 D4
Fagurhólsmýri [IS] 192 B3
Faial [P] 100 A3
Fai della Paganella [I] 72 C4
Faido [CH] 70 F2
Fains le Sources [F] 44 D4
Faistós [GR] 140 E5
Fajã do Ouvidor [P] 100 C3
Fajã dos Cubres [P] 100 C3
Faja Grande [P] 100 B3
Fakenham [GB] 14 G1
Fåker [S] 182 G3
Fakija [BG] 148 E5
Fakse [DK] 156 G4
Fakse Ladeplads [DK] 156 G4
Falaise [F] 26 F4
Falásarna [GR] 140 B4
Falatádos [GR] 138 E2
Falcade [I] 72 E4
Falconara, Castello di- [I] 126 E4
Falconara Marittima [I] 112 C6
Falcone [I] 124 A7
Falcsut [H] 76 B1
Faldsled [DK] 156 D4
Falerii Novi [I] 114 H4
Falerna [I] 124 D5
Falerna Marina [I] 124 D5
Falerum [S] 162 G1
Falileevo [RUS] 178 F6
Faliráki [GR] 154 D3
Falkenberg [D] 34 E5
Falkenberg [D] 60 G3
Falkenberg [S] 160 H4
Falkenstein [A] 62 F3
Falkenstein [A] 62 F3
Falkenstein [D] 34 A4
Falkenstein [D] 44 F1
Falkenstein [D] 48 C6
Falkenstein [D] 48 C2
Falkenstein, Château de- [F] 44 H5
Falkirk [GB] 8 E3
Falköping [S] 166 E6
Fałków [PL] 38 A6
Falla [S] 168 A5
Fållen [S] 162 D5
Fallersleben [D] 32 H2
Fallet [N] 172 C5
Fallet [N] 180 H5
Fällfors [S] 196 A4
Fallingbostel [D] 18 F6
Falmouth [GB] 12 C5
Falset [E] 90 H6
Falsterbo [S] 156 H3
Fălticeni [RO] 204 D3
Falträsk [S] 190 G4
Faludden [S] 168 G6
Falun [S] 174 C4
Faluszliget [H] 76 G2
Fámjin [FR] 160 A3
Fana [N] 170 B4
Fanano [I] 110 E4
Fanári [GR] 130 F3
Fanári [GR] 132 F2
Fanbyn [S] 184 D4
Fáncs [H] 76 B3
Fanefjord [DK] 156 G5
Fångåmon [S] 182 F2
Fanjeaux [F] 106 B4
Fannrem [N] 180 H1
Fano [I] 112 C5
Fanós [GR] 128 G3
Fântânele [RO] 148 B2
Fanthyttan [S] 166 H2
Farad [H] 62 G6
Fara Novarese [I] 70 F4
Fårbo [S] 162 G3
Farcheville, Château de- [F] 42 F5
Farébersviller [F] 44 G4
Fareham [GB] 12 H5
Fårevejle [DK] 156 F2
Farfa, Abbazia di- [I] 116 A4
Färgaryd [S] 162 B4
Färgelanda [S] 166 C5
Färila [S] 184 C6
Faringdon [GB] 12 H3
Faringe [S] 168 E1
Fåringtofta [S] 158 C1
Farini [I] 110 C2
Färjestaden [S] 162 G5
Farkadóna [GR] 132 F2
Farkasgyepü [H] 74 H2
Farkaždin [SRB] 142 G1
Farlete [E] 90 F4
Fărliug [RO] 76 H6
Färlöv [S] 158 D1
Färna [S] 168 B2
Färnäs [S] 172 G3
Farnese [I] 114 G3
Farnham [GB] 14 D4
Faro [P] 94 C6
Fårö [S] 168 H3
Fårösund [S] 168 H3
Farranfore [IRL] 4 B4
Farre [DK] 160 D6
Fársala [GR] 132 G3
Farsø [DK] 160 D4
Farstad [N] 180 E2
Farstorp [S] 158 D1
Farsund [N] 164 C5
Farum [DK] 156 G2
Fårvang [DK] 160 D6
Fasanerie, Schloss- [D] 46 E2
Fasano [I] 122 E3
Fåset [N] 182 B4
Fasgar [E] 78 G5
Fasovka [UA] 202 D7
Faster [DK] 156 B1
Fasterholt [DK] 156 C1
Fastov [UA] 202 D7
Fatezh [RUS] 202 F5
Fátima [E] 100 H4
Fátima [P] 86 C3
Fatjas [S] 190 H1
Fatnica [BIH] 144 D3
Fättjaur [S] 190 E3
Faucille, Col de la- [F] 70 B1
Faucogney-et-la-Mer [F] 58 C3
Faulbach [D] 46 D4
Faulensee [CH] 70 E1
Faulquemont [F] 44 F4

Fuhrberg [D] 32 G1
Fulda [D] 46 E2
Fulnek [CZ] 50 E5
Fülöpszállás [H] 76 C3
Fulpmes [A] 72 D1
Fulunäs [S] 172 E2
Fumay [F] 30 C6
Fumel [F] 66 F5
Funäsdalen [S] 182 E4
Funchal [P] 100 A3
Fundão [P] 86 F2
Fundres / Pfundres [I] 72 E2
Furadouro [P] 80 B4
Furculeşti [RO] 148 B2
Fure [N] 170 B1
Furnas [P] 100 E3
Furnes (Veurne) [B] 28 F1
Fürnitz [A] 72 H3
Fursest [N] 180 D4
Furset [N] 180 E2
Fürstenau [D] 32 C1
Fürstenberg [D] 20 D5
Fürstenfeld [A] 74 E2
Fürstenfeldbruck [D] 60 D4
Fürstenwalde [D] 34 F2
Fürstenwerder [D] 20 D5
Fürstenzell [D] 60 H3
Furta [H] 76 G2
Furtan [S] 166 E2
Fürth [D] 46 G5
Furth im Wald [D] 48 D6
Furtwangen [D] 58 F3
Furuby [S] 162 E4
Furudal [S] 172 H2
Furuflaten [N] 192 G2
Furusjö [S] 162 D1
Furusund [S] 168 F2
Furutangvik [N] 190 D4
Furuvik [S] 174 E4
Fusa [N] 170 B4
Fuscaldo [I] 124 D4
Fusch [A] 72 G1
Fushë Arrëz [AL] 128 B1
Fushë-Krujë [AL] 128 B2
Fushë-Kuqe [AL] 128 B2
Fushë Muhurr [AL] 128 C2
Fusio [CH] 70 F2
Füssen [D] 60 C6
Futog [SRB] 142 F1
Futrikelv [N] 192 F2
Füzesabony [H] 64 E5
Füzesgyarmat [H] 76 G2
Fuzeta [P] 94 D6
Fyláki [GR] 132 G3
Fylákio [GR] 130 H1
Fylakopi [GR] 138 D4
Fylí [GR] 134 B6
Fylí [GR] 134 C6
Fyllinge [S] 162 B5
Fynshav [DK] 156 D4
Fyresdal [N] 164 E3
Fyrkat [DK] 160 D5
Fyteíes [GR] 132 E4

G

Gaas [A] 74 F2
Gaasbeek [B] 28 H3
Gabarc [BG] 146 G3
Gabarret [F] 66 D6
Gabčíkovo [SK] 62 H5
Gabela [BIH] 144 C3
Gaber [BG] 146 F4
Gabicce Mare [I] 112 B5
Gąbin [PL] 36 H2
Gąbino [PL] 22 B2
Gaboš [HR] 142 E1
Gabrovica [BG] 146 G5
Gabrovka [SLO] 74 C5
Gabrovo [BG] 148 C4
Gać [PL] 24 D6
Gacé [F] 26 G5
Gacko [BIH] 144 D2
Gäda [S] 184 C5
Gäddede [S] 190 E5
Gäddeholm [S] 168 C2
Gadebusch [D] 18 H4
Gadna [H] 64 F4
Gádor [E] 102 G5
Gádoros [H] 76 F3
Gadžin Han [SRB] 146 D4
Gæidno [N] 194 D2
Gæidnovuoppe [N] 194 B4
Gaël [F] 26 B5
Găeşti [RO] 204 D5
Gaeta [I] 120 C2
Gaflenz [A] 62 C5
Gagarin [RUS] 202 E3
Gaggenau [D] 58 F1
Gagliano Castelferrato [I] 126 F3
Gagliano del Capo [I] 122 G6
Gagnef [S] 172 H4
Gahro [D] 34 E4
Gaildorf [D] 46 E6
Gaillac [F] 106 B2
Gaillimh / Galway [IRL] 2 C5
Gaillon [F] 28 C6
Gainsborough [GB] 10 F5
Gairloch [GB] 6 C4
Gairo [I] 118 E5
Gaj [HR] 142 B1
Gaj [SRB] 142 H2
Gajary [SK] 62 G4
Gajdobra [SRB] 142 F1
Gakovo [SRB] 76 C5
Gålå [N] 170 H1
Galåbodarna [S] 182 F3
Galan [F] 84 F4
Galanádo [GR] 138 F3
Galanito [N] 194 B4
Galanta [SK] 62 H4
Galapagar [E] 88 F5
Galashiels [GB] 8 E4
Galata [BG] 148 F3
Galatáki, Moní- [GR] 134 B4
Galatás [GR] 136 G2
Galaţi [RO] 204 E4
Galatia (Mehmetcik) [CY] 154 G4
Galati Marina [I] 124 B7
Galatina [I] 122 G5
Galátista [GR] 130 B5
Galatone [I] 122 G5
Galaxídi [GR] 132 G5
Galbally [IRL] 4 D4
Gålborget [S] 184 F1
Galdakao [E] 82 G4
Gáldar [E] 100 C6
Galeata [I] 110 G5
Galera [E] 102 G3
Galéria [F] 114 A3
Galgaguta [H] 64 D5
Galgagyörk [H] 64 D5
Galgamácsa [H] 64 D6
Galicea Mare [RO] 146 F1
Galinóporni (Kaleburnu) [CY] 154 H4
Galiny [PL] 22 H3
Galipsós [GR] 130 C4
Galissás [GR] 138 D2
Galisteo [E] 86 H4
Galižana [HR] 112 D2
Galizano [E] 82 F3
Gallarate [I] 70 F4
Gällared [S] 162 B4
Gallargues [F] 106 F4
Gallarus Oratory [IRL] 4 A3
Gallegos del Río [E] 80 G4
Gallegos de Solmirón [E] 88 C4
Gallenstein [A] 62 C6
Galliate [I] 70 F5
Gallípoli [I] 122 G5
Gällivare [S] 192 G6
Gallneukirchen [A] 62 B4
Gällö [S] 182 H3
Gällstad [S] 162 C2
Gallur [E] 90 D3
Galovo [BG] 146 G2
Gålsjö bruk [S] 184 F2
Galston [GB] 8 D3
Galtelli [I] 118 E4
Galten [DK] 156 D1
Galten [N] 182 D6
Gåltjärn [S] 184 E4
Galtström [S] 184 F5
Galtür [A] 72 B2
Galveias [P] 86 D5
Gálvez [E] 96 E2
Gałwany [PL] 24 B3
Galway / Gaillimh [IRL] 2 C5
Galyatető [H] 64 E5
Gamaches [F] 28 C4
Gambara [I] 110 D1
Gambárie [I] 124 C7
Gambatesa [I] 120 F1
Gambolò [I] 70 F5
Gaming [A] 62 D5
Gamla Gränome [S] 168 D1
Gamla Uppsala [S] 168 D1
Gamleby [S] 162 G2
Gammalsälen [S] 172 F4
Gammel Estrup [DK] 160 E5
Gammel Skagen [DK] 160 E2
Gammelskolla [N] 172 B2
Gammelstaden [S] 196 B3
Gammertingen [D] 58 H3
Gams [CH] 58 H5
Gamvik [N] 194 D1
Gamzigrad [SRB] 146 D2
Gan [F] 84 E3
Ganacker [D] 60 G3
Ganagobie, Prieuré- [F] 108 C3
Gand (Gent) [B] 28 G2
Gandal [N] 164 B3
Gândara [P] 86 E2
Ganderkesee [D] 18 D5
Gandesa [E] 90 G6
Gandía [E] 98 F6
Gandino [I] 70 H4
Gandrup [DK] 160 E4
Gandvik [N] 194 E2
Ganges [F] 106 E3
Gangi [I] 126 E3
Gângiova [RO] 146 G2
Gangkofen [D] 60 G3
Gannat [F] 68 D1
Gänserndorf [A] 62 F4
Gap [F] 108 D2
Gaperhult [S] 166 E4
Gara [H] 76 C5
Garaballa [E] 98 D3
Garabonc [H] 74 G3
Garafía [E] 100 A4
Garaguso [I] 122 C4
Gara Khitrino [BG] 148 E2
Garani [BY] 202 B5
Garavac [BIH] 142 D2
Garbagna [I] 110 B2
Garbno [PL] 24 B3
Garbów [PL] 38 D5
Garbsen [D] 32 F2
Garching [D] 60 G4
Garcia [E] 90 H6
Garciaz [E] 96 B2
Garčin [HR] 142 D2
Gârcov [RO] 148 A2
Gard, Pont du- [F] 106 G3
Garda [I] 72 C6
Gardanne [F] 108 B5
Gårdby [S] 162 G5
Gardeja [PL] 22 E4
Gardelegen [D] 34 B2
Gardíki [GR] 132 F4
Gårding [D] 18 E2
Gärdnäs [S] 190 E5
Gardone Riviera [I] 72 B5
Gardone Val Trómpia [I] 72 B5
Gárdony [H] 76 B2
Gärdsby [S] 162 E4
Gårdsjöbäcken [S] 190 F3
Gårdskär [S] 174 F4
Gärdslösa [S] 162 G5
Gardstad [N] 190 C4
Gårdstånga [S] 158 C2
Garein [F] 66 C5
Gårelehöjden [S] 184 E1
Garen [N] 170 D4
Gares / Puente la Reina [E] 84 B4
Garešnica [HR] 74 G6
Garéssio [I] 108 G3
Gargaliánoi [GR] 136 C4
Gargas, Grotte de- [F] 84 F4
Gargaur [S] 190 G3
Gargellen [A] 72 A2
Gargilesse-Dampierre [F] 54 H5
Gargnano [I] 72 C5
Gargoles de Abajo [E] 90 A5
Gargyán [H] 76 D4
Gargždai [LT] 200 D4
Gari [MK] 128 D2
Garibaldi, Tomba di- [I] 118 E2
Garípa [GR] 140 E5
Garkalne [LV] 198 D5
Garlasco [I] 70 F5
Garlin [F] 84 E2
Garlstorf [D] 18 F5
Garmisch Partenkirchen [D] 60 D6
Garmo [N] 180 F5
Garnish Gardens [IRL] 4 B5
Garoza [LV] 198 D5
Garpenberg [S] 174 D5
Garraf [E] 92 D5
Garrafe de Torío [E] 78 H5
Garray [E] 90 B2
Garrel [D] 18 C5
Garristown [IRL] 2 F5
Garrotxa, Zona Volcànica de la- [E] 92 F2
Garrovillas [E] 86 G4
Garrucha [E] 102 H5
Gars am Kamp [A] 62 E3
Garsås [S] 172 G3
Garsnas [S] 158 D3
Gartland [N] 190 C5
Gartow [D] 20 A6
Gartringen [D] 58 G1
Gartz [D] 20 E5
Garvão [P] 94 C3
Garwolin [PL] 38 C4
Garz [D] 20 D2
Gåsborn [S] 166 G1
Gåsbue [N] 180 F4
Gaschurn [A] 72 B2
Gascueña [E] 98 B1
Gasen [A] 74 D1
Gaskeluokta [S] 190 F4
Gąski [PL] 24 D3
Gąsocin [PL] 38 B1
Gaspoltshofen [A] 62 A4
Gässåsen [S] 184 D5
Gasteiner Klamm [A] 72 G1
Gastes [F] 66 B4
Gastoúni [GR] 136 B2
Gasztony [H] 74 F2
Gata [N] 172 C4
Gata de Gorgos [E] 104 F1
Gatchina [RUS] 178 H6
Gatehouse of Fleet [GB] 8 D5
Gátér [H] 76 E3
Gateshead [GB] 8 G6
Gátova [E] 98 E4
Gatta [I] 110 D3
Gattendorf [A] 62 G5
Gattinara [I] 70 E4
Gaubert [F] 42 E5
Gaucín [E] 100 H4
Gaukås [N] 164 E3
Gaulstad [N] 190 C5
Gaupne [N] 170 D1
Gaushach [D] 46 E3
Gausvik [N] 192 E4
Gautefall [N] 164 F3
Gautestad [N] 164 D4
Gauville [F] 26 G5
Gavaloú [GR] 132 E5
Gavardo [I] 72 B6
Gavarnie [F] 84 E5
Gavarnie, Cirque de- [F] 84 E5
Gávavencsellő [H] 64 G4
Gaverina Terme [I] 70 H4
Gavi [I] 110 A2
Gavião [P] 86 E4
Gavirate [I] 70 F4
Gävle [S] 174 E4
Gavnø Slot [DK] 156 F4
Gavoi [I] 118 D4
Gavorrano [I] 114 F2
Gavray [F] 26 D4
Gavrilov- Yam [RUS] 202 F1
Gávrio [GR] 134 E6
Gávros [GR] 128 E5
Gavry [RUS] 198 G5
Gåvsta [S] 168 D1
Gävunda [S] 172 G4
Gåxsjö [S] 190 E6
Gaziköy [TR] 150 C4
Gazimağusa (Ammóchostos) [CY] 154 G5
Gazoldo degli Ippoliti [I] 110 E1
Gázoros [GR] 130 C3
Gbelce [SK] 64 B5
Gdańsk [PL] 22 E2
Gdov [RUS] 202 A2
Gdów [PL] 52 B4
Gdynia [PL] 22 E2
Gea de Albarracín [E] 98 D1
Geashill [IRL] 2 E6
Geaune [F] 84 E2
Gebesee [D] 32 H6
Geblar [D] 46 F1
Gebze [TR] 150 F3
Geçitkale (Lefkónikon) [CY] 154 G5
Geçkinli [TR] 150 B2
Gedem [D] 46 D2
Gedesby [DK] 20 B1
Gedinne [B] 44 D1
Gediz [TR] 152 G2
Gedser [DK] 20 B1
Gedsted [DK] 160 D4
Gedved [DK] 156 D1
Geel [B] 30 D3
Geertruidenberg [NL] 16 D6
Geeste [D] 16 H4
Geesthacht [D] 18 G4
Gefell [D] 48 B2
Gefrees [D] 46 H3
Gefýra [GR] 128 H4
Gefýria [GR] 132 F3
Gehren [D] 46 G2
Geijersholm [S] 172 F6
Geilenkirchen [D] 30 F4
Geilo [N] 170 E4
Geiranger [N] 180 E4
Geisa [D] 46 E1
Geiselhöring [D] 60 F2
Geiselwind [D] 46 F4
Geisenfeld [D] 60 E3
Geisenhausen [D] 60 F3
Geisingen [D] 58 G3
Geislingen [D] 60 B3
Geisnes [N] 190 C4
Geithain [D] 34 D6
Geithus [N] 170 G6
Gela [I] 126 E5
Geldern [D] 30 G2
Geldrop [NL] 30 E2
Geleen [NL] 30 F4
Gelej [H] 64 F5
Gelembe [TR] 152 D2
Gelgaudiškis [LT] 200 E5
Gelibolu [TR] 150 B5
Gelibolu [TR] 154 D1
Gelida [E] 92 D4
Gelnhausen [D] 46 D3
Gelnica [SK] 64 F2
Gelsa [E] 90 F4
Gelsenkirchen [D] 30 H3
Gelting [D] 156 C5
Gelu [RO] 76 G5
Gembloux [B] 30 D5
Gémenos [F] 108 B5
Gemerská Poloma [SK] 64 E3
Gemerská Ves [SK] 64 E3
Gemert [NL] 30 F2
Gemikonağı (Karavostasi) [CY] 154 F5
Gemiş [TR] 152 H5
Gemlik [TR] 150 F4
Gemmenich [B] 30 F4
Gemona del Friuli [I] 72 G4
Gémozac [F] 54 C6
Gemünd [D] 30 F5
Gemünden [D] 32 E6
Gemünden [D] 44 H2
Gemunden [D] 46 E3
Genappe [B] 30 C4
Génave [E] 96 G6
Genazzano [I] 116 B5
Gençay [F] 54 E4
Gencsapáti [H] 74 F1
Génelard [F] 56 F5
General Inzovo [BG] 148 D5
Generalski Stol [HR] 112 G1
General Toshevo [BG] 148 F1
Generli [TR] 150 C3
Genevad [S] 162 B5
Genève [CH] 70 B2
Gengenbach [D] 58 F2
Genillé [F] 54 G3
Genk [B] 30 E4
Genlis [F] 56 H4
Gennádio [GR] 154 D4
Genna Maria, Nuraghe- [I] 118 C6
Gennep [NL] 16 F6
Gennes [F] 54 E2
Génolhac [F] 68 D6
Génova [I] 110 B3
Genshagen [D] 34 E3
Gent (Gand) [B] 28 G2
Genthin [D] 34 C2
Gentioux [F] 68 A2
Genzano di Lucánia [I] 120 H3
Genzano di Roma [I] 116 A6
Georgianoí [GR] 128 G5
Georgioúpoli [GR] 140 C4
Georgi Traykov [BG] 148 F3
Georgsheil [D] 18 B4
Geotermia, Museo della- [I] 114 F1
Gera [D] 48 C1
Geraardsbergen [B] 28 H3
Gerabronn [D] 46 E5
Gerace [I] 124 D7
Gerakarou [GR] 130 B4
Gérakas [GR] 136 F4
Geráki [GR] 136 E4
Gerakiní [GR] 130 B5
Gérardmer [F] 58 D2
Geras [A] 62 E3
Gerasdorf bei Wien [A] 62 F4
Gerbéviller [F] 44 F6
Gerbstedt [D] 34 B4
Gérce [H] 74 G2
Gerchsheim [D] 46 E4
Geremeas [I] 118 D7
Gerena [E] 94 G5
Gerês [P] 78 B6
Geretsried [D] 60 E5
Gérgal [E] 102 G4
Gerince [TR] 154 C2
Gerlos [A] 72 E1
Germaringen [D] 60 C5
Germasogeia [CY] 154 F6
Germay [F] 44 D6
Gemencik [TR] 152 D5
Germering [D] 60 C4
Germering [D] 60 D4
Germersheim [D] 46 B5
Germigny-des-Pres [F] 42 F6
Gernika-Lumo [E] 82 H4
Gernrode [D] 34 A4
Gernsbach [D] 58 F1
Gernsheim [D] 46 C4
Gerola Alta [I] 70 H3
Geroliménas [GR] 136 E5
Gerolstein [D] 30 G6
Gerolzhofen [D] 46 F4
Gerona / Girona [E] 92 F3
Geroskípou [CY] 154 F6
Gerovo [HR] 112 F1
Gerri de la Sal [E] 92 C1
Gersfeld [D] 46 E2
Gersthofen [D] 60 D3
Gerswalde [D] 20 D6
Gesäter [S] 166 C4
Gesäuse [A] 62 C6
Gescher [D] 16 G6
Geseke [D] 32 D4
Gespunsart [F] 44 C2
Gestelnburg [CH] 70 E2
Gesualdo [I] 120 F3
Gesunda [S] 172 G3
Geta [FIN] 176 A5
Getafe [E] 88 F6
Getaria [E] 84 A2
Gettlinge [S] 162 G6
Gettorf [D] 18 F2
Getxo [E] 82 G3
Gévezé [F] 26 C5
Gevgelija [MK] 128 G3
Gevigney-et-Mercey [F] 58 B3
Gevrey-Chambertin [F] 56 G4
Gevsjön [S] 182 E1
Gex [F] 70 B2
Gey [D] 30 F5
Geyikli [TR] 130 H6
Geyre [TR] 152 F5
Geysir [IS] 192 B3
Geyve [TR] 150 G3
Geziq [AL] 128 B1
Gföhl [A] 62 D3
Ghedi [I] 72 B6
Gheorghieni [RO] 204 D4
Ghilarza [I] 118 C4
Ghimpaţi [RO] 148 C1
Ghisonaccia [F] 114 C4
Ghisoni [F] 114 B4
Giáltra [GR] 132 H4
Giannitsá [GR] 128 G4
Giannoúli [GR] 130 H2
Giardinetto [I] 120 G2
Giardini-Naxos [I] 124 B8
Giarmata [RO] 76 G5
Giarratana [I] 126 F5
Giarre [I] 124 A8
Giat [F] 68 B2
Giba [I] 118 B7
Gibellina [I] 126 B2
Gibellina, Ruderi di- [I] 126 C2
Gibilmanna, Santuario di- [I] 126 E2
Gibostad [N] 192 F2
Gibraleón [E] 94 E5
Gibraltar [GBZ] 100 G5
Gic [H] 74 H1
Gidböle [S] 184 G1
Gideå [S] 184 G1
Gideåkroken [S] 190 G5
Gidle [PL] 50 G1
Gieboldehausen [D] 32 G4
Giedraičiai [LT] 200 G5
Gielas [S] 190 E3
Gielniów [PL] 38 A5
Gien [F] 56 C2
Giengedal [N] 180 C5
Giengen [D] 60 C3
Giens [F] 108 C6
Giera [RO] 142 H1
Gierałtowice [PL] 50 G4
Gieselwerder [D] 32 F4
Giessen [D] 46 C1
Gieten [NL] 16 G3
Giethoorn [NL] 16 F3
Gietrzwałd [PL] 22 G4
Giffoni [I] 120 F3
Gifhorn [D] 32 H2
Gigen [BG] 148 A2
Giglio Porto [I] 114 E4
Gignac [F] 106 E4
Gijón / Xixón [E] 82 B1
Giksi [LV] 198 E4
Gilford [NIR] 2 G4
Gilja [N] 164 B3
Gilleleje [DK] 156 G1
Gillhov [S] 182 G4
Gills [GB] 6 F2
Gillstad [S] 166 E5
Gilserberg [D] 32 E6
Gilze [NL] 30 D2
Gimat [F] 84 G2
Gimdalen [S] 184 C3
Gimel-les-Cascades [F] 66 H3
Gimenells, Castell de- [E] 90 G4
Gimmestad [N] 180 C5
Gimo [S] 174 F5
Gimont [F] 84 G3
Ginci [BG] 146 F4
Gingst [D] 20 D2
Ginosa [I] 122 D4
Ginzling [A] 72 E2
Ginzo de Limia / Xinzo de Limia [E] 78 C6
Giões [P] 94 D4
Gióia del Colle [I] 122 E3
Gióia Táuro [I] 124 C6
Gioiosa Marea [I] 124 A7
Giornico [CH] 70 G2
Giove Anxur, Tempio di- [I] 120 C2
Giovinazzo [I] 122 D2
Giraltovce [SK] 52 D6
Girgantai [LT] 24 E2
Girifalco [I] 124 D5
Girne (Kerýneia) [CY] 154 G5
Girolata [F] 114 A3
Giromagny [F] 58 C3
Girona / Gerona [E] 92 F3
Gironella [E] 92 E2
Girvan [GB] 8 C4
Gisholt [N] 164 F3
Gislaved [S] 162 C3
Gislev [DK] 156 E3
Gisors [F] 28 C6
Gisselås [S] 190 E6
Gisselfeld [DK] 156 F3
Gissi [I] 116 E5
Gisslarbo [S] 168 B2
Gistaín [E] 84 F5
Gistel [B] 28 F1
Gistrup [DK] 160 E4
Gittun [S] 190 G2
Giugliano In Campania [I] 120 D3
Giuliano di Roma [I] 120 C1
Giulianova [I] 116 D3
Giulvăz [RO] 76 G6
Giurgiţa [RO] 146 G2
Giurgiu [RO] 148 C1
Give [DK] 156 C2
Givet [F] 30 D6
Givors [F] 68 F3
Givry [B] 28 H4
Givry [F] 56 E3
Givry [F] 56 G5
Givry-en-Argonne [F] 44 C4
Giżałki [PL] 36 E3
Gizdavac [HR] 144 A1
Gizeux [F] 54 F2
Giżycko [PL] 24 C3
Gizzeria [I] 124 D5
Gjakove / Đakovica [SRB] 146 B6
Gjelten [N] 182 B5
Gjemnes [N] 180 F2
Gjerbës [AL] 128 C5
Gjerde [N] 180 D6
Gjermundshamn [N] 170 B5
Gjern [DK] 160 D6
Gjerrild [DK] 160 F5
Gjerstad [N] 164 F4
Gjersvik [N] 190 D4
Gjesvær [N] 194 C1
Gjeving [N] 164 F4
Gjinar [AL] 128 C3
Gjirokastër [AL] 128 C6
Gjølme [N] 180 H1
Gjøra [N] 180 G3
Gjóv [FR] 160 B1
Gjøvik [N] 172 B3
Gjøvik [N] 192 E3
G. Konjare [MK] 128 F1
Gkoritsá [GR] 136 E4
Gkoúra [GR] 136 D1
Gla [GR] 134 A5
Gladbeck [D] 30 H2
Gladenbach [D] 32 D6
Gladhammar [S] 162 G2
Gladstad [N] 190 C3
Glamoč [BIH] 142 B4
Glåmos [N] 182 C3
Glamsbjerg [DK] 156 D3
Glandorf [D] 32 D2
Glanmire [IRL] 4 C5
Glanworth [IRL] 4 D4
Glarus [CH] 58 G6
Glasgow [GB] 8 D3
Glashütte [D] 48 E1
Glashütten [A] 74 C3
Glastonbury [GB] 12 F4
Glauchau [D] 48 C1
Glava [BG] 148 A3
Glava [S] 166 D2
Glavan [BG] 148 D5
Glavanovtsi [BG] 146 E4
Glavičice [BIH] 142 E3
Glavinitsa [BG] 148 E1
Glavnik [SRB] 146 C4
Gleann Cholm Cille / Glencolumbkille [IRL] 2 D2
Gleann na Muaidhe / Glenamoy [IRL] 2 C3
Głębock [PL] 22 G2
Glebychevo [RUS] 178 F3
Gleichen [D] 46 G1
Gleina [D] 48 C1
Gleinalm Tunnel [A] 74 D1
Gleisdorf [A] 74 E2
Glenamaddy [IRL] 2 D4
Glenamoy / Gleann na Muaidhe [IRL] 2 C3
Glencoe [GB] 6 C6
Glencolumbkille / Gleann Cholm Cille [IRL] 2 D2
Glendalough [IRL] 4 G3
Glenealy [IRL] 4 G4
Glengarriff [IRL] 4 B5
Glénic [F] 54 H5
Glenmore [IRL] 4 E4
Glenrothes [GB] 8 E3
Glenties [IRL] 2 E2
Glenville [IRL] 4 D5
Glesne [N] 170 G5
Gletsch [CH] 70 F2
Gletscher Garten [D] 60 G5
Glewitz [D] 20 C3
Glimåkra [S] 158 D1
Glimmingehus [S] 158 D3
Glin [IRL] 4 C3
Glina [HR] 112 H1
Glinka [PL] 50 G5
Glinojeck [PL] 38 A1
Glinsce / Glinsk [IRL] 2 B4
Glinsk / Glinsce [IRL] 2 B4
G. Lisina [SRB] 146 E5
Glissjöberg [S] 182 G5
Glitterheim [N] 180 F6
Gliwice [PL] 50 F3
Gllavë [AL] 128 B5
Globitsy [RUS] 178 F5
Globočica [SRB] 146 C6
Głodowa [PL] 22 B3
Gloggnitz [A] 62 E6
Głogoczów [PL] 50 H4
Glogovac [HR] 74 G5
Głogów [PL] 36 B5
Głogówek [PL] 50 E3
Głogów Małopolski [PL] 52 E3
Glomfjord [N] 190 E1
Glommen [S] 160 H4
Glommersträsk [S] 190 H4
Glömminge [S] 162 G5
Glorup [DK] 156 E4
Glóssa [GR] 134 B3
Glössbo [S] 174 E2
Glossop [GB] 10 E4
Glostrup [DK] 156 G2
Glöte [S] 182 F5
Gloucester [GB] 12 G2
Głowaczów [PL] 38 C4
Główczyce [PL] 22 C2
Glowe [D] 20 D2
Glöwen [D] 20 B6
Głowno [PL] 36 H4
Gložan [SRB] 142 F1
Glozhene [BG] 146 G2
Glozhene [BG] 148 A4
Glozhenski Manastir [BG] 148 A4
Głubczyce [PL] 50 E3
Głuchołazy [PL] 50 D3
Głuchów [PL] 36 F4
Głuchów [PL] 36 H4
Głuchowo [PL] 36 C3
Glücksburg [D] 156 C4
Glückstadt [D] 18 E3
Gluda [LV] 198 D5
Glumsø [DK] 156 F3
Glušci [SRB] 142 F2
Głuszyca [PL] 50 B2
Glýfa [GR] 132 H3
Glyfáda [GR] 132 F5
Glyfáda [GR] 136 G1
Glykí [GR] 132 C3
Glyngøre [DK] 160 C4
Gmünd [A] 62 C3
Gmünd [A] 72 H2
Gmund [D] 60 E5
Gmunden [A] 62 A5
Gnarp [S] 184 E5
Gnarrenburg [D] 18 E4
Gnas [A] 74 E3
Gnesau [A] 74 B3
Gnesta [S] 168 D4
Gneux [F] 44 B3
Gniechowice [PL] 50 C1
Gniew [PL] 22 E4
Gniewkowo [PL] 36 E1
Gniezno [PL] 36 D2
Gnisvärd [S] 168 F4
Gnjilane [SRB] 146 D5
Gnocchetta [I] 110 H2
Gnoien [D] 20 C3
Gnojnice [BIH] 144 C2
Gnosjö [S] 162 C3
Göbel [TR] 150 D5
Göçbeyli [TR] 152 C2
Göçek [TR] 154 F2
Goch [D] 16 F6
Göd [H] 64 C6
Godafoss [IS] 192 C2
Godalming [GB] 14 D5
Godby [FIN] 176 A5
Godech [BG] 146 F4
Godegard [S] 166 H5
Godelheim [D] 32 F4
Gödenroth [D] 44 H1
Goderville [F] 26 G2
Godętowo [PL] 22 D2
Godkowo [PL] 22 G3
Gödöllő [H] 64 D6
Godovič [SLO] 74 B5
Godowa [PL] 52 D4
Godøynes [N] 192 D6
Gödre [H] 76 A4
Godziesze Wielkie [PL] 36 E5
Godziszewo [PL] 22 E3
Goes [NL] 16 B6
Góglio [I] 70 E2
Gogolin [PL] 50 E2
Gógolo [I] 72 C3
Göhren [D] 20 E2
Goirle [NL] 30 E2
Góis [P] 86 E2
Góito [I] 110 E1
Goizueta [E] 84 B3
Gojani i Madh [AL] 128 B1
Gojsalići [BIH] 142 E4
Gökçedağ [TR] 152 F1
Gökçek [TR] 152 H4
Gökçen [TR] 152 D4
Gökçeören [TR] 152 E3
Gokels [D] 18 F2
Gökova [TR] 154 D1
Gökpınar [TR] 154 H1
Göksholm [S] 166 H3
Göktepe [TR] 150 H3
Göktepe [TR] 152 F6
Gol [N] 170 F3
Gola [HR] 74 G4
Gołąb [PL] 38 D5
Gołańcz [PL] 36 D1
Gölbent [TR] 154 F3
Gölby [FIN] 176 A5
Golchen [D] 20 D4
Gölcük [TR] 150 C4
Gölcük [TR] 150 G3
Gölcük [TR] 152 D2
Gölcük [TR] 152 E4

Golçük [TR] 154 E1
Golčův Jeníkov [CZ] 48 H4
Golczewo [PL] 20 F4
Gołdap [PL] 24 D2
Goldbach [D] 46 D3
Goldberg [D] 20 B4
Goldelund [D] 156 B5
Golden [IRL] 4 D4
Goldenstedt [D] 18 D6
Gölecik [TR] 150 D4
Goleen [IRL] 4 B5
Golegã [P] 86 D4
Goleim [AL] 128 B6
Golema Crcorija [MK] 146 E6
Golemo Selo [SRB] 146 D5
Goleniów [PL] 20 F5
Goleniowy [PL] 50 H2
Golfe-Juan [F] 108 E5
Golfo Aranci [I] 118 E2
Golfo di Sogno [F] 114 B6
Gölhisar [TR] 152 G6
Golina [PL] 36 E3
Goliševa [LV] 198 G5
Golizyno [RUS] 202 F3
Goljam Dervent [BG] 150 B1
Goljamo Belovo [BG] 148 A6
Goljamo Kamenjane [BG] 130 G2
Goljan Man. [BG] 148 D5
Gollden [N] 194 B4
Göllersdorf [A] 62 E3
Gollhofen [D] 46 F4
Golling [A] 60 G6
Gölmarmara [TR] 152 D3
Golmayo [E] 90 B3
Golnice [PL] 36 A5
Golnik [SLO] 74 B4
Golodskoye [RUS] 202 F4
Gölova [TR] 154 H1
Gölpazarı [TR] 150 H4
Golpejas [E] 80 G6
Golspie [GB] 6 E4
Golssen [D] 34 E4
Göltarla [TR] 154 H2
Golub Dobrzyń [PL] 22 E6
Golubovci [MNE] 144 E4
Gołuchów [PL] 36 E4
Golvesh [BG] 148 F1
Gölyaka [TR] 150 D5
Golyalo Krushevo [BG] 148 E5
Golyam porovec [BG] 148 E2
Gölyazi [TR] 150 E5
Gołymin-Ośrodek [PL] 38 B1
Golzow [D] 34 D3
Gómara [E] 90 C3
Gombasecká Jaskyňa [SK] 64 E3
Gombe [TR] 154 G2
Gombo [I] 110 D5
Gömeç [TR] 152 B2
Gomes Aires [P] 94 C4
Gommern [D] 34 B3
Gomunice [PL] 36 G6
Gönc [H] 64 G3
Goncelin [F] 70 A4
Gondomar [P] 80 C4
Gondrecourt [F] 44 D5
Gondrin [F] 66 D6
Gönen [TR] 150 D5
Goni, Nuraghe- [I] 118 D6
Goniá [GR] 140 B4
Goniądz [PL] 24 E4
Gónnoi [GR] 132 G1
Gonnosfanádiga [I] 118 C6
Gönyű [H] 64 A6
Gonzaga [I] 110 E2
Gooik [B] 28 H3
Goole [GB] 10 F4
Goor [NL] 16 G5
Göpfritz [A] 62 D3
Goppenstein [CH] 70 E2
Göppingen [D] 60 B2
Góra [PL] 36 C5
Góra [PL] 36 H2
Góra Kalwaria [PL] 38 C3
Goransko [MNE] 144 D3
Góra Puławska [PL] 38 D5
Góra Świętej Anny [PL] 50 E3
Goražde [BIH] 144 E1
Gorbachevo [RUS] 202 F4
Gördalen [S] 172 E1
Gordaliza del Pino [E] 82 B5
Gordes [F] 106 H3
Gördes [TR] 152 E3
Goren Chiflik [BG] 148 F3
Gorenja Vas [SLO] 74 B5
Goresbridge [IRL] 4 F4
Gorey [IRL] 4 F4
Görgeteg [H] 74 H5
Gorgier [CH] 58 C6
Gorgonzola [I] 70 G5
Gorica [BG] 148 F4
Gorica [BIH] 144 B2
Gorica [HR] 112 F4
Gorica [SLO] 74 D4
Gorica Jamnička [HR] 74 E6
Goričan [HR] 74 F4
Goricë [AL] 128 D4
Gorinchem [NL] 16 D5
Gorino Veneto [I] 110 H3
Goritsy [RUS] 202 E2
Göritz [D] 20 E5
Gorízia [I] 72 H5
Gorjão [P] 86 D4
Gørlev [DK] 156 F3
Gorlice [PL] 52 C5
Görlitz [D] 34 G6
Gormanston Castle [IRL] 2 F5
Gormund [CH] 58 F5
Gorna Beshovica [BG] 146 G3
Gorna Cerovene [BG] 146 F3
Gorna Dikanja [BG] 146 F5
Gorna Kremena [BG] 146 G3
Gorna Mitropoliya [BG] 148 A3
Gorna Oryakhovitsa [BG] 148 C3
Gorna Studena [BG] 148 C3
Gornij [HR] 112 H4
Gorni Tsibur [BG] 146 F2
Gornja Grabovica [BIH] 144 C2
Gornjak, Manastir- [SRB] 146 C1
Gornja Klina [SRB] 146 B5
Gornja Ploča [HR] 112 G4
Gornja Radgona [SLO] 74 E3
Gornja Sabanta [SRB] 146 C2
Gornja Toponica [SRB] 146 D3
Gornja Tuzla [BIH] 142 E3
Gornja Vrijeska [HR] 74 G6
Gornji Lapac [HR] 112 H4
Gornji Milanovac [SRB] 146 B2
Gornji Podgradci [BIH] 142 B2
Gornji Ravno [BIH] 144 B1
Górno [PL] 52 C1
Gorno Alexandrovo [BG] 148 E4
Gorno Novo Selo [BG] 148 C5
Gorno Yabălkovo [BG] 148 E5
Gorobinci [MK] 128 F1
Gorodets [RUS] 198 H2
Gorodno [RUS] 198 H3
Górowo Iławeckie [PL] 22 G2
Gorredijk [NL] 16 F2
Gorron [F] 26 E5
Gørslev [DK] 156 G3
Gort [IRL] 2 C5
Górtys [GR] 136 D2
Górtys [GR] 140 E5
Görükle [TR] 150 E4
Gorv [N] 180 B5
Görvik [S] 184 C1
Gorzanów [PL] 50 C3
Görzke [D] 34 C3
Gorzkowice [PL] 36 G6
Gorzków-Osada [PL] 38 F6
Górzna [PL] 22 B5
Górzno [PL] 22 F6
Górzno [PL] 36 E4
Gorzów Śląski [PL] 50 F1
Gorzów Wielkopolski [PL] 34 H2
Górzyca [PL] 34 G2
Gorzyce [PL] 52 D2
Gorzyń [PL] 36 B2
Gorẑẑam [N] 194 D3
Gosaldo [I] 72 E4
Gosau [A] 60 H6
Göschenen [CH] 70 F1
Gościno [PL] 20 G3
Gosdorf [A] 74 E3
Goslar [D] 32 G3
Goślice [PL] 36 H2
Gósol [E] 92 D2
Gospari [LV] 198 F6
Gospić [HR] 112 G4
Gosport [GB] 12 H5
Gossau [CH] 58 H5
Gosselies [B] 30 C5
Gossensass / Colle Isarco [I] 72 D2
Gössl [A] 62 B6
Gössweinstein [D] 46 G4
Gosticy [RUS] 198 G1
Gostilicy [RUS] 178 G5
Gostivar [MK] 128 D1
Gostków [PL] 36 F4
Göstling [A] 62 C5
Gostomia [PL] 22 A6
Gostun [SRB] 146 A4
Gostycyn [PL] 22 C5
Gostyń [PL] 36 C4
Gostynin [PL] 36 G2
Goszcz [PL] 36 D5
Goszczanowo [PL] 36 A2
Göteborg [S] 160 G2
Götene [S] 166 E5
Gotenica [SLO] 74 C6
Gotha [D] 32 H6
Gothem [S] 168 G4
Götlunda [S] 168 A3
Gotse Delchev [BG] 130 C1
Gottböle [FIN] 186 A4
Gottby [FIN] 176 A5
Gotthard Tunnel [CH] 70 F2
Göttingen [D] 32 F4
Gottne [S] 184 G1
Gottolengo [I] 110 D1
Gottröra [S] 168 E2
Göttweig [A] 62 D4
Götzis [A] 58 H5
Gouarec [F] 26 A5
Gouda [NL] 16 D5
Goules, Col des- [F] 68 C2
Goulven [F] 40 B1
Gouménissa [GR] 128 G3
Goumois [CH] 58 C5
Gourdon [F] 66 G4
Gourin [F] 40 C3
Gournay-en-Bray [F] 28 C5
Goúrnes [GR] 140 E4
Gourniá [GR] 140 G5
Gourville [F] 54 D6
Gout-Rossignol [F] 66 E2
Gouveia [P] 80 D6
Goúves [GR] 140 F4
Gouvets [F] 26 E4
Gouviá [GR] 132 B2
Gouzon [F] 56 B6
Govedartsi [BG] 146 G6
Govedjari [HR] 144 B3
Gøvstdal [N] 170 F5
Goworowo [PL] 24 C6
Gowran [IRL] 4 F4
Göynükbelen [TR] 150 F5
Gózd [PL] 38 C5
Gozdnica [PL] 34 H5
Gózd – Zaszosie [PL] 52 B1
Gözler [TR] 152 G4
Graal-Müritz [D] 20 B2
Grab [BIH] 144 D4
Grab [PL] 36 D4
Grabarka [PL] 38 E2
Grabaţ [RO] 76 F5
Graberje [HR] 142 A1
Gråbo [S] 160 H2
Gråborg [S] 162 G5
Grabovac [SRB] 146 C1
Grabow [D] 20 A5
Grabów [PL] 36 F3
Grabowiec [PL] 52 G1
Grabówka [PL] 24 F5
Grabów nad Prosną [PL] 36 E5
Grabownica Starzeńska [PL] 52 E4
Grabowskie [PL] 24 D5
Gračac [HR] 112 H4
Gračanica [BIH] 142 D3
Gračanica [SRB] 142 F4
Gračanica [SRB] 146 C5
Graçay [F] 54 H3
Grächen [CH] 70 E2
Gračišće [HR] 112 D2
Gradac [BIH] 144 C3
Gradac [HR] 144 B3
Gradac [MNE] 144 E2
Gradac [MNE] 144 E4
Gradac, Manastir- [SRB] 146 B3
Gradačac [BIH] 142 D2
Graddis [N] 190 F1
Gräddö [S] 168 F2
Gradec [BG] 146 E2
Gradec Prokupski [HR] 112 H1
Gradefes [E] 82 C4
Graderas, Cueva de las- [E] 90 E6
Gradešnika [MK] 128 F3
Gradets [BG] 148 D4
Gradignan [F] 66 C3
Gradin [SLO] 112 D1
Gradina [HR] 112 F3
Gradina [SRB] 146 E4
Gradinarovo [BG] 148 E3
Gradisca d'Isonzo [I] 72 H5
Gradishte [BG] 148 B3
Gradište [HR] 142 E2
Gradište [SRB] 146 E3
Gradki [PL] 22 H3
Grado [E] 78 G3
Grado [I] 72 G6
Gradówek [PL] 34 H6
Gradsko [MK] 128 F2
Græsted [DK] 156 G1
Grafenau [D] 60 H2
Gräfenberg [D] 46 G4
Grafenegg [A] 62 E4
Gräfenhainichen [D] 34 C4
Grafenwöhr [D] 48 B4
Grafenwörth [A] 62 E4
Grafing [D] 60 E4
Grafrath [D] 60 D4
Gräfsnäs [S] 160 H1
Graglia, Santuário di- [I] 70 E4
Gragnano [I] 120 E3
Gråhaugen [N] 180 G2
Grahovo [MNE] 144 D4
Grahovo [SLO] 74 B6
Graiguenamanagh [IRL] 4 F4
Grainetière, Abbaye de la- [F] 54 C3
Graja, Cueva de la- [E] 102 E2
Grajewo [PL] 24 D4
Gralhos [P] 80 D3
Gralla [A] 74 D3
Grallagh [IRL] 2 D4
Gram [DK] 156 B3
Gramada [BG] 146 E2
Gramat [F] 66 G4
Gramatikovo [BG] 148 F5
Grambow [D] 20 E5
Grametten [A] 62 D2
Gramkow [D] 20 A3
Grammatikó [GR] 132 G3
Gramméni Oxyá [GR] 132 F4
Gramméno [GR] 132 C2
Grammichele [I] 126 F4
Gramsh [AL] 128 C4
Gram Slot [DK] 156 B3
Gramzda [LV] 198 B6
Gramzow [D] 20 D6
Gramzow [D] 20 E5
Gran [N] 172 B4
Granåbron [S] 172 F5
Granada [E] 102 E4
Granadilla de Abona [E] 100 B5
Granard [IRL] 2 E4
Granarolo dell'Emilia [I] 110 F3
Granåsen [S] 190 F5
Granátula de Calatrava [E] 96 F4
Granberget [S] 190 F5
Granboda [FIN] 176 B6
Grancey-le-Château [F] 56 G3
Grandas de Salime [E] 78 F3
Grandcamp-Maisy [F] 26 E2
Grand-Champ [F] 26 A6
Grand Chartreuse, Couvent de la- [F] 68 H4
Grande-Fougeray [F] 40 F5
Grandjouan [F] 40 F5
Grándola [P] 94 C2
Grandpré [F] 44 C3
Grandrieu [F] 68 D5
Grand Roc [F] 66 F3
Grand-Rozoy [F] 42 H3
Grandson [CH] 58 C6
Grand-St-Bernard, Col du- [CH/I] 70 C3
Grand-St-Bernard, Tunnel du- [CH/I] 70 C3
Grandvilliers [F] 28 D5
Grañén [E] 90 F3
Grangärde [S] 172 H5
Grange [IRL] 2 D3
Grange-Bleneau, Château de la- [F] 42 G4
Grange-le-Bocage [F] 42 H5
Grängesberg [S] 172 H6
Granges-sur-Vologne [F] 58 D2
Grängsjö [S] 184 E5
Granhult [S] 192 H6
Graninge [S] 184 E2
Granitola Torretta [I] 126 B3
Granitz, Jagdschloss- [D] 20 E2
Granja [P] 80 B4
Granja [P] 94 E3
Granja de Moreruela [E] 80 H4
Granja de Torrehermosa [E] 96 B5
Grankulla / Kauniainen [FIN] 176 H5
Grankullavik [S] 162 H3
Gränna [S] 162 D1
Grannäs [S] 190 F3
Granne [PL] 38 E2
Grannes [N] 190 E3
Gränninngen [S] 184 C2
Granollers [E] 92 E4
Granowo [PL] 36 C3
Gransee [D] 20 D6
Gränsgård [S] 190 G3
Gransherad [N] 164 F1
Gransjö [S] 196 A2
Gränsjön [S] 166 D2
Gran Tarajal [E] 100 E6
Grantham [GB] 10 F6
Grantown-on-Spey [GB] 6 E5
Granträsk [S] 190 G5
Granvik [S] 166 G5
Granvika [N] 182 C5
Granville [F] 26 D4
Granvin [N] 170 C3
Granvollen [N] 172 B4
Grao / el Grau [E] 98 F6
Grasbakken [N] 194 E2
Gråsberg [S] 172 H5
Graševo [BG] 148 A6
Grašišće [SLO] 72 H6
Gräsmark [S] 166 E1
Gräsmyr [S] 190 H6
Gräso [S] 174 F5
Grassac [F] 66 F1
Grassano [I] 122 C4
Grassau [D] 60 F5
Grasse [F] 108 E4
Gråssjön [S] 184 C3
Gråsten [DK] 156 C4
Grästorp [S] 166 D6
Gratangen [N] 192 F4
Gråtanliden [S] 190 F4
Gratkorn [A] 74 D2
Gråträsk [S] 190 H3
Graulhet [F] 106 B3
Graun im Vinschgau / Curon Venosta [I] 72 B2
Graus [E] 90 H3
Grava [S] 166 E2
Grávalos [E] 84 A5
Gravberget [N] 172 D3
Gravdal [N] 164 B4
Gravdal [N] 192 C4
Grave [NL] 16 E6
Gravedona [I] 70 G3
Gravelines [F] 14 H6
Gravellona Toce [I] 70 F3
Gravens [DK] 156 C2
Gravesend [GB] 14 F4
Gravhaug [N] 180 C5
Graviá [GR] 132 G4
Gravina in Púglia [I] 122 D3
Gravítsa [GR] 132 E3
Gravmark [S] 196 A5
Gravoúna [GR] 130 E3
Gray [F] 58 A4
Grayan-et-Hôpital [F] 54 B6
Graz [A] 74 D2
Grazalema [E] 100 H4
Gražiškiai [LT] 24 E2
Grazzanise [I] 120 D2
Grazzano Visconti [I] 110 C2
Grčak [SRB] 146 C3
Grčarice [SLO] 74 C6
Grdelica [SRB] 146 D4
Greaca [RO] 148 D1
Greaker [N] 164 H2
Great Dunmow [GB] 14 F3
Great Malvern [GB] 12 G2
Great Torrington [GB] 12 D3
Great Yarmouth [GB] 14 H2
Grebbestad [S] 166 B4
Grebenhain [D] 46 D2
Grebenstein [D] 32 F5
Grębkowo [PL] 38 D3
Grębocin [PL] 22 E6
Greding [D] 46 G6
Greencastle [NIR] 2 G5
Greenock [GB] 8 D3
Greetsiel [D] 16 H1
Gregolímano [GR] 132 H4
Greifenburg [A] 72 G3
Greiffenberg [D] 20 E6
Greifswald [D] 20 D3
Greillenstein [A] 62 D3
Grein [A] 62 C4
Greiz [D] 48 C2
Grenaa [DK] 160 F5
Grenade [F] 66 C6
Grenade [F] 84 H2
Grenchen [CH] 58 D5
Grenctale [LV] 198 E6
Grenoble [F] 68 H4
Grense-Jakobselv [N] 194 F3
Grenzland-Turm [CZ] 48 C4
Gréolières [F] 108 E4
Gréoux-les-Bains [F] 108 C4
Gressoney-la-Trinité [I] 70 E3
Gressoney-St-Jean [I] 70 E4
Gresten [A] 62 D5
Gretna Green [GB] 8 E5
Grettstadt [D] 46 F3
Greussen [D] 32 H5
Greux [F] 44 D6
Grevbäck [S] 166 G6
Greve in Chianti [I] 110 F6
Greven [D] 32 C2
Grevená [GR] 128 E6
Grevenbroich [D] 30 G4
Grevenbrück [D] 32 C5
Grevenmacher [L] 44 F2
Grevesmühlen [D] 18 H3
Greve Strand [DK] 156 G3
Greyabbey [NIR] 2 H4
Greystones [IRL] 4 G3
Grez-en-Bouère [F] 40 H5
Grezzana [I] 72 C6
Grianan of Aileach [IRL] 2 F2
Gries-am-Brenner [A] 72 D2
Griesbach [D] 60 H3
Gries in Sellrain [A] 72 D1
Grieskirchen [A] 62 A4
Griffen [A] 74 C3
Grignan [F] 106 H2
Grignols [F] 66 D5
Grigoriopol [UA] 204 E3
Grillby [S] 168 C2
Grimaldi [I] 124 D5
Grimaud [F] 108 D5
Grimdalen [N] 164 E2
Grimma [D] 34 D6
Grimmen [D] 20 D3
Grimo [N] 170 C4
Grimsås [S] 162 C3
Grimsbu [N] 180 H5
Grimsby [GB] 10 G4
Grimsdalshytta [N] 180 H5
Grimslöv [S] 162 D5
Grímsstaðir [IS] 192 C2
Grimstad [N] 164 E5
Grindaheim [N] 170 F2
Grindal [N] 180 H2
Grindavík [IS] 192 A3
Grindelwald [CH] 70 E1
Grindjorda [N] 192 E4
Grindsted [DK] 156 B2
Grinkiškis [LT] 200 F4
Griñón [E] 88 F6
Grinzane Cavour [I] 108 G2
Gripenberg [S] 162 E1
Gripenberg [S] 162 E1
Grisignano di Zocco [I] 72 D6
Grisolles [F] 84 H2
Grisslehamn [S] 174 G6
Grisvåg [N] 180 F1
Grivitsa [BG] 148 B3
Grivy [RUS] 198 G4
Grizáno [GR] 132 F2
Grižkabūdis [LT] 200 E5
Grøa [N] 180 G3
Gröbers [D] 34 C5
Grobina [LV] 198 B6
Gröbming [A] 74 B1
Grocka [SRB] 142 H3
Gródek [PL] 24 F5
Gródek [PL] 38 G1
Gródek nad Dunajcem [PL] 52 C4
Gröditz [D] 34 E5
Gródki [PL] 52 F1
Grodków [PL] 50 D2
Grodno [PL] 50 B2
Grodzeń [PL] 36 G1
Grodziec [PL] 36 A6
Grodziec [PL] 50 F4
Grodzisk Mazowieki [PL] 38 B3
Grodzisk Wielkopolski [PL] 36 B3
Groenlo [NL] 16 G5
Groix [F] 40 C4
Grojdibodu [RO] 148 A2
Grójec [PL] 36 D3
Grójec [PL] 38 B4
Grömitz [D] 18 H3
Gromnik [PL] 52 C4
Gromo [I] 72 A4
Gromovo [RUS] 178 G2
Gromovo [RUS] 200 D5
Grøna [N] 180 F5
Gronau [D] 16 G5
Gronau [D] 32 F3
Grönbo [S] 196 A4
Grønbua [N] 180 F6
Grøndal [N] 180 B5
Grong [N] 190 C5
Grönhögen [S] 158 G1
Grønhøj [DK] 160 C5
Gröningen [D] 34 A3
Groningen [NL] 16 G2
Grønnes [N] 180 E3
Grönskåra [S] 162 F4
Grönsö [S] 168 C2
Gropen [S] 166 G3
Grósio [I] 72 B4
Grossarl [A] 72 G1
Grossbeeren [D] 34 E2
Grossbreitenbach [D] 46 G2
Grossburgwedel [D] 32 G2
Grossenbrode [D] 18 H2
Grossenhain [D] 34 E5
Grossenkneten [D] 18 C5
Grossenzersdorf [A] 62 F4
Grosseto [I] 114 F3
Gross-Gerau [D] 46 C3
Gross-Gerungs [A] 62 C3
Grossglobnitz [A] 62 D3
Grosshabersdorf [D] 46 F5
Grossharras [A] 62 F3
Grosshöchstetten [CH] 58 E6
Gross Mohrdorf [D] 20 C2
Gross Oesingen [D] 32 H1
Gross-Pertenschlag [A] 62 C4
Gross-Pertholz [A] 62 C3
Grosspetersdorf [A] 74 F2
Grossraming [A] 62 C5
Gross Räschen [D] 34 F5
Gross Schönebeck [D] 34 E1
Gross-Siegharts [A] 62 D3
Gross-Umstadt [D] 46 D3
Grosswoltersdorf [D] 20 C6
Grostenquin [F] 44 F4
Grosuplje [SLO] 74 C5
Grøtavær [N] 192 E3
Grötholen [S] 182 E6
Grotli [N] 180 E5
Grotnes [S] 170 C4
Grottaglie [I] 122 F4
Grottaminarda [I] 120 F2
Grottammare [I] 116 D2
Grotteria [I] 124 D7
Grouw [NL] 16 F2
Grova [N] 164 F3
Grövelsjön [S] 182 D5
Grovfjord [N] 192 E4
Grozd'ovo [BG] 148 F3
Grožnjan [HR] 112 D1
Gr. Strömkendorf [D] 20 A3
Grua [N] 172 B5
Grubben [N] 190 E3
Grube [D] 18 H2
Grubišno Polje [HR] 74 G6
Gruda [HR] 144 D4
Grude [BIH] 144 B2
Grude [S] 162 B1
Grudusk [PL] 22 H6
Grudziądz [PL] 22 E5
Gruemirë [AL] 144 E5
Gruia [RO] 146 E1
Gruibingen [D] 60 B3
Gruissan [F] 106 D5
Grumentum [I] 120 H5
Grums [S] 166 E3
Grünau [A] 62 B5
Grünberg [D] 46 D1
Grünburg [A] 62 B5
Grundfors [S] 190 E4
Grundforsen [S] 172 E2
Grundlsee [A] 62 A6
Grundsel [S] 190 H3
Grundsjö [S] 190 F4
Grundsjö [S] 190 F5
Grundsjön [S] 184 C5
Grundsund [S] 166 C6
Grundsunda [S] 184 H2
Grundtjärn [S] 184 E1
Grünenplan [D] 32 F3
Grungedal [N] 164 E1
Grünheide [D] 34 F2
Grünhof [D] 20 E4
Grünstadt [D] 46 B4
Grunwald [PL] 22 G5
Grupčin [MK] 128 D1
Grüsch [CH] 58 H6
Gruškovje [SLO] 74 E4
Gruvberget [S] 174 D3
Gruyères [CH] 70 C1
Gruža [SRB] 146 B2
Gruzdžiai [LT] 200 E3
Grybów [PL] 52 C5
Grycksbo [S] 172 H4
Gryfice [PL] 20 G4
Gryfino [PL] 20 F5
Gryfów Śląski [PL] 48 H1
Grykë [AL] 128 A4
Gryllefjord [N] 192 E2
Grymyr [N] 170 H5
Gryneion [TR] 152 C3
Gryt [S] 168 C4
Gryt [S] 168 C6
Grytgöl [S] 166 H4
Grythyttan [S] 166 G2
Grytsjö [S] 190 E4
Grytstorp [S] 166 H5
Gryzy [PL] 24 D3
Grzmiąca [PL] 22 A4
Grzybno [PL] 22 F5
Gschnitz [A] 72 D2
Gschöder [A] 62 D6
Gschwend [D] 46 E6
Gstaad [CH] 70 D2
Gstadt [D] 60 F5
Gsteig [CH] 70 D2
Guadahortuna [E] 102 E3
Guadajoz [E] 94 H6
Guadalajara [E] 88 G5
Guadalcanal [E] 94 H4
Guadalcázar [E] 102 B1
Guadalerzas [E] 96 F3
Guadalest [E] 104 E2
Guadalmez [E] 96 C4
Guadalmina [E] 102 A5
Guadalupe [E] 96 C2
Guadalupe, Monasterio de- [E] 96 C2
Guadalupe, Santuario de- [E] 102 F1
Guadamur [E] 96 E2
Guadarrama [E] 88 F5
Guadix [E] 102 F4
Guagno [F] 114 B4
Gualdo Cattáneo [I] 116 A2
Gualdo Tadino [I] 116 B2
Guarcino [I] 116 C6
Guarda [CH] 72 B2
Guarda [P] 86 G2
Guardamar del Segura [E] 104 D3
Guardavalle [I] 124 D6
Guardiagrele [I] 116 D5
Guardialfiera [I] 116 E6
Guardia Lombardi [I] 120 F3
Guardia Piemontese [I] 124 C4
Guardia Sanframondi [I] 120 E2
Guardias Viejas [E] 102 F5
Guardo [E] 82 C4
Guareña [E] 94 H2
Guarromán [E] 96 E6
Guasila [I] 118 C6
Guastalla [I] 110 E2
Guazzora [I] 70 F6
Gubanitsy [RUS] 178 G6
Gubbhägen [S] 190 E5
Gúbbio [I] 116 A1
Gubbmyran [S] 172 E2
Gubbträsk [S] 190 G4
Guben [D] 34 G4
Guber [BIH] 144 B1
Guberevac [SRB] 146 B2
Gubin [PL] 34 G4
Guča [SRB] 146 B2
Gücenoluk [TR] 152 H1
Gudavac [BIH] 142 A2
Guddal [N] 170 B1
Guderup [DK] 156 C4
Gudhjem [DK] 158 E4
Gudow [D] 18 G4
Gudvangen [N] 170 D2
Guebwiller [F] 58 D3
Güéjar Sierra [E] 102 E4
Guémené-Penfao [F] 40 F5
Guémené-sur-Scorff [F] 40 D3
Guenange [F] 44 F3
Guer [F] 26 B6
Guérande [F] 40 D6
Guéret [F] 54 H6
Guérigny [F] 56 D4
Guethary [F] 84 C2
Gueugnon [F] 56 E5
Güglingen [D] 46 C6
Guglionesi [I] 116 F5
Gugny [PL] 24 E5
Guía de Isora [E] 100 B5
Guichen [F] 26 C6
Guidonia [I] 116 A5
Guíglia [I] 110 E3
Guignes [F] 42 G4
Guijuelo [E] 88 C4
Guildford [GB] 14 D4
Guillaumes [F] 108 E3
Guillena [E] 94 G5
Guillestre [F] 108 E2
Guils [E] 92 D1
Guilvinec [F] 40 B3
Güímar [E] 100 C5
Guimarães [P] 80 C3
Guimerà [E] 92 C3
Guimiliau [F] 40 C2
Guincho [P] 86 A5
Guînes [F] 14 G6
Guingamp [F] 26 A4
Guipry [F] 40 F4
Guísamo [E] 78 D2
Guisborough [GB] 10 G2
Guise [F] 28 G5
Guissény [F] 40 B1
Guissona [E] 92 C3
Guitalens [F] 106 B3
Guitiriz [E] 78 D2
Guîtres [F] 66 D3
Gujan-Mestras [F] 66 B3
Gükçeyazı [TR] 152 D1
Gulbene [LV] 198 F4
Guldborg [DK] 156 F5
Gülec [TR] 150 C5
Gulgofjorden [N] 194 D1
Gulla [N] 180 G2
Gullabo [S] 162 F6
Gullaskruv [S] 162 F4
Gullbrå [N] 170 C2
Gulleråsen [S] 172 H3
Gullfoss [IS] 192 B3
Gullhaug [N] 164 H2
Gullringen [S] 162 F2
Gullsby [S] 172 E6
Gullspång [S] 166 F4
Gullstein [N] 180 F1
Güllü [TR] 152 F4
Güllüce [TR] 150 E5
Güllük [TR] 154 C1
Gülpınar [TR] 134 G1
Gulsele [S] 190 F6
Gulsrud [N] 170 H5
Gulsvik [N] 170 G4
Gülübintsi [BG] 148 D5
Gülübovo [BG] 148 D5
Gulyantsi [BG] 148 B2
Gumboda [S] 196 A5
Gumhöjden [S] 166 F1
Gumiel de Hizán [E] 88 G2
Gumlösa [S] 158 D1
Gummersbach [D] 32 C5
Gumpoldskirchen [A] 62 F5
Gumtow [D] 20 B6
Gümüldür [TR] 152 C5
Gümüşpınar [TR] 150 D2
Gümüşsu [TR] 152 H4
Gümüşsuyu [TR] 150 D3
Gümüşyeni [TR] 150 G5
Gümzovo [BG] 146 E2
Gundelfingen [D] 60 C3
Gundelsheim [D] 46 D5
Güneşli [TR] 152 E2
Güney [TR] 152 F4
Güney [TR] 152 G5
Güneyköy [TR] 152 F2
Güngör (Koutsovéntis) [CY] 154 G5
Güngörmez [TR] 152 D1
Gunja [HR] 142 E2
Günlüce [TR] 152 F1
Gunnarn [S] 190 G4
Gunnarp [S] 162 B4
Gunnarsbyn [S] 196 B2
Gunnarskog [S] 166 D1
Gunnarskulla [FIN] 176 G5
Gunnarvattnet [S] 190 E5
Gunnebo [S] 162 G2
Gunnilbo [S] 168 B2
Gunten [CH] 70 E1
Güntersberge [D] 32 H4
Gunterslubn [D] 46 C4
Guntersdorf [A] 62 E3
Guntertshausen [A] 60 G4
Guntín [E] 78 D3
Günzburg [D] 60 C3
Gunzenhausen [D] 46 F6
Gurçeşme [TR] 150 C5
Gurcz [PL] 22 E4

Hermo [E] 78 F4
Hermsdorf [D] 48 B1
Hernani [E] 84 B2
Herne [D] 30 H3
Herne Bay [GB] 14 G5
Herning [DK] 160 C6
Hernstein [A] 62 E5
Heroldsberg [D] 46 G5
Herøya [N] 164 G3
Herøysund [N] 170 B5
Herråkra [S] 162 E4
Herräng [S] 174 G5
Herraskylä [FIN] 186 D4
Herre [N] 164 G3
Herrenberg [D] 58 G1
Herrenchiemsee [D] 60 F5
Herrera [E] 96 E4
Herrera [E] 102 B2
Herrera del Duque [E] 96 C3
Herrera de los Navarros [E] 90 D5
Herrera de Pisuerga [E] 82 D5
Herrería [E] 90 C5
Herreruela [E] 86 G5
Herrestad [S] 166 C5
Herrgotts Kirche [D] 46 E5
Herrljunga [S] 162 B1
Herrnburg [D] 18 G3
Herrnhut [D] 48 G1
Herrösskatan [FIN] 168 G1
Herrsching [D] 60 D4
Herrskog [S] 184 F3
Herrvik [S] 168 G5
Hersbruck [D] 46 H5
Herselt [B] 30 D3
Hertford [GB] 14 E3
Hertník [SK] 52 C6
Hervás [E] 88 B5
Hervik [N] 164 B2
Herzberg [D] 20 B4
Herzberg [D] 32 G4
Herzberg [D] 34 D1
Herzberg [D] 34 E4
Herzberg [D] 46 E1
Herzfeld [D] 32 D4
Herzfelde [D] 34 F2
Herzlake [D] 18 B6
Herzogenaurach [D] 46 G5
Herzogenburg [A] 62 E4
Herzsprung [D] 20 C6
Hesdin [F] 28 D3
Hesel [D] 18 C4
Heskestad [N] 164 B4
Heskestad [N] 164 C5
Hesnæs [DK] 20 B1
Hessel [DK] 160 C4
Hesselagergård [DK] 156 E4
Hessich-Lichtenau [D] 32 F5
Hess Oldendorf [D] 32 F2
Hessvik [N] 170 C4
Hestad [N] 170 C1
Hestenesøyri [N] 180 C5
Hestra [S] 162 C3
Hestra [S] 162 E1
Hetin [SRB] 76 F6
Het Loo [NL] 16 F5
Hettange-Grande [F] 44 E3
Hettstedt [D] 34 B4
Hetvehely [H] 76 A5
Heustreu [D] 46 F2
Heverlee [B] 30 D4
Heves [H] 64 E6
Hévíz [H] 74 G3
Hevlin [CZ] 62 F3
Hexentanzplatz [D] 34 A4
Hexham [GB] 8 F6
Heyrieux [F] 68 G3
Heysham [GB] 10 D3
Hidas [H] 76 B4
Hidasnémeti [H] 64 G3
Hieflau [A] 62 C6
Hiendelaencina [E] 88 H4
Hierapolis [TR] 152 G5
Hiersac [F] 54 D6
Hietakylä [FIN] 188 C3
Hietanen [FIN] 188 C6
Hietaniemi [FIN] 194 F6
Hietaperä [FIN] 196 F5
High Cross [IRL] 4 F3
High Wycombe [GB] 14 D4
Higuera, Torre de la- [E] 100 F2
Higuera de la Serena [E] 96 B4
Higuera de Vargas [E] 94 F2
Higuera la Real [E] 94 F3
Higueruela [E] 98 C5
Hihnavaara [FIN] 194 E6
Hiirola [FIN] 188 C5
Hiitinen / Hitis [FIN] 176 E6
Híjar [E] 90 F5
Hilchenbach [D] 32 C5
Hildal [N] 170 C5
Hildburghausen [D] 46 G2
Hilden [D] 30 G4
Hilders [D] 46 E2
Hildesheim [D] 32 G3
Hildre [N] 180 D3
Hilertshausen [D] 60 E3
Hilkerode [D] 32 G4
Hilla [FIN] 176 G5
Hille [S] 174 E4
Hillegom [NL] 16 D4
Hillerød [DK] 156 G2
Hillerstorp [S] 162 C3
Hillesøy [N] 192 F2
Hillilä [FIN] 196 C5
Hillion [F] 26 B4
Hillsand [S] 190 E5
Hillsborough [NIR] 2 G4
Hillswick [GB] 6 G3
Hilltown [NIR] 2 G4
Hilmo [N] 182 C2
Hilpoltstein [D] 46 G6
Hilterfingen [CH] 70 E1
Hiltulanlahti [FIN] 188 C2
Hilvarenbeek [NL] 30 E2
Hilversum [NL] 16 E4
Himanka [FIN] 196 C5
Himankakylä [FIN] 196 C5
Himarë [AL] 128 B6
Himlštejn [CZ] 48 D3
Himmelkoron [D] 46 H3
Himmelpforten [D] 18 E4
Hinckley [GB] 10 E6
Hindås [S] 160 H2
Hindelang [D] 60 C6
Hinderburg [D] 34 C1
Hindsig [DK] 156 B2
Hinnerjoki [FIN] 176 D3
Hinnerup [DK] 160 D6
Hinneryd [S] 162 C5
Hinojal [E] 86 H4
Hinojos [E] 94 F6
Hinojosa del Duque [E] 96 C4
Hinojosa del Valle [E] 94 H3
Hinterbichl [A] 72 F2
Hinterrhein [CH] 70 G2
Hintersee [D] 20 E4
Hinterstoder [A] 62 B6
Hinterthal [A] 72 G1
Hintertux [A] 72 D1
Hinterweidenthal [D] 44 H4
Hinterzarten [D] 58 F3
Hío [E] 78 B4
Hırkalı [TR] 152 E3
Hirnsdorf [A] 74 E2
Hirnyk [UA] 52 H2
Hirrlingen [D] 58 G2
Hirschaid [D] 46 G4
Hirschau [D] 48 B5
Hirschberg [D] 48 B2
Hirschegg [A] 60 B6
Hirschhorn [D] 46 C5
Hirsch-Stein [D] 48 B3
Hirsilä [FIN] 186 E6
Hirsingue [F] 58 D4
Hirson [F] 28 G5
Hîrşova [RO] 204 E5
Hirtshals [DK] 160 E2
Hirvassalmi [FIN] 194 D5
Hirvasvaara [FIN] 194 E7
Hirvensalmi [FIN] 186 H6
Hirvihaara [FIN] 176 H4
Hirvijärvi [S] 194 B8
Hirvijoki [FIN] 186 D2
Hirvisalo [FIN] 178 B2
Hisarcık [TR] 152 F2
Hisardžik [SRB] 146 A3
Hisarlık [TR] 150 G4
Hisartepe Dascylium [TR] 150 E4
Histria [RO] 204 F5
Hita [E] 88 H5
Hitchin [GB] 14 E3
Hitiaş [RO] 76 H6
Hitis / Hiitinen [FIN] 176 E6
Hitovo [BG] 148 F1
Hittarp [S] 156 H1
Hitterdal [N] 182 D4
Hitzacker [D] 18 H5
Hiukkajoki [FIN] 188 F5
Hjallerup [DK] 160 E3
Hjällstad [S] 172 E4
Hjälmseryd [S] 162 D3
Hjältanstorp [S] 184 D4
Hjärnarp [DK] 162 B6
Hjartåsen [N] 190 E2
Hjärtum [S] 166 C6
Hjelle [N] 180 C5
Hjelle [N] 180 D5
Hjellestad [N] 170 A4
Hjelmeland [N] 164 B2
Hjelset [N] 180 E3
Hjerkinn [N] 180 G4
Hjerpsted [DK] 156 B4
Hjerting [DK] 156 A2
Hjo [S] 166 F6
Hjøllund [DK] 156 C1
Hjørring [DK] 160 E2
Hjorte [DK] 156 D3
Hjorted [S] 162 G2
Hjorteset [N] 180 C5
Hjortkvarn [S] 166 H4
Hjortsberga [S] 158 F1
Hjortsberga [S] 162 D4
Hjulsbro [S] 168 A6
Hjulsjö [S] 166 G2
Hlinsko [CZ] 50 B4
Hlobyne [UA] 202 F7
Hlohovec [SK] 62 H4
Hluboká nad Vltavou [CZ] 62 C2
Hlučín [CZ] 50 E4
Hluk [CZ] 62 H2
Hlukhiv [UA] 202 E6
Hlusk [BY] 202 C6
Hlybokaya [BY] 202 B4
Hlyniany [UA] 52 G4
Hniezdne [SK] 52 B6
Hnilec [SK] 64 E2
Hnúšťa [SK] 64 D3
Hobermayer-Hofen [A] 74 E2
Hobol [H] 76 A5
Hobro [DK] 160 D5
Hocalar [TR] 152 H3
Hoče [SLO] 74 D4
Hoces del Cabriel [E] 98 C4
Hoces del Duratón [E] 88 G3
Hoces del Riaza [E] 88 G2
Höchberg [D] 46 E4
Hochburg [A] 60 G4
Hochburg [D] 58 E2
Hochdonn [D] 18 E3
Hochdorf [CH] 58 F5
Höchenschwand [D] 58 F4
Hochfelden [F] 44 H5
Hochosterwitz [A] 74 B3
Hochspeyer [D] 46 B4
Höchst [D] 46 D4
Höchstadt [D] 46 G4
Höchstädt [D] 60 C3
Hochstatten [D] 46 B3
Höckendorf [D] 48 E1
Hockenheim [D] 46 C5
Hoczew [PL] 52 E5
Hodal [N] 182 C4
Hodalen [N] 182 C4
Hodejov [SK] 64 E4
Hodenhagen [D] 18 E6
Hodkovice nad Mohelkou [CZ] 48 G2
Hódmezővásárhely [H] 76 E4
Hodøl [N] 182 D4
Hodonín [CZ] 62 G2
Hodoš [SLO] 74 F3
Hodošan [HR] 74 F4
Hoedekenskerke [NL] 28 H1
Hoei (Huy) [B] 30 D5
Hoek van Holland [NL] 16 C5
Hoenzethen [D] 18 G6
Hof [D] 48 B3
Hof [D] 58 F1
Hofgeismar [D] 32 F4
Hofheim [D] 46 F3
Hofles [N] 190 C4
Höfn [IS] 192 C3
Hofors [S] 174 D4
Hofstad [N] 190 B5
Högakustenbron [S] 184 F3
Höganäs [S] 156 H1
Hogdal [S] 166 B4
Högé [S] 184 B2
Högerud [S] 166 E2
Högfors [S] 166 H1
Högfors / Karkkila [FIN] 176 G4
Höghult [S] 162 F2
Högklint [S] 168 F4
Höglunda [S] 184 D2
Högnabba [FIN] 186 D1
Högsäter [S] 166 D5
Högsby [S] 162 F4
Høgset [N] 180 E2
Högsjö [S] 184 F3
Høgstadgård [N] 192 G3
Hogstorp [S] 166 C5
Högvålen [S] 182 E5
Hőgyész [H] 76 B4
Hohenau [A] 62 G3
Hohenbachschlucht [A] 72 B1
Hohenberg [A] 62 E5
Hohenbrunn [D] 60 E4
Hohenburg [D] 46 H5
Hoheneck [D] 46 F5
Hohenems [A] 58 H5
Hohenfels [D] 46 B4
Hohenhewen [D] 58 G4
Höhenkirchen [D] 60 E4
Hohenlimburg [D] 32 C4
Hohenlinden [D] 60 F4
Hohenlockstedt [D] 18 F3
Hohenneuffen [D] 58 H2
Hohenpeissenberg [D] 60 D5
Hohenschwangau [D] 60 C6
Hohenstein [D] 46 B2
Hohensyburg [D] 32 C4
Hohentauern [A] 74 C1
Hohentwiel [D] 58 G4
Hohen Wehrda [D] 46 E1
Hohenwerfen [A] 60 G6
Hohenwestedt [D] 18 F2
Hohenzollern [D] 58 G2
Hohne [D] 32 G1
Hohneck [F] 58 D3
Hohrodberg [F] 58 D3
Hohwacht [D] 18 G2
Hoikhankylä [FIN] 186 H3
Hoilola [FIN] 188 H3
Hoisko [FIN] 186 D2
Højby [DK] 156 F2
Højer [DK] 156 B4
Højerup [DK] 156 G4
Højslev Stby [DK] 160 C5
Hojsova Stráž [CZ] 48 D6
Hok [S] 162 D3
Hökåsen [S] 168 B2
Hökhuvud [S] 174 F5
Hokka [FIN] 186 H5
Hokksund [N] 164 G1
Hökön [S] 162 D6
Hoks Herrgård [S] 162 D3
Hokusukoski [FIN] 186 E4
Hol [N] 170 F3
Hol [S] 162 B1
Holand [N] 190 D5
Hola Prystan' [UA] 204 G3
Holašovice [CZ] 62 B2
Holbæk [DK] 156 F2
Holbeach [GB] 10 G6
Holbøl [DK] 156 C4
Holckenhavn [DK] 156 E3
Holdorf [D] 32 D1
Hole [S] 172 F5
Holeby [DK] 20 A1
Holedeč [CZ] 48 E3
Holešov [CZ] 50 D6
Holíč [SK] 62 G3
Holice [CZ] 50 B4
Hölick [S] 174 E1
Holiseva [FIN] 186 F5
Holja [FIN] 176 G2
Höljes [S] 172 E3
Hollabrunn [A] 62 E3
Hollád [H] 74 G3
Høllen [N] 164 D6
Hollenbach [D] 60 D3
Hollenegg [A] 74 D3
Hollenstedt [D] 18 F4
Hollerath [D] 30 F5
Hollestein [A] 62 C5
Hollfeld [D] 46 G4
Hollingsholm [N] 180 E2
Hollola [FIN] 176 H2
Hollolan [FIN] 176 H2
Hollum [NL] 16 F1
Höllviken [S] 156 H3
Holm [DK] 156 C4
Holm [FIN] 196 B6
Holm [N] 166 B3
Holm [N] 190 C4
Holm [S] 184 D4
Hólmavík [IS] 192 B2
Holmec [SLO] 74 C3
Holmedal [S] 166 D2
Holmegil [N] 166 C3
Holmestrand [N] 164 H2
Holmfirth [GB] 10 E4
Holmfors [S] 190 G4
Holmfors [S] 196 A3
Holmön [S] 196 A6
Holmsjö [S] 162 F6
Holmsjö [S] 184 C3
Holmsjö [S] 190 G6
Holmsund [S] 196 A6
Holmsveden [S] 174 E3
Holmudden [S] 168 H3
Holm-Zhirkovskij [RUS] 202 D3
Holoby [UA] 202 B7
Holovanivs'k [UA] 204 F2
Holovne [UA] 38 G5
Holøydal [N] 182 C5
Holsætra [N] 170 H2
Holsbybrunn [S] 162 E3
Holsen [N] 170 C1
Holsljunge [S] 162 B3
Holstebro [DK] 160 B5
Holsted [DK] 156 B2
Holsworthy [GB] 12 D4
Holt [GB] 14 G1
Holt [N] 164 F4
Holt [N] 192 F3
Holten [NL] 16 G5
Holtet [N] 166 C4
Holtet [N] 172 D4
Holtsås [N] 164 F2
Holtsee [D] 18 F2
Holtslåstten [N] 172 C4
Holwerd [NL] 16 F1
Holycross [IRL] 4 E4
Holyhead [GB] 10 B3
Holywell [GB] 10 C4
Holywood [NIR] 2 G3
Holzdorf [D] 34 D4
Holzgau [A] 72 B1
Holzkirchen [D] 60 E5
Holzleitensattel [A] 72 C1
Holzminden [D] 32 F3
Holzschlag [D] 58 F3
Homberg [D] 32 F6
Homberg [D] 46 D1
Homborsund [N] 164 E5
Hombukt [N] 192 H1
Homburg [D] 44 G4
Hommelstø [N] 190 D3
Hommelvik [N] 182 C1
Hommersåk [N] 164 B3
Homokszentgyörgy [H] 74 H5
Homps [F] 106 C4
Homyel' [BY] 202 D6
Honaz [TR] 152 G5
Hondarribia / Fuenterrabía [E] 84 B2
Hönebach [D] 32 F6
Hønefoss [N] 170 H5
Honfleur [F] 26 G3
Hong [DK] 156 F3
Honiton [GB] 12 F4
Honkajoki [FIN] 186 C5
Honkakoski [FIN] 186 B6
Honkola [FIN] 186 G3
Hønning [DK] 156 B3
Honningsvåg [N] 180 B4
Honningsvåg [N] 194 C1
Honrubia [E] 98 B3
Honrubia de la Cuesta [E] 88 G3
Hontalbilla [E] 88 F3
Hontoria de la Cantera [E] 82 E6
Hontoria del Pinar [E] 90 A2
Hoofddorp [NL] 16 D4
Hoogerheide [NL] 30 C2
Hoogeveen [NL] 16 G3
Hoogezand [NL] 16 G2
Hoogkarspel [NL] 16 E3
Hoogstraten [B] 30 D2
Hooksiel [D] 18 C3
Höör [S] 158 C2
Hoorn [NL] 16 E3
Hopfgarten [A] 60 F6
Hoplandsjøen [N] 170 A2
Hopovo, Manastir- [SRB] 142 F2
Hopperstad Stavkirke [N] 170 C2
Hopseldet [N] 194 D1
Hopsten [D] 32 C2
Hoptrup [DK] 156 C3
Hora-Sv-Šebestiána [CZ] 48 E2
Horažd'ovice [CZ] 48 E6
Horb [D] 58 G2
Horbelev [DK] 20 B1
Hörby [S] 158 C2
Horcajo de los Montes [E] 96 D3
Horcajo de Santiago [E] 96 H2
Horche [E] 88 H5
Horda [S] 162 D4
Hörda [S] 162 D4
Hordain [F] 28 F4
Hordalia [N] 170 C5
Horgen [CH] 58 F5
Horgevik [N] 164 E2
Horgoš [SRB] 76 E5
Horgoū [MNE] 204 A5
Horia [RO] 76 G4
Hořice [CZ] 50 A3
Horitschon [A] 62 F6
Hörja [S] 158 C1
Horjul [SLO] 74 B5
Hörken [S] 166 G1
Horki [BY] 202 D4
Hormogos [E] 88 E6
Horn [A] 62 E3
Horn [D] 32 E3
Horn [D] 58 G4
Horn [N] 170 H4
Horn [N] 190 D3
Horn [S] 162 F2
Hornachos [E] 94 H3
Hornachuelos [E] 96 B6
Horna Štubňa [SK] 64 C3
Hornbæk [DK] 156 G1
Hornberg [D] 46 D5
Hornberg [D] 58 F2
Hornburg [D] 32 H3
Horncastle [GB] 10 G5
Horndal [S] 174 D5
Hörne [D] 18 E3
Horne [DK] 156 D4
Horneburg [D] 18 F4
Hörnefors [S] 190 H6
Hornesund [N] 164 D5
Horní Benešov [CZ] 50 D4
Horní Cerekev [CZ] 48 H6
Horní Lideč [CZ] 50 E6
Horní Loděnice [CZ] 50 D4
Hornindal [N] 180 D5
Hørning [DK] 156 D1
Horní Planá [CZ] 62 B3
Horní Vltavice [CZ] 62 A2
Hornnes [N] 164 D4
Hornos [E] 102 G1
Hornos de Peal [E] 102 F2
Hornoy [F] 28 D5
Hornsea [GB] 10 G4
Hornslet [DK] 160 E6
Hörnum [D] 156 A4
Hornum [DK] 160 D4
Horný Tisovník [SK] 64 C4
Horodenka [UA] 204 D2
Horodło [PL] 38 G6
Horodnytsia [UA] 202 C7
Horodok [UA] 52 G4
Horodyshche [UA] 202 E8
Horokhiv [UA] 202 B8
Horonkylä [FIN] 186 B4
Hořovice [CZ] 48 E4
Horred [S] 160 H3
Hörröd [S] 158 D2
Horrskog [S] 174 E5
Horsens [DK] 156 D2
Horsham [GB] 14 E5
Hørsholm [DK] 156 G2
Horslunde [DK] 156 E4
Horsmanaho [FIN] 188 E2
Horšovský Týn [CZ] 48 D5
Horst [B] 30 D4
Horst [D] 18 G5
Horst [NL] 30 F3
Hörstel [D] 32 C2
Horstmar [D] 16 H5
Horsunlu [TR] 152 F5
Hort [H] 64 D6
Horta [P] 100 C3
Horten [N] 164 H2
Hortezuela [E] 90 A3
Hortigüela [E] 88 H1
Hortobágy [H] 64 G6
Hörup [D] 156 B5
Hørve [DK] 156 F2
Horven [N] 190 C4
Horw [CH] 58 F6
Hosby [DK] 156 D2
Hoscheid [L] 44 F2
Hosenfeld [D] 46 E2
Hoset [N] 192 D6
Hoshtevë Vithkuq [AL] 128 C6
Hosjö [S] 174 C4
Hoslemo [N] 164 D2
Hospental [CH] 70 F1
Hospice de France [F] 84 F5
Hospital [IRL] 4 D4
Hospital de Orbigo [E] 78 G6
Hossa [FIN] 196 F3
Hossegor [F] 66 A6
Hosszúpályi [H] 76 H1
Hosszú-Pereszteg [H] 74 G2
Hostalric [E] 92 F4
Hoštejn [CZ] 50 C4
Hostens [F] 66 C4
Hostěradice [CZ] 62 F2
Hostianské Nemce [SK] 64 C4
Hostinné [CZ] 50 A2
Hostomice [CZ] 48 F4
Hoston [N] 180 H2
Hostouň [CZ] 48 D5
Hostovice [SK] 52 E6
Hostýn [CZ] 50 D6
Hotagen [S] 190 E5
Hotarele [RO] 148 D1
Hoting [S] 190 F5
Hotton [B] 30 E6
Hötzelsdorf [A] 62 E3
Hou [DK] 160 E4
Houdain [F] 28 E3
Houdan [F] 42 E3
Houdelaincourt [F] 44 D5
Houeillès [F] 66 D5
Houffalize [B] 30 E6
Houlbjerg [DK] 160 D5
Houlgate [F] 26 F3
Hourtin [F] 66 C2
Hourtin-Plage [F] 66 C2
Houthalen [B] 30 E3
Houtsala [FIN] 176 C5
Houtskär / Houtskari [FIN] 176 C5
Houtskari / Houtskär [FIN] 176 C5
Hov [DK] 156 D1
Hov [N] 170 H3
Hov [S] 166 G6
Hova [S] 166 F4
Hovborg [DK] 156 B2
Hovda [N] 170 G3
Hovdala [S] 158 C1
Hovden [N] 164 D1
Hovden [N] 192 D3
Høve [DK] 156 F2
Hove [DK] 160 B5
Hove [N] 180 C6
Hövelhof [D] 32 E3
Hoven [DK] 156 B1
Hoverberg [S] 182 G3
Hovet [N] 170 E3
Hovi [FIN] 188 C2
Hovin [N] 164 F1
Hovin [N] 182 B2
Hovinsholm [N] 172 B4
Hovland [N] 164 B4
Hovland [N] 170 C4
Hovmantorp [S] 162 E5
Hovsta [S] 166 H3
Howard, Castle- [IRL] 4 G4
Howth [IRL] 2 F6
Höxter [D] 32 F4
Hoya [D] 18 E6
Hoya-Gonzalo [E] 98 C5
Høyanger [N] 170 C1
Høydalen [N] 164 F3
Høydalsmo [N] 164 E2
Høydalsseter [N] 180 E6
Hoyerswerda [D] 34 F5
Høyjord [N] 164 H2
Høylandet [N] 190 C4
Hoym [D] 34 B4
Hoyos [E] 86 G3
Hoyos del Espino [E] 88 C5
Höytiä [FIN] 186 F4
Hozha [BY] 24 F3
Hrabaw [RUS] 202 C6
Hrachovo [SK] 64 D3
Hrad Beckov [SK] 64 A3
Hradec Králové [CZ] 50 A3
Hradec nad Moravicí [CZ] 50 E4
Hradec nad Svitavou [CZ] 50 B5
Hrádek [CZ] 48 F2
Hrádek [CZ] 50 A3
Hrádek [CZ] 62 F3
Hrádek nad Nisou [CZ] 48 G1
Hradhoviště [CZ] 62 C2
Hradvz'k [UA] 202 F8
Hranice [CZ] 50 E5
Hranovnica [SK] 64 E2
Hrastik [SLO] 74 D5
Hrastovlje [SLO] 72 H6
Hrebenne [PL] 52 G3
Hredino [RUS] 198 H3
Hřensko [CZ] 48 F1
Hriňová [SK] 64 D3
Hrob [CZ] 48 E2
Hrochův Týnec [CZ] 50 B4
Hrodna [BY] 24 F4
Hronov [CZ] 50 B2
Hrotovice [CZ] 62 E2
Hrtkovci [SRB] 142 F2
Hrubieszów [PL] 52 G1
Hrubov [SK] 52 E6
Hrubý Rohozec [CZ] 48 H2
Hrud [PL] 38 F3
Hrušov [SK] 64 B4
Hrušovany [CZ] 62 F3
Hrvace [HR] 144 A1
Hrvatska Kostajnica [HR] 142 B2
Huaröd [S] 158 D2
Huarte [E] 84 B4
Huben [A] 72 C2
Huben [A] 72 F2
Hubertusburg [D] 34 D5
Hubertusstock, Jagdschloss- [D] 20 D6
Hucqueliers [F] 28 D3
Huda Luknja [SLO] 74 D4
Huddersfield [GB] 10 E4
Huddinge [S] 168 D3
Huddunge [S] 174 E6
Hudiksvall [S] 174 E1
Huedin [RO] 204 C4
Huélago [E] 102 F3
Huélamo [E] 98 C2
Huelgoat [F] 40 C2
Huelma [E] 102 E3
Huelva [E] 94 E6
Huércal de Almería [E] 102 G5
Huércal-Overa [E] 102 H4
Huerta del Rey [E] 88 H2
Huerta de Valdecarábanos [E] 96 G2
Huérteles [E] 90 C2
Huerto [E] 90 G3
Huesa [E] 102 F2
Huesca [E] 84 D6
Huéscar [E] 102 G3
Hueselgau [D] 32 G6
Huete [E] 98 A1
Huétor Tájar [E] 102 D3
Hüfingen [D] 58 F3
Hufthamar [N] 170 A4
Huhdasjärvi [FIN] 178 C2
Huhla [BG] 130 G1
Huhtala [FIN] 196 D2
Huhtapuhto [FIN] 196 D5
Huhti [FIN] 176 F2
Huhtilampi [FIN] 188 G3
Huhus [FIN] 188 G2
Huissinkylä [FIN] 186 C3
Huittinen [FIN] 176 E2
Huizen [NL] 16 D3
Huizen [NL] 16 E4
Huizingen [B] 28 H3
Hujakkala [FIN] 178 E3
Hukkala [FIN] 188 E2
Hukvaldy [CZ] 50 E5
Hulderbo [N] 180 G5
Hulín [CZ] 50 D6
Huljen [S] 184 E4
Hulle [N] 180 G1
Hullsjön [S] 184 D4
Hulsing [DK] 160 E2
Hulst [NL] 28 H1
Hult [S] 162 E2
Hult [S] 166 F3
Hultanäs [S] 162 E4
Hultsfred [S] 162 F3
Hultsjö [S] 162 D3
Hum [BIH] 144 D2
Hum [HR] 112 E1
Humada [E] 82 E5
Humanes [E] 88 H5
Humble [DK] 156 E5
Humenné [SK] 64 H2
Humla [S] 162 C1
Humlebæk [DK] 156 G2
Humlum [DK] 160 B5
Hümme [D] 32 F4
Hummelsta [S] 168 C2
Hummelvik [N] 192 H1
Humpolec [CZ] 48 H5
Humppi [FIN] 186 F2
Humppila [FIN] 176 F3
Humprecht [CZ] 48 H2
Hunaudaye, Château de- [F] 26 B4
Hundåla [N] 190 D2
Hunderdorf [D] 60 G2
Hundested [DK] 156 G2
Hundorp [N] 170 H1
Hunedoara [RO] 204 C5
Hünfeld [D] 46 E1
Hunge [S] 182 H3
Hungen [D] 46 D2
Hungerford [GB] 12 H3
Hunnebostrand [S] 166 B5
Hunspach [F] 46 B6
Hunstanton [GB] 10 H6
Huntingdon [GB] 14 E2
Huntly [GB] 6 F5
Huopanankoski [FIN] 186 F2
Hurbanovo [SK] 64 B5
Hurdal [N] 172 B4
Hurdal Verk [N] 172 C4
Hurez, Mănăstirea- [RO] 204 C5
Huriel [F] 56 C5
Hurissalo [FIN] 188 D6
Hurskaala [FIN] 188 C4
Hŭrsovo [BG] 148 E2
Hurtanmaa [FIN] 178 D2
Hurup [DK] 160 B4
Hurva [S] 158 C2
Hus [CZ] 62 B2
Husa [N] 170 B5
Huså [S] 182 F1
Husaby [S] 166 E5
Húsavík [IS] 192 C2
Husbondliden [S] 190 G4
Husby [DK] 160 B5
Husbygård [S] 168 C4
Husby Långhundra [S] 168 D2
Husby-Sjuhundra [S] 168 E2
Huşi [RO] 204 E3
Husinec [CZ] 62 B2
Huskvarna [S] 162 D2
Husnes [N] 170 B5
Husö [FIN] 176 C6
Hustopeče [CZ] 62 F2
Husum [D] 18 E1
Husum [S] 184 G2
Husvika [N] 190 D3
Huta [PL] 52 C5
Huta Zawadzka [PL] 38 A4
Hutovo [BIH] 144 C3
Hüttenberg [A] 74 C2
Hüttschlag [A] 72 G1
Huttwil [CH] 58 E5
Huutijärvi [FIN] 176 F1
Huwniki [PL] 52 F4
Huy (Hoei) [B] 30 D5
Hvalba [FR] 160 A3
Hvalpsund [DK] 160 C4
Hvalvík [FR] 160 B1
Hvam [N] 172 B6
Hvammstangi [IS] 192 B2
Hvar [HR] 144 A2
Hveragerði [IS] 192 A3
Hvidbjerg [DK] 160 B4
Hvide Sande [DK] 156 A1
Hvittingfoss [N] 164 G2
Hvolsvöllur [IS] 192 A3
Hvoznitsa [BY] 38 G4
Hybo [S] 184 D6
Hycklinge [S] 162 F2
Hyde [GB] 10 E4
Hyen [N] 180 C5
Hyères [F] 108 C6
Hyervyaty [BY] 200 H5
Hyggen [N] 164 H1
Hylestad [N] 164 D3
Hyllested Skovgårde [DK] 160 F6
Hyltebruk [S] 162 B4
Hynnekleiv [N] 164 E4
Hyry [FIN] 196 D3
Hyrynsalmi [FIN] 196 F4
Hyssna [S] 160 H2
Hythe [GB] 14 F5
Hyttegrend [N] 192 F3
Hytti [FIN] 178 E2
Hyvinge / Hyvinkää [FIN] 176 H4
Hyvinkää / Hyvinge [FIN] 176 H4
Hyypiö [FIN] 194 D7
Hyżne [PL] 52 E4

I

Ialissós [GR] 154 D3
Ianca [RO] 148 A2
Iaşi [RO] 204 E3
Íasmos [GR] 130 F2

Jošanička Banja [SRB] 146 B3
Jošavka [BIH] 142 C3
Josefov [CZ] 50 B3
Jøsenfjorden [N] 164 C2
Joševa [SRB] 142 F3
Josipdol [HR] 112 G2
Josipovac [HR] 76 B6
Jössefors [S] 166 D2
Josselin [F] 26 B6
Jøssund [N] 190 C5
Jostedal [N] 180 D6
Jósvafő [H] 64 F3
Jouarre [F] 42 H4
Jõuga [EST] 198 F1
Jougne [F] 58 B6
Joukio [FIN] 188 F6
Joukokylä [FIN] 196 F3
Joure [NL] 16 F3
Journaankylä [FIN] 178 B4
Joutsa [FIN] 186 G6
Joutseno [FIN] 178 E2
Joutsijärvi [FIN] 194 E7
Jovan [S] 190 G4
Joviac [F] 68 F6
Jøvik [N] 192 G2
Jovsa [SK] 64 H2
Joyeuse [F] 68 E6
Józefów [PL] 38 C3
Józefów [PL] 38 D6
Józefów [PL] 52 F2
Józsa [H] 64 G6
Juankoski [FIN] 188 D1
Juan–les–Pins [F] 108 E5
Judaberg [N] 164 B2
Judenburg [A] 74 C2
Judinsalo [FIN] 186 G6
Juelsminde [DK] 156 D2
Jugendburg [D] 46 C1
Jugon–les–Lacs [F] 26 B5
Jugorje [SLO] 74 D6
Juhtimäki [FIN] 186 D6
Juillac [F] 66 G3
Juist [D] 16 H1
Jukkasjärvi [S] 192 G5
Juknaičiai [LT] 200 D5
Juktån [S] 190 G4
Jule [N] 190 D5
Jülich [D] 30 F4
Julierpass [CH] 70 H2
Julita [S] 168 B3
Jullouville [F] 26 D4
Jumièges [F] 26 H3
Jumilla [E] 104 C1
Juminen [FIN] 196 F6
Jumisko [FIN] 194 E8
Jumkersrott [D] 18 B3
Jumkil [S] 168 D1
Jung [S] 166 E6
Jungsund [FIN] 186 B2
Junibodsand [S] 184 F5
Juniville [F] 44 C3
Junnikkala [FIN] 178 E1
Junosuando [S] 194 B7
Junqueira [P] 80 E4
Junsele [S] 190 F6
Juntusranta [FIN] 196 F3
Juodupė [LT] 198 F6
Juojärvi [FIN] 188 E3
Juoksengi [S] 194 B8
Juokslahti [FIN] 186 F5
Juorkuna [FIN] 196 E4
Jupiter [RO] 148 G1
Jurbarkas [LT] 200 E5
Jurignac [F] 66 E1
Jurklošter [SLO] 74 D5
Jurków [PL] 52 B4
Jūrmala [LV] 198 D5
Jurmo [FIN] 176 C4
Jurmo [FIN] 176 D6
Jurovski Brod [HR] 74 D6
Jurowce [PL] 24 E5
Jurva [FIN] 186 B3
Jurvala [FIN] 178 D2
Jurvansalo [FIN] 186 G2
Jushkino [RUS] 198 G2
Jushkozero [RUS] 196 H3
Jussey [F] 58 B3
Juszkowy Gród [PL] 24 F6
Juta [H] 74 H4
Jüterbog [D] 34 D3
Jutis [S] 190 F2
Jutrosin [PL] 36 D5
Jutsajaura [S] 192 G6
Juujärvi [FIN] 194 E8
Juuka [FIN] 188 E1
Juupajoki [FIN] 186 E6
Juurikka [FIN] 188 G4
Juva [FIN] 176 D4
Juva [FIN] 188 D5
Juvanum [I] 116 D5
Juvigny–le–Tertre [F] 26 E4
Juvola [FIN] 188 E4
Juvre [DK] 156 B3
Juzennecourt [F] 44 C6
Južnyj [RUS] 22 H2
Jyderup [DK] 156 F2
Jylhä [FIN] 186 G1
Jyllinge [DK] 156 G2
Jyrkäntoski [FIN] 194 F8
Jyrkha [FIN] 196 F5
Jyväskylä [FIN] 186 G4

K

Kaalamo [RUS] 188 G4
Kaalasjärvi [S] 192 G5
Kaalinen / Ikalis [FIN] 186 D6
Kaamanen [FIN] 194 D4
Kaanaa [FIN] 186 E6
Kääntöjärvi [S] 192 H5
Kaarela [FIN] 196 D3
Kaaresuvanto [FIN] 192 H4
Kaarina [FIN] 176 D4
Kaarma [EST] 198 C3
Käärmelahti [FIN] 188 F5
Kaarssen [D] 18 H5
Kaartilankoski [FIN] 188 E5
Kaatsheuvel [NL] 16 D6
Kaavi [FIN] 188 D2
Kaba [H] 76 G1
Kabakca [TR] 150 D2
Kabalar [TR] 152 G4
Kabaltepe [TR] 130 H5
Kabböle [FIN] 178 B4
Kåbdalis [S] 190 H2
Kabelvåg [N] 192 D4
Kabile [LV] 198 C5
Kableshkovo [BG] 148 F4
Kać [SRB] 142 F1
Kačanik [SRB] 146 C6
Kacelovo [BG] 148 D2
Kaceřov [CZ] 48 E4
Kachanovo [RUS] 198 G4
Kačikol [SRB] 146 C5
Kačina [CZ] 48 H4
Kácov [CZ] 48 G4
Kaczorów [PL] 50 B1
Kadaň [CZ] 48 E3
Kadarkút [H] 74 H4
Kadikalesi [TR] 152 D5
Kadıköy [TR] 150 B4
Kadıköy [TR] 152 F4
Kadıköy [TR] 154 G2
Kadłubówka [PL] 38 E1
Kadłub Turawski [PL] 50 E2
Kadrifakovo [MK] 128 F1
Kadyanda [TR] 154 F2
Kadzidło [PL] 24 C5
Käenkoski [FIN] 188 G1
Kåfjord [N] 194 C1
Kaga [S] 166 H5
Kåge [S] 196 A4
Kågeröd [S] 158 C2
Kagkádi [GR] 136 C1
Kaharlyk [UA] 202 D7
Kahla [D] 46 H1
Kaïáfas [GR] 136 C2
Kaïméni Chóra [GR] 136 G2
Käina [EST] 198 C2
Kainach bei Voitsberg [A] 74 D2
Kainasto [FIN] 186 B4
Kaindorf [A] 74 E2
Kainu [FIN] 186 D1
Kainulasjärvi [S] 194 B7
Kaipiainen [FIN] 178 C2
Kairahta [FIN] 186 G4
Kairala [FIN] 194 E7
Kairila [FIN] 176 D1
Kaisepakte [S] 192 F4
Kaiserbach [D] 46 D6
Kaisersesch [D] 30 G6
Kaiserslautern [D] 44 H3
Kaiser–Wilhelm–Koog [D] 18 E3
Kaisheim [D] 60 D2
Kaišiadoris [LT] 200 F5
Kaitainsalmi [FIN] 196 F5
Kaitsor [FIN] 186 B2
Kaivanto [FIN] 196 E4
Kaivomäki [FIN] 188 D5
Kajaani / Kajana [FIN] 196 E5
Kajana / Kajaani [FIN] 196 E5
Kajánújfalu [H] 76 E3
Kajetans–Brücke [A] 72 C2
Kajoo [FIN] 188 E1
Kájov [CZ] 62 B2
Kajraly [RUS] 194 F7
Kakanj [BIH] 142 D4
Kakarriq [AL] 128 A1
Kakavi [AL] 132 C1
Kakerbeck [D] 34 B1
Kakhovka [UA] 204 G3
Käkilahti [FIN] 196 E5
Kaklıç [TR] 152 C4
Kaklik [TR] 152 G5
Kaklik [TR] 152 G5
Kakmå [HR] 112 G5
Kąkolewnica Wschodnia [PL] 38 E4
Kakopetriá [CY] 154 F5
Kakóvatos [GR] 136 C3
Kăkrina [BG] 148 B3
Kakslauttanen [FIN] 194 D5
Kaktyni [LV] 198 E5
Kakuåsen [S] 190 E6
Kakushöhle [D] 30 G5
Kál [H] 64 E6
Kälä [FIN] 186 H5
Kalaja [FIN] 196 D6
Kalajoki [FIN] 196 C5
Kalak [N] 194 D2
Kalakoski [FIN] 186 D4
Kalamáki [GR] 132 H2
Kalamáki [GR] 134 A2
Kalamariá [GR] 128 H4
Kalamáta [GR] 136 D4
Kalámi [GR] 140 C4
Kalamítsi [GR] 130 D6
Kálamos [GR] 134 C5
Kalamotí [GR] 134 G5
Kalampáki [GR] 130 D3
Kalampáki [GR] 132 E2
Kalanchak [RUS] 204 G3
Kalándra [GR] 130 B6
Kalá Nerá [GR] 132 H2
Kalanti [FIN] 176 C3
Kälarne [S] 184 D3
Kálathos [GR] 154 D4
Kalavárda [GR] 154 D3
Kalávryta [GR] 136 D1
Kalax [FIN] 186 A4
Kalbe [D] 34 B1
Kalce [SLO] 74 B5
Kalčevo [BG] 148 E5
Káld [H] 74 G2
Kaldfarnes [N] 192 E3
Kaldhusseter [N] 180 E4
Kale [TR] 152 D1
Kale [TR] 152 F6
Kale [TR] 154 H3
Kaleburnu (Galinóporni) [CY] 154 H4
Kalekovets [BG] 148 B5
Kaleköy [TR] 130 G5
Kalela [FIN] 176 D3
Kalenić, Manastir– [SRB] 146 C2
Kálergo [GR] 134 D5
Kalesija [BIH] 142 E3
Kalety [PL] 50 F2
Kalétzi [GR] 132 D2
Kalétzi [GR] 136 C1
Kaleva [FIN] 176 E4
Kalí [GR] 128 G4
Kaliánoi [GR] 136 E1
Kalidón [GR] 132 E5
Kaliningrad [RUS] 22 G1
Kalinkavichy [BY] 202 C6
Kalinovik [BIH] 144 D2
Kalinovka [RUS] 24 C1
Kalinovo [PL] 24 D3
Kalinovo [SK] 64 D4
Kalirráchi [GR] 128 E6
Kalisty [PL] 22 G3
Kalisz [PL] 36 E4
Kalisz Pomorski [PL] 20 H5
Kalivári [GR] 134 E6
Kalix [S] 196 C2
Kaljord [N] 192 D4
Kalkan [TR] 154 G3
Kalkar [D] 16 F6
Kalkbrugger [DK] 160 C5
Kalkım [TR] 152 C1
Kalkkinen [FIN] 178 A2
Kall [D] 30 G5
Kall [S] 182 F1
Källa [S] 162 H4
Kallarat [AL] 128 B6
Källarbo [S] 174 C5
Kallaste [EST] 198 F2
Källbäck [FIN] 178 A4
Källberget [S] 182 F3
Kållered [S] 160 H2
Kalli [EST] 198 D3
Kallimasiá [GR] 134 G5
Kallinge [S] 158 F1
Kallio [FIN] 186 D5
Kallio [FIN] 196 F5
Kalliojoki [FIN] 196 G4
Kallislahti [FIN] 188 E5
Kallithéa [GR] 128 G6
Kallithéa [GR] 130 C3
Kallithéa [GR] 130 C6
Kallithéa [GR] 136 D2
Kallithéa [GR] 154 D3
Kalliuskoski [FIN] 196 E4
Kallmünz [D] 48 B6
Kálló [H] 64 D5
Kallön [S] 190 G3
Kalloní [GR] 134 G2
Kalloní [GR] 136 F2
Kállósemjén [H] 64 H5
Kallsedet [S] 190 D6
Kallträsk [FIN] 186 B5
Källunga [S] 162 B1
Kallunki [FIN] 194 F7
Kalmakattio [FIN] 194 C5
Kálmánháza [H] 64 G5
Kalmar [S] 162 G5
Kalmari [FIN] 186 F3
Kalná [CZ] 48 G4
Kalna [SRB] 146 E3
Kalná nad Hronom [SK] 64 B4
Kalnciems [LV] 198 D5
Kalnik [PL] 22 G3
Kalochóri [GR] 128 E5
Kaló Chorió [GR] 140 F5
Kalocsa [H] 76 C4
Kalofer [BG] 148 B5
Kalogriá [GR] 132 E6
Kaloí Liménes [GR] 140 E5
Kalókastro [GR] 130 B3
Kalonéri [GR] 128 E5
Kaló Nero [GR] 136 C3
Kalopanagiótis [CY] 154 F5
Kaloskopí [GR] 132 G4
Kalotina [BG] 146 F4
Kaloyan [BG] 148 F2
Kaloyanovo [BG] 148 B5
Káloz [H] 76 B2
Kalpáki [GR] 132 C1
Kalpio [FIN] 196 E4
Kals [A] 72 F2
Kalsdorf [A] 74 D2
Kalsdorf [A] 74 E2
Kalsvik [S] 168 E3
Kaltanenai [LT] 200 G4
Kaltenkirchen [D] 18 F5
Kaltennordheim [D] 46 F2
Kaltinėnai [LT] 200 E4
Kaluga [RUS] 202 F4
Kalugerovo [BG] 148 A5
Kalundborg [DK] 156 E2
Kalush [UA] 204 C2
Kałuszyn [PL] 38 C3
Kalv [S] 162 B3
Kalvåg [N] 180 B5
Kalvarija [LT] 24 E2
Kalvatn [N] 180 D4
Kalvehave [DK] 156 G4
Kalven [N] 194 B1
Kälviä / Kelviå [FIN] 196 C6
Kälvik [S] 162 G2
Kalvitsa [FIN] 188 C5
Kalvola [FIN] 176 G2
Kalwang [A] 74 C1
Kalwaria Zebrzydowska [PL] 50 H4
Kalyazin [RUS] 202 F2
Kálymnos [GR] 154 A2
Kalynivka [UA] 202 C8
Kalývia [GR] 132 E4
Kám [H] 74 G2
Kamanski Vučiak [HR] 142 C1
Kamáres [GR] 138 D3
Kamáres [GR] 138 E3
Kamáres [GR] 140 E5
Kamariótissa [GR] 130 F4
Kamburovo [BG] 148 D3
Kamchiya [BG] 148 F3
Kámeiros [GR] 154 D4
Kámen [CZ] 48 G5
Kamen [D] 32 C4
Kamenari [MNE] 144 D4
Kaména Voúrla [GR] 132 H4
Kamen Bryag [BG] 148 G2
Kamengrad [BIH] 142 B2
Kamenica [MK] 146 E6
Kamenice nad Lipou [CZ] 48 G6
Kamenichý Hrad [SK] 52 C6
Kameničná [SK] 64 A5
Kamenka [RUS] 178 F3
Kamennogorsk [RUS] 178 F2
Kamenný Újezd [CZ] 62 C2
Kameno [BG] 148 F4
Kamenovo [BG] 148 D2
Kamensko [HR] 142 C1
Kamensko [HR] 144 B2
Kamenz [D] 34 F6
Kamëz [AL] 128 B2
Kamianets'–Podil's'kyi [UA] 204 D2
Kamianka [UA] 202 E8
Kamianka–Dniprovs'ka [UA] 204 H2
Kamičak [BIH] 142 B3
Kamień [PL] 52 E3
Kamienica [PL] 52 B5
Kamieniec Ząbkowicki [PL] 50 C2
Kamienka [SK] 52 B5
Kamień Krajeński [PL] 22 C5
Kamienna Góra [PL] 50 B2
Kamień Pomorski [PL] 20 F3
Kamieńsk [PL] 36 G6
Kamínia [GR] 130 F6
Kamínia [GR] 132 D1
Kamion [PL] 38 A2
Kammerstein [A] 74 C1
Kamnica [SLO] 74 C5
Kamnik [SLO] 74 C4
Kampánis [GR] 128 H4
Kampen [D] 156 A4
Kampen [NL] 16 F4
Kamperland [NL] 16 B6
Kampiá [GR] 134 G4
Kampinos [PL] 38 A3
Kamp Lintfort [D] 30 G3
Kampor [HR] 112 F3
Kámpos [GR] 132 F5
Kámpos [GR] 136 D4
Kámpos [GR] 138 H2
Kámpos [GR] 140 B4
Kamula [FIN] 196 E5
Kamyanyets [BY] 38 G2
Kamyanyuki [BY] 38 G2
Kamýk nad Vltavou [CZ] 48 F5
Kanal [SLO] 72 H5
Kanala [FIN] 186 E1
Kanála [GR] 138 C2
Kanália [GR] 132 H2
Kanalláki [GR] 132 C3
Kanatlarci [MK] 128 E3
Kańczuga [PL] 52 E3
Kandava [LV] 198 C5
Kandel [D] 46 B5
Kandern [D] 58 E4
Kandersteg [CH] 70 D2
Kandestederne [DK] 160 E2
Kandíla [GR] 136 E2
Kandira [TR] 150 G2
Kanepi [EST] 198 F3
Kanestraum [N] 180 F2
Kanfanar [HR] 112 D2
Kangas [FIN] 196 D5
Kangasaho [FIN] 186 E3
Kangasala [FIN] 176 F1
Kangashäkki [FIN] 186 G3
Kangaskylä [FIN] 186 F1
Kangaslampi [FIN] 188 D4
Kangasniemi [FIN] 186 H5
Kanin [PL] 22 B2
Kaninkola [FIN] 176 E4
Kaniv [UA] 202 E7
Kanižarica [SLO] 74 D6
Kanjiža [SRB] 76 E5
Kanjon Cetine [HR] 144 A2
Kanjon Ugar [BIH] 142 C3
Kankaanpää [FIN] 186 C6
Kankainen [FIN] 186 G4
Kankova [SLO] 74 E3
Kånna [S] 162 C5
Kannonkoski [FIN] 186 F2
Kannus [FIN] 196 C5
Kannuskoski [FIN] 178 D2
Kanpaneta / Campanas [E] 84 B4
Kansız [TR] 150 E5
Kanstad [N] 192 E4
Kantala [FIN] 188 C4
Kántanos [GR] 140 B5
Kanteemaa [FIN] 176 E3
Kántia [GR] 136 F2
Kantojoki [FIN] 194 F8
Kantokylä [FIN] 196 D5
Kantomaanpää [FIN] 194 C8
Kantornes [N] 192 F2
Kantorp [S] 168 B4
Kantti [FIN] 186 C5
Kanturk [IRL] 4 C4
Kányavár [H] 74 F3
Kaolinovo [BG] 148 E2
Kaona [SRB] 146 B3
Kaonik [BIH] 142 D4
Kaonik [SRB] 146 C3
Kąp [PL] 24 C3
Kapaklı [TR] 150 E4
Kapaklı [TR] 152 D3
Kapandríti [GR] 134 C5
Kāpas [LV] 198 C5
Kapčiamiestis [LT] 24 F3
Kapellludden [S] 162 G5
Kapfenberg [A] 74 D1
Kapıkaya [TR] 152 F2
Kapıkırı [TR] 152 D6
Kapinci [HR] 74 H6
Kapitan Andreevo [BG] 150 A2
Kaplıca (Davlós) [CY] 154 G4
Kaplice [CZ] 62 C3
Kapolcs [H] 74 H2
Kápolna [H] 64 E5
Kaposfüred [H] 74 H4
Kaposvár [H] 76 A4
Kapp [N] 172 B4
Kappel [D] 44 H2
Kappel [D] 58 E2
Kappeln [D] 18 F1
Kappelshamn [S] 168 G3
Kappelskär [S] 168 F2
Kappl [A] 72 B1
Kaprun [A] 72 F1
Kapsáli [GR] 136 F6
Kápsas [GR] 136 E2
Kapušany [SK] 64 G2
Kapuvár [H] 62 G6
Karaağaç [TR] 150 G2
Karabayır [TR] 154 F1
Karabeylı [TR] 152 G3
Karabiga [TR] 150 C4
Karabörtlen [TR] 154 E1
Karaburun [TR] 134 H4
Karaburun [TR] 150 E2
Karacaali [TR] 150 F4
Karacabey [TR] 150 E5
Karacaköy [TR] 150 D2
Karacalar [TR] 152 D2
Karacalar [TR] 152 E2
Karaçalı [TR] 150 G2
Karaçam [TR] 152 D2
Karacaoğlan [TR] 150 B2
Karacaşehir [TR] 150 H5
Karacasu [TR] 152 F5
Karaçulha [TR] 154 F2
Karád [H] 76 A3
Karahallı [TR] 152 G4
Karahisar [TR] 152 F5
Karainebeyli [TR] 150 B5
Karaisen [BG] 148 C3
Karakadağ [TR] 150 C1
Karakagür [TR] 150 B3
Karakamza [TR] 150 B1
Karakaya [TR] 152 D6
Karakiani [GR] 136 G1
Karakoumi (Karakum) [CY] 154 G5
Karaköy [TR] 152 B1
Karaköy [TR] 152 D4
Karaköy [TR] 152 F4
Karakum (Karakoumi) [CY] 154 G5
Karakür [TR] 152 F2
Karakurt [TR] 152 D2
Karakuzu [TR] 152 C3
Karala [EST] 198 C3
Karalaks [N] 194 C3
Karali [RUS] 188 H3
Karalin [BY] 24 H5
Karamanci [BG] 148 C6
Karamandere [TR] 150 D2
Karamanlı [TR] 152 H6
Karamürsel [TR] 150 F3
Karamyshevo [RUS] 198 H3
Karancslapujtő [H] 64 D4
Karaova [TR] 154 C1
Karapazar [TR] 150 H5
Karapelit [BG] 148 F2
Karapürçek [TR] 150 H3
Karasjok [N] 194 C3
Karasu [TR] 150 H2
Kárász [H] 76 B4
Karataş [TR] 152 E3
Karats [S] 190 G1
Karavás [GR] 136 F6
Karaveliler [TR] 152 C2
Karavelovo [BG] 148 E5
Káravos [GR] 134 C5
Karavostasi (Gemikonağı) [CY] 154 F5
Karavostásis [GR] 138 E4
Karavukovo [SRB] 142 E1
Karawankeni Predor [A/SLO] 74 B4
Karayakuplu [TR] 150 G3
Karbasan [TR] 152 G4
Karbenning [S] 168 B1
Kårböle [S] 182 H6
Karby [DK] 160 C4
Karby [S] 168 E2
Karcag [H] 76 F1
Karczowiska [PL] 36 B5
Kardakáta [GR] 132 C6
Kardam [BG] 148 G1
Kardámaina [GR] 154 B2
Kardámyla [GR] 134 G4
Kardamýli [GR] 136 D4
Kardašova–Řečice [CZ] 48 G6
Kardítsa [GR] 132 F2
Kärdla [EST] 198 C2
Kardos [H] 76 F3
Kardoskút [H] 76 F4
Käremo [S] 162 G5
Karersee / Carezza al Lago [I] 72 D3
Karesuando [S] 192 H4
Kärevere [EST] 198 F2
Kargalı [TR] 150 F2
Kargı [TR] 154 F2
Kargów [PL] 52 C2
Kargowa [PL] 36 B3
Karhujärvi [FIN] 194 E7
Karhukangas [FIN] 196 D5
Karhula [FIN] 178 C4
Kårhus [N] 164 B1
Karhusjärvi [FIN] 178 E2
Kari [FIN] 188 D1
Kariani [GR] 130 C4
Karigasniemi [FIN] 194 C3
Karijoki / Bötom [FIN] 186 B4
Karine [TR] 152 C6
Karinkanta [FIN] 196 D4
Karis / Karjaa [FIN] 176 F5
Karise [DK] 156 G3
Karítaina [GR] 136 D2
Karjaa / Karis [FIN] 176 F5
Karjala [FIN] 176 D3
Karjalohja [FIN] 176 F5
Kärjenkoski [FIN] 186 B5
Kärkäälä [FIN] 186 G3
Karkaloú [GR] 136 D2
Kärki [LV] 198 E4
Karkkila / Högfors [FIN] 176 G4
Karkku [FIN] 176 E1
Karklampi [FIN] 186 F6
Kärkölä [FIN] 176 F4
Kärkölä [FIN] 176 H3
Karksi–Nuia [EST] 198 E3
Karlby [FIN] 168 H1
Karleby / Kokkola [FIN] 196 C6
Karlevistenen [S] 162 G5
Karlewo [PL] 22 F6
Karl Gustav [S] 160 H3
Karlholmsbruk [S] 174 F4
Karlino [PL] 20 H3
Karlö / Hailuoto [FIN] 196 D4
Karlobag [HR] 112 F4
Karlovac [HR] 112 G1
Karlóvasi [GR] 152 C5
Karlova Studánka [CZ] 50 D4
Karlovo [BG] 148 B4
Karlovy Vary [CZ] 48 D3
Karłowice [PL] 50 D1
Karlsberg [D] 44 H2
Karlsberg [S] 162 D1
Karlsberg [S] 172 H1
Karlsborg [S] 166 G5
Karlsborg [S] 196 C3
Karlshamn [S] 158 E1
Karlshöfen [D] 18 E4
Karlskoga [S] 166 G3
Karlskrona [S] 158 F1
Karlslunde Strand [DK] 156 G3
Karlsrud [N] 170 F5
Karlsruhe [D] 46 B6
Karlstad [S] 166 F3
Karlstadt [D] 46 E3
Karlštejn [CZ] 48 F4
Karlštejn [CZ] 50 B5
Karlstift [A] 62 C3
Karlstorp [S] 162 E3
Karmas [S] 192 F6
Kärnä [FIN] 186 D2
Kärnä [FIN] 186 G2
Kärnåsens Hembygdsgård [S] 166 F1
Karniszyn [PL] 22 G6
Karnobat [BG] 148 E4
Karojba [HR] 112 D1
Karousádes [GR] 132 A2
Karow [D] 20 B4
Karpacz [PL] 50 A2
Karpasolo [FIN] 188 F3
Kárpathos [GR] 140 H3
Karpenísi [GR] 132 F4
Karperó [GR] 132 E1
Karpuzlu [TR] 152 E6
Karrantza / Carranza [E] 82 F3
Kärrbackstrand [S] 172 E3
Kärrbö [S] 168 A1
Karrebæksminde [DK] 156 F4
Kärsämä [FIN] 196 D4
Kärsämäki [FIN] 196 D5
Kārsava [LV] 198 G5
Karsibór [PL] 20 E4
Karşıyaka [TR] 150 D4
Karsjö [S] 174 D1
Karstädt [D] 20 A5
Karst en Yesos [E] 102 H5
Kärstna [EST] 198 E3
Karstø [N] 164 A2
Karstula [FIN] 186 F3
Kartal [TR] 150 F3
Kartala [BG] 146 G6
Kartena [LT] 200 D4
Kartéri [GR] 132 C3
Karteros [GR] 140 E4
Karthaía [GR] 138 C2
Karttula [FIN] 186 H2
Kartuzy [PL] 22 D2
Karungi [S] 196 C2
Karunki [FIN] 196 C2
Karup [DK] 160 C5
Karuse [EST] 198 D2
Karvala [FIN] 186 D2
Kärväskylä [FIN] 186 G1
Kårvatn [N] 180 G3
Karvia [FIN] 186 C5
Karvik [N] 192 H2
Kårvikhamn [N] 192 F2
Karviná [CZ] 50 F4
Karvio [FIN] 188 E3
Karvounári [GR] 132 C3
Karwia [PL] 22 D1
Karwica [PL] 24 C4
Karyá [GR] 128 G6
Karyá [GR] 132 C4
Karyá [GR] 136 E2
Karyés [GR] 130 D5
Karyés [GR] 132 G3
Karyés [GR] 136 E3
Karyótissa [GR] 128 G4
Karyoúpoli [GR] 136 E5
Kárystos [GR] 134 D6
Kås [DK] 160 D3
Kaş [TR] 154 G3
Kasaba [TR] 154 G3
Kašalj [SRB] 146 B4
Kascyukovichy [BY] 202 D5
Kåseberga [S] 158 D3
Kasejovice [CZ] 48 E5
Kashin [RUS] 202 E2
Kashirskoye [RUS] 200 C5
Kašina [HR] 74 E5
Kasinka Wielka [PL] 52 B4
Kåskats [S] 190 H2
Kaski [FIN] 176 F5
Kaskii [FIN] 188 D5
Kaskinen / Kaskö [FIN] 186 A4
Kaskö / Kaskinen [FIN] 186 A4
Kas'kovo [RUS] 178 G5
Kaslania Pass [GR] 128 F5
Käsmu [EST] 198 E1
Kasnäs [FIN] 176 E6
Káspakas [GR] 130 F6
Kašperk [CZ] 48 E6
Kašperské Hory [CZ] 48 E6
Kaspichan [BG] 148 E3
Kassa [FIN] 194 B7
Kassándreia [GR] 130 B6
Kassari [EST] 198 C2
Kassel [D] 32 F5
Kassiópi [GR] 132 B2
Kassópi [GR] 132 C3
Kastabos [TR] 154 D2
Kastaniá [GR] 128 G5
Kastaniá [GR] 132 E2
Kastaniá [GR] 132 F3
Kastaniá [GR] 136 E4
Kastaniá [GR] 136 E1
Kastaniá [GR] 136 F5
Kastaniés [GR] 150 A2
Kastelholms [FIN] 176 B5
Kastellaun [D] 44 H2
Kastélli [GR] 140 B4
Kastélli [GR] 140 F5
Kaštel Stari [HR] 142 A5
Kaštel Žegarski [HR] 112 H5
Kasterlee [B] 30 D3
Kastl [D] 46 H5
Kastlösa [S] 162 G6
Kastneshamn [N] 192 E3
Kastorf [D] 18 G4
Kastoriá [GR] 128 E5
Kastráki [GR] 132 E4
Kastre [EST] 198 F3
Kastri [GR] 140 C6
Kástro [GR] 134 A5
Kástro [GR] 134 B3
Kástro [GR] 136 B1
Kastrosykiá [GR] 132 C3
Kastrup [DK] 156 H3
Kaszaper [H] 76 F4
Katáfyto [GR] 130 C2
Katákolo [GR] 136 B2
Kataloinen [FIN] 176 H2
Kätänjoki [FIN] 186 D3
Katápola [GR] 138 G4
Katará Pass [GR] 132 D1
Katastári [GR] 136 A2
Kåtaviken [S] 190 E2
Katerbow [D] 20 C6
Kateríni [GR] 128 G5
Kateřinská [CZ] 50 C6
Katerloch [A] 74 D2
Katerma [FIN] 196 F5
Kätkasuvanto [FIN] 194 B6
Kätkesuando [S] 194 B6
Katlanovo [MK] 128 E1
Katlanovska Banja [MK] 128 F1
Katlenburg–Duhm [D] 32 G4
Káto Achaïa [GR] 132 E6
Káto Alepochóri [GR] 134 B6
Káto Aséa [GR] 136 D3
Katochí [GR] 132 E5
Káto Dolianá [GR] 136 E3
Káto Kleitoría [GR] 136 D1
Káto Makrinoú [GR] 132 E5
Káto Nevrokópi [GR] 130 C2
Káto Pýrgos [CY] 154 F5
Káto Samikó [GR] 136 C2
Káto Tithoréa [GR] 132 H5
Katoúna [GR] 132 D4
Káto Velitsés [GR] 136 C1
Káto Vérmio [GR] 128 F5
Katovice [CZ] 48 E6
Káto Vlasía [GR] 136 D1
Káto Vrontoú [GR] 130 C2
Katowice [PL] 50 G3
Káto Zákros [GR] 140 H5
Katrineberg [S] 174 D3
Katrineholm [S] 168 B4
Katschberg Tunnel [A] 72 H2
Kattavía [GR] 154 C5
Katthammarsvik [S] 168 G5
Kattilakoski [FIN] 186 D1
Kättilstad [S] 162 F1
Kattisavan [S] 190 G4
Kattlunds [S] 168 G6
Kattuvuoma [S] 192 G4
Katumäki [FIN] 188 C3
Katundi i Ri [AL] 128 A2
Katuntsi [BG] 130 B2
Katwijk aan Zee [NL] 16 C4
Katy [PL] 20 F4
Kąty [PL] 52 E2
Katyčiai [LT] 200 D5
Katymár [H] 76 C5
Kąty Wrocławskie [PL] 50 C1
Kaub [D] 46 B3
Kaufbeuren [D] 60 C5
Kaufering [D] 60 D4
Kaufungen [D] 32 F5
Kauhajärvi [FIN] 186 C5
Kauhajärvi [FIN] 186 D2
Kauhajoki [FIN] 186 B4
Kauhava [FIN] 186 C2
Kaukalampi [FIN] 176 H3
Kaukela [FIN] 176 H1
Kaukonen [FIN] 194 C6
Kauksi [EST] 198 F2
Kaukuri [FIN] 176 F5
Kaulbach [D] 44 H3
Kaunas [LT] 200 F5
Kaunata [LV] 198 G5

Kauniainen / Grankulla [FIN] 176 H5
Kaunos [TR] 154 E2
Kauns [A] 72 C1
Kaupanger [N] 170 D2
Kaurajärvi [FIN] 186 C2
Kauria [FIN] 178 D1
Kauša [LV] 198 F6
Kausala [FIN] 178 B3
Kaustby / Kaustinen [FIN] 196 C6
Kaustinen / Kaustby [FIN] 196 C6
Kautokeino [N] 194 B4
Kauttua [FIN] 176 D3
Káva [H] 76 D1
Kavacık [TR] 150 B3
Kavacık [TR] 152 E1
Kavacık [TR] 152 H5
Kavadarci [MK] 128 F2
Kavajë [AL] 128 A3
Kavak [TR] 150 B4
Kavakdere [TR] 150 C2
Kavakköy [TR] 152 E6
Kavakli [TR] 130 H2
Kavaklı [TR] 150 B2
Kavaklı [TR] 150 E3
Kavaklıdere [TR] 152 E6
Kavála [GR] 130 D3
Kavarna [BG] 148 G2
Kavaröskaten [S] 174 G5
Kåvenvallen [S] 182 E4
Kävlinge [S] 158 C2
Kávos [GR] 132 B3
Kavoúsi [GR] 140 G5
Kavşit [TR] 152 E5
Kavýli [GR] 130 H1
Kaxholmen [S] 162 D2
Kayabaşı [TR] 154 G1
Kayaköy [TR] 152 D4
Kayaköy [TR] 154 F2
Kayalar [TR] 150 D6
Kayapa [TR] 150 B1
Kayapa [TR] 152 C1
Käyhtiönmaa [FIN] 176 D2
Kayı [TR] 150 C3
Käylä [FIN] 194 F8
Kaymakçi [TR] 152 E4
Kaymaz [TR] 150 G2
Kaynarca [TR] 150 G2
Käyrämö [FIN] 194 D7
Kayran [TR] 152 F5
Kaysersberg [F] 58 D2
Kazaklar [TR] 152 F4
Kazanci [BIH] 142 B4
Kažani [MK] 128 E3
Kazanka [UA] 204 G2
Kazanlŭk [BG] 148 C4
Kazárma [GR] 136 D4
Kazichene [BG] 146 G5
Kazimierza Wielka [PL] 52 B3
Kazimierz Biskupi [PL] 36 E3
Kazimierz Dolny [PL] 38 D5
Kâzımpaşa [TR] 150 G3
Kazincbarcika [H] 64 F4
Kazlu–Rūda [LT] 24 F1
Kaznějov [CZ] 48 E4
Kaz'yany [BY] 200 H4
Kcynia [PL] 22 C6
Kdyně [CZ] 48 D5
Kéa [GR] 138 C2
Keadue [IRL] 2 D4
Keady [NIR] 2 F4
Kebrene [TR] 152 B1
Kecel [H] 76 C4
Kecskemét [H] 76 D2
Kėdainiai [LT] 200 F5
Kédros [GR] 132 F3
Kędzierzyn–Koźle [PL] 50 E3
Keel [IRL] 2 B3
Keenagh [IRL] 2 D5
Kefalári [GR] 136 E1
Kéfalos [GR] 154 A3
Kefalóvryso [GR] 132 C1
Kefalóvryso [GR] 132 F1
Kefermarkt [A] 62 C4
Kefken [TR] 150 G2
Keflavík [IS] 192 A3
Kehidakustány [H] 74 G3
Kehl [D] 44 H6
Kehra [EST] 198 E1
Kehrig [D] 30 H6
Kehtna [EST] 198 E2
Keighley [GB] 10 E3
Keihärinkoski [FIN] 186 F2
Keihäskoski [FIN] 176 E3
Keikyä [FIN] 176 E2
Keila–Joa [EST] 198 D1
Keipene [LV] 198 E5
Keisala [FIN] 186 E2
Keitele [FIN] 186 G1
Keith [GB] 6 F5
Kekava [LV] 198 D5
Kékestető [H] 64 E5
Kelankyla [FIN] 196 E2
Kelberg [D] 30 G6
Kelbra [D] 32 H5
Këlcyrë [AL] 128 C6
Kelebia [H] 76 D4
Kelebija [SRB] 76 D5
Kelefá [GR] 136 E5
Kelekçi [TR] 152 G6
Kelemér [H] 64 E4
Keler [TR] 152 C5
Keles [TR] 150 F5
Kelheim [D] 60 E2
Kell [D] 44 G3
Kélla [GR] 128 F4
Kellenberg [D] 30 F4
Kellenhusen [D] 18 H2
Kellerberg [D] 32 D5
Kellinghusen [D] 18 F3
Kelloselkä [FIN] 194 F7
Kells [IRL] 2 F5
Kells [IRL] 4 B4
Kelmė [LT] 200 E4
Kelottijärvi [FIN] 192 H4
Kelso [GB] 8 F4
Keltaniemi [FIN] 178 B2
Kelujärvi [FIN] 194 D6
Kelvä [FIN] 188 F1
Kelviä / Kälviä [FIN] 196 C6
Kemaliye [TR] 152 E3
Kemalpaşa [TR] 152 D4
Kemberg [D] 34 D4
Kemecse [H] 64 H4
Kemence [H] 64 C5
Kemenesmagasi [H] 74 G1
Kemer [TR] 150 C4
Kemer [TR] 152 F5
Kemer [TR] 154 F2
Kemerburgaz [TR] 150 E2
Kemerköy [TR] 154 G3
Kémes [H] 76 A5
Kemi [FIN] 196 C3
Kemihaara [FIN] 194 E5
Kemijärvi [FIN] 194 E7
Keminmaa [FIN] 196 C2
Kemiö / Kimito [FIN] 176 E5
Kemnath [D] 48 B4
Kemnitz [D] 20 D3
Kemnitz [D] 34 D3
Kempele [FIN] 196 D4
Kempen [D] 30 G3
Kempolovo [RUS] 178 G5
Kempten [D] 60 C5
Kendal [GB] 10 E2
Kenderes [H] 76 F1
Kendice [SK] 64 G2
Kengis [S] 194 B7
Kengyel [H] 76 E2
Kenmare [IRL] 4 B4
Kentrikó [GR] 128 H3
Kéntro [GR] 136 C1
Kenyeri [H] 74 G1
Kenzingen [D] 58 E2
Kepez [TR] 150 B5
Kępice [PL] 22 B3
Kepno [PL] 36 E6
Kepsut [TR] 152 D1
Kerameía [GR] 134 H2
Keramídi [GR] 132 H2
Keramítsa [GR] 132 C2
Keramos [TR] 154 C1
Keramotí [GR] 130 E3
Keräntöjärvi [S] 194 B6
Kerasiá [GR] 134 B4
Kerasochóri [GR] 132 E3
Kerasóna [GR] 132 D3
Keratéa [GR] 136 H1
Keratókampos [GR] 140 F5
Kerava / Kervo [FIN] 176 H4
Kerecsend [H] 64 E5
Kerekegyháza [H] 76 D2
Kerí [GR] 136 A2
Kerien [F] 26 A4
Kerimäki [FIN] 188 F5
Kerisalo [FIN] 188 D4
Kerjean, Château de– [F] 40 B1
Kerken [D] 30 G3
Kerkíni [GR] 128 H3
Kerkonkoski [FIN] 186 H3
Kerkrade [NL] 30 F4
Kérkyra [GR] 132 B2
Kerma [FIN] 188 E3
Kermen [BG] 148 D4
Kernascléden [F] 40 C3
Kerpen [D] 30 G4
Kerpiçlik [TR] 152 F2
Kërrabë [AL] 128 B3
Kersilö [FIN] 194 D6
Kerstimbo [S] 174 E5
Kerteminde [DK] 156 E3
Kertészsziget [H] 76 G2
Kertil [TR] 152 D2
Kervo / Kerava [FIN] 176 H4
Kerýneia (Girne) [CY] 154 G5
Kerzers [CH] 58 D6
Kesälahti [FIN] 188 G5
Keşan [TR] 150 B3
Kesarevo [BG] 148 D3
Kesasjärv [S] 194 B8
Kesh [NIR] 2 E3
Keskastel [F] 44 G5
Keskikylä [FIN] 196 D4
Keskinen [FIN] 196 F4
Kesselfall [A] 72 F1
Kesselsdorf [D] 34 E6
Kesten'ga [RUS] 196 H2
Kesteren [NL] 16 E5
Kesti [FIN] 186 B4
Kestilä [FIN] 196 E5
Keswick [GB] 8 E6
Keszthely [H] 74 G3
Kétegyháza [H] 76 G3
Ketenovo [MK] 146 E6
Ketomella [FIN] 194 B5
Kętrzyn [PL] 24 C3
Kétsoproni [H] 76 F3
Kettering [GB] 14 E2
Kettilsby [S] 166 D3
Kettwig [D] 30 G3
Kęty [PL] 50 G4
Ketzin [D] 34 D2
Keula [D] 32 G5
Keuruu [FIN] 186 F4
Keväjärvi [FIN] 194 E4
Kevelaer [D] 30 F2
Kevo [FIN] 194 D3
Kežmarok [SK] 52 B6
Khaapalampi [RUS] 188 H5
Khadziloni [BY] 24 H3
Kharava [BY] 38 H1
Kharmanli [BG] 148 D6
Khaskovo [BG] 148 C6
Kherson [UA] 204 G3
Khisariya [BG] 148 B5
Khiytola [RUS] 178 G1
Khlebarovo [BG] 148 D2
Khmel'nyts'kyi [UA] 202 C8
Khmil'nyk [UA] 202 C8
Khodoriv [UA] 204 C2
Kholm [RUS] 202 C3
Kholm–Zhirkovskiy [RUS] 202 D3
Khorol [UA] 202 F7
Khotyn [UA] 204 D2
Khoyniki [BY] 202 D6
Khust [UA] 204 C3
Khvoynaya [RUS] 202 D1
Khyriv [UA] 52 F5
Kiáto [GR] 136 F1
Kiaunoriai [LT] 200 E4
Kibæk [DK] 156 B1
Kiberg [N] 194 F2
Kiburi [LV] 198 B6
Kibyra [TR] 152 G6
Kičevo [MK] 128 D2
Kichenitsa [BG] 148 D2
Kichevo [BG] 148 F2
Kidałowice [PL] 52 F3
Kidderminster [GB] 12 G1
Kidlington [GB] 14 D3
Kidričevo [SLO] 74 E4
Kidsgrove [GB] 10 E5
Kidwelly [GB] 12 E2
Kiefersfelden [D] 60 F6
Kiel [D] 18 G2
Kielajoki [FIN] 194 D4
Kielce [PL] 52 B1
Kienberg [A] 72 F2
Kienberg [CH] 58 E5
Kiental [CH] 70 E1
Kierinki [FIN] 194 C7
Kiernozia [PL] 36 H3
Kiesilä [FIN] 178 D1
Kietävälä [FIN] 188 E6
Kietrz [PL] 50 E4
Kiezmark [PL] 22 E3
Kifisiá [GR] 134 C6
Kifjord [N] 194 D1
Kihelkonna [EST] 198 C3
Kihniö [FIN] 186 D5
Kihtelysvaara [FIN] 188 G3
Kiikala [FIN] 176 F4
Kiikka [FIN] 176 E2
Kiikoinen [FIN] 176 E1
Kiiminki [FIN] 196 D3
Kiiskilä [FIN] 196 D6
Kiistala [FIN] 194 C6
Kije [PL] 52 B2
Kijevo [BIH] 144 D1
Kijevo [HR] 142 A4
Kijevo [SRB] 146 B5
Kijmajärvi [FIN] 176 E2
Kikerino [RUS] 178 G6
Kikinda [MNE] 204 B5
Kikinda [SRB] 76 F5
Kikół [PL] 36 G1
Kikut [N] 170 E4
Kil [N] 164 F4
Kil [S] 166 E2
Kil [S] 166 H3
Kila [GR] 128 F5
Kila [S] 166 E3
Kila [S] 168 B1
Kilafors [S] 174 D2
Kılavuzlar [TR] 152 H6
Kilbaha [IRL] 2 A6
Kilbeggan [IRL] 2 E5
Kilberry [IRL] 2 F5
Kilboghamn [N] 190 D2
Kilcar / Cill Charthaigh [IRL] 2 D2
Kilcock [IRL] 2 F6
Kilcolman Castle [IRL] 4 C4
Kilconnell [IRL] 2 D5
Kilcoole [IRL] 4 G3
Kilcooley Abbey [IRL] 4 E4
Kilcormac [IRL] 2 D6
Kilcullen [IRL] 2 E6
Kilcurry [IRL] 2 F4
Kildare [IRL] 2 E6
Kilderss [NIR] 2 F3
Kildorrery [IRL] 4 D4
Kilebygd [N] 164 G3
Kilen [N] 164 F2
Kilfenora [IRL] 2 B5
Kilfinnane [IRL] 4 D4
Kilgarvan [IRL] 4 B4
Kilifarevo [BG] 148 C4
Kilingi–Nõmme [EST] 198 E3
Kilitbahir [TR] 130 H5
Kilkee [IRL] 2 B6
Kilkeel [NIR] 2 G4
Kilkenny / Cill Chainnigh [IRL] 4 E4
Kilkieran / Cill Chiaráin [IRL] 2 B4
Kilkinkylä [FIN] 188 C6
Kilkinlea [IRL] 4 C3
Kilkís [GR] 128 H3
Kill [IRL] 4 E5
Killadysert [IRL] 2 B6
Killala [IRL] 2 C3
Killaloe [IRL] 2 C6
Killarney / Cill Airne [IRL] 4 B4
Killashandra [IRL] 2 E4
Killashee [IRL] 2 D5
Killeberg [S] 162 C6
Killeigh [IRL] 2 E6
Killenaule [IRL] 4 E4
Killimer [IRL] 2 B6
Killimor [IRL] 2 D5
Killin [GB] 8 D2
Killinge [S] 192 G5
Killinkoski [FIN] 186 D4
Killorglin [IRL] 4 B4
Killybegs [IRL] 2 D2
Killyleagh [NIR] 2 G4
Kilmacduagh Cathedral [IRL] 2 C5
Kilmacrenan [IRL] 2 E2
Kilmacthomas [IRL] 4 E5
Kilmaganny [IRL] 4 E4
Kilmaine [IRL] 2 C4
Kilmallock [IRL] 4 D4
Kilmanahan [IRL] 4 E4
Kilmarnock [GB] 8 D3
Kilmartin [GB] 8 C2
Kilmeaden [IRL] 4 E5
Kilmeage [IRL] 2 E6
Kilmeedy [IRL] 4 C4
Kilmelford [GB] 8 C2
Kilmichael [IRL] 4 C5
Kilmore Quay [IRL] 4 F5
Kilnaleck [IRL] 2 E4
Kilpisjärvi [FIN] 192 G3
Kilpola [FIN] 188 D5
Kilrush [IRL] 2 B6
Kilshannig [IRL] 4 B3
Kilsmo [S] 166 H4
Kilsyth [GB] 8 D3
Kiltealy [IRL] 4 F4
Kilternan [IRL] 4 G3
Kiltimagh [IRL] 2 C4
Kilvakkala [FIN] 186 D6
Kilvo [S] 196 A1
Kilwinning [GB] 8 C3
Kilyos [TR] 150 E2
Kimási [GR] 134 B4
Kimasozero [RUS] 196 H4
Kiminki [FIN] 186 E2
Kimito / Kemiö [FIN] 176 E5
Kimle [H] 62 H5
Kimméria [GR] 130 E2
Kimola [FIN] 178 B2
Kímolos [GR] 138 D4
Kimonkylä [FIN] 178 B3
Kimovaara [RUS] 196 H5
Kimry [RUS] 202 E2
Kincardine [GB] 8 E3
Kindberg [A] 62 D6
Kindelbrück [D] 32 H5
Kinding [D] 46 G6
Kindsjön [S] 172 E4
Kinéta [GR] 134 B6
Kingisepp [RUS] 198 G1
Kingsbridge [GB] 12 D5
Kingscourt [IRL] 2 F5
King's Lynn [GB] 14 F1
Kingston upon Hull [GB] 10 G4
Kington [GB] 12 F1
Kınık [TR] 150 F5
Kınık [TR] 152 C2
Kınık [TR] 154 F3
Kınık [TR] 154 G1
Kınıkyeri [TR] 152 G6
Kinlochbervie [GB] 6 D2
Kinlochewe [GB] 6 C4
Kinlochleven [GB] 6 C6
Kinlough [IRL] 2 D3
Kinna [S] 162 B3
Kinnadoohy [IRL] 2 B4
Kinnarp [S] 162 C1
Kinnbäck [S] 196 B4
Kinnegad [IRL] 2 E5
Kinni [FIN] 178 C1
Kinnitty [IRL] 2 D6
Kinnula [FIN] 186 F1
Kinnuranlahti [FIN] 188 C1
Kinrooi [B] 30 E3
Kinross [GB] 8 E2
Kinsale [IRL] 4 C5
Kinsarvik [N] 170 C4
Kintai [LT] 200 D4
Kintaus [FIN] 186 F4
Kinvarra [IRL] 2 C5
Kióni [GR] 132 D5
Kiónia [GR] 138 E2
Kipen' [RUS] 178 G5
Kipi [EST] 198 C3
Kipilahti [FIN] 178 B4
Kipina [FIN] 196 E3
Kipoureío [GR] 132 E1
Kirakkaköngäs [FIN] 194 D4
Kiralan [TR] 152 G4
Királyegyháza [H] 76 A5
Kıranköy [TR] 152 F3
Kirawsk [BY] 202 C5
Kiraz [TR] 152 E4
Kirazlı [TR] 150 B5
Kirbla [EST] 198 D2
Kircasalih [TR] 150 B2
Kirchbach [A] 72 G3
Kirchbach [A] 74 E2
Kirchberg [A] 60 F6
Kirchberg [D] 44 H2
Kirchberg [D] 46 E5
Kirchberg an der Pielach [A] 62 D5
Kirchbichl [A] 60 F6
Kirchdorf [D] 20 A3
Kirchdorf [D] 32 E1
Kirchdorf an der Krems [A] 62 B5
Kirchen [D] 18 C3
Kirchenlamitz [D] 48 B3
Kirchen–tellinsfurt [D] 58 H2
Kirchenthumbach [D] 46 H4
Kirchhain [D] 32 E6
Kirchheim [D] 32 F6
Kirchheimbolanden [D] 46 B4
Kirchheim unter Teck [D] 58 H1
Kirchhm i.I. [A] 60 H4
Kirchlauter [D] 46 F3
Kirchlinteln [D] 18 E6
Kirchschlag [A] 62 F6
Kirchseeon [D] 60 E4
Kirchundem [D] 32 C5
Kirchzell [D] 46 D4
Kircubbin [NIR] 2 H4
Kireç [TR] 152 E1
Kiriküla [EST] 198 D1
Kırıklar [TR] 152 C1
Kiriou, Roche de– [F] 40 D2
Kiriši [RUS] 202 C1
Kir'jamo [RUS] 178 E6
Kirjaluokta [S] 192 F5
Kırkağaç [TR] 152 D2
Kirkby Lonsdale [GB] 10 E2
Kirkcaldy [GB] 8 E3
Kirkcudbright [GB] 8 D5
Kirkeby [N] 182 D1
Kirkehamn [N] 164 B5
Kirke Hvalsø [DK] 156 F3
Kirkenær [N] 172 D4
Kirkenes [N] 194 E3
Kirkholt [DK] 160 E3
Kirki [GR] 130 G3
Kirkjubæjarklaustur [IS] 192 B3
Kirkjubøur [FR] 160 B2
Kirkkolati [RUS] 188 H4
Kirkkonummi / Kyrkslätt [FIN] 176 G5
Kırklareli [TR] 150 B1
Kirkonkylä [FIN] 176 E4
Kırkpınar [TR] 152 H6
Kirkvollen [N] 182 D2
Kirkwall [GB] 6 G2
Kirn [D] 44 H2
Kirov [RUS] 202 E4
Kirovohrad [UA] 202 E8
Kirovsk [RUS] 202 B1
Kirovskoye [RUS] 178 G3
Kirriemuir [GB] 8 F2
Kirtorf [D] 46 D1
Kiruna [S] 192 G5
Kisa [S] 162 F1
Kisbér [H] 64 A6
Kisdobsza [H] 74 H5
Kiseljak [BIH] 144 C1
Kishartyán [H] 64 D5
Kisielice [PL] 22 F4
Kisielnica [PL] 24 D5
Kisko [FIN] 176 F5
Kisköre [H] 64 F6
Kiskőrös [H] 76 D3
Kiskundorozsma [H] 76 E4
Kiskunfélegyháza [H] 76 E3
Kiskunhalas [H] 76 D4
Kiskunlacháza [H] 76 C2
Kiskunmajsa [H] 76 D4
Kişla [TR] 152 F3
Kisláng [H] 76 B2
Kisslegg [D] 60 B5
Kisszállás [H] 76 D4
Kist [D] 46 E4
Kistanje [HR] 112 H5
Kistelek [H] 76 E4
Kisterenye [H] 64 D5
Kisújszállás [H] 76 F1
Kisvárda [H] 64 H4
Kiszkowo [PL] 36 D2
Kiszombor [H] 76 F4
Kitajaur [S] 190 H2
Kitee [FIN] 188 G4
Kiten [BG] 148 F5
Kítion [CY] 154 G5
Kitkiöjärvi [S] 194 B6
Kitkiöjoki [S] 194 B6
Kítros [GR] 128 G5
Kitsi [FIN] 196 H6
Kittelfjäll [S] 190 E4
Kittendorf [D] 20 C4
Kittilä [FIN] 194 C6
Kittsee [A] 62 G5
Kitula [FIN] 176 F4
Kitula [FIN] 186 G5
Kitzbühel [A] 60 F6
Kitzingen [D] 46 F4
Kitzloch–Klamm [A] 72 G1
Kiukainen [FIN] 176 D2
Kiurujärvi [FIN] 194 E6
Kiuruvesi [FIN] 196 E6
Kiutaköngäs [FIN] 194 F8
Kivadár [H] 74 H5
Kivéri [GR] 136 E2
Kivesjärvi [FIN] 196 E4
Kiviapaja [FIN] 188 E5
Kivijärvi [FIN] 186 F2
Kivik [S] 158 D3
Kivikangas [FIN] 186 E1
Kivilahti [FIN] 188 G1
Kivilompolo [FIN] 194 B5
Kivilompolo [FIN] 194 C8
Kivioja [FIN] 194 C8
Kiviõli [EST] 198 F1
Kivisalmi [FIN] 186 H3
Kivisuo [FIN] 186 G5
Kivivaara [FIN] 196 G5
Kivi–Vigala [EST] 198 D2
Kivotós [GR] 128 E6
Kıyıkışlacık [TR] 154 C1
Kıyıköy [TR] 150 D1
Kızılca [TR] 152 G6
Kızılcabölük [TR] 152 F5
Kızılcasöğüt [TR] 152 G3
Kızılinler [TR] 150 H5
Kızılkoltuk [TR] 152 F2
Kızılören [TR] 152 H3
Kızılyaka [TR] 154 D1
Kjeeringvika [N] 192 E4
Kjelda [N] 190 C4
Kjeldebotn [N] 192 E4
Kjelfossen [N] 170 D2
Kjellerup [DK] 160 D6
Kjellmyra [N] 172 D4
Kjernmoen [N] 172 D3
Kjerrengvoll [N] 182 C3
Kjerret [N] 166 D1
Kjerringvåg [N] 190 A6
Kjerringvik [N] 190 C6
Kjerstad [N] 180 D3
Kjøllefjord [N] 194 D1
Kjølsdal [N] 180 C5
Kjøpsvik [N] 192 E4
Kjøra [N] 180 H1
Kjulo / Köyliö [FIN] 176 D2
K. Kamila [GR] 130 B3
Klacka–Lerberg [S] 166 G2
Kläckeberga [S] 162 G5
Kladanj [BIH] 142 E4
Kladnica [SRB] 146 A3
Kladnice [HR] 142 A5
Kladno [CZ] 48 F3
Kladovo [SRB] 204 C6
Kladruby [CZ] 48 D4
Klæbu [N] 182 B1
Klaffer [A] 62 B3
Klagenfurt [A] 74 B3
Klaipėda [LT] 200 D4
Klakegg [N] 180 D6
Klaksvík [FR] 160 B1
Klamila [FIN] 178 D3
Klana [HR] 112 E1
Klanac [HR] 112 G4
Klanjec [HR] 74 E5
Klanxbüll [D] 156 B4
Kläpen [N] 192 E3
Kläppen [S] 190 G3
Klarabro [S] 172 E4
Klärke [S] 184 E3
Klarup [DK] 160 E4
Klašnice [BIH] 142 C2
Klässbol [S] 166 E2
Klášterec nad Ohří [CZ] 48 D3
Klášter Teplá [CZ] 48 D4
Kláštor pod Znievom [SK] 64 C2
Klatovy [CZ] 48 D5
Klaukkala [FIN] 176 G4
Klaus an der Pyhrnbahn [A] 62 B5
Klausdorf [D] 20 D2
Klausdorf [D] 34 E3
Klausen / Chiusa [I] 72 D3
Klazienaveen [NL] 16 H3
Klazomenai [TR] 152 C4
Kłębowiec [PL] 22 A5
Klecko [PL] 36 D2
Kleczew [PL] 36 E3
Klein Glödnitz [A] 74 B3
Kleinhau [D] 30 F5
Kleinhaugsdorf [A] 62 E3
Klein Vielen [D] 20 C5
Kleinzell [A] 62 E5
Kleisoúra [GR] 132 D3
Kleive [N] 180 E3
Kleivegrend [N] 164 E2
Kleivstua [N] 170 H5
Klejniki [PL] 24 F6
Klemensker [DK] 158 E4
Klement [A] 62 F3
Klempenow [D] 20 D4
Klempicz [PL] 36 C1
Klenčí pod Čerchovem [CZ] 48 D5
Klenike [SRB] 146 D5
Klenjë [AL] 128 C2
Klenovica [HR] 112 F2
Kleppe [N] 164 A3
Kleppestø [N] 170 A3
Klerken [B] 28 F2
Klešno [PL] 36 A1
Kleszczele [PL] 38 F2
Kletnya [RUS] 202 E5
Kleve [D] 16 F6
Klevshult [S] 162 D3
Klezeno [RUS] 198 G4
Klichaw [RUS] 202 C5
Kliczków [PL] 34 H5
Klietz [D] 34 C1
Klimátia [GR] 132 C2
Kliment [BG] 148 E2
Klimontów [PL] 52 B3
Klimontów [PL] 52 D2
Klimovo [RUS] 178 F3
Klimpfjäll [S] 190 E4
Klin [RUS] 202 E2
Klina [SRB] 146 B5
Klinča Sela [HR] 74 E6
Klingenbach [A] 62 F6
Klingenmunster [D] 46 B5
Klingenthal [D] 48 C3
Klink [D] 20 C5
Klintehamn [S] 168 F5
Klintfors [S] 196 A4
Klintholm [DK] 156 G4
Klintsy [RUS] 202 D5
Kliplev [DK] 156 C4
Klippan [S] 158 C1
Klippen [S] 190 E3
Klippen [S] 190 G5
Klippinge [DK] 156 G3
Klírou [CY] 154 G5
Klis [HR] 144 A2
Klisino [PL] 50 E3
Klisura [BG] 148 A4
Klisura [SRB] 146 E5
Klisura Sutjeske [BIH] 144 D2
Klitmøller [DK] 160 C3
Klixbüll [D] 156 B4
Kljajićevo [SRB] 76 D6
Ključ [BIH] 142 B3
Klobouky u Brna [CZ] 62 G2
Kłobuck [PL] 50 F1
Kłobuczyn [PL] 36 B5
Klobuk [BIH] 144 B2
Klockestrand [S] 184 F3
Kłoczew [PL] 38 D4
Kłodawa [PL] 34 H1
Kłodawa [PL] 36 F3
Kłodzko [PL] 50 C3
Kløfta [N] 172 B5
Klokkarvik [N] 170 A4
Klokkervik [N] 194 C2
Klokočevac [SRB] 146 D1
Klokočevci [HR] 76 B6
Klokotnica [BIH] 142 D3
Klooster [NL] 16 G4
Klos [AL] 128 B2
Klos [AL] 128 B1
Kloštar Ivanić [HR] 74 F6
Kloštar Podravski [HR] 74 G5
Kloster [S] 174 D5
Kloster Arnstein [D] 46 B2
Kloster Chorin [D] 34 F1
Klosterkirche in Altenmarkt [D] 60 G3
Klösterle [A] 72 B1
Klosterneuburg [A] 62 F4
Klosterruiner [N] 180 B4
Klosters [CH] 72 A2
Kloster Schäftlarn [D] 60 E5
Kloster Zella [D] 32 G5
Kloster Zinna [D] 34 D3
Kloten [S] 166 H1
Klötze [D] 34 A1
Klöverträsk [S] 196 B3
Klövimoen [N] 190 D3
Klövsjö [S] 182 G4
Kl. Plasten [D] 20 C4
Kluczbork [PL] 50 E1
Klucze [PL] 50 G3
Kluczewsko [PL] 50 H1
Kluis [D] 20 D2
Kluki [PL] 22 C1
Kluki [PL] 36 G5
Klukowa Huta [PL] 22 D3
Klupe [BIH] 142 C3
Klusy [PL] 24 D4
Klutsjön [S] 182 E5
Klütz [D] 18 H3
Klyastsitsy [BY] 198 H6
Knaben [N] 164 C4
Knäm [S] 166 B4
Knapphus [N] 164 B1
Knäred [S] 162 B5
Knaresborough [GB] 10 F3
Knarvik [N] 170 B3
Knäsjö [S] 190 G6
Knätten [S] 182 G5
Knebel [DK] 160 E6
Knetzgau [D] 46 F3
Kneža [SLO] 72 H4
Knežak [SLO] 74 B6
Kneževi Vinogradi [HR] 76 C6
Kneževo [HR] 76 B5
Knezha [BG] 146 G3
Knežica [BIH] 142 B2
Knić [SRB] 146 B2
Knídi [GR] 128 F6
Knidos [TR] 154 B3
Kniebis [D] 58 F2
Knighton [GB] 10 C6
Knights Town [IRL] 4 A4
Knin [HR] 142 A4
Knislinge [S] 158 D1
Knittelfeld [A] 74 C2
Knivsta [S] 168 D2
Knjaževac [SRB] 146 E3
Knock [IRL] 2 C4
Knockcroghery [IRL] 2 D5
Knocknalina / Cnocán na Líne [IRL] 2 B2
Knocktopher [IRL] 4 E4
Knokke–Heist [B] 28 G1
Knosós [GR] 140 E4
Knottingley [GB] 10 F4
Knudshoved [DK] 156 E3
Knurów [PL] 50 F3
Knurowiec [PL] 38 C1
Knutby [S] 168 E1
Knutsford [GB] 10 D4
Knyazevo [RUS] 198 H5
Knyazhevo [BG] 148 E5
Knyazhicy [RUS] 198 G3
Knyszyn [PL] 24 E5
Kobarid [SLO] 72 H4
Kobbelveid [N] 192 E5
Kobeliaky [UA] 202 F7
København [DK] 156 H2
Koberg [S] 166 D6
Kobeřice [CZ] 50 E4
Kobiele Wlk. [PL] 36 H6
Kobilyane [BG] 130 F1
Kobišnica [SRB] 146 E1
Koblenz [D] 30 H6
Kobryn [BY] 38 G2
Kobułty [PL] 24 B4
Kobylany [PL] 38 F3
Kobylin [PL] 36 D4
Kobyłka [PL] 38 C2
Kobyl'nik [BY] 200 H5
Kocaali [TR] 150 B4
Kocaali [TR] 150 H2
Kocabaş [TR] 152 G5
Kocaburgaz [TR] 150 D4
Kocaçeşme [TR] 150 B4
Kocaeli (İzmit) [TR] 150 G3
Kocakaymaz [TR] 150 G2
Kočani [MK] 128 G1
Kocapınar [TR] 150 D5
Koçarlı [TR] 152 D5
Kocbeře [CZ] 50 A2
Koceljevo [SRB] 146 A1
Kočerin [BIH] 144 B2
Kočevje [SLO] 74 C6
Kočevska Reka [SLO] 74 C6
Kochel [D] 60 D5
Kocherinovo [BG] 146 F6
Kocherov [UA] 202 D7
Kochmar [BG] 148 F2
Kock [PL] 38 E4
Kocs [H] 64 B6
Kocsér [H] 76 E2
Kocsola [H] 76 B4
Kócsújfalu [H] 64 F6
Koczała [PL] 22 B4
Kodal [N] 164 H3
Kodeń [PL] 38 F3
Kodersdorf [D] 34 G6
Kodesjärvi [FIN] 186 B5
Kodrąb [PL] 36 H6
Koetschette [L] 44 E2
Kofçaz [TR] 150 B1
Köflach [A] 74 D2
Kögbo [S] 174 E4
Køge [DK] 156 G3
Kogila [MK] 128 E3
Kogula [EST] 198 C3
Kohfidisch [A] 74 F2
Kohila [EST] 198 D2
Kohtla–Järve [EST] 198 F1
Koigi [EST] 198 E2
Koijärvi [FIN] 176 F3
Koikkala [FIN] 188 D5

L'Ampolla [E] 92 B5
Lamporecchio [I] 110 E5
Lamppi [FIN] 176 C1
Lamprechtshausen [A] 60 G5
Lamprechtsofenloch [A] 60 G6
Lämsänkylä [FIN] 196 F2
Lamsfeld [D] 34 F4
Lamstedt [D] 18 E4
La Mudarra [E] 88 E1
La Muela [E] 90 E4
La Mure [F] 68 H5
Lamure-sur-Azergues [F] 68 F2
La Murta [E] 98 E5
Lana [I] 72 C3
Lanaja [E] 90 F4
La Napoule-Plage [F] 108 E5
Lanark [GB] 8 D4
La Nava [E] 94 F4
La Nava de Ricomalillo [E] 96 D1
La Nava de Santiago [E] 86 G6
Lancaster [GB] 10 D2
Lanciano [I] 116 E5
Łańcut [PL] 52 E3
Landau [D] 46 B5
Landau [D] 60 G3
Landeck [A] 72 C1
Landedo [P] 80 F3
Landendorf [A] 62 F3
Landepéreuse [F] 26 G4
Landerneau [F] 40 B2
Landersfjorden [N] 194 D2
Landeryd [S] 162 B4
Landesbergen [D] 32 E1
Landete [E] 98 D3
Landévennec [F] 40 B2
Landivisiau [F] 40 C2
Landivy [F] 26 D5
Landkirchen [D] 18 H2
Landön [S] 182 G1
Landquart [CH] 58 H6
Landrecies [F] 28 G4
Landsberg [D] 34 C5
Landsberg [D] 60 D4
Landsbro [S] 162 E3
Landshut [D] 60 F3
Landshut, Ruine- [D] 44 G2
Landskrona [S] 156 H2
Landštejn [CZ] 62 D2
Landstuhl [D] 44 H3
Landudec [F] 40 B3
Landvetter [S] 160 H2
Lane [N] 170 C1
Lanersbach [A] 72 E1
Lanesborough [IRL] 2 D5
La Neuve-Lyre [F] 26 H5
La Neuveville [CH] 58 D5
Langa [DK] 160 D5
Långå [S] 182 F4
Langa de Duero [E] 88 H2
Långåminne [FIN] 186 B3
Langangen [N] 164 G3
Langballig [D] 156 C5
Långban [S] 166 G1
Långbo [S] 174 D2
Langdal [N] 180 E4
Langeac [F] 68 D4
Langeais [F] 54 F2
Langehauk [N] 170 F3
Langeid [N] 164 D3
Långe Jan [S] 158 G1
Längelmäki [FIN] 186 F6
Langelsheim [D] 32 G3
Långemåla [S] 162 G4
Langen [A] 72 B1
Langen [D] 18 D4
Langen [D] 46 C3
Langenargen [D] 58 H4
Långenäs [S] 166 E1
Langenau [D] 60 B3
Langenburg [D] 46 E5
Langenes [N] 192 D3
Längenfeld [A] 72 C2
Langenfeld [D] 30 G4
Langenhahn [D] 46 B1
Langenhorn [D] 156 B5
Langenisarhofen [D] 60 G3
Langenlois [A] 62 E4
Langennaundorf [D] 34 E5
Langenorla [D] 46 H1
Langenselbold [D] 46 D3
Langenthal [CH] 58 E5
Langenwang [A] 62 E6
Langenzenn [D] 46 F5
Langeoog [D] 18 B3
Langeskov [DK] 156 E3
Langesø [DK] 156 D3
Langesund [N] 164 G3
Langevåg [N] 164 A1
Langevåg [N] 180 C3
Langewiese [D] 32 D5
Langfjord [N] 192 H1
Langfjordnes [N] 194 D1
Långflon [S] 172 E3
Langhammars [S] 168 H3
Langhirano [I] 110 D3
Langholm [GB] 8 E5
Långjöby [S] 190 F4
Långlöt [S] 162 G5
Långnäs [FIN] 176 B5
Langnau im Emmental [CH] 58 E6
Langø [DK] 156 E5
Langogne [F] 68 D5
Langoiran [F] 66 D3
Langon [F] 66 D4
Langquaid [D] 60 F2
Langraiz Oka / Nanclares de la Oca [E] 82 G5
Langreo / Langréu [E] 78 H4
Langres [F] 56 H2
Langréu / Langreo [E] 78 H4
Långron [S] 184 H1
Långsel [S] 194 A8
Långsele [S] 184 E2
Långsele [S] 190 F5
Långserud [S] 166 D3
Långshyttan [S] 174 D5
Langstrand [N] 194 B2
Långträsk [S] 190 H4
Långträsk [S] 196 A3
Languidou, Chapelle de- [F] 40 B3
Langula [D] 32 G5
Långvattnet [S] 190 H4
Langviken [S] 196 A4
Långviksmon [S] 184 G1
Långvind [S] 174 E2
Langwarden [D] 18 D4
Langwedel [D] 18 E6
Langweid [D] 60 D3
Langweiler [D] 44 H3
Langwies [CH] 70 H1
Lanhelas [P] 78 A5
Lanjarón [E] 102 E5
Lankas [LV] 198 B5
Lankila [FIN] 178 D3
Länkipohja [FIN] 186 F6
Lankojärvi [FIN] 194 C7
Lankoori [FIN] 176 C2
Lankosi [FIN] 186 B6
Lanleff, Temple de- [F] 26 A3
Lanmeur [F] 40 C1
Lanna [S] 162 C3
Länna [S] 168 C3
Lannabruk [S] 166 G3
Lannavaara [S] 192 H4
Lannemezan [F] 84 F4
Lannevesi [FIN] 186 F3
Lannilis [F] 40 B1
Lannion [F] 40 D1
Lanobre [F] 68 B3
La Noguera [E] 98 D1
Lanouaille [F] 66 G2
Lansån [S] 194 B8
Lansikylä [FIN] 186 D3
Lansjärv [S] 194 A8
Lanškroun [CZ] 50 C4
Lanslebourg-Mont-Cenis [F] 70 C5
Lanšperk [CZ] 50 B4
Lantosque [F] 108 F4
Lanusei [I] 118 E5
Lanvollon [F] 26 A4
Lánycsók [H] 76 B5
Lanzá [E] 78 C2
Lanzendorf [A] 62 F5
Lanžhot [CZ] 62 G3
Lanzo d'Intelvi [I] 70 G3
Lanzo Torinese [I] 70 D5
Lao [EST] 198 D3
Laodikeia [TR] 152 G5
La Oliva [E] 84 B5
La Oliva [E] 100 E6
Laon [F] 28 G6
La Orotava [E] 100 B5
La Paca [E] 104 B3
La Pacaudière [F] 68 E1
Lápafő [H] 76 A4
Lapalisse [F] 56 D6
La Pallice [F] 54 B4
La Palma [E] 104 C4
La Palma del Condado [E] 94 F6
Lapalme [F] 106 D5
La Palud-sur-Verdon [F] 108 D4
la Panouse [F] 68 D5
Łapanów [PL] 52 B4
Lápas [GR] 132 E6
La Pelechaneta / Pelejaneta [E] 98 F3
La Peraleja [E] 98 B1
la Péruse [F] 54 E6
La Petite-Pierre [F] 44 G5
Lapeyrade [F] 66 D5
Lapinjärvi / Lappträsk [FIN] 178 B3
Lapinlahti [FIN] 188 C1
Lapinsaari [FIN] 186 C3
Lapistó [H] 76 E3
Lápithos (Lâpta) [CY] 154 F5
La Plagne [F] 70 B4
la Plaine-Sur-Mer [F] 40 E6
La Plaza / Teverga [E] 78 G4
Laplume [F] 66 E5
la Pobla de Lillet [E] 92 E2
La Pobla de Massaluca [E] 90 G6
la Pobla de Segur [E] 92 C1
la Pobla de Vallbona [E] 98 E4
La Pobla Llarga [E] 98 E6
la Pobla Tornesa [E] 98 G3
La Pola de Gordón [E] 78 H5
La Portera [E] 98 D4
Lapoutroie [F] 58 D2
Lapovo [SRB] 146 C2
Lappach / Lappago [I] 72 E2
Lappago / Lappach [I] 72 E2
Lappajärvi [FIN] 186 D2
Lappäjärvi [FIN] 194 B5
Läppe [S] 168 B3
Lappeenranta / Villmanstrand [FIN] 178 E2
Lappfjärd / Lapväärtti [FIN] 186 B5
Lappfors [FIN] 186 C1
Lappi [FIN] 176 D3
Lappo [FIN] 176 C5
Lappo / Lapua [FIN] 186 C2
Lappohja / Lappvik [FIN] 176 F6
Lappträsk [S] 196 C2
Lappträsk / Lapinjärvi [FIN] 178 B3
Lappvattnet [S] 196 A5
Lappvik / Lappohja [FIN] 176 F6
la Primaude [F] 68 B6
Lapseki [TR] 150 B5
Lâpta (Lápithos) [CY] 154 F5
Laptevo [RUS] 198 H5
Lapua / Lappo [FIN] 186 C2
La Puebla de Almoradiel [E] 96 G3
La Puebla de Castro [E] 90 H3
La Puebla de Cazalla [E] 102 A3
La Puebla de Híjar [E] 90 F5
La Puebla de los Infantes [E] 96 B6
La Puebla del Río [E] 94 G6
La Puebla de Montalbán [E] 96 E1
La Puebla de Valdavia [E] 82 D4
La Puebla de Valverde [E] 98 E2
La Pueblanueva [E] 96 E1
La Puerta del Segura [E] 102 G1
La Punt [CH] 72 A3
Lapušnik [MNE] 146 C5
Lapväärtti / Lappfjärd [FIN] 186 B5
Łapy [PL] 24 E6
Laqueuille [F] 68 C2
L'Aquila [I] 116 C4
La Rábita [E] 102 E5
Laracha [E] 78 C2
Laragh [IRL] 4 G3
Laragne-Montéglin [F] 108 C2
La Rambla [E] 102 C2
l'Arbre [F] 54 E6
L'Arbresle [F] 68 F2
Lärbro [S] 168 G4
Larceveau-Arros-Cibits [F] 84 C3
Larche [F] 66 G3
Larche [F] 108 E2
Lärdal [N] 164 E2
Lardaro [I] 72 C4
Larderello [I] 114 F1
Lardero [E] 82 G6
Lárdos [GR] 154 D4
Lardosa [P] 86 F3
Laredo [E] 82 F3
La Réole [F] 66 D4
La Restinga [E] 100 A5
Largentière [F] 68 E6
L'Argentière-la-Bessée [F] 70 B6
Largs [GB] 8 C3
La Rhune [E] 84 B2
Lariano [I] 116 B6
La Rinconada [E] 94 G6
Larino [I] 116 F6
Larionovo [RUS] 178 G2
Lárisa [GR] 132 G2
Larissa [TR] 152 C3
Larkollen [N] 166 B3
L'Armelliere [F] 106 G4
Larmor [F] 40 C4
Lárnaka [CY] 154 G5
Larne [NIR] 2 G3
La Robla [E] 78 H5
La Roca de la Sierra [E] 86 G6
la Roca del Vallès [E] 92 E4
La Roche [CH] 70 D1
La Roche-Bernard [F] 40 E5
La Roche-Chalais [F] 66 E2
La Roche-de-Rame [F] 70 B6
La Roche-Derrien [F] 26 A3
La Roche-en-Ardenne [B] 30 E6
La Rochefoucauld [F] 54 E6
La Rochelle [F] 54 C4
La Roche-Posay [F] 54 F3
La Roche-sur-Foron [F] 70 B2
La Roche-sur-Yon [F] 54 B3
La Rochette [F] 70 A4
Larochette [L] 44 F2
La Roda [E] 98 B4
La Roda de Andalucía [E] 102 B3
Laroquebrou [F] 68 A4
La Roquebrussanne [F] 108 C5
Laroque-des-Arcs [F] 66 G5
Laroque-d'Olmes [F] 106 A5
La Roque-Gageac [F] 66 G4
La Rösa [CH] 72 B3
La Rouche-Courbon [F] 54 C5
Larraga [E] 84 B4
Larrau [F] 84 D3
Larret [F] 58 A3
Larroque [F] 106 B2
Larsmo / Luoto [FIN] 196 C6
Larsnes [N] 180 C4
l'Artigue [F] 84 H5
La Rubia [E] 90 B2
Laruns [F] 84 D4
Larvik [N] 164 G3
Lárymna [GR] 134 B5
La Salceda [E] 88 F4
la Salles-les Alpes [F] 70 B6
La Salvetat [F] 66 H6
La Salvetat-sur-Agout [F] 106 C3
Läsänkoski [FIN] 188 C5
Las Anorias [E] 98 C6
Lasarte-Oria [E] 84 B2
La Sauceda [E] 100 G4
Las Bárdenas Reales [E] 84 B6
Las Batuecas [E] 88 B4
Låsby [DK] 160 D6
Las Cabezas de San Juan [E] 100 G3
Las Caldas de Besaya [E] 82 E3
Lascaux, Grotte de- [F] 66 G3
la Selve [F] 106 C2
la Sénia [E] 92 A6
Lasenice [CZ] 62 C2
La Señuela [E] 100 G2
La Serna Del Monte [E] 88 G4
la Seu d'Urgell [E] 92 D1
La Seyne [F] 108 C6
Las Fuentes [E] 98 C5
Las Huelgas [E] 82 E6
Łasin [PL] 22 E5
Łask [PL] 36 G5
Łaskarzew [PL] 38 C4
Laski [PL] 22 B3
Laski [PL] 36 E6
Łasko [PL] 20 H6
Laško [SLO] 74 D5
Laskowa [PL] 52 B4
Laskowice [PL] 22 D5
Laskowice [PL] 50 D3
Laslovo [HR] 142 E1
Las Marías [E] 102 F5
Las Médulas [E] 78 E5
Las Mesas [E] 96 H3
Las Navas de la Concepción [E] 96 B6
Las Navas del Marqués [E] 88 E5
Las Negras [E] 102 H5
La Solana [E] 96 G4
La Souche [F] 68 E6
La Souterraine [F] 54 G5
Lasovo [SRB] 146 D2
Las Palas [E] 104 C4
Las Palmas de Gran Canaria [E] 100 C6
Las Pedroñeras [E] 96 H3
La Spézia [I] 110 C4
Las Rozas [E] 88 F5
Lassan [D] 20 E3
Lassay [F] 26 E5
Lassemoen [N] 190 D4
Lassigny [F] 28 E6
Lastein [N] 164 B2
La Sterza [I] 110 E6
Las Torcas [E] 98 C2
Las Torres de Cotillas [E] 104 C3
Lastovo [HR] 144 A3
Lastra a Signa [I] 110 E5
Lastras de Cuéllar [E] 88 F3
Lastres [E] 82 C2
Lästringe [S] 168 D4
Lastrup [D] 18 C6
Lastuk [FIN] 188 D1
Lastulahti [FIN] 188 D1
Lastva [BIH] 144 D4
La Suze-sur-Sarthe [F] 42 B5
Lašva [BIH] 142 D4
Las Veguillas [E] 88 C3
Las Ventas con Peña Aguilera [E] 96 E2
Las Ventas de S. Julián [E] 88 C6
Łaszczów [PL] 52 G2
Laszki [PL] 52 F3
la Tannière [F] 26 D5
Låtefossen [N] 170 C5
Latera [I] 114 G3
Laterza [I] 122 D4
Lathen [D] 16 H3
La Thuile [I] 70 C4
Latiano [I] 122 F4
Latikberg [S] 190 F5
Latina [I] 120 B1
Latinac [SRB] 146 D3
Latisana [I] 72 G5
Látky [SK] 64 D3
Lató [GR] 140 F5
Latorpsbruk [S] 166 H3
la Torre [E] 98 D4
la Torre Baixa [E] 98 D2
La Torre de Esteban Hambrán [E] 88 E6
La Torresaviñán [E] 90 A5
La Tour-du-Pin [F] 68 G3
La Tranche-sur-Mer [F] 54 B4
Latresne [F] 66 D3
La Trimouille [F] 54 G4
La Trinité [F] 40 D5
La Trinité-Porhoët [F] 26 B5
Latronico [I] 120 H5
Latronquière [F] 66 H4
Latte, Fort la- [F] 26 B4
Latteluokta [S] 192 G4
Lattuna [FIN] 194 E6
La Turbie [F] 108 F4
Latva [FIN] 196 D5
Latvalampi [FIN] 188 E3
Laubrières [F] 40 G5
Laucha [D] 34 B5
Lauchdorf [D] 60 C4
Lauchhammer [D] 34 E5
Laudal [N] 164 D5
Lauder [GB] 8 F4
Laudio / Llodio [E] 82 G4
Laudona [LV] 198 F5
Lauenau [D] 32 F2
Lauenbrück [D] 18 E5
Lauenburg [D] 18 G5
Lauenstein [D] 48 E2
Lauf [D] 46 G5
Laufen [CH] 58 D4
Laufen [D] 60 G5
Laufenburg [CH] 58 F4
Laufenburg (Baden) [D] 58 F4
Lauffen [D] 46 D6
Laugnac [F] 66 E5
Laugratte [F] 66 E4
Lauingen [D] 60 C3
Laujar de Andarax [E] 102 F5
Laukaa [FIN] 186 G4
Laukeland [N] 170 B1
Laukka [FIN] 196 D4
Laukkala [FIN] 186 G1
Lauksundskaret [N] 192 G1
Laukuluspa [S] 192 G5
Laukuva [LT] 200 E4
Laukvik [N] 192 F2
Laukvik [N] 194 B3
Laukvika [N] 192 D5
Launceston [GB] 12 D4
La Unión [E] 104 C4
Laupen [CH] 58 D6
Laupheim [D] 60 B4
Lauragh [IRL] 4 B5
Laureana di Borrello [I] 124 D6
Laurencetown [IRL] 2 D5
Laurenzana [I] 120 H4
Lauria [I] 120 H5
Laurière [F] 54 G6
Laurino [I] 120 G4
Lausanne [CH] 70 C1
Laussig [D] 34 D5
Lautaporras [FIN] 176 F3
Lautenburg [D] 30 F4
Lauter [S] 168 H3
Lauterbach [D] 46 E1
Lauterbourg [F] 46 B6
Lauterbrunnen [CH] 70 E1
Lautere [LV] 198 F5
Lauterecken [D] 44 H3
Lauterhofen [D] 46 H5
Lautrec [F] 106 B3
Lauvåsen [N] 182 B2
Lauvsjølia [N] 190 D5
Lauvsnes [N] 190 C5
Lauvstad [N] 180 C4
Lauvuskylä [FIN] 196 G5
Lauvvik [N] 164 B3
Lauwersoog [NL] 16 G1
Lauzerte [F] 66 F5
Lauzun [F] 66 E4
La Vácherie [F] 68 G5
Lavagna [I] 110 B3
Laval [F] 26 E6
la Vall d'Uixó [E] 98 F4
La Vallivana [E] 98 G2
Lavamünd [A] 74 C3
Lavangnes [N] 192 E3
Lávara [GR] 130 H2
Lavardac [F] 66 E5
Lavardin [F] 42 C6
Lavardin [F] 42 C6
Lavarone [I] 72 D5
Lavaur [F] 106 B3
La Vecilla [E] 82 B3
Lavelanet [F] 106 A5
Lavello [I] 120 H3
Lavelsloh [D] 32 E2
La Venta [E] 102 F4
La Verna [I] 110 G6
la Veurdre [F] 56 D4
Lavia [FIN] 176 E1
Laviano [I] 120 G3
Lavik [N] 170 B2
la Vila Joiosa / Villajoyosa [E] 104 E2
la Villa / Stern [I] 72 E3
Lavinio-Lido di Enea [I] 120 A1
La Virgen del Camino [E] 78 H5
Lavis [I] 72 C4
Lavit [F] 66 F6
Lavong [N] 190 D2
Lavos [P] 86 C2
La Voulte-sur-Rhône [F] 68 F5
Lavoûte-Chilhac [F] 68 D4
Lavoûte-Polignac, Château de- [F] 68 D4
Lavoûte-sur-Loire [F] 68 D4
Lavoye [F] 44 D4
Lavra [E] 80 B3
Lavre [P] 86 C6
Lávrio [GR] 136 H1
Lavry [RUS] 198 G4
Lavsjö [S] 190 F5
La Wantzenau [F] 44 H6
Ławszowa [PL] 34 H5
Laxå [S] 166 G4
Laxe [E] 78 B2
Laxne [S] 168 C3
Laxsjö [S] 190 E6
Laxsjön [S] 184 E3
Laxtjärn [S] 172 G5
Laxviken [S] 190 E6
La Yedra [E] 102 F2
La Yesa [E] 98 E3
Läyliäinen [FIN] 176 G4
La Yunta [E] 90 C5
Laza [E] 78 D6
Lazarevac [SRB] 146 B1
Lazarevac [SRB] 204 B6
Lazarevo [SRB] 142 G1
Lazdijai [LT] 24 F2
Laze [SLO] 74 C4
Lázi [H] 76 A1
Laži [LV] 198 C4
Laziale [I] 116 B5
Lazise [I] 72 C6
Łaziska Górne [PL] 50 F3
Lazisko [SK] 64 D2
Lazkao [E] 84 A3
Lázně Bělohrad [CZ] 50 A3
Lázně Kynžvart [CZ] 48 C4
Laz Stubički [HR] 74 E5
La Zubia [E] 102 E4
Łazy [PL] 22 A2
Leacanabuaile Stone Fort [IRL] 4 A4
Leamington Spa [GB] 14 D2
Leap [IRL] 4 B5
Leatherhead [GB] 14 E4
Łeba [PL] 22 C1
Lebach [D] 44 G3
Le Ballon [F] 26 D6
Lebane [SRB] 146 D4
Lebanza [E] 82 D3
Le Bar [F] 108 E4
Le Barp [F] 66 C4
Le Beausset [F] 108 C5
Lebedin [UA] 202 F7
Lébényimiklós [H] 62 H6
Lebesby [N] 194 D2
Le Biot [F] 70 C2
Le Blanc [F] 54 G4
Łebno [PL] 22 D2
Le Boréon [F] 108 F3
Lębork [PL] 22 C2
Le Boulou [F] 92 G1
Le Bourg d'Oisans [F] 68 H5
Le Bourget [F] 68 H3
le Bousquet-d'Orb [F] 106 D3
Le Bouveret [CH] 70 C2
Lebrija [E] 100 G3
Lebring [A] 74 D3
Le Bugue [F] 66 F3
Lebus [D] 34 G2
Lebyazh'e [RUS] 178 G5
Le Calanche [F] 114 A4
le Caloy [F] 66 C6
Le Cap-d'Agde [F] 106 E5
Le Cateau-Cambrésis [F] 28 G4
Le Catelet [F] 28 F5
Le Caylar [F] 106 E3
Lecce [I] 122 G4
Lecco [I] 70 G4
Lécera [E] 90 E5
Lech [A] 72 B1
Lechainá [GR] 136 B1
L'Echalp [F] 70 C6
le Chambon-sur-Lignon [F] 68 E4
Le Chateau-d'Oléron [F] 54 B5
Le Châtelard [F] 70 A3
Le Châtelet [F] 56 B4
Le Chesne [F] 44 C2
Le Cheylard [F] 68 E5
Lechlade on Thames [GB] 12 H3
Lechmühlen [D] 60 D4
Lechovice [CZ] 62 F2
Léchovo [GR] 128 E5
Lēči [LV] 198 B5
Leciñena [E] 90 F3
Leck [D] 156 B4
Le Conquet [F] 40 A2
Le Coteau [F] 68 E2
Le Creusot [F] 56 F5
Le Croisic [F] 40 D6
Le Crotoy [F] 28 D3
Lectoure [F] 66 E6
Łęczna [PL] 38 E5
Łęczyca [PL] 20 G5
Łęczyca [PL] 36 G3
Ledal [N] 180 G1
Ledaña [E] 98 C4
Ledbury [GB] 12 G2
Ledeč nad Sázavou [CZ] 48 H5
Ledena Pećina [MNE] 144 E2
Ledenika Peštera [BG] 146 F3
Ledesma [E] 80 G6
Ledge [D] 20 B6
Lédignan [F] 106 F3
Ledigos [E] 82 C5
Leding [S] 184 G1
Ledmozero [RUS] 196 H4
Lednica [SK] 50 E6
Lednica [SK] 50 E6
Lednice [CZ] 62 G3
Le Donjon [F] 56 E6
Le Dorat [F] 54 F5
Ledreborg [DK] 156 G3
Łędyczek [PL] 22 B5
Leeds [GB] 10 F3
Leek [GB] 10 E5
Leek [NL] 16 G2
Leenane [IRL] 2 B4
Leens [NL] 16 G2
Leer [D] 18 B4
Leerdam [NL] 16 D5
Leese [D] 32 E1
Leesi [EST] 198 E1
Leeuwarden [NL] 16 F2
Le Faou [F] 40 B2
Le Faouët [F] 40 C3
le Fayet [F] 70 C3
Lefka [BG] 150 A1
Léfka (Lefke) [CY] 154 F5
Lefkáda [GR] 132 D4
Lefkádia [GR] 128 F4
Lefkadíti [GR] 132 G5
Lefke (Léfka) [CY] 154 F5
Léfkes [GR] 138 E3
Lefkími [GR] 132 B3
Lefkógeia [GR] 130 C2
Lefkónikon (Geçitkale) [CY] 154 G5
Lefkoşa (Lefkosía) [CY] 154 G5
Lefkosía (Lefkoşa) [CY] 154 G5
Léfktra [GR] 134 A5
le Folgoet [F] 40 B1
Le Folgoët [F] 40 B1
Le Fossat [F] 84 H4
Le Freney [F] 70 B5
le Fuilet [F] 54 C1
Leganés [E] 88 F6
Le-Gault-St-Denis [F] 42 E5
Legbąd [PL] 22 D4
Legden [D] 16 H5
Legé [F] 54 B2
Legionowo [PL] 38 B2
Léglise [B] 44 E2
Legnago [I] 110 F1
Legnano [I] 70 F4
Legnica [PL] 36 B6
Legnickie Pole [PL] 36 B6
Legoland [DK] 156 B2
le Gouray [F] 26 B5
Łęgowo [PL] 22 E3
Legrad [HR] 74 G4
Le Grand-Bourg [F] 54 G6
Le Grand-Lucé [F] 42 C5
Le Grand-Pressigny [F] 54 F3
Le Grau-du-Roi [F] 106 F4
Legrená [GR] 136 H2
le Gressier [F] 66 B3
Leguatiano [E] 82 G4
Léguevin [F] 84 H3
Łęg Wygoda [PL] 52 C3
Le Havre [F] 26 G3
Lehelitz [D] 34 C5
Le-Hérie-La Vieville [F] 28 G5
Lehmäjoki [FIN] 186 C2
Lehmen [D] 30 H6
Lehmo [FIN] 188 F2
Lehnice [SK] 62 H5
Lehnin [D] 34 D3
Le Hohwald [F] 44 G6
Le Houga [F] 66 C6
Lehrberg [D] 46 F5
Lehre [D] 32 H2
Lehrte [D] 32 G2
Lehtimäki [FIN] 186 D3
Lehtmetsa [EST] 198 E1
Lehtola [FIN] 194 E7
Lehtomäki [FIN] 196 F5
Lehtovaara [FIN] 188 H2
Lehtovaara [FIN] 196 F5
Leianokládi [GR] 132 G4
Leibnitz [A] 74 D3
Leicester [GB] 10 F6
Leiden [NL] 16 D4
Leie [EST] 198 E3
Leiferde [D] 32 G2
Leighlinbridge [IRL] 4 F4
Leighton Buzzard [GB] 14 E3
Leikanger [N] 170 D2
Leikanger [N] 180 B4
Leinefelde [D] 32 G5
Leinelä [FIN] 176 H2
Leinesodden [N] 190 D2
Leini [I] 70 D5
Leipalingis [LT] 24 F3
Leipämäki [FIN] 188 E4
Leipheim [D] 60 C3
Leipojärvi [S] 192 H6
Leipsoí [GR] 138 H2
Leipzig [D] 34 C5
Leira [N] 170 G3
Leira [N] 180 F1
Leira [N] 190 D3
Leirbotn [N] 194 B3
Leirfall [N] 182 C1
Leirgulen [N] 180 B5
Leiria [P] 86 C3
Leiro [E] 78 C4
Leirosa [P] 86 C2
Leirpollskogen [N] 194 D2
Leirvik [FR] 160 B1
Leirvik [N] 170 B1
Leirvik [N] 170 B5
Leirvik [N] 192 F4
Leirvika [N] 190 D2
Leisi [EST] 198 C3
Leisnig [D] 34 D6
Leissigen [CH] 70 E1
Leitir Mealláin / Lettermullan [IRL] 2 B5
Leitzkau [D] 34 C3
Leivadia [CY] 154 G5
Leivadítis [GR] 130 E2
Leivonmäki [FIN] 186 G5
Lejasciems [LV] 198 F4
Lekáni [GR] 130 D2
Łękawa [PL] 36 G6
Lekeitio / Lequeitio [E] 82 H4
Lekenik [HR] 74 E6
Lekeryd [S] 162 D2
Lekhchevo [BG] 146 F3
Łęki Górne [PL] 52 C4
Leknes [N] 180 D4
Leknes [N] 192 C4
Łęknica [PL] 34 G5
Leksand [S] 172 H4
Leksberg [S] 166 F5
Leksvik [N] 190 B6
Lekunberri [E] 84 B3
Lekvattnet [S] 172 E5
Leland [N] 190 D2
Le Lauzet-Ubaye [F] 108 D2
Le Lavandou [F] 108 D6
L'Elefante [I] 118 C2
Lelice [PL] 36 H1
Le Liège [F] 54 G2
Le Lion-D'Angers [F] 40 H6
Lelkowo [PL] 22 G2
Lelle [EST] 198 E2
Le Locle [CH] 58 C5
Le Logis-du-Pin [F] 108 D4
Le Loroux-Bottereau [F] 54 C1
Le Louroux [F] 40 G6
Lelów [PL] 50 H2
Le Luc [F] 108 D5
Le Ludd [F] 42 B6
Lelystad [NL] 16 E4
Lem [DK] 156 B1
Le Mans [F] 42 B5
Le Markstein [F] 58 D3
Le Mas-d'Azil [F] 84 H4
Le Mayet [F] 68 D1
Lembach [F] 44 H5
Lembeck [D] 16 G6
Lembeye [F] 84 E3
Lemele [NL] 16 G4
Le Merlerault [F] 26 G5
Le-Mesnil-Vigot [F] 26 D3
Lemesos (Limassol) [CY] 154 F6
Lemetinvaara [FIN] 196 F5
Lemförde [D] 32 D1
Lemgo [D] 32 E3
Lemi [FIN] 178 D2
Lemke [D] 32 F1
Lemland [FIN] 176 B6
Lemmenjoki [FIN] 194 D4
Lemmer [NL] 16 F3
Lemnhult [S] 162 E3
Le Monastier [F] 68 E5
Le Monêtier-les-Bains [F] 70 B5
Le Mont-Dore [F] 68 C2
Le Monteix [F] 56 C6
Le Montet [F] 56 D5
Le Mont-St-Michel [F] 26 D4
Le Mont-St-Michel [F] 26 D4
Le Moulin du Pali [F] 108 E4
le Mouret [CH] 58 D6
Lemovzha [RUS] 198 H1
Lempäälä [FIN] 176 F2

Lempdes [F] 68 C3
Lempdes [F] 68 D2
Lempyy [FIN] 188 C3
le Mulins [F] 68 E2
Le Muret [F] 66 C4
Le Muy [F] 108 D5
Lemvig [DK] 160 B5
Lena [N] 172 B4
Lenart V Slovenskih Goricah [SLO] 74 E3
Lencloître [F] 54 E3
Lencouacq [F] 66 C5
Lend [A] 72 G1
Lendava [SLO] 74 F3
Lendery [RUS] 196 H6
Lendinara [I] 110 G2
Lendum [DK] 160 E3
Lenes [N] 180 G1
Le Neubourg [F] 26 H4
Lengefeld [D] 46 H1
Lengerich [D] 32 C1
Lengerich [D] 32 C2
Lenggries [D] 60 E5
Lengnau [CH] 58 F4
Lengyeltóti [H] 74 H3
Lenhovda [S] 162 E4
Leni [I] 124 B5
Lenina [BY] 202 D6
Léning [F] 44 F4
Lenk [CH] 70 D2
Lenna [I] 70 H3
Lennartsfors [S] 166 C3
Lenningen [N] 170 G2
Lenno [I] 70 G3
Leno [I] 72 B6
Lenola [I] 120 C1
Lenora [CZ] 62 B2
Le Nouvion-en-Thiérache [F] 28 G5
Lenovo [BG] 148 B6
Lens [F] 28 F3
Lensahn [D] 18 H2
Lensvik [N] 180 H1
Léntas [GR] 140 E5
Lentföhrden [D] 18 F3
Lenti [H] 74 F3
Lentiira [FIN] 196 G4
Lenting [D] 60 E2
Lentini [I] 126 G4
Lentvaris [LT] 24 H1
Lenungen [S] 166 D2
Lenzburg [CH] 58 F5
Lenzen [D] 20 A6
Lenzerheide [CH] 70 H1
Lenzkirch [D] 58 F3
Leoben [A] 72 H2
Leoben [A] 74 D1
Leogang [A] 60 G6
Leominster [GB] 12 G1
León [E] 78 H5
Léon [F] 66 B5
Leonarisso (Ziyamet) [CY] 154 G4
Leonberg [D] 58 G1
Leonessa [I] 116 B3
Leonessa [I] 120 G2
Leonforte [I] 126 F3
Leonídio [GR] 136 F3
Leontári [GR] 136 D3
Leóntio [GR] 136 E2
Leontýnský Zámek [CZ] 48 E4
Leopoldsburg [B] 30 E3
Leopoldsdorf [A] 62 F4
Leopovina [HR] 74 F5
Le Palais [F] 40 C5
Le Palmyre [F] 54 B6
L'Epau, Abbaye de- [F] 42 B5
Lepe [E] 94 E5
Le-Péage-de-Roussillon [F] 68 F4
Lepenica [SRB] 146 D5
Lepenicë [AL] 128 B6
Lepenoú [GR] 132 E4
Le Perthus [F] 92 G2
Lepetane [MNE] 144 D4
Le Pin-au-Haras [F] 26 G5
l'Epine [F] 44 C4
Lepistönmäki [FIN] 186 D1
le Pleynet [F] 70 A5
Lepoglava [HR] 74 E4
Le Poiré-sur-Vie [F] 54 B3
Le Pont [F] 70 A3
Le Pont-de-Beauvoisin [F] 68 H4
Le Pont-de-Claix [F] 68 H5
le Pont-de-Montvert [F] 68 D6
Le Pontet [F] 66 D2
Leporano [I] 122 E4
Le Porge [F] 66 C3
Le Portel [F] 28 D2
Leposavić [SRB] 146 C4
Le Pouldu [F] 40 C4
Lépoura [GR] 134 C5
Le Pouzin [F] 68 F5
Leppäkoski [FIN] 186 G6
Leppälä [FIN] 178 E2
Leppälahti [FIN] 186 H1
Leppälahti [FIN] 188 F3
Leppämäki [FIN] 188 C3
Leppäselkä [FIN] 186 G2
Leppävesi [FIN] 186 G4
Leppävirta [FIN] 188 D3
Lépreo [GR] 136 C3
Lepsény [H] 76 B2
Leptokaryá [GR] 128 G6
Lëpushë [AL] 146 A5
Le Puy-en-Velay [F] 68 D4
Lequeitio / Lekeitio [E] 82 H4
Leques, Col des- [F] 108 D4
Le Quesnoy [F] 28 G4
Ler [N] 182 B2
Le Rabot [F] 56 B2
Lerbäck [S] 166 H4
Lercara Friddi [I] 126 D3
Lerchenborg [DK] 156 E2
Lerdala [S] 166 F5
Lerga [E] 84 B4
Lerici [I] 110 C4
Lérida / Lleida [E] 90 H4
Lerín [E] 84 A4
Lerma [E] 88 G1
Lerm-et-Musset [F] 66 D5
Lermoos [A] 60 D6
Lérni [GR] 136 E2
Le Rozier [F] 106 E2
Lerresfjord [N] 194 B2
Lerum [S] 160 H2
Le Russey [F] 58 C5
Lerwick [GB] 6 G4
Lés [E] 84 F5
Leş [RO] 76 H2
Lesa [I] 70 F4
Les Abrets [F] 68 H3
Les Adrets [F] 108 E5
Les Aix-d'Angillon [F] 56 C3
Lešak [SRB] 146 B4
Lesaka [E] 84 B3
les Aldudes [F] 84 C3
Les Andelys [F] 28 C6
Les Antiques [F] 106 G4
Les Arcs [F] 70 B3
Les Arcs [F] 108 D5
les Avants [CH] 70 C1
les Avellanes [E] 92 B2
Les Baux-de-Provence [F] 106 G4
les Borges Blanques [E] 92 B3
Les Bouchoux [F] 70 A2
Les Boulay Lue [F] 44 F4
Les Cabannes [F] 84 H5
L'Escala [E] 92 G3
Les Calanques [F] 106 H5
Lescar [F] 84 E3
L'Escarène [F] 108 F4
Les Cases d'Alcanar [E] 92 A6
Lesce [SLO] 74 B4
Les Contamines-Montjoie [F] 70 C3
les Coves de Vinromà [E] 98 G2
Les Deux-Alpes [F] 70 A5
Les Diablerets [CH] 70 D2
Lesdins [F] 28 F5
Les Echarmeaux [F] 68 F1
Les Echelles [F] 68 H4
Le Sentier [CH] 70 B1
Les Epesses [F] 54 C2
Les Escaldes [AND] 84 H6
Les Essarts [F] 54 C3
Les Eyzies-de-Tayac [F] 66 F3
Les-Fins [F] 58 C5
Les Forges [F] 26 A5
Les Gets [F] 70 C2
Les Halles [F] 68 F3
Les Haudères [CH] 70 D3
Les Hayons [F] 28 C5
Les Herbiers [F] 54 C2
Les Houches [F] 70 C3
Lesichovo [BG] 148 A5
Lésina [I] 116 F6
Les Issambres [F] 108 D5
Lesja [N] 180 G5
Lesjärvi [FIN] 176 F3
Lesjaskog [N] 180 F4
Lesjaverk [N] 180 F4
Lesjöfors [S] 166 F1
Leskelä [FIN] 196 D5
Lesko [PL] 52 E5
Leskovac [SRB] 146 D4
Leskova Dolina [SLO] 74 B6
Leskovik [AL] 128 D6
Leskovo [BG] 148 F1
Les Laumes [F] 56 F3
Les Lecques [F] 108 B5
Les Menuires [F] 70 B4
Lesmont [F] 44 B5
Lésna [PL] 48 H1
Lesneven [F] 40 B1
Lešnica [PL] 50 E3
Lešnica [SRB] 142 F3
Leśniów Wielki [PL] 34 H4
Lesnovo [MK] 128 F1
Lesogorskiy [RUS] 178 F2
Lesparre-Médoc [F] 66 C2
Lesperon [F] 66 B5
Les Pieux [F] 26 D2
Les Planches-en-Montagne [F] 58 B6
les Planes d'Hostoles [E] 92 F3
l'Espluga de Francolí [E] 92 C4
Les Ponts-de-Cé [F] 40 H6
Lesquin [F] 28 F3
Les Riceys [F] 56 F1
Les Rosiers [F] 54 E1
les Rotes [E] 104 F1
Les Rousses [F] 70 B1
Les Sables-d'Olonne [F] 54 B3
Les Saisies [F] 70 B3
Les Salles [F] 68 E2
Lessay [F] 26 D3
Lessebo [S] 162 E5
Lessila [FIN] 176 D1
Lessines [B] 28 G3
Lestards [F] 66 H2
l'Estartit [E] 92 G3
Lestelle Bétharram [F] 84 E4
Les-Thilliers-en-Vexin [F] 28 C6
Lestijärvi [FIN] 196 D6
Les Trois-Epis [F] 58 D2
Les Trois-Moutiers [F] 54 E2
Lesum [D] 18 D5
Lesura [BG] 146 G3
les Useres / Useras [E] 98 F3
Les Vans [F] 68 E6
Leszno [PL] 36 C4
Leszno [PL] 38 B3
Leszno Górne [PL] 36 A5
Létavértes [H] 76 H1
Letchworth [GB] 14 E3
Le Teil [F] 68 F6
Le Teilleul [F] 26 E5
le Temple [F] 66 C3
Letenye [H] 74 F4
Le Thillot [F] 58 C3
Letkés [H] 64 C5
Letku [FIN] 176 F4
Letmathe [D] 32 C4
Letnitsa [BG] 148 B3
Letohrad [CZ] 50 B4
Letoon [TR] 154 F3
Le Touquet-Paris-Plage [F] 28 D3
Le Touvet [F] 68 H4
Letovice [CZ] 50 C5
Le Trayas [F] 108 E5
Le Tremblade [F] 54 B5
Le Tréport [F] 28 C4
Letreros, Cueva de los- [E] 102 H3
Letsbo [S] 184 D6
Letschin [D] 34 G2
Letterfrack [IRL] 2 B4
Letterkenny [IRL] 2 E2
Lettermullan / Leitir Mealláin [IRL] 2 B5
Letur [E] 104 A1
Letychiv [UA] 202 C8
Letzlingen [D] 34 B2
Leu [RO] 146 G1
Leucate [F] 106 D6
Leuchtenburg [D] 46 H1
Leuglay [F] 56 G2
Leuk [CH] 70 D2
Leukerbad [CH] 70 D2
Leun [D] 46 C1
Leuna [D] 34 C5
Leussow [D] 18 H5
Leutasch [A] 60 D6
Leutenberg [D] 46 H2
Leutkirch [D] 60 B5
Leutschach [A] 74 D3
Leuven (Louvain) [B] 30 D4
Leuze [B] 28 G3
Levajok [N] 194 C3
Le Val-André [F] 26 B4
Levan [AL] 128 A4
Levänen [FIN] 178 D1
Levanger [N] 190 C6
Levanto [FIN] 176 H3
Lévanto [I] 110 C4
Levanzo [I] 126 A2
Leväranta [FIN] 194 E7
Levashovo [RUS] 178 H4
Leväsjoki [FIN] 186 B6
Le Vast [F] 26 E2
Le Vaudreuil [F] 28 B6
Levdun [N] 194 B2
Leven [GB] 8 F3
Levens [F] 108 E4
Le Verdon [F] 54 B6
Leverkusen [D] 30 G4
Levern [D] 32 D2
Le Vernet [F] 108 D3
Levet [F] 56 C4
Levice [SK] 64 B4
Levico Terme [I] 72 D5
Levídi [GR] 136 D2
Levie [F] 114 B5
Levier [F] 58 B5
Le Vigan [F] 106 E3
Levoča [SK] 64 E2
Levroux [F] 54 H3
Levski [BG] 148 B3
Levunovo [BG] 130 B2
Lewes [GB] 14 E5
Lewin Brzeski [PL] 50 D2
Leyburn [GB] 10 F2
Leysin [CH] 70 C2
Leżajsk [PL] 52 E3
Ležáky [CZ] 50 B4
Lézardrieux [F] 26 A3
Lézat [F] 70 A1
Lezay [F] 54 E5
Lezhë [AL] 128 B1
Lézignan-Corbières [F] 106 C5
Lezoux [F] 68 D2
Lezuza [E] 98 A5
Lgota [PL] 50 G3
L'gov [RUS] 202 F6
L'hermitage-Lorge [F] 26 A5
L'Hospitalet de l'Infant [E] 92 B5
l'Hospitalet de Llobregat [E] 92 E4
l'Hospitalet-l'Andorre [F] 92 E1
Liapádes [GR] 132 B2
Liatorp [S] 162 D5
Libáň [CZ] 48 H3
Liběchov [CZ] 48 F3
Liberec [CZ] 48 G2
Libiąż [PL] 50 G3
Libochovice [CZ] 48 F3
Libohovë [AL] 132 C1
Libourne [F] 66 D3
Libramont [B] 44 D1
Librazhd [AL] 128 C3
Librilla [E] 104 C3
Libusza [PL] 52 C4
Licata [I] 126 E4
Licciana Nardi [I] 110 D4
Lich [D] 46 C2
Licháda [GR] 132 H4
Lichfield [GB] 10 E6
Lichnice [CZ] 48 H4
Lichtenau [A] 62 D3
Lichtenau [D] 32 E4
Lichtenberg [D] 46 H2
Lichtenberg [F] 44 H5
Lichtenfels [D] 32 E5
Lichtenfels [D] 46 G3
Lichtensteig [CH] 58 G5
Lichtenstein [CH] 70 H1
Lichtenstein [D] 48 C2
Lichtenstein [D] 58 H2
Lichtenvoorde [NL] 16 G5
Lickershamn [S] 168 G4
Lički Osik [HR] 112 G3
Ličko Lešće [HR] 112 G3
Licodia Eubea [I] 126 F4
Licques [F] 14 G6
Lid [S] 166 F1
Lida [BY] 202 A5
Liden [S] 162 E2
Liden [S] 184 E4
Liden [S] 190 F4
Liden [S] 196 A4
Lidhult [S] 162 C5
Lidice [CZ] 48 F3
Lidingö [S] 168 E3
Lidköping [S] 166 E5
Lido degli Estensi [I] 110 H3
Lido delle Nazioni [I] 110 H3
Lido di Camaiore [I] 110 D5
Lido di Castel Fusano [I] 114 H6
Lido di Fermo [I] 116 D2
Lido di Jésolo [I] 72 F6
Lido di Latina [I] 120 B1
Lido di Metaponto [I] 122 D4
Lido di Óstia [I] 114 H6
Lido di Pomposa [I] 110 H3
Lido di Rivoli [I] 120 H1
Lido di Scanzano [I] 122 D5
Lido di Spina [I] 110 H3
Lido di Torre Mileto [I] 116 G5
Lido di Venézia [I] 110 H1
Lidoríki [GR] 132 G5
Lido Silvana [I] 122 F4
Lidsjöberg [S] 190 E5
Lidzbark [PL] 22 G5
Lidzbark Warmiński [PL] 22 H3
Liebegg [CH] 58 F5
Liebenau [A] 62 C3
Liebenau [D] 32 E1
Liebenwalde [D] 34 E1
Lieberose [D] 34 F4
Liebling [RO] 76 G6
Liechtenstein Klamm [A] 72 G1
Liedakkala [FIN] 196 C2
Liedenpohja [FIN] 186 D4
Lieg [D] 44 H1
Liège (Luik) [B] 30 E5
Lieksa [FIN] 196 G6
Lielvārde [LV] 198 E5
Lienz [A] 72 F2
Liepāja [LV] 198 B6
Liepna [LV] 198 G4
Lier [B] 30 D3
Lier [N] 164 H1
Lierbyen [N] 164 H1
Liérganes [E] 82 F3
Liernais [F] 56 F4
Lierville [F] 42 F2
Liesa [E] 84 D6
Liesjärvi [FIN] 186 E4
Lieskau [D] 34 E5
Lieske [D] 34 G5
Liesniemi [FIN] 176 E5
Liesse [F] 28 G6
Liestal [CH] 58 E4
Lieto / Lundo [FIN] 176 E4
Liétor [E] 98 B6
Lieu-Restauré, Abbaye de- [F] 42 G3
Lieurey [F] 26 G4
Lievestuore [FIN] 186 G4
Lievikoski [FIN] 176 D2
Liezen [A] 62 B6
Liezere [LV] 198 F5
Lifford [IRL] 2 F2
Liffré [F] 26 C6
Liggavägen [S] 190 H1
Ligieri [LV] 198 E5
Lignano Pineta [I] 72 G6
Lignano Sabbiadoro [I] 72 G6
Ligneuville [B] 30 F6
Lignières [F] 56 B4
Ligny-en-Barrois [F] 44 D5
Ligourió [GR] 136 F2
Ligueil [F] 54 F3
Ligugé, Abbaye de- [F] 54 E4
Lihjamo [FIN] 186 F4
Lihme [DK] 160 C5
Lihula [EST] 198 D2
Liiansaari [FIN] 178 D1
Liinahamari [RUS] 194 F3
Liitsola [FIN] 176 E2
Liiva [EST] 198 C2
Lijärvi [FIN] 194 D3
Lijeva Rijeka [MNE] 144 E4
Likavský Hrad [SK] 64 C2
Likenäs [S] 172 E4
Likosoúra [GR] 136 D3
Liland [S] 184 F3
Lilaste [LV] 198 D5
Lild Strand [DK] 160 C3
L'Ile-Bouchard [F] 54 F2
L'Ile-Rousse [F] 114 B3
Lilienfeld [A] 62 D5
Liljendal [FIN] 178 B4
Lilla Edet [S] 166 D6
Lillåfors [S] 194 A8
Lillafüred [H] 64 F4
Lillaz [I] 70 D4
Lillbo [S] 174 D1
Lillby [FIN] 186 C1
Lille [DK] 156 G3
Lille [F] 28 F3
Lillebo [N] 182 D6
Lillebonne [F] 26 H3
Lillefjord [N] 194 B2
Lillehammer [N] 172 B2
Lillerød [DK] 156 G2
Lillers [F] 28 E3
Lillesand [N] 164 E5
Lillestrøm [N] 166 C1
Lille Værløse [DK] 156 G2
Lillhaga [S] 172 H1
Lillhärad [S] 168 B2
Lillhärdal [S] 182 G6
Lillholmsjö [S] 182 G1
Lillkågeträsk [S] 196 A4
Lillkyro / Vähäkyro [FIN] 186 B2
Lillo [E] 96 G2
Lillögda [S] 190 G5
Lillpite [S] 196 A3
Lillsele [S] 190 H5
Lillviken [S] 190 F2
Limáni Chersonísou [GR] 140 F4
Limanköy [TR] 150 D1
Limanowa [PL] 52 B5
Limassol (Lemesos) [CY] 154 F6
Limatola [I] 120 E2
Limavady [NIR] 2 F2
Limbaži [LV] 198 E4
Limbourg [B] 30 F5
Limburg [D] 46 B2
Limedsforsen [S] 172 F3
Limenária [GR] 130 E4
Liménas [GR] 134 C4
Liméni [GR] 136 E5
Limerick / Luimneach [IRL] 4 D3
Limhamn [S] 156 H3
Limingo / Liminka [FIN] 196 D4
Liminka / Limingo [FIN] 196 D4
Liminkakylä [FIN] 196 D5
Limín Litochórou [GR] 128 G6
Liminpuro [FIN] 196 E4
Limmared [S] 162 C2
Limna [UA] 52 F6
Limnae [TR] 130 H5
Límnes [GR] 136 F2
Límni [GR] 134 B4
Limniá [GR] 130 D3
Limnitsa [GR] 132 F5
Limoges [F] 66 G1
Limogne-en-Quercy [F] 66 G5
Limone Piemonte [I] 108 F3
Limonest [F] 68 F2
Limone sul Garda [I] 72 C5
Limosano [I] 116 E6
Limours [F] 42 F4
Limoux [F] 106 B5
Lin [AL] 128 D3
Lina älv [S] 192 G6
Linares [E] 102 E1
Linares de Mora [E] 98 F2
Linares de Riofrío [E] 88 B4
Linariá [GR] 134 D3
Lincoln [GB] 10 G5
Lind [DK] 156 B1
Lindärva [S] 166 E5
Lindås [N] 170 B3
Lindås [S] 162 F5
Lindau [D] 34 C3
Lindau [D] 60 B5
Lindaunis [D] 18 F1
Linddalen [S] 166 G4
Linde [DK] 160 B5
Lindefallet [S] 174 E2
Lindefjell [N] 164 C4
Lindelbrunn [D] 46 B5
Lindelse [DK] 156 E4
Linden [BG] 130 C2
Linden [D] 44 H4
Lindenberg [D] 34 E2
Lindenberg [D] 60 B5
Lindenfels [D] 46 C4
Lindenholz [CH] 58 E5
Linderbach [D] 32 H6
Linderhof [D] 60 D6
Lindern [D] 18 C6
Linderöd [S] 158 D2
Lindesberg [S] 166 H2
Lindesnäs [S] 172 G5
Lindkoski [FIN] 178 B3
Lindlia [N] 170 G4
Lindome [S] 160 H2
Líndos [GR] 154 D4
Lindoso [P] 78 B6
Lindow [D] 20 C6
Lindsås [N] 164 E4
Lindum [DK] 160 D5
Lindved [DK] 156 C2
Líně [CZ] 48 D4
Lingbo [S] 174 E3
Linge [N] 180 E4
Lingen [D] 16 H4
Linghed [S] 174 D4
Linghem [S] 168 A5
Linguaglossa [I] 124 A8
Linken [D] 20 E5
Linköping [S] 168 A5
Linkvarnen [S] 184 A5
Linna [FIN] 186 F3
Linnankylä [FIN] 186 D5
Linnanperä [FIN] 186 F1
Linnerud [N] 172 C3
Linneryd [S] 162 E5
Linnes [N] 172 E1
Linnés Hammarby [S] 168 D1
Linosa [I] 126 B5
Linova [BY] 38 H2
Linovo [RUS] 198 G4
Linsdal [S] 162 G5
Linsell [S] 182 F5
Linthal [CH] 58 G6
Lintzel [D] 18 F6
Linum [D] 34 D1
Linz [A] 62 B4
Linz [D] 30 H5
Liomseter [N] 170 G2
Lioni [I] 120 F3
Lióprasο [GR] 132 F2
Lipa [BIH] 144 B1
Lípa [CZ] 50 E6
Lipa [PL] 52 E2
Lipany [SK] 52 C6
Lipar [SRB] 76 D6
Lipari [I] 124 B6
Lipcani [MD] 204 D3
Liperi [FIN] 188 F3
Liperonmäki [FIN] 188 C4
Lipiany [PL] 20 F6
Lipica [SLO] 72 H6
Lipik [HR] 142 B1
Lipinki Łużyckie [PL] 34 G5
Lipka [PL] 22 C5
Lipljan [SRB] 146 C5
Lipnica [BG] 146 G3
Lipnica [PL] 22 C3
Lipnica [PL] 22 E6
Lipnice nad Sázavou [CZ] 48 H5
Lipnik [PL] 52 D2
Lipník nad Bečvou [CZ] 50 D5
Lipno [PL] 36 G1
Lipno nad Vltavou [CZ] 62 B3
Lipova [CZ] 50 E6
Lipova [RO] 76 H4
Lipovac [HR] 142 E2
Lipová-Lázně [CZ] 50 D3
Lipovci [SLO] 74 F3
Lipovica [SRB] 146 D4
Lipovka [RUS] 24 C1
Lipovljani [HR] 142 B1
Lipovo Polje [HR] 112 G3
Lipowina [PL] 22 G2
Lipowo [PL] 22 G4
Lippborg [D] 32 D4
Lippstadt [D] 32 D4
Lipsheim [F] 44 H6
Lipsk [PL] 24 F4
Lipsko [PL] 38 C6
Lipsko [PL] 52 F2
Liptovská Osada [SK] 64 C2
Liptovská Teplička [SK] 64 E2
Liptovské Matiašovce [SK] 50 H6
Liptovský-Mikuláš [SK] 64 D2
Lipusz [PL] 22 C3
Lis [AL] 128 B2
Lisboa [P] 86 B5
Lisburn [NIR] 2 G4
Liscarroll [IRL] 4 C4
Lisdoonvarna [IRL] 2 B5
Lisec [MK] 128 D1
Liseleje [DK] 156 G1
Liselund [DK] 156 G4
Liselund [DK] 156 G4
Lisia Góra [PL] 52 C3
Lisieux [F] 26 G4
Lisinki [FIN] 194 C7
Liskeard [GB] 12 D4
Lisland [N] 164 E2
L'Isle [CH] 70 B1
Lisle [F] 66 F2
L'Isle-Adam [F] 42 F3
L'Isle-de-Noé [F] 84 F3
L'Isle-en-Dodon [F] 84 G3
l'Isle-Jourdain [F] 54 F5
L'Isle-Jourdain [F] 84 H3
Lisleset [N] 170 F4
L'Isle-sur-la-Sorgue [F] 106 H3
L'Isle-sur-le-Doubs [F] 58 C4
Lisle-sur-Tarn [F] 106 B2
Lisma [FIN] 194 C5
Lismore [IRL] 4 D5
Lišnja [BIH] 142 C2
Lison, Source du- [F] 58 B5
Lišov [CZ] 62 C2
Lisów [PL] 34 G2
Lisse [NL] 16 D4
Lissewege [B] 28 G1
Lisskogsbrändan [S] 172 F4
List [D] 156 A4
Lista [S] 168 B3
Lişteava [RO] 146 G2
Listerby [S] 158 F1
Lištica [BIH] 144 C2
Listowel [IRL] 4 C3
Lit [S] 182 H2
Litene [LV] 198 F4
Litér [H] 76 A2
Liternum [I] 120 D3
Lit-et-Mixe [F] 66 B5
Lithakiá [GR] 136 A2
Lithínes [GR] 140 G5
Lití [GR] 128 H4
Litice [CZ] 50 B4
Litija [SLO] 74 C5
Litke [H] 64 D4
Litmalahti [FIN] 188 D2
Litmaniemi [FIN] 188 D2
Litóchoro [GR] 128 G6
Litoměřice [CZ] 48 F2
Litomyšl [CZ] 50 B4
Litovel [CZ] 50 C5
Litslena [S] 168 C2
Littlehampton [GB] 14 D5
Littleport [GB] 14 F2
Litultovice [CZ] 50 D4
Litvínov [CZ] 48 E2
Liubar [UA] 202 C8
Liubech [UA] 202 D6
Liubeshiv [UA] 202 B7
Liuboml' [UA] 38 G5
Liukoniai [LT] 200 G5
Liusselstugan [S] 190 H2
Livada de Bihor [RO] 76 H2
Livade [HR] 112 D1
Livadeiá [GR] 132 H5
Livaderó [GR] 130 D2
Livadhja [AL] 132 B1
Livádi [GR] 128 G6
Livádi [GR] 130 B5
Livádi [GR] 136 F6
Livádi [GR] 138 D3
Livádia [GR] 154 B3
Livadochóri [GR] 130 F6
Līvāni [LV] 198 F6
Livari [MNE] 144 E5
Livarot [F] 26 G4
Liverá [GR] 128 F5
Livera (Sadrazamköy) [CY] 154 F5
Livernon [F] 66 H5
Liverpool [GB] 10 D4
Livigno [I] 72 B3
Livingston [GB] 8 E3
Livno [BIH] 144 B1
Livo [FIN] 196 E3
Livold [SLO] 74 C6
Livorno [I] 110 D6
Livorno Ferraris [I] 70 E5
Livov [SK] 52 C6
Livron-sur-Drôme [F] 68 F5
Liw [PL] 38 D2
Lixa [P] 80 C4
Lixoúri [GR] 132 C6
Lizard [GB] 12 B5
Lizarra / Estella [E] 84 A4
Lizartza [E] 84 B3
Lizy [F] 42 G3
Lizzano [I] 122 F4
Lješane [SRB] 146 B5
Ljig [SRB] 146 B1
Ljørdalen [N] 172 E2
Ljosland [N] 164 D4
Ljuba [SRB] 142 F2
Ljuban' [BY] 202 C6
Ljuban' [RUS] 202 C1
Ljubaništa [MK] 128 D4
Ljubenovo [BG] 148 D5
Ljubinje [BIH] 144 C3
Ljubljana [SLO] 74 B5
Ljubno [SLO] 74 B4
Ljubno [SLO] 74 C4
Ljubogošta [BIH] 144 D1
Ljubostinja, Manastir- [SRB] 146 C3
Ljubovija [MNE] 204 A6
Ljubovija [SRB] 142 F4
Ljubovo [BIH] 144 D4
Ljubuški [BIH] 144 B2
Ljubytino [RUS] 202 C1
Ljudinovo [RUS] 202 E4
Ljugarn [S] 168 G5
Ljungby [S] 162 C5
Ljungbyhed [S] 158 C1
Ljungbyholm [S] 162 F5
Ljungdalen [S] 182 E3
Ljunghusen [S] 156 H3
Ljungsarp [S] 162 C2
Ljungsbro [S] 166 H5
Ljungskile [S] 166 C6
Ljusdal [S] 184 D6
Ljusfallshammar [S] 166 H4
Ljusne [S] 174 E2
Ljustero [S] 168 E2
Ljustorp [S] 184 E4
Ljusträsk [S] 190 H3
Ljutići [MNE] 144 E2
Ljuti Dol [BG] 146 G4
Ljutomer [SLO] 74 E4
Llafranc [E] 92 G3
Llagostera [E] 92 F3
Llanberis [GB] 10 B4
Llançà [E] 92 G2
Llandeilo [GB] 12 E2
Llandovery [GB] 12 E1
Llandrindod Wells [GB] 10 C6
Llandudno [GB] 10 C4
Llanelli [GB] 12 E2
Llanes [E] 82 D2
Llangefni [GB] 10 B4
Llangollen [GB] 10 C5
Llangurig [GB] 10 C6
Llanidloes [GB] 10 C6
Llantwit Major [GB] 12 E3
Llanuwchllyn [GB] 10 C5
Llavorsí [E] 84 G6
Lleida / Lérida [E] 90 H4
Llera [E] 94 H3
Llerena [E] 94 H4
Lles de Cerdanya [E] 92 D1
Llíria [E] 98 E4
Llivia [F] 92 E1
Llodio / Laudio [E] 82 G4
Lloret de Mar [E] 92 F4
Lluc, Monestir de- [E] 104 E4
Llucena / Lucena del Cid [E] 98 F3
Llucmajor [E] 104 E5
Lnáře [CZ] 48 E5
Lniano [PL] 22 D5
Loano [I] 108 G3
Loarre, Cast. de- [E] 84 D6
Löbau [D] 34 G6
Lobenstein [D] 46 H2
Łobez [PL] 20 G4
Lobios [E] 78 C6
Löbnitz [D] 20 C2
Łobodno [PL] 50 G1
Lobón [E] 94 G2
Lobonäs [S] 172 H1
Loborika [HR] 112 D2
Lobosh [BG] 146 F5
Loburg [D] 34 C3
Łobżenica [PL] 22 C5
Locana [I] 70 D4
Locarno [CH] 70 F3
Loccum [D] 32 E2
Lochaline [GB] 6 B6
Loch Baghasdail / Lochboisdale [GB] 6 A4
Lochboisdale / Loch Baghasdail [GB] 6 A4
Lochearnhead [GB] 8 D2
Lochem [NL] 16 F5
Loches [F] 54 G3
Loch Garman / Wexford [IRL] 4 F5
Lochgilphead [GB] 8 C2
Lochinver [GB] 6 D3
Lochmaddy / Loch nam Madadh [GB] 6 A3
Loch nam Madadh / Lochmaddy [GB] 6 A3
Łochocin [PL] 36 G1

Magyarmecske [H] 76 A5
Magyarszombatfa [H] 74 F3
Maheriv [UA] 52 G3
Mahide [E] 80 G3
Mahilyow [BY] 202 C5
Mahlow [D] 34 E2
Mahlsdorf [D] 34 B1
Mahlu [FIN] 186 F3
Mahmutlar [TR] 152 D4
Mahmutsevketpaşa [TR] 150 F2
Mahnala [FIN] 176 E1
Mahón / Maó [E] 104 H5
Mahora [E] 98 C4
Mahovo [HR] 74 F6
Maia [P] 80 B3
Maia [P] 100 E3
Maia [P] 100 E4
Maials [E] 90 H5
Maîche [F] 58 C5
Máida [I] 124 D5
Maidenhead [GB] 14 D4
Maidstone [GB] 14 F5
Maienfeld [CH] 58 H6
Maierato [I] 124 D6
Maijanen [FIN] 194 C7
Maillezais [F] 54 C4
Mailly-le-Camp [F] 44 B5
Mailly-le-Château [F] 56 E2
Mainburg [D] 60 E3
Mainhardt [D] 46 D6
Maintenon [F] 42 E4
Mainua [FIN] 196 E5
Mainz [D] 46 C3
Maiori [I] 120 E4
Maiori, Nuraghe- [I] 118 D2
Mair de Diu de Montgarri [E] 84 G5
Mairena del Alcor [E] 94 H6
Mairena del Aljarafe [E] 94 G6
Maisach [D] 60 D4
Maishofen [A] 72 F1
Maišiogala [LT] 200 G5
Maison-Neuve [F] 44 C6
Maissau [A] 62 E3
Máistir Gaoithe / Mastergeeby [IRL] 4 A4
Maja [HR] 142 A1
Majadahonda [E] 88 F5
Majadas [E] 86 H6
Majadas [E] 88 B6
Majaelrayo [E] 88 H4
Majavatn [N] 190 D4
Majdan [MK] 128 F3
Majdanek [PL] 38 E5
Majdan Królewski [PL] 52 D2
Majdanpek [SRB] 146 D1
Majdanpek [SRB] 204 B6
Majtum [S] 190 H2
Majur [SRB] 142 F2
Makarska [HR] 144 B2
Makaševičy [BY] 202 B6
Makedonski Brod [MK] 128 E2
Mäkela [FIN] 194 F8
Makhnovka [RUS] 198 H4
Mäkikylä [FIN] 186 F5
Mäkitalo [FIN] 194 C6
Mäkkilkylä [FIN] 186 E4
Makkola [FIN] 188 E4
Makljenovac [BIH] 142 D3
Makó [H] 76 F4
Makó-Rákos [H] 76 F4
Makov [SK] 50 F6
Maková Hora [CZ] 48 F5
Makoviš [SRB] 146 A2
Makovo [MK] 128 E3
Maków [PL] 50 H3
Mąkowarsko [PL] 22 C5
Maków Mazowiecki [PL] 38 B1
Maków Podhalański [PL] 50 H4
Makrakómi [GR] 132 F4
Makreš [MK] 146 D6
Mákri [GR] 130 G3
Mákri [GR] 136 E2
Makrochóri [GR] 128 G5
Makrýammos [GR] 130 E4
Makrygialós [GR] 140 G5
Makrynítsa [GR] 132 H2
Makryplágio [GR] 130 D2
Maksamaa / Maxmo [FIN] 186 B2
Maksatiha [RUS] 202 E2
Malå [S] 190 G4
Mala Bosna [SRB] 76 D5
Malacky [SK] 62 G4
Mala Domaša [SK] 64 G2
Maladzyechna [BY] 202 B5
Málaga [E] 102 C4
Malagón [E] 96 F3
Malahide [IRL] 2 F6
Málainn Mhóir / Malin More [IRL] 2 D2
Mała Karczma [PL] 22 E4
Mala Kladuša [BIH] 112 H2
Malăk Porovec [BG] 148 E2
Mala Krsna [SRB] 142 H3
Malalbergo [I] 110 F3
Malá Lehota [SK] 64 B3
Malamoneda [E] 96 E2
Malandríno [GR] 132 G5
Mälarhusen [S] 158 D3
Malaryta [BY] 38 G4
Mala Subotica [HR] 74 F4
Malaucène [F] 106 H3
Malax / Maalahti [FIN] 186 B3
Malaya Vishera [RUS] 202 C1
Malbork [PL] 22 E3
Malbouzon [F] 68 C5
Malbuisson [F] 58 B6
Malcésine [I] 72 C5
Malchin [D] 20 C4
Malchow [D] 20 C5
Malcocinado [E] 96 A5
Malcontenta [I] 110 H1
Malcov [SK] 52 C6
Maldegem [B] 28 G1
Maldon [GB] 14 F4
Małdyty [PL] 22 F4
Malé [I] 72 C4
Malechowo [PL] 22 B3
Máleme [GR] 140 B4
Malenovice [CZ] 50 D6
Malente-Gremsmühlen [D] 18 G2
Måleräs [S] 162 F4
Máles [GR] 140 F5
Malesco [I] 70 F3
Malesherbes [F] 42 F5
Malesína [GR] 134 B4
Malestroit [F] 26 B6
Maletto [I] 124 A8
Malexander [S] 162 E1
Malfourat, Mine de- [F] 66 E4
Malgovik [S] 190 F5
Malhadas [P] 80 G4
Malhao [P] 86 F2
Mália [GR] 140 F4
Malicorne [F] 42 B5
Mali Idjos [SRB] 76 D6
Malikovo [HR] 144 A1
Målilla [S] 162 F3
Mali Lošinj [HR] 112 E4
Malin [IRL] 2 F1
Malin [UA] 202 D7
Málinec [SK] 64 D3
Malines (Mechelen) [B] 30 C3
Malingsbo [S] 166 H1
Maliniec [PL] 36 E3
Malin More / Málainn Mhóir [IRL] 2 D2
Malinska [HR] 112 E2
Mali Prolog [HR] 144 B3
Maliq [AL] 128 D4
Mališevo / Malisheve [SRB] 146 B5
Malisheve / Mališevo [SRB] 146 B5
Maliskylä [FIN] 196 D5
Mali Štupelj [MNE] 146 B5
Malix [CH] 70 H1
Mali Zvornik [SRB] 142 E3
Maljevac [HR] 112 H2
Maljovica [BG] 146 G6
Malkara [TR] 150 B3
Małkinia Górna [PL] 38 D1
Malkkila [FIN] 188 E3
Malko Gradishte [BG] 148 D6
Malko Tŭrnovo [BG] 150 C1
Mal'kovo [RUS] 198 H5
Mallaig [GB] 6 B5
Mallersdorf [D] 60 F2
Málles Venosta / Mals im Vinschgau [I] 72 B2
Malling [DK] 156 D1
Mallnitz [A] 72 G2
Mallow [IRL] 4 C4
Malm [N] 190 C5
Malmbäck [S] 162 D2
Malmberget [S] 192 G6
Malmédy [B] 30 F5
Malmesbury [GB] 12 G3
Malmköping [S] 168 C3
Malmö [S] 156 H3
Malmslätt [S] 166 H5
Malo [I] 72 D5
Małogoszcz [PL] 52 B1
Maloja [CH] 70 H2
Malo-les-Bains [F] 14 H6
Malomirovo [BG] 148 E5
Malónas [GR] 154 D4
Malonno [I] 72 B4
Małopolski [PL] 52 A2
Malorad [BG] 146 G3
Małowidz [PL] 24 B5
Måløy [N] 180 B5
Maloyaroslavets [RUS] 202 F3
Malpartida de Cáceres [E] 86 G5
Malpartida de Plasencia [E] 88 B5
Malpica de Bergantiños [E] 78 C1
Malpica de Tajo [E] 96 E1
Mālpils [LV] 198 E5
Målsåker [S] 168 D3
Malšice [CZ] 48 G6
Mals im Vinschgau / Málles Venosta [I] 72 B2
Malsjö [S] 166 E3
Malsjöbodarna [S] 182 H4
Målsnes [N] 192 F2
Malta [A] 72 H2
Malta [LV] 198 G6
Maltat [F] 56 E5
Maltepe [TR] 150 C5
Maltepe [TR] 150 F3
Maltesholm [S] 158 D2
Malton [GB] 10 G3
Malu [RO] 146 G1
Malung [S] 172 F4
Malungen [N] 172 C4
Malungen [S] 184 E5
Malungsfors [S] 172 F4
Maluszyn [PL] 50 H1
Malva [E] 88 D1
Malveira [P] 86 B4
Malvik [N] 182 C1
Mályi [H] 64 F5
Mały Płock [PL] 24 D5
Malyye Rozhki [RUS] 198 G1
Mamaia [RO] 204 F5
Mamarrosa [P] 80 B6
Mamers [F] 26 G6
Mammola [I] 124 D7
Mamone [I] 118 E3
Mamonovo [RUS] 22 G2
Mám Trasna / Maumtrasna [IRL] 2 B4
Mamure Kalesi [TR] 154 F4
Mamyra [N] 190 B5
Mána [GR] 136 E1
Maňa [SK] 64 B4
Manacor [E] 104 F5
Manamansalo [FIN] 196 E4
Manasija, Manastir- [SRB] 146 C2
Mancha Real [E] 102 E2
Manchester [GB] 10 E4
Manching [D] 60 E2
Manciano [I] 114 G3
Mancier [F] 66 D6
Mandal [N] 164 D6
Måndalen [N] 180 E3
Mándas [I] 118 D6
Mandelieu [F] 108 E5
Mandello del Lario [I] 70 G3
Mandelsloh [D] 32 F1
Manderscheid [D] 44 G1
Mandira [TR] 150 B2
Mándra [GR] 130 H2
Mándra [GR] 134 B6
Mandráki [GR] 154 B3
Mandrikó [GR] 154 C4
Manduria [I] 122 F4
Manerba del Garda [I] 72 B6
Manérbio [I] 72 A6
Manětín [CZ] 48 D4
Mánfa [H] 76 B5
Manfredónia [I] 120 H1
Mangalia [RO] 148 G1
Mangen [N] 166 C1
Manger [N] 170 A3
Mangfall Brücke [D] 60 E5
Mångsbodarna [S] 172 F3
Mangskog [S] 166 E1
Mangualde [P] 80 C6
Manguilla [E] 96 A4
Máni [GR] 130 H1
Maniago [I] 72 F4
Manisa [TR] 152 D3
Manita Peć [HR] 112 G4
Mank [A] 62 D5
Månkarbo [S] 174 E5
Mańki [PL] 22 G4
Manlleu [E] 92 E3
Mannheim [D] 46 C4
Mano [F] 66 C4
Manoláda [GR] 136 B1
Mañón [E] 78 E1
Manorhamilton [IRL] 2 D3
Manosque [F] 108 C4
Manresa [E] 92 D3
Månsåsen [S] 182 G2
Manschnow [D] 34 G2
Mansfeld [D] 34 B4
Mansfield [GB] 10 F5
Mansilla de las Mulas [E] 78 H6
Mansle [F] 54 E6
Manso [F] 114 A3
Mansoniemi [FIN] 186 C6
Mantamádos [GR] 134 H2
Manteigas [P] 86 F2
Mantes-la-Jolie [F] 42 E3
Mantila [FIN] 186 C4
Mantíneia [GR] 136 E2
Mäntlahti [FIN] 178 D4
Mantorp [S] 166 H6
Mantoúdi [GR] 134 B4
Mantova [I] 110 E1
Mäntsälä [FIN] 176 H3
Mänttä [FIN] 186 F5
Mäntyharju [FIN] 178 C1
Mäntyjärvi [FIN] 194 E8
Mäntylahti [FIN] 188 C1
Mäntyluoto [FIN] 176 C1
Manyas [TR] 150 D5
Manzanares [E] 96 F4
Manzanares el Real [E] 88 F5
Manzaneda [E] 78 E5
Manzanera [E] 98 E3
Manzanilla [E] 94 F6
Manzat [F] 68 C1
Maó / Mahón [E] 104 H5
Maqueda [E] 88 E6
Maranchón [E] 90 B5
Maranello [I] 110 E3
Marano di Napoli [I] 120 D3
Marano Lagunare [I] 72 G5
Marans [F] 54 C4
Maratea [I] 120 G5
Marateca [P] 86 B6
Marathiás [GR] 132 F5
Marathókampos [GR] 152 C6
Marathónas [GR] 134 C6
Marathópoli [GR] 136 C4
Maráthos [GR] 140 E4
Marathóvounos (Ulukışla) [CY] 154 G5
Maravillas, Cueva de las- [E] 94 F4
Marbach [D] 46 D6
Marbäck [S] 162 C2
Marbäck [S] 162 E2
Mårbacka [S] 166 E1
Mårbacken [S] 172 E5
Marbella [E] 102 B5
Marboz [F] 68 G1
Marburg [D] 32 D6
Marcali [H] 74 H3
Marčana [HR] 112 D2
Marceddí [I] 118 B5
Marcenais [F] 66 D3
March [GB] 14 F2
Marchaux [F] 58 B4
Marche-en-Famenne [B] 30 D6
Marchegg [A] 62 G4
Marchena [E] 102 A2
Marchenilla [E] 94 G6
Marcheprime [F] 66 C3
Marciac [F] 84 F3
Marciana Marina [I] 114 D2
Marcianise [I] 120 E3
Marcigny [F] 56 E6
Marcilla [E] 84 B5
Marcillac-Vallon [F] 68 B5
Marcillat-en-Combraille [F] 56 C6
Marcilly-le-Hayer [F] 42 H5
Marcinowice [PL] 50 C1
Marciszów [PL] 50 B1
Marckolsheim [F] 58 E2
Mardalsfoss [N] 180 F4
Mardie [F] 42 E6
Mårdsele [S] 190 H4
Mårdsjö [S] 184 C2
Mårdsund [S] 182 G2
Marebbe / St Vigil [I] 72 E3
Máre de Déu de la Balma [E] 98 G1
Mare de Déu del Toro [E] 104 H4
Mårem [N] 170 F5
Måren [N] 170 C2
Marennes [F] 54 B5
Maréttimo [I] 126 A2
Mareuil [F] 54 C3
Mareuil [F] 66 F2
Marevo [RUS] 202 C2
Margarítes [GR] 140 D4
Margaríti [GR] 132 C3
Margate [GB] 14 G5
Margecany [SK] 64 F2
Margherita di Savoia [I] 120 H2
Margonin [PL] 22 B6
Marhaň [SK] 52 D6
Marhanets' [UA] 204 H2
Marhet [B] 44 E1
María [E] 102 H3
Maria Birnbaum [D] 60 D3
Maria de la Salut [E] 104 E5
Maria Dreierchen [A] 62 E3
Mariager [DK] 160 D5
Maria Laach [D] 30 H6
Maria Laach [D] 30 H6
Marialva [P] 80 E5
Maria Martenthal [D] 30 G6
Mariannelund [S] 162 F2
Marianopoli [I] 126 E3
Marianos [P] 86 C4
Mariánské Lázně [CZ] 48 D4
Máriapócs [H] 64 H5
Maria Saal [A] 74 B3
Mariastein [A] 60 F6
Maria Taferl [A] 62 D4
Maria Trost [A] 74 D2
Maria Wörth [A] 74 B3
Mariazell [A] 62 D5
Maribo [DK] 20 A1
Maribor [SLO] 74 E3
Marieby [S] 182 G2
Mariedal [S] 166 E5
Mariedamm [S] 166 H4
Mariefred [S] 168 C3
Mariehamn / Maarianhamina [FIN] 176 A5
Marieholm [S] 158 C2
Marieholm [S] 162 C3
Marielyst [DK] 20 B1
Mariëmont [F] 28 H4
Marienberg [D] 48 D2
Marienberg, Kloster- / Monte Maria, Abbazia di- [I] 72 B2
Marienborn [D] 34 A3
Marienburg [D] 44 G2
Marienheide [D] 32 C5
Marienstatt [D] 32 C6
Marienthal [D] 32 C6
Mariestad [S] 166 F5
Marieux [F] 28 E4
Marifjøra [N] 170 D1
Marignane [F] 106 H5
Marigny-le-Châtel [F] 44 A5
Marihn [D] 20 C4
Marija Bistrica [HR] 74 E5
Marijampolė [LT] 24 E1
Marikostinovo [BG] 130 B2
Marilles [B] 30 D4
Marín [E] 78 B4
Marina [EST] 198 E3
Marina [HR] 116 H1
Marina [I] 108 H3
Marina [I] 118 B6
Marina di Alberese [I] 114 F3
Marina di Amendolara [I] 122 D6
Marina di Árbus [I] 118 B6
Marina di Ardea [I] 116 A6
Marina di Camerota [I] 120 G5
Marina di Campo [I] 114 D3
Marina di Caronía [I] 126 F2
Marina di Carrara [I] 110 D4
Marina di Castagneto-Donorático [I] 114 E1
Marina di Chiéuti [I] 116 F5
Marina di Gáiro [I] 118 E6
Marina di Ginosa [I] 122 E4
Marina di Gioiosa Iónica [I] 124 D7
Marina di Grosseto [I] 114 F3
Marina di Léuca [I] 122 G6
Marina di Massa [I] 110 D4
Marina di Pietrasanta [I] 110 D5
Marina di Pisa [I] 110 D5
Marina di Ragusa [I] 126 F5
Marina di Ravenna [I] 110 H3
Marina di Schiavonea [I] 124 E3
Marina di Vasto [I] 116 E5
Mar'ina Horka [BY] 202 C5
Marinaleda [E] 102 B2
Marina Palmense [I] 116 D2
Marina Romea [I] 110 H3
Marine de Sisco [F] 114 C2
Marinella [I] 126 B3
Marineo [I] 126 D2
Marines [F] 42 F2
Maringues [F] 68 D2
Marinha Grande [P] 86 C3
Marinhais [P] 86 C5
Marinkainen [FIN] 196 C5
Mar'insko [RUS] 198 G2
Mariotto [I] 122 D3
Maristella [I] 118 B3
Maristova [N] 170 E2
Marjalija [E] 96 F2
Marjamaa [EST] 198 D2
Marjaniemi [FIN] 196 C4
Marjovaara [FIN] 188 G2
Markabygd [N] 190 C6
Markaryd [S] 162 C6
Markdorf [D] 58 H4
Marke [B] 28 G2
Market Deeping [GB] 14 E1
Market Drayton [GB] 10 D5
Market Harborough [GB] 14 E2
Markethill [NIR] 2 F4
Market Rasen [GB] 10 G5
Market Weighton [GB] 10 G4
Marki [PL] 38 B2
Markina-Xemein [E] 82 H4
Märkisch Buchholz [D] 34 E3
Markitta [S] 192 H6
Markkina [FIN] 192 H4
Markleugast [D] 46 H3
Markneukirchen [D] 48 C3
Markop [N] 194 B2
Markópoulo [GR] 136 A1
Markópoulo [GR] 136 H1
Markovac [SRB] 146 C1
Markova Sušica [MK] 128 E1
Markovci pri Ptuju [SLO] 74 E4
Markov Manastir [MK] 128 E1
Markovo [BG] 148 E3
Markovo Kale [SRB] 146 D5
Markranstädt [D] 34 C5
Marksburg [D] 46 B2
Markt Bibart [D] 46 F4
Marktbreit [D] 46 E4
Markt Erlbach [D] 46 F5
Marktheidenfeld [D] 46 E4
Markt-Indersdorf [D] 60 E3
Marktjärn [S] 184 D4
Marktl [D] 60 G4
Marktoberdorf [D] 60 C5
Marktredwitz [D] 48 C4
Markt St Florian [A] 62 B4
Markt St Martin [A] 62 F6
Marktzeuln [D] 46 G3
Markušica [HR] 142 E1
Markušovce [SK] 64 F2
Markvarec [CZ] 62 D2
Marl [D] 30 H2
Marlborough [GB] 12 H3
Marle [F] 28 G5
Marlenheim [F] 44 G6
Marlens [F] 70 B3
Marlow [D] 20 C3
Marma [S] 174 E4
Marmande [F] 66 E4
Marmara [TR] 150 C4
Marmaraereğlisi [TR] 150 D3
Marmári [GR] 134 D6
Marmaris [TR] 154 D2
Mármaro [GR] 134 G4
Marmelete [P] 94 B4
Marmolejo [E] 102 D1
Marmore, Cascata delle- [I] 116 A3
Marmoutier [F] 44 G5
Marmuri, Grotta su- [I] 118 D5
Marnay [F] 58 A4
Marne [D] 18 E3
Marnitz [D] 20 B5
Maróneia [GR] 130 F3
Maroslele [H] 76 E4
Maróstica [I] 72 D5
Marotta [I] 112 C6
Marpíssa [GR] 138 E3
Marquartstein [D] 60 F5
Marquion [F] 28 F4
Marquise [F] 14 G6
Marradi [I] 110 F5
Marrebæk [DK] 20 B1
Marrúbiu [I] 118 C5
Marsala [I] 126 B2
Mărşani [RO] 146 G2
Marsberg [D] 32 E4
Marschlins [CH] 58 H6
Marsciano [I] 116 A2
Marseillan [F] 106 E4
Marseillan-Plage [F] 106 E5
Marseille [F] 106 H5
Marseille-en-Beauvaisis [F] 28 D5
Marshavitsy [RUS] 198 H4
Marsico Nuovo [I] 120 G4
Marsico Vetere [I] 120 H4
Marsiliana [I] 114 F3
Marsjö [S] 168 A4
Marsliden [S] 190 E4
Märsta [S] 168 D2
Marstal [DK] 156 D4
Marstrand [S] 160 G1
Märsylä [FIN] 196 C5
Marta [I] 114 G3
Martano [I] 122 G5
Martel [F] 66 G4
Martelange [B] 44 E2
Mártély [H] 76 E4
Marten [BG] 148 D1
Martfű [H] 76 E2
Marthille [F] 44 F5
Marthon [F] 66 F1
Martigné-Ferchaud [F] 40 G5
Martigny [CH] 70 C2
Martigues [F] 106 H5
Martim Longo [P] 94 D4
Martin [SK] 64 C2
Martina / Martinsbruck [CH] 72 B2
Martina Franca [I] 122 E3
Martinci Čepinski [HR] 142 D1
Martín de la Jara [E] 102 B3
Martín de Yeltes [E] 88 B3
Martinet [E] 92 D1
Martinje [SLO] 74 E3
Martíno [GR] 134 B5
Martinsbruck / Martina [CH] 72 B2
Martinsicuro [I] 116 D3
Martinszell [D] 60 E3
Martinvast [F] 26 D2
Mártis [I] 118 C3
Martjanci [SLO] 74 E3
Martna [EST] 198 D2
Martock [GB] 12 F4
Martofte [DK] 156 E3
Martonvaara [FIN] 188 F1
Martonvásár [H] 76 C1
Martorell [E] 92 D4
Martos [E] 102 D2
Mårtsviken [S] 172 E3
Martti [FIN] 194 E6
Marttila [FIN] 176 E4
Maruflar [TR] 152 C3
Maruševec [HR] 74 E4
Marvão [P] 86 F5
Marvejols [F] 68 C5
Marvik [S] 164 B2
Marwałd [PL] 22 G5
Marxwalde [D] 34 F2
Marxzell [D] 46 B6
Marynin [PL] 38 F5
Maryport [GB] 8 D6
Marzabotto [I] 110 F4
Marzahna [D] 34 D3
Marzahne [D] 34 D2
Marzamemi [I] 126 G6
Marzocca [I] 112 C6
Mâsca [RO] 76 H4
Maschen [D] 18 F5
Mas d'Azil, Grotte du- [F] 84 H4
Mas de Barberans [E] 92 A5
Mas de las Matas [E] 90 F6
Masegoso de Tajuña [E] 90 A5
Maser [I] 72 E5
Masevaux [F] 58 D3
Masfjordnes [N] 170 B2
Mashan [AL] 128 C4
Masi [N] 194 B4
Maside [E] 78 C4
Masi Torello [I] 110 G3
Maskjok [N] 194 D2
Masku [FIN] 176 D4
Maslarevo [BG] 148 C3
Maslenica [HR] 112 G4
Maslinica [HR] 116 H1
Maslovare [BIH] 142 C3
Maso [FIN] 186 G3
Maspalomas [E] 100 C6
Massa [I] 110 D4
Massa Fiscaglia [I] 110 G3
Massafra [I] 122 E4
Massa Lubrense [I] 120 E4
Massamagrell [E] 98 F4
Massa Marittima [I] 114 F2
Massat [F] 84 H5
Massay [F] 56 B3
Masseret [F] 66 G2
Masseube [F] 84 G3
Massiac [F] 68 C3
Mastaura [TR] 152 E5
Masterelv [N] 194 B2
Mastergeeby / Máistir Gaoithe [IRL] 4 A4
Masterud [N] 172 D5
Mas Thibert [F] 106 G4
Mastichári [GR] 154 B2
Mästocka [S] 162 B5
Masty [BY] 24 G4
Masugnsbyn [S] 192 H5
Maszewo [PL] 20 G5
Maszewo [PL] 34 G3
Matabuena [E] 88 G4
Mata de Alcántara [E] 86 G4
Mátala [GR] 140 D5
Matalascañas [E] 100 F2
Matalebreras [E] 84 A6
Matallana de Torío [E] 82 B5
Matallana de Toríos [E] 82 B3
Mataporquera [E] 82 E4
Matara [FIN] 188 E1
Matarágka [GR] 132 F2
Mataró [E] 92 E4
Mataruška Banja [SRB] 146 B3
Mätäsvaara [FIN] 196 G6
Matejče, Manastir- [MK] 146 D6
Matelica [I] 116 B2
Matera [I] 122 D4
Matersdalen [N] 170 B5
Mateševo [MNE] 144 E3
Matfors [S] 184 E5
Matha [F] 54 D5
Mathay [F] 58 C4
Mathildedal [FIN] 176 E5
Matignon [F] 26 B4
Matīši [LV] 198 E4
Matka, Manastir- [MK] 128 E1
Matkavaara [FIN] 196 F4
Matlock [GB] 10 E5
Matochina [BG] 150 A1
Matos [P] 94 B2
Matosinhos [P] 80 B4
Matour [F] 56 F6
Mátrafüred [H] 64 E5
Mátraháza [H] 64 E5
Mátraszentimre [H] 64 D5
Mátraterenye [H] 64 E5
Mátraverebély [H] 64 D5
Matre [N] 170 B5
Matre [N] 170 B2
Matrei am Brenner [A] 72 D1
Matrei in Osttirol [A] 72 F2
Matrosovo [RUS] 200 D5
Mattaur [S] 190 G2
Matteröd [S] 158 C1
Mattersburg [A] 62 F6
Mattighofen [A] 60 G4
Mattila [FIN] 188 E6
Mattilanmäki [FIN] 194 E7
Mattinata [I] 116 H6
Mattinen [FIN] 176 C4
Mattmar [S] 182 F2
Mattsee [A] 60 G5
Måttsund [S] 196 B3
Matulji [HR] 112 E1
Matyli [BY] 24 G3
Matzen [A] 60 E6
Matzen [A] 62 F4
Maubeuge [F] 28 G4
Maubourguet [F] 84 F3
Mauchline [GB] 8 D4
Mauerkirchen [A] 60 H4
Maukdal [N] 192 F3
Maula [FIN] 196 C2
Maulbronn [D] 46 C6
Mauléon [F] 54 D2
Mauléon-Licharre [F] 84 D3
Maulévrier [F] 54 D2
Maumtrasna / Mám Trasna [IRL] 2 B4
Maunujärvi [FIN] 194 C6
Maupas, Château de- [F] 56 C3
Maupertus-sur-Mer [F] 26 D2
Maura [N] 172 B5
Maurach [A] 60 E6
Maure [F] 26 B6
Mauriac [F] 68 B3
Maurnes [N] 192 D3
Mauron [F] 26 B6
Maurs [F] 66 H5
Maurstad [N] 180 B5
Maurvangen [N] 170 F1
Maury [F] 106 C6
Mautern [A] 74 C1
Mauterndorf [A] 72 H2
Mauth [D] 62 A2
Mauthausen [A] 62 C4
Mauvezin [F] 84 G2
Mauvoisin [CH] 70 D3
Mauzé-sur-le-Mignon [F] 54 C4
Mavréli [GR] 132 F1
Mavrochóri [GR] 128 E5
Mavrokklísi [GR] 130 H2
Mavroléfki [GR] 130 D3
Mavromáta [GR] 132 F3
Mavromáti [GR] 136 D3
Mavrothálassa [GR] 130 C3
Mavrovi Hanovi [MK] 128 D2
Mavrovo [MK] 128 D2
Mavrovoúni [GR] 132 G2
Mavrovoúni [GR] 136 E5
Maximiliana [E] 102 C4
Maximilians-Grotte [D] 46 H5
Maxmo / Maksamaa [FIN] 186 B2
Maybole [GB] 8 C4
Mayen [D] 30 H6
Mayenne [F] 26 E6
Mayet [F] 42 B6
Maynooth [IRL] 2 F6
Mayoralgo [E] 86 H5
Mayorga [E] 82 B5
Mayrhofen [A] 72 E1
Mäyry [FIN] 186 D3
Mazagón [E] 94 E6
Mazagran [F] 44 C3
Mazamet [F] 106 C4
Mazara del Vallo [I] 126 B3
Mazarrón [E] 104 B4
Mažeikiai [LT] 198 C6
Mazères [F] 106 A4
Mazerulles [F] 44 F5
Mázia [GR] 132 D2
Mazières-en-Gâtine [F] 54 D4
Mazıköy [TR] 154 C2
Mazilmaja [LV] 198 B6
Mazirbe [LV] 198 C4
Mazotos [CY] 154 G6
Mazsalaca [LV] 198 E3
Mazurki [PL] 38 C4
Mazyr [BY] 202 C6
Mazzalve [LV] 198 E6
Mazzarino [I] 126 E4
Mazzarò [I] 124 B8
Mazzarrone [I] 126 F5
M. Bondone [I] 72 C4
Mchowo [PL] 22 H6
M. D. de la Salut [E] 92 F3
M. D. de Pinós [E] 92 D3
M. D. de Queralt [E] 92 D2
Mdzewo [PL] 22 G6
Mealhada [P] 80 B6
Méandre de Queuille [F] 68 C1
Meaux [F] 42 G3
Mechelen (Malines) [B] 30 C3
Mechernich [D] 30 G5
Mechka [BG] 148 C2
Mechowo [PL] 20 F4
Mecidiye [TR] 152 D3
Męcikał [PL] 22 C4
Meckenbeuren [D] 60 A5
Mecsér [H] 62 H5
Meda [P] 80 E5
Medak [HR] 112 G4
Mede [I] 70 F6
Medebach [D] 32 D5
Medelim [P] 86 F3
Medellín [E] 96 A3
Medelser Schlucht [CH] 70 G1
Medemblik [NL] 16 E3
Medena Selišta [BIH] 142 B4
Meden Rudnik [BG] 148 F4
Medenychi [UA] 52 H5
Medet [TR] 152 G6
Medetli [TR] 150 G4
Medevi [S] 166 G5
Medgidia [RO] 204 E5
Medgyesháza [H] 76 G3
Medhamn [S] 166 F3

Murchin [D] 20 E3
Murcia [E] 104 C3
Murciélagos, Cueva de los- [E] 102 C2
Murcielagos, Cueva de los- [E] 102 E5
Murczyn [PL] 36 E1
Mur-de-Barrez [F] 68 B4
Mur-de-Bretagne [F] 26 A5
Mureck [A] 74 E3
Mürefte [TR] 150 C4
Muret [F] 84 H3
Murga [H] 76 B4
Murgados [E] 78 D1
Murgaševo [MK] 128 E3
Murgia / Murguía [E] 82 G5
Murg-Kraftwerk [D] 58 F1
Murguía / Murgia [E] 82 G5
Muri [CH] 58 F5
Murias de Paredes [E] 78 G4
Murieta [E] 82 H6
Murighiol [RO] 204 F5
Murino [MNE] 146 A5
Muriquan [AL] 128 A1
Murjek [S] 196 A2
Murlo [I] 114 F2
Murnau [D] 60 D5
Muro [E] 104 E4
Muro [F] 114 B3
Muro de Alcoy / Muro del Comtat [E] 104 E1
Muro del Comtat / Muro de Alcoy [E] 104 E1
Murole [FIN] 186 E6
Muro Lucano [I] 120 G3
Murony [H] 76 G3
Muros [E] 78 B3
Murowana Goślina [PL] 36 C2
Mürren [CH] 70 E2
Murrhardt [D] 46 D6
Murrisk Abbey [IRL] 2 B4
Murru [EST] 198 D3
Murska Sobota [SLO] 74 E3
Mursko Središće [HR] 74 F4
Murta [RO] 146 G2
Murtas [E] 102 E5
Murten [CH] 58 D6
Murter [HR] 112 G6
Murtinheira [P] 80 A6
Murtolahti [FIN] 188 D1
Murtosa [P] 80 B5
Murtovaara [FIN] 196 F2
Murvica [HR] 112 G5
Mürzsteg [A] 62 D6
Mürzzuschlag [A] 62 E6
Musamaa [FIN] 186 C2
Musasău de Tinca [RO] 76 H2
Musetrene [N] 180 G6
Mussalo [FIN] 178 C4
Musselkanaal [NL] 16 H3
Mussidan [F] 66 E3
Mussomeli [I] 126 D3
Mussy [F] 56 G2
Mustafa Kemal Paşa [TR] 150 E5
Müstair [CH] 72 B3
Mustajärvi [FIN] 186 E5
Mustajõe [EST] 198 G1
Mustalahti [FIN] 186 F5
Mustasaari / Korsholm [FIN] 186 B2
Mustér / Disentis [CH] 70 G1
Mustikkaperä [FIN] 186 F2
Mustinmäki [FIN] 188 D3
Mustinsalo [FIN] 188 D3
Mustjala [EST] 198 C3
Mustla [EST] 198 E3
Mustola [FIN] 194 E4
Mustvee [EST] 198 F2
Muszaki [PL] 22 H5
Muszyna [PL] 52 C5
Muszynka [PL] 52 C5
Muta [SLO] 74 D3
Mutalahti [FIN] 188 H3
Mutanj [SRB] 146 B2
Mutilva [E] 84 B4
Mutlangen [D] 60 B2
Mutriku [E] 82 H4
Muttalip [TR] 150 H5
Mutterstadt [D] 46 B5
Muurame [FIN] 186 G5
Muurasjärvi [FIN] 196 D6
Muurikkala [FIN] 178 D3
Muurla [FIN] 176 F5
Muurola [FIN] 178 D3
Muurola [FIN] 194 C8
Muuruvesi [FIN] 188 D2
Muxía [E] 78 B2
Múzeum Oravskej Dediny [SK] 50 H6
Muzillac [F] 40 E5
Mužla [SK] 64 B5
Mužlja [SRB] 142 G1
Myakishevo [RUS] 198 H5
Mybotn [N] 192 E3
Myckelgensjö [S] 184 F1
Myczków [PL] 52 E5
Myggenäs [S] 160 G1
Myhinpää [FIN] 186 H3
Myjava [SK] 62 H3
Mykínes [GR] 136 E2
Myking [N] 170 F4
Myklebust [N] 180 B5
Myklebust [N] 180 D3
Myklestøyl [N] 164 D3
Mykolaïv [UA] 52 H5
Mykolaïv [UA] 204 G3
Mýkonos [GR] 138 E2
Myllyaho [FIN] 186 F1
Myllykoski [FIN] 178 C3
Myllykselä [FIN] 176 H2
Myllymaa [FIN] 176 E2
Myllymäki [FIN] 186 E4
Mýloi [GR] 136 E2
Mylopótamos [GR] 136 F6
Mylund [DK] 160 E3
Mynämäki [FIN] 176 D4
Myndos [TR] 154 B2
Myonnesos [TR] 152 C5
Myos [TR] 152 D6
Myra [TR] 154 H3
Myrane [N] 164 B4
Myrås [S] 190 G3
Myrdal [N] 170 D3
Myre [N] 192 D3
Myre [N] 192 E3
Myren [S] 172 E5
Myrhorod [UA] 202 F7
Mýrina [GR] 130 F6
Myrina [TR] 152 C3
Myrkky [FIN] 186 B4
Myrmoen [N] 182 D3
Myrnes [N] 192 H1
Myrnyi [UA] 204 G4
Myronivka [UA] 202 E8
Myrskylä / Mörskom [FIN] 178 B3
Myrtiés [GR] 154 A2
Mýrtos [GR] 140 F5
Mýrtou (Çamlıbel) [CY] 154 F5
Myrvika [N] 190 C4
Myrviken [S] 182 G3
Mysen [N] 166 C2
Myšenec [CZ] 48 F6
Myshall [IRL] 4 F4
Myshuryn Rih [UA] 202 F8
Myšlenice [PL] 50 H4
Myślibórz [PL] 34 G1
Myślice [PL] 22 F4
Mysłowice [PL] 50 G3
Mysovka [RUS] 200 D5
Mystegná [GR] 134 H2
Mystrás [GR] 136 E4
Mysubyttseter [N] 180 E5
Myszków [PL] 50 G2
Myszyniec [PL] 24 C5
Mýtikas [GR] 132 D5
Mytilíni [GR] 134 H2
Mytishchi [RUS] 202 F3
Mýtna [SK] 64 D3
Myto [BY] 24 H3
Mýto [CZ] 48 E4
Mzdowo [PL] 22 B3
Mzurki [PL] 36 G5

N

Nå [N] 170 C4
Naamijoki [FIN] 194 B7
Naantali / Nådend [FIN] 176 D4
Naarajärvi [FIN] 188 C4
Naarden [NL] 16 E4
Naarva [FIN] 188 G1
Nääs [S] 160 H2
Naas / An Nás [IRL] 2 F6
Nabaskoze / Navascués [E] 84 C4
Nabbelund [S] 162 H3
Nabburg [D] 48 C5
Náchod [CZ] 50 B3
Nacıvelioba [TR] 150 D5
Nacka [S] 168 E3
Nădab [RO] 76 G3
Nadarzyn [PL] 38 B3
Nadăş [RO] 76 H4
Naddvik [N] 170 E2
Nadela [E] 78 E3
Nådend / Naantali [FIN] 176 D4
Nădlac [RO] 76 F4
Nădlac [RO] 204 B5
Nadrin [B] 30 E6
Nádudvar [H] 76 G1
Nærbø [N] 164 A4
Næstved [DK] 156 F4
Näfels [CH] 58 G6
Náfpaktos [GR] 132 F5
Náfplio [GR] 136 F2
Naggen [S] 184 D5
Naglarby [S] 174 C5
Nagłowice [PL] 52 A2
Nagold [D] 58 G2
Nagu / Nauvo [FIN] 176 D5
Nagyatád [H] 74 H4
Nagybajom [H] 74 H4
Nagybaracska [H] 76 C5
Nagycenk [H] 62 F6
Nagycserkesz [H] 64 G5
Nagydorog [H] 76 B3
Nagyér [H] 76 F4
Nagyfüged [H] 64 E6
Nagygyanté [H] 76 G2
Nagygyimót [H] 74 H1
Nagyhalász [H] 64 H4
Nagyhegyes [H] 64 G6
Nagyhomok [H] 64 H4
Nagyigmánd [H] 64 A6
Nagyiván [H] 64 F6
Nagykálló [H] 64 H5
Nagykanizsa [H] 74 G4
Nagykáta [H] 76 D1
Nagykereki [H] 76 H1
Nagykőllked [H] 74 F2
Nagykónyi [H] 76 B3
Nagykőrös [H] 76 D2
Nagylak [H] 76 F4
Nagylóc [H] 64 D5
Nagymágocs [H] 76 F3
Nagymaros [H] 64 C5
Nagyoroszi [H] 64 C5
Nagypuszta [H] 74 H4
Nagyrábé [H] 76 G1
Nagyszénás [H] 76 F3
Nagyvázsony [H] 74 H2
Naharros [E] 90 A4
Naharros [E] 98 B2
Nahe [D] 18 F3
Nahkiaisoja [FIN] 194 C8
Naila [D] 46 H3
Nailloux [F] 106 A4
Nailsworth [GB] 12 G3
Naipu [RO] 148 C1
Nairn [GB] 6 E5
Najac [F] 66 H6
Nájera [E] 82 G6
Näkkälä [FIN] 194 B5
Nakkesletta [N] 192 G1
Nakkila [FIN] 176 D2
Naklik [PL] 52 E2
Naklo [SLO] 74 B4
Nakło nad Notecią [PL] 22 C6
Nakovo [SRB] 76 F5
Nakskov [DK] 156 E5
Nälden [S] 182 G2
Nałęczów [PL] 38 D5
Nálepkovo [SK] 64 F2
Näljänkä [FIN] 196 F3
Nalkki [FIN] 196 E4
Nalzen [F] 106 A5
Nalžovské Hory [CZ] 48 E6
Nalžovské Hory [CZ] 48 E6
Nambroca [E] 96 F2
Namen (Namur) [B] 30 D5
Náměšť nad Oslavou [CZ] 50 B6
Námestovo [SK] 50 G5
Namlos [A] 60 C6
Namma [N] 172 D4
Nämpnäs [FIN] 186 A4
Namsos [N] 190 C5
Namsskogan [N] 190 D4
Namsvassgardån [N] 190 D4
Namur (Namen) [B] 30 D5
Namysłów [PL] 36 D6
Nanclares de la Oca / Langraiz Oka [E] 82 G5
Nancy [F] 44 E5
Nangis [F] 42 G4
Nannestad [N] 172 B5
Nans-les-Pins [F] 108 C5
Nant [F] 106 E3
Nantes [F] 40 F6
Nanteuil-le-Haudouin [F] 42 G3
Nantiat [F] 54 G6
Nantua [F] 68 H2
Nantwich [GB] 10 D5
Naours, Grottes de- [F] 28 E4
Náousa [GR] 128 F4
Náousa [GR] 138 E3
Näpagård [N] 170 F6
Napi [EST] 198 C2
Naples [TR] 150 C3
Nápoli [I] 120 E3
Na Pomezí [CZ] 50 C3
Naposenaho [FIN] 186 E2
När [S] 168 G5
Nåra [N] 170 A2
Narach [BY] 200 H5
Naraio, Castelo de- [E] 78 D2
Narberth [GB] 12 D1
Narbolía [I] 118 C5
Narbonne [F] 106 D5
Narbonne-Plage [F] 106 D5
Narbuvollen [N] 182 C4
Narcao [I] 118 B7
Nardis, Cascata di- [I] 72 C4
Nardò [I] 122 G5
Narechenski Bani [BG] 148 B6
Narew [PL] 24 F6
Narewka [PL] 24 F6
Närhilä [FIN] 186 G3
Narila [FIN] 188 D5
Narjordet [N] 182 C4
Narkaus [FIN] 194 D8
Narlıca [TR] 150 F4
Narni [I] 116 A4
Naro [I] 126 D4
Naro-Fominsk [RUS] 202 F3
Narol [PL] 52 G2
Narón [E] 78 D4
Närpes / Närpiö [FIN] 186 A4
Närpiö / Närpes [FIN] 186 A4
Narta [HR] 74 G6
Nartháki [GR] 132 G3
Nartkowo [PL] 20 G3
Närtuna [S] 168 E2
Naruska [FIN] 194 F6
Narva [EST] 198 G1
Narva [FIN] 176 F2
Närvä [FIN] 186 G6
Närvä [S] 192 H4
Narva-Jõesuu [EST] 198 G1
Närvijoki [FIN] 186 B3
Narvik [N] 192 E4
Näs [S] 162 D1
Näs [S] 166 G2
Näs [S] 168 F6
Nås [S] 172 G5
Naşa [TR] 152 F2
Näsåker [S] 184 E1
N. Åsarp [S] 162 C1
Năsăud [RO] 204 C3
Nasbinals [F] 68 C5
Näsby [S] 158 G1
Näsbyholm [S] 162 D3
Nascimiento del Río Cuervo [E] 98 C1
Näset [S] 184 D4
Näshulta [S] 168 B3
Našice [HR] 142 D1
Nasielsk [PL] 38 B2
Näsinge [S] 166 C4
Näsland [S] 190 H5
Následovice [CZ] 62 G2
Naso [I] 124 B6
Na Špičáku [CZ] 50 D3
Nassau [D] 46 B2
Nassereith [A] 72 C1
Nässja [S] 166 G5
Nässjö [S] 162 D2
Nässjö [S] 184 D1
Nässvallen [S] 182 F4
Nasswald [A] 62 E6
Nastan [BG] 130 D1
Nästansjö [S] 190 F4
Nastazin [PL] 20 G5
Násteln [S] 182 G4
Nästi [FIN] 176 D3
Nastola [FIN] 178 B3
Nasüm [S] 158 E1
Näsviken [S] 174 E1
Näsviken [S] 190 E6
Nata [CY] 154 F6
Natalinci [SRB] 146 B1
Nätra Fjällskog [S] 184 F2
Nattavaara [S] 196 A1
Nättraby [S] 158 F1
Nattvatn [N] 194 C3
Naturno / Naturns [I] 72 C3
Naturns / Naturno [I] 72 C3
Naucelle [F] 66 H6
Nauders [A] 72 B2
Nauen [D] 34 D2
Naujoji Akmenė [LT] 198 C6
Naul [IRL] 2 F5
Naumburg [D] 34 B6
Naumestis [LT] 200 F4
Naunhof [D] 34 D5
Nausta [S] 190 H2
Naustbukta [N] 190 C4
Naustdal [N] 180 C6
Nauste [N] 180 F3
Naustvika [N] 180 F4
Nautijaure [S] 190 H1
Nautsung [N] 170 B1
Nauvo / Nagu [FIN] 176 D5
Nava [E] 82 C2
Navacelles, Cirque de- [F] 106 E3
Navacerrada [E] 88 F4
Nava de la Asunción [E] 88 E3
Nava del Rey [E] 88 D2
Navahermosa [E] 96 E2
Navahrudak [BY] 202 B5
Navalagamella [E] 88 E5
Navalcán [E] 88 C6
Navalcarnero [E] 88 F6
Navaleno [E] 90 A2
Navalguijo [E] 88 C5
Navalmanzano [E] 88 F3
Navalmoral [E] 88 D5
Navalmoral de la Mata [E] 88 B6
Navalón [E] 98 D6
Navalperal de Pinares [E] 88 E5
Navalpino [E] 96 D3
Navalvillar de Ibor [E] 96 C1
Navalvillar de Pela [E] 96 B3
Navan / An Uaimh [IRL] 2 F5
Nävårdalen [N] 182 B3
Navarredonda de Gredos [E] 88 C5
Navarrenx [F] 84 D3
Navarrés [E] 98 E5
Navarrete [E] 82 G6
Navàs [E] 92 E3
Navascués / Nabaskoze [E] 84 C4
Navas de Estena [E] 96 E2
Navas del Madroño [E] 86 G4
Navas del Rey [E] 88 E5
Navas de Oro [E] 88 E3
Navas de San Juan [E] 102 F1
Navata [E] 92 G2
Navatalgordo [E] 88 D5
Nävekvarn [S] 168 C5
Navelsaker [N] 180 C5
Nave Redonda [P] 94 B4
Näverkärret [S] 166 H2
Navelli [I] 116 C4
Naverstad [S] 166 C4
Naveta des Tudons [E] 104 G4
Navia [E] 78 F2
Navilly [F] 56 G5
Navit [N] 192 H2
Navlya [RUS] 202 E5
Navruz [TR] 150 C5
Naxås [S] 182 F1
Náxos [GR] 138 E3
Naxos [I] 124 B8
Nazaré [P] 86 C3
Nazifoaşa [TR] 150 G5
Nazilli [TR] 152 E5
Nazimovo [RUS] 198 H4
N. Bukovica [HR] 74 H6
N.-D. de Clausis [F] 108 E2
N.-D. de Kerdevot [F] 40 B3
N.-D. de la Salette [F] 68 H5
N.-D. de Lure [F] 108 C3
N.-D. de Miracles [F] 108 E3
N.-D.-du-Haut [F] 58 C3
N.-D. du Mai [F] 108 C6
Ndroq [AL] 128 B3
Néa Anchíalos [GR] 132 H3
Néa Artáki [GR] 134 B5
Néa Epídavros [GR] 136 F2
Néa Fókaia [GR] 130 B6
Néa Kallikráteia [GR] 130 B5
Néa Karváli [GR] 130 D3
Néa Kerdýllia [GR] 130 C4
Néa Koróni [GR] 136 D4
Neale [IRL] 2 C4
Néa Liosia [GR] 134 C6
Néa Mádytos [GR] 130 C4
Néa Makri [GR] 134 C6
Néa Michanióna [GR] 128 H5
Néa Moní [GR] 134 G4
Néa Moudaniá [GR] 130 B5
Neamţ, Mănăstirea- [RO] 204 D3
Neandria [TR] 130 H6
Néa Péramos [GR] 130 D3
Néa Péramos [GR] 134 B6
Néa Plágia [GR] 130 B5
Neápoli [GR] 128 E5
Neápoli [GR] 136 F5
Neápoli [GR] 140 F4
Neapolis [TR] 152 E5
Néa Poteídaia [GR] 130 B5
Néa Róda [GR] 130 C5
Néa Roúmata [GR] 140 B4
Néa Sánta [GR] 130 G2
Néa Stýra [GR] 134 D5
Neath [GB] 12 E2
Néa Tríglia [GR] 130 B5
Néa Výssa [GR] 130 H1
Néa Zíchni [GR] 130 C3
Nebiler [TR] 152 C2
Nebolchi [RUS] 202 C1
Nebra [D] 34 B5
Nechanice [CZ] 50 A3
Neckarelz [D] 46 D5
Neckargemünd [D] 46 C5
Neckargerach [D] 46 D5
Neckarsteinach [D] 46 C5
Neckarsulm [D] 46 D5
Neckenmarkt [A] 62 F6
Necşeşti [RO] 148 B1
Nečtiny [CZ] 48 D4
Neda [E] 78 D1
Nedansjö [S] 184 E4
Nedde [F] 66 H2
Neddemin [D] 20 D4
Neded [SK] 64 A5
Nedelišće [HR] 74 F4
Nederhögen [S] 182 G4
Nedervetil / Alaveteli [FIN] 196 C6
Neder Vindinge [DK] 156 F4
Nedre Eggedal [N] 170 G5
Nedre Gärdsjö [S] 172 H3
Nedre Soppero [S] 192 H4
Nedstrand [N] 164 B2
Nedvědice [CZ] 50 B5
Nędza [PL] 50 E3
Neede [NL] 16 G5
Neermoor [D] 18 B4
Neeroeteren [B] 30 E3
Nefyn [GB] 10 B4
Negorci [MK] 128 G3
Negoslavci [HR] 142 E1
Negotin [SRB] 146 E1
Negotin [SRB] 204 C6
Negotino [MK] 128 F2
Negovanovci [BG] 146 E2
Negrar [I] 72 C6
Negreira [E] 78 B3
Negren-Tino [CH] 70 G2
Négrondes [F] 66 F2
Negru Vodă [RO] 148 G1
Neheim-Hüsten [D] 32 C4
Nehoiu [RO] 204 D5
Neiden [N] 194 E3
Neitisuanto [S] 192 G5
Neittävä [FIN] 196 E4
Nejdek [CZ] 48 D3
Nekromanteío [GR] 132 C3
Neksø [DK] 158 E4
Nelas [P] 80 C6
Nelidovo [RUS] 202 D3
Nellim [FIN] 194 E4
Nellingen [D] 60 B3
Neltaa [FIN] 176 G4
Neman [RUS] 200 D5
Nembro [I] 70 H4
Neméa [GR] 136 E1
Neméa [GR] 136 E1
Nemenčinė [LT] 200 G5
Nemesnádudvar [H] 76 C4
Nemesszalók [H] 74 G1
Németkér [H] 76 C3
Nemila [BIH] 142 D4
Nemours [F] 42 G5
Nemrutkale [TR] 152 C3
Nemška Loka [SLO] 74 C6
Nemšová [SK] 64 A2
Nemti [H] 64 D5
Nemyriv [UA] 52 G3
Nenagh [IRL] 2 D6
Nendeln [FL] 58 H5
Neochóri [GR] 132 E5
Neochóri [GR] 132 F3
Neochóri [GR] 132 F2
Neochóri [GR] 134 A2
Neochóri [GR] 134 C5
Neochóri [GR] 136 B1
Néo Monastíri [GR] 132 G3
Néos Marmarás [GR] 130 C6
Nepi [I] 114 H4
Nepomuk [CZ] 48 E5
Neptun [RO] 148 G1
Nérac [F] 66 E5
Neratovice [CZ] 48 G3
Néré [F] 54 D5
Neresheim [D] 60 C2
Nereta [LV] 198 E6
Nereto [I] 116 D3
Neretva Kanjon [BIH] 144 C2
Nerezine [HR] 112 E3
Nerežišća [HR] 144 A2
Neringa-Nida [LT] 200 D5
Néris-les-Bains [F] 56 C6
Nerja [E] 102 D5
Nerja, Cueva de- [E] 102 D5
Nérondes [F] 56 C4
Nerpio [E] 102 H2
Nerpio, Cuevas de- [E] 102 H2
Nersingen [D] 60 B3
Nerskogen [N] 180 H3
Nerva [E] 94 F5
Nervesa della Battaglia [I] 72 E5
Nervi [I] 110 B3
Nerviano [I] 70 G4
Nes [N] 164 F2
Nes [N] 170 D1
Nes [N] 170 H4
Nes [N] 180 C6
Nes [NL] 16 F1
Nesactium [HR] 112 D2
Nesaseter [N] 190 D4
Nesbyen [N] 170 G4
Nesebŭr [BG] 148 F4
Neset [N] 190 E2
Nesflaten [N] 164 C1
Nesheim [N] 170 C3
Neskaupstaður [IS] 192 D3
Neslandsvatn [N] 164 F3
Nesle [F] 28 F5
Nesna [N] 190 D2
Nesoddtangen [N] 166 B1
Nespereira [P] 80 C3
Nesseby [N] 194 E2
Nesselwang [D] 60 C5
Nestáni [GR] 136 E2
Nestavoll [N] 180 H4
Nesterov [RUS] 24 D1
Nestório [GR] 128 D5
Nesttun [N] 170 B4
Nesvik [N] 164 B2
Neszmély [H] 64 B6
Netolice [CZ] 62 B2
Netretić [HR] 112 G1
Nettancourt [F] 44 C4
Netta Pierwsza [PL] 24 E4
Nettetal [D] 30 F3
Nettuno [I] 120 B1
Nettuno, Grotta di- [I] 118 B3
Neubeckum [D] 32 D3
Neuberg [A] 74 E1
Neuberg an der Mürz [A] 62 D6
Neubrandenburg [D] 20 D4
Neubukow [D] 20 A3
Neubulach [D] 58 G1
Neuburg [D] 60 D2
Neuburg [D] 60 H3
Neuchâtel [CH] 58 C5
Neu Darchau [D] 18 G5
Neudorf [D] 34 A4
Neudorf [D] 46 C5
Neudorf-Platendorf [D] 32 H2
Neuenburg [D] 18 C4
Neuenbürg [D] 46 C6
Neuenburg [D] 58 E3
Neuenhaus [D] 16 G4
Neuenkirchen [D] 18 F5
Neuenstein [D] 32 F6
Neuenstein [D] 46 D5
Neuenstein [D] 46 D5
Neuenwalde [D] 18 D3
Neuer Weg [D] 18 C4
Neufahrn [D] 60 F3
Neuf-Brisach [F] 58 E3
Neufchâteau [B] 44 D2
Neufchâteau [F] 44 D6
Neufchâtel-en-Bray [F] 28 C5
Neufchâtel-sur-Aisne [F] 44 B2
Neufeld [D] 18 E3
Neufelden [A] 62 B3
Neuffen [D] 58 H2
Neugersdorf [D] 48 G1
Neuhaus [D] 18 E3
Neuhaus [D] 18 H5
Neuhaus [D] 32 F4
Neuhaus [D] 46 G2
Neuhaus [D] 46 H4
Neuhaus [D] 60 H3
Neuhausen am Rheinfall [CH] 58 F4
Neuhof [D] 34 E3
Neuhofen an der Krems [A] 62 B4
Neuillé Port-Pierre [F] 54 F1
Neuilly-l'Évêque [F] 58 A3
Neuilly-St-Front [F] 42 H3
Neu-Isenburg [D] 46 C3
Neukalen [D] 20 C4
Neukirch [D] 34 F6
Neukirchen [A] 60 G4
Neukirchen [A] 72 F1
Neukirchen [D] 32 E6
Neukirchen [D] 156 B4
Neukloster [D] 20 A3
Neuland [D] 18 E3
Neulengbach [A] 62 E4
Neulingen [D] 46 C6
Neu Lübbennau [D] 34 F3
Neum [BIH] 144 C3
Neumarkt [A] 60 H5
Neumarkt [A] 74 B2
Neumarkt [D] 46 H5
Neumarkt / Egna [I] 72 D4
Neumarkt-St Veit [D] 60 F4
Neu-Moresnet [B] 30 F5
Neumorschen [D] 32 F6
Neu Mukran [D] 20 D2
Neumünster [D] 18 F3
Neunagelberg [A] 62 C3
Neunburg [D] 48 C5
Neung-sur-Beuvron [F] 56 B2
Neunkirchen [A] 62 E6
Neunkirchen [D] 44 G3
Neunkirchen-Seelscheid [D] 30 H4
Neuötting [D] 60 G4
Neupölla [A] 62 D3
Neuruppin [D] 20 C6
Neu Schrepkow [D] 20 B6
Neuschwanstein [D] 60 C6
Neusiedl am See [A] 62 G5
Neuss [D] 30 G3
Neustadt [D] 18 H3
Neustadt [D] 32 E6
Neustadt [D] 34 C1
Neustadt [D] 34 F6
Neustadt [D] 46 E3
Neustadt [D] 46 G2
Neustadt [D] 48 B1
Neustadt [D] 58 F3
Neustadt [D] 60 E2
Neustadt am Rübenberge [D] 32 F2
Neustadt an der Aisch [D] 46 F5
Neustadt an der Waldnaab [D] 48 C4
Neustadt an der Weinstrasse [D] 46 B5
Neustadt-Glewe [D] 20 A5
Neustift [A] 72 D1
Neustift / Novacella [I] 72 D2
Neustrelitz [D] 20 C5
Neu-Ulm [D] 60 B3
Neuvéglise [F] 68 C4
Neuves-Maisons [F] 44 E5
Neuvic [F] 66 E3
Neuvic [F] 68 B3
Neuville [F] 54 E3
Neuville [F] 68 F2
Neuville-aux-Bois [F] 42 E5
Neuvilly-en-Argonne [F] 44 D3
Neuvola [FIN] 186 H4
Neuvy [F] 54 H4
Neuvy-Bouin [F] 54 D3
Neuvy-sur-Barangeon [F] 56 C3
Neuwied [D] 30 H6
Neuzelle [D] 34 G3
Neveklov [CZ] 48 G4
Nevel' [RUS] 202 C3
Neverfjord [N] 194 B2
Nevers [F] 56 D4
Nevès [E] 92 D2
Nevesinje [BIH] 144 C2
Nevlunghavn [N] 164 G3
Nevossuo [FIN] 178 C3
New Alresford [GB] 12 H4
Newark-on-Trent [GB] 10 F5
Newbiggin-by-the-Sea [GB] 8 G5
Newbliss [IRL] 2 F4
Newbridge / Droichead Nua [IRL] 2 E6
Newburgh [GB] 8 E2
Newbury [GB] 12 H4
Newcastle [NIR] 2 G4
Newcastle Emlyn [GB] 10 A6
Newcastle-under-Lyme [GB] 10 E5
Newcastle upon Tyne [GB] 8 G6
Newcastle West [IRL] 4 C3
New Galloway [GB] 8 D5
Newgrange [IRL] 2 F5
Newhaven [GB] 14 E6
Newinn [IRL] 4 D4
Newmarket [GB] 14 F3
Newmarket [IRL] 4 C4
Newmarket-on-Fergus [IRL] 2 C6
Newport [GB] 10 D5
Newport [GB] 12 F3
Newport [GB] 12 H5
Newport [IRL] 2 C3
Newport [IRL] 4 D3
Newport-on-Tay [GB] 8 F2
Newport Pagnell [GB] 14 E3
New Quay [GB] 10 B6
Newquay [GB] 12 C4
New Romney [GB] 14 F5
New Ross / Ros Mhic Thriúin [IRL] 4 F4
Newry [NIR] 2 F4
Newton Abbot [GB] 12 E5
Newton Le Willows [GB] 10 D4
Newtonmore [GB] 6 D6
Newton Stewart [GB] 8 C5
Newtown [GB] 10 C6
Newtownabbey [NIR] 2 G3
Newtownards [NIR] 2 G3
Newtown Butler [NIR] 2 E4
Newtownhamilton [NIR] 2 F4
Newtownmountkennedy [IRL] 4 G3
Newtownstewart [NIR] 2 F3
Nexon [F] 66 G2
Nežilovo [MK] 128 E2
Niadinge [LT] 24 G2
Niana [I] 70 E4
Nianfors [S] 174 E1
Niaux, Grotte de- [F] 84 H5
Nibe [DK] 160 D4
Nicaj-Shalë [AL] 146 A6
Nicaj Shoshë [AL] 146 A6
Nicastro [I] 124 D5
Nice [F] 108 E4
Nickelsdorf [A] 62 G5
Nicknoret [S] 190 H4
Nicolosi [I] 126 G3
Nicopolis ad Istrum [BG] 148 C3
Nicosia [I] 126 F3
Nicotera [I] 124 C6
Nidda [D] 46 D2
Nidderau [D] 46 D2
Nideck, Château du- [F] 44 G6
Nideggen [D] 30 F5
Nidzica [PL] 22 G5
Niebla [E] 94 F5
Nieborow [PL] 36 H3
Niebüll [D] 156 B4
Nieby [D] 156 C5
Niechanowo [PL] 36 D2
Niechorze [PL] 20 G3
Niedalino [PL] 20 H3
Niederalben [D] 44 H3
Niederalteich [D] 60 G3
Niederau [A] 60 F6
Niederaula [D] 46 E1
Niederbronn-les-Bains [F] 44 H5
Niederelsungen [D] 32 E5
Niederkleen [D] 46 C2
Niederkrüchten [D] 30 F3
Niederndorf [A] 60 F6
Niederoderwitz [D] 48 G1
Nieder Stotzingen [D] 60 C3
Niederwinkling [D] 60 G2
Nieder-Wöllstadt [D] 46 C2
Niederwölz [A] 74 B2
Niedrzwica Duża [PL] 38 E6
Niedźwiedź [PL] 22 E5
Niemce [PL] 38 E5
Niemcza [PL] 50 C2
Niemegk [D] 34 D3
Niemica [PL] 22 A3

Odoyev [RUS] 202 F4
Odranci [SLO] 74 F3
Odry [CZ] 50 E5
Odrzywół [PL] 38 B5
Ødsted [DK] 156 C2
Odum [DK] 160 E6
Odžaci [SRB] 142 E1
Odžak [BIH] 142 D2
Odžak [MNE] 144 E2
Ödzemirci [TR] 152 H4
Odziena [LV] 198 E5
Oebisfelde [D] 34 A2
Oederan [D] 48 D1
Oeding [D] 16 G6
Oeijenbraak [B] 30 D3
Oelde [D] 32 D3
Oelsnitz [D] 48 C2
Oensinger Klus [CH] 58 E5
Oersberg [D] 18 F1
Oetmannshausen [D] 32 F5
Oëtre, Roche d'– [F] 26 F4
Oettingen [D] 46 F6
Oetz [A] 72 C1
Öfehértó [H] 64 H5
Offenbach [D] 46 C3
Offenburg [D] 44 H6
Offenheim [D] 46 B4
Offida [I] 116 C2
Ofir [P] 80 B3
Oforsen [S] 172 F6
Ofte [N] 164 E2
Ogenbargen [D] 18 C4
Oğlansini [TR] 154 F1
Ogliastro Cilento [I] 120 F4
Ognica [PL] 20 E6
Ognjanovo [BG] 130 C1
Ogre [LV] 198 E5
Ogrodzieniec [PL] 50 G2
Ogrosen [D] 34 F4
O Grove [E] 78 B4
Ogulin [HR] 112 G2
Ohat [H] 64 F6
Oheb [CZ] 50 A4
Ohlava [FIN] 196 D3
Ohordorf [D] 32 H1
Ohrdruf [D] 46 G1
Ohrid [MK] 128 D3
Öhringen [D] 46 D5
Ohtola [FIN] 186 D4
Ohuta [H] 64 G4
Oia [GR] 138 F5
Oiã [P] 80 B5
Oia / Arrabal [E] 78 A5
Oijärvi [FIN] 196 D3
Oikarainen [FIN] 194 D8
Oímbra [E] 78 D6
Oinasjärvi [FIN] 176 F4
O Incio [E] 78 E4
Oinoanda [TR] 154 G2
Oinói [GR] 134 B6
Oinoskylä [FIN] 186 F2
Oiron [F] 54 E3
Oirschot [NL] 30 E2
Oisemont [F] 28 D4
Oissel [F] 28 B6
Oisterwijk [NL] 16 D6
Oitti [FIN] 176 H3
Oitylo [GR] 136 E5
Oivu / Äivo [FIN] 196 C6
Öja [FIN] 196 C6
Öjaby [S] 162 D4
Ojakylä [FIN] 196 D5
Ojakylä [FIN] 196 E4
Ojala [FIN] 186 D2
Öjarn [S] 190 E6
Ojców [PL] 50 H3
Öje [S] 172 F3
Öjebyn [S] 196 B3
Ojén [E] 102 B5
Ojo Guareña [E] 82 F4
Ojós [E] 104 C2
Ojos Negros [E] 90 C6
Ojrzeń [PL] 38 A1
Öjung [S] 174 C1
Öjvasslan [S] 182 F6
Okalewo [PL] 22 F6
Okalewo [PL] 22 F6
Okány [H] 76 G2
Økdal [N] 182 B3
Okehampton [GB] 12 D4
Oker [D] 32 G3
Okhtyrka [UA] 202 F7
Okkelberg [N] 182 C1
Oklaj [HR] 112 H5
Oklubalı [TR] 150 H5
Okol [AL] 146 A6
Okonek [PL] 22 B5
Okonin [PL] 22 E5
Okopy [PL] 38 G5
Okoř [CZ] 48 F3
Okors [BG] 148 E2
Okrug [HR] 116 H1
Oksajärvi [S] 192 H5
Oksakoski [FIN] 186 E1
Oksava [FIN] 196 D6
Oksböl [DK] 156 A2
Oksdøl [N] 190 C5
Øksendalen [N] 170 H1
Øksendrup [DK] 156 E4
Øksfjord [N] 192 H1
Oksfjordhamn [N] 192 G1
Øksna [N] 172 C3
Øksnes [N] 192 D4
Okstad [N] 182 C2
Oktiabrs'ke [UA] 204 H4
Oktoniá [GR] 134 C4
Okučani [HR] 142 C1
Okulovka [RUS] 202 D2
Okuninka [PL] 38 F4
Ólafsfjörður [IS] 192 C2
Ólafsvík [IS] 192 A2
Ö. Lagnö [S] 168 E2
Olargues [F] 106 D4
Olaszfalu [H] 76 A2
Oława [PL] 50 D1
Olazagutia / Olazti [E] 82 H5
Olazti / Olazagutia [E] 82 H5
Olba [E] 98 E3
Olbasa [TR] 152 H6
Olbernhau [D] 48 E2
Olbia [I] 118 E3
Olbięcin [PL] 52 E1
Oldcastle [IRL] 2 E5
Oldeberkoop [NL] 16 F3
Oldeide [N] 180 B5
Olden [N] 180 D5
Oldenburg [D] 18 C5
Oldenburg [D] 18 H2
Oldenzaal [NL] 16 G5
Olderdalen [N] 192 G2
Olderfjord [N] 194 C2
Oldervik [N] 192 G2
Oldham [GB] 10 E4
Oldmeldrum [GB] 6 F6
Old Mellifont Abbey [IRL] 2 F5
Oldřichovice [CZ] 50 F5
Oleby [S] 172 E5
Olecko [PL] 24 D3
Oléggio [I] 70 F4
Oleiros [E] 78 B3
Oleiros [E] 78 C2
Oleiros [P] 86 E3
Oleksandriia [UA] 202 F8
Oleksandrivka [UA] 202 E8
Oleksandrivka [UA] 204 G2
Olen [B] 30 D3
Ølen [N] 164 B1
Olèrdola [E] 92 D4
Olesa de Montserrat [E] 92 D4
Oleśnica [PL] 36 D6
Olešnice [CZ] 50 B5
Olesno [PL] 50 F1
Oleszno [PL] 50 H1
Oleszyce [PL] 52 F3
Oletta [F] 114 C3
Olette [F] 92 F1
Olevs'k [UA] 202 C7
Ølgod [DK] 156 B2
Olhain, Château Féodal d'– [F] 28 E3
Olhão [P] 94 C6
Ol'hopil' [UA] 204 E2
Oliana [E] 92 D2
Olia Speciosa [I] 118 D7
Olíena [I] 118 D4
Olingdal [S] 182 G6
Olingsjövallen [S] 182 G6
Olite [E] 84 B5
Oliva [E] 98 F6
Oliva de la Frontera [E] 94 F3
Oliva de Mérida [E] 94 H2
Olivadi [I] 124 D6
Olivares [E] 94 G6
Olivares de Júcar [E] 98 B3
Oliveira de Azeméis [P] 80 B5
Oliveira de Frades [P] 80 C5
Oliveira do Bairro [P] 80 B5
Oliveira do Hospital [P] 86 E2
Olivenza [E] 94 F2
Olivet [F] 42 E6
Olivone [CH] 70 G2
Ol'Ka [SK] 52 D6
Olkkala [FIN] 176 G4
Olkusz [PL] 50 G3
Ollerup [DK] 156 D4
Olliergues [F] 68 D2
Ollikkala [FIN] 178 C1
Ollila [FIN] 176 E4
Öllölä [FIN] 188 G3
Ölmbrotorp [S] 166 H3
Ölme [S] 166 F3
Olmedilla de Alarcón [E] 98 B3
Olmedillo de Roa [E] 88 G2
Olmedo [E] 88 E3
Olmedo [I] 118 B3
Olmeto [F] 114 B5
Ölmhult [S] 166 F2
Olmillos de Sasamón [E] 82 E5
Olocau del Rey [E] 98 F1
Olofsfors [S] 184 H1
Olofström [S] 158 E1
Olombrada [E] 88 F3
Olomouc [CZ] 50 D5
Olon / Oyon [E] 82 H6
Olonzac [F] 106 C4
Oloron–Ste–Marie [F] 84 D3
Olos Fthiotidos [GR] 132 G4
Olost [E] 92 E3
Olot [E] 92 F2
Olovo [BIH] 142 E4
Ołownik [PL] 24 C2
Olpe [D] 32 C5
Øls [DK] 160 D5
Olsätter [S] 166 F2
Olsberg [D] 32 D5
Olsborg [N] 192 F3
Olseröd [S] 158 D2
Ölserud [S] 166 E4
Ol'sha–Dolgaya [RUS] 202 D4
Olshammar [S] 166 G4
Olší [CZ] 50 B5
Ölsremma [S] 162 C2
Olst [NL] 16 F4
Ølstykke [DK] 156 G2
Olszowa Wola [PL] 38 B4
Olsztyn [PL] 22 H4
Olsztyn [PL] 50 G2
Olsztynek [PL] 22 G4
Olszyna [PL] 34 G4
Olszyna [PL] 34 H6
Oltedal [N] 164 B3
Olten [CH] 58 E5
Olteni [RO] 148 D3
Olteniţa [RO] 148 D1
Olteren [N] 192 G3
Oltre il Colle [I] 70 H4
Ölüdeniz [TR] 154 F2
Oluklu [TR] 150 H5
Olula del Río [E] 102 H4
Ólvega [E] 90 C3
Olvera [E] 102 A3
Olympía [GR] 136 C2
Olympiáda [GR] 130 C4
Ólympos [GR] 140 H2
Ólynthos [GR] 130 B5
Olza [PL] 50 E4
Oma, Bosque de– [E] 82 H4
Omagh [NIR] 2 F3
Omalí [GR] 128 E6
Omalós [GR] 140 C5
Oman [BG] 148 E5
Omarska [BIH] 142 B2
Ombygget Stavkirke [N] 170 D2
Omegna [I] 70 F3
Ömerköy [TR] 150 D5
Ömerli [TR] 150 F2
Omiš [HR] 144 A2
Omišalj [HR] 112 E2
Ommen [NL] 16 G4
Ommunddallen [N] 190 B5
Omodos [CY] 154 F6
Omoljica [SRB] 142 H2
Ömossa / Metsälä [FIN] 186 B5
Omsjö [S] 184 E1
Omurtag [BG] 148 D3
Øn [N] 170 B1
Oña [E] 82 F5
Oñati [E] 82 H4
Onda [E] 98 F3
Ondara [E] 104 F1
Ondarroa [E] 82 H4
Ondić [HR] 112 H4
Ö Nësberg [S] 172 F5
Onești [RO] 204 D4
Onguera [E] 82 D2
Onil [E] 104 D1
Onkamo [FIN] 188 G3
Onkamo [FIN] 194 F7
Onkiniemi [FIN] 178 B1
Onnaing [F] 28 G4
Önneköp [S] 158 D2
Onoranza [I] 120 G1
Onsaker [N] 170 H4
Onsevig [DK] 156 E4
Ontiñena [E] 90 G4
Ontinyent [E] 98 E6
Ontojoki Porokylä [FIN] 196 F5
Ontur [E] 98 C6
Önusberg [S] 196 A3
Onuškis [LT] 24 G1
Onzonilla [E] 78 H6
Ooidonk [B] 28 G2
Oola [IRL] 4 D4
Oostburg [NL] 28 G1
Oostduinkerke [B] 28 F1
Oostende (Ostende) [B] 28 F1
Oosterbeek [NL] 16 F5
Oosterend [NL] 16 E1
Oosterhout [NL] 16 D6
Oosterwolde [NL] 16 G3
Oostmalle [B] 30 D3
Ootmarsum [NL] 16 G4
Opaka [BG] 148 D2
Opalenica [PL] 36 B3
Opařany [CZ] 48 F5
Oparić [SRB] 146 C3
Opatija [HR] 112 E1
Opatów [PL] 36 E6
Opatów [PL] 52 D1
Opatówek [PL] 36 E4
Opatowiec [PL] 52 B3
Opava [CZ] 50 E4
Ope [S] 182 G2
Opglabbek [B] 30 E4
Opi [I] 116 C6
O Pino [E] 78 C3
O Pino [E] 78 C3
Opinogóra Górna [PL] 38 B1
Opishnia [UA] 202 F7
Opladen [D] 30 G4
Oplenac, Manastir– [SRB] 146 B1
Opletnya [BG] 146 F4
Oploo [NL] 30 F2
Oplotnica [SLO] 74 D4
Opochka [RUS] 198 H5
Opočno [CZ] 50 B3
Opoczno [PL] 38 A5
Opole [PL] 50 E2
Opole Lubelskie [PL] 38 D6
Opol'ye [RUS] 178 F6
Oporów [PL] 36 G3
O Porriño [E] 78 B5
Opovo [SRB] 142 G2
Oppach [D] 34 G6
Oppaker [N] 172 C5
Oppdal [N] 180 H3
Oppdøl [N] 180 F3
Oppeby [S] 162 F1
Oppedal [N] 170 B2
Oppegård [N] 166 B1
Oppenau [D] 58 F2
Oppenheim [D] 46 C3
Oppheim [N] 170 C3
Opphus [N] 172 C2
Oppido Lucano [I] 120 H3
Oppido Mamertina [I] 124 C7
Oppidum d'Ensérune [F] 106 D4
Oppola [RUS] 188 G5
Opponitz [A] 62 C5
Oppsal [N] 164 B3
Opsa [BY] 200 H4
Ópusztaszer [H] 76 E4
Opuzen [HR] 144 B3
Orá [CY] 154 G6
Öra [S] 162 C1
Ora / Auer [I] 72 D4
Oradea [RO] 76 H2
Orahovac [SRB] 146 B6
Orahov Do [BIH] 144 C3
Orahovica [HR] 142 D1
Orahovlje [BIH] 144 B2
Oraison [F] 108 C3
Orajärvi [FIN] 194 C7
Orange [F] 106 G3
Orani [I] 118 D4
Oranienbaum [D] 34 C4
Oranienburg [D] 34 E1
Oranmore [IRL] 2 C5
Oraovica [SRB] 146 D4
Öras [N] 182 C2
Orašac [BIH] 112 H3
Orašac [MK] 146 D6
Orašac [SRB] 146 D4
Orasi [F] 114 B6
Orašje [BIH] 142 E2
Orăştie [RO] 204 C5
Oravainen / Oravais [FIN] 186 C2
Oravais / Oravainen [FIN] 186 C2
Öravan [S] 190 G5
Oravasaari [FIN] 186 G4
Oravi [FIN] 188 E4
Oravijoki [FIN] 196 E5
Oravikoski [FIN] 188 D3
Oravisalo [FIN] 188 F3
Oraviţa [RO] 204 B5
Oravská Lesná [SK] 50 G5
Oravská Polhora [SK] 50 G5
Oravský Podzámok [SK] 50 G6
Orba [E] 104 F1
Ørbæk [DK] 156 E3
Orbassano [I] 70 D6
Orbe [CH] 58 C6
Orbeasca [RO] 148 B1
Orbec [F] 26 G4
Orbetello [I] 114 F4
Orbey [F] 58 D2
Ørby [DK] 156 E1
Örbyhus [S] 174 F5
Örbyhus [S] 174 F5
Orca [P] 86 F3
Orcera [E] 102 G1
Orches [F] 54 F3
Orchies [F] 28 F3
Orchomenós [GR] 132 H5
Orchomenós [GR] 132 H5
Orchomenós [GR] 136 D2
Orcières [F] 70 A6
Orderud [N] 166 C2
Ordes [E] 78 C2
Ordino [AND] 84 H6
Orduña [E] 82 G4
Ore [S] 184 H1
Orebić [HR] 144 B3
Örebro [S] 166 H3
Öregrund [S] 174 G5
Orehova vas Rače [SLO] 74 E4
Orehoved [DK] 156 F4
Orehovica [BG] 148 A2
Orehovno [RUS] 198 H2
Oreiní [GR] 130 C3
Orel [RUS] 202 F5
Ören [TR] 152 C2
Ören [TR] 152 G2
Ören [TR] 154 C1
Ören [TR] 154 F2
Örencık [TR] 150 C6
Örencik [TR] 152 G1
Örenkaya [TR] 152 H3
Orense / Ourense [E] 78 C5
Oreoí [GR] 134 A3
Oresak [BG] 148 B4
Oreshari [BG] 130 G1
Orestiáda [GR] 130 H1
Öreström [S] 190 H5
Oresvika [N] 190 D2
Öreyd [S] 162 C3
Orgáni [GR] 130 G2
Organyà [E] 92 D2
Orgaz [E] 96 F2
Orgelet [F] 56 H6
Orgenvika [N] 170 G5
Orgeval [F] 42 F3
Orgjost [AL] 128 C1
Orgnac–l'Aven [F] 106 G2
Orgon [F] 106 H4
Orgosolo [I] 118 D4
Orgovány [H] 76 D3
Orhaneli [TR] 150 F5
Orhangazi [TR] 150 F4
Orhanıye [TR] 130 H3
Orhanlar [TR] 150 D5
Orhanli [TR] 152 C4
Orhei [MD] 204 E3
Ør. Hvidbjerg [DK] 160 C4
Oria [E] 102 H4
Oria [I] 122 F4
Orihuela [E] 104 D3
Orihuela del Tremedal [E] 98 D1
Orikhiv [UA] 204 H2
Orikum [AL] 128 A6
Orikum [AL] 128 A6
Orimattila [FIN] 178 B3
Orio [E] 84 B2
Oriolo [I] 122 D5
Oripää [FIN] 176 E3
Orismala [FIN] 186 C3
Orissaare [EST] 198 C3
Oristano [I] 118 C5
Őriszentpéter [H] 74 F3
Orivesi [FIN] 186 E6
Orizare [BG] 148 F4
Ørjarvik [N] 180 E2
Ørje [N] 166 C2
Órjiva [E] 102 E5
Orkanger [N] 180 H1
Örkelljunga [S] 158 C1
Örkény [H] 76 D2
Orléans [F] 42 E6
Orlík nad Vltavou [CZ] 48 F5
Orlík nad Vltavou [CZ] 48 F5
Orlovat [SRB] 142 G1
Orly [F] 42 F4
Orly [RUS] 178 E6
Orlya [BY] 24 H4
Orlyak [BG] 148 F2
Orlyane [BG] 148 A3
Ormanlı [TR] 150 D2
Ormea [I] 108 G3
Ormemyr [N] 164 F1
Örménykút [H] 76 F2
Ormestad [N] 164 D6
Órmos [GR] 128 H5
Órmos [GR] 138 D1
Órmos Panagías [GR] 130 C5
Órmos Prínou [GR] 130 E4
Ormož [SLO] 74 E4
Ormsjö [S] 190 F5
Ormskirk [GB] 10 D4
Ornans [F] 58 B5
Ornäs [S] 174 C4
Ornavasso [I] 70 F3
Örnberg [FIN] 186 B2
Ornes [N] 190 D4
Orneta [PL] 22 G3
Ørnhøj [DK] 160 B6
Örnsköldsvik [S] 184 G2
Orolik [HR] 142 E1
Oron–la–Ville [CH] 70 C1
Oropa, Santuário d'– [I] 70 E4
Oropesa [E] 88 C6
Oropesa del Mar / Orpesa [E] 98 G3
Orošac [HR] 144 C4
Orosei [I] 118 E4
Orosháza [H] 76 F3
Oroso [E] 78 C3
Oroszlány [H] 64 B6
Oroszló [H] 76 B4
Ørpen [N] 170 G5
Orpesa / Oropesa del Mar [E] 98 G3
Orpington [GB] 14 E4
Orre [N] 164 A3
Orrefors [S] 162 F5
Orrfors [S] 194 B8
Orrliden [S] 172 E2
Orrviken [S] 182 G2
Orsa [S] 172 G3
Orsala [S] 172 G5
Orsara di Púglia [I] 120 G2
Örsås [S] 162 B3
Orscholz [D] 44 F3
Örsebo [S] 162 E1
Örserum [S] 162 D1
Orsha [BY] 202 C4
Orsières [CH] 70 C3
Örsjö [S] 162 F5
Ørskog [N] 180 D3
Ørslev [DK] 156 G4
Örslösa [S] 166 E5
Ørsnes [N] 180 D3
Orsogna [I] 116 D5
Orsomarso [I] 120 H6
Orşova [RO] 204 C6
Orsoya [BG] 146 F2
Ørsta [N] 180 C4
Orsta [S] 168 A2
Ørsted [DK] 160 E5
Örsundsbro [S] 168 D2
Ort [A] 60 H4
Ortaca [TR] 150 B5
Ortaca [TR] 154 E2
Ortakent [TR] 154 B2
Ortaklar [TR] 152 D5
Ortaköy [TR] 150 H3
Ortaköy [TR] 152 E6
Orta Nova [I] 120 G2
Ortaoba [TR] 150 C5
Orta San Giúlio [I] 70 F4
Orte [I] 116 A4
Ortenberg [D] 46 D2
Ortenburg [D] 60 H3
Orth [A] 62 F4
Orthez [F] 84 D2
Orthovoúni [GR] 132 E1
Ortigueira [E] 78 E1
Ørting [DK] 156 D1
Ortisei / St Ulrich [I] 72 D3
Orţişoara [RO] 76 G5
Ortnevik [N] 170 C2
Orto [F] 114 B4
Örtomta [S] 168 B5
Ortona [I] 116 E4
Ortrand [D] 34 E5
Orträsk [S] 190 H5
Ortu [I] 118 C6
Ortueri [I] 118 C5
Öru [EST] 198 F3
Oruçoğlu [TR] 150 F2
Ørum [DK] 160 D5
Ørum [DK] 160 E5
Orume [I] 118 D4
Orup [S] 158 D3
Orval, Abbaye d'– [B] 44 D2
Orvalho [P] 86 E3
Ørvella [N] 164 F2
Orvieto [I] 114 H3
Örviken [S] 196 A4
Orvinio [I] 116 B5
Oryahovec [BG] 130 E1
Oryakhovo [BG] 146 G2
Ö. Ryd [S] 168 B5
Orzechowo [PL] 22 E6
Orzesze [PL] 50 F3
Orzhytsia [UA] 202 E7
Orzinuovi [I] 70 H5
Orzola [E] 100 E5
Orzysz [PL] 24 C4
Os [N] 182 C4
Os [S] 162 D4
Osa [N] 170 D3
Osby [S] 162 C6
Oschatz [D] 34 D5
Oschersleben [D] 34 B3
Öschiri [I] 118 D3
Ościłowo [PL] 38 A1
Ose [N] 164 D3
Øse [N] 192 F4
Osečina [SRB] 142 F3
Oseja de Sajambre [E] 82 C3
Osen [N] 190 B5
Osenets [BG] 148 D2
Osera de Ebro [E] 90 F4
Osidda [I] 118 D4
Osie [PL] 22 D4
Osieczna [PL] 22 D4
Osieczna [PL] 36 C4
Osiecznica [PL] 34 H3
Osiek [PL] 22 E4
Osiek [PL] 52 D2
Osijek [HR] 76 C6
Osikovitsa [BG] 146 G4
Osilo [I] 118 C3
Osimo [I] 116 C1
Osinja [BIH] 142 C2
Osinów [PL] 34 F1
Osíou Louká, Moní– [GR] 132 H5
Osipaonica [SRB] 142 H3
Osjaków [PL] 36 F6
Osječenica [MNE] 144 D4
Oskal [N] 194 B4
Oskar [S] 162 F5
Oskar–Fredriksborg [S] 168 E3
Oskarshamn [S] 162 G3
Oskarström [S] 162 B5
Øskendalsøra [N] 180 F3
Oskowo [PL] 22 C2
Osl'any [SK] 64 B3
Osli [H] 62 G6
Oslo [N] 166 B1
Øsløs [DK] 160 C3
Osma [FIN] 194 D3
Osmancalı [TR] 152 C3
Osmaneli [TR] 150 G4
Osmankalfalar [TR] 152 H6
Osmanlar [TR] 152 C1
Osmanli [TR] 150 B2
Os'mino [RUS] 198 H1
Osmjany [BY] 202 A5
Ösmo [S] 168 D4
Osmoy–St–Valery [F] 28 C4
Osnabrück [D] 32 D2
Osnäs [FIN] 176 C4
Ośno Lubuskie [PL] 34 G2
Osoblaha [CZ] 50 D3
Osor [E] 92 F3
Osor [HR] 112 E3
Osorno la Mayor [E] 82 D5
Osowiec [PL] 24 E4
Osowo Lęborskie [PL] 22 C2
Osowo Leśne [PL] 22 D4
Osøyro [N] 170 B4
Os Peares [E] 78 D5
Ospedaletti [I] 108 F4
Ospitaletto [I] 72 A6
Ossa [GR] 130 B4
Ossa de Montiel [E] 96 H5
Ossiach [A] 74 B3
Ossjøen [N] 170 E4
Östansjö [S] 166 G4
Östansjö [S] 182 G6
Östansjö [S] 190 G3
Östanvik [S] 172 H3
Ostarije [HR] 112 G2
Ostashkov [RUS] 202 D2
Ostaszewo [PL] 22 E3
Östavall [S] 184 C4
Ostbevern [D] 32 C3
Østbirk [DK] 156 C1
Østby [N] 172 E2
Osted [DK] 156 G3
Ostellato [I] 110 G3
Østenå [N] 164 F2
Ostende (Oostende) [B] 28 F1
Østerbo [N] 166 C3
Østerbø [N] 170 E3
Osterburg [D] 34 B1
Osterburken [D] 46 D5
Österbybruk [S] 174 F5
Østerby Havn [DK] 160 F3
Österbymo [S] 162 E2
Osterede [S] 184 D3
Österfärnebo [S] 174 E5
Österforse [S] 184 E2
Östergraninge [S] 184 E3
Osterhever [D] 18 E2
Osterhofen [D] 60 G3
Osterholz–Scharmbeck [D] 18 D5
Øster Hurup [DK] 160 E4
Østerild [DK] 160 C3
Østerlars [DK] 158 E4
Österlövsta [S] 174 F5
Østermarie [DK] 158 E4
Östermark / Teuva [FIN] 186 B4
Östermiething [A] 60 G4
Osterncappeln [D] 32 D2
Östernoret [S] 190 F5
Österö [FIN] 186 B1
Osterode [D] 32 G4
Österreichisches Freilichtmuseum [A] 74 D2
Östersund [S] 182 G2
Östersundom [FIN] 176 H5
Østerud [N] 164 G1
Øster Ulslev [DK] 20 B1
Österunda [S] 168 C2
Östervåla [S] 174 E5
Östervallskog [S] 166 C2
Øster Vrå [DK] 160 E3
Ostfildern [D] 58 H1
Östfora [S] 168 C1
Östhammar [S] 174 G5
Ostheim [D] 46 F2
Osthofen [D] 46 B4
Ostia [I] 114 H6
Ostíglia [I] 110 F2
Ostiz [E] 84 B3
Ostland [D] 16 G1
Östloning [S] 184 E4
Östmark [S] 172 E5
Östnäs [S] 196 A6
Östomsjön [S] 172 E1
Ostra [I] 112 C6
Östraby [S] 158 C2
Ostrach [D] 58 H3
Östra Ed [S] 162 G1
Östra Frölunda [S] 162 B3
Östra Husby [S] 168 B5
Östra Kärne [S] 166 G2
Östra Luka [BIH] 142 B2
Ostrava [CZ] 50 E4
Östra Yttermark [FIN] 186 A4
Østre Kile [N] 164 E3
Ostrelj [BIH] 142 A3
Ostritz [D] 48 G1
Ostróda [PL] 22 G4
Ostrog, Manastir– [MNE] 144 E4
Ostroh [UA] 202 B8
Ostrołęka [PL] 24 C6
Ostromecko [PL] 22 D6
Ostroróg [PL] 36 B2
Ostros [MNE] 128 A1
Ostrov [CZ] 48 D3
Ostrov [RUS] 178 F2
Ostrov [RUS] 198 G4
Ostrovcy [RUS] 198 G2
Ostrov nad Oslavou [CZ] 50 B5
Ostrovo [BG] 148 D2
Ostrowice [PL] 20 G4
Ostrowiec [PL] 22 B3
Ostrowiec Świętokrzyski [PL] 52 C1
Ostrowite [PL] 22 D5
Ostrowite [PL] 36 E2
Ostrów Lubelski [PL] 38 E5
Ostrów Mazowiecka [PL] 38 D1
Ostrów Wielkopolski [PL] 36 E5
Ostrožac [BIH] 112 H3
Ostrožac [BIH] 144 C1
Ostrožany [PL] 38 E2
Ostrzeszów [PL] 36 E5
Ostuni [I] 122 F3
Ostvik [S] 196 A4
Østvika [N] 190 D4
Ostwald [F] 44 H6
Osuna [E] 102 B3
Oswestry [GB] 10 C5
Oświęcim [PL] 50 G4
Osztopán [H] 74 H4
Otalampi [FIN] 176 G4
Otanmäki [FIN] 196 E5
Otanów [PL] 20 F6
Otava [FIN] 188 C6
Otelec [RO] 76 F6
Otepää [EST] 198 F3
Oteren [N] 192 G2
Oterma [FIN] 196 E4
Otero de Bodas [E] 80 H3
Oteševo [MK] 128 D4
Otivar [E] 102 D5
Otley [GB] 10 F3
Otmuchów [PL] 50 D3
Otnes [N] 182 C6
Otočac [HR] 112 G3
Otočec [SLO] 74 D5
Otok [HR] 142 E2
Otok [SLO] 74 B6
Otoka [BIH] 142 A2
Otorowo [PL] 36 C2
Otradnoye [RUS] 178 G2
Otranto [I] 122 H5
Otrić [HR] 112 H4
Otrokovice [CZ] 50 D6
Otsa [EST] 198 F3
Otsagi / Ochagavía [E] 84 C4
Otta [N] 180 G6
Ottana [I] 118 D4
Ottaviano [I] 120 E3
Ottenby [S] 158 G1
Ottenschlag [A] 62 D4
Ottensheim [A] 62 B4
Ottenstein [A] 62 D3
Otterbach [D] 44 H3
Otterbäcken [S] 166 F4
Otterlo [NL] 16 E5
Otterndorf [D] 18 E3
Ottersberg [D] 18 E5
Otterup [DK] 156 D3
Öttevény [H] 62 H6
Ottnang [A] 62 A4
Ottobeuren [D] 60 C4
Ottobiano [I] 70 F5
Ottone [I] 110 B3
Ottsjö [S] 182 E2
Ottweiler [D] 44 G3
Ö. Tvärásel [S] 196 A3
Otwock [PL] 38 C3
Ouanne [F] 56 E2
Oucques [F] 42 D6
Oud Beijerland [NL] 16 C5
Ouddorp [NL] 16 B5
Oudenaarde (Audenarde) [B] 28 G2
Oude–Pekela [NL] 16 H2
Oudewater [NL] 16 D5
Oughterard [IRL] 2 C4
Ouistreham [F] 26 F3
Oulainen [FIN] 196 D5
Oullins [F] 68 F3
Oulu / Uleåborg [FIN] 196 D4
Oulunsalo [FIN] 196 D4
Oulx [I] 70 B5
Ounas [FIN] 196 E5
Oundle [GB] 14 E2
Oura [P] 80 E3
Ouranoúpoli [GR] 130 D5
Ourense / Orense [E] 78 C5
Ourique [P] 94 C4
Ourol [E] 78 E2
Ourscamps, Abbaye d'– [F] 28 F6
Oust [F] 84 G5
Outes [E] 78 B3
Outokumpu [FIN] 188 E2
Ouzouer–le–Marché [F] 42 D6
Ovabaşı [TR] 154 F4
Ovacık [TR] 152 E4
Ovacık [TR] 152 F4
Ovacık [TR] 154 H1

Schlaitz [D] 34 C4
Schlanders / Silandro [I] 72 C3
Schlangenbad [D] 46 B3
Schleching [D] 60 F5
Schleiden [D] 30 F5
Schleiz [D] 48 B2
Schleswig [D] 18 F1
Schleusingen [D] 46 G2
Schlieben [D] 34 E4
Schlierbach [A] 62 B5
Schliersee [D] 60 E5
Schlitz [D] 20 C4
Schlitz [D] 46 E1
Schllerten [D] 32 G3
Schloss [D] 46 C5
Schlosshof [A] 62 G4
Schlosspark [F] 44 H5
Schlotheim [D] 32 H5
Schluchsee [D] 58 F3
Schlüchtern [D] 46 E2
Schluderbach / Carbonin [I] 72 E3
Schluderns / Sluderno [I] 72 C3
Schlüssberg [A] 62 B4
Schlüsselfeld [D] 46 F4
Schlutup [D] 18 H3
Schmalkalden [D] 46 F1
Schmallenberg [D] 32 D5
Schmidmühlen [D] 48 B6
Schmilka [D] 48 F1
Schmölln [D] 20 E5
Schmölln [D] 48 C1
Schnackenburg [D] 20 A6
Schnaittenbach [D] 48 B5
Schneeberg [D] 48 D2
Schneverdingen [D] 18 F5
Schober Pass [A] 74 C1
Schöder [A] 74 B2
Schöllkrippen [D] 46 D3
Schönau [D] 58 E3
Schönbach [A] 62 D4
Schönbeck [D] 20 D4
Schönberg [A] 72 D1
Schönberg [D] 18 G2
Schönberg [D] 18 H3
Schönberg [D] 48 C3
Schönberg [D] 60 H2
Schönbergerstrand [D] 18 G2
Schönborn [A] 62 E4
Schönebeck [D] 20 B6
Schönebeck [D] 34 B3
Schönecken [D] 44 F1
Schongau [D] 60 D5
Schönhagen [D] 18 G1
Schöningen [D] 32 H3
Schönleiten [D] 60 D3
Schönmünzach [D] 58 F1
Schöntal [D] 46 D5
Schönthal [D] 48 C5
Schönwald [D] 58 F3
Schönwalde [D] 18 H2
Schönwalde [D] 34 E2
Schoondijke [NL] 28 G1
Schoonebeek [NL] 16 G4
Schoonhoven [NL] 16 D5
Schoonoord [NL] 16 G3
Schopfheim [D] 58 E4
Schopfloch [D] 46 F6
Schöppenstedt [D] 32 H3
Schoppernau [A] 60 B6
Schöppingen [D] 16 H5
Schorndorf [D] 60 B2
Schotten [D] 46 D2
Schramberg [D] 58 F2
Schrems [A] 62 D3
Schriesheim [D] 46 C4
Schrobenhausen [D] 60 D3
Schröcken [A] 72 B1
Schruns [A] 72 A1
Schull [IRL] 4 B5
Schüpfheim [CH] 58 E6
Schuttertal [D] 58 E2
Schüttorf [D] 16 H5
Schwaan [D] 20 B3
Schwabach [D] 46 G5
Schwabhausen [D] 46 G1
Schwabhausen [D] 60 D4
Schwäbisch Gmünd [D] 60 B2
Schwäbisch Hall [D] 46 E6
Schwabmünchen [D] 60 C4
Schwaförden [D] 18 D6
Schwaigern [D] 46 D5
Schwalenberg [D] 32 E3
Schwalmstadt-Treysa [D] 32 E6
Schwalmstadt-Ziegenhain [D] 32 E6
Schwanbeck [D] 20 D4
Schwanden [CH] 58 G6
Schwandorf [D] 48 B5
Schwanebeck [D] 34 A3
Schwanenstadt [A] 62 A5
Schwanewede [D] 18 D5
Schwaney [D] 32 E4
Schwarmstedt [D] 32 F1
Schwarzach [A] 72 G1
Schwarzburg [D] 46 G2
Schwarzenau [A] 62 D3
Schwarzenbach [D] 48 B3
Schwarzenbek [D] 18 G4
Schwarzenberg [D] 48 D2
Schwarzenfeld [D] 48 B5
Schwarzenfels [D] 46 E2
Schwarze Pumpe [D] 34 F5
Schwarzsee [CH] 70 D1
Schwaz [A] 72 E1
Schwechat [A] 62 F4
Schweden-Stein [D] 34 C5
Schwedt [D] 20 E6
Schwegenheim [D] 46 B5
Schweich [D] 44 G2
Schweinfurt [D] 46 F3
Schweitenkirchen [D] 60 E3
Schwelm [D] 30 H3
Schwenningen [D] 58 F3
Schwerin [D] 20 A4
Schwerte [D] 32 C4
Schwetzingen [D] 46 C5
Schwittersdorf [D] 34 B4
Schwuelper [D] 32 G2
Schwyz [CH] 58 F6
Sciacca [I] 126 C3
Sciara del Fuoco [I] 124 C5
Scicli [I] 126 F5
Scilla [I] 124 C7
Ścinawa [PL] 36 B5
Scoglitti [I] 126 F5
S. Colombano al Lambro [I] 70 G6
Scopello [I] 70 E4
Scopello [I] 126 B1
Scordia [I] 126 F4
Scorzè [I] 72 E6
Scotch Corner [GB] 10 F2
Scourie [GB] 6 D2
Scrabster [GB] 6 F2
Scrignac [F] 40 C2
Scritto [I] 116 A1
Scunthorpe [GB] 10 G4
Scuol [CH] 72 B2
Scupi [MK] 128 E1
S. Damiano Macra [I] 108 F2
S. Doménico [I] 70 E2
Seaford [GB] 14 E6
Seaham [GB] 8 G6
Seara [E] 78 E5
Seatoller [GB] 10 D1
Seaton [GB] 12 F4
Sebbersund [DK] 160 D4
Sebečevo [SRB] 146 B4
Sebeş [RO] 204 C5
Sebezh [RUS] 198 H5
Sebnitz [D] 48 F1
Seč [CZ] 48 E5
Seč [CZ] 50 A4
Sećanj [SRB] 142 H1
Secemin [PL] 50 H2
Séchault [F] 44 C3
Seckau [A] 74 C1
Seclin [F] 28 F3
Secondigny [F] 54 D3
Sečovce [SK] 64 G3
Sečovlje [SLO] 112 D1
Seda [LT] 200 D3
Sedan [F] 44 D2
Sedbergh [GB] 10 E2
Sedelsberg [D] 18 C5
Sedemte Prestola, Manastir– [BG] 146 F4
Séderon [F] 108 B2
Sédico [I] 72 E4
Sédilo [I] 118 C4
Sédini [I] 118 C3
Sedlčany [CZ] 48 F5
Sedlec [CZ] 48 H4
Sedlec-Prčice [CZ] 48 G5
Sedlice [CZ] 48 E5
Sedrun [CH] 70 F1
Šeduva [LT] 200 F4
Sędziszów [PL] 52 D3
See [A] 72 B1
Seebach [A] 74 B2
Seeboden [A] 72 H2
Seebruck [D] 60 F5
Seefeld in Tyrol [A] 72 D1
Seehausen [D] 20 A6
Seehausen [D] 34 B3
Seehausen [D] 34 D4
Seehof [A] 62 D5
Seekirchen [A] 60 G5
Seelbach [D] 58 E2
Seeling-stadt [D] 48 C1
Seelisberg Tunnel [CH] 58 F6
Seelow [D] 34 F2
Seem [DK] 156 B3
Seeon [D] 60 F5
Seeon [D] 60 F5
Seerhausen [D] 34 E5
Sées [F] 26 F5
Seesen [D] 32 G3
Seeshaupt [D] 60 D5
Seethal [A] 74 B2
Seewalchen [A] 60 H5
Seewiesen [A] 62 D6
Seferihisar [TR] 152 C5
Sefrivatnet [N] 190 D3
Segalstad [N] 170 H2
Segarcea [RO] 146 G1
Segård [N] 172 B3
Segelvik [N] 192 G1
Segerstad [S] 162 G6
Segesd [H] 74 G4
Segesta [I] 126 B2
Seget [HR] 116 H1
Seggau [A] 74 D3
Seglinge [FIN] 176 B5
Segmon [S] 166 E3
Segni [I] 116 B6
Segóbriga [E] 96 H2
Segonzac [F] 54 D6
Segorbe [E] 98 E3
Segovia [E] 88 F4
Segré [F] 40 G5
Seğucak [TR] 150 E5
Ségur [F] 68 B6
Segura [E] 102 G1
Segura [P] 86 G4
Segura de León [E] 94 G4
Segura de los Baños [E] 90 E6
Segurilla [E] 88 D6
Şehirlioğlu [TR] 152 F3
Sehnde [D] 32 G2
Şehvarmaz [TR] 150 G3
Seia [P] 86 F2
Seiches-sur-le-Loir [F] 40 H6
Seifhennersdorf [D] 48 G1
Seilhac [F] 66 H3
Seilleraye, Château de la– [F] 40 F6
Seim [N] 170 B3
Seinäjoki [FIN] 186 C3
Seira [E] 84 F6
Seis / Siusi [I] 72 D3
Seissan [F] 84 G3
Seitenstetten Markt [A] 62 C5
Seixal [P] 86 B5
Seixo [P] 80 C6
Sejerby [DK] 156 E2
Sejny [PL] 24 E3
Sejs [DK] 156 C1
Seki [TR] 154 G2
Sela [N] 190 B5
Seland [N] 164 E5
Selanovtsi [BG] 146 G2
Selänpää [FIN] 178 C2
Selargius [I] 118 D7
Selb [D] 48 C3
Selbitz [D] 46 H3
Selbu [N] 182 C2
Selby [GB] 10 F4
Selca [SLO] 74 B4
Selce [HR] 112 F2
Selchow [D] 34 F3
Selçuk [TR] 152 D5
Selde [DK] 160 C4
Selendi [TR] 152 D3
Selendi [TR] 152 F3
Selenicë [AL] 128 B5
Selent [D] 18 G2
Sélestat [F] 58 E2
Selet [S] 196 A4
Seleuş [RO] 76 H4
Seleuš [SRB] 142 H2
Selevac [SRB] 146 B1
Selfjorden [N] 192 C4
Selfoss [IS] 192 A3
Selgua [E] 90 G3
Séli [GR] 128 F5
Selianítika [GR] 132 F6
Seligenstadt [D] 46 D3
Selimağa [TR] 152 E1
Selimiye [TR] 152 D6
Selínia [GR] 136 G1
Selinunte [I] 126 B3
Selishtë [AL] 128 C2
Selishte [BG] 146 F6
Selište [SRB] 146 D2
Selitë [AL] 128 B4
Selizharovo [RUS] 202 D3
Selje [N] 180 B4
Seljestad [N] 170 C5
Seljord [N] 164 F2
Selkie [FIN] 188 G2
Selkirk [GB] 8 E4
Selkisaray [TR] 152 H2
Selkopp [N] 194 B2
Sella [E] 104 E2
Sella di Corno [I] 116 B4
Sellasía [GR] 136 E3
Selles [F] 54 H2
Sellía [GR] 140 D5
Sellières [F] 56 H5
Sellin [D] 20 E2
Sellye [H] 76 A5
Selm [D] 32 C3
Šelmberk [CZ] 48 G5
Selmsdorf [D] 18 H3
Selnes [N] 190 B5
Selnica [SLO] 74 D3
Selongey [F] 56 H3
Selonnet [F] 108 D2
S. Elpidio a Mare [I] 116 C2
Selsälandet [S] 184 D2
Selseng [N] 170 D1
Selsingen [D] 18 E4
Selsjön [S] 184 E2
Selsø Slot [DK] 156 G2
Selsverket [N] 180 G5
Seltjärn [S] 184 F1
Seltz [F] 46 B6
Selva di Cadore [I] 72 E3
Selva di Val Gardena / Wolkenstein in Gröden [I] 72 E3
Selvik [N] 180 B6
Selvino [I] 70 H4
Sem [N] 164 H3
Šember [CZ] 48 G4
Semblana [P] 94 C4
Semeljci [HR] 142 D1
Semeyskoye [RUS] 178 F5
Semily [CZ] 48 H2
Semizovac [BIH] 144 D1
Semmering [A] 62 E6
Semmering Pass [A] 62 E6
Sempas [SLO] 72 H5
Sempeter [SLO] 72 H5
Šempeter v savinjski dolini [SLO] 74 C4
Semur-en-Auxois [F] 56 F3
Seňa [SK] 64 G3
Sena de Luna [E] 78 G4
Sénas [F] 106 H4
Şencöy [TR] 150 F3
Sencur [SLO] 74 B4
Senden [D] 16 H6
Sendenhorst [D] 32 C3
Sendim [P] 80 G5
Senec [SK] 62 H4
Seneffe [B] 28 H3
Senez [F] 108 D4
Senftenberg [D] 34 F5
Senica [SK] 62 G3
Senigállia [I] 112 C6
Senise [I] 122 C5
Senj [HR] 112 F2
Senlis [F] 42 G3
Sennecey-le-Grand [F] 56 G5
Sennelager [D] 32 E3
Sennestadt [D] 32 D3
Sennewitz [D] 34 C5
Sennik [BG] 148 B4
Sénnori [I] 118 C3
Senohrad [SK] 64 C4
Senoji Varena [LT] 24 G2
Senokos [BG] 148 G2
Senonches [F] 26 H6
Senoncourt [F] 58 B3
Senones [F] 44 G6
Senorbì [I] 118 D6
Señorío de Bértiz [E] 84 B3
Senovo [BG] 148 D2
Senovo [SLO] 74 D5
Senožaty [CZ] 48 H5
Senožeče [SLO] 74 B6
Sens [F] 42 G6
Sens-de-Bretagne [F] 26 D5
Senseruth [B] 44 D2
Senta [MNE] 204 A5
Senta [SRB] 76 E5
Senterada [E] 84 G6
Šentilj [SLO] 74 D3
Šentjanž [SLO] 74 D5
Šentjur [SLO] 74 D4
Šentvid pri Zavodnju [SLO] 74 C4
Senum [N] 164 D4
Sepekov [CZ] 48 F5
Sepino [I] 120 E1
Sępólno Krajeńskie [PL] 22 C5
Sępopol [PL] 22 H2
Şepreuş [RO] 76 H3
Septemvri [BG] 148 A6
Septemvriyci [BG] 146 F3
Sept-Saulx [F] 44 B3
Sepúlveda [E] 88 G3
Sequeros [E] 88 B4
Serain [F] 28 F5
Seraincourt [F] 28 H6
Seraing [B] 30 E5
Seraserli [TR] 152 H4
Seravezza [I] 110 D5
Serceören [TR] 150 E5
Serebryanskiy [RUS] 198 H2
Sered' [SK] 62 H4
Seredka [RUS] 198 G3
Seregélyes [H] 76 B2
Seregno [I] 70 G4
Sérent [F] 26 B6
Serfaus [A] 72 C2
Sergen [TR] 150 C1
Sergiyev Posad [RUS] 202 F2
Serhat [TR] 152 B1
Seriaji [LT] 24 F2
Seriate [I] 70 H4
Sérifos [GR] 138 D3
Serinhisar [TR] 152 G5
Serino [I] 120 F3
Sermaize-les-Bains [F] 44 C4
Sermenin [MK] 128 G3
Sérmide [I] 110 F2
Sermoneta [I] 120 B1
Serock [PL] 38 B2
Seroczyn [PL] 38 D3
Seroick Jezioro Zegrzyńskie [PL] 38 B2
Serón [E] 102 G4
Serón de Nágima [E] 90 C3
Seròs [E] 90 G5
Serpa [P] 94 E3
Serpins [P] 86 E2
Serpukhov [RUS] 202 F3
Serra [E] 98 E4
Serracapriola [I] 116 F6
Serrada [E] 88 E2
Serra de Agua [P] 100 A3
Serra dè Conti [I] 112 C6
Serradifalco [I] 126 D3
Serradilla [E] 88 A6
Serramazzoni [I] 110 E3
Serra Nova [E] 104 F5
Serrant, Château de– [F] 40 G6
Serra Orrios [I] 118 E4
Serra San Bruno [I] 124 D6
Serra San Quirico [I] 116 B1
Serrastretta [I] 124 D5
Serravalle [CH] 70 G2
Serravalle Pistoiese [I] 110 E5
Serrenti [I] 118 C6
Serres [F] 108 C2
Sérres [GR] 130 C3
Serreta [P] 100 D3
Serri [I] 118 D6
Serrières [F] 68 F4
Sersale [I] 124 E5
Sertã [P] 86 E3
Sertolovo [RUS] 178 H4
Sertolovo [RUS] 178 H4
Seruci, Nuraghe– [I] 118 B7
Sérvia [GR] 128 F6
Servian [F] 106 D4
Servianá [GR] 132 D2
Servigliano [I] 116 C2
Serwy [PL] 24 E3
Sesa [E] 90 F3
Seseña Nuevo [E] 96 G1
Sesimbra [P] 86 B6
Seskinore [NIR] 2 F3
Sésklo [GR] 132 H2
Sesma [E] 82 H6
Sessa Aurunca [I] 120 D2
Sessvatn [N] 164 D1
Šestani [MNE] 144 E5
Šestanovac [HR] 144 B2
Sestao [E] 82 G3
Sesto / Sexten [I] 72 F3
Sesto al Reghena [I] 72 F5
Sesto Calende [I] 70 F4
Sesto Fiorentino [I] 110 F5
Sestola [I] 110 E4
Sesto S. Giovanni [I] 70 G5
Sestriere [I] 70 C5
Sestri Levante [I] 110 B4
Sestroretsk [RUS] 178 G4
Sestu [I] 118 C7
Sesué [E] 84 F5
Sesvete [HR] 74 E5
Séta [GR] 134 C4
Šeta [LT] 200 F4
Setcases [E] 92 F2
Sète [F] 106 E4
Seter [N] 182 D5
Seter [N] 190 B6
Setermoen [N] 192 F3
Setihovo [BIH] 144 E1
Setpsindiği [TR] 150 A1
Setså [N] 192 D6
Settebagni [I] 116 A5
Settimo Torinese [I] 70 D5
Settle [GB] 10 E3
Setúbal [P] 86 B6
Seui [I] 118 D5
Seulo [I] 118 D5
Seurre [F] 56 G4
Sevar [BG] 148 D1
Sevaster [AL] 128 B5
Sevastopol' [UA] 204 H4
Sevast'yanovo [RUS] 178 G1
Sevel [DK] 160 C5
Sevenoaks [GB] 14 E5
Sever [P] 80 C5
Sévérac-le-Château [F] 68 C6
Severin [D] 20 B4
Severin [HR] 74 G5
Ševětín [CZ] 62 C2
Sevettijärvi [FIN] 194 E3
Sevilla [E] 94 G6
Sevilleja de la Jara [E] 96 D2
Şevketiye [TR] 150 B5
Şevketiye [TR] 150 D5
Sevlievo [BG] 148 B4
Sevnica [SLO] 74 D5
Sevojno [SRB] 146 A2
Sevrier [F] 70 B3
Sevsk [RUS] 202 E5
Sexdrega [S] 162 B2
Sexten / Sesto [I] 72 F3
Seyches [F] 66 E4
Seyda [D] 34 D4
Seydiköy [TR] 152 C4
Seydisfjördur [IS] 192 D3
Seyitömer [TR] 150 G6
Seymen [TR] 150 D3
Seyne [F] 108 D2
Seynod [F] 70 A3
Seyssel [F] 68 H2
Seysses [F] 84 H3
Şeytan Sofrasi [TR] 134 H2
Sežana [SLO] 72 H6
Sézanne [F] 44 A4
Sezimovo Ústí [CZ] 48 G5
Sezze [I] 120 B1
S. Fågelås [S] 166 F6
Sfáka [GR] 140 G5
Sfakiá [GR] 140 C5
Sfântu Gheorghe [RO] 204 D4
S. Felices de los Gallegos [E] 80 F6
Sforzacosta [I] 116 C2
S. Geraldo [P] 86 D6
S. Ginés de la Jara, Monasterio de– [E] 104 C4
S. Giorgio della Richinvelda [I] 72 F5
S. Giorgio d. Sannio [I] 120 F2
S. Giovanni Bianco [I] 70 H4
S. Giusta [I] 118 C5
S. Gregório [I] 118 D7
S. Gregorio Magno [I] 120 G4
S. Gusmé [I] 114 G1
Shabla [BG] 148 G2
Shaftesbury [GB] 12 G4
Shahovskaja [RUS] 202 E3
Shakhovskaya [RUS] 202 E3
Shanagolden [IRL] 4 C3
Shanklin [GB] 12 H5
Shannon [IRL] 2 C6
Shannonbridge [IRL] 2 D5
Sharashova [BY] 38 G1
Sharnevo [BG] 148 D5
Shatalovo [RUS] 202 D4
Shatsk [BY] 202 B5
Shats'k [UA] 38 G4
Shchors [UA] 202 D6
Shchors'k [UA] 204 F2
Shchuchin [BY] 24 H4
Shchuchyn [BY] 202 A6
's Heerenberg [NL] 16 F6
Sheerness [GB] 14 F4
Sheffield [GB] 10 F4
Shefford [GB] 14 E3
Shëmhill [AL] 128 B3
Shëngjergj [AL] 128 B3
Shëngjergj [AL] 146 A6
Shëngjin [AL] 128 A1
Shënmëri [AL] 146 B6
Shepetivka [UA] 202 C8
Shepton Mallet [GB] 12 F4
Sherborne [GB] 12 G4
Shercock [IRL] 2 F4
Sheringham [GB] 14 G1
's-Hertogen-Bosch [NL] 16 E6
Shetaj [AL] 128 A2
Shijak [AL] 128 A3
Shiki [RUS] 198 H4
Shilkovci [BG] 148 C4
Shillelagh [IRL] 4 F4
Shimsk [RUS] 202 C2
Shinrone [IRL] 2 D6
Shipchenski Manastir [BG] 148 C4
Shipchenski Prokhad [BG] 148 C4
Shipka [BG] 148 C4
Shipkovo [BG] 148 B4
Shiroka Lŭka [BG] 130 D1
Shirokë [AL] 128 A1
Shirokoye [RUS] 22 H2
Shivatsevo [BG] 148 D4
Shkalle [AL] 132 B2
Shklow [BY] 202 C5
Shkodër [AL] 128 A1
Shkorpilovtsi [BG] 148 F3
Shmoylovo [RUS] 198 H3
Shoshan [AL] 146 A6
Shostka [UA] 202 E6
Shpola [UA] 202 E8
Shranamanragh Bridge [IRL] 2 B3
Shrewsbury [GB] 10 D5
Shrule [IRL] 2 C4
Shtëpëz [AL] 128 C6
Shtërmen [AL] 128 B4
Shumen [BG] 148 E3
Shumsk [UA] 202 B8
Shyroke [UA] 204 G2
Shyshchytsy [BY] 202 B6
Siána [GR] 154 C4
Sianów [PL] 22 A3
Siare [EST] 198 D3
Siátista [GR] 128 E6
Šiauliai [LT] 200 E4
Sibabravas [LT] 200 F4
Sibari [I] 122 D6
Sibbhult [S] 158 D1
Sibbo / Sipoo [FIN] 176 H4
Šibenik [HR] 112 H6
Sibilla, Ruderi di– [I] 120 C1
Sibinj [HR] 142 D2
Sibiu [RO] 204 C5
Sibo [S] 174 D2
Sićevo [SRB] 146 D3
Sicignano degli Alburni [I] 120 G4
Siculiana [I] 126 D4
Šid [MNE] 204 A5
Šid [SRB] 142 E2
Sidári [GR] 132 A2
Siddeburen [NL] 16 H2
Sideby / Siipyy [FIN] 186 A5
Sidensjö [S] 184 F2
Siderno [I] 124 D7
Sidertjärn [S] 172 G1
Sidiró [GR] 130 G2
Sidirókastro [GR] 130 B3
Sidirónero [GR] 130 D2
Sidmouth [GB] 12 E4
Sidra [PL] 24 F4
Sidra [PL] 24 F4
Sidyma [TR] 154 F3
Sidzina [PL] 50 D2
Siebe [N] 194 B4
Siebenberg [D] 30 G6
Siecq [F] 54 D6
Siedlce [PL] 38 D3
Siedlinghausen [D] 32 D5
Siedlisko [PL] 22 A6
Siedlisko [PL] 36 A4
Siegburg [D] 30 H5
Siegen [D] 32 C6
Siegenburg [D] 60 E2
Sieggraben [A] 62 F6
Siegsdorf [D] 60 G5
Siekierki [PL] 34 F1
Siekkinen [FIN] 196 E2
Sielec [PL] 38 F6
Sielpia Wlk [PL] 38 A6
Siemiany [PL] 22 F4
Siemiatycze [PL] 38 E2
Siena [I] 114 F1
Sieniawa [PL] 52 F3
Sieniawka [PL] 48 G1
Sieniec [PL] 36 F6
Siennica [PL] 38 C3
Siennica Różana [PL] 38 F6
Sienno [PL] 38 C6
Sieppijärvi [FIN] 194 C7
Sieradz [PL] 36 F5
Sieraków [PL] 36 B2
Sieraków [PL] 50 F2
Sierakowice [PL] 22 D2
Sierck-les-Bains [F] 44 F3
Sierentz [F] 58 D4
Sierning [A] 62 B5
Sierpc [PL] 36 G1
Sierra Bermeja [E] 100 H4
Sierra de Fuentes [E] 86 H5
Sierra de Luna [E] 84 C6
Sierra de Yeguas [E] 102 B3
Sierra Nevada [E] 102 E4
Sierre [CH] 70 D2
Siete Aguas [E] 98 D4
Sievi [FIN] 196 D5
Siewierz [PL] 50 G2
Sifferbo [S] 172 H4
Siğacik [TR] 152 C5
Sigean [F] 106 D5
Sigena, Monasterio de– [E] 90 G4
Siggjarvåg [N] 170 A5
Sighetu Marmaţiei [RO] 204 C3
Sighişoara [RO] 204 D4
Siglufjördur [IS] 192 B2
Sigmaringen [D] 58 H3
Signes [F] 108 C5
Signy-l'Abbaye [F] 28 H6
Sígri [GR] 134 G2
Sigtuna [S] 168 D2
Sigüeiro [E] 78 C3
Sigüenza [E] 90 A4
Sigües [E] 84 C4
Sigulda [LV] 198 E5
Sihtuuna [FIN] 194 C8
Siikainen [FIN] 186 B6
Siikajoki [FIN] 196 D4
Siikakoski [FIN] 188 E5
Siikala [FIN] 176 G4
Siilinjärvi [FIN] 188 C2
Siipyy / Sideby [FIN] 186 A5
Siivikko [FIN] 196 E3
Sijarinska Banja [SRB] 146 D5
Sikeå [S] 196 A5
Sikfors [S] 196 A3
Síkinos [GR] 138 E4
Siklós [H] 76 B5
Sikopokh'ya [RUS] 188 H5
Sikórz [PL] 36 G2
Sikovuono [FIN] 194 D4
Siksjö [S] 190 F5
Siksjön [S] 190 H3
Sil [S] 190 F6
Šilale [LT] 200 D4
Silandro / Schlanders [I] 72 C3
Silánus [I] 118 C4
Silbaš [SRB] 142 F1
Silberstedt [D] 18 F1
Şile [TR] 150 F2
Siles [E] 102 H1
Şilindia [RO] 76 H4
Silíqua [I] 118 C7
Silivri [TR] 150 D3
Siljan [N] 164 G3
Siljansnäs [S] 172 G4
Silkås [S] 182 H1
Silkeborg [DK] 160 D6
Silla [E] 98 E5
Silla de Felipe II [E] 88 F5
Sillamäe [EST] 198 F1
Sillans-la-Cascade [F] 108 C4
Silleda [E] 78 C3
Sillé-le-Guillaume [F] 26 F6
Sillerud [S] 166 D3
Sillian [A] 72 F3
Sillre [S] 184 E3
Silnica [PL] 50 H1
Silno [PL] 22 C4
Šilo [HR] 112 F2
Sils [E] 92 F3
Silsand [N] 192 F3
Sils-Maria [CH] 70 H2
Siltakylä Broby [FIN] 178 C4
Siltala [FIN] 196 E5
Šilutė [LT] 200 D5
Šiluva [LT] 200 E4
Silva [E] 78 C2
Silvacane [F] 106 H4
Silvaplana [CH] 70 H2
Silvares [P] 86 F2
Silvenski Bani [BG] 148 D4
Silverdalen [S] 162 F3
Silvermines [IRL] 4 D3
Silves [P] 94 B5
Silvi Marina [I] 116 D4
Silz [A] 72 C1
Simagino [RUS] 178 G4
Simagino [RUS] 178 G4
Simanala [FIN] 188 E4
Simancas [E] 88 E2
Şimand [RO] 76 G4
Simaság [H] 74 G1
Simav [TR] 152 F2
Simaxis [I] 118 C5
Simbach [D] 60 G4
Simbach [D] 60 G3
Simena [TR] 154 H3
Simeonovgrad [BG] 148 D6
Simferopol' [UA] 204 H4
Simići [BIH] 142 E4
Simitli [BG] 128 H1
Šimkaičiai [LT] 200 E5
Simlångsdalen [S] 162 B5
Şimleu Silvaniei [RO] 204 C4
Simmelkaer [DK] 160 C6
Simmerath [D] 30 F5
Simmerberg [D] 60 B5
Simmern [D] 44 H2
Simnas [LT] 24 F2
Simo [FIN] 196 D3
Símonos Pétras, Moní– [GR] 130 D5
Simonstorp [S] 168 B4
Simontornya [H] 76 B3
Simorre [F] 84 G3
Simpele [FIN] 188 F6
Simplon Dorf [CH] 70 E2
Simplonpass [CH] 70 E2
Simrishamn [S] 158 D3
Simuna [EST] 198 F2
Šimuni [HR] 112 F4
Sinaia [RO] 204 D5
Sinalunga [I] 114 G2
Sinanaj [AL] 128 B5
Sinanoğlu [TR] 150 H2
Sinarcas [E] 98 D3
Sincanlı [TR] 152 H2
Sincansarnıç [TR] 150 E5
Sindal [DK] 160 E2
Sindelfingen [D] 58 G1
Sindi [EST] 198 D3
Sındırgı [TR] 152 E2
Sinekçi [TR] 150 C5
Sinekli [TR] 150 D2
Sinemorets [BG] 148 G5
Sines [P] 94 B2
Sinettä [FIN] 194 C7
Sineu [E] 104 E5
Sinevo [RUS] 178 G2
Singen [D] 58 G4
Singerin [A] 62 E5
Singsås [N] 182 B2
Singusdal [N] 164 F3
Sinilähde [FIN] 178 B2
Siniscola [I] 118 E4
Sinj [HR] 144 A1
Sinnai [I] 118 D7
Sinnes [N] 164 C3
Sinópoli [I] 124 C7
Sinsen [A] 72 B1
Sinsen [CH] 72 B1
Sinsheim [D] 46 C5
Sintea Mare [RO] 76 H3
Sintra [P] 86 A5
Sintsi [FIN] 188 F3
Sinuessa [I] 120 D2
Sinyaya Nikola [RUS] 198 G4
Sinzig [D] 30 H5
Siófok [H] 76 A2
Sion [CH] 70 D2
Sion [CZ] 48 H4
Sion [F] 44 E6
Siorac-en-Périgord [F] 66 F4
Sipahi [TR] 150 B3
Šipči [SRB] 146 B4
Sipiren [FIN] 196 F4
Šipkovica [MK] 128 G1
Sipoo / Sibbo [FIN] 176 H4
Šipovo [BIH] 142 B4
Sippola [FIN] 178 C3
Sira [N] 164 C4

Sirač [HR] 142 C1
Siracusa [I] 126 G5
Siret [RO] 204 D3
Sirevåg [N] 164 B4
Şiria [RO] 76 H4
Sirig [SRB] 142 F1
Sirishtnik [BG] 146 F5
Širitovci [HR] 112 H5
Sirkka [FIN] 194 C6
Sirkön [S] 162 D5
Sirma [N] 194 D2
Sirmione [I] 72 B6
Sirnach [CH] 58 G5
Sirok [H] 64 E5
Široké [SK] 64 F2
Široki Brijeg [BIH] 144 B2
Sirolo [I] 116 C1
Siruela [E] 96 C3
Širvintos [LT] 200 G5
Sisak [HR] 142 A1
Sisamón [E] 90 C4
Sisante [E] 98 B4
Sisättö [FIN] 186 D6
Sisbacka [FIN] 186 C1
S. Isidoro del Campo [E] 94 G6
Šišljavić [HR] 112 H1
Sissa [I] 110 D2
Sissach [CH] 58 E4
Sissonne [F] 28 G6
Şiştarovăţ [RO] 76 H5
Sisteron [F] 108 C3
Sistiana [I] 72 H5
Sistranda [N] 190 A6
Sit. Anna [S] 168 C6
Sitasjaurestugorna [S] 192 F5
Siteía [GR] 140 G4
Sitges [E] 92 D5
Sitno [HR] 142 A5
Sitovo [BG] 148 E1
Sitrama de Tera [E] 80 H3
Sittard [NL] 30 F4
Sitten [D] 34 D6
Sittensen [D] 18 E5
Sittersdorf [A] 74 C3
Sittingbourne [GB] 14 F5
Sitzendorf [A] 62 E3
Siuntiol / Sjundea [FIN] 176 G5
Siurua [FIN] 196 D3
Siusi / Seis [I] 72 D3
Sivac [SRB] 76 D6
Sivakka [FIN] 196 F5
Sivakka [FIN] 196 G5
Sivakkavaara [FIN] 188 E2
Sivaslı [TR] 152 G3
Siverskiy [RUS] 178 H6
Síviri [GR] 130 B6
Sivriler [TR] 150 C1
Sivry-sur-Meuse [F] 44 D3
Six-Fours-les-Plages [F] 108 C6
Sixmilebridge [IRL] 2 C6
Sizun [F] 40 B2
Sjenica [SRB] 146 A4
S. Jeroni, Monestir de- [E] 98 E6
Sjisjka [S] 192 G5
Sjoa [N] 180 G6
Sjøåsen [N] 190 C5
Sjöberg [S] 190 F3
Sjöbo [S] 158 C3
Sjøholt [N] 180 D3
Sjøli [N] 172 C1
Sjørring [DK] 160 C4
Sjørup [DK] 160 C5
Sjötofta [S] 162 B3
Sjötorp [S] 166 F4
Sjoutnäset [S] 190 E5
Sjøvegan [N] 192 F3
Sjövik [S] 160 H1
S. Juan, Castillo de- [E] 104 B4
S. Juan de la Peña [E] 84 D5
Sjundea / Siuntiol [FIN] 176 G5
Sjursjok [N] 194 D2
Sjursvika [N] 192 E3
Sjusjøen [N] 172 B2
Skabland [N] 172 B4
Skåbu [N] 170 G1
Skadovs'k [UA] 204 G3
Skælskør [DK] 156 F3
Skærbæk [DK] 156 B3
Skafídia [GR] 136 B2
Skaftafell [IS] 192 B3
Skaftung [FIN] 186 A5
Skagaströnd [IS] 192 B2
Skage [N] 190 C5
Skagen [DK] 160 F2
Skaidi [N] 194 B2
Skaistkalne [LV] 198 E6
Skakavac [HR] 112 H1
Skála [GR] 134 A4
Skála [GR] 134 G2
Skála [GR] 136 A1
Skála [GR] 136 E4
Skála [GR] 138 H2
Skała [PL] 50 H3
Skalabiňa [SK] 64 C2
Skála Eresoú [GR] 134 G2
Skála Kalliráchis [GR] 130 E4
Skålan [S] 182 G4
Skála Oropoú [GR] 134 C5
Skala-Podil's'ka [UA] 204 D2
Skálavík [FR] 160 B2
Skalbmierz [PL] 52 B3
Skaldö [FIN] 176 F6
Skalica [SK] 62 G3
Skalité [SK] 50 F5
Skalitsa [BG] 148 D5
Skallelv [N] 194 F2
Skällerőd [S] 166 B4
Skällerud [S] 166 D4
Skallerup Kit [DK] 160 E2
Skallskog [S] 172 G4
Skalmodal [S] 190 E3
Skalmsiö [S] 184 F1
Skalochóri [GR] 128 E5
Skalotí [GR] 130 D2
Skalotí [GR] 140 C5
Skals [DK] 160 D5
Skålsjön [S] 174 D3
Skalstugan [S] 182 E1
Skammestein [N] 170 G2
Skän [S] 184 D5
Skandáli [GR] 130 F6
Skanderborg [DK] 156 D1
Skånes Fagerhult [S] 162 C6
Skåne-Tranås [S] 158 D3
Skånevik [N] 170 B6
Skåningbukt [N] 192 G1
Skänninge [S] 166 H6
Skanör [S] 156 H3
Skansbachen [S] 172 G5
Skansen [N] 190 C6
Skansholm [S] 190 F4
Skansnäs [S] 190 F3
Skåpafors [S] 166 D4
Skąpe [PL] 34 H3
Skar [N] 170 D2
Skara [S] 166 E5
Skäran [S] 196 A5
Skarberget [N] 192 E4
Skärblacka [S] 168 A5
Skarda [S] 190 G5
Skåre [S] 166 E2
Skäret [N] 172 E1
Skärhamn [S] 160 G1
Skarhult [S] 158 C2
Skarínou [CY] 154 G6
Skarjenfossen [N] 164 D2
Skärlöv [S] 162 G6
Skarmunken [N] 192 G2
Skarnes [N] 172 C5
Skarpengland [N] 164 D5
Skärplinge [S] 174 F4
Skarsfjord [N] 192 F1
Skarstein [N] 192 E3
Skarszewy [PL] 22 D3
Skårup [DK] 156 E4
Skärvången [S] 190 E6
Skarvberg-Tunnelen [N] 194 C2
Skarveberg [N] 194 B2
Skarvsjö [S] 190 F4
Skaryszew [PL] 38 C5
Skarżynek [PL] 38 B1
Skarżysko-Kamienna [PL] 38 B6
Skasberget [N] 172 D4
Skata [FIN] 176 E6
Skattungbyn [S] 172 G2
Skatval [N] 182 C1
Skaudvilė [LT] 200 E4
Skave [DK] 160 C5
Skavik [N] 194 B2
Skawina [PL] 50 H4
Skeda udde [S] 166 H6
Skedevi [S] 168 B4
Skedshult [S] 162 G1
Skedsmokorset [N] 172 B6
Skee [S] 166 C4
Skegness [GB] 10 H5
Skehobruk [S] 168 E1
Skei [N] 180 D6
Skei [N] 180 G2
Skeie [N] 164 C5
Skela [SRB] 142 G3
Skelani [BIH] 142 F4
Skelde [DK] 156 C4
Skellefteå [S] 196 A4
Skelleftehamn [S] 196 A4
Skelleftestrand [S] 196 A4
Skelmersdale [GB] 10 D4
Skender Vakuf [BIH] 142 C3
Skene [S] 162 B3
Skenshyttan [S] 172 H5
Skepastó [GR] 130 B4
Skępe [PL] 36 G1
Skeppshult [S] 162 C4
Skeppsmyra [S] 168 F1
Skeppsvik [S] 196 A6
Skerping [DK] 160 D3
Skerries [IRL] 2 F6
Ski [N] 166 B1
Skiáthos [GR] 134 B3
Skibbereen [IRL] 4 B5
Skibbild [DK] 160 C6
Skibby [DK] 156 G2
Skibniew-Podawce [PL] 38 D2
Skibotn [N] 192 G2
Skidal' [BY] 24 G4
Skien [N] 164 G3
Skierbieszów [PL] 52 G1
Skierniewice [PL] 36 H4
Skiippagurra [N] 194 D2
Skille [N] 190 D3
Skillingarid [S] 162 D3
Skillingaryd [S] 162 D3
Skillinge [S] 158 D3
Skillingmark [S] 166 D1
Skiniás [GR] 140 F5
Skinnarbu [N] 164 E1
Skinnerup [DK] 160 C3
Skinnskatteberg [S] 168 A1
Skiønne [N] 170 F5
Skipnes [N] 180 G1
Skipton [GB] 10 E3
Skiptvet [N] 166 B2
Skirö [S] 162 E3
Skivarp [S] 158 C3
Skive [DK] 160 C5
Skiveren [DK] 160 E2
Skivjane [SRB] 146 B5
Skjærhalden [N] 166 B3
Skjånes [N] 194 D1
Skjåvika [N] 190 D3
Skjeberg [N] 166 B3
Skjeggedal [N] 164 E4
Skjelbreid [N] 190 D5
Skjelstad [N] 190 C5
Skjelten [N] 180 D3
Skjelvik [N] 194 C2
Skjern [DK] 156 B1
Skjervefossen [N] 170 C3
Skjervøy [N] 192 G1
Skjold [N] 164 B1
Skjoldastraumen [N] 164 B1
Skjolden [N] 170 E1
Skjønhaug [N] 166 C2
Skjøtningberg [N] 194 D1
Sklíthro [GR] 132 H2
Skoby [S] 168 D1
Skočivir [MK] 128 F3
Škocjanske Jame [SLO] 74 B6
Skoczów [PL] 50 F4
Skodje [N] 180 D3
Skødstrup [DK] 160 E6
Škofije [SLO] 72 H6
Škofja Loka [SLO] 74 B4
Škofljica [SLO] 74 C5
Skog [S] 174 E3
Skógafoss [IS] 192 B3
Skoganvarre [N] 194 C3
Skogar [IS] 192 B3
Skogen [S] 166 D3
Skoger [N] 164 H2
Skogfoss [N] 194 E3
Skoghall [S] 166 E3
Skogli [N] 170 F4
Skogly [N] 194 E3
Skogn [N] 190 C6
Skogså [S] 196 B2
Skogsby [S] 162 G5
Skogstad [N] 170 F2
Skogstorp [S] 160 H4
Skogstorp [S] 168 B3
Skogvatnet [N] 192 F4
Skoki [PL] 36 D2
Skokloster [S] 168 D2
Skole [UA] 52 G6
Skollenborg [N] 164 G2
Sköllersta [S] 166 H3
Skomdal [N] 164 E3
Skomielna Biała [PL] 50 H5
Skomlin [PL] 36 F6
Skönberga [S] 168 B5
Skópelos [GR] 134 B3
Skópelos [GR] 134 H2
Skopí [GR] 140 G4
Skopiá [GR] 132 G3
Skopje [MK] 128 E1
Skopós [GR] 128 E4
Skopun [FR] 160 A2
Skor [N] 164 B2
Skórcz [PL] 22 E4
Skórka [PL] 22 B6
Skoroszów [PL] 36 D5
Skorovatn [N] 190 D4
Skorped [S] 184 F2
Skørping [DK] 160 D4
Skörstorp [S] 162 C1
Skórzec [PL] 38 D3
Skotnes [N] 190 C4
Skotnoye [RUS] 178 H4
Skotoússa [GR] 130 B3
Skoträsk [S] 190 G4
Skotselv [N] 164 G1
Skotterud [N] 166 D1
Skoulikariá [GR] 132 E3
Skoúra [GR] 136 E4
Skoútari [GR] 136 D3
Skovballe [DK] 156 D4
Skovby [DK] 156 D4
Skövde [S] 166 F6
Skra [GR] 128 G3
Skrad [HR] 112 F1
Skradin [HR] 112 H6
Skradinski Buk [HR] 112 H6
Skråmestø [N] 170 A3
Skravena [BG] 146 G4
Skrea [S] 160 H4
Skrede [N] 180 C5
Skreia [N] 172 B4
Skrīveri [LV] 198 E5
Skröven [S] 194 A8
Skrunda [LV] 198 C5
Skucku [S] 182 G3
Skudeneshavn [N] 164 A2
Skulsk [PL] 36 E2
Skulte [LV] 198 D4
Skultorp [S] 166 F6
Skultuna [S] 168 B2
Skuodas [LT] 198 B6
Skurugata [S] 162 E2
Skurup [S] 158 C3
Škušava [LV] 198 G5
Skute [N] 170 H4
Skuteč [CZ] 50 B4
Skutskär [S] 174 E4
Skutvik [N] 192 D5
Skvyra [UA] 202 D8
Skwierzyna [PL] 34 H2
Skýcov [SK] 64 B3
Skýdra [GR] 128 G4
Skylloura (Yılmaköy) [CY] 154 F5
Skýros [GR] 134 D3
Skyttmon [S] 184 C1
Skyttorp [S] 168 D1
Sládkovičovo [SK] 62 H4
Sladów [PL] 38 A2
Slagavallen [S] 182 E5
Slagelse [DK] 156 F3
Slagnäs [S] 190 G3
Slane [IRL] 2 F5
Slangerup [DK] 156 G2
Slănic Moldova [RO] 204 D4
Slano [HR] 144 C3
Slantsy [RUS] 198 G1
Slaný [CZ] 48 F3
Šlapanice [CZ] 48 F3
Slåstad [N] 172 C5
Slatina [HR] 74 H6
Slatina [MNE] 144 E3
Slatina [RO] 204 D6
Slatina [SRB] 142 F3
Slatina [SRB] 146 B2
Slatina [SRB] 146 E1
Slatiňany [CZ] 50 A4
Slatino [MK] 146 C6
Slatinski Drenovac [HR] 74 H6
Slättåkra [S] 162 B5
Slättberg [S] 172 G3
Slättberg [S] 194 A8
Slåttevik [N] 164 A2
Slätthog [S] 162 D4
Slattum [N] 172 B6
Slåttvik [N] 190 D4
Slavětín [CZ] 50 C5
Slavhostice [CZ] 48 H3
Slavičín [CZ] 64 A2
Slavín [CZ] 48 G2
Slavkovichi [RUS] 198 H3
Slavkov u Brna (Austerlitz) [CZ] 50 C6
Slavonice [CZ] 62 D2
Slavonski Brod [HR] 142 D2
Slavotin [BG] 146 F3
Slavsk [RUS] 200 D5
Slavuta [UA] 202 B8
Slavutych [UA] 202 D6
Slavyanovo [BG] 148 B3
Sława [PL] 36 B4
Sławatycze [PL] 38 F4
Slawharad [BY] 202 D5
Sławków [PL] 50 G3
Sławno [PL] 22 B2
Sławoborze [PL] 20 H4
Sleaford [GB] 10 G6
Sleme [SLO] 74 C4
Slemmestad [N] 164 H1
Slepač Most [MNE] 146 A4
Slepčević [SRB] 142 F3
Ślesin [PL] 22 C6
Ślesin [PL] 36 E3
Śleszów [PL] 50 C1
Sletta [N] 194 A2
Slettafoss [N] 180 F4
Slette [N] 180 E5
Slettestrand [DK] 160 D3
Slettmo [N] 192 F2
Sliač [SK] 64 C3
Sliedrecht [NL] 16 D5
Sliema [M] 126 C6
Sligeach / Sligo [IRL] 2 D3
Sligo / Sligeach [IRL] 2 D3
Slinde [N] 170 D2
Slipra [N] 190 C6
Slite [S] 168 G4
Sliven [BG] 148 D4
Slivnica [SLO] 74 D4
Slivnitsa [BG] 146 F4
Slivno [HR] 144 B2
Slivo Pole [BG] 148 D1
Slivovo [SRB] 146 C5
Śliwa [PL] 22 F4
Śliwice [PL] 22 D4
Slobozia [RO] 148 C2
Slobozia Mândra [RO] 148 B2
Słomniki [PL] 52 A3
Slonim [BY] 202 A6
Słonowice [PL] 20 G4
Słońsk [PL] 34 G2
Sloten [NL] 16 F3
Slottsbron [S] 166 E3
Slough [GB] 14 E4
Sloup [CZ] 50 C5
Sloupsko – Šošuvské Jeskyně [CZ] 50 C5
Slovac [SRB] 146 A1
Slovenj Gradec [SLO] 74 D4
Slovenska Bistrica [SLO] 74 D4
Slovenská L'upča [SK] 64 C3
Slovenske Konjice [SLO] 74 D4
Slovenské Nové Mesto [SK] 64 G3
Slovinci [HR] 142 B1
Słubice [PL] 34 G3
Słubice [PL] 36 H2
Sluderno / Schluderns [I] 72 C3
Sluis [NL] 16 C6
Sluis [NL] 28 G1
Slŭnchev Bryag [BG] 148 F4
Slunj [HR] 112 G2
Słupca [PL] 36 E3
Słupia [PL] 52 C3
Słupiec [PL] 50 C2
Słupno [PL] 36 H2
Słupsk [PL] 22 B2
Slutsk [BY] 202 B6
Służewo [PL] 36 F1
Småge [N] 180 D2
Smålandsstenar [S] 162 C4
Smalåsen [N] 190 D4
Smalininkai [LT] 200 E5
Smârdioasa [RO] 148 C2
Smarhon' [BY] 200 H5
S. Maria della Versa [I] 70 G6
S. Maria in Calanca [CH] 70 G2
S. Marina Salina [I] 124 B5
Šmarje [SLO] 72 H6
Šmarje [SLO] 74 D4
S. Martino in Pensilis [I] 116 F6
Šmartno [SLO] 74 C5
Šmartno [SLO] 74 D4
S. Mauro Forte [I] 122 C4
S. M. de Naranco [E] 78 H3
Smedås [N] 182 C4
Smedbyn [S] 166 E3
Smědeč [CZ] 62 B2
Smederevo [SRB] 142 H3
Smederevo [SRB] 204 B6
Smederevska-Palanka [SRB] 146 C1
Smedjebacken [S] 172 H5
Smedjeviken [S] 182 E1
Smedstorp [S] 158 D3
Smęgorzów [PL] 52 C3
Smeland [N] 164 E3
Smelror [N] 194 F2
S. Michele di Ganzaria [I] 126 F4
Smidary [CZ] 48 H3
Śmigiel [PL] 36 C4
S. Miguel [E] 84 B3
S. Miguel de Escalada [E] 78 H6
S. Miguel del Arroyo [E] 88 F2
S. Miguel de las Victorias [E] 90 B6
Smila [UA] 202 E8
Smilde [NL] 16 G3
Smiljan [BG] 130 E1
Śmiłowo [PL] 22 B6
Smiltene [LV] 198 F4
Smínthi [GR] 130 E2
Smirnenski [BG] 146 F3
Smögen [S] 166 B5
Smogulec [PL] 22 C6
Smokvica [MK] 128 G3
Smołdzino [PL] 22 C1
Smoleń [PL] 50 H3
Smolensk [RUS] 202 D4
Smolevitschi [BY] 202 B5
Smolnica [PL] 34 G1
Smolník [SK] 64 F3
Smolyan [BG] 130 E1
Smolyanovtsi [BG] 146 F3
Smørfjord [N] 194 C2
Smørhamn [N] 180 B5
Smuka [SLO] 74 C6
Smyadovo [BG] 148 E3
Smygehamn [S] 158 C3
Snappertuna [FIN] 176 F5
Snaptun [DK] 156 D2
Snartemo [N] 164 C5
Snarup [DK] 156 D4
Snåsa [N] 190 C5
Snausen [N] 180 H1
Snavlunda [S] 166 G4
Snedsted [DK] 160 C4
Sneek [NL] 16 F2
Sneem [IRL] 4 B4
Snefjord [N] 194 B2
Snerta [N] 182 D6
Snesudden [S] 196 A2
Sněžné [CZ] 50 B5
S. Nicola da Crissa [I] 124 D6
S. Nicolás del Puerto [E] 96 A5
Snihurivka [UA] 204 G3
Snilldal [N] 180 H1
Snina [SK] 64 H2
Snjatyn [UA] 204 D3
Šnjegotina Gornja [BIH] 142 C3
Snogebæk [DK] 158 E4
Snössvallen [S] 182 F6
Snöstorp [S] 162 B5
S. Ny [S] 166 E3
Soajo [P] 78 B6
Soanlakhti [RUS] 188 H4
Soave [I] 72 C6
Söbbön [S] 166 C4
Sober [E] 78 D5
Soběslav [CZ] 48 G6
Sobibór [PL] 38 G5
Sobieszewo [PL] 22 E2
Sobieszów [PL] 50 A1
Sobki [PL] 36 G5
Sobków [PL] 52 B2
Sobotín [CZ] 50 C4
Sobotište [SK] 62 H3
Sobotka [CZ] 48 H2
Sobótka [PL] 50 C1
Sobowidz [PL] 22 E3
Sobra [HR] 144 C3
Sobrado [E] 78 D3
Sobrado dos Monxes [E] 78 D3
Sobral da Adiça [P] 94 E3
Sobral de Monte Agraço [P] 86 B4
Sobran [TR] 150 H5
Sobrance [SK] 64 H2
Sobreira Formosa [P] 86 E3
Søby [DK] 156 D4
Soča [SLO] 72 H4
Sočanica [SRB] 146 C4
Sočerga [SLO] 112 D1
Sochaczew [PL] 38 A3
Sochaux [F] 58 C4
Sochocin [PL] 38 A2
Sochós [GR] 130 B4
Socodor [RO] 76 G3
Socovos [E] 104 B2
Socuéllamos [E] 96 H4
Sodankylä [FIN] 194 D6
Söderåkra [S] 162 F6
Söderala [S] 174 E2
Söderås [S] 172 H3
Söderbärke [S] 168 A1
Söderboda [S] 174 G5
Söderby [FIN] 178 C4
Söderby-Karl [S] 168 E1
Söderfors [S] 174 E5
Söderhamn [S] 174 E2
Söderköping [S] 168 B5
Södertälje [S] 168 D3
Söderudden [FIN] 186 A2
Södra Vallgrund [FIN] 186 A2
Södra Vi [S] 162 F2
Sodražica [SLO] 74 C6
Sødring [DK] 160 E5
Soest [D] 32 D4
Soest [NL] 16 E5
Soestdijk [NL] 16 E5
Sofádes [GR] 132 F3
Sofiero [S] 156 H1
Sofiïvka [UA] 202 F8
Sofikó [GR] 136 F1
Sofiya [BG] 146 F5
Sofó [GR] 132 G2
Sögel [D] 18 B6
Sogge bru [N] 180 E3
Sogliano al Rubicone [I] 110 H5
Sogndal [N] 170 D1
Sogndalstrand [N] 164 B5
Søgne [N] 164 D6
Sogn Folkemuseum [N] 170 D2
Sogn Gions [CH] 70 G1
Söğütdüdere [TR] 154 F2
Soğukpınar [TR] 150 F5
Soğuksu [TR] 150 H2
Söğüt [TR] 150 H4
Söğüt [TR] 154 D2
Söğüt [TR] 154 G1
Söğütalan [TR] 150 E5
Söğütyaylası [TR] 152 H1
Sohren [D] 44 H2
Soidinkumpu [FIN] 194 F8
Soidinvaara [FIN] 196 F5
Soignies [B] 28 H3
Soini [FIN] 186 E3
Soissons [F] 42 H2
Sokal' [UA] 52 H2
Söke [TR] 152 D5
Soklot [FIN] 186 B1
Sokna [N] 170 H5
Soknedal [N] 182 B2
Soko Banja [SRB] 146 D3
Sokolac [BIH] 112 H3
Sokolac [BIH] 142 E4
Sokolany [PL] 24 F4
Sokółka [PL] 24 F5
Sokolniki [PL] 36 E5
Sokolov [CZ] 48 C3
Sokolovo [BG] 148 B4
Sokolovo [BG] 148 G2
Sokołów Małopolski [PL] 52 E3
Sokołów Podlaski [PL] 38 D2
Sokoły [PL] 24 E6
Sokovaara [FIN] 188 G1
Sol [SK] 64 G2
Sola [N] 164 A3
Solana de los Barros [E] 94 G2
Solana del Pino [E] 96 E5
Solánas [I] 118 D7
Solares [E] 82 F3
Solarolo [I] 110 G4
Solbacken [S] 168 E3
Solberg [N] 164 G2
Solberg [S] 190 G6
Solberga [S] 162 E2
Solbjerg [DK] 160 C4
Solbjerg [DK] 160 E4
Solčava [SLO] 74 C4
Solda / Sulden [I] 72 C3
Sölden [A] 72 C2
Soldeu [AND] 84 H6
Solec Kujawski [PL] 22 D6
Solec nad Wisłą [PL] 38 D6
Solec-Zdrój [PL] 52 C3
Solem [N] 190 C5
Solenzara [F] 114 B5
Solera del Gabaldón [E] 98 C3
Solesmes [F] 28 G4
Solesmes, Abbaye de- [F] 42 A5
Solevåg [N] 180 D3
Solf / Sulva [FIN] 186 B2
Solfonn [N] 170 C5
Solheim [N] 170 B2
Solignac [F] 66 G1
Solihull [GB] 12 H1
Solin [HR] 144 A2
Solingen [D] 30 H4
Solivella [E] 92 C4
Söll [A] 60 F6
Sollana [E] 98 E5
Sollebrunn [S] 162 B1
Sollefteå [S] 184 E2
Sollenau [A] 62 F5
Sollentuna [S] 168 D3
Soller [D] 30 G5
Sóller [E] 104 E4
Sóller / el Port [E] 104 E4
Søllerød [DK] 156 G2
Sollerön [S] 172 G3
Søllested [DK] 156 E5
Sollia [N] 182 B6
Solliden [S] 162 G5
Solliès-Pont [F] 108 C5
Sollihøgda [N] 170 H6
Solmaz [TR] 152 F6
Solmyra [S] 168 B2
Solna [S] 168 D3
Solnechnogorsk [RUS] 202 E3
Solnhofen [D] 60 D2
Solnice [CZ] 50 B3
Solojärvi [FIN] 194 D4
Solonka [UA] 202 A8
Solosancho [E] 88 D4
Sološnica [SK] 62 G4
Solothurn [CH] 58 D5
Solovi [RUS] 198 G3
Solovychi [UA] 38 H6
Solrød Strand [DK] 156 G3
Solsa [S] 168 D4
Solsnes [N] 180 E3
Solsona [E] 92 D2
Solsvik [N] 170 A3
Solt [H] 76 C3
Soltau [D] 18 F6
Sol'tsy [RUS] 202 C2
Soltvadkert [H] 76 D3
Solum [N] 170 G5
Solunto [I] 126 D2
Solutré, Roche de- [F] 56 F6
Solvang [N] 180 H5
Sölvesborg [S] 158 E1
Solvik [S] 166 D3
Solvorn [N] 170 D1
Soma [TR] 152 D2
Somådal [N] 182 D5
Somaglia [I] 70 H6
Somåseter [N] 182 D5
Sombernon [F] 56 G3
Sombor [MNE] 204 A5
Sombor [SRB] 76 C6
Someren [NL] 30 E3
Somerniemi [FIN] 176 F4
Somero [FIN] 176 F4
Somino [RUS] 202 D1
Sommariva del Bosco [I] 108 G2
Sommarset [N] 192 D5
Sommatino [I] 126 E4
Sommen [S] 162 E1
Sommepy-Tahure [F] 44 C3
Sömmerda [D] 34 A6
Sommerfeld [D] 34 D1
Sommersted [DK] 156 C3
Sommery [F] 28 C5
Sommesous [F] 44 B4
Sommières [F] 106 F3
Somo [E] 82 F3
Somogyacsa [H] 76 A3
Somogyapáti [H] 74 H5
Somogyjád [H] 74 H4
Somogyszob [H] 74 G4
Somogytarnóca [H] 74 H5
Somogyvár [H] 74 H3
Somosierra [E] 88 G4
Somosierra, Puerto de- [E] 88 G4
Somovit [BG] 148 B2
Sompolno [PL] 36 F2
Somport, Túnel de- [E/F] 84 D4
Sompuis [F] 44 B5
Sompujärvi [FIN] 196 D2
Somvik [S] 162 E1
Son [N] 166 B2
Son Bou [E] 104 H4
Sonceboz [CH] 58 D5
Soncillo [E] 82 E4
Soncino [I] 70 H5
Sóndalo [I] 72 B3
Sondby [FIN] 178 B4
Søndeled [N] 164 F4
Sønder Balling [DK] 160 C5
Sønderborg [DK] 156 C4
Sønderby [DK] 156 C4
Sønderby [DK] 156 F4
Sønderby [DK] 160 B6
Sønder Dråby [DK] 160 C4
Sønder Felding [DK] 156 B1
Sønderho [DK] 156 A3
Sønder Omme [DK] 156 B1
Sondershausen [D] 32 H5
Sønderså [DK] 156 D3
Søndervig [DK] 160 B6
Søndervika [N] 182 D4
Sondrio [I] 70 H3
Söndrum [S] 162 B5
Sonekulla [S] 158 E1
Songe [N] 164 F4
Songesand [N] 164 B3
Sonkaja [FIN] 188 G2
Sonkajärvi [FIN] 196 E6
Sonneberg [D] 46 G2
Sonntagberg [A] 62 C5
Sonogno [CH] 70 F2
Sonsbeck [D] 30 G2
Sonseca [E] 96 F2
Sonta [SRB] 76 C6
Sonthofen [D] 60 B6
Sontra [D] 32 F6
Son Xoriguer [E] 104 G4
Söörmarkku [FIN] 176 D1
Sopeira [E] 84 F6
Sopela [E] 82 G3
Sophienhöhle [D] 46 H4
Sople [PL] 52 F3
Sopoćani [SRB] 146 B4
Sopoćani, Manastir- [SRB] 146 B4
Soponya [H] 76 B2
Šoporňa [SK] 64 A4
Sopot [BG] 148 B4
Sopot [MK] 146 D6
Sopot [PL] 22 E2
Sopot [SRB] 146 B1
Sopotnica [MK] 128 D3
Sopparjok [N] 194 C3
Sopron [H] 62 F6
Sora [I] 116 C6
Soragna [I] 110 D2
Söråker [S] 184 F4
Sorano [I] 114 G3
Sorbas [E] 102 H5
Sorbie [GB] 8 C5
Sørbø [N] 164 B2
Sörbo [S] 166 C5
Sørbotn [N] 192 F2
Sörbygden [S] 184 D3
Sørbymagle [DK] 156 F3
Sørdal [N] 190 E1
Sore [F] 66 C4
Söréd [H] 76 B1
Søre Herefoss [N] 164 E5
Soreide [N] 170 C2
Søre Moen [N] 190 C6
Sørenget [N] 190 C5
Soresina [I] 70 H5
Sörfjärden [S] 184 E5
Sør-Flatanger [N] 190 B5
Sörforsa [S] 174 E1
Sórgono [I] 118 D5
Sorgues [F] 106 G3
Sörgutvik [N] 190 C4
Sørhella [N] 180 G4
Soria [E] 90 B3
Soriano Calabro [I] 124 D6
Soriano nel Cimino [I] 114 H4
Sorica [SLO] 74 B4
Sorihuela del Guadalimar [E] 102 G1
Sorita [E] 98 G1
Sørkjosen [N] 192 G2

Sorkun [TR] 152 H3
Sorkwity [PL] 24 B4
Sörmjöle [S] 190 H6
Sørmo [N] 192 F3
Sorø [DK] 156 F3
Soroca [MD] 204 E2
Soroní [GR] 154 D3
Sorpe [E] 84 G5
Sørreisa [N] 192 F3
Sorrento [I] 120 E4
Sorsakoski [FIN] 188 D3
Sorsele [S] 190 G3
Sörsjön [S] 172 E2
Sorso [I] 118 C3
Sort [E] 84 G6
Sortavala [RUS] 188 H5
Sortino [I] 126 G4
Sörtjärn [S] 182 G4
Sortland [N] 192 D3
Sør-Tverrfjord [N] 192 H1
Sørumsand [N] 166 C1
Sorunda [S] 168 D4
Sörup [D] 156 C5
Sørup [DK] 160 D4
Sørvær [N] 194 A2
Sørværøy [N] 192 C5
Sørvågen [N] 192 C5
Sørvágur [FR] 160 A1
Sörvattnet [S] 182 E5
Sørvik [N] 190 B6
Sørvik [N] 192 E3
Sörviken [S] 184 D1
Sørvollen [N] 182 C5
Sösdala [S] 158 C2
Sos del Rey Católico [E] 84 C5
Soses [E] 90 H5
Sošice [HR] 74 D6
Sośnica [PL] 50 G2
Sośnica [PL] 22 A5
Sośnicowice [PL] 50 F3
Sosnicy [RUS] 198 H1
Sosnivka [UA] 52 H2
Sosnove [UA] 202 B7
Sosnovo [RUS] 178 G3
Sosnovo [RUS] 198 H1
Sosnovskoye [RUS] 178 E2
Sosnovyy [RUS] 196 H1
Sosnovyy Bor [RUS] 178 F5
Sosnowica [PL] 38 F5
Sosnowiec [PL] 50 G3
Sospel [F] 108 F4
Sossano [I] 110 F1
Šoštanj [SLO] 74 D4
Sóstis [GR] 130 F2
Søstrefoss [N] 180 D4
Sostrup [DK] 160 F5
Sot [SRB] 142 F2
Sotaseter [N] 180 E5
Soteska [SLO] 74 C6
Søtholmen [N] 166 C4
Sotillo de la Adrada [E] 88 E5
Sotillo de las Palomas [E] 88 D6
Sotin [HR] 142 E1
Sotkamo [FIN] 196 F5
Sotkuma [FIN] 188 F2
Sotobañado y Priorato [E] 82 D5
Soto del Barco [E] 78 H3
Soto de los Infantes [E] 78 G3
Soto del Real [E] 88 F5
Sotos [E] 98 C2
Sotresgudo [E] 82 D5
Sotrondio / San Martín del Rey Aurelio [E] 78 H4
Sotta [F] 114 B6
Sotteville les Rouen [F] 28 B5
Sottomarina [I] 110 H1
Sottrum [D] 18 E5
Sottunga [FIN] 176 B5
Sotuélamos [E] 96 H4
Soual [F] 106 B3
Soúda [GR] 140 C4
Souesmes [F] 56 C2
Soufflenheim [F] 46 B6
Souflí [GR] 130 H2
Soúgia [GR] 140 B5
Souillac [F] 66 G4
Souilly [F] 44 D4
Soulac-sur-Mere [F] 54 B6
Soulaines-Dhuys [F] 44 C6
Soulópoulo [GR] 132 C2
Soultz [F] 44 H5
Soultz [F] 58 D3
Soumoulou [F] 84 E3
Soúnio [GR] 130 E2
Soúnio [GR] 136 H2
Souppes-sur-Loing [F] 42 G5
Sourdeval [F] 26 E4
Sourdon [F] 28 E5
Soure [P] 86 D2
Sournia [F] 92 F1
Sourotí [GR] 130 B5
Soúrpi [GR] 132 H3
Sousceyrac [F] 66 H4
Sousel [P] 86 E6
Soustons [F] 66 A6
Soutelo [E] 78 C4
Southampton [GB] 12 H5
Southend-on-Sea [GB] 14 F4
South Molton [GB] 12 E4
Southport [GB] 10 D3
South Shields [GB] 8 G6
Southwold [GB] 14 H3
Soutomaior, Cast. de- [E] 78 B4
Souvála [GR] 136 G1
Souvigny [F] 56 D5
Søvang [DK] 156 B4
Søvassli [N] 180 H1
Sovata [RO] 204 D4
Sövdeborg [S] 158 C3
Söve [TR] 150 D5
Sover [I] 72 D4
Soverato [I] 124 E6
Soveria Mannelli [I] 124 D5
Sövestad [S] 158 D3
Sovetsk [RUS] 200 D5
Sovetskiy [RUS] 178 F3
Søvik [N] 180 D3
Sovinec [CZ] 50 D4
Sovjan [AL] 128 D4
Sowia Góra [PL] 36 B2
Sowiniec [PL] 20 G6
Soyen [D] 60 F4
Søyland [N] 164 A4
Sozaro [TR] 150 C1
Sozopol [BG] 148 F4
Spa [B] 30 E5
Spacco della Regina [I] 114 F4
Spaichingen [D] 58 G3
Spakenburg [NL] 16 E4
Spalding [GB] 10 G6
Spálené Poříčí [CZ] 48 E5
Spalt [D] 46 G6
Spanchevci [BG] 146 F3
S. Pancrázio [I] 72 C3
Spandau [D] 34 E2
Spånga [S] 168 C3
Spangenberg [D] 32 F5
Spangereid [N] 164 C6
Spannberg [A] 62 F4
Španovica [HR] 142 C1
S. Pantaleón de Losa [E] 82 F4
Sparanise [I] 120 D2
Spare [LV] 198 C5
Sparreholm [S] 168 C4
Sparresholm [DK] 156 F4
Spárta [GR] 134 B6
Spartà [I] 124 B7
Spárti [GR] 136 E4
Spárto [GR] 132 D4
Spas [AL] 146 B6
Spasovo [BG] 148 G1
Spasskaya Polist' [RUS] 202 C1
Spáta [GR] 134 C6
Spatharaíoi [GR] 138 H1
Spean Bridge [GB] 6 C6
Specke [S] 166 D2
S. Pedro [P] 94 E2
S. Pedro de Cardeña [E] 82 E6
S. Pedro de Teverga [E] 78 G4
Speinshart [D] 48 B4
Spekedalssetra [N] 182 C5
Spello [I] 116 A2
Spenge [D] 32 D2
Spennymoor [GB] 10 F1
Spenshult [S] 162 B4
Spentrup [DK] 160 E5
Spercheiáda [GR] 132 F4
S. Pere de Ribes [E] 92 D4
Sperlonga [I] 120 C2
Spétses [GR] 136 F3
Speyer [D] 46 C5
Spezzano Albanese [I] 124 D3
Spicino [RUS] 198 G2
Spickendorf [D] 34 C5
Spiddal / An Spidéal [IRL] 2 B5
Spiegelau [D] 60 H2
Spiekeroog [D] 18 C3
Spielbg [D] 46 F5
Spielfeld [A] 74 D3
S. Pietro al Natisone [I] 72 H4
Spiez [CH] 70 E1
Spijkenisse [NL] 16 C5
Spílaia Diroú [GR] 136 E5
Spíli [GR] 140 D5
Spilimbergo [I] 72 F4
Spilja Hrustovača [BIH] 142 B3
Spillum [N] 190 C5
Spina, Necropoli di- [I] 110 G3
Spinalógka [GR] 140 F4
Spinazzola [I] 120 H3
Spincourt [F] 44 E3
Spind [N] 164 C5
Špindlerův-Mlýn [CZ] 50 A2
Spineta Nuova [I] 120 F4
Špionica Donja [BIH] 142 D3
Špišić Bukovica [HR] 74 G5
Spiss [A] 72 B2
Spišská Belá [SK] 52 B6
Spišská Nová Ves [SK] 64 E2
Spišské Podhradie [SK] 64 F2
Spišský Hrad [SK] 64 F2
Spišský Štvrtok [SK] 64 E2
Spital am Pyhrn [A] 62 B6
Spittal an der Drau [A] 72 H3
Spitz [A] 62 D4
Spjærøy [N] 166 B3
Spjald [DK] 160 B6
Spjelkavik [N] 180 D3
Spjutsund [FIN] 178 B4
Split [HR] 144 A2
Splügen [CH] 70 G2
Spodnja Idrija [SLO] 74 B5
Spodsbjerg [DK] 156 E4
Špogi [LV] 198 F6
Spohle [D] 18 C4
Spoleto [I] 116 B3
Spoltore [I] 116 D4
Spotorno [I] 108 H3
Spøttrup [DK] 160 C4
Sprakensehl [D] 32 H1
Spręcowo [PL] 22 G4
Spreenhagen [D] 34 F3
Spremberg [D] 34 F5
Spresiano [I] 72 E5
Springe [D] 32 F2
Sproge [S] 168 F5
Spy [B] 30 D5
Spychowo [PL] 24 C4
Spydeberg [N] 166 B2
Spytkowice [PL] 50 H5
Squillace [I] 124 E6
Squinzano [I] 122 G4
Srahmore [IRL] 2 C3
Srb [HR] 112 H4
Srbac [BIH] 142 C2
Srbica [SRB] 146 C5
Srbobran [MNE] 204 A5
Srbobran [SRB] 76 E6
Srđevići [BIH] 144 B1
Srdiečko [SK] 64 D2
Srebărna [BG] 148 E1
Srebrenica [BIH] 142 F4
Srebrenik [BIH] 142 D3
Sredets [BG] 148 C5
Sredets [BG] 148 F5
Središče ob Dravi [SLO] 74 F4
Sredishte [BG] 148 F1
Srednje [BIH] 142 D4
Srednogortsi [BG] 130 E1
Sredno Gradishte [BG] 148 C5
Sredogriv [BG] 146 E3
Śrem [PL] 36 C3
Sremska Kamenica [SRB] 142 F1
Sremska Mitrovica [MNE] 204 A6
Sremska Mitrovica [SRB] 142 F2
Sremska Rača [SRB] 142 F2
Sremski Karlovci [SRB] 142 F2
Sribne [UA] 202 E7
Srní [CZ] 62 A2
Środa Śląska [PL] 36 C6
Środa Wielkopolska [PL] 36 D3
Srokowo [PL] 24 C3
S. Roque do P. [P] 100 C3
Srpci [MK] 128 E3
Srp. Itebej [SRB] 76 F6
Srpska Crnja [SRB] 76 F6
Srpski Miletić [SRB] 76 C6
S. Salvador de Leyre [E] 84 C4
S. Silvestre de Guzmán [E] 94 E5
S. Stefano d'Aveto [I] 110 C3
Sta [S] 182 E1
Staaken [D] 34 E2
Sta. Ana, Monasterio de- [E] 104 C2
Staatz [A] 62 F3
Stabbestad [N] 164 F4
Stabbursnes [N] 194 C2
Stabekk [N] 166 B1
Sta. Casilda [E] 82 F5
Stachy [CZ] 48 E6
Sta. Coloma [AND] 84 H6
Sta. Coloma de G. [E] 92 E4
Sta. Cristina de Lena [E] 78 H4
Stade [D] 18 E4
Stadl a. d. Mur [A] 74 B2
Stadra [S] 166 G2
Stadskanaal [NL] 16 H3
Stadt Allendorf [D] 32 E6
Stadthagen [D] 32 F2
Stadtilm [D] 46 G1
Stadtkyll [D] 30 F6
Stadtlauringen [D] 46 F3
Stadtlohn [D] 16 G5
Stadtoldendorf [D] 32 F3
Stadtroda [D] 48 B1
Stadtsteinach [D] 46 H3
St Aegyd [A] 62 D5
Sta. Elena [E] 84 E5
Sta. Espina, Monasterio de- [E] 88 E1
Stäfa [CH] 58 G5
Staffanstorp [DK] 158 C3
Staffarda, Abbazia di- [I] 108 F2
Staffelstein [D] 46 G3
Stafford [GB] 10 E5
St-Affrique [F] 106 D3
Stágeira [GR] 130 C4
St-Agnant [F] 54 C5
St-Agrève [F] 68 E5
Stahle [D] 32 F3
Stai [N] 172 C1
Staicele [LV] 198 E4
St-Aignan [F] 40 G5
St-Aignan [F] 54 H2
Staigue Fort [IRL] 4 B4
Stainach [A] 62 B6
Staines [GB] 14 E4
Stainsland [N] 164 D4
Stainville [F] 44 D5
Stainz [A] 74 D2
Stakčín [SK] 64 H2
Stakenjokk [S] 190 E4
Stakkvik [N] 192 G1
Stalać [SRB] 146 C3
St-Alban [F] 68 C5
St Albans [GB] 14 E3
Stalden [CH] 70 E2
Stalheim [N] 170 D3
Stalheims-Kleivene Museum [N] 170 C3
Stalída [GR] 140 F4
Stall [A] 72 G2
Stallarholmen [S] 168 C3
Stallberg [D] 20 E4
Ställberg [S] 166 G1
Ställdalen [S] 166 G1
Stalon [S] 190 F4
Stalowa Wola [PL] 52 E2
St-Amand-en-Puisaye [F] 56 D2
St-Amand-les-Eaux [F] 28 G3
St-Amand-Longpré [F] 42 C6
St-Amand-Montrond [F] 56 C4
St-Amans [F] 68 C5
St-Amant-Roche-Savine [F] 68 D3
Sta. Maria da Real [E] 78 C4
Sta. Maria de Conxo [E] 78 C3
Sta. Maria de la Vega [E] 88 D2
Sta. María de Lebeña [E] 82 D3
Sta. Maria de Melque [E] 96 E2
Sta. Maria de Mezonzo [E] 78 D3
Sta. Maria la Real [E] 82 D4
Sta. Maria la Real [E] 84 A6
Stambolovo [BG] 148 C3
St-Ambroix [F] 106 F2
Sta. M. de Bellpuig de les Avellanes [E] 92 B2
St-Amé [F] 58 C3
Stameriena [LV] 198 F4
Stamford [GB] 14 E1
Stamná [GR] 132 E5
St-Amour [F] 56 H6
Stampfen [A] 72 G2
Stams [A] 72 C1
Stamsund [N] 192 D4
St Andrä [A] 74 C3
St-André [F] 42 D3
St Andreasberg [D] 32 G4
St-André-de-Cubzac [F] 66 D3
St-André-les-Alpes [F] 108 D3
St Andrews [GB] 8 F2
Stänga [S] 168 G5
Stange [N] 172 C4
Stangerum [DK] 160 E5
Stanghelle [N] 170 B3
Staniewice [PL] 22 B2
Stanišić [SRB] 76 C5
Stanisławów [PL] 38 C3
Štanjel [SLO] 72 H5
Stanjevci [MK] 128 F1
Staňkov [CZ] 48 D5
St Annaparochie [NL] 16 F2
Stanós [GR] 130 C4
Stans [CH] 58 F6
Stansstad [CH] 58 F6
St-Anthème [F] 68 E3
St-Antoine [F] 68 G4
St.-Antoine, Chapelle- [F] 84 D3
St Anton [A] 72 B1
St-Antonin-Noble-Val [F] 66 G6
St. Antonino [F] 114 B3
Stany [PL] 52 D2
Stanzach [A] 60 C6
St-Août [F] 54 H4
Stapar [SRB] 76 C6
Staphorst [NL] 16 F3
Stapnes [N] 164 B4
Stąporków [PL] 38 B6
Stara [PL] 36 H6
Stará Bystrica [SK] 50 G6
Stara Cerkev [SLO] 74 C6
Starachowice [PL] 38 B6
Stara Gradiška [HR] 142 C2
Stara Krašnica [PL] 50 B1
Stará L'ubovňa [SK] 52 C6
Stara Moravica [SRB] 76 D5
Stara Novalja [HR] 112 F3
Stara Pazova [SRB] 142 G2
Stara Reka [BG] 148 D4
Stará Turá [SK] 62 H3
Stará Voda [CZ] 48 C4
Staravolya [BY] 38 G1
Stara Wrona [PL] 38 B2
Staraya Russa [RUS] 202 C2
Staraya Toropa [RUS] 202 C3
Stara Zagora [BG] 148 C5
Starcevo [BG] 130 E2
Stare Czarnowo [PL] 20 F5
Stare Dębno [PL] 20 H4
Staré Hory [SK] 64 C2
Stare Jeżewo [PL] 24 E5
Staré Město [CZ] 50 C3
Staré Město [CZ] 50 C4
Staré Město [CZ] 62 H2
Stare Osieczno [PL] 20 H6
Stargard-Szczeciński [PL] 20 F5
Stårheim [N] 180 C5
Stari Bar [MNE] 144 E5
Stari Dojran [MK] 128 H3
Starigrad [HR] 112 F3
Stari Grad [HR] 144 A2
Stari Gradac [HR] 74 G5
Starigrad Paklenica [HR] 112 G4
Stari Mikanovci [HR] 142 D1
Stari Slankamen [SRB] 142 G2
Staritsa [RUS] 202 E3
Starjak [HR] 74 E6
Starkov [CZ] 50 B5
Starnberg [D] 60 D4
Starod [SLO] 112 E1
Starodub [RUS] 202 E5
Starogard [PL] 20 G4
Starogard Gdański [PL] 22 E3
Starokostiantyniv [UA] 202 C8
Staromieście [PL] 50 H2
Staro Nagoričane, Manastir- [MK] 146 D6
Staro Oryakhovo [BG] 148 F3
Staropol'ye [RUS] 198 G1
Starosel [BG] 148 B5
Staroselci [BG] 148 A3
Staro selo [BG] 148 A4
Staro Selo [BG] 148 D1
Starożreby [PL] 36 H2
Starup [DK] 156 B2
Starup [DK] 156 C3
Starý Bernštejn [CZ] 48 G2
Stary Borek [PL] 52 E4
Starychi [UA] 52 G3
Stary Dzierzgoń [PL] 22 F4
Stary Gózd [PL] 38 B5
Starý Hrozenkov [CZ] 64 A2
Staryi Sambir [UA] 52 F5
Stary Plzenec [CZ] 48 E5
Stary Sącz [PL] 52 B5
Starý Smokovec [SK] 52 B6
Stary Szelków [PL] 38 B1
Starý Vestec [CZ] 48 G3
Stary Wieś [PL] 38 E6
Staryya Darohi [BY] 202 C6
Starzyny [PL] 50 H2
St-Astier [F] 66 F3
Staszów [PL] 52 C2
Stat. Angístis [GR] 130 C3
Stathelle [N] 164 G3
Statland [N] 190 C5
Statte [I] 122 E4
St-Aubane [F] 108 E4
St-Auban-sur-l'Ouvèze [F] 108 B2
St-Aubin-d'Aubigné [F] 26 C5
St-Aubin-du-Cormier [F] 26 D5
St-Aubin-sur-Mer [F] 26 F3
St.-Augustin, Château de- [F] 56 D4
St-Aulaye [F] 66 E2
Staume [N] 180 C5
Staupitz [D] 34 E5
St Austell [GB] 12 C5
Stava [S] 162 D1
Stavang [N] 180 B6
Stavanger [N] 164 B3
Stavaträsk [S] 196 A4
Stave [N] 192 E3
Staveley [GB] 10 F5
Stavelot [B] 30 E5
Stavenisse [NL] 16 C6
Staveren [NL] 16 E3
Stavern [D] 16 H3
Stavern [N] 164 G3
Stavertsi [BG] 148 A3
Stavkirke [N] 164 F2
Stavkirke [N] 170 E1
St-Avold [F] 44 F4
Stavre [S] 182 H3
Stavreviken [S] 184 E4
Stavrochóri [GR] 140 G5
Stavrodrómi [GR] 136 D2
Stavrós [GR] 128 G4
Stavrós [GR] 130 C4
Stavrós [GR] 132 C5
Stavrós [GR] 132 G3
Stavrós [GR] 134 B4
Stavrós [GR] 134 C6
Stavrós [GR] 140 C4
Stavrós tis Psókas [CY] 154 F5
Stavroúpoli [GR] 130 E2
Stavsjø [N] 172 B3
Stavsnäs [S] 168 E3
Stawiguda [PL] 22 G4
Stawiski [PL] 24 D5
Stawiszyn [PL] 36 E4
St-Aygulf [F] 108 D5
St-Bard [F] 68 B1
St. Barthélemy [CH] 70 C1
St.-Barthélemy [F] 26 E4
St. Bartholomä [D] 60 G6
St-Béat [F] 84 F5
St-Beauzély [F] 106 D2
St-Benin [F] 56 D4
St-Benoît-du-Sault [F] 54 G5
St-Benoît-sur-Loire [F] 42 F6
St-Bertrand-de-Comminges [F] 84 F4
St.-Blaise [F] 106 G5
St Blasien [D] 58 F4
St-Blin [F] 44 D6
St-Bonnet-de-Joux [F] 56 F6
St-Bonnet-en-Champsaur [F] 68 H6
St-Bonnet-le-Château [F] 68 E3
St-Brevin-les-Pins [F] 40 E6
St-Brice-en-Coglès [F] 26 D5
St-Brieuc [F] 26 B4
St-Calais [F] 42 C5
St-Cast-le-Guildo [F] 26 B4
St-Céré [F] 66 H4
St-Cergue [CH] 70 B1
St-Cernin [F] 68 B4
St-Chamas [F] 106 H4
St-Chamond [F] 68 F3
St-Chély-d'Apcher [F] 68 C5
St-Chély-d'Aubrac [F] 68 B5
St-Chinian [F] 106 D4
St Christina / Santa Cristina [I] 72 D3
St Christoph [A] 72 B1
St. Christophe-en-Oisans [F] 70 A5
St-Ciers-sur-Gironde [F] 66 D2
St-Cirq-Lapopie [F] 66 G5
St.-Clair [F] 26 F3
St-Clar [F] 66 E6
St-Claud [F] 54 E6
St-Claude [F] 70 A1
St Clears [GB] 12 D2
St-Clément [F] 44 F6
St-Clément-sur-Durance [F] 108 E2
St-Côme-d'Olt [F] 68 B5
St.-Cosme-en-Vairais [F] 26 G6
St-Cyprien [F] 66 F4
St-Cyprien-Plage [F] 92 G1
St. David's [GB] 12 D1
St-Denis [F] 42 F3
St-Denis-d'Oléron [F] 54 B5
St-Denis d'Orques [F] 42 A5
St-Didier-en-Velay [F] 68 E4
St-Dié [F] 58 D2
St-Dizier [F] 44 C5
St-Donat-sur-l'Herbasse [F] 68 F4
St. Doulagh's Church [IRL] 2 F6
Steane [N] 164 E2
Ste-Anne-d'Auray [F] 26 A6
Ste-Anne-la-Palud [F] 40 B2
Ste.-Barbe [F] 40 C3
Stechelberg [CH] 70 E2
Štěchovice [CZ] 48 F4
Steckborn [CH] 58 G4
Ste-Croix [CH] 58 C6
Ste-Croix-Volvestre [F] 84 G4
Steeg [A] 72 B1
Steenbergen [NL] 16 C6
Ste.-Engrâce [F] 84 D4
Ste-Enimie [F] 68 C6
Steenvoorde [F] 28 E2
Steenwijk [NL] 16 F3
Stefáni [GR] 132 D3
Štefanikova Mohyla [SK] 62 H3
Stefaniná [GR] 130 C4
Stefanovo [BG] 148 F2
Ste-Foy-la-Grande [F] 66 E3
Stegaros [N] 170 E5
Ste-Gauburge-Ste-Colombe [F] 26 G5
Stege [DK] 156 G4
Stegeborg [S] 168 B5
Stegersbach [A] 74 E2
Stegna [PL] 22 E2
St-Egrève [F] 68 H4
Ste-Hélène [F] 66 C3
Ste-Hermine [F] 54 C3
Stehnovo [RUS] 198 H4
Steigen [N] 192 D5
Steilwände [D] 60 B5
Stein [A] 62 D4
Stein [D] 46 G5
Stein [N] 170 H5
Stein [N] 190 B5
Steinaberg bru [N] 170 C5
Stein am Rhein [CH] 58 G4
Steinau [D] 46 E2
Steinbach [D] 46 H2
Steinberg [A] 74 F1
Steinberg [D] 156 C5
Steinberg am Rofan [A] 60 E6
Steine [N] 170 B2
Steinestø [N] 170 B3
Steinfeld [A] 72 G3
Steinfeld [D] 30 G5
Steinfeld [D] 32 D1
Steinfurt [D] 16 H5
Steingaden [D] 60 D5
Steinhagen [D] 20 C3
Steinhausen [D] 60 B4
Steinheim [D] 32 E3
Steinhorst [D] 32 G1
Steinibach [CH] 58 G6
Steinkjer [N] 190 C5
Steinløysa [N] 180 E2
Stein Pass [A/D] 60 G6
Steinsåsen [N] 182 D4
Steinsberg [D] 46 C5
Steinsburg [D] 46 F2
Steinsdal [N] 190 B6
Steinshøle [N] 170 F5
Steinsholt [N] 164 G2
Steinsøynes [N] 180 F1
Steinsvik [N] 180 C4
Ste.- Jalle [F] 108 B2
Steknica [PL] 22 C1
Ste-Livrade-sur-Lot [F] 66 E5
Stellendam [NL] 16 C5
St-Eloy-les-Mines [F] 56 C6
Ste-Marie-aux-Mines [F] 58 D2
Ste-Marie-de-Campan [F] 84 F4
Ste-Marie-du-Mont [F] 26 E2
Ste-Maure-de-Touraine [F] 54 F3
Ste-Maxime [F] 108 D5
Ste-Menehould [F] 44 C4
Ste-Mère-Eglise [F] 26 E2
St-Emilion [F] 66 D3
Sten [S] 162 D1
Stenay [F] 44 D3
Stenbjerg [DK] 160 B4
Stenbo [S] 162 G3
Stendal [D] 34 C2
Stende [LV] 198 C5
Steneby [S] 166 D4
Stengelsrud [N] 164 G1
St Englmar [D] 60 G2
Stenhammar [S] 168 B4
Stenhamra [S] 168 D3
Stení [GR] 134 C4
Steninge [S] 160 H5
Steninge [S] 168 D2
Stenlille [DK] 156 F3
Stenløse [DK] 156 G2
Stennäs [S] 190 G6
Stenó [GR] 136 E2
Sténoma [GR] 132 F4
Stensele [S] 190 F4
Stensjö [S] 162 G3
Stensjön [S] 162 E2
Stenstorp [S] 166 F6
Stensträsk [S] 190 H4
Stenstrup [DK] 156 D4
Stensund [S] 190 G2
Stensund [S] 190 G3
Stensunda [S] 168 E1
Stenträsk [S] 190 H2
Stenudden [S] 190 G2
Stenungsund [S] 160 G1
Steornabhagh / Stornoway [GB] 6 C2
Stepanci [MK] 128 E2
Stepnica [PL] 20 F4
Stepojevac [SRB] 146 B1
Sterdyń-Osada [PL] 38 D2
Sterehushche [UA] 204 G3
Sterlawki Wielkie [PL] 24 C3
Stern, Manastir- [BIH] 142 C2
Stern / la Villa [I] 72 E3
Stérna [GR] 130 D2
Sternberg [D] 20 B4
Šternberk [CZ] 48 H6
Šternberk [CZ] 50 D5
Stérnes [GR] 140 C4
Stérnia [GR] 138 E1
Sterringi [N] 180 F5
Sterzing / Vipiteno [I] 72 D2
Ste-Sévère [F] 56 B5
Stes-Maries-de-la-Mer [F] 106 F5
St. Estèphe [F] 66 C2
Ste-Suzanne [F] 42 A4
Stęszew [PL] 36 C3
Štětí [CZ] 48 F2
St-Étienne [F] 68 E3
St-Étienne [F] 108 C3
St-Étienne-de-Baïgorry [F] 84 C3
St-Étienne-de-St-Geoirs [F] 68 G4
St-Etienne-de-Tinée [F] 108 E3
Ste-Tulle [F] 108 C4
Stevenage [GB] 14 E3
Stevrek [BG] 148 D3
Stewarton [GB] 8 D3
Steyerberg [D] 32 E1
Steyersberg [A] 62 E6
Steyr [A] 62 B5
Steyr-Durchbruch [A] 62 B5
Stezherovo [BG] 148 B2
St-Fargeau [F] 56 D2
St.-Fiacre [F] 40 C3
St-Firmin [F] 68 H6
St-Florent [F] 40 G6
St-Florent [F] 56 B3
St-Florent [F] 114 C3
St.-Florent-des-Bois [F] 54 C3
St-Florentin [F] 42 H6
St. Florian [A] 60 H4
St-Flour [F] 68 C4
St-Fort-sur-Gironde [F] 66 D1
St.-Fort-sur-le-Né [F] 66 D1
St-Fulgent [F] 54 C2
St Gallen [A] 62 C6
St Gallen [CH] 58 H5
St Gallenkirch [A] 72 B1
St-Galmier [F] 68 E3
St. Gangolf [D] 44 F3
St-Gaudens [F] 84 G4
St-Gaultier [F] 54 G4
St-Geniez-d'Olt [F] 68 B6
St-Genis-de-Saintonge [F] 66 D1
St-Genix-sur-Guiers [F] 68 H3
St. George [CH] 70 B1
St Georgen [A] 60 H5
St Georgen [A] 74 C2
St Georgen [D] 58 F3
St-Georges [F] 40 G6
St-Georges-de-Didonne [F] 54 C6
St. Georges-on-Couzan [F] 68 E2
St-Geours-de-Maremne [F] 66 B6
St-Germain [F] 42 F3
St-Germain [F] 66 G2
St-Germain-de-Calberte [F] 106 F2
St-Germain-de-Joux [F] 68 H2
St-Germain-des-Fossés [F] 56 D6
St-Germain-des-Vaux [F] 26 D1
St-Germain-du-Bois [F] 56 G5
St-Germain-du-Plain [F] 56 G5
St-Germain-Laval [F] 68 E2
St-Germain-Lembron [F] 68 C3
St-Germain-l'Herm [F] 68 D3
St-Germain-Plage [F] 26 D3
St-Germer-de-Fly [F] 28 D6
St-Gervais [F] 106 D3
St-Gervais-d'Auvergne [F] 68 C1
St-Gervais-les-Bains [F] 70 C3
St-Géry [F] 66 G5
St-Gildas-des-Bois [F] 40 E5
St Gilgen [A] 60 H5
St-Gilles [F] 106 G4
St-Gilles-Croix-de-Vie [F] 54 B2
St-Gilles-Pligeaux [F] 26 A4
St-Gingolph [CH] 70 C2
St-Girons [F] 84 G5
St-Girons-en-Marensin [F] 66 B5
St-Girons-Plage [F] 66 A5
St Goar [D] 46 B2
St Goarshausen [D] 46 B2
St-Gobain [F] 28 F6
St-Gorgon-Main [F] 58 B5
St-Guénolé [F] 40 B3
St-Guilhem-le-Desert [F] 106 E3
St Helens [GB] 10 D4
St Helier [GBJ] 26 C3
St. Hilaire Cottes [F] 28 E3
St-Hilaire-de-Villefranche [F] 54 C5
St-Hilaire-du-Harcouët [F] 26 D5
St-Hippolyte [F] 58 C5
St-Hippolyte-du-Fort [F] 106 F3
St. Höga [S] 160 G1
St-Honoré les-Bains [F] 56 E4
St-Hubert [B] 44 D1
Stia [I] 110 G5
Sticciano Scalo [I] 114 F2
Stiefern [A] 62 E3
Stiens [NL] 16 F2
Stift Zwettl [A] 62 D3
Stigen [N] 172 E2
Stigen [S] 166 D5
Stigfoss [N] 180 E3
Stigliano [I] 122 C4
Stigliano, Bagni di- [I] 114 H5
Stignano [I] 124 D7
Stigsjö [S] 184 F4
Stigtomta [S] 168 C4

Sunnansjö [S] 184 D4
Sunnaryd [S] 162 C4
Sunndal [N] 170 C5
Sunndalsøra [N] 180 F3
Sunne [S] 166 E1
Sunnemo [S] 166 F1
Sunnersta [S] 168 D2
Suntaži [LV] 198 E5
Suodenniemi [FIN] 176 E1
Suojoki [FIN] 186 B5
Suokonmäki [FIN] 186 D3
Suolahti [FIN] 186 G3
Suolovuobme [N] 194 B3
Suomenlinna / Sveaborg [FIN] 176 H5
Suomenniemi [FIN] 178 D1
Suomijärvi [FIN] 186 C5
Suomusjärvi [FIN] 176 F4
Suonenjoki [FIN] 188 C3
Suontaka [FIN] 176 D3
Suontee [FIN] 188 C3
Suopelto [FIN] 176 H1
Suorva [S] 192 F5
Šuoššjávri [N] 194 B4
Suotuperä [FIN] 196 D5
Suovanlahti [FIN] 186 G2
Superga [I] 70 D5
Supetar [HR] 144 A2
Supino [I] 116 B6
Supraśl [PL] 24 F5
Surahammar [S] 168 B2
Šurany [SK] 64 B5
Suraż [PL] 24 E6
Surazh [BY] 202 C4
Surazh [RUS] 202 D5
Surbo [I] 122 G4
Surčin [SRB] 142 G2
Surduk [SRB] 142 G2
Surdulica [SRB] 146 E5
Surgères [F] 54 C5
Súria [E] 92 D3
Šurice [SK] 64 E4
Surju [EST] 198 E3
Šurlane [SRB] 146 D6
Surnadalsöra [N] 180 G2
Sŭrnitsa [BG] 130 C1
Sursee [CH] 58 E5
Surtainville [F] 26 D2
Surte [S] 160 H2
Survilliers [F] 42 G3
Susa [I] 70 C5
Šušara [SRB] 142 H2
Susch [CH] 72 B2
Suscinio, Château de- [F] 40 D5
Susek [SRB] 142 F1
Suševo [MK] 128 G2
Sushitsa [BG] 148 C3
Sušice [CZ] 48 E6
Suso y Yuso, Monasterios de- [E] 82 G6
Süssen [D] 60 B2
Susurluk [TR] 150 D5
Susz [PL] 22 F4
Sutivan [HR] 144 A2
Sutjeska [SRB] 142 H1
Sütlaç [TR] 152 H4
Sutomore [MNE] 144 E5
Sutri [I] 114 H4
Sutrieu [F] 68 H2
Sutton Coldfield [GB] 10 E6
Süttorf [D] 18 G6
Suure-Jaani [EST] 198 E2
Suurejõe [EST] 198 E2
Suuremõisa [EST] 198 C2
Suurlahti [FIN] 178 D1
Suurmäki [FIN] 188 E3
Suva Reka [SRB] 146 C6
Suvekas [LT] 200 G3
Suvereto [I] 114 E2
Suvorove [UA] 204 F4
Suvorovo [BG] 148 F2
Suvorovo [RUS] 202 E3
Suwałki [PL] 24 E3
Suystamo [RUS] 188 H4
Suzzara [I] 110 E2
Svabensverk [S] 174 C3
Svalöv [S] 158 C2
Svalyava [UA] 204 C3
Svanabyn [S] 190 F5
Svaneholm [S] 158 C3
Svanehölm [S] 166 H6
Svaneke [DK] 158 E4
Svanesund [S] 166 C6
Svängsta [S] 158 E1
Svaningen [S] 190 E5
Sv. Anna [CZ] 50 A5
Svannäs [S] 190 G2
Svanskog [S] 166 D3
Svanvik [N] 194 F3
Svappavaara [S] 192 G5
Svarar [FIN] 186 B3
Svärdsjo [S] 174 D4
Svarstad [N] 164 G2
Svartå [S] 166 G3
Svärta [S] 168 C4
Svartå Mustio [FIN] 176 F5
Svartberget [S] 194 B8
Svartbyn [S] 194 B8
Svarte [S] 158 C3
Svärtinge [S] 168 B5
Svartisdalen [N] 190 E2
Svartlå [S] 196 A2
Svartnäs [S] 174 D3
Svartnäs [S] 190 H4
Svartnes [N] 192 D6
Svartnes [N] 194 F2
Svarttjärn [S] 190 F3
Svartvik [S] 184 E5
Svatá Hora [CZ] 48 F5
Svatá Kateřina [CZ] 48 C5
Svategjel [N] 170 E2
Svätý Anton [SK] 64 C4
Svätý Jur [SK] 62 G4
Svätý Mikuláš [CZ] 50 B4
Svätý Peter [SK] 64 B5
Sv. Barbora [CZ] 48 G6
Sveaborg / Suomenlinna [FIN] 176 H5
Svedala [S] 158 C3
Svedasai [LT] 200 G4
Svedje [S] 184 E5
Svedje [S] 184 G1
Svedje [S] 190 E5
Sveg [S] 182 G5
Sveindal [N] 164 D4
Sveio [N] 164 A1
Švėkšna [LT] 200 D4
Svelgen [N] 180 B5
Svellingen [N] 190 A6
Svelvik [N] 164 H2
Svenarum [S] 162 D3
Švenčionėliaj [LT] 200 H4
Švenčionys [LT] 200 H5
Svendborg [DK] 156 E4
Svenes [N] 164 E4
Svenkerud [N] 170 G3
Svenljunga [S] 162 B3
Svennevad [S] 166 H4
Svensby [N] 192 G2
Svenskby [FIN] 176 F5
Svensköp [S] 158 D2
Svenstavik [S] 182 G3
Svenstorp [S] 158 C2
Svenstrup [DK] 160 D4
Sveom [N] 180 G5
Švermov [CZ] 48 F3
S. Vero Milis [I] 118 C5
Sveta Petka [SRB] 146 D2
Sveti Andrejaš [MK] 128 E1
Sveti Ivan Žabno [HR] 74 F5
Sveti Jovan Bigorski [MK] 128 C2
Sveti Konstantin [BG] 148 A6
Sveti Naum [AL] 128 D4
Sveti Nikita [MK] 146 C6
Sveti Nikole [MK] 128 F1
Sveti Pantelejmon [MK] 128 E1
Sveti Rok [HR] 112 G4
Sveti Stefan [MNE] 144 E5
Světlá nad Sázavou [CZ] 48 H5
Svetlen [BG] 148 D3
Svetlice [SK] 52 E6
Svetlina [BG] 148 D5
Svetlina [BG] 148 E5
Svetlogorsk [RUS] 200 C5
Svetlyy [RUS] 22 G1
Svetlyy [RUS] 194 E4
Svetogorsk [RUS] 178 F2
Svetozar Miletic [SRB] 76 C5
Svetvinčenat [HR] 112 D2
Svežen [BG] 148 B5
Svib [HR] 144 B2
S. Vicente de la Cabeza [E] 80 G4
Svidnik [SK] 52 D5
Švihov [CZ] 48 D5
Svilajnac [SRB] 146 C1
Svilengrad [BG] 150 A2
Sviljojevo [SRB] 76 C6
Svinesund [S] 166 C3
Svinesundbrö [N/S] 166 B3
Svingstad [N] 170 H3
Svingvoll [N] 170 H2
Svinhult [S] 162 E2
Svinná [SK] 64 B3
Svinndal [N] 166 B2
Svinninge [DK] 156 F2
Svir [BY] 200 H5
Svishtov [BG] 148 C2
Svislach [BY] 24 G5
Svitavy [CZ] 50 B4
Svitlovods'k [UA] 202 F8
Sv. Juraj [HR] 112 F2
Sv. Jurij [SLO] 74 E3
Sv. Martin [HR] 74 F4
Sv. Nikola [MNE] 128 A1
Svoboda [BG] 148 F1
Svoboda [RUS] 24 C2
Svobodnoye [RUS] 178 F2
Svode [BG] 146 G4
Svodín [SK] 64 B5
Svodje [SRB] 146 E4
Svoge [BG] 146 F4
Svolvær [N] 192 D4
Svorkmo [N] 180 H2
Svormuseet [N] 180 D5
Svratka [CZ] 50 B5
Svrčinovec [SK] 50 F5
Svrljig [SRB] 146 D3
Svullrya [N] 172 D5
Sv. Vid [HR] 112 F2
Svyetlahorsk [BY] 202 C6
Swaffham [GB] 14 G2
Swalmen [NL] 30 F3
Swanage [GB] 12 G5
Swanlinbar [IRL] 2 E4
Swansea [GB] 12 E2
Swarożyn [PL] 22 E3
Swarzędz [PL] 36 C2
Swarzewo [PL] 22 D1
Świdnica [PL] 34 H4
Świdnica [PL] 50 B1
Świdnik [PL] 38 E5
Świdwin [PL] 20 H4
Świebodzice [PL] 50 B1
Świebodzin [PL] 36 A3
Świecie [PL] 22 D5
Świecko [PL] 34 G3
Świeradów-Zdrój [PL] 48 H1
Świerczów [PL] 50 E1
Świerki [PL] 50 B2
Świerzawa [PL] 50 B1
Świerzno [PL] 20 F3
Święta [PL] 20 F4
Święta Anna [PL] 50 G1
Święta Lipka [PL] 24 B3
Święte [PL] 36 E3
Świętno [PL] 36 B4
Swindon [GB] 12 H3
Swinford [IRL] 2 C4
Świnoujście [PL] 20 E3
Swords [IRL] 2 F6
Swornegacie [PL] 22 C4
Swory [PL] 38 E3
Syalyets [BY] 38 H1
Sybaris-Copia [I] 124 D3
Sychevka [RUS] 202 E3
Sycöw [PL] 36 D6
Sydanmää [FIN] 176 D2
Sykaminéa [GR] 134 G2
Sykäräinen [FIN] 196 D6
Syke [D] 18 D6
Sykéa [GR] 136 F4
Sykéa [GR] 140 G5
Sykiá [GR] 130 D6
Sykiá [GR] 132 F1
Sykióna [GR] 136 E1
Sykkylven [N] 180 D4
Sykoúri [GR] 132 G1
Sylling [N] 164 H1
Sylte [N] 180 E2
Symbister [GB] 6 H4
Sými [GR] 154 C3
Synsiö [FIN] 186 H5
Syötekylä [FIN] 196 E2
Sypnievo [PL] 22 C5
Sypniewo [PL] 24 C6
Syrau [D] 48 C2
Syrävaara [FIN] 196 G5
Sysmä [FIN] 178 A1
Sysslebäck [S] 172 E4
Syston [GB] 10 F6
Syväjärvi [FIN] 194 D7
Syvänniemi [FIN] 188 C2
Syvärinpää [FIN] 196 F6
Syvde [N] 180 C4
Sývota [GR] 132 C2
Syvsten [DK] 160 E3
Syyspohja [FIN] 178 E1
Szabadegyháza [H] 76 B2
Szabadszállás [H] 76 C3
Szabolcsbáka [H] 64 H4
Szada [H] 64 D6
Szadek [PL] 36 F4
Szakály [H] 76 B4
Szakcs [H] 76 B3
Szakmár [H] 76 C3
Szalánta [H] 76 B5
Szalkszentmárton [H] 76 C2
Szalonna [H] 64 F3
Szamocin [PL] 22 B6
Szamotuły [PL] 36 C2
Szandaszőlős [H] 76 E2
Szank [H] 76 D3
Szany [H] 74 G1
Szápár [H] 76 A1
Szarvas [H] 76 F2
Szarvasi Arboretum [H] 76 F2
Szarvaskő [H] 64 E5
Szászvár [H] 76 B4
Százhalombatta [H] 76 C1
Szczaniec [PL] 36 A3
Szczawne [PL] 52 E5
Szczawnica [PL] 52 B5
Szczebrzeszyn [PL] 52 F1
Szczecin [PL] 20 F5
Szczecinek [PL] 22 B4
Szczekociny [PL] 50 H2
Szczercöw [PL] 36 G5
Szczucin [PL] 52 C3
Szczuczyn [PL] 24 D4
Szczurowa [PL] 52 B3
Szczyrk [PL] 50 G5
Szczytna [PL] 50 B3
Szczytno [PL] 24 B4
Szécsény [H] 64 D5
Szederkény [H] 76 B5
Szedres [H] 76 B4
Szeged [H] 76 E4
Szeghalom [H] 76 G2
Szegvár [H] 76 E3
Székely [H] 64 H4
Székesfehérvár [H] 76 B2
Székkutas [H] 76 F3
Szekszárd [H] 76 C4
Szemere [H] 64 F3
Szendehely [H] 64 C5
Szendrő [H] 64 F4
Szendrölád [H] 64 F4
Szentendre [H] 64 C6
Szentes [H] 76 E3
Szentliszló [H] 74 G3
Szentliszló [H] 76 A5
Szentlőrinc [H] 76 A5
Szenyér [H] 74 H4
Szephalom [H] 64 G3
Szerencs [H] 64 G4
Szestno [PL] 24 B3
Szetlew [PL] 36 E3
Szigetszentmiklós [H] 76 C1
Szigetvár [H] 76 A5
Szigliget [H] 74 H3
Szikszó [H] 64 F4
Szil [H] 62 G6
Szilvágy [H] 74 F3
Szilvásvárad [H] 64 E4
Szirák [H] 64 D5
Szittyóürbő [H] 76 C2
Szklarska Poręba [PL] 48 H1
Szklary [PL] 52 E4
Szklary Górne [PL] 36 B5
Szlichtyngowa [PL] 36 B4
Szob [H] 64 C5
Szolnok [H] 76 E2
Szombathely [H] 74 F2
Szonowice [PL] 50 E3
Szőny [H] 64 B6
Szpetal Górny [PL] 36 G2
Szprotawa [PL] 34 H5
Szreńsk [PL] 22 G6
Szropy [PL] 22 F3
Sztabin [PL] 24 E4
Sztum [PL] 22 E4
Sztutowo [PL] 22 F2
Sztynort [PL] 24 C3
Szubin [PL] 22 C6
Szűcs [H] 64 E5
Szulmierz [PL] 22 H6
Szumirad [PL] 50 E1
Szumowo [PL] 24 D6
Szurdokpüspöki [H] 64 D5
Szwecja [PL] 22 B5
Szydłów [PL] 36 G5
Szydłów [PL] 52 C2
Szydłowiec [PL] 38 B6
Szydłowo [PL] 22 B6
Szymbark [PL] 22 F4
Szypliszki [PL] 24 E2

T

Taalintehdas / Dalsbruk [FIN] 176 E6
Taastrup [DK] 156 G2
Taavetti [FIN] 178 D2
Tab [H] 76 A3
Tabaja [BIH] 144 C3
Tábara [E] 80 H4
Taberg [S] 162 D2
Tabernas [E] 102 G5
Tabiano Bagni [I] 110 D2
Taboada [E] 78 D4
Tábor [CZ] 48 G5
Tábua [P] 86 E2
Tabuaço [P] 80 D5
Tabuenca [E] 90 D3
Täby [S] 168 D2
Tachov [CZ] 48 C4
Tackåsen [S] 172 H2
Tadcaster [GB] 10 F3
Tädene [S] 166 E5
Tafalla [E] 84 B4
Tafira [E] 100 C6
Tafjord [N] 180 E4
Täfteå [S] 184 G2
Tagaranna [EST] 198 C3
Tagenac [F] 68 C4
Taggia [I] 108 G4
Taghmon [IRL] 4 F5
Tagliacozzo [I] 116 B5
Táglio di Po [I] 110 H2
Tahal [E] 102 G4
Tahitótfalu [H] 64 C6
Tahivilla [E] 100 G5
Tahtacı [TR] 152 C2
Tahtaköprü [TR] 150 G5
Tai di Cadore [I] 72 F4
Tailfingen [D] 58 G2
Taillebois [F] 26 F4
Taimoniemi [FIN] 186 G2
Tain [GB] 6 E4
Taininiemi [FIN] 196 D2
Tain-l'Hermitage [F] 68 F4
Taipadas [P] 86 C5
Taipale [FIN] 176 E1
Taipale [FIN] 186 F3
Taipale [FIN] 186 H2
Taipaleenharju [FIN] 196 E3
Taipaleenkyla [FIN] 186 D4
Taipalsaari [FIN] 178 D2
Tairbeart / Tarbert [GB] 6 B3
Taivalkoski [FIN] 196 F3
Taivalmaa [FIN] 186 C4
Taivassalo / Tövsala [FIN] 176 C4
Taizé [F] 56 F6
Tajada, Cuevas de la- [E] 98 D2
Tajcy [RUS] 178 H5
Tajo de las Figuras, Cueva del- [E] 100 G5
Takácsi [H] 74 H1
Takamaa [FIN] 176 F1
Takene [S] 166 F3
Takmak [TR] 152 F3
Talachyn [BY] 202 C5
Talalaïvka [UA] 202 F6
Talamone [I] 114 F3
Tál ar Groaz [F] 40 B2
Talarrubias [E] 96 C3
Talaván [E] 86 H4
Talavera de la Reina [E] 88 D6
Talavera la Real [E] 94 G1
Talaveruela [E] 88 C5
Talayuela [E] 88 B6
Talayuelas [E] 98 D3
Talcy [F] 42 D6
Tali [EST] 198 E3
Táliga [E] 94 F2
Talinen [S] 194 B7
Talla [I] 110 G6
Tallaght [IRL] 2 F6
Tallaki [RUS] 24 B1
Tallard [F] 108 D2
Tällas [S] 190 G3
Tallåsen [S] 172 D3
Tallåsen [S] 184 D6
Tällberg [S] 172 H3
Tallhed [S] 172 G2
Tallinn [EST] 198 D1
Talloires [F] 70 B3
Tallow [IRL] 4 D5
Tallsjö [S] 190 G5
Tallträsk [S] 190 G5
Talluskylä [FIN] 186 H2
Tallvik [S] 194 B8
Tállya [H] 64 G4
Talmont [F] 54 C6
Talmont-St-Hilaire [F] 54 B3
Talpaki [RUS] 24 B1
Talsi [LV] 198 C5
Tałty [PL] 24 C4
Talvik [N] 192 H1
Tamajón [E] 88 H4
Tamames [E] 88 B3
Tamanes [N] 194 D2
Tamarë [AL] 144 F4
Tamarino [BG] 148 E5
Tamarit [E] 92 C5
Tamarite de Litera [E] 90 H4
Tamási [H] 76 B3
Tambohuse [DK] 160 C4
Taminaschlucht [CH] 58 H6
Tamis [TR] 134 G1
Tammela [FIN] 176 F3
Tammensiel [D] 18 E1
Tammerfors / Tampere [FIN] 176 F1
Tammijärvi [FIN] 186 G5
Tammilahti [FIN] 186 G5
Tammisaari / Ekenäs [FIN] 176 F6
Tamnič [SRB] 146 E2
Tampere / Tammerfors [FIN] 176 F1
Tamsalu [EST] 198 E1
Tamsweg [A] 72 H2
Tämta [S] 162 B1
Tamworth [GB] 10 E6
Tanabru [N] 194 D2
Tanágra [GR] 134 B5
Tananger [N] 164 A3
Tancarville [F] 26 G3
Tanda [SRB] 146 D1
Tandö [S] 172 F3
Tandragee [NIR] 2 G4
Tandsbyn [S] 182 G3
Tandsjöborg [S] 172 G1
Tånga [S] 155 H1
Tångaberg [S] 160 H3
Tangen [N] 166 B3
Tangen [N] 166 C1
Tangen [N] 172 C4
Tangen [N] 192 F3
Tanger [AFR] 100 F6
Tangerhütte [D] 34 B2
Tangermünde [D] 34 C2
Tanhua [FIN] 194 E6
Taninges [F] 70 B2
Tankolampi [FIN] 186 G3
Tanlay [F] 56 F2
Tann [D] 46 F1
Tannåker [S] 162 C4
Tännäs [S] 182 E4
Tänndalen [S] 182 D4
Tanne [D] 32 H4
Tannenhof [D] 20 C5
Tännforsen [S] 182 E1
Tannheim [A] 60 C6
Tannila [FIN] 196 D3
Tänno [S] 162 D4
Tanowo [PL] 20 F5
Tanttila [FIN] 176 H2
Tanum [N] 164 G3
Tanum [S] 166 C4
Tanumshede [S] 166 C4
Tanus [F] 106 C2
Tanvald [CZ] 48 H2
Taormina [I] 124 B8
Tapa [EST] 198 E1
Tapanivaara [FIN] 196 F4
Tapfheim [D] 60 C2
Tapia de Casariego [E] 78 F2
Tapionkylä [FIN] 194 C7
Tápiószecső [H] 76 D1
Tápiószele [H] 76 D1
Tápiószentmárton [H] 76 D1
Tápiószölös [H] 76 D1
Tapojärvi [FIN] 194 B6
Tapolca [H] 74 H3
Tapolcafő [H] 74 H1
Taponas [F] 68 F2
Tapperøje [DK] 156 G4
Taps [DK] 156 C3
Tapsony [H] 74 G4
Tapsony [H] 76 C1
Tara [IRL] 2 F5
Taraguilla [E] 100 G5
Tarajalejo [E] 100 D6
Tara Kanjon [MNE] 144 E3
Tara Kanjon [MNE] 144 E2
Taraklı [TR] 150 H4
Taramundi [E] 78 F2
Tarancón [E] 96 H2
Táranto [I] 122 E4
Tarare [F] 68 F2
Tarascon [F] 106 G4
Tarascon-sur-Ariège [F] 84 H5
Tarasp [CH] 72 B2
Tarazona [E] 84 A6
Tarazona de la Mancha [E] 98 B4
Tårbæk [DK] 156 H2
Tarbert [GB] 8 C3
Tarbert [IRL] 2 B6
Tarbert / Tairbeart [GB] 6 B3
Tarbes [F] 84 F3
Tarcento [I] 72 G4
Tarčin [BIH] 144 C1
Tarczyn [PL] 38 B4
Tardets-Sorholus [F] 84 D3
Tardienta [E] 90 F3
Tärendö [S] 194 B7
Târgovişte [RO] 204 D5
Târgu Frumos [RO] 204 D3
Târgu Jiu [RO] 204 C5
Târgu Lăpuş [RO] 204 C3
Târgu Mureş [RO] 204 C4
Târgu Neamţ [RO] 204 D3
Târgu Secuiesc [RO] 204 D4
Tarhos [H] 76 G3
Tarhos [H] 76 G3
Tarifa [E] 100 G6
Tarján [H] 64 B6
Tarło [PL] 38 E5
Tarm [DK] 156 B1
Tarmstedt [D] 18 E5
Tärna [S] 168 C1
Tärnaby [S] 190 E3
Tarnala [FIN] 188 G5
Tarnalelesz [H] 64 E5
Tarnaméra [H] 64 E6
Tärnamo [S] 190 E3
Tarnaörs [H] 64 E6
Tarnaszentmiklós [H] 64 E6
Tărnăveni [RO] 204 C4
Tarnawa Duża [PL] 52 F1
Tarnawatka [PL] 52 G2
Tarnawka [PL] 52 E1
Tärnet [N] 194 F3
Tarnobrzeg [PL] 52 D2
Tarnogród [PL] 52 F2
Tárnok [H] 76 C1
Tarnos [F] 66 A6
Tărnova [RO] 76 H4
Tărnovci [BG] 148 D1
Tarnów [PL] 34 G1
Tarnów [PL] 38 C4
Tarnów [PL] 52 C4
Tarnów Jez. [PL] 36 B4
Tarnowo Podgórne [PL] 36 C2
Tarnowskie Góry [PL] 50 F3
Tärnsjö [S] 174 E5
Tärnvik [N] 192 D5
Tarouca [P] 80 D5
Tarp [D] 18 F1
Tarquinia [I] 114 G4
Tarquínia [I] 114 G4
Tarquinia Lido [I] 114 G4
Tarragona [E] 92 C5
Tärrajur [S] 190 H2
Tarrasa / Terrassa [E] 92 E4
Tàrrega [E] 92 C3
Tårs [DK] 156 E4
Tårs [DK] 160 E3
Tarsia [I] 124 D3
Tartas [F] 66 B6
Tartu [EST] 198 F3
Tårup [DK] 156 E3
Tarutino [UA] 204 F4
Tarvainen [FIN] 176 D4
Tarvasjoki [FIN] 176 E4
Tarvisio [I] 72 H3
Tarvola [FIN] 186 D2
Tasapää [FIN] 188 G4
Taşbükü [TR] 154 D2
Täsch [CH] 70 E3
Täsjö [S] 190 F5
Taşköy [TR] 152 F3
Taşkule [TR] 152 C3
Taşlıca [TR] 154 D3
Tasovice [CZ] 62 F3
Tassjö [S] 162 B6
Tata [H] 64 B6
Tatabánya [H] 64 B6
Tataháza [H] 76 D4
Tatarbunary [UA] 204 F4
Tatárszentgyörgy [H] 76 D2
Tatlısu (Akanthoú) [CY] 154 G5
Tatranská Kotlina [SK] 52 B6
Tatranská Lomnica [SK] 52 B6
Tau [N] 164 B3
Taubenlochschlucht [CH] 58 D5
Tauberbischofsheim [D] 46 E4
Taucha [D] 34 C5
Tauerntunnel [A] 72 G2
Tauern Tunnel [A] 72 H1
Taufers / Tubre [I] 72 B3
Taufkirchen [A] 60 H4
Taufkirchen [D] 60 F4
Taujėnai [LT] 200 G4
Taüll [E] 84 G6
Taunton [GB] 12 F4
Taunusstein [D] 46 B3
Tauplitz [A] 62 B6
Taurage [LT] 200 E5
Taurasi [I] 120 F3
Taurianova [I] 124 C7
Taurine, Terme- [I] 114 G5
Taurisano [I] 122 G6
Taurkains [LV] 198 E5
Tauros [GR] 134 C6
Tauste [E] 90 E3
Tauves [F] 68 B2
Tavaklı [TR] 134 G1
Tavannes [CH] 58 D5
Tavarnelle Val di Pesa [I] 110 F6
Tavas [TR] 152 G5
Tavascan [E] 84 G6
Tavastehus / Hämeenlinna [FIN] 176 G3
Tavastila [FIN] 178 C3
Tavastkenka [FIN] 196 E5
Tavastkyro / Hämeenkyrö [FIN] 176 E1
Tavaux [F] 56 H4
Tavelsjö [S] 190 H5
Taverna [I] 124 E5
Tavernelle [I] 114 H2
Tavernes [F] 108 C4
Tavernes de la Valldigna [E] 98 E6
Taviano [I] 122 G6
Tavira [P] 94 D5
Tavistock [GB] 12 D4
Tavna, Manastir- [BIH] 142 E3
Tavole Palatine [I] 122 D4
Tavşancil [TR] 150 F3
Tavşanlı [TR] 152 G1
Taxan [S] 190 F6
Taxenbach [A] 72 G1
Taxiarchón, Moní- [GR] 138 D3
Tayfur [TR] 150 B5
Taytan [TR] 152 E3
Tazha [BG] 148 B4
Tázlár [H] 76 D3
Tazones [E] 82 C1
Tczew [PL] 22 E3
Tczów [PL] 38 C5
Teano [I] 120 D2
Tearce [MK] 146 C6
Teascu [RO] 146 G1
Techendorf [A] 72 G3
Teck [D] 58 H2
Tecklenburg [D] 32 C2
Tecuci [RO] 204 E4
Teerijärvi / Terjärv [FIN] 196 C6
Teféli [GR] 140 E5
Tefenni [TR] 152 H6
Tegéa [GR] 136 E3
Tegelen [NL] 30 F3
Tegelträsk [S] 190 G6
Tegernsee [D] 60 E5
Teggiano [I] 120 G4
Téglás [H] 64 H5
Teglaszin [H] 74 F2
Teglio [I] 72 A4
Teguise [E] 100 E6
Tehi [FIN] 176 H1
Teichel [D] 46 H1
Teichiussa [TR] 152 D6
Teignmouth [GB] 12 E5
Teillay [F] 40 F5
Teillet [F] 106 C3
Teisendorf [D] 60 G5
Teisko [FIN] 186 E6
Teixeiro [E] 78 D2
Tejeda [E] 100 C6
Tejn [DK] 158 E4
Teke [TR] 150 F2
Tekeriš [SRB] 142 F3
Tekin [TR] 152 H4
Tekirdağ [TR] 150 C3
Tekmen [TR] 154 F4
Tekovské Lužany [SK] 64 B5
Telana [I] 118 E5
Telavåg [N] 170 A4
Telč [CZ] 48 H6
Teldau [D] 18 G5
Telde [E] 100 C6
Teleborg [S] 162 E5
Telekháza [H] 64 F6
Telese Terme [I] 120 E2
Telford [GB] 10 D6
Telfs [A] 72 C1
Telgte [D] 32 C3
Telheiro [P] 94 B3
Telish [BG] 148 A3
Teljo [FIN] 196 G5
Tellingstedt [D] 18 E2
Tellskap [CH] 58 F6
Telmessos [TR] 154 F2
Telšiai [LT] 200 E4
Telti [I] 118 D3
Tembleque [E] 96 G2
Temelín [CZ] 48 F6
Temerin [SRB] 142 F1
Temerin [SRB] 204 A5
Temmes [FIN] 196 D4
Temnata Dupka [BG] 146 F4
Témpi [GR] 132 G1
Témpio Pausánia [I] 118 D3
Templemore [IRL] 4 E3
Templetouhy [IRL] 4 E3
Templin [D] 20 D6
Templom [H] 64 C5
Temse [B] 30 C3
Temska [SRB] 146 E3
Tenala / Tenhola [FIN] 176 F5
Tenby [GB] 12 D2
Tence [F] 68 E4
Tenda, Colle di - / Tende, Col de- [F/I] 108 F3
Tende [F] 108 F3
Tende, Col de- / Tenda, Colle di - [F/I] 108 F3
Tendilla [E] 88 H6
Tenebrón [E] 88 A3
Tenero [CH] 70 F3
Tenevo [BG] 148 E5
Tenhola / Tenala [FIN] 176 F5
Tenhult [S] 162 D2
Tenja [HR] 142 E1
Tenk [H] 64 E6
Tennänget [S] 172 F3
Tennevol [N] 192 F3
Tenterden [GB] 14 F5
Tentudia, Mon. de- [E] 94 G4
Teo / Ramallosa [E] 78 C3
Teofipol' [UA] 202 B8
Teolo [I] 110 G1
Teos [TR] 152 C5
Teovo [MK] 128 E2
Tepasto [FIN] 194 C6
Tepecik [TR] 150 E5
Tepecik [TR] 150 F5
Tepecik [TR] 150 F3
Tepecik [TR] 152 G1
Tepeköy [TR] 152 E4
Tepelenë [AL] 128 B6
Tepeören [TR] 150 F3
Teplá [CZ] 48 D4
Teplice [CZ] 48 E2
Teplice nad Metují [CZ] 50 B2
Tepsa [FIN] 194 C6
Téramo [I] 116 C3
Ter Apel [NL] 16 H3
Teratyn [PL] 38 G6
Terchová [SK] 50 G6
Terebiń [PL] 52 G1
Terebišče [RUS] 198 G3
Terebovlia [UA] 202 B8
Teremia Mare [RO] 76 F5
Terena [P] 94 E2
Teresa de Confrentes [E] 98 D5
Teresin [PL] 38 A3
Teresin [PL] 38 G6
Terespol [PL] 38 F3
Terezín [CZ] 48 F2
Terezino Polje [HR] 74 H5
Tergnier [F] 28 F6
Terjärv / Teerijärvi [FIN] 196 C6
Terkoz [TR] 150 E2
Terland [N] 164 B4
Terlizzi [I] 122 D2
Termal [TR] 150 F3
Termas de Monfortinho [P] 86 G3
Terme di Lurisia [I] 108 F3
Terme di Valdieri [I] 108 F3
Terme Luigiane [I] 124 C4
Termes-d'Armagnac [F] 84 F2
Terme S. Lucia [I] 116 C2
Terme Vigliatore [I] 124 A7

Términi Imerese [I] 126 D2
Terminillo [I] 116 B4
Terminón [E] 82 E5
Térmoli [I] 116 F5
Termolovo [RUS] 178 G3
Termonde (Dendermonde) [B] 28 H2
Termonfeckin [IRL] 2 F5
Ternberg [A] 62 B5
Terndrup [DK] 160 E4
Terneuzen [NL] 28 H1
Terni [I] 116 A3
Ternitz [A] 62 E6
Ternopil' [UA] 202 B8
Térovo [GR] 132 D2
Terpan [AL] 128 B5
Terpezita [RO] 146 F1
Terpilitsy [RUS] 178 G6
Terpní [GR] 130 B3
Terracina [I] 120 C2
Terradillos de los Templarios [E] 82 C5
Terråk [N] 190 D4
Terralba [I] 118 C5
Terra Mala [I] 118 D7
Terra Mitica [E] 104 E2
Terranova di Pollino [I] 122 C6
Terrassa / Tarrasa [E] 92 E4
Terrasson-la-Villedieu [F] 66 G3
Terrateig [E] 98 E6
Terrazos [E] 82 F5
Terriente [E] 98 D2
Terskanperä [FIN] 196 D5
Tersløse [DK] 156 F3
Tertenía [I] 118 E6
Teruel [E] 98 E2
Tervahauta [FIN] 176 E1
Tervakoski [FIN] 176 G3
Tervel [BG] 148 F1
Tervo [FIN] 186 H2
Tervola [FIN] 196 C2
Tervuren [B] 30 C4
Terz [A] 62 D5
Terzaga [E] 90 C6
Tesárske Mlyňany [SK] 64 B4
Tesejerague [E] 100 D6
Těškovice [CZ] 50 E4
Teslić [BIH] 142 C3
Teslui [RO] 146 G1
Tessenberg [A] 72 F3
Tesseosen [N] 180 G6
Tessin [D] 20 C3
Tessy-sur-Vire [F] 26 E4
Tét [H] 62 H6
Tetbury [GB] 12 G3
Teterow [D] 20 C4
Teteven [BG] 148 A4
Tetovo [BG] 148 D2
Tetovo [MK] 128 D1
Tetrálofo [GR] 128 F5
Tettnang [D] 58 H4
Teuchrania [TR] 152 C3
Teufelshöhle [D] 46 H4
Teufen [CH] 58 H5
Teulada [E] 104 F2
Teulada [I] 118 C7
Teupitz [D] 34 E3
Teurnia [A] 72 H3
Teuro [FIN] 176 F3
Teuva / Östermark [FIN] 186 B4
Tevaniemi [FIN] 186 D6
Tevel [H] 76 B4
Teverga / La Plaza [E] 78 G4
Tevfikiye [TR] 130 H5
Tewkesbury [GB] 12 G2
Tewli [BY] 38 G2
Texeiro [E] 78 E3
Texing [A] 62 D5
Teysset [F] 66 E5
Thal [A] 72 F3
Thale [D] 34 A4
Thalfang [D] 44 G2
Thalheim [D] 48 D2
Thalmässing [D] 46 G6
Thalwil [CH] 58 F5
Thame [GB] 14 D3
Thann [F] 58 D3
Thannhausen [D] 60 C3
Tharandt [D] 48 E1
Tharigné-sur-Dué [F] 42 C5
Thárros [I] 118 B5
Tharsis [E] 94 E5
Thásos [GR] 130 E4
Thatcham [GB] 12 H4
Thaumiers [F] 56 C4
Theessen [D] 34 C3
Them [DK] 156 C1
Themar [D] 46 F2
Thénezay [F] 54 E3
Thenon [F] 66 F3
Theológos [GR] 130 E4
Theológos [GR] 134 A4
Théoule [F] 108 E5
Thera [TR] 154 E2
Thermá [GR] 130 G4
Thérma [GR] 138 G1
Thérmi [GR] 130 B4
Thermí [GR] 134 H2
Thermisía [GR] 136 G2
Thérmo [GR] 132 F5
Thermopýles [GR] 132 G4
Thermopýles [GR] 132 G4
Thernberg [A] 62 E6
Thérouanne [F] 28 E2
Thespiés [GR] 134 A5
Thesprotia [GR] 132 C2
Thessaloníki [GR] 128 H4
Thetford [GB] 14 G2
The Turoe Stone [IRL] 2 C5
Theuley [F] 58 B3
Theux [B] 30 E5
Thevet-St-Julien [F] 56 B4
Theze [F] 84 E3
Thiaucourt-Regniéville [F] 44 E4
Thiberville [F] 26 G4
Thiélbemont-Farémont [F] 44 C5
Thiendorf [D] 34 E5
Thiene [I] 72 D5
Thiers [F] 68 D2
Thiersee [A] 60 F6
Thiersheim [D] 48 C3
Thiesi [I] 118 C3
Thiessow [D] 20 E2
Thingvellir [IS] 192 A3
Thionville [F] 44 E3
Thíra [GR] 138 F5
Thíra / Firá [GR] 138 F5
Thirette [F] 68 H1
Thirsk [GB] 10 F3
Thisted [DK] 160 C4
Thísvi [GR] 132 H5
Thíva [GR] 134 B5
Thivars [F] 42 D4
Thiviers [F] 66 F2
Thizy [F] 68 F2
Tho, Pieve del- [I] 110 G4
Thoard [F] 108 D3
Thoissey [F] 68 G1
Tholey [D] 44 G3
Tholó [GR] 136 C3
Thomasberg [A] 62 E6
Thomas Street [IRL] 2 D5
Thomastown [IRL] 4 E4
Thônes [F] 70 B3
Thonon-les-Bains [F] 70 B2
Thorens-Glières, Château de- [F] 70 B3
Thorigné-en-Charnie [F] 42 A5
Thorikó [GR] 136 H1
Thörl [A] 62 D6
Thornbury [GB] 12 G3
Thorney [GB] 14 F2
Thornhill [GB] 8 D4
Thoronet, Abbaye du- [F] 108 D5
Thors [F] 44 C6
Thórshöfn [IS] 192 C2
Thouarcé [F] 54 D2
Thouars [F] 54 E2
Thouría [GR] 136 D4
Thoúrio [GR] 130 H1
Thueyts [F] 68 E5
Thuin [B] 28 H4
Thuir [F] 92 G1
Thum [D] 48 D2
Thun [CH] 70 D1
Thuret [F] 68 D2
Thürkow [D] 20 C4
Thurles / Durlas [IRL] 4 E3
Thurnau [D] 46 H3
Thurn Pass [A] 72 F1
Thurso [GB] 6 F2
Thury-Harcourt [F] 26 F4
Thusis [CH] 70 H1
Thyborøn [DK] 160 B4
Thymariá [GR] 130 H3
Thymianá [GR] 134 G5
Thyregod [DK] 156 C1
Tiana [I] 118 D5
Tibaes [P] 80 C3
Tibarrié [F] 106 C3
Tibava [SK] 64 H2
Tiberio, Grotta di- [I] 120 C2
Tibro [S] 166 F5
Ticha [BG] 148 D3
Tidaholm [S] 166 F6
Tidan [S] 166 F5
Tidersrum [S] 162 F1
Tidö [S] 168 B2
Tiefenbronn [D] 58 G1
Tiefencastel [CH] 70 H2
Tiefensee [D] 34 F2
Tiel [NL] 16 E5
Tielt [B] 28 G2
Tiemassaari [FIN] 188 D4
Tienen (Tirlemont) [B] 30 D4
Tiengen [D] 58 F4
Tiercé [F] 40 H6
Tierga [E] 90 D3
Tiermas [E] 88 H3
Tierp [S] 174 F5
Tieva [FIN] 194 C6
Tigănaşi [RO] 146 E1
Tighina [MD] 204 F3
Tigkáki [GR] 154 B2
Tignes [F] 70 C4
Tihany [H] 76 A2
Tihilä [FIN] 196 E5
Tihusniemi [FIN] 188 D4
Tiironkyla [FIN] 186 F2
Tiistenjoki [FIN] 186 D3
Tijarafe [E] 100 A4
Tíjola [E] 102 G4
Tikhvin [RUS] 202 C1
Tikkakoski [FIN] 186 G4
Tikkala [FIN] 186 F5
Tikkala [FIN] 188 G3
Tilberga [S] 168 C2
Tilburg [NL] 30 E2
Tilbury [GB] 14 F4
Til-Châtel [F] 56 H3
Tilloy Lès Mofflaines [F] 28 F4
Tiltagals [LV] 198 F5
Tilži [LV] 198 G5
Timahoe [IRL] 4 F3
Time [N] 164 A3
Tími [CY] 154 F6
Timiryazevo [RUS] 200 D5
Timişoara [RO] 76 G5
Timişoara [RO] 204 B5
Timmel [D] 18 B4
Timmele [S] 162 C2
Timmendorfer Strand [D] 18 H3
Timmernabben [S] 162 G4
Timmersdala [S] 166 F5
Timmervik [S] 166 D5
Timoleague [IRL] 4 C5
Timoniemi [FIN] 196 G5
Timovaara [FIN] 188 E1
Timrå [S] 184 E4
Timsfors [S] 162 C6
Tinahely [IRL] 4 F4
Tinajo [E] 100 E5
Tinca [RO] 76 H3
Tinchebray [F] 26 E4
Tindaya [E] 100 E6
Tineo [E] 78 G3
Tingelstad [N] 170 H4
Tinglev [DK] 156 B4
Tingnes [N] 172 B3
Tingsryd [S] 162 E5
Tingstad [S] 168 B5
Tingstäde [S] 168 G4
Tingvoll [N] 180 F2
Tinnoset [N] 164 F1
Tínos [GR] 138 E2
Tiñosillos [E] 88 E4
Tintern Abbey [IRL] 4 F5
Tintigni [B] 44 E2
Tinuži [LV] 198 E5
Tiobraid Arann / Tipperary [IRL] 4 D4
Tione di Trento [I] 72 C4
Tipasoja [FIN] 196 F5
Tipperary / Tiobraid Arann [IRL] 4 D4
Tiranë [AL] 128 B3
Tirano [I] 72 B4
Tiraspol [MD] 204 F3
Tire [TR] 152 D5
Tirgo [E] 82 G6
Tiriolo [I] 124 E5
Tirlemont (Tienen) [B] 30 D4
Tirmo [FIN] 178 B4
Tirol / Tirolo [I] 72 C3
Tirolo / Tirol [I] 72 C3
Tirrénia [I] 110 D6
Tirschenreuth [D] 48 C4
Tirstrup [DK] 160 E6
Tíryntha [GR] 136 F2
Tišća [BIH] 142 E4
Tiscar-Don Pedro [E] 102 F2
Tishevica [BG] 146 G3
Tishino [RUS] 22 H2
Tismana, Mănăstirea- [RO] 204 C5
Tisno [HR] 112 G6
Tišnov [CZ] 50 B6
Tisovec [SK] 64 D3
Tistrup [DK] 156 B2
Tisvilde [DK] 156 G1
Tiszaalpár [H] 76 E3
Tiszabábolna [H] 64 F6
Tiszabúra [H] 76 F1
Tiszacsege [H] 64 F6
Tiszacsermely [H] 64 H4
Tiszadob [H] 64 G5
Tiszaföldvár [H] 76 E2
Tiszafüred [H] 64 F6
Tiszajenő [H] 76 E2
Tiszakécske [H] 76 E2
Tiszalök [H] 64 G5
Tiszalúc [H] 64 F5
Tiszanána [H] 64 F6
Tiszaörs [H] 64 F6
Tiszaroff [H] 76 E1
Tiszasüly [H] 76 E1
Tiszaszőlős [H] 64 F6
Tiszatelek [H] 64 H4
Tiszaújváros [H] 64 F5
Tiszavasvári [H] 64 G5
Titaguas [E] 98 D3
Titel [SRB] 142 G1
Titisee [D] 58 F3
Tito [I] 120 G4
Tito Bustillo, Cueva de- [E] 82 C2
Titova Spilja [BIH] 142 A3
Titov Veles [MK] 128 F1
Titran [N] 190 A6
Tittling [D] 60 H3
Tittmoning [D] 60 G4
Titz [D] 30 F4
Tiuccia [F] 114 A4
Tiukka / Tjöck [FIN] 186 B4
Tiurajärvi [FIN] 194 C6
Tivat [MNE] 144 D4
Tived [S] 166 G4
Tiverton [GB] 12 E4
Tivoli [I] 116 B5
Tizzano [F] 114 A6
Tjæreborg [DK] 156 B2
Tjällmo [S] 166 H5
Tjalme [S] 192 G4
Tjåmotis [S] 190 G1
Tjautjas [S] 192 G6
Tjeldnes [N] 192 E4
Tjele [DK] 160 D5
Tjelle [N] 180 F3
Tjentište [BIH] 144 D2
Tjöck / Tiukka [FIN] 186 B4
Tjolöholm [S] 160 H3
Tjøme [N] 164 H3
Tjong [N] 190 D1
Tjønnefoss [N] 164 E3
Tjørhom [N] 164 C3
Tjørnhom [N] 164 C5
Tjørnuvik [FR] 160 A1
Tjøtta [N] 190 D3
Tjugum [N] 170 C1
Tjultrask [S] 190 F2
Tjuvkil [S] 160 G1
Tkon [HR] 112 G5
Tlachene [BG] 146 G3
Tleń [PL] 22 D4
Tlmače [SK] 64 B4
Tlos [TR] 154 G2
Tłuchowo [PL] 36 G1
Tlumačov [CZ] 50 D6
Tłuszcz [PL] 38 C2
Tobarra [E] 98 B6
Tobercurry [IRL] 2 D3
Tobermory [GB] 6 B6
Tobias [A] 62 D5
Toblach / Dobbiaco [I] 72 E3
Tocha [P] 80 A6
Tocina [E] 94 H5
Töcksfors [S] 166 C2
Todal [N] 180 G2
Todalen [N] 180 G3
Todi [I] 116 A3
Todorići [BIH] 142 B4
Tødsø [DK] 160 C4
Todtmoos [D] 58 E4
Todtnau [D] 58 E3
Tödva [EST] 198 D1
Tofftbyn [S] 174 C4
Tofte [N] 164 H2
Tofterup [DK] 156 B2
Tofteryd [S] 162 D3
Tofteseter [N] 170 H1
Toftesetra [N] 180 G5
Toftir [FR] 160 B2
Toftlund [DK] 156 B3
Togher [IRL] 2 D5
Tóház [H] 76 B3
Tohmajärvi [FIN] 188 G3
Toholampi [FIN] 196 C6
Tohvri [EST] 198 E3
Toichío [GR] 128 E5
Toijala [FIN] 176 F2
Toijola [FIN] 188 D6
Toikkala [FIN] 178 C2
Toikkala [FIN] 178 D2
Toirano, Grotte di- [I] 108 G3
Toitz [D] 20 C3
Toivakka [FIN] 186 G5
Toivola [FIN] 178 C1
Töjby [FIN] 186 A4
Tojšići [BIH] 142 E3
Tokačka [BG] 130 F2
Tokagjelet [N] 170 B4
Tokaj [H] 64 G4
Tokarnia [PL] 50 H4
Tokarnia [PL] 52 B2
Tokary [PL] 36 F4
Tokary [PL] 38 F2
Tokmak [UA] 204 H2
Tokod [H] 64 B6
Toksovo [RUS] 178 H4
Tolcsva [H] 64 G4
Toledo [E] 96 F1
Tolentino [I] 116 C2
Tolfa [I] 114 G4
Tolfta [S] 174 F5
Tolg [S] 162 E4
Tolga [N] 182 C4
Tolkis / Tolkkinen [FIN] 178 B4
Tolkkinen / Tolkis [FIN] 178 B4
Tolkmicko [PL] 22 F2
Tollarp [S] 158 D2
Tølløse [DK] 156 F3
Tolmachevo [RUS] 198 H1
Tolmezzo [I] 72 G4
Tolmin [SLO] 72 H4
Tolna [H] 76 C4
Tolne [DK] 160 E2
Toló [GR] 136 F2
Tolob [GB] 6 G4
Tolonen [FIN] 194 D5
Tolosa [E] 84 B3
Tolosa [P] 86 E4
Tolosenmäki [FIN] 188 G4
Tolox [E] 102 B4
Tolve [I] 120 H4
Tomar [P] 86 D3
Tomaševac [SRB] 142 G1
Tomaševo [MNE] 146 A4
Tomášikovo [SK] 62 H5
Tomaszów Lubelski [PL] 52 G2
Tomaszów Mazowiecki [PL] 36 H5
Tomatin [GB] 6 E5
Tombebœuf [F] 66 E4
Tomelilla [S] 158 D3
Tomelloso [E] 96 G4
Tomerdingen [D] 60 B3
Tomintoul [GB] 6 E5
Tomislavgrad [BIH] 144 B1
Tømmernes [N] 192 E5
Tommerup [DK] 156 D3
Tømmervåg [N] 180 F2
Tommola [FIN] 178 C1
Tompa [H] 76 D4
Tømra [N] 182 C2
Tomrefjord [N] 180 D3
Tomter [N] 166 B2
Tona [E] 92 E3
Tonara [I] 118 D5
Tonbridge [GB] 14 E5
Tondela [P] 80 C6
Tønder [DK] 156 B4
Tongeren (Tongres) [B] 30 E4
Tongres (Tongeren) [B] 30 E4
Tongue [GB] 6 E2
Tonnay-Boutonne [F] 54 C5
Tonnay-Charente [F] 54 C5
Tonneins [F] 66 E5
Tonnerre [F] 56 F2
Tonnes [N] 190 D1
Tönning [D] 18 E2
Tonquédec, Château de- [F] 40 D1
Tønsberg [N] 164 H3
Tonstad [N] 164 C4
Toomyvara [IRL] 2 D6
Toormakeady / Tuar Mhic Éadaigh [IRL] 2 C4
Topares [E] 102 H3
Topchii [BG] 148 D2
Töpchin [D] 34 E3
Topczewo [PL] 24 E6
Topli Dol [SRB] 146 E3
Toplița [RO] 204 D4
Toplou [GR] 140 G4
Topo [P] 100 C3
Topola [SRB] 146 B1
Topola [SRB] 204 B6
Topolčani [MK] 128 E3
Topoľčany [SK] 64 B3
Topoľčiansky Hrad [SK] 64 A3
Topólia [GR] 140 B4
Topolnica [SRB] 146 D1
Topolovățu Mare [RO] 76 H5
Topolovec [BG] 146 F2
Topolovgrad [BG] 150 A1
Topolovica [HR] 74 G6
Topolovo [BG] 148 B6
Toporu [RO] 148 C1
Topusko [HR] 112 H1
Toques [E] 78 D3
Torà [E] 92 D3
Toral de los Vados [E] 78 F5
Torbalı [TR] 152 D4
Tørberget [N] 172 D2
Torbole [I] 72 C5
Torcello [I] 72 F6
Tordera [E] 92 F4
Tordesillas [E] 88 E2
Tordesilos [E] 90 C6
Töre [S] 196 B2
Töreboda [S] 166 F5
Toreby [DK] 20 A1
Torekov [S] 160 H6
Torelló [E] 92 E3
Toreno [E] 78 F5
Toresund [S] 168 C3
Torf [A] 74 B2
Torfyanovka [RUS] 178 E3
Torgåsmon [S] 172 F3
Torgau [D] 34 D5
Torgelow [D] 20 E4
Torgiano [I] 116 A2
Torhamn [S] 158 G1
Torhout [B] 28 F2
Tori [EST] 198 E3
Torigni-sur-Vire [F] 26 E3
Torija [E] 88 H5
Toril [E] 98 D2
Torino [I] 70 D5
Torino di Sangro [I] 116 E5
Torino di Sangro Marina [I] 116 E5
Torís / Turís [E] 98 E5
Torla [E] 84 E5
Torma [EST] 198 F2
Tormac [RO] 76 H6
Törmäkylä [FIN] 196 E4
Tormänki [FIN] 194 C7
Tormänmäki [FIN] 196 E4
Tormos [E] 84 D6
Tornal'a [SK] 64 E4
Tornavacas [E] 88 B5
Tornby [DK] 160 E2
Torneå / Tornio [FIN] 196 C2
Tørnes [N] 164 F3
Tørnes [N] 180 E2
Torneträsk [S] 192 G4
Tornio / Torneå [FIN] 196 C2
Tornioniemi [FIN] 188 E4
Tornjoš [SRB] 76 E5
Toro [E] 88 D1
Törökszentmiklós [H] 76 E2
Toróni [GR] 130 C6
Torony [H] 74 F2
Toropec [RUS] 202 C3
Toropets [RUS] 202 C3
Toros [BG] 148 A4
Toros de Guisando [E] 88 E5
Torp [FIN] 174 H5
Torp [S] 166 C5
Torpa [S] 162 C5
Torpa Stenhus [S] 162 B2
Torpo [N] 170 F3
Torpoint [GB] 12 D5
Torpsbruk [S] 162 D4
Torpshammar [S] 184 D4
Torquay [GB] 12 E5
Torquemada [E] 82 D6
Torralba [E] 90 B4
Torralba [E] 96 F4
Torralba de el Burgo [E] 90 A3
Torralba de Oropesa [E] 88 C6
Torrão [P] 94 D2
Torre [E] 102 D5
Torre Annunziata [I] 120 E3
Torre Beretti [I] 70 F6
Torreblanca [E] 98 G3
Torrecaballeros [E] 88 F4
Torrecampo [E] 96 D5
Torre Canne [I] 122 F3
Torrechiara, Castello di- [I] 110 D3
Torrecilla [E] 98 C1
Torrecilla de la Orden [E] 88 D2
Torrecilla del Pinar [E] 90 B5
Torrecillas de la Tiesa [E] 96 B1
Torreciudad, Santuario de- [E] 90 H3
Torre de D. Chama [P] 80 F3
Torre de Juan Abad [E] 96 G5
Torre del Bierzo [E] 78 F5
Torre del Compte [E] 102 E2
Torre del Greco [I] 120 E3
Torre del Lago Puccini [I] 110 D5
Torre dell'Impiso [I] 126 B1
Torre del Mar [E] 102 C5
Torredembarra [E] 92 C5
Torre de Moncorvo [P] 80 E5
Torre de' Pàsseri [I] 116 D4
Torre de Sta. María [E] 86 H6
Torredonjimeno [E] 102 D2
Torre Faro [I] 124 C7
Torrefarrera [E] 90 H4
Torregamones [E] 80 G4
Torre Grande [I] 118 B5
Torreguadiaro [E] 100 H5
Torreiglesias [E] 88 F3
Torreira [P] 80 B5
Torrejoncillo [E] 86 H4
Torrejón de Ardoz [E] 88 G6
Torrejón de la Calzada [E] 88 F6
Torrejón del Rey [E] 88 G5
Torrejón el Rubio [E] 88 A6
Torrelaguna [E] 88 G4
Torrelapaja [E] 90 C3
Torrelavega [E] 82 E3
Torrelobatón [E] 88 E1
Torrelodones [E] 88 F5
Torremaggiore [I] 116 F6
Torremejia [E] 94 H2
Torre Melissa [I] 124 F4
Torremocha [E] 86 H6
Torremocha de Jiloca [E] 98 D1
Torremocha del Pinar [E] 90 B5
Torremolinos [E] 102 B5
Torremormojón [E] 82 C6
Torrenostra [E] 98 G3
Torrent [E] 98 E5
Torrente de Cinca [E] 90 G5
Torrenueva [E] 96 F5
Torrenueva [E] 102 E5
Torre Orsaia [I] 120 G5
Torre-Pacheco [E] 104 C4
Torre Pellice [I] 70 C6
Torreperogil [E] 102 F2
Torrequemada [E] 86 H5
Torre Santa Susanna [I] 122 F4
Torres Cabrera [E] 102 C1
Torre S. Gennaro [I] 122 G4
Torres Novas [P] 86 C4
Torre S. Sabina [I] 122 F3
Torres Vedras [P] 86 B4
Torretta [I] 124 F4
Torrette di Fano [I] 112 C6
Torre Vã [P] 94 C3
Torrevieja [E] 104 D3
Torrflonäs [S] 184 C5
Torricella [I] 122 F5
Torri del Benaco [I] 72 C6
Torríglia [I] 110 B3
Torrijas [E] 98 E3
Torrijos [E] 96 E1
Tørring [DK] 156 C2
Tørring [N] 190 C5
Torrita di Siena [I] 114 G2
Torroella de Montgrí [E] 92 G3
Torrox [E] 102 D5
Torrubia [E] 96 D5
Torsåker [S] 168 D4
Torsåker [S] 174 D4
Torsången [S] 166 E5
Torsås [S] 162 F6
Torsborg [S] 182 F3
Torsburgen [S] 168 G5
Torsby [S] 166 E1
Torsby [S] 172 E5
Torshälla [S] 168 B3
Tórshavn [FR] 160 B2
Torslanda [S] 160 G2
Torsminde [DK] 160 B5
Törtel [H] 76 E2
Tortinmäki [FIN] 176 E4
Tórtola de Henares [E] 88 H5
Tórtoles de Esgueva [E] 88 G2
Tortolì [I] 118 E5
Tortona [I] 110 B2
Tortora [I] 120 H6
Tortoreto [I] 116 D3
Tortoreto Lido [I] 116 D3
Tortorici [I] 126 F2
Tortosa [E] 92 A5
Tortosendo [P] 86 F2
Toruń [PL] 22 E6
Torup [S] 158 C3
Torup [S] 162 B4
Torup Strand [DK] 160 C3
Tõrva [EST] 198 E3
Tor Vaiánica [I] 116 A6
Torvikbukt [N] 180 F2
Tørvikbygd [N] 170 C4
Torvinen [FIN] 194 D7
Torvsjö [S] 190 F5
Torvund [N] 170 B1
Torzhok [RUS] 202 E2
Torzym [PL] 34 H3
Tosbotn [N] 190 D3
Toscolano Maderno [I] 72 B5
Tösens [A] 72 C2
Toses, Collado de- [E] 92 E2
Tosno [RUS] 202 B1
Toso [N] 170 H5
Tossa de Mar [E] 92 F4
Tossåsen [S] 182 G3
Tossavanlahti [FIN] 186 G1
Tösse [S] 166 D4
Tostedt [D] 18 F5
Tosterup [S] 158 D3
Tószeg [H] 76 E2
Toszek [PL] 50 F3
Totana [E] 104 B3
Totebo [S] 162 F2
Tôtes [F] 28 B5
Tótkomlós [H] 76 F4
Tøtlandsvik [N] 164 C2
Totleben [BG] 148 B3
Totnes [GB] 12 E5
Tøttdal [N] 190 C5
Tottijärvi [FIN] 176 F2
Totvázsony [H] 74 H2
Toucy [F] 56 E2
Touffou [F] 54 F4
Toul [F] 44 E5
Toulon [F] 108 C6
Toulon sur Allier [F] 56 D5
Toulon-sur-Arroux [F] 56 F5
Toulouse [F] 84 H3
Tourcoing [F] 28 F3
Tourmalet, Col du- [F] 84 E4
Tournai (Doornik) [B] 28 G3
Tournan [F] 42 G4
Tournay [F] 84 F4
Tournon [F] 68 F5
Tournon-d'Agenais [F] 66 F5
Tournon-St-Martin [F] 54 G4
Tournus [F] 56 G6
Tourny [F] 28 C6
Tours [F] 54 F2
Tourves [F] 108 C5
Toury [F] 42 E5
Toutes Aures, Col de- [F] 108 D4
Touvois [F] 54 B2
Toužim [CZ] 48 D3
Tovačov [CZ] 50 D5
Tovarnik [HR] 142 E2
Tøvik [N] 180 E2
Tövsala / Taivassalo [FIN] 176 C4
Tovste [UA] 204 D2
Towcester [GB] 14 D2
Töysä [FIN] 186 D3
Trabada [E] 78 F2
Trabadelo [E] 78 E5
Trabanca [E] 80 G5
Trabazos [E] 80 G4
Traben-Trarbach [D] 44 G2
Trabía [I] 126 D2
Trabotivište [MK] 128 H1
Trabuc, Grottes de- [F] 106 F3
Tracheiá [GR] 136 F2
Trachíli [GR] 134 C5
Tracino [I] 126 A5
Trädet [S] 162 C1
Trælleborg [DK] 156 F3
Trafaria [P] 86 A5
Trafoi [I] 72 B3
Tragacete [E] 98 C1
Traian [RO] 148 B2
Traiguera [E] 92 A6
Traisen [A] 62 D5
Traiskirchen [A] 62 F5
Traismauer [A] 62 E4
Trajano [E] 100 G3
Trakai [LT] 24 H1
Trakošćan [HR] 74 E4
Tralee / Trá Lí [IRL] 4 B3
Trá Lí / Tralee [IRL] 4 B3
Tralleis [TR] 152 E5
Tramaríglio [I] 118 B3
Tramelan [CH] 58 D5
Tramonti di Sopra [I] 72 F4
Tramore [IRL] 4 E5
Tranås [S] 162 E1
Tranby [N] 164 H1
Tranco [E] 102 G1
Trancoso [P] 80 D6
Tranderup [DK] 156 D4
Tranekær [DK] 156 E4
Tranekær Slot [DK] 156 E4
Tranemo [S] 162 C3
Trångmon [S] 190 E4
Trångslet [S] 172 F2
Trångsviken [S] 182 G2
Tranhult [S] 162 C3
Trani [I] 122 D2
Trankil [S] 166 C3
Tranóvalto [GR] 128 F6
Tranøya [N] 192 E4
Transtrand [S] 172 F3
Tranum Strand [DK] 160 D3
Tranvik [S] 168 E3
Trápani [I] 126 B2
Trapishte [BG] 148 D3
Trappe d'Aiguebelle, Monastère de la- [F] 68 F6
Trappes [F] 42 F4
Traryd [S] 162 C5
Träskända / Järvenpää [FIN] 176 H4
Träskvik [FIN] 186 B5
Träslövsläge [S] 160 H4
Trasmiras [E] 78 D6
Trassem [D] 44 F3
Trästenik [BG] 148 A3
Trate [SLO] 74 E3
Tratzberg [A] 60 E6
Traun [A] 62 B4
Traunkirchen [A] 62 A5
Traunreut [D] 60 G5
Traunstein [D] 60 G5
Trautenfels [A] 62 B6
Trautmannsdorf [A] 62 F5
Travemünde [D] 18 H3
Travers [CH] 58 C6
Travnik [BIH] 142 C4
Travo [F] 114 B5
Travo [I] 110 C2
Trazo [E] 78 C2
Trbovlje [SLO] 74 C5
Tréban [F] 56 D5
Trebatsch [D] 34 F3
Trebbin [D] 34 E3
Třebechovice pod Orebem [CZ] 50 B3
Trebenice [CZ] 48 F2
Trébeurden [F] 40 D1
Třebíč [CZ] 50 A6
Trebija [SLO] 74 B5
Trebinje [BIH] 144 D3
Trebisacce [I] 122 D6
Trebišov [SK] 64 G3
Trebnje [SLO] 74 C5
Třeboň [CZ] 62 C2
Tréboul [F] 40 B3
Trebovice [CZ] 50 B4
Trebujena [E] 100 F3
Trecastagni [I] 126 G3
Trecate [I] 70 F5
Trecenta [I] 110 F2
Trecesson, Château de- [F] 26 B6
Treffurt [D] 32 G5
Tregaron [GB] 10 B6
Trégastel [F] 40 D1
Tregnago [I] 72 C6
Tréguier [F] 26 A3
Trehörna [S] 162 E1
Treia [D] 18 E1
Treibach [A] 74 B3
Treignac [F] 66 H2
Treillieres [F] 40 F6

Treis [D] 44 H1
Trekanten [S] 162 F5
Trelde [DK] 156 C2
Trelleborg [S] 158 C3
Tremês [P] 86 C4
Tremestieri [I] 124 B7
Tremezzo [I] 70 G3
Tremisht [AL] 128 C6
Třemošná [CZ] 48 E4
Tremp [E] 92 C2
Trenčianska Turná [SK] 64 A2
Trenčianske Bohuslavice [SK] 64 A3
Trenčianske Teplice [SK] 64 B2
Trenčín [SK] 64 A2
Trend [DK] 160 C4
Trendelburg [D] 32 F4
Trengereid [N] 170 B4
Trent [CH] 70 C3
Trenta [SLO] 72 H4
Trento [I] 72 C4
Treppeln [D] 34 G3
Trept [F] 68 G3
Tres Cantos [E] 88 F5
Trescore Balneario [I] 70 H4
Tresenda [I] 72 B4
Tresfjord [N] 180 E3
Tresigallo [I] 110 G2
Treski [EST] 198 G3
Treskog [S] 166 D1
Treskovec, Manastir- [MK] 128 E2
Tresnurághes [I] 118 B4
Trespaderne [E] 82 F5
Třešť [CZ] 48 H6
Tresta [GB] 6 H3
Tresta Rzadowa [PL] 36 H5
Trets [F] 108 B5
Tretten [N] 170 H2
Treuchtlingen [D] 60 D2
Treuenbrietzen [D] 34 D3
Treungen [N] 164 E3
Trevélez [E] 102 E4
Tréveray [F] 44 D5
Trevi [I] 116 B3
Treviglio [I] 70 H5
Trevignano Romano [I] 114 H4
Treviño [E] 82 G5
Treviso [I] 72 E6
Trévoux [F] 68 F2
Trezelles [F] 56 D6
Trezzano sul Naviglio [I] 70 G5
Trezzo sull'Adda [I] 70 G4
Trgovište [SRB] 146 E5
Trhomné [CZ] 48 D4
Trhová Kamenice [CZ] 50 A4
Trhové Sviny [CZ] 62 C2
Trhoviště [SK] 64 H3
Triacastela [E] 78 E4
Triaize [F] 54 C4
Triánta [GR] 154 D3
Triaucourt–en–Argonne [F] 44 D4
Tribanj Kruščica [HR] 112 G4
Triberg [D] 58 F3
Tribsees [D] 20 C3
Tricárico [I] 120 H4
Tricase [I] 122 G6
Tricesimo [I] 72 G4
Trichiana [I] 72 E4
Trie [F] 84 F3
Trieben [A] 62 C6
Trier [D] 44 F2
Trieste [I] 72 H6
Trifels [D] 46 B5
Trignac [F] 40 E6
Trígono [GR] 128 E4
Trigueros [E] 94 F5
Tríkala [GR] 128 G4
Tríkala [GR] 132 F2
Tríkala [GR] 136 E1
Trikéri [GR] 134 A3
Tríkomon (Iskele) [CY] 154 G5
Trilj [HR] 144 A1
Trillevallen [S] 182 F2
Trillo [E] 90 A5
Trílofo [GR] 132 G3
Trim [IRL] 2 F5
Trimburg [D] 46 E3
Trindade [P] 80 E4
Trindade [P] 94 D3
Třinec [CZ] 50 F5
Trinidad [E] 84 A4
Trinità d'Agultu e Vignola [I] 118 D2
Trinitápoli [I] 120 H2
Trinité, Ermitage de la– [F] 114 B6
Trino [I] 70 E5
Triollo [E] 82 D4
Triora [I] 108 F4
Trípoli [GR] 136 E2
Triponzo [I] 116 B3
Tripótama [GR] 136 D1
Triptis [D] 48 B1
Trisanna–Brücke [A] 72 B1
Trisulti, Abbazia di– [I] 116 C6
Trittau [D] 18 G4
Trittenheim [D] 44 G2
Trivento [I] 116 E6
Trnava [CZ] 50 B6
Trnava [SK] 62 H4
Trnovec nad Váhom [SK] 64 A4
Trnovo [BIH] 144 D1
Trnovo ob Soci [SLO] 72 H4
Troarn [F] 26 F3
Trocnov [CZ] 62 C2
Trödje [S] 174 E3
Troense [DK] 156 E4
Trofa [P] 80 B5
Trofaiach [A] 74 C1
Trofimovo [RUS] 198 H4
Trofors [N] 190 D3
Trogir [HR] 116 H1
Troia [I] 120 G2
Tróia [P] 86 B6
Troina [I] 126 F3
Troisdorf [D] 30 H5
Trois Fontaines, Abbaye des– [F] 44 C5
Trois–Ponts [B] 30 E5
Troïts'ke [UA] 204 F3
Troizína [GR] 136 G2
Trojane [SLO] 74 C4
Trøjborg [DK] 156 B4
Trolla [N] 182 B1
Trollböle [FIN] 176 F6
Trolleholm [S] 158 C2
Trolle Ljungby [S] 158 D2
Trollenäs [S] 158 C2
Trollhättan [S] 166 D6
Trollkyrkja [N] 180 E2
Trollvik [N] 192 G2
Tromello [I] 70 F5
Tromøy [N] 164 F5
Tromsø [N] 192 F2
Tromvik [N] 192 F2
Tronco [P] 80 E3
Trondheim [N] 182 B1
Trones [N] 190 E1
Trönninge [S] 162 A4
Trönninge [S] 162 B5
Tronvik [N] 190 B6
Trôo [F] 42 C6
Troódos [CY] 154 F6
Troon [GB] 8 C3
Tropea [I] 124 C6
Tropfstein–Höhle [A] 74 C3
Tropojë [AL] 146 B5
Trosa [S] 168 D4
Troškūnai [LT] 200 G4
Trosky [CZ] 48 H2
Trössing [A] 74 E3
Trossingen [D] 58 G3
Tröstau [D] 48 B3
Trostberg [D] 60 F4
Trosterud [N] 166 C2
Trostianets' [UA] 202 F7
Trostianets' [UA] 204 E2
Trouville [F] 26 G3
Trowbridge [GB] 12 G3
Troyan [BG] 148 B4
Troyanovo [BG] 148 E4
Troyanski Manastir [BG] 148 B4
Troyanski Pateka [BG] 148 B4
Trøyen [N] 182 B2
Troyes [F] 44 B6
Troyon [F] 44 D4
Trpanj [HR] 144 B3
Trpinja [HR] 142 E1
Tršić [SRB] 142 F3
Trstená [SK] 50 H6
Trstena [SRB] 146 D5
Trstenik [SRB] 146 C3
Trsteno [HR] 144 C3
Trstín [SK] 62 H3
Trubchevsk [RUS] 202 E5
Trubia [E] 78 H3
Truchas [E] 78 F6
Truchtersheim [F] 44 H5
Trud [BG] 148 B5
Trujillo [E] 96 B1
Trulben [D] 44 H4
Trün [BG] 146 E4
Trun [CH] 70 G1
Trun [F] 26 F4
Truro [GB] 12 C5
Truskavets' [UA] 52 G5
Trustrup [DK] 160 F6
Trutnov [CZ] 50 B2
Trutnowy [PL] 22 E3
Truva [TR] 130 H5
Tryavna [BG] 148 C4
Trydal [N] 164 D2
Tryde [S] 158 D3
Tryggelev [DK] 156 E5
Tryggestad [N] 180 D4
Tryńcza [PL] 52 E3
Trýpi [GR] 136 E4
Trypití [GR] 130 C5
Trysa [TR] 154 H3
Tryserum [S] 162 G1
Tryšiai [LT] 200 E3
Trysil Innbygda [N] 172 D2
Tryszczyn [PL] 22 D5
Trzcianka [PL] 22 A6
Trzciel [PL] 36 B3
Trzcinna [PL] 34 H1
Trzcińsko Zdrój [PL] 20 F6
Trzebiatów [PL] 20 G3
Trzebiel [PL] 34 G5
Trzebież [PL] 20 F4
Trzebina [PL] 50 D3
Trzebinia [PL] 50 G3
Trzebnica [PL] 36 C6
Trzebów [PL] 34 H2
Trzemeszno [PL] 36 E2
Trzepnica [PL] 36 H6
Trzepowo [PL] 22 D3
Trzešcianka [PL] 24 F6
Tržič [SLO] 74 B4
Trzin [SLO] 74 C5
Tržišče [SLO] 74 D5
Tsagkaráda [GR] 134 A2
Tsamandás [GR] 132 C1
Tsampíka, Moní– [GR] 154 D4
Tsangário [GR] 132 C3
Tsapel'ka [RUS] 198 H3
Tsarevets [BG] 148 C2
Tsarevo [BG] 148 G5
Tsaritsani [GR] 132 G1
Tschernitz [D] 34 G5
Tschierv [CH] 72 B3
Tsenovo [BG] 148 C2
Tsiurupyns'k [UA] 204 G3
Tsotíli [GR] 128 E6
Tsoútsouros [GR] 140 F5
Tsvelodubovo [RUS] 178 G3
Tua [N] 190 C5
Tua [P] 80 E4
Tuaim / Tuam [IRL] 2 C4
Tuam / Tuaim [IRL] 2 C4
Tuar Mhic Éadaigh / Toourmakeady [IRL] 2 C4
Tubilla del Agua [E] 82 E5
Tübingen [D] 58 G2
Tubre / Taufers [I] 72 B3
Tučepi [HR] 144 B2
Tuchan [F] 106 C5
Tüchen [D] 20 B6
Tuchola [PL] 22 D4
Tuchomie [PL] 22 C3
Tuchów [PL] 52 C4
Tuckur [FIN] 186 B2
Tuczno [PL] 20 H6
Tuddal [N] 164 F1
Tudela [E] 84 B6
Tudela de Duero [E] 88 E2
Tudu [EST] 198 F1
Tudulinna [EST] 198 F2
Tuffé [F] 42 C5
Tufjord [N] 194 B1
Tuhkakylä [FIN] 196 F5
Tuhkala [RUS] 196 G2
Tui [E] 78 B5
Tuin [MK] 128 D2
Tuineje [E] 100 E6
Tuiskula [FIN] 186 C3
Tuixén [E] 92 D2
Tūja [LV] 198 D4
Tukums [LV] 198 D5
Tulare [SRB] 146 D5
Tuławki [PL] 22 H3
Tulca [RO] 76 H3
Tulcea [RO] 204 F5
Tul'chyn [UA] 204 E2
Tulešice [CZ] 62 F2
Tuliszków [PL] 36 E3
Tulla [IRL] 2 C6
Tullamore [IRL] 2 E6
Tulle [F] 66 H3
Tullebølle [DK] 156 E4
Tulleråsen [S] 182 G1
Tullgarn [S] 168 D4
Tullinge [S] 168 D3
Tullins [F] 68 G4
Tulln [A] 62 E4
Tullow [IRL] 4 F4
Tułowice [PL] 50 D2
Tulppio [FIN] 194 F6
Tulsk [IRL] 2 D4
Tum [PL] 36 G3
Tumba [S] 168 D3
Tummsjøen [N] 190 D4
Tumulus de Gavrinis [F] 40 D5
Tun [S] 166 D5
Tuna [S] 162 F3
Tunaberg [S] 168 C5
Tuna Hästberg [S] 172 H5
Tunbridge Wells [GB] 14 E5
Tunbyn [S] 184 E5
Tunçbilek [TR] 150 G6
Tune [DK] 156 G3
Tunge [S] 160 H1
Tungelsta [S] 168 E4
Tungozero [RUS] 196 G2
Tunhovd [N] 170 F4
Tunnerstad [S] 162 D1
Tunnsjørørvika [N] 190 D4
Tunø By [DK] 156 D1
Tuntsa [FIN] 194 F6
Tunvågen [S] 182 G3
Tuohikotti [FIN] 178 C2
Tuohittu [FIN] 176 F5
Tuomioja [FIN] 196 D4
Tuonj [HR] 112 G2
Tuorila [FIN] 186 B6
Tuornoel, Château de– [F] 68 C2
Tupadły [PL] 36 E2
Tupitsyno [RUS] 198 G2
Tuplice [PL] 34 G4
Tuppurinmäki [FIN] 188 D3
Tura [H] 64 D6
Turaj [AL] 128 C1
Turalići [BIH] 142 E4
Turan [TR] 150 F4
Turanlı [TR] 152 C2
Turany [SK] 50 G6
Türas [TR] 150 G2
Turawa [PL] 50 E2
Turba [EST] 198 D2
Turbe [BIH] 142 C4
Turčianske Teplice [SK] 64 C2
Turckheim [F] 58 D3
Turda [RO] 204 C4
Turégano [E] 88 F3
Turek [PL] 36 F4
Turenki [FIN] 176 G3
Turenne [F] 66 G3
Turgeliai [LT] 200 G6
Türgovishte [BG] 148 D3
Turgut [TR] 152 E6
Turgutbey [TR] 150 C2
Turgutlu [TR] 152 D4
Turgutreis [TR] 154 B2
Turhala [FIN] 196 E6
Türi [EST] 198 E2
Turi [I] 122 E3
Turiis'k [UA] 38 H5
Turís / Torís [E] 98 E5
Turjaci [HR] 144 A1
Turjak [SLO] 74 C5
Turka [PL] 38 G5
Turka [UA] 52 F6
Türkeli [TR] 150 C4
Túrkeve [H] 76 F2
Türkheim [D] 60 C4
Türkmen [TR] 152 C3
Turkovići [BIH] 144 D1
Turku / Åbo [FIN] 176 D4
Turleque [E] 96 F2
Turlough [IRL] 2 C4
Turmantas [LT] 200 H4
Turňa nad Bodvou [SK] 64 F3
Turnberry [GB] 8 C4
Turnhout [B] 30 D3
Türnitz [A] 62 D5
Turnov [CZ] 48 H2
Turnu Măgurele [RO] 148 B2
Turo [FIN] 194 D4
Turobin [PL] 52 F1
Túrony [H] 76 B5
Turośl [PL] 24 C5
Turów [PL] 38 E4
Turrach [A] 74 A2
Turre [E] 102 H5
Turriff [GB] 6 F5
Turtagrø [N] 170 E1
Turtel [MK] 128 G1
Turunç [TR] 154 D2
Turunçova [TR] 154 H3
Turzovka [SK] 50 F5
Tusa [I] 126 E2
Tusby / Tuusula [FIN] 176 H4
Tuscánia [I] 114 G4
Tušilovic [HR] 112 G1
Tuskö [S] 174 G5
Tustervatnet [N] 190 D3
Tuszów Narodowy [PL] 52 D2
Tuszyn [PL] 36 G5
Tuszyny [PL] 22 D5
Tutajev [RUS] 202 F1
Tutayev [RUS] 202 F1
Tutin [SRB] 146 B4
Tutjunniemi [FIN] 188 F3
Tutrakan [BG] 148 D1
Tutting [D] 60 H4
Tuttlingen [D] 58 G3
Tútugi [E] 102 G3
Tutzing [D] 60 D5
Tützpatz [D] 20 D4
Tuukkala [FIN] 186 H6
Tuukkala [FIN] 188 C6
Tuulos [FIN] 176 G2
Tuupovaara [FIN] 188 G3
Tuuruniemi [FIN] 194 D4
Tuusjärvi [FIN] 188 D2
Tuuski [FIN] 178 C4
Tuusniemi [FIN] 188 E2
Tuusula / Tusby [FIN] 176 H4
Tuv [N] 170 F3
Tuvas [FIN] 186 B4
Tuzi [MNE] 144 E4
Tuzla [BIH] 142 E3
Tuzla [TR] 134 G1
Tuzla [TR] 150 F3
Tuzlata [BG] 148 G2
Tuzsér [H] 64 H4
Tvååker [S] 160 H4
Tväråbäck [S] 190 H5
Tvärålund [S] 190 H5
Tvärminne [FIN] 176 F6
Tvärskog [S] 162 F5
Tvärud [S] 166 D1
Tvede [DK] 160 E5
Tvedestrand [N] 164 F4
Tveit [N] 164 B2
Tveita [N] 170 B4
Tveitsund [N] 164 E3
Tver' [RUS] 202 E2
Tverai [LT] 200 D4
Tverrå [N] 164 C3
Tverrå [N] 190 E2
Tverrelvmo [N] 192 G3
Tversted [DK] 160 E2
Tvinde [N] 170 C3
Tvindehaugen [N] 170 F1
Tving [S] 158 F1
Tvis [DK] 160 C5
Tvøroyri [FR] 160 A3
Tvrdošovce [SK] 64 A5
Tv–Torony [H] 74 G3
Tvŭrditsa [BG] 148 D4
Twann–Schlucht [CH] 58 D5
Twardogóra [PL] 36 D5
Tweng [A] 72 H1
Twimberg [A] 74 C2
Twist [D] 16 H4
Twistringen [D] 18 D6
Tworków [PL] 50 E4
Tworóg [PL] 50 F2
Tyamsha [RUS] 198 G3
Tychowo [PL] 22 A4
Tychy [PL] 50 G3
Tyczyn [PL] 52 E4
Tyfjord [N] 194 D1
Tyfors [S] 172 G5
Tyholland [NIR] 2 F4
Tyin [N] 170 F2
Tyinosen [N] 170 E2
Tykocin [PL] 24 E5
Tylawa [PL] 52 D5
Týlisos [GR] 140 E4
Tylldal [N] 182 B5
Tylösand [S] 162 B5
Tylstrup [DK] 160 E3
Tymbark [PL] 52 B4
Tymfristós [GR] 132 F4
Tympáki [GR] 140 D5
Tyndaris [I] 124 A7
Tynderö [S] 184 F4
Tyndrum [GB] 8 D2
Týnec nad Labem [CZ] 48 H4
Tynemouth [GB] 8 G6
Tyngsjö [S] 172 F5
Tyniec [PL] 50 H4
Týniště nad Orlicí [CZ] 50 B3
Tynkä [FIN] 196 C5
Týn nad Vltavou [CZ] 48 F6
Tynnelsö [S] 168 C3
Tynset [N] 182 B4
Tyresö [S] 168 E3
Tyringe [S] 158 C1
Tyrislöt [S] 168 C6
Tyristrand [N] 170 H5
Tyrjänsaari [FIN] 188 G1
Tyrnävä [FIN] 196 D4
Týrnavos [GR] 132 G1
Tyrós [GR] 136 F3
Týřov [CZ] 48 E4
Tyrrellspass [IRL] 2 E5
Tyry [FIN] 186 F6
Tysdal [N] 164 B2
Tysken [N] 172 D4
Tysse [N] 170 B1
Tysse [N] 170 B4
Tyssebotn [N] 170 B3
Tyssedal [N] 170 C5
Tystberga [S] 168 C4
Tyszki–Nadbory [PL] 24 D6
Tytuvėnai [LT] 200 E4
Tyulenovo [BG] 148 G2
Tyvsen [DK] 156 B4
Tywyn [GB] 10 B5
Tzermiádo [GR] 140 F5
Tzummarum [NL] 16 F2

U

Ub [SRB] 146 A1
Úbeda [E] 102 F2
Ubergsmoen [N] 164 F4
Überhamn [D] 18 E5
Überlingen [D] 58 G4
Ubli [HR] 144 A3
Ubrique [E] 100 H4
Uçarı [TR] 154 F4
Uccellina, Torre dell–' [I] 114 F3
Ucero [E] 90 A2
Uchanie [PL] 38 G6
Uchorowo [PL] 36 C2
Uchte [D] 32 E1
Uckange [F] 44 E3
Uckfield [GB] 14 E5
Uclés [E] 96 H2
Uçmakdere [TR] 150 C3
Üçpınar [TR] 152 D3
Ucria [I] 124 A7
Udavské [SK] 64 H2
Udbina [HR] 112 H4
Udbyhøj [DK] 160 E5
Udbyhøj Vasehuse [DK] 160 E5
Uddeholm [S] 166 F1
Uddel [NL] 16 F4
Uddel [NL] 16 F4
Udden [S] 166 D5
Uddevalla [S] 166 C5
Uddheden [S] 166 E1
Uden [NL] 16 E6
Udine [I] 72 G5
Údlice [CZ] 48 E2
Udorpie [PL] 22 C3
Udovo [MK] 128 G2
Ūdrupij [LV] 198 F4
Udvar [H] 76 B5
Ueckermünde [D] 20 E4
Ueffeln [D] 32 C1
Uelsen [D] 16 G4
Uelzen [D] 18 G6
Uetersen [D] 18 F4
Uetze [D] 32 G2
Uffenheim [D] 46 F5
Uga [E] 100 E6
Ugāle [LV] 198 C5
Ugao [SRB] 146 A4
Ugao–Miraballes [E] 82 G4
Ugento [I] 122 G6
Ugerløse [DK] 156 F3
Uggdal [N] 170 B5
Uggerby [DK] 160 E2
Uggersjev [DK] 156 D3
Ugglarps havsbad [S] 160 H4
Ugíjar [E] 102 F5
Ugine [F] 70 B3
Uglich [RUS] 202 F1
Ugljan [HR] 112 F5
Ugljane [HR] 144 A2
Ugny–sur–Meuse [F] 44 D5
Ugrinovci [SRB] 146 B2
Uğürchin [BG] 148 A4
Uğurluca [TR] 152 G2
Uğurlutepe [TR] 130 G5
Uherčice [CZ] 62 E2
Uherse Mineralne [PL] 52 E5
Uherské Hradiště [CZ] 62 H2
Uherský Brod [CZ] 62 H2
Uherský Ostroh [CZ] 62 H2
Uhlířské Janovice [CZ] 48 G4
Uhniv [UA] 52 G2
Uhřiněves [CZ] 48 G4
Uhrovec [SK] 64 B3
Uhrovský Hrad [SK] 64 B3
Uhrsleben [D] 34 B3
Uhyst [D] 34 G5
Uig [GB] 6 B4
Uihartyán [H] 76 D2
Uimaharju [FIN] 188 G1
Uimila [FIN] 178 B2
Uitelep [H] 76 B3
Uithoorn [NL] 16 D4
Uithuizen [NL] 16 G1
Ujazd [PL] 36 H5
Ujazd [PL] 50 E3
Ujazd [PL] 52 C2
Újfehértó [H] 64 H5
Újiráz [H] 76 G2
Újkígyós [H] 76 G3
Újléta [H] 64 H6
Ujma Duża [PL] 36 F2
Újmajor [H] 74 H1
Újpetre [H] 76 B5
Ujście [PL] 22 B6
Újszász [H] 76 E1
Ujué [E] 84 B5
Ukk [H] 74 G2
Ukkola [FIN] 188 F1
Ukmergė [LT] 200 G5
Ükmez [TR] 152 C5
Ukonvaara [FIN] 188 E1
Ukri [LV] 198 D6
Ukta [PL] 24 C4
Ula [BY] 202 C4
Ula [TR] 154 D1
Ul'anka [SK] 64 C3
Ulan Majorat [PL] 38 E4
Ulanów [PL] 52 E2
Ulaş [TR] 150 C2
Ulbjerg [DK] 160 D5
Ulcinj [MNE] 144 E5
Uldum [DK] 156 C2
Uleåborg / Oulu [FIN] 196 D4
Ulefoss [N] 164 F2
Uleila del Campo [E] 102 H4
Ulëzë [AL] 128 B2
Ulfborg [DK] 160 B5
Ulgardereköyü [TR] 150 B5
Ulhówek [PL] 52 G2
Úlibice [CZ] 48 H3
Ulinia [PL] 22 C1
Ulivar [RO] 76 F6
Uljanik [HR] 142 B1
Uljma [SRB] 142 H2
Ullånger [S] 184 F3
Ullapool [GB] 6 D3
Ullared [S] 162 B4
Ullatti [S] 192 H6
Ullava [FIN] 196 C6
Ulldecona [E] 92 A6
Ulldemolins [E] 90 H5
Ullene [S] 166 E6
Ullerslev [DK] 156 E3
Ullervad [S] 166 F5
Üllés [H] 76 E4
Ullisjaur [S] 190 F4
Üllő [H] 76 D1
Ulm [D] 60 B3
Ulme [P] 86 D4
Ulmen [D] 44 G1
Ulmeni [RO] 148 D1
Ulnes [N] 170 G2
Ulog [BIH] 144 D2
Ulpiana [SRB] 146 C5
Ulpia Traiana [RO] 204 C5
Ulricehamn [S] 162 C2
Ulrika [S] 162 E1
Ulriksfors [S] 190 E6
Ulsberg [N] 180 H3
Ulsrud [N] 166 C1
Ulsted [DK] 160 E4
Ulsteinvik [N] 180 C4
Ulstrup [DK] 156 E2
Ulstrup [DK] 160 D5
Uluabat [TR] 150 E5
Ulubey [TR] 152 G3
Ulüçayır [TR] 150 H5
Uludağ [TR] 150 F5
Ulukışla (Marathóvounos) [CY] 154 G5
Uluköy [TR] 150 H6
Ulvåla [N] 172 D3
Ulvåsa [S] 166 H5
Ulverston [GB] 10 D2
Ülvesbüll [D] 18 E1
Ulvestad [N] 170 D1
Ulvik [N] 170 D3
Ulvika [N] 192 E4
Ulvila / Ulvsby [FIN] 176 D2
Ulvsby / Ulvila [FIN] 176 D2
Ulvsjön [S] 172 G1
Ulvsvåg [N] 192 E4
Umag [HR] 112 D1
Uman' [UA] 202 D8
Umasjö [S] 190 E2
Umbertide [I] 116 A1
Umbukta [N] 190 E2
Umčari [SRB] 142 H3
Umeå [S] 196 A6
Umfors [S] 190 E2
Umgransele [S] 190 G4
Umhausen [A] 72 C1
Umka [SRB] 142 G3
Umkirch [D] 58 E3
Umurbey [TR] 150 B5
Umurbey [TR] 150 F4
Umurlu [TR] 152 E5
Uña [E] 98 C2
Unaja [FIN] 176 C3
Unari [FIN] 194 D7
Unbyn [S] 196 B3
Uncastillo [E] 84 C5
Undenäs [S] 166 G5
Undersåker [S] 182 F2
Undva [EST] 198 C3
Úněšov [CZ] 48 D4
Ungheni [MD] 204 E3
Unhošť [CZ] 48 F3
Unichowo [PL] 22 C3
Uničov [CZ] 50 C4
Uniejów [PL] 36 F4
Unirea [RO] 146 F1
Unisław [PL] 22 D6
Unna [D] 32 C4
Unnaryd [S] 162 C4
Unserfrau / Madonna di Senales [I] 72 C2
Unset [N] 182 C5
Unsholtet [N] 182 C3
Untamala [FIN] 186 C2
Unterach [A] 60 H5
Unterbergen [A] 74 E1
Unterlüss [D] 18 G6
Unterradlberg [A] 62 E4
Unterschächen [CH] 70 G1
Unter–Schleissheim [D] 60 E4
Unteruhldingen [D] 58 H4
Unterwasser [CH] 58 H5
Unterweissenbach [A] 62 C4
Unterwössen [D] 60 F5
Untorp [S] 172 G2
Uors [CH] 70 G1
Úpice [CZ] 50 B2
Upiłka [PL] 22 C4
Upper Largo [GB] 8 F3
Upphärad [S] 166 D6
Upplands Väsby [S] 168 D2
Uppsala [S] 168 D1
Uppsete [N] 170 D3
Upyna [LT] 200 E4
Urachi, Nuraghe s'– [I] 118 C5
Uraiújfalu [H] 74 G1
Úras [I] 118 C6
Ura Vajgurore [AL] 128 B4
Urbánia [I] 110 H6
Urbeis [F] 58 D2
Úrbel del Castillo [E] 82 E5
Urbino [I] 112 B6
Urbise [F] 56 E6
Urbœ [S] 164 E1
Urçay [F] 56 C5
Urda [E] 96 F3
Urdaibai [E] 82 H3
Urdos [F] 84 D4
Uriage–les–Bains [F] 68 H5
Uriz / Arze–Arce [E] 84 C4
Urjala [FIN] 176 F2
Urjalankylä [FIN] 176 F2
Urk [NL] 16 E3
Úrkút [H] 74 H2
Urla [TR] 152 C4
Urlingford [IRL] 4 E3
Urnäsch [CH] 58 H5
Urnes [N] 170 D1
Uroševac [SRB] 146 C6
Urpila [FIN] 186 F1
Urroz [E] 84 B4
Urshult [S] 162 E5
Ursus [PL] 38 B3
Urtimjaur [S] 196 A1
Ürünlü [TR] 150 B2
Ururi [I] 116 F6
Ury [F] 42 F5
Urzędów [PL] 38 D6
Urzelina [P] 100 C3
Urziceni [RO] 204 E5
Urzicuța [RO] 146 F2
Urzulei [I] 118 E5
Usagre [E] 94 H3
Uşak [TR] 152 G3
Ušće [SRB] 146 B3
Uścìe Gorlickie [PL] 52 C5
Usedom [D] 20 E4
Usélus [I] 118 C5
Useras / les Useres [E] 98 F3
Ushakovo [RUS] 22 G2
Uši [MK] 128 F2
Ušinci [BG] 148 D2
Usingen [D] 46 C2
Uskali [FIN] 188 G3
Uskedal [N] 170 B5
Uski [FIN] 178 D3
Uskopolje [BIH] 144 B1
Üsküdar [TR] 150 E3
Üsküp [TR] 150 C1
Usküpdere [TR] 150 C1
Uslar [D] 32 F4
Usma [LV] 198 C5
Usmate Velate [I] 70 G4
Úsov [CZ] 50 C4
Uspen'ye [RUS] 202 B3
Ussé [F] 54 F2
Usseglio [I] 70 C5
Ussel [F] 68 B2
Ussel [I] 70 D4
Usseln [D] 32 D5
Usson–du–Poitou [F] 54 F5
Usson–en–Forez [F] 68 E3
Usson–les–Bains [F] 106 B6
Ustaoset [N] 170 E4
Ustaritz [F] 84 C2
Úštěk [CZ] 48 F2
Uster [CH] 58 G5
Ústí [CZ] 50 E6
Ustibar [BIH] 144 E2
Ústí nad Labem [CZ] 48 F2
Ústí nad Orlicí [CZ] 50 B4
Ustiprača [BIH] 144 E1
Ustje [RUS] 198 H1
Ustjuzha [RUS] 202 E1
Ustka [PL] 22 B2
Ust'–Luga [RUS] 178 E6
Ustrem [BG] 150 A1
Ustroń [PL] 50 F5
Ustronie Morskie [PL] 20 H3
Ustrzyki Dolne [PL] 52 F5
Ustrzyki Górne [PL] 52 F6
Ustyluh [UA] 38 G6
Ustyuzhna [RUS] 202 E1
Ususău [RO] 76 H5
Usvaty [RUS] 202 C4
Usvyaty [RUS] 202 C4
Utajärvi [FIN] 196 E4
Utåker [N] 170 B5
Utansjö [S] 184 F3
Utbjoa [N] 164 B1
Utebo [E] 90 E3
Utena [LT] 200 G4
Utersum [D] 156 A5
Uthlede [D] 18 D4
Utiel [E] 98 D4
Utne [N] 170 C4
Utrecht [NL] 16 D5
Utrera [E] 100 G2
Utrillas [E] 90 E6
Utrine [SRB] 76 E5
Utsjö [S] 172 F4
Utsjoki [FIN] 194 D3
Utstein [N] 164 A2
Uttendorf [A] 60 G4
Uttendorf [A] 72 F1
Uttermossa [FIN] 186 B5
Uttersberg [S] 168 A2
Utti [FIN] 178 C3
Utting [D] 60 D4
Uttoxeter [GB] 10 E5
Utula [FIN] 178 E1
Utvalnäs [S] 174 E4
Utvängstorp [S] 162 C1
Utvik [N] 180 D5
Utvorda [N] 190 C4
Uukuniemen Kk. [FIN] 188 G5
Uukuniemi [FIN] 188 G5
Uurainen [FIN] 186 F4
Uuro [FIN] 186 B5
Uuro [FIN] 188 F2
Uusijoki [FIN] 194 E5

Uusikaarlepyy / Nykarleby [FIN] 186 C1
Uusikartano [FIN] 176 D3
Uusikaupunki / Nystad [FIN] 176 C3
Uusikylä [FIN] 178 B3
Uusi-Värtsilä [FIN] 188 G3
Uutela [FIN] 194 D6
Uva [FIN] 196 F4
Uvac [BIH] 144 E1
Úvaly [CZ] 48 G4
Uvanå [S] 172 F5
Uvarovka [RUS] 202 E3
Uvdal [N] 170 F4
Uvernet-Fours [F] 108 D2
Uyeasound [GB] 6 H3
Uzdowo [PL] 22 G5
Uzel [F] 26 A5
Uzerche [F] 66 G2
Uzès [F] 106 G3
Uzeste [F] 66 D4
Uzhorod [UA] 204 B3
Užice [SRB] 146 A2
Uzlovoye [RUS] 200 E5
Uzhots'kyi, Pereval- [UA] 52 F6
Užpaliai [LT] 200 G4
Üzümlü [TR] 154 F2
Uzunköprü [TR] 150 B3
Uzunkuyu [TR] 152 B4
Uzunpınar [TR] 152 G4
Uzuntarla [TR] 150 G3
Užventis [LT] 200 E4

V

Vä [N] 164 E1
Vä [S] 158 D2
Vaajakoski [FIN] 186 G4
Vaajasalmi [FIN] 186 H3
Vääkiö [FIN] 196 F3
Vääksy [FIN] 178 A2
Vaala [FIN] 196 E4
Vaalajärvi [FIN] 194 D6
Vaalimaa [FIN] 178 D3
Vaaljoki [FIN] 176 D3
Vaarakylä [FIN] 196 F3
Vaaraniva [FIN] 196 F3
Väärinmaja [FIN] 186 E5
Vaas [F] 42 B6
Vaasa / Vasa [FIN] 186 B2
Vaassen [NL] 16 F4
Väätäiskylä [FIN] 186 E3
Vabalninkas [LT] 200 F3
Vabres-l'Abbaye [F] 106 D3
Vác [H] 64 C5
Vacha [D] 46 F1
Váchartyán [H] 64 C6
Väckelsång [S] 162 E5
Vad [S] 168 A1
Vădastra [RO] 148 A2
Vadépuszta [H] 76 A3
Väderstad [S] 166 G6
Vadheim [N] 170 C1
Vadili (Vatili) [CY] 154 G5
Vadna [H] 64 F4
Vado Ligure [I] 108 H3
Vadsø [N] 194 E2
Vadstena [S] 166 G5
Vaduz [FL] 58 H6
Væggerløse [DK] 20 B1
Vafaíka [GR] 130 E3
Vafiochóri [GR] 128 G3
Vág [H] 74 G1
Våga [N] 164 A2
Vågåmo [N] 180 G5
Vagan [BIH] 142 B4
Våge [N] 164 A1
Våge [N] 164 C6
Våge [N] 170 B5
Vage [N] 180 E3
Vågen [N] 190 A6
Vägeva [EST] 198 F2
Vaggeryd [S] 162 D3
Vaggsvik [N] 192 F3
Vágia [GR] 134 B5
Vagiónia [GR] 140 E5
Vaglio Basilicata [I] 120 H4
Vagnhärad [S] 168 D4
Vagos [P] 80 B5
Vågsbygd [N] 164 D6
Vägsele [S] 190 G5
Vågsjöfors [S] 172 E5
Vågslid [N] 164 D1
Vágur [FR] 160 A3
Vähäkyro / Lillkyro [FIN] 186 B2
Vahanka [FIN] 186 E3
Vahastu [EST] 198 E2
Vaheri [FIN] 186 G5
Väi [GR] 140 H4
Vaiano [I] 110 F5
Vaiges [F] 40 H5
Vaiguva [LT] 200 E4
Vaihingen [D] 46 C6
Väike-Maarja [EST] 198 F1
Väike Rakke [EST] 198 F3
Vailly [F] 56 C2
Vainikkala [FIN] 178 E2
Vainupea [EST] 198 E1
Vainutas [LT] 200 D5
Vaison-la-Romaine [F] 106 H3
Vaite [F] 58 A3
Vajmat [S] 190 H2
Vajnede [LV] 198 C6
Vajont [I] 72 F4
Vajszló [H] 76 A5
Vajza [AL] 128 B5
Vakarel [BG] 146 G5
Vakern [S] 172 F5
Vakıflar [TR] 150 C2
Vaksdal [N] 170 B3
Vaksevo [BG] 146 F6
Vakumonë [AL] 128 B3
Vålådalen [S] 182 E2
Valajanaapa [FIN] 196 D2
Valajaskoski [FIN] 194 D8
Valandovo [MK] 128 G2
Valanhamn [N] 192 G1
Valareña [E] 84 B6
Valaská Belá [SK] 64 B2
Valašská Polanka [CZ] 50 E6
Valašské Klobouky [CZ] 50 E6
Valašské Meziříčí [CZ] 50 E5
Valbella [CH] 70 H1
Valberg [F] 108 E3
Vålberg [S] 166 E3
Valbiska [HR] 112 E2
Valbo [S] 174 E4
Valbondione [I] 72 A4
Valbonë [AL] 146 A5
Valbonnais [F] 68 H5
Vâlcani [RO] 76 F5
Valcarlos / Luzaide [E] 84 C3
Val-Claret [F] 70 C4
Valcum [H] 74 G3
Valdagno [I] 72 D6
Valdahon [F] 58 B5
Valdaj [RUS] 202 D2
Valdalen [N] 182 D5
Valday [RUS] 202 D2
Valdeazores [E] 96 D2
Valdecaballeros [E] 96 C2
Valdecabras [E] 98 C2
Valdecarros [E] 88 C3
Valdedios [E] 82 C2
Valdeganga [E] 98 C5
Valdeinfierno [E] 96 B5
Valdelacas de Tajo [E] 96 C1
Val del Charco del Agua Amarga, Cueva de la- [E] 90 F6
Valdeltormo [E] 90 G6
Valdemadera [E] 84 A6
Valdemārpils [LV] 198 C4
Valdemarsvik [S] 168 C6
Valdemorillo [E] 88 F5
Valdemoro [E] 88 F6
Valdemoro Sierra [E] 98 C2
Valdenoceda [E] 82 F4
Valdepeñas [E] 96 F5
Valdepeñas de Jaén [E] 102 E3
Valdepolo [E] 82 C4
Valderas [E] 82 B5
Valderice [I] 126 B2
Valderoure [F] 108 D4
Valderöy [N] 180 C3
Valderrobres [E] 98 G1
Valdesalor [E] 86 H5
Val d'Esquières [F] 108 D5
Valdeverdeja [E] 96 C1
Valdieri [I] 108 F3
Val d'Isère [F] 70 C4
Val-d'Izé [F] 26 D6
Valdobbiádene [I] 72 E5
Valdoviño [E] 78 D1
Valdštejn [CZ] 48 H2
Valdunquillo [E] 82 B6
Valea lui Mihai [RO] 204 B3
Valea Rea [RO] 148 F1
Valebø [N] 164 F2
Valečov [CZ] 48 G2
Vale da Rosa [P] 94 C5
Vale de Açor [P] 94 D3
Vale de Cambra [P] 80 C5
Vale de Lobos [P] 94 C5
Vale de Santarém [P] 86 C4
Vale do Arco [P] 86 D4
Vale do Côa, Parque Arqueológico do- [P] 80 E5
Vale do Poço [P] 94 D4
Válega [P] 80 B5
Valéggio sul Míncio [I] 110 E1
Valen [N] 170 B5
Valença do Minho [P] 78 B5
Valençay [F] 54 H3
Valence [F] 66 E6
Valence [F] 66 F6
Valence [F] 68 F5
Valence d'Albigeois [F] 106 C2
Valence-sur-Baïse [F] 66 D6
Valencia [E] 98 E4
Valencia de Alcántara [E] 86 F5
Valencia de Don Juan [E] 82 B5
Valencia de las Torres [E] 94 H3
Valencia del Ventoso [E] 94 G3
Valencia de Mombuey [E] 94 F3
Valenciennes [F] 28 G4
Văleni [RO] 148 B1
Vălenii de Munte [RO] 204 D5
Valensole [F] 108 C4
Valentano [I] 114 G3
Valentigney [F] 58 C4
Valenza [I] 70 F6
Våler [N] 166 B2
Våler [N] 172 D4
Valeria [E] 98 B3
Vales Mortos [P] 94 E4
Valevåg [N] 170 B6
Valfábbrica [I] 116 A2
Valga [EST] 198 F4
Valgeristi [EST] 198 D2
Valgrisenche [I] 70 C4
Valguarnera Caropepe [I] 126 F3
Välijoki [FIN] 178 D2
Välijoki [FIN] 194 D8
Valimítika [GR] 132 G6
Välivaara [FIN] 196 G6
Valjevo [SRB] 146 A1
Valjevo [SRB] 204 A6
Valjimena [E] 88 C4
Valjok [N] 194 C3
Valka [LV] 198 F4
Valkeajärvi [FIN] 186 E4
Valkeakoski [FIN] 176 F2
Valkeala [FIN] 178 C2
Valkeavaara [FIN] 188 G4
Valkenburg [NL] 30 F4
Valkenswaard [NL] 30 E3
Valkiamäki [FIN] 188 E6
Valkininkai [LT] 24 H2
Valko / Valkom [FIN] 178 B4
Valkom / Valko [FIN] 178 B4
Valla [S] 182 F1
Valla [S] 184 D3
Vallada [E] 78 F4
Valladolid [E] 88 E2
Vallåkra [S] 156 H2
Vallargärdet [S] 166 F2
Vallata [I] 120 F3
Vallbona de les Monges [E] 92 C4
Valldal [N] 180 E4
Valldemossa [E] 104 E4
Valle [LV] 198 E6
Valle [N] 164 D2
Valle de Abdalajís [E] 102 B4
Valle de Cabuérniga [E] 82 E3
Valle dei Templi [I] 126 D4
Valle de la Serena [E] 96 A3
Valle de los Caidos [E] 88 F5
Valle de Matamoros [E] 94 F3
Valledoria [I] 118 C2
Vallehermoso [E] 100 B5
Vallelunga Pratameno [I] 126 D3
Vallen [S] 184 D1
Vallentuna [S] 168 E2
Valleraugue [F] 106 E2
Vallet [F] 54 C2
Valletta [M] 126 C6
Vallfogona de Ripollès [E] 92 E2
Vallheim [N] 190 D4
Vallivana [E] 98 G2
Vallo di Lucania [I] 120 F5
Valloire [F] 70 B5
Valloires, Abbaye de- [F] 28 D3
Vallombrosa [I] 110 F5
Vallon-en-Sully [F] 56 C5
Vallon-Pont-d'Arc [F] 68 E6
Vallorbe [CH] 58 B6
Vallorcine [F] 70 C3
Vallø Slot [DK] 156 G3
Vallouise [F] 70 B6
Valls [E] 92 C4
Vallsbo [S] 174 D3
Vallset [N] 172 C4
Vallsta [S] 174 D1
Vallter 2000 [E] 92 E2
Vallvik [S] 174 E2
Valmadrid [E] 90 E4
Valmiera [LV] 198 E4
Valmigère [F] 106 C5
Valmojado [E] 88 E6
Valmontone [I] 116 B6
Valmorel [F] 70 B4
Val Moutier [CH] 58 D5
Valö [S] 174 F5
Valognes [F] 26 D2
Valongo [P] 80 C4
Valoria la Buena [E] 88 F1
Valøya [N] 190 C5
Valozhyn [BY] 200 H6
Valpaços [P] 80 E3
Valpelline [I] 70 D3
Valporquero de Torío [E] 78 H5
Valpovo [HR] 76 B6
Valras-Plage [F] 106 D5
Valréas [F] 106 H2
Vals [CH] 70 G2
Valsamónero [GR] 140 E5
Valsavarenche [I] 70 C4
Valsebo [S] 166 C3
Valset [N] 190 B6
Valsinni [I] 122 D5
Valsjöbyn [S] 190 E5
Valsjön [S] 184 D5
Valskog [S] 168 B3
Vals-les-Bains [F] 68 E6
Valsøybotn [N] 180 G2
Välsta [S] 184 E6
Val-Suzon [F] 56 G3
Valtesíniko [GR] 136 D2
Val Thorens [F] 70 B5
Valtiendas [E] 88 G3
Valtierra [E] 84 B5
Valtimo [FIN] 196 F5
Valtola [FIN] 178 C2
Váltos [GR] 130 H1
Valtournenche [I] 70 D3
Valvanera, Monasterio de- [E] 90 B1
Valverde [E] 100 A5
Valverde, Santuario di- [I] 118 B3
Valverde de Cervera [E] 84 A6
Valverde de Júcar [E] 98 B3
Valverde del Camino [E] 94 F5
Valverde de Leganés [E] 94 F2
Valverde del Fresno [E] 86 G3
Valzul [LT] 72 B2
Vama Veche [RO] 148 G1
Vamberk [CZ] 50 B3
Vamdrup [DK] 156 C3
Våmhus [S] 172 G3
Vamlingbo [S] 168 F6
Vammala [FIN] 176 E2
Vámos [GR] 140 C4
Vámosmikola [H] 64 C5
Vámospércs [H] 64 H6
Vámosszabadi [H] 62 H6
Vampula [FIN] 176 E3
V. Ämtervik [S] 166 E2
Vamvakoú [GR] 132 G2
Vanås [S] 158 D1
Vana-Vigala [EST] 198 D2
Vanda / Vantaa [FIN] 176 H5
Vandel [DK] 156 C2
Vandellós [E] 90 H6
Vandenesse [F] 56 E4
Vandoies / Vintl [I] 72 E2
Vändra [EST] 198 E2
Vandžegala [LT] 200 F5
Väne [LV] 198 C5
Vanebu [N] 164 G2
Vänersborg [S] 166 D5
Väne-Ryr [S] 166 D6
Vaneskoski [FIN] 186 C6
Vånga [S] 158 D1
Vangaži [LV] 198 E5
Vängel [S] 190 F6
Vangsnes [N] 170 D2
Vanha-Kihlanki [S] 194 B6
Vanhakylä [FIN] 186 B5
Vanhamäki [FIN] 188 C5
Vänjaurbäck [S] 190 G5
Vänjaurträsk [S] 190 G5
Vânju Mare [RO] 146 E1
Vankiva [S] 158 D1
Vännacka [S] 166 D2
Vännäs [S] 190 H6
Vännäsberget [S] 194 B8
Vännäsby [S] 190 H6
Vannes [F] 40 D5
Vansbro [S] 172 G4
Vanse [N] 164 C5
Vansjö [S] 168 B1
Vänsjö [S] 182 H6
Vanstad [S] 158 D3
Vantaa / Vanda [FIN] 176 H5
Vanttauskoski [FIN] 194 D8
Vanvik [N] 164 C1
Vanvikan [N] 190 B6
Vanyarc [H] 64 D5
Vaplan [S] 182 G2
Vara [S] 166 E6
Varabla [EST] 198 D3
Varades [F] 40 G6
Varages [F] 108 C4
Varakļāni [LV] 198 F5
Varaldsøy [S] 170 B5
Varallo [I] 70 E4
Varanava [BY] 200 G6
Varangerbotn [N] 194 E2
Varano de' Melegari [I] 110 D3
Varaždin [HR] 74 F4
Varaždinske Toplice [HR] 74 F4
Varazze [I] 108 H3
Varberg [S] 160 H4
Varbola [EST] 198 D2
Vărbovo [BG] 148 D6
Varbyane [BG] 148 E2
Varces [F] 68 H5
Várda [GR] 136 B1
Varde [DK] 156 B2
Vardim [BG] 148 C2
Vardiste [BIH] 144 E1
Vårdö [FIN] 176 B5
Vardø [N] 194 F2
Várdomb [H] 76 C4
Vårdsberg [S] 168 A5
Varduva [LT] 200 D3
Varekil [S] 166 C6
Varel [D] 18 C4
Varellaíoi [GR] 134 D5
Varena [LT] 24 G2
Varengeville-sur-Mer [F] 28 C4
Varenna [I] 70 G3
Varennes-en-Argonne [F] 44 D3
Varennes-sur-Allier [F] 56 D6
Vareš [BIH] 142 D4
Varese [I] 70 F4
Varese Ligure [I] 110 C3
Vårgårda [S] 162 B1
Vargön [S] 166 D5
Vargträsk [S] 190 G5
Varhaug [N] 164 A4
Värhus [N] 182 C3
Vári [GR] 138 D2
Varias [RO] 76 G5
Varilhes [F] 84 H5
Varín [SK] 50 F6
Väring [S] 166 F5
Váris [GR] 128 F6
Varjakka [FIN] 196 D4
Varjisträsk [S] 190 H2
Varkaus [FIN] 188 D4
Várkiza [GR] 136 H1
Varland [N] 164 E1
Värmdö [S] 168 E3
Värmlandsbro [S] 166 E3
Varmo [I] 72 G5
Värmskog [S] 166 E2
Varna [BG] 148 F3
Varna [SRB] 142 F3
Varna (Vahrn) [I] 72 D2
Värnamo [S] 162 D4
Varnany [BY] 200 H5
Varnhem [S] 166 F5
Varniai [LT] 200 E4
Varnja [EST] 198 F2
Varnsdorf [CZ] 48 G1
Varntresk [N] 190 E3
Väröbacka [S] 160 H3
Városerdő [H] 76 G3
Városföld [H] 76 D3
Varoška Rijeka [BIH] 112 H2
Városlőd [H] 74 H2
Varovnik [BG] 148 F5
Varp [S] 166 C4
Varpaisjärvi [FIN] 196 F6
Várpalota [H] 76 B2
Varpanen [FIN] 178 C1
Varparanta [FIN] 188 E4
Varparanta [FIN] 188 F2
Varpsjö [S] 190 F5
Värriö [FIN] 194 E6
Vars [F] 108 E2
Varşand [RO] 76 G3
Värsås [S] 166 F6
Varshko [RUS] 178 G3
Varsi [I] 110 C3
Varsseveld [NL] 16 F6
Vartdal [N] 180 C4
Vartemyagi [RUS] 178 H4
Vartius [FIN] 196 G4
Vărtoapele [RO] 148 B1
Vărtopu [RO] 146 F1
Värtsilä [FIN] 188 G3
Varv [S] 166 H5
Varvara [BG] 148 A6
Varvara [BG] 148 G5
Varvára [GR] 130 C4
Varzi [I] 110 B2
Varzy [F] 56 E3
Vasa / Vaasa [FIN] 186 B2
Vasalemma [EST] 198 D1
Vasankari [FIN] 196 C5
Vasarapera [FIN] 194 F8
Vasarás [GR] 136 E3
Vasbotna [N] 190 C5
Väse [S] 166 F3
Vasiláki [GR] 136 C2
Vasilevo [BG] 148 G2
Vasil'evskoye [RUS] 198 H4
Vasiliká [GR] 130 B5
Vasiliká [GR] 134 B3
Vasiliká [GR] 134 G2
Vasilikí [GR] 132 C5
Vasilikó [GR] 134 B5
Vasilikós [GR] 136 B2
Vasilishki [BY] 24 H3
Vasilítsi [GR] 136 D5
Vasil Levski [BG] 148 D5
Vaškai [LT] 198 D6
Vaskelovo [RUS] 178 H3
Vaskio [FIN] 176 E4
Vaskivesi [FIN] 186 D5
Vasknarva [EST] 198 G2
Vaskút [H] 76 C5
Vasles [F] 54 E4
Vaslui [RO] 204 E4
Vassbø [N] 164 B4
Vassbotten [S] 166 C4
Vassenden [N] 170 G1
Vassenden [N] 180 C6
Vásses [GR] 136 D3
Vassli [N] 180 G1
Vassmolösa [S] 162 F5
Vassnäs [S] 182 E1
Vasstrand [N] 192 F2
Vassurány [H] 74 F1
Vassy [F] 26 E4
Västan [S] 184 E5
Västansfors [S] 168 A1
Västansjö [S] 184 F3
Västansjö [S] 190 E3
Västansjö [S] 190 F4
Västansjön [S] 184 E5
Västbacka [S] 172 G1
Västbacken [S] 182 F1
Västeräker [S] 168 D2
Väster-Arådalen [S] 182 F3
Västerås [S] 168 B2
Västerby [S] 168 D4
Västerfärnebo [S] 168 B1
Västergärn [S] 168 F5
Västerhaninge [S] 168 E3
Västerhus [S] 184 G2
Västermyckeläng [S] 172 F2
Västermyrriset [S] 190 G5
Västerrottna [S] 166 E1
Västersel [S] 184 G2
Västervik [S] 162 G2
Vastila [FIN] 178 C3
Västilä [FIN] 186 F6
Västland [S] 174 F5
Vasto [I] 116 E5
Västra Frölunda [S] 160 G2
Västra Yttermark [FIN] 186 A4
Västrum [S] 162 G2
Vasvár [H] 74 G2
Vasylivka [UA] 204 H2
Vasyl'kiv [UA] 202 D7
Vasyl'kivka [UA] 204 F3
Vát [H] 74 G1
Vatan [F] 54 H3
Vaterá [GR] 134 G3
Váthi [GR] 128 H3
Vathý [GR] 134 B5
Vathý [GR] 138 H4
Vathý [GR] 152 C6
Vathýlakkos [GR] 128 F5
Vathýlakkos [GR] 130 D2
Vathýpetro [GR] 140 E5
Vatili (Vadili) [CY] 154 G5
Vatne [N] 164 B3
Vatne [N] 164 D4
Vatne [N] 180 C4
Vatne [N] 180 D3
Vatnstraum [N] 164 E5
Vatólakkos [GR] 128 E6
Vatopedíou, Moní- [GR] 130 D5
Vatoúsa [GR] 134 G2
Vatra Dornei [RO] 204 D3
Vatta [H] 64 F5
Vättershus [S] 162 D1
Vattjom [S] 184 E4
Vattlång [S] 184 E6
Vattnäs [S] 172 G3
Vatvet [N] 166 C3
Vau [P] 94 B5
Vaucelles, Abbaye de- [F] 28 F4
Vauclaix [F] 56 E3
Vaucluse [F] 58 C5
Vaucouleurs [F] 44 D5
Vaudoy en Brie [F] 42 G4
Vau i Dejës [AL] 128 B1
Vauldalen [N] 182 D3
Vauvenargues [F] 108 B4
Vauvert [F] 106 F4
Vauville [F] 26 D1
Vauvillers [F] 58 B3
Vaux-Le Vicomte [F] 42 G4
Vavylás (Güzelyalı) [CY] 154 F5
Vawkavysk [BY] 24 G5
Vaxholm [S] 168 E3
Växjö [S] 162 E4
Växtorp [S] 162 B6
Vayrac [F] 66 H4
Vaysal [TR] 150 B1
Važecká Jaskyňa [SK] 64 D2
V. Bodarna [S] 160 H1
Vean [N] 180 G1
Vebbestrup [DK] 160 D4
Veberöd [S] 158 C3
Veblungsnes [N] 180 E3
Vebomark [S] 196 A5
Vecbebri [LV] 198 E5
Večelkov [SK] 64 E4
Vechta [D] 18 C6
Vecilla de Valderaduey [E] 82 C4
Vecinos [E] 88 B3
Veckholm [S] 168 D2
Vecpiebalga [LV] 198 F5
Vecsés [H] 76 C1
Vecumnieki [LV] 198 E5
Vedavågen [N] 164 A2
Vedbæk [DK] 156 G2
Veddelev [DK] 156 G2
Veddige [S] 160 H3
Vedea [RO] 148 C1
Vedelago [I] 72 E5
Vedersø Klit [DK] 160 B5
Vedevåg [S] 166 H2
Vedjeön [S] 190 E5
Vedum [S] 166 E6
Veendam [NL] 16 H2
Veenendaal [NL] 16 E5
Veere [NL] 16 B6
Vegacervera [E] 78 H5
Vega de Espinareda [E] 78 F4
Vega de los Árboles [E] 96 G4
Vegadeo [E] 78 F2
Vega de Pas [E] 82 F3
Vega de Valcarce [E] 78 E4
Vegårshei [N] 164 F4
Vegas de Coria [E] 88 B4
Vegas del Condado [E] 78 H5
Vegger [DK] 160 D4
Veggli [N] 170 F5
Veghel [NL] 16 E6
Veglie [I] 122 G5
Vegset [N] 190 C5
Vegusdal [N] 164 E4
Vehkajärvi [FIN] 176 G1
Vehkalah [FIN] 178 B1
Vehkaperä [FIN] 186 E3
Vehmaa [FIN] 176 D4
Vehmaa [FIN] 188 D5
Vehmasmäki [FIN] 188 C3
Vehmersalmi [FIN] 188 D2
Vehniä [FIN] 186 G4
Vehu [FIN] 186 E3
Vehuvarpee [FIN] 186 C6
Veidnesklubben [N] 194 C2
Veikkola [FIN] 176 G5
Veinge [S] 162 B5
Veio [I] 114 H5
Veiros [P] 86 E6
Veisiejai [LT] 24 F3
Veitshöchheim [D] 46 E4
Veiviržėnai [LT] 200 D4
Vejano [I] 114 H4
Vejby [DK] 156 G1
Vejbystrand [S] 162 B6
Vejen [DK] 156 B2
Vejer de la Frontera [E] 100 F5
Vejers Strand [DK] 156 A2
Vejinac [BIH] 112 H2
Vejle [DK] 156 C2
Vejprty [CZ] 48 D2
Vekilski [BG] 148 F2
Velada [E] 88 D6
Velagići [BIH] 142 B3
Vela Luka [HR] 144 A3
Velanídia [GR] 136 F5
Velas [P] 100 C3
Velbert [D] 30 H3
Velburg [D] 46 H6
Velbuzhdki Pateka (Velbuzhdki Prolaz) [BG/MK] 146 E6
Velbuzhdki Prolaz (Velbuzhdki Pateka) [BG/MK] 146 E6
Velchevo [BG] 148 B4
Velden [A] 74 B3
Velden [D] 46 H4
Velden [D] 60 F4
Veldhoven [NL] 30 E2
Velebit [SRB] 76 E5
Velefique [E] 102 G4
Velehrad [CZ] 62 G2
Velēna [LV] 198 F4
Velence [H] 76 B2
Velenje [SLO] 74 D4
Velešín [CZ] 62 C2
Velešta [MK] 128 D3
Velestíno [GR] 132 H2
Vélez-Blanco [E] 102 H3
Vélez-Málaga [E] 102 C5
Vélez-Rubio [E] 102 H3
Velgošti [MK] 128 D3
Vel. Grđevac [HR] 74 G6
Velhartice [CZ] 48 E6
Vel. Horozhanka [UA] 52 H4
Veličani [BIH] 144 C3
Velika [HR] 142 C1
Velika Brusnica [BIH] 142 D2
Velika Dapčevica [HR] 74 G6
Velika Drenova [SRB] 146 C3
Velika Gorica [HR] 74 E6
Velika Kladuša [HR] 112 H2
Velika Kopanica [HR] 142 D2
Velika Kruša [SRB] 146 B6
Velika Plana [SRB] 146 C1
Velika Remeta, Manastir- [SRB] 142 F2
Velika Slatina [SRB] 146 C5
Velike Lašče [SLO] 74 C5
Veliki Preslav [BG] 148 E3
Veliki Šiljegovac [SRB] 146 D3
Veliki Tabor [HR] 74 D5
Veliki Zdenci [HR] 74 G6
Velikiye Luki [RUS] 202 C3
Veliko Orašje [SRB] 146 C1
Veliko Tŭrnovo [BG] 148 C3
Veli Lošinj [HR] 112 E4
Velimlje [MNE] 144 D3
Velingrad [BG] 148 A6
Velipojë [AL] 128 A1
Veliternë [AL] 128 D4
Velizh [RUS] 202 C4
Veljun [HR] 112 G2
Velká Bíteš [CZ] 50 B6
Velká Hleďsebe [CZ] 48 C4
Velká nad Veličkou [CZ] 62 H2
Velké Bílovice [CZ] 62 G3
Velké Brezno [CZ] 48 F2
Velké Heraltice [CZ] 50 D4
Veľké Kapušany [SK] 64 H3
Velké Karlovice [CZ] 50 E6
Veľké Leváre [SK] 62 G3
Velké Losiny [CZ] 50 C4
Velké Meziříčí [CZ] 50 B6
Velké Němčice [CZ] 62 F2
Velké Opatovice [CZ] 50 C5
Veľké Raškovce [SK] 64 H3
Veľke Ripňany [SK] 64 A3
Veľké Uherce [SK] 64 B3
Velkua [FIN] 176 D4
Velkuanmaa [FIN] 176 D5
Velký Beranov [CZ] 50 A5
Velký Bor [CZ] 48 E5
Veľký Folkmar [SK] 64 F2
Veľký Krtíš [SK] 64 D4
Veľký Meder [SK] 62 H5
Veľký Šariš [SK] 64 G2
Velký Újezd [CZ] 50 D5
Velle [N] 180 D4
Velleclaire [F] 58 B4
Velleia [I] 110 C2
Velles [F] 54 H4
Velletri [I] 116 A6
Vellinge [S] 156 H3
Vel. Ljubin [UA] 52 G4
Velp [NL] 16 F5
Velpke [D] 32 H2
Velta [N] 172 D4
Vel. Trnovac [SRB] 146 D5
Veltrusy [CZ] 48 F3
Veluće [SRB] 146 C3
Velušina [MK] 128 E4
Velvary [CZ] 48 F3
Velventós [GR] 128 F5
Vel'ye [RUS] 198 H4
Velyka Lepetykha [UA] 204 G2
Velyki Mosty [UA] 52 H3
Velykyi Bereznyi [UA] 204 B2
Vemb [DK] 160 B5
Vemdalen [S] 182 F4
Vemhån [S] 182 G5
Vemmelv [DK] 156 F3
Vemmenæs [DK] 156 E4
Ven [N] 164 B3
Vena [S] 162 F3
Venabu [N] 170 H1
Venaco [F] 114 B4
Venafro [I] 120 D1
Venäjä [FIN] 176 F3
Venaria Reale [I] 70 D5
Venåsen [N] 180 H6
Venčane [SRB] 146 B1
Vence [F] 108 E4
Venda Nova [P] 80 D3
Vendargues [F] 106 F4
Vendas de Galizes [P] 86 E2
Vendas Novas [P] 86 C6
Vendays-Montalivet [F] 66 C1
Vendel [S] 174 F5
Vendelsö [S] 168 E3
Vendeuvre [F] 44 B6
Vendinha [E] 94 E2
Vendôme [F] 42 D6
Vendranges [F] 68 E2
Veneheitto [FIN] 196 E4
Veneskoski [FIN] 186 C3
Venets [BG] 148 C5
Venets [BG] 148 E5
Venets [BG] 148 E2
Venevere [EST] 198 F2
Venézia [I] 72 E6
Venialbo [E] 80 H5
Venjan [S] 172 F3
Venlo [NL] 30 F3
Venn [N] 182 B2
Vénna [GR] 130 F3
Vennesla [N] 164 D5
Vennesund [N] 190 C4
Venngarn [S] 168 D2
Venosa [I] 120 H3
Venoy [F] 56 E2
Venray [NL] 30 F2
Vent [A] 72 C2
Venta de Arraco [E] 84 D4
Venta de Baños [E] 88 F1
Venta del Moro [E] 98 D4
Venta de los Santos [E] 96 G6
Venta del Pobre [E] 102 H5
Ventadour, Château de- [F] 68 A3
Venta el Alto [E] 94 G5
Venta Nueva [E] 78 F4
Ventas de Huelma [E] 102 D4
Ventas de Zafarraya [E] 102 C4
Ventė [LT] 200 D5
Ventimíglia [I] 108 F4
Ventiseri [F] 114 B5
Ventnor [GB] 12 H5
Vento, Grotta del- [I] 110 D5
Ventosa de Pisuerga [E] 82 D5
Ventspils [LV] 198 B4
Venus [RO] 148 G1
Venzone [I] 72 G4
Vepsä [FIN] 196 D4

Virttaa [FIN] 176 E3
Virvoru [RO] 146 F1
Vis [HR] 116 H2
Visaginas [LT] 200 H4
Visbek [D] 18 C6
Visby [DK] 156 B4
Visby [S] 168 G4
Visé [B] 30 E4
Višegrad [BIH] 144 E1
Visegrád [H] 64 C5
Viseu [P] 80 C6
Vishaj [AL] 128 B3
Vishnyeva [BY] 200 H6
Vishovgrad [BG] 148 C3
Vishtytis [LT] 24 D2
Visiedo [E] 90 D6
Vişina Veche [RO] 148 A2
Visingsborg [S] 162 D1
Viskafors [S] 162 B2
Viskinge [DK] 156 F2
Viškovci [HR] 142 D1
Viškovo [HR] 112 E1
Visland [N] 164 C4
Vislanda [S] 162 D5
Višnja Gora [SLO] 74 C5
Visočka Ržana [SRB] 146 E4
Viso del Marqués [E] 96 F5
Visoka [SRB] 146 A3
Visoki Dečani, Manastir- [SRB] 146 B5
Visoko [BIH] 142 D4
Visoko [SLO] 74 B4
Visp [CH] 70 E2
Vissefjärda [S] 162 F5
Visselhövede [D] 18 E6
Visseltofta [S] 162 C6
Vissenbjerg [DK] 156 D3
Visso [I] 116 B2
Vistdal [N] 180 F3
Vistheden [S] 196 A3
Vistino [RUS] 178 F5
Visuvesi [FIN] 186 E5
Visz [H] 74 H3
Visz [H] 76 A3
Vitalahti [FIN] 186 G5
Vităneşti [RO] 148 C1
Vitanovac [SRB] 146 B3
Vitberget [S] 190 H2
Vitemölla [S] 158 D2
Viterbo [I] 114 H4
Viterbo, Bagni di- [I] 114 H4
Vithkuq [AL] 128 C5
Vitigudino [E] 80 F6
Vitina [BIH] 144 B2
Vitina [SRB] 146 C6
Vitis [A] 62 D3
Vitkov [CZ] 50 E4
Vitkovo [SRB] 146 C3
Vitolište [MK] 128 F3
Vitomirica [SRB] 146 B5
Vitoria-Gasteiz [E] 82 G5
Vitré [F] 26 D6
Vitry-le-François [F] 44 C5
Vitsand [S] 172 E5
Vitskøl Kloster [DK] 160 D4
Vitsyebsk [BY] 202 C4
Vittangi [S] 192 H5
Vittarp [DK] 156 A2
Vittaryd [S] 162 C4
Vitteaux [F] 56 G3
Vittel [F] 58 B2
Vittinge [S] 168 C1
Vittjärn [S] 172 D5
Vittjärv [S] 196 B3
Vittória [I] 126 F5
Vittoriosa [M] 126 C6
Vittório Véneto [I] 72 E5
Vitträsk [S] 194 A8
Vittsjö [S] 162 C6
Vittskövle [S] 158 D2
Vitvattnet [S] 196 C2
Vitzenburg [D] 34 B5
Vitznau [CH] 58 F6
Viù [I] 70 D5
Viuhkola [FIN] 178 D2
Vivario [F] 114 B4
Viveiro [E] 78 E1
Vivel del Río Martín [E] 90 E6
Viver [E] 98 E3
Viverols [F] 68 E3
Viverone [I] 70 E5
Viveros [E] 96 H5
Vivier, Château du- [F] 42 G4
Viviers [F] 68 F6
Vivonne [F] 54 E4
Vivungi [S] 192 H5
Vixía Herbeira [E] 78 D1
Vize [TR] 150 C2
Vizica [BG] 148 F5
Vizille [F] 68 H5
Vižinada [HR] 112 D1
Vizovice [CZ] 50 E6
Vizsoly [H] 64 G4
Vizzavona [F] 114 B4
Vizzini [I] 126 F4
Vjazy [RUS] 178 E3
Vjetrenica [BIH] 144 C3
Vlaardingen [NL] 16 C5
Vlacháva [GR] 132 E1
Vlacherná [GR] 132 D3
Vlachiótis [GR] 136 E4
Vlachokerasiá [GR] 136 E3
Vlachovo Březí [CZ] 48 E6
Vladičin Han [SRB] 146 D5
Vlădila [RO] 148 A1
Vladimir [MNE] 128 A1
Vladimirescu [RO] 76 G4
Vladimirovac [SRB] 142 H2
Vladimirovka [RUS] 178 H2
Vladimirovo [BG] 146 F3
Vladimirovo [BG] 148 F2
Vladimirskiy [RUS] 198 H3
Vlagtweed [NL] 16 H3
Vlahovo [BG] 130 E1
Vlaković [HR] 142 A1
V. Laole [SRB] 146 C1
Vlas [BG] 148 F4
Vlasenica [BIH] 142 E4
Vlašim [CZ] 48 G5
Vlaşin [RO] 148 C1
Vlasina Okruglica [SRB] 146 E5
Vlasotince [SRB] 146 D4
Vlieland [NL] 16 E1
Vlissingen [NL] 16 B6
Vlkava [CZ] 48 G3
Vlkolinec [SK] 64 C2
Vllahinë [AL] 128 B5
Vlochós [GR] 132 F2
Vlorë [AL] 128 A5
Vlotho [D] 32 E2
Vlychó [GR] 132 D5
V. Nedelja [SLO] 74 E4
Voćin [HR] 74 H6
Vöcklabruck [A] 62 A5
Voden [BG] 150 B1
Vodice [HR] 112 H6
Vodice [SLO] 74 B4
Vođinci [HR] 142 E1
Voditsa [BG] 148 D3
Vodňany [CZ] 48 F6
Vodnjan [HR] 112 D2
Vodskov [DK] 160 E3
Voergård [DK] 160 E3
Voerså [DK] 160 E3
Vogatsikó [GR] 128 E5
Vogelsdorf [D] 34 F2
Voghera [I] 70 F6
Vognillan [N] 180 H3
Vogogna [I] 70 E3
Vogorno [CH] 70 F3
Vogorno [CH] 70 G2
Vogošća [BIH] 144 D1
Vohburg [D] 60 E2
Vohenstrauss [D] 48 C5
Võhma [EST] 198 C3
Võhma [EST] 198 E2
Vöhringen [D] 60 B4
Void [F] 44 D5
Voikoski [FIN] 178 C2
Voiluoto [FIN] 176 C3
Voïnka [UA] 204 H3
Voiron [F] 68 H4
Voise [F] 42 E4
Võiske [EST] 198 D3
Voitsberg [A] 74 D2
Voix [F] 108 C3
Vojakkala [FIN] 176 G3
Vojany [SK] 64 H3
Vojčice [SK] 64 G3
Vojens [DK] 156 C3
Vojlovica [SRB] 142 H2
Vojmån [S] 190 F4
Vojnić [HR] 112 H1
Vojnik [SLO] 74 D4
Vojtanov [CZ] 48 C3
Vojtjajaure [S] 190 E3
Voknavolok [RUS] 196 G3
Voláda [GR] 140 H2
Vólakas [GR] 130 C2
Volary [CZ] 62 B2
Volda [N] 180 C4
Voldby [DK] 160 F5
Volders [A] 72 D1
Volendam [NL] 16 E4
Volfštejn [CZ] 48 D4
Volgosovo [RUS] 198 G2
Volimes [GR] 136 A2
Volissós [GR] 134 G4
Volkach [D] 46 F4
Völkermarkt [A] 74 C3
Volkhov [RUS] 202 C1
Völklingen [D] 44 G4
Volkmarsen [D] 32 E5
Volkovija [MK] 128 D2
Vollenhove [NL] 16 F3
Volmsjö [S] 190 G5
Volochys'k [UA] 202 B8
Volodarka [UA] 202 D8
Volodymyr-Volyns'kyi [UA] 38 H6
Volokolamsk [RUS] 202 E3
Voloma [RUS] 196 H5
Vólos [GR] 132 H2
Voloshovo [RUS] 198 H2
Volosovo [RUS] 178 G6
Volovo [BG] 148 C2
Volpiano [I] 70 D5
Volterra [I] 114 F1
Volterraio [I] 114 E2
Voltri [I] 110 A3
Voltti [FIN] 186 C2
Volturara Appula [I] 120 F1
Volvic [F] 68 C2
Volyně [CZ] 48 E6
Vonêche [B] 30 D6
Voneshta voda [BG] 148 C4
Vónitsa [GR] 132 D4
Võnnu [EST] 198 F3
Vönöck [H] 74 G1
Voorschoten [NL] 16 C4
Voorst [NL] 16 F5
Vopnafjörður [IS] 192 C2
Vörå / Vöyri [FIN] 186 B2
Vorau [A] 74 E1
Vorbasse [DK] 156 B2
Vorbourg [CH] 58 D4
Vorchdorf [A] 62 B5
Vörden [D] 32 D1
Vordernberg [A] 62 C6
Vorderriss [D] 60 D6
Vordingborg [DK] 156 F4
Vorë [AL] 128 B3
Voreinó [GR] 128 F3
Voreppe [F] 68 H4
Vorey [F] 68 E4
Vøringsfossen [N] 170 D4
Vormsele [S] 190 G4
Vormstad [N] 180 H2
Vormsund [N] 172 C5
Voroneţ, Mănăstirea- [RO] 204 D3
Voronkova Niva [RUS] 198 H4
Vorontsovo [RUS] 198 H4
Vorsfelde [D] 32 H2
Võru [EST] 198 F3
Voruća [BIH] 142 D3
Voskopojë [AL] 128 C5
Voss [N] 170 C3
Vossijatskoje [UA] 204 G2
Votice [CZ] 48 G5
Votonósi [GR] 132 D1
Vouillé [F] 54 E3
Voukoliés [GR] 140 B4
Voúla [GR] 136 G1
Vouliagméni [GR] 136 G1
Voulpaix [F] 28 G5
Voúlpi [GR] 132 E3
Voulx [F] 42 G5
Vourkári [GR] 138 C2
Vourvouroú [GR] 130 C5
Voutás [GR] 134 A4
Vouvant [F] 54 C3
Vouvray [F] 54 G2
Vouzela [P] 80 C5
Vouziers [F] 44 C3
Voves [F] 42 E5
Vovoúsa [GR] 132 D1
Vowpa [BY] 24 G5
Voxna [S] 174 C2
Voxtorp [S] 162 D4
Vöylä [FIN] 194 D4
Voynica [BG] 146 E2
Voynitsa [RUS] 196 G3
Voynovo [BG] 148 F1
Vöyri / Vörå [FIN] 186 B2
Voz [HR] 112 F2
Vozarci [MK] 128 F2
Voznesens'k [UA] 204 F2
Vozrozhdenie [RUS] 178 F2
Vrå [DK] 160 E3
Vrå [S] 162 C5
Vrabinec [CZ] 48 F2
Vráble [SK] 64 B4
Vračevšnica [SRB] 146 B2
Vrachnaíika [GR] 132 F6
Vrådal [N] 164 E2
Vråliosen [N] 164 E2
Vrams Gunnarstorp [S] 156 H1
Vrana [HR] 112 E3
Vrana [HR] 112 F5
Vranduk [BIH] 142 D4
Vranilovci [BG] 148 C4
Vranino [BG] 148 G2
Vranisht [AL] 146 B6
Vranja [HR] 112 E1
Vranjak [HR] 112 F3
Vranje [SRB] 146 D5
Vranjina [MNE] 144 E4
Vranjska Banja [SRB] 146 D5
Vranov nad Dyjí [CZ] 62 E2
Vranov nad Topl'ou [SK] 64 G2
Vransko [SLO] 74 C4
Vrapčići [BIH] 144 C2
Vrapčište [MK] 128 D1
Vrástama [GR] 130 C5
Vratarnica [SRB] 146 E2
Vratkovići [BIH] 144 D3
Vrátna [SK] 50 G6
Vratna, Manastir- [SRB] 146 E1
Vratnica [MK] 146 C6
Vratno [HR] 74 E4
Vratsa [BG] 146 G3
Vravróna [GR] 134 C6
Vražogrnac [SRB] 146 E2
Vrba [SLO] 74 B4
Vrbanja [BIH] 142 C3
Vrbanja [HR] 142 E2
Vrbanje [MNE] 144 D4
Vrbas [MNE] 204 A5
Vrbas [SRB] 76 D6
Vrbaška [BIH] 142 C2
Vrbnica [SRB] 146 B6
Vrbnik [HR] 112 F2
Vrbno pod Pradědem [CZ] 50 D3
Vrboska [HR] 144 A2
Vrbovce [SK] 62 H3
Vrbové [SK] 62 H3
Vrbovec [HR] 74 F5
Vrbovsko [HR] 112 F1
Vrchlabí [CZ] 50 A2
Vrčice [SLO] 74 D6
Vrčin [SRB] 142 G3
Vrdnik [SRB] 142 F2
Vreden [D] 16 G5
Vrees [D] 18 C5
Vrelo [HR] 112 G3
Vrelo Bune [BIH] 144 C2
Vrena [S] 168 C4
Vreoci [SRB] 146 B1
Vresovo [BG] 148 E4
Vresse [B] 44 D1
Vreta Kloster [S] 166 H5
Vretstorp [S] 166 G4
Vrgorac [HR] 144 B2
Vrhnika [SLO] 74 B5
Vrhpolje [BIH] 142 B3
Vriezenveen [NL] 16 G4
Vrigny [F] 44 B3
Vrigstad [S] 162 D3
Vrilisia [GR] 134 C6
Vrilissia [GR] 132 G3
Vrin [CH] 70 G1
Vrlika [HR] 142 A4
Vrnjačka Banja [SRB] 146 C3
Vron [F] 28 D3
Vrontádos [GR] 134 G4
Vrontoú [GR] 128 G6
Vroomshoop [NL] 16 G4
Vrosína [GR] 132 C2
Vrouchás [GR] 140 F4
Vroutek [CZ] 48 E3
Vroville [F] 44 E6
Vrpolje [HR] 112 H6
Vrpolje [HR] 142 D1
Vršac [SRB] 204 B5
Vršani [BIH] 142 E2
Vrsar [HR] 112 D2
Vrtoče [BIH] 142 A3
Vrtojba [SLO] 72 H5
Vrútky [SK] 50 F6
Vrŭv [BG] 146 E1
Vry [F] 44 F4
Vrýses [GR] 140 C4
Vrysoúla [GR] 132 C3
Vrytaína [GR] 132 H3
Vsetín [CZ] 50 E6
V. Sjulsmark [S] 196 A5
V. Torsås [S] 162 D5
V. Trebeljevo [SLO] 74 C5
V. Trgovišće [HR] 74 E5
Vučitrn [SRB] 146 C5
Vučjavas [SLO] 74 E3
Vučkovci [BIH] 142 D2
Vuckovica [SRB] 146 B2
Vue [F] 54 B1
Vufflens, Château de- [CH] 70 B1
Vught [NL] 16 E6
Vŭglevtsi [BG] 148 C4
Vujanovo [SRB] 146 D4
Vuka [HR] 142 D1
Vukojevica [HR] 142 D1
Vukovar [HR] 142 E1
Vukovec [HR] 74 F5
Vulcăneşti [MD] 204 E4
Vŭlchedrŭm [BG] 146 F2
Vŭlchidol [BG] 148 F2
Vulci [I] 114 G4
Vuobmaved [FIN] 194 C4
Vuojalahti [FIN] 186 H5
Vuojärvi [FIN] 194 D7
Vuokatti [FIN] 196 F5
Vuolenkoski [FIN] 178 B2
Vuolijoki [FIN] 196 E5
Vuolle [FIN] 196 C5
Vuollerim [S] 196 A2
Vuonislahti [FIN] 188 F1
Vuorenkylä [FIN] 186 G6
Vuorenmaa [FIN] 176 E3
Vuorenmaa [FIN] 188 D5
Vuorijärvi [FIN] 186 C5
Vuorilahti [FIN] 186 F2
Vuoriniemi [FIN] 188 F5
Vuostimojärvi [FIN] 194 E7
Vuotner [S] 190 H3
Vuotsino [FIN] 194 E7
Vuotso [FIN] 194 D5
Vuottas [S] 194 A8
Vuottolahti [FIN] 196 E5
Vŭrbitsa [BG] 148 E3
Vŭrshets [BG] 146 F3
Vyalikaryta [BY] 38 G3
Vyanta [LT] 198 C6
Vyartsilya [RUS] 188 G3
Vyaz'ma [RUS] 202 E3
Vybor [RUS] 198 H4
Vyborg [RUS] 178 F3
Vyerkhnyadzvinsk [BY] 202 B4
Vyhonochy [RUS] 202 E5
Vynnyky [UA] 52 H4
Vynohradiv [UA] 204 C3
Vyra [RUS] 178 H6
Vyritsa [RUS] 178 H6
Vyróneia [GR] 130 B2
Vyshgorodok [RUS] 198 G4
Vyshhorod [UA] 202 D7
Vyshniy Volochek [RUS] 202 D2
Vyškov [CZ] 50 C6
Vyskytná [CZ] 48 H5
Vyšná Revúca [SK] 64 C2
Vysock [RUS] 178 E3
Vysoká [CZ] 48 H4
Vysoká u Příbr. [CZ] 48 E5
Vysokaye [BY] 38 F2
Vysoké Mýto [CZ] 50 B4
Vysokoe [RUS] 24 C1
Vysokoye [RUS] 198 G2
Vysoký Chlumec [CZ] 48 F5
Vysoký Hrádek [CZ] 62 C2
Vyšší Brod [CZ] 62 B3
Vyssineá [GR] 128 E5
Vytína [GR] 136 D2

W

Waabs [D] 18 F1
Waalwijk [NL] 16 D6
Wabern [D] 32 E5
Wąbrzeźno [PL] 22 E5
Wachenroth [D] 46 F4
Wąchock [PL] 38 B6
Wachow [D] 34 D2
Wächtersbach [D] 46 D2
Wachtum [D] 18 C6
Wackersdorf [D] 48 C5
Wadebridge [GB] 12 C4
Wädenswil [CH] 58 F5
Wadlew [PL] 36 G5
Wadowice [PL] 50 G4
Wagenfeld [D] 32 E1
Wageningen [NL] 16 E5
Waging [D] 60 G5
Wagrain [A] 72 G1
Wągrowiec [PL] 36 D1
Wahlwies [D] 58 G4
Wahrenholz [D] 32 H1
Waiblingen [D] 58 H1
Waidhaus [D] 48 C5
Waidhofen an der Thaya [A] 62 D3
Waidhofen an der Ybbs [A] 62 C5
Waidring [A] 60 F6
Waischenfeld [D] 46 G4
Wakefield [GB] 10 F4
Walbeck [D] 34 A2
Wałbrzych [PL] 50 B2
Walchensee [D] 60 D6
Walchsee [A] 60 F5
Walcourt [B] 28 H4
Wałcz [PL] 22 A5
Wald [A] 72 E1
Wald [CH] 58 G5
Wald-angelloch [D] 46 C5
Waldbröl [D] 32 C6
Waldburg [D] 60 B5
Waldeck [D] 32 E5
Waldenbuch [D] 58 H1
Waldenburg [D] 46 D6
Waldenburg [D] 48 C1
Waldfischbach [D] 44 H4
Waldhausen [D] 46 D5
Waldheim [D] 34 D6
Waldkirch [D] 58 E3
Waldkirchen [D] 62 A3
Waldkraiburg [D] 60 F4
Waldmünchen [D] 48 C5
Waldowice [PL] 34 H2
Waldsassen [D] 48 C4
Waldshut [D] 58 F4
Waldweiler [D] 44 G3
Walenstadt [CH] 58 H6
Walhalla [D] 48 C6
Wallasey [GB] 10 D4
Walldorf [D] 46 C5
Walldürn [D] 46 D4
Wallenfels [D] 46 H3
Wallern [A] 62 G6
Wallersdorf [D] 60 G3
Wallerstein [D] 60 C2
Wallfahrtskirche [D] 60 C2
Wallingford [GB] 14 D3
Wallsbüll [D] 156 B4
Wals [A] 60 G5
Walsall [GB] 10 E6
Walsrode [D] 18 E6
Waltrop [D] 30 H2
Waltsberg [A] 74 E3
Wambach [D] 32 E6
Wambierzyce [PL] 50 B2
Wanderup [D] 18 E1
Wanditz [D] 34 E1
Wanfried [D] 32 G5
Wangen [D] 60 B5
Wangenbourg [F] 44 G6
Wangerooge [D] 18 C3
Wangersen [D] 18 E4
Wängi [CH] 58 G5
Wankendorf [D] 18 G2
Wantage [GB] 12 H3
Wanzleben [D] 34 B3
Warburg [D] 32 E4
Wardenburg [D] 18 C5
Ware [GB] 14 E3
Waregem [B] 28 G2
Wareham [GB] 12 G5
Waremme [B] 30 E4
Waren [D] 20 C4
Warendorf [D] 32 D3
Warin [D] 20 A4
Warka [PL] 38 C4
Warlubie [PL] 22 E4
Warmbad Villach [A] 72 H3
Warmensteinach [D] 84 B4
Warminster [GB] 12 G4
Warmsen [D] 32 E2
Warnemünde [D] 20 B3
Warner Bros Park [E] 88 F6
Warnice [PL] 20 F5
Warnice [PL] 34 G1
Warnsveld [NL] 16 F5
Warrenpoint [NIR] 2 G4
Warrington [GB] 10 D4
Warstein [D] 32 D4
Warszawa [PL] 38 B3
Warszkowo [PL] 22 B2
Warta [PL] 36 F4
Warta Bolesławiecka [PL] 36 A6
Wartburg [D] 32 G6
Wartensee [CH] 58 F5
Wartenstein [A] 62 E6
Warth [A] 72 B1
Wartha [D] 32 G6
Warwick [GB] 12 H2
Washington [GB] 8 G6
Wasigenstein, Château de- [F] 44 H4
Wasilków [PL] 24 E5
Wąsosz [PL] 24 D4
Wąsosz [PL] 36 C5
Wasselonne [F] 44 G6
Wassen [CH] 70 F1
Wassenaar [NL] 16 C4
Wassenberg [D] 30 F4
Wasseralfingen [D] 60 C2
Wasserbillig [L] 44 F2
Wasserburg [D] 60 F4
Wasserfall Groppenstn. [A] 72 G2
Wasserkuppe [D] 46 E2
Wasserleonberg [A] 72 H3
Wasserschloss [D] 32 C3
Wasserschloss [D] 34 D4
Wassertrüdingen [D] 46 F6
Wassy [F] 44 C5
Wastl am Wald [A] 62 D5
Wasungen [D] 46 F1
Waterford / Port Lairge [IRL] 4 E5
Watergrasshill [IRL] 4 D5
Waterloo [B] 30 C4
Waterlooville [GB] 12 H5
Waterville / An Coireán [IRL] 4 A4
Watford [GB] 14 E4
Watten [F] 14 H6
Wattens [A] 72 D1
Watton [GB] 14 G4
Wattwil [CH] 58 G5
Watzelsdorf [A] 62 E3
Waulsort [B] 30 D6
Waver (Wavre) [B] 30 D4
Wavre (Waver) [B] 30 D4
Waxenberg [A] 62 B4
Waxweiler [D] 44 F1
Ważne Młyny [PL] 36 G6
Wda [PL] 22 D4
Wdzydze Kiszewskie [PL] 22 D3
Węchadłów [PL] 52 B2
Wechselburg [D] 34 D6
Weddelsborg [DK] 156 C3
Wedel [D] 18 F4
Wedemark [D] 32 F1
Weener [D] 18 B5
Weert [NL] 30 E3
Weesen [CH] 58 G6
Weeze [D] 30 F2
Wegberg [D] 30 F3
Wegeleben [D] 34 A4
Wegenstedt [D] 34 B2
Weggis [CH] 58 F6
Węgliniec [PL] 34 H6
Węgorzewo [PL] 24 C2
Węgorzyno [PL] 20 G5
Węgrów [PL] 38 D2
Węgrzynice [PL] 34 H3
Wegscheid [D] 62 A3
Wehr [D] 30 H6
Wehr [D] 58 E4
Weichselboden [A] 62 D6
Weichshofen [D] 60 F3
Weida [D] 48 C1
Weiden [D] 48 C4
Weidenberg [D] 46 H4
Weidensees [D] 46 H4
Weidenstetten [D] 60 B3
Weigetschlag [A] 62 B3
Weikersheim [D] 46 E5
Weil [D] 58 G1
Weilar [D] 46 F1
Weilburg [D] 46 C2
Weilheim [D] 60 D5
Weilmünster [D] 46 C2
Weimar [D] 32 D6
Weimar [D] 34 A6
Weinfelden [CH] 58 G4
Weingarten [D] 60 B5
Weinheim [D] 46 C4
Weinsberg [D] 46 D5
Weintor [D] 46 B5
Weirenstein [A] 72 F2
Weismain [D] 46 G3
Weissbriach [A] 72 G3
Weissenbach [A] 60 C6
Weissenbach [A] 72 H3
Weissenbach / Riobianco [I] 72 D2
Weissenberg [D] 34 G6
Weissenburg [D] 46 G6
Weissenegg [A] 74 D2
Weissenfels [D] 34 C6
Weissenhorn [D] 60 B3
Weissenkirchen [A] 62 D4
Weissensee [D] 32 H5
Weissenstadt [D] 48 B3
Weissenstein [D] 46 G4
Weisskirchen [A] 74 C2
Weisstannen [CH] 58 H6
Weisswasser [D] 34 G5
Weitensfeld [A] 74 B3
Weitersfelden [A] 62 C3
Weitra [A] 62 C3
Weiz [A] 74 D2
Wejherowo [PL] 22 D2
Welden [D] 60 C3
Wełdkowo [PL] 22 A3
Well [NL] 30 F2
Wellaune [D] 34 D5
Welle [D] 18 F5
Wellin [B] 30 D6
Wellingborough [GB] 14 E2
Wellington [GB] 12 F4
Wells [GB] 12 F4
Wells-next-the-Sea [GB] 14 G1
Wels [A] 62 B4
Welsberg / Monguelfo [I] 72 E3
Welschnofen / Nova Levante [I] 72 D3
Welshpool [GB] 10 C5
Weltenburg [D] 60 E2
Welwyn Garden City [GB] 14 E3
Welzheim [D] 60 B2
Wemding [D] 60 D2
Wemperhaardt [L] 30 F6
Wenddorf [D] 34 B2
Wendlingen [D] 58 H1
Wenecja [PL] 36 D1
Wengen [CH] 70 E1
Wennigsen [D] 32 F2
Wenns [A] 72 C1
Wépion [B] 30 D5
Weppersdorf [A] 62 F6
Werben [D] 34 C1
Werbomont [B] 30 E5
Werdau [D] 48 C2
Werder [D] 34 D2
Werdohl [D] 32 C5
Werfen [A] 60 G6
Werl [D] 32 C4
Werlte [D] 18 B6
Wermelskirchen [D] 30 H4
Wernberg [D] 48 C5
Werne [D] 32 C4
Werneck [D] 46 E3
Werneuchen [D] 34 F2
Wernigerode [D] 32 H4
Wertach [D] 60 C5
Wertheim [D] 46 D4
Werther [D] 32 D3
Wertingen [D] 60 C3
Wesel [D] 30 G2
Wesenberg [D] 20 C5
Wesendorf [D] 32 H1
Wesoła [PL] 52 C3
Wesselburen [D] 18 E2
Wesseling [D] 30 G4
Wessobrunn [D] 60 D5
West Bridgford [GB] 10 F5
West Bromwich [GB] 10 E6
Westbury [GB] 12 G4
Westende-Bad [B] 28 F1
Westendorf [A] 60 F6
Westenholz [D] 18 F6
Westensee [D] 18 F2
Westerhever [D] 18 D2
Westerholt [D] 18 B3
Westerland [D] 156 A4
Westerlo [B] 30 D3
Westerstede [D] 18 C4
Westkapelle [NL] 16 B6
Weston-super-Mare [GB] 12 F3
Westport [IRL] 2 C4
West Sandwick [GB] 6 H3
West-Terschelling [NL] 16 E1
Wetherby [GB] 10 F3
Wetlina [PL] 52 E6
Wetter [D] 30 H3
Wetter [D] 32 D6
Wetteren [B] 28 H2
Wettringen [D] 16 H5
Wetzikon [CH] 58 G5
Wetzlar [D] 46 C1
Wexford / Loch Garman [IRL] 4 F5
Weyer [A] 74 D1
Weyerburg [A] 72 F1
Weyer-Markt [A] 62 C5
Weyhausen [D] 32 G1
Weymouth [GB] 12 F5
Weyregg [A] 60 H5
Whitby [GB] 10 G2
Whitchurch [GB] 10 D5
Whitegate [IRL] 4 D5
Whitehead [NIR] 2 H3
Whithorn [GB] 8 C5
Whiting Bay [GB] 8 C3
Whitley Bay [GB] 8 G6
Whitstable [GB] 14 F5
Wiartel [PL] 24 C4
Wiązownica [PL] 52 F3
Wiblingen [D] 60 B3
Wicie [PL] 22 A2
Wicimice [PL] 20 G4
Wick [GB] 6 F3
Wickham Market [GB] 14 G3
Wicklow [IRL] 4 G4
Wicko [PL] 22 C1
Widawa [PL] 36 C6
Widawa [PL] 36 F5
Widdern [D] 46 D5
Widnes [GB] 10 D4
Widoma [PL] 52 A3
Widuchowa [PL] 20 E6
Więcbork [PL] 22 C5
Wiechowice [PL] 50 E4
Wiedenbrück [D] 32 D3
Wiefelstede [D] 18 C5
Wiehe [D] 34 B5
Wiehler Tropfsteinhöle [D] 30 H4
Wiek [D] 20 D1
Większyce [PL] 50 E3
Wielbark [PL] 22 H5
Wiele [PL] 22 D4
Wieleń [PL] 36 B1
Wielgie [PL] 36 F5
Wielgie [PL] 38 C6
Wielichowo [PL] 36 B3
Wieliczka [PL] 52 A4
Wieliczki [PL] 24 D3
Wielka Piaśnica [PL] 22 D1
Wielogłowy [PL] 52 B5
Wielogóra [PL] 38 C5
Wielowieś [PL] 50 F2
Wieluń [PL] 36 F6
Wien [A] 62 F4
Wiener Neustadt [A] 62 F5
Wienhausen [D] 32 G1
Wieniawa [PL] 38 B5
Wiepke [D] 34 B2
Wierden [NL] 16 G4
Wieruszów [PL] 36 E6
Wierzbica [PL] 38 B5
Wierzbice [PL] 50 C1
Wierzbowo [PL] 22 G5
Wierzchowo [PL] 22 B4
Wierzchucin Krolewski [PL] 22 C5
Wierzchucino [PL] 22 D1
Wies [D] 60 D5
Wiesau [D] 48 C4
Wiesbaden [D] 46 B3
Wiesberg [A] 72 B1
Wieselburg [A] 62 D4
Wiesen [CH] 70 H1
Wiesenburg [D] 34 C3
Wiesentheid [D] 46 F4
Wieskirche [D] 60 D5
Wiesloch [D] 46 C5
Wiesmath [A] 62 F6
Wiesmoor [D] 18 C4
Wietze [D] 32 G1
Wietzendorf [D] 18 F6
Wigan [GB] 10 D4
Wigston [GB] 10 F6
Wigton [GB] 8 E6
Wigtown [GB] 8 C5
Wijhe [NL] 16 F4
Wikingerburg [D] 44 F2
Wil [CH] 58 G5
Wilanów [PL] 38 B3
Wilczków [PL] 36 C6
Wilczkowo [PL] 22 G3
Wilczyska [PL] 52 C5
Wildalpen [A] 62 C6
Wildbad [D] 58 G1
Wildberg [D] 58 G1
Wildeck [D] 46 D6
Wildenburg [D] 44 G2

Wildenburg [D] 46 D4
Wildenrath [D] 30 F4
Wildenstein [CH] 58 E4
Wildenstein [D] 58 G3
Wildenstein Wasserfall [A] 74 C3
Wildeshausen [D] 18 D6
Wildhaus [CH] 58 H5
Wildkirchli [CH] 58 H5
Wildon [A] 74 D3
Wilfersdorf [A] 62 F3
Wilga [PL] 38 C4
Wilhelmsburg [A] 62 D5
Wilhelmsh [D] 32 F5
Wilhelmshaven [D] 18 C4
Wilhelmsthal [D] 32 F5
Wilhering [A] 62 B4
Wilków [PL] 38 B4
Wilków [PL] 50 H2
Wilkowo [PL] 34 H3
Willebroek [B] 30 C3
Willemstad [NL] 16 C6
Willingen [D] 32 D5
Willisau [CH] 58 E5
Willsbach [D] 46 D6
Wilnsdorf [D] 32 C6
Wilsin [NL] 16 D4
Wilster [D] 18 E3
Wilsum [D] 16 G4
Wilton [GB] 12 G4
Wiltz [L] 44 E2
Wimborne Minster [GB] 12 G5
Wimereux [F] 14 G6
Wincanton [GB] 12 G4
Winchester [GB] 12 H4
Windeck [D] 32 C6
Windermere [GB] 10 D2
Windisch [D] 48 C4
Windischgarsten [A] 62 B6
Windsbach [D] 46 G5
Wingen-sur-Moder [F] 44 G5
Winklern [A] 72 G2
Winnenden [D] 58 H1
Winnica [PL] 38 B2
Winnigstedt [D] 32 H3
Winnweiler [D] 46 B4
Winschoten [NL] 16 H2
Winsen [D] 18 G5
Winsen [D] 32 G1
Wińsko [PL] 36 C5
Winsum [NL] 16 G2
Winterberg [D] 32 D5
Winterfeld [D] 34 B1
Wintermoor [D] 18 F5
Winterstein [D] 32 G6
Winterswijk [NL] 16 G5
Winterthur [CH] 58 G4
Wipperfürth [D] 30 H4
Wippra [D] 34 A4
Wiry [PL] 50 C1
Wisbech [GB] 14 F2
Wischhafen [D] 18 E3
Wisełka [PL] 20 F3
Wiskitki [PL] 38 A3
Wisła [PL] 50 F5
Wiślica [PL] 52 B3
Wismar [D] 20 A3
Wiśniewo Ełckie [PL] 24 D4
Wiśniowa [PL] 52 A4
Wiśniowa [PL] 52 D4
Wissant [F] 14 G6
Wissembourg [F] 46 B6
Wissen [D] 32 C6
Wisznice [PL] 38 F4
Witham [GB] 14 F4
Withernsea [GB] 10 H4
Witków [PL] 52 H2
Witkowice [PL] 50 G1
Witkowo [PL] 36 E2
Witney [GB] 12 H3
Witnica [PL] 34 G1
Witnica [PL] 34 G2
Witostowice [PL] 50 C2
Witowo [PL] 36 F2
Wittdün [D] 18 D1
Witten [D] 30 H3
Wittenberge [D] 20 A6
Wittenborn [D] 18 G3
Wittenburg [D] 18 H4
Wittgenstein [D] 46 B4
Wittichenau [D] 34 F5
Wittingen [D] 32 H1
Wittislingen [D] 60 C3
Wittlich [D] 44 G2
Wittmund [D] 18 C4
Wittstock [D] 20 C5
Witzenhausen [D] 32 F5
Wiżajny [PL] 24 E2
Wizna [PL] 24 D5
Władysławowo [PL] 22 D1
Wleń [PL] 50 A1
Włocławek [PL] 36 G2
Włodawa [PL] 38 F4
Włoszczowa [PL] 50 H1
Włoszczowice [PL] 52 B2
Wodzisław [PL] 52 B2
Wodzisław Śląski [PL] 50 F4
Woerden [NL] 16 D5
Woerth [F] 44 H5
Woesten [B] 28 F2
Wohlen [CH] 58 F5
Wohra [D] 32 E6
Wojtowice [PL] 50 D2
Wojcieszków [PL] 38 D4
Wojcieszów [PL] 50 B1
Wójcin [PL] 36 E2
Wojnicz [PL] 52 C4
Wojsławice [PL] 38 F6
Wojtokiemie [PL] 24 E2
Woking [GB] 14 D4
Wola Idzikowska [PL] 38 F6
Wola Klasztorna [PL] 38 D5
Wola Obszańska [PL] 52 F2
Wola Rakowa [PL] 36 G4
Wola Uhruska [PL] 38 G5
Wola Wierzbowska [PL] 22 H6
Wolbórz [PL] 36 H5
Wolbrom [PL] 50 H3
Wołczyn [PL] 50 E1
Woldegk [D] 20 D5
Wolenice [PL] 36 D4
Wolfach [D] 58 F2
Wolfegg [D] 60 B5
Wolfen [D] 34 C4
Wolfenbüttel [D] 32 H3
Wolfhagen [D] 32 E5
Wolframs-Eschenbach [D] 46 F6
Wolfratshausen [D] 60 E5
Wolfsberg [A] 74 C3
Wolfsburg [D] 32 H2
Wolfstein [D] 44 H3
Wolgast [D] 20 E3
Wolhusen [CH] 58 E6
Wolibórz [PL] 50 C2
Wolica [PL] 52 B2
Wolin [PL] 20 F4
Wolin [PL] 20 F3
Wólka [PL] 52 A1
Wólka Dobryńska [PL] 38 F3
Wólka Łabuńska [PL] 52 G2
Wolkenstein [D] 48 D2
Wolkenstein in Gröden / Selva di Val Gardena [I] 72 E3
Wolkersdorf [A] 62 F4
Wollenberg [D] 34 F1
Wöllersdorf [A] 62 E5
Wollin [D] 34 C3
Wolmirstedt [D] 34 B3
Wolnzach [D] 60 E3
Wołomin [PL] 38 C2
Wołosate [PL] 52 F6
Wołów [PL] 36 C5
Wolsingham [GB] 10 F1
Wolsztyn [PL] 36 B3
Wolvega [NL] 16 F3
Wolverhampton [GB] 10 D6
Woodbridge [GB] 14 G3
Woodford [IRL] 2 C6
Wooler [GB] 8 F4
Wootton Bassett [GB] 12 G3
Worb [CH] 58 D6
Worbis [D] 32 G5
Worcester [GB] 12 G2
Worden-Sankt Andra [A] 62 F4
Wörgl [A] 60 F6
Workington [GB] 8 D6
Worksop [GB] 10 F5
Workum [NL] 16 E2
Wörlitz [D] 34 C4
Wormerveer [NL] 16 D4
Wormhout [F] 14 H6
Worms [D] 46 C4
Wörnitz [D] 46 F5
Worpswede [D] 18 E5
Wörrstadt [D] 46 B3
Wörth [A] 72 G1
Wörth [D] 46 B6
Wörth [D] 46 D4
Wörth [D] 60 F2
Wörth [D] 60 F3
Worthing [GB] 14 D5
Wożławki [PL] 22 H3
Woźniki [PL] 50 G2
Wożuczyn [PL] 52 G2
Wragby [GB] 10 G5
Wręczyca Wielka [PL] 50 F1
Wredenhagen [D] 20 C5
Wrexham [GB] 10 D5
Wriezen [D] 34 F2
Wróblew [PL] 36 F5
Wroblewo [PL] 36 B2
Wrocki [PL] 22 F5
Wrocław [PL] 36 C6
Wroniniec [PL] 36 B4
Wronki [PL] 24 D3
Wronki [PL] 36 B2
Wrząca Wielka [PL] 36 F3
Września [PL] 36 D3
Wschowa [PL] 36 B4
Wulfen [D] 30 H2
Wulkau [D] 34 C1
Wullersdorf [A] 62 E3
Wullowitz [A] 62 C3
Wünnenberg [D] 32 D4
Wunsiedel [D] 48 B3
Wunstorf [D] 32 F2
Wuppertal [D] 30 H3
Würgau [D] 46 G4
Wurmlinger Kapelle [D] 58 G2
Wurzbach [D] 46 H2
Würzbrunnen [CH] 58 E6
Würzburg [D] 46 E4
Wurzen [D] 34 D5
Wust [D] 34 C2
Wusterhausen [D] 34 D1
Wüstermarke [D] 34 E4
Wustrow [D] 20 C2
Wustrow [D] 20 C5
Wuustwezel [B] 30 D2
Wybcz [PL] 22 D6
Wydminy [PL] 24 D3
Wygoda [PL] 52 D4
Wyk [D] 156 A5
Wymondham [GB] 14 G2
Wyrzysk [PL] 22 C6
Wyśmierzyce [PL] 38 B4
Wysoka [PL] 22 B6
Wysokie [PL] 52 F1
Wysokie Mazowieckie [PL] 24 D6
Wysowa [PL] 52 C5
Wyszanów [PL] 36 E5
Wyszki [PL] 24 E6
Wyszków [PL] 38 C2
Wyszogród [PL] 38 A2
Wyszyna [PL] 36 F3

X

Xàbia [E] 104 F1
Xàbia / Jávea [E] 104 F1
Xabier / Javier [E] 84 C4
Xanten [D] 30 G2
Xánthi [GR] 130 E2
Xanthos [TR] 154 F3
Xàtiva [E] 98 E6
Xeraco [E] 98 F6
Xeresa [E] 98 E6
Xert [E] 98 G2
Xerta [E] 92 A5
Xertigny [F] 58 C2
Xesta, Puerto de la- [E] 78 E2
Xhoffraix [B] 30 F5
Xilopároiko [GR] 132 E2
Xinzo de Limia / Ginzo de Limia [E] 78 C6
Xirokámpi [GR] 136 E4
Xirókampos [GR] 154 A2
Xivert, Castell de- [E] 98 G3
Xixón / Gijón [E] 83 B2
Xixona / Jijona [E] 104 E2
Xodos / Chodos [E] 98 F2
Xove [E] 78 E1
Xubia [E] 78 D1
Xunqueira de Ambia [E] 78 D5
Xunqueira de Espadanedo [E] 78 D5
Xylaganí [GR] 130 F3
Xylofagou [CY] 154 G5
Xylókastro [GR] 132 H6
Xylópoli [GR] 130 B3
Xyniás [GR] 132 G3
Xynó Neró [GR] 128 E4

Y

Yablanitsa [BG] 148 A4
Yablanovo [BG] 148 D3
Yablonovka [RUS] 178 H2
Yacimiento de Botorrita [E] 90 E4
Yacimientos de Icnitas [E] 90 C2
Yağcılar [TR] 152 E1
Yağcılı [TR] 152 D2
Yağlılar [TR] 152 C1
Yagoda [BG] 148 C5
Yahotyn [UA] 202 E7
Yaiza [E] 100 E6
Yakimovo [BG] 146 F2
Yakkima [FIN] 188 G4
Yakoruda [BG] 146 G6
Yalakdere [TR] 150 F3
Yalıkavak [TR] 154 B1
Yalıköy [TR] 150 D2
Yalova [TR] 150 F3
Yalta [UA] 204 H4
Yaman [TR] 152 G4
Yambol [BG] 148 E5
Yamm [RUS] 198 G2
Yampil' [UA] 202 B8
Yampil' [UA] 202 E6
Yampil' [UA] 204 E2
Yancıklar [TR] 150 C2
Yanguas [E] 90 C2
Yanjukalns [LV] 198 F5
Yantarnyy [RUS] 22 G1
Yaraş [TR] 154 D1
Yarbasan [TR] 152 F2
Yarema [BG] 146 F5
Yarımca [TR] 150 G3
Yariş [TR] 152 G1
Yarm [GB] 10 F2
Yarmolyntsi [UA] 204 D2
Yarmouth [GB] 12 H5
Yartsevo [RUS] 202 D4
Yasen [BG] 148 A3
Yasna Polyana [BG] 148 F5
Yassıören [TR] 150 E2
Yassıören [TR] 152 F1
Yatağan [TR] 152 E6
Yavorets [BG] 148 B4
Yavoriv [UA] 52 G3
Yaylabayır [TR] 152 E2
Yayladamı [TR] 152 C2
Yaylaköy [TR] 152 H6
Yazhelbitsy [RUS] 202 C2
Yazıkent [TR] 152 E5
Yazıköy [TR] 154 B3
Yazıköy [TR] 152 H5
Yazır [TR] 152 G6
Yazır [TR] 154 H2
Yazırköy [TR] 152 F5
Ybbs an der Donau [A] 62 D4
Ybbsitz [A] 62 C5
Ychoux [F] 66 B4
Yderby [DK] 156 F1
Ýdra [GR] 136 G3
Ydrefors [S] 162 F2
Yecla [E] 104 D1
Yecla de Yeltes [E] 80 F6
Yeleğen [TR] 152 F4
Yelizavetino [RUS] 178 G6
Yel'na [RUS] 202 D4
Yel'nya [RUS] 202 D4
Yelo [E] 90 B4
Yel'tsy [RUS] 202 D3
Yelverton [GB] 12 D5
Yemel'yanovka [RUS] 196 G5
Yemikaraağac [TR] 150 E4
Yemişendere [TR] 152 F6
Yemişli [TR] 152 F2
Yenibogaziçi (Ay. Seryios) [CY] 154 G5
Yenice [TR] 130 H3
Yenice [TR] 150 C1
Yenice [TR] 150 C5
Yenice [TR] 150 D4
Yenice [TR] 152 F5
Yenice [TR] 152 H2
Yenicekent [TR] 152 F4
Yeniçiftlik [TR] 150 D3
Yeniçöy [TR] 152 D3
Yenidoğan [TR] 152 D5
Yenierenköy (Aigialoúsa) [CY] 154 G4
Yenifoça [TR] 152 C3
Yeni Karpuzlu [TR] 130 H3
Yeniköy [TR] 130 H6
Yeniköy [TR] 150 C3
Yeniköy [TR] 150 D6
Yeniköy [TR] 150 E2
Yeniköy [TR] 150 F6
Yeniköy [TR] 150 F4
Yeniköy [TR] 150 G3
Yeniköy [TR] 152 E3
Yeniköy [TR] 152 F2
Yeniköy [TR] 154 G3
Yenipazar [TR] 150 H4
Yenipazar [TR] 152 E5
Yenişakran [TR] 152 C3
Yenisarıbey [TR] 150 D5
Yenişehir [TR] 150 G4
Yenişehir [TR] 152 F3
Yenişehir [TR] 152 F3
Yenne [F] 68 H3
Yeovil [GB] 12 F4
Yerkesik [TR] 154 D1
Yershi [RUS] 202 E4
Yerville [F] 26 H3
Yesa / Esa [E] 84 C4
Yeşilçay / Ağva [TR] 150 G2
Yeşilköy [TR] 150 E3
Yesilköy [TR] 152 F2
Yesilköy [TR] 154 G3
Yeşiller [TR] 150 F5
Yeşilova [TR] 150 D5
Yeşilova [TR] 152 H5
Yeşilvadi [TR] 150 F2
Yeşilyurt [TR] 152 F4
Yeşilyurt [TR] 154 D1
Yeşilyuva [TR] 152 G5
Yeste [E] 102 H1
Yevpatoria [UA] 204 H4
Yezyaryshcha [BY] 202 C4
Yiğitler [TR] 152 B1
Yılmazköy (Skylloura) [CY] 154 F5
Yılmazlı [TR] 154 G1
Ylakiai [LT] 198 C6
Ylä-Kuona [FIN] 188 F4
Ylämaa [FIN] 178 E3
Ylämylly [FIN] 188 F2
Yläne [FIN] 176 D3
Ylihärmä [FIN] 186 C2
Yli-li [FIN] 196 D3
Yli-Kärppä [FIN] 196 D2
Ylikiiminki [FIN] 196 D4
Ylikiä [FIN] 176 D5
Ylikylä [FIN] 186 B4
Ylikylä [FIN] 186 C2
Ylikylä [FIN] 186 E1
Yli-Lesti [FIN] 186 E1
Yli-li [FIN] 196 D3
Ylimarkku / Övermark [FIN] 186 B4
Yli-Nampa [FIN] 194 D7
Yli-Olhava [FIN] 196 D3
Ylistaro [FIN] 186 C3
Ylitornio / Övertorneå [FIN] 194 B8
Ylivieska [FIN] 196 D5
Ylläsjärvi [FIN] 194 C6
Ylöjärvi [FIN] 176 F1
Ylönkylä [FIN] 176 E5
Yngsjö [S] 158 D2
Yoğuntas [TR] 150 B1
Yolağzı [TR] 130 H4
Yolüstü [TR] 152 F5
Yordankino [BG] 146 G4
York [GB] 10 F3
Youghal [IRL] 4 D5
Ypáti [GR] 132 G2
Yport [F] 26 G2
Yppäri [FIN] 196 C5
Ypres (Ieper) [B] 28 F2
Ýpso [GR] 132 B2
Ypsoús [GR] 136 D2
Yquem, Château- [F] 66 D4
Yrittäperä [FIN] 196 E3
Yrkje [N] 164 B2
Yrouerre [F] 56 F2
Yset [N] 182 B4
Yssandon, Puy d'- [F] 66 G3
Yssingeaux [F] 68 E4
Ystad [S] 158 D3
Ystebrød [N] 164 B4
Ytre Arna [N] 170 B3
Ytre Enebakk [N] 166 B1
Ytre Kjæs [N] 194 C2
Ytre Snillfjord [N] 180 G1
Ytterån [S] 182 G2
Ytterås [N] 182 C1
Ytteråträsk [S] 196 A5
Ytterberg [S] 182 G5
Ytterbyn [S] 172 H4
Ytterby [S] 160 G1
Ytterhogdal [S] 182 H5
Ytterjeppo [FIN] 186 C1
Yttermalung [S] 172 F4
Yttersélö [S] 168 C3
Ytterturingen [S] 182 H4
Yttervik [S] 190 E3
Yukarıkızılca [TR] 152 D4
Yukhavichy [BY] 198 H6
Yukhnov [RUS] 202 E4
Yuminda [EST] 198 E1
Yuncos [E] 96 F1
Yundola [BG] 146 G6
Yunquera [E] 102 B4
Yunquera de Henares [E] 88 H5
Yuntdağ [TR] 152 C3
Yunuseli [TR] 150 F4
Yuratsishki [BY] 200 H6
Yüreğil [TR] 152 E2
Yürücekler [TR] 150 F5
Yuste, Monasterio de- [E] 88 B5
Yusufça [TR] 152 G6
Yuvacık [TR] 154 D2
Yuzhnoukrains'k [UA] 204 F2
Yverdon-les-Bains [CH] 58 C6
Yvetot [F] 26 H3
Yvoir [B] 30 D5
Yvoire [F] 70 B2
Yxnerum [S] 168 B6

Z

Zaandam [NL] 16 D4
Zabalats' [BY] 24 H3
Žabalj [SRB] 142 G1
Zăbalt [RO] 76 H5
Zabar [H] 64 E4
Žabari [SRB] 146 C1
Žabice [PL] 36 B5
Zabierzów [PL] 50 H3
Zabki [PL] 38 B3
Ząbkowice Śląskie [PL] 50 C2
Žabljak [HR] 112 H6
Žabljak [MNE] 144 E2
Zabłudów [PL] 24 F6
Žabno [PL] 52 C3
Zabok [HR] 74 E5
Zabolottia [UA] 38 G4
Zabór [PL] 36 A4
Zábřeh [CZ] 50 C4
Zabrodzie [PL] 38 C2
Zabrze [PL] 50 F3
Zabrzeż [PL] 52 B5
Zabzun [AL] 128 C3
Zacháro [GR] 136 C3
Zachloroú [GR] 132 G6
Zadar [HR] 112 G5
Zadní Chodov [CZ] 48 C4
Zadvarje [HR] 144 A2
Zadzyezhzha [BY] 198 H6
Zafferana Etnea [I] 126 G3
Zafirovo [BG] 148 E1
Zafra [E] 94 G3
Žaga [SLO] 72 H4
Żagań [PL] 34 H5
Žagare [LT] 198 D6
Zagklivéri [GR] 130 B4
Żaglav [HR] 112 F5
Zaglavak [SRB] 146 A2
Zagorá [GR] 132 H2
Zagorje [HR] 112 G1
Zagorje [SLO] 74 C5
Zagórów [PL] 36 E3
Zagórz [PL] 52 E5
Zagórzany [PL] 52 C4
Zagoska [RUS] 198 H3
Zagreb [HR] 74 E6
Žagubica [SRB] 146 D1
Zagvozd [HR] 144 B2
Zagwiździe [PL] 50 E1
Zagyvapálfalva [H] 64 D5
Zahara [E] 100 H3
Zahara de los Atunes [E] 100 G5
Zahinos [E] 94 F3
Zahna [D] 34 D4
Zahody [RUS] 198 G3
Záhoří [CZ] 48 F6
Záhorská Ves [SK] 62 G4
Zahrádky [CZ] 48 G2
Zaiceva [LV] 198 G4
Zaidin [E] 90 G4
Zaisenhausen [D] 46 C5
Zajas [MK] 128 D2
Zaječar [SRB] 146 E2
Zaječar [SRB] 204 C6
Zákas [GR] 128 E6
Zakliczyn [PL] 52 C4
Zaklików [PL] 52 E1
Zakopane [PL] 50 H6
Zakroczym [PL] 38 B2
Zakrós [GR] 140 H5
Zakrós [GR] 140 H5
Zakrzewo [PL] 36 F1
Zakrzówek [PL] 38 C5
Zákupy [CZ] 48 G2
Zákynthos [GR] 136 B2
Zalaapáti [H] 74 G3
Zalabaksa [H] 74 F3
Zalabér [H] 74 G2
Zalaegerszeg [H] 74 G3
Zalakaros [H] 74 G3
Zalakomár [H] 74 G4
Zalaksáni [H] 74 G3
Zalalövő [H] 74 F3
Zalamea de la Serena [E] 96 B4
Zalamea la Real [E] 94 F5
Zalaszabar [H] 74 G3
Zalaszántó [H] 74 G3
Zalaszentbalázs [H] 74 G3
Zalaszentgrót [H] 74 G2
Zălau [RO] 204 C4
Žalec [SLO] 74 D4
Zalewo [PL] 22 F4
Załęże [PL] 22 H5
Zalishchyky [UA] 204 D2
Zalivnoye [RUS] 200 D5
Zalla [E] 82 G4
Zaltbommel [NL] 16 E6
Załuski [PL] 38 A2
Załuż [PL] 52 E5
Zalužnica [HR] 112 G3
Zamárdi [H] 76 A3
Zamarte [PL] 22 C4
Žamberk [CZ] 50 B4
Zambrana [E] 82 G5
Zambrów [PL] 24 D6
Zambujal [P] 86 B6
Zambujeira do Mar [P] 94 B4
Zamora [E] 80 H5
Zamość [PL] 24 C6
Zamość [PL] 24 C6
Zamość [PL] 52 F1
Zamostne [PL] 22 D2
Zandhoven [B] 30 D3
Zandvoort [NL] 16 D4
Zangoza / Sangüesa [E] 84 C5
Zaniemyśl [PL] 36 D3
Zánka [H] 74 H3
Zan'kovo [RUS] 198 G4
Zante [LV] 198 C5
Zaorejas [E] 90 B5
Zaostrog [HR] 144 B3
Zaostrov'ye [RUS] 178 H2
Zaozernoye [RUS] 24 C2
Zapadnaja Dvina [RUS] 202 D3
Zapadnaya Dvina [RUS] 202 C3
Zapałów [PL] 52 F3
Zapfendorf [D] 46 G3
Zaplyus'ye [RUS] 198 H2
Zapole [PL] 36 F5
Zapolyarnyy [RUS] 194 F3
Zapol'ye [RUS] 198 H2
Zaporizhzhia [UA] 204 H2
Zaporozhskoye [RUS] 178 H3
Záppeio [GR] 132 G2
Zapponeta [I] 120 H1
Zaprešić [HR] 74 E5
Zaprudy [BY] 38 H2
Zapyškis [LT] 200 F5
Zapytiv [UA] 52 H3
Zaragoza [E] 90 E4
Zárakes [GR] 134 D5
Zărand [RO] 76 H4
Zarańsko [PL] 20 H5
Zarasai [LT] 200 H4
Zarautz [E] 84 A2
Zarcilla de los Ramons [E] 104 B3
Zaręby-Warchoły [PL] 38 D1
Zarech'e [RUS] 198 H4
Zarechnyy [RUS] 196 G4
Zarenthien [D] 18 H6
Żarki [PL] 50 G2
Zárkos [GR] 132 F2
Zărnești [RO] 204 D5
Žarnovica [SK] 64 B3
Żarnów [PL] 38 A6
Żarnowiec [PL] 50 H2
Zarós [GR] 140 E5
Žarošice [CZ] 62 G2
Żarów [PL] 50 B1
Zarrentin [D] 18 H4
Żarska Wieś [PL] 34 H6
Zarszyn [PL] 52 E5
Żary [PL] 34 H5
Zarza-Capilla [E] 96 C4
Zarza de Alange [E] 94 H2
Zarzadilla de Totana [E] 104 B3
Zarza la Mayor [E] 86 G4
Zarzecze [PL] 38 D5
Zarzecze [PL] 52 E2
Zás [E] 78 B2
Zasa [LV] 198 F6
Zasieki [PL] 34 G4
Žatec [CZ] 48 E3
Zatom [PL] 20 H6
Zator [PL] 50 G4
Zaube [LV] 198 E5
Zauchwitz [D] 34 D3
Zavala [BIH] 144 C3
Zavet [BG] 148 D2
Zavidovići [BIH] 142 D3
Zavlaka [SRB] 142 F3
Zavoya [BG] 130 F2
Zavrc [SLO] 74 E4
Zawada [PL] 36 A4
Zawada [PL] 50 E2
Zawady [PL] 50 F1
Zawadzkie [PL] 50 F2
Zawichost [PL] 52 D1
Zawidów [PL] 48 G1
Zawiercie [PL] 50 G2
Zawoja [PL] 50 H5
Zawonia [PL] 36 D5
Zawroty [PL] 22 G4
Zayan'e [RUS] 198 G2
Zayan'ye [RUS] 198 G2
Zaytsevo [RUS] 178 F2
Žažina [HR] 142 A1
Zázriva [SK] 50 G6
Zbąszyń [PL] 36 B3
Zbąszynek [PL] 36 A3
Zblewo [PL] 22 D4
Zboj [SK] 52 F6
Zbojno [PL] 22 F6
Zborište [BIH] 112 H2
Zborov [SK] 52 D5
Zborowice [PL] 52 C4
Zbrachlin [PL] 22 D5
Zbraslav [CZ] 48 F4
Zbraslavice [CZ] 48 H4
Zbrašovske Aragonitové Jeskyně [CZ] 50 D5
Zbucz [PL] 38 F1
Zbuczyn Poduchowny [PL] 38 D3
Zdala [HR] 74 G5
Žďár [CZ] 48 E3
Žďár nad Sázavou [CZ] 50 B5
Zdenci [HR] 76 A6
Zdenska Vas [SLO] 74 C5
Zdiby [CZ] 48 F3
Zdice [CZ] 48 F4
Ždírec nad Doubravou [CZ] 50 A5
Zdounky [CZ] 50 D6
Zdunje [MK] 128 D1
Zduńska Wola [PL] 36 F5
Zduny [PL] 36 D5
Zduny [PL] 36 H3
Zdziechowice [PL] 52 E1
Zdzieszowice [PL] 50 E3
Žebrák [CZ] 48 E4
Zebreira [P] 86 G4
Zebrzydowa [PL] 34 H6
Zeddiani [I] 118 C5
Žednik [SRB] 76 D5
Zeebrugge [B] 28 G1
Zeewolde [NL] 16 E4
Zefyría [GR] 138 D4
Żegiestów-Zdrój [PL] 52 C5
Zehdenick [D] 20 D6
Zeil [D] 60 B5
Zeist [NL] 16 E5
Zeitz [D] 34 C6
Żelazna [PL] 22 D1
Żelazna Góra [PL] 22 G2
Żelechów [PL] 38 D4
Zelená Hora [CZ] 48 E5
Zelena morava [BG] 148 D3
Zelenika [MNE] 144 D4
Zelenogorsk [RUS] 178 G4
Zelenogradsk [RUS] 200 C5
Želetava [CZ] 50 A6
Železná [CZ] 48 C5
Železná Ruda [CZ] 48 D6
Železnik [SRB] 142 G3
Železniki [SLO] 74 B4
Železný Brod [CZ] 48 H2
Zelhem [NL] 16 F5
Želiezovce [SK] 64 B5
Želin [SLO] 74 A5
Zelina [HR] 74 F5
Zélio [GR] 132 H4
Želiv [CZ] 48 H5
Želizna [PL] 38 E4
Żelkowo [PL] 22 C2
Zell [A] 62 A4
Zell [A] 44 G2
Zell [D] 58 E4
Zella [D] 32 G5
Zella-Mehlis [D] 46 G2
Zell am See [A] 72 F1
Zell am Ziller [A] 72 E1
Želnava [CZ] 62 B2
Zelów [PL] 36 G5
Zeltini [LV] 198 F4
Zeltweg [A] 74 C2
Želva [LT] 200 G5
Zelwa [PL] 24 F3
Zelzate [B] 28 H1
Žemaičių Naumiestis [LT] 200 D5
Žemberovce [SK] 64 C4
Zemblak [AL] 128 D4
Zeme [I] 70 F5
Zemen [BG] 146 F5
Zemite [LV] 198 C5
Zemmer [D] 44 G2
Zemplinske Jastrabie [SK] 64 H3
Zemplínska Teplica [SK] 64 G3
Zemun [SRB] 142 G2
Zenica [BIH] 142 D4
Žepa [BIH] 142 E4
Žepče [BIH] 142 D3
Zerbst [D] 34 C3
Żerczyce [PL] 38 E2
Zerevna [BG] 148 D4
Zerf [D] 44 F3
Zeri [I] 110 C3
Zerind [RO] 76 G3
Zermatt [CH] 70 D3
Zernez [CH] 72 B2
Zernien [D] 18 H6
Żerniki [PL] 36 C6
Zerqan [AL] 128 C2
Zestoa / Cestona [E] 84 A2
Žetale [SLO] 74 E4
Zetel [D] 18 C4
Zeulenroda [D] 48 B2
Zeven [D] 18 E5
Zevenaar [NL] 16 F5
Zevenergen [NL] 16 C6
Zevgaráki [GR] 132 E5
Zeybekçayırı [TR] 150 C6
Zeytinbağı [TR] 150 E4
Zeytindağ [TR] 152 C3
Zeytinli [TR] 152 C1
Zgierz [PL] 36 G4
Zg. Jezersko [SLO] 74 B4
Zgniłocha [PL] 22 H4
Zgórsko [PL] 52 C3
Zgorzelec [PL] 34 G6
Zg. Polskava [SLO] 74 D4
Zg. Polskava [SLO] 74 D4
Zhabinka [BY] 38 G2
Zhaludok [BY] 24 H4
Zhashkiv [UA] 202 D8
Zhedricy [RUS] 198 H4
Zhelezna [BG] 146 F3
Zheleznitsa [BG] 146 F5
Zheleznodorozhnyj [RUS] 24 B2
Zheleznogorsk [RUS] 202 F5
Zheleznya [RUS] 202 F4
Zhilentsi [BG] 146 E6
Zhitnica [BG] 148 B5
Zhitom i Madh [AL] 128 B5
Zhitosvyat [BG] 148 E4
Zhlobin [BY] 202 C6
Zhmerynka [UA] 202 C8
Zhodzina [BY] 202 C5
Zhoř [CZ] 48 D5
Zhovkva [UA] 52 H3
Zhovten' [UA] 204 F3
Zhovtneve [UA] 52 H1
Zhuprany [BY] 200 H6
Zhvtkavichy [BY] 202 C6
Zhydachiv [UA] 52 H5
Zhytomyr [UA] 202 C7
Žiar nad Hronom [SK] 64 C3
Zicavo [F] 114 B5
Zickhusen [D] 20 A4
Zidani Most [SLO] 74 D5
Ziddorf [D] 20 C4
Židlochovice [CZ] 62 F2
Ziębice [PL] 50 C2
Ziegenrück [D] 46 H2
Zieleniec Duży [PL] 24 B5
Zielona Chocina [PL] 22 C4
Zielona Góra [PL] 34 H4
Zielonczyn [PL] 20 F4

9th edition November 2007

© ISTITUTO GEOGRAFICO DE AGOSTINI, Novara and
© Automobile Association Developments Limited, Basingstoke.

Original edition printed 1996

 This product includes mapping data licensed from Ordnance Survey® with the permission of the Controller of Her Majesty's Stationery Office. © Crown copyright 2007. All rights reserved. Licence number 100021153.

 This product includes mapping based upon data licensed from Ordnance Survey of Northern Ireland® reproduced by permission of the Chief Executive, acting on behalf of the Controller of Her Majesty's Stationery Office. © Crown copyright 2007. Permit No. 70038.

Republic of Ireland mapping based on Ordnance Survey Ireland.
Permit No. MP000106 © Ordnance Survey Ireland and Government of Ireland

Published by ISTITUTO GEOGRAFICO DE AGOSTINI, Novara
and Automobile Association Developments Limited whose registered office is Fanum House, Basing View, Basingstoke, Hampshire RG21 4EA, UK. Registered number 1878835.

ISBN-13: 978 0 7495 5451 4 (flexibound)
ISBN-10: 0 7495 5451 7
ISBN-13: 978 0 7495 5450 7 (wire bound)
ISBN-10: 0 7495 5450 9

A CIP catalogue record for this book is available from The British Library.

Printed in Italy by Canale & C. S.P.A., Torino on paper from EMAS (Eco Management and Audit Scheme) registered paper mills.
Paper: 90gsm Presto Silk.